Trademarks and Their Role in Innovation, Entrepreneurship and Industrial Organization

T0300228

Trademarks are the most widely used intellectual property right by companies worldwide. Their strategic importance is increasing, as reputational assets become more relevant for companies than ever, in national and global markets. Trademarks also represent key tools for companies to profit from innovation and can make the difference for start-ups and entrepreneurial firms by allowing them to gain legitimacy and fostering fund raising from investors.

This book *Trademarks and Their Role in Innovation, Entrepreneurship and Industrial Organization* takes stock of the emerging academic research on how companies use trademarks. It collects a rich set of contributions from several research perspectives and disciplines and proposes an integrated view bridging different levels of analysis: individual, firm, industry, and country level. Specifically, the book combines an industrial organization, innovation, and entrepreneurship perspective to understand why, when and with what effects entrepreneurs, innovators, and firms use trademarks. The book is targeted toward academic readers to gain a better understanding of the emerging and interdisciplinary field of trademark research as well as interested practitioners from the area of intellectual property (IP) management and policy-making.

The chapters in this book were originally published in *Industry and Innovation*.

Carolina Castaldi is Full Professor in Geography of Innovation at Utrecht University, the Netherlands.

Joern Block is Full Professor at University of Trier, Germany and Erasmus University Rotterdam, the Netherlands.

Meindert J. Flikkema is Professor in the School of Business & Economics at Vrije Universiteit Amsterdam, the Netherlands.

Trademarks and Their Role in Innovation, Entrepreneurship and Industrial Organization

Edited by
Carolina Castaldi, Joern Block and
Meindert J. Flikkema

Routledge
Taylor & Francis Group

LONDON AND NEW YORK

First published 2021
by Routledge
2 Park Square, Milton Park, Abingdon, Oxon, OX14 4RN

and by Routledge
605 Third Avenue, New York, NY 10158

Routledge is an imprint of the Taylor & Francis Group, an informa business

British Library Cataloguing-in-Publication Data
A catalogue record for this book is available from the British Library

ISBN13: 978-0-367-70664-7 (hbk)
ISBN13: 978-0-367-70666-1 (pbk)
ISBN13: 978-1-003-14744-2 (ebk)

Typeset in Minion Pro
by codeMantra

Publisher's Note
The publisher accepts responsibility for any inconsistencies that may have arisen during the conversion of this book from journal articles to book chapters, namely the inclusion of journal terminology.

Disclaimer
Every effort has been made to contact copyright holders for their permission to reprint material in this book. The publishers would be grateful to hear from any copyright holder who is not here acknowledged and will undertake to rectify any errors or omissions in future editions of this book.

Contents

Citation Information

The following chapters were originally published in different issues of *Industry and Innovation*. When citing this material, please use the original citations and page numbering for each article, as follows:

Chapter 1
Why and when do firms trademark? Bridging perspectives from industrial organisation, innovation and entrepreneurship
Carolina Castaldi, Joern Block and Meindert J Flikkema
Industry and Innovation, volume 27, issue 1–2 (2020) pp. 1–10

Chapter 2
Which firms use trademarks? Firm-level evidence from Germany on the role of distance, product quality and innovation
Dirk Crass
Industry and Innovation, volume 27, issue 7 (2020) pp. 730–755

Chapter 3
Are trademark counts a valid indicator of innovation? Results of an in-depth study of new Benelux trademarks filed by SMEs
Meindert Flikkema, Ard-Pieter De Man and Carolina Castaldi
Industry and Innovation, volume 21, issue 4 (2014) pp. 310–331

Chapter 4
Innovation activities and business cycles: are trademarks a leading indicator?
Charles A. W. deGrazia, Amanda Myers and Andrew A. Toole
Industry and Innovation, volume 27, issue 1–2 (2020) pp. 184–203

Chapter 5
On the price elasticity of demand for trademarks
Gaétan de Rassenfosse
Industry and Innovation, volume 27, issue 1–2 (2020) pp. 11–24

Chapter 6
From a distinctive sign to an exchangeable asset: exploring the U.S. market for trademark licensing
Edoardo Ferrucci, Maria Isabella Leone, Manuel Romagnoli and Andrea Toros
Industry and Innovation, volume 27, issue 1–2 (2020) pp. 25–51

For any permission-related enquiries please visit:
http://www.tandfonline.com/page/help/permissions

Contributors

Suma Athreye Management Science and Entrepreneurship Group, Essex Business School, Southend-on-Sea, UK.

Joern Block Department of Management, University of Trier, Germany. Department of Applied Economics, Erasmus School of Economics, Erasmus University Rotterdam, the Netherlands.

Mónica Carmona Department of Business Management and Marketing, University of Huelva, Spain.

Carolina Castaldi Department of Human Geography and Planning, Utrecht University, the Netherlands.

Emilio Congregado Department of Economics, University of Huelva, Spain.

Dirk Crass Economics of Innovation and Industrial Dynamics, Centre for European Economic Research (ZEW), Mannheim, Germany.

Charles A. W. deGrazia Ecole de Management Léonard De Vinci, Paris, France.

Ard-Pieter de Man Department of Management and Organization, VU University, Amsterdam, the Netherlands.

Gaétan de Rassenfosse Ecole polytechnique fédérale de Lausanne, College of Management of Technology, Lausanne, Switzerland.

Geertjan De Vries Department of Applied Economics, Erasmus School of Economics, Erasmus University Rotterdam, the Netherlands. Tinbergen Institute, Rotterdam, the Netherlands.

Mafini Dosso European Commission, Joint Research Centre, Edificio Expo, Seville, Spain.

Claudio Fassio School of Economics and Management & CIRCLE, Lund University, Sweden. BRICK, Collegio Carlo Alberto, Torino, Italy.

Edoardo Ferrucci Department of Business and Management, LUISS Guido Carli, Rome, Italy. GREThA UMR CNRS 5113- Université de Bordeaux, France.

Christian Fisch Trier University, Germany. Erasmus School of Economics, Erasmus University Rotterdam, the Netherlands.

Meindert J. Flikkema School of Business & Economics at Vrije Universiteit Amsterdam, the Netherlands.

Marco Grazzi Department of Economic Policy, Università Cattolica del Sacro Cuore, Milano, Italy.

Maria Isabella Leone Department of Business and Management, LUISS Guido Carli, Rome, Italy.

Patrick Llerena Bureau d'Economie théorique et Appliquée, Université de Strasbourg, France.

Serhiy Lyalkov International University of Andalusia, Santa María de la Rábida Campus, Huelva, Spain.

Ana Millán Department of Financial Economics and Accounting, Pablo de Olavide University, Sevilla, Spain.

José María Millán Department of Economics, University of Huelva, Spain.

Valentine Millot Organisation for Economic Co-Operation and Development (OECD), Paris, France. Bureau d'Economie théorique et Appliquée, Université de Strasbourg, France.

Amanda Myers Booz Allen Hamilton.

Enrico Pennings Department of Applied Economics, Erasmus School of Economics, Erasmus University Rotterdam, the Netherlands. Tinbergen Institute, Rotterdam, the Netherlands. Erasmus Institute of Management (ERIM), Erasmus University, Rotterdam, the Netherlands.

Chiara Piccardo Department of Economics, University of Verona, Italy.

Manuel Romagnoli Department of Business and Management, LUISS Guido Carli, Rome, Italy.

Szabolcs Szilárd Sebrek Department of Business Studies, Institute of Business Economics, Corvinus Business School, Budapest, Hungary.

Grid Thoma Computer Science Division, University of Camerino, Italy.

Andrew A. Toole United States Patent and Trademark Office, Alexandria, USA. Centre for European Economic Research, Mannheim, Germany.

Andrea Toros Department of Business and Management, LUISS Guido Carli, Rome, Italy.

Cecilia Vergari Department of Economics and Management, University of Pisa, Italy.

Antonio Vezzani Department of Economics, Roma Tre University, Italy.

Preface

Carolina Castaldi, Joern Block and Meindert J. Flikkema

Trademarks are the most widely used intellectual property right by companies worldwide. According to the World Intellectual Property Organization (WIPO) a trademark is 'a sign capable of distinguishing the goods or services of one enterprise from those of other enterprises'. The strategic importance of trademark protection is increasing, as reputational assets and brand equity become more relevant for companies than ever in national and global markets. Trademarks also represent key tools for companies to profit from innovation and can make the difference for start-ups and entrepreneurial firms by allowing them to gain legitimacy and fostering fund raising from investors.

In economic terms, trademarks contribute to economic efficiency by reducing consumer search costs (Landes and Posner, 1987). Rather than having to inquire into the source and qualities of every potential purchase, consumers can look at trademarks as shorthand indicators (Dogan and Lemley, 2007). 'By protecting established trademarks against confusing imitation, the law ensures a reliable vocabulary for communications between producers and consumers. Both sellers and buyers benefit from the ability to trust this vocabulary to mean what it says. Sellers benefit because they can invest in goodwill with the knowledge that others will not appropriate it. Consumers benefit because they do not have to do exhaustive research or even spend extra time looking at labels before making a purchase; they can know, based on a brand name, that a product has the features they are seeking' (Dogan and Lemley, 2007, p. 1226). Increasingly, this informational role of trademarks has given space to new functions, as trademarks have become strategic tools in corporate market strategies and even commodities to exchange in specialized markets (Ramello, 2006).

Despite their increasing relevance, academic research on trademarks has been long scattered and confined within the boundaries of specific disciplines. As a striking comparison, research on patents has been extensive and occupies a steady position within research on the economics and management of innovation. Within the same domain, studies on trademarks have only been a handful, but are now becoming more commonplace, as an emerging new strand of both theoretical and empirical research. We, the three editors of this book, have played a leading role in pushing research on trademarks to be central within economics and management research. Historically, few researchers had opened the way for this to happen. As a brief history of trademark research, let us mention here a few, at the risk of forgetting many others.

Christine Greenhalgh has been one of the pioneers on the economics side: she initiated several projects where she pushed for looking at the whole range of intellectual property rights that firms use, not only patents (Schautschick and Greenhalgh, 2016). She conceptualized trademark strategies and the role of trademarks in corporate differentiation strategies, and she also studied whether trademarks hinder or promote dynamic competition (Greenhalgh and Rogers, 2012).

Andrea Fosfuri and Marco Giarratana promoted the use of trademark data within management research: they used trademarks to construct original indicators of market competition (Fosfuri and Giarratana, 2009) and commercialization capabilities (Fosfuri et al., 2008).

Sandro Mendonça led the way for investigating the potential of trademarks as indicators of innovation and industrial dynamics, in his seminal paper in Research Policy (Mendonça et al., 2004).

Finally, we should mention former Chief Economists at the USPTO, particularly Stuart Graham and Alan Marco, and their colleague Amanda Myers, who made it possible to have access to the entire database of trademark filings at the USPTO, the first trademark office to make trademark data publicly available to researchers and others (Graham et al., 2013). Their initiative has been followed by many other offices and commercial databases are also increasingly including information on trademarks.

We all three take pride in having put forward the seminal work of these and other pioneers of trademark research in our works.

Carolina Castaldi has contributed to the understanding of how firms across different economic sectors leverage trademarks (Castaldi, 2018). She recently offered a plea for exploiting trademarks more systematically in management research (Castaldi, 2020). She is also the driving force behind another special issue on trademarks in the making at Regional Studies, co-edited with Sandro Mendonça.

Joern Block has played a leading role in researching trademarks from an entrepreneurship perspective. He co-authored several studies revealing how trademarks allow start-ups to attract investment and gain legitimacy (Block et al., 2014, 2015). He also investigated the market valuation of trademarks (Sandner and Block, 2011).

Meindert Flikkema has focused on collecting micro data and testing the validity of EU and national trademarks as innovation indicators. He was one of the first to link innovation studies to marketing research on branding strategies for innovation (Flikkema et al., 2014, 2019).

This book originates from our project for a special issue in *Industry and Innovation*. This relatively new journal profiled itself from the very start as an outlet open to contributions about other forms of innovation than just the traditional technology-based and patent-protected innovation in R&D intensive sectors. As such, the journal felt like the right place for attracting research on trademarks. The call for papers attracted both researchers that were already working on trademarks and others who saw the special issue as an opportunity to do so. We received a large number of submissions and eventually collected papers filling two full issues of *Industry and Innovation*. Let us thank here the support that we received from Christopher Grimpe and Bram Timmermans from the editorial team.

This book collects all the papers included in the special issue and other key papers on trademarks that appeared in *Industry and Innovation*. As such, this book takes stock of the emerging academic research on how companies use trademarks. The rich set of contributions come from several research perspectives and disciplines and proposes an integrated view bridging different levels of analysis: individual, firm, industry, and country level.

The book contains four parts, including several chapters.

Part I: Bridging perspectives on trademarks and firms

The first part contains foundational papers, both conceptual and empirical, that combine different perspectives to understand trademarking activity.

In the first chapter we offer a conceptual framework to understand different corporate motives to file trademarks. We combine an industrial organization, innovation and entrepreneurship perspective to understand why, when and with what effects entrepreneurs, innovators and firms use trademarks. The chapter by Dirk Crass is complementary to our conceptual work and offers empirical evidence from Germany on the motives and propensity to trademark.

The other two chapters concern the use of trademark indicators to measure innovation and economic activity. Meindert Flikkema, Ard-Pieter de Man and Carolina Castaldi showed that 60% of trademarks filed at the Benelux office referred to some form of innovation, providing the first trademark-level study on the relation between trademarks and innovation. Charles DeGrazia, Amanda Myers and Andrew O'Toole argue in their chapter that trademark metrics can be added to the toolbox of leading indicators of economies.

Part II: Trademarks as assets

The second part includes chapters that shed light on the extent to which trademarks are valuable assets for companies. Gaetan De Rassenfosse finds that trademark filing demand is not price elastic, indicating that cost consideration do not play a dominant role in the decision to trademark. Edoardo Ferrucci, Maria Isabella Leone, Manuel Romagnoli and Andrea Toros offer the very first empirical study on the market for brands, i.e. on transactions where trademarks are traded as commodities. Finally, Mafini Dosso and Andrea Vezzani show that the market value of R&D intensive companies depends on both trademark-protected reputational assets, as well as on patent-protected technological assets.

Part III: Trademarks and IP strategies of innovative firms

The third part collects chapters focusing on how trademarks are part of IP strategies of innovative firms. All three studies by Marco Grazzi, Chiara Piccardo and Cecilia Vergari, by Patrick Llerena and Valentine Millot and by Grid Thoma, demonstrate that combining patents and trademarks in a synergetic way pays off. Yet, the sectoral context matters significantly for the effect size.

Suma Athreye and Claudio Fassio provide an original take by investigating factors leading innovative firms not to trademark, or at least not to file a new trademark. They find collaborative innovation projects to be one of the instances where firms might avoid filing new trademarks.

Part IV: Trademarks and entrepreneurship

The final part offers a collection of studies focused on how entrepreneurs leverage trademarks. Serhiv Lyalkov, Mónica Carmona, Emilio Congregado, Ana Millán, and José María Millán reveal that trademarks can be associated with Kirznerian entrepreneurship and hence used them to measure it accordingly on a country level. Szabolcs Szilárd Sebrek focuses on the technology search activities of entrepreneurial firms in the security software industry and finds that the breadth of the trademark portfolio matters for the geographical spread of technology search.

Finally, Geertjan de Vries, Enrico Pennings, Joern Block and Christian Fisch looked at the timing of the IPR filings of start-ups, to understand why and under which conditions trademarks are filed prior to patents.

To conclude, we are happy to see the many original trademark studies published in *Industry and Innovation* bundled in this volume. Let us stress that the book is targeted towards academic readers to gain a better understanding of the emerging and interdisciplinary field of trademark research as well as interested practitioners from the area of intellectual property (IP) management and policy-making. We see much potential for further researching trademarks and for leveraging them as original and novel data source in academic and policy work.

References

Block, J. H., De Vries, G., Schumann, J. H., & Sandner, P. (2014). Trademarks and venture capital valuation. *Journal of Business Venturing*, 29(4), 525–542.

Block, J. H., Fisch, C. O., Hahn, A., & Sandner, P. G. (2015). Why do SMEs file trademarks? Insights from firms in innovative industries. *Research Policy*, 44(10), 1915–1930.

Castaldi, C. (2018). To trademark or not to trademark: The case of the creative and cultural industries. *Research Policy*, 47(3), 606–616.

Castaldi, C. (2020). All the great things you can do with trademark data: Taking stock and looking ahead. *Strategic Organization*, 18(3), 472–484.

Dogan, S. L., & Lemley, M. A. (2007). A search-costs theory of limiting doctrines in trademark law. *Trademark Reporter*, 97, 1223.

Flikkema, M., Castaldi, C., de Man, A. P., & Seip, M. (2019). Trademarks' relatedness to product and service innovation: A branding strategy approach. *Research Policy*, 48(6), 1340–1353.

Flikkema, M., De Man, A. P., & Castaldi, C. (2014). Are trademark counts a valid indicator of innovation? Results of an in-depth study of new Benelux trademarks filed by SMEs. *Industry and Innovation*, 21(4), 310–331.

Fosfuri, A., & Giarratana, M. S. (2009). Masters of war: Rivals' product innovation and new advertising in mature product markets. *Management Science*, 55(2), 181–191.

Fosfuri, A., Giarratana, M. S., & Luzzi, A. (2008). The penguin has entered the building: The commercialization of open source software products. *Organization Science*, 19(2), 292–305.

Graham, S. J., Hancock, G., Marco, A. C., & Myers, A. F. (2013). The USPTO trademark case files dataset: Descriptions, lessons, and insights. *Journal of Economics & Management Strategy*, 22(4), 669–705.

Greenhalgh, C., & Rogers, M. (2012). Trade marks and performance in services and manufacturing firms: Evidence of Schumpeterian competition through innovation. *Australian Economic Review*, 45(1), 50–76.

Landes, W. M., & Posner, R. A. (1987). Trademark law: An economic perspective. *The Journal of Law and Economics*, 30(2), 265–309.

Mendonça, S., Pereira, T. S., & Godinho, M. M. (2004). Trademarks as an indicator of innovation and industrial change. *Research Policy*, 33(9), 1385–1404.

Ramello, G. B. (2006). What's in a sign? Trademark law and economic theory. *Journal of Economic Surveys*, 20(4), 547–565.

Sandner, P., & Block, J. (2011). The market value of R&D, patents and trademarks. *Research Policy*, 40(7), 969–985.

Schautschick, P., & Greenhalgh, C. (2016). Empirical studies of trade marks–the existing economic literature. *Economics of Innovation and New Technology*, 25(4), 358–390.

Part I

Bridging perspectives on trademarks and firms

Why and when do firms trademark? Bridging perspectives from industrial organisation, innovation and entrepreneurship

Carolina Castaldi ⓘ, Joern Block and Meindert J. Flikkema

ABSTRACT

This editorial to the special issue on "Trademarks and their role in innovation, entrepreneurship and industrial organization" proposes a novel framework to understand why and when firms file trademarks. The three perspectives at the core of the special issue offer several insights on trademark motives but have not been linked for understanding the underlying strategies and contingencies. We propose to study trademark motives in relation to the firm and the innovation life cycle stage. Inspired by the framework, we outline avenues for further research.

1. Introduction

Research on trademarks is gaining significant momentum[1]. According to Castaldi (2019), one of the challenges for further research is that we still miss a comprehensive theory of why firms choose to file trademarks and which contingencies explain specific strategies. At the same time, trademark research is growing within three distinct domains: industrial organisation (IO), innovation and entrepreneurship studies (see Table 1 for an overview).

The IO perspective is the oldest and has focused on the cost/benefit considerations behind the use of trademarks by firms (Economides 1988). Trademarks are information signals that can reduce transaction and search costs (Milgrom and Roberts 1986). Increasingly, trademarks have become 'signs above signs' (Ramello 2006). They allow firms to pursue differentiation strategies that translate into premium pricing, hence bring significant private returns to firms (Greenhalgh and Rogers 2012). As such, the IO perspective views firms as highly strategic in their decision to trademark. Trademarks allow securing market positions by avoiding imitation and deterring market entry (Lunney, 1999, Appelt 2009, Fosfuri and Giarratana 2009). Relatedly, a key motive for firms to file and maintain trademark portfolios is that they represent assets (Castaldi 2019), with a clear impact on firm market value and profitability (Schautschick and

---

[1]Another trademark-focused special issue on 'The Brand and its history: Part I: Trademarks and Branding' has appeared in 2018 in *Business History* (Saiz and Castro 2018) and one on 'Regions and Trademarks' is in the making at *Regional Studies*, edited by Carolina Castaldi and Sandro Mendonça.

Table 1. Overview of motives and contingencies discussed in the IO, innovation and entrepreneurship domains.

Perspectives	Why do firms trademark?	When? Contingencies, triggers
Industrial Organisation [focus is on strategic motives and securing market positions]	• To enable differentiation strategies and premium pricing • To safeguard market positions, by fighting imitation and erecting barriers to entry • To build valuable asset positions • To participate in markets for brands	• B2C markets with stronger differentiation levels more likely to have high trademark use • Large firms in specific sectors skilfully enacting IPR bundling/stacking to counteract patent and/or copyright expiration cliffs (pharma, media)
Innovation [focus is on appropriation strategies by innovative firms]	• To flag the market introduction of innovation • To secure the benefits from branding strategies for innovation in home markets and beyond. • To prolong other IP rights, predominantly patents. • To enable the franchising of innovative concepts.	• Before the market introduction of innovations to signal their market orientation to VCs (R&D stage) or to preview a new product or service. • After the market introduction of innovations: conditional on market success.
Entrepreneurship [focus is on resource attraction by young firms]	• Resource attraction through signalling to external stakeholders (e.g. entrepreneurial finance providers) • Other motives and explanations: marketing myopia, founder ambitions, IP subsidies for startups	• Depends to a strong degree on founder team composition • Existence of resource constraints • Role of VC ($\rightarrow$ professionalisation of the startup) • Innovativeness of the product

Greenhalgh 2016). Trademark assets often complement technological assets (Sandner and Block 2011, Grazzi, Piccardo, and Vergari 2019; Dosso and Vezzani 2017).

From an innovation perspective, filing a new trademark is a means for firms to announce the introduction of new products (Flikkema, de Man, and Castaldi 2014; Flikkema et al. 2019). Next to signalling, trademarks act as complementary specialised assets helping firms to appropriate the economic rents from innovation through compelling branding, distribution and franchising strategies (Teece 1986, Hoffman, Munemo, and Watson 2016). Trademarks are used both as complements to patents and instead of patents, for the 'protection' of incremental or new-to-the-firm innovation and of non-technological innovation, like service and organisational innovation (Mendonça, Pereira, and Godinho 2004).

More recently, the entrepreneurship perspective has focused on trademarking decisions in young and small firms. Trademarks filed by startups constitute a valuable signal to external stakeholders such as (potential) customers and investors. Startups, particularly in their early phases, do not have a track record of satisfied customers and successful products and are typically not known to the market. They may suffer from severe liabilities of newness (Gruber 2004) and hence may file a trademark as a way to signal their seriousness and professionalism towards external stakeholders (Block et al. 2015a). When it comes to investors, De Vries et al. (2017) found that VC involvement is an important driver of trademark filing and the building of brand assets (Forti, Munari, and Zhang 2019).

In this paper we argue that bridging the three perspectives and combining insights from IO, innovation and entrepreneurship research on trademarks can shape the contours of a theory on the motives behind trademarking and their underlying corporate practices. Hence our guiding question is the broad one of *why and when do firms trademark?* We propose that motives to trademark depend both on the phase in the *firm* and *innovation lifecycle*. These two dimensions allow connecting the insights from the three perspectives in an organic way. The papers collected in the special issue offer clues to define and test elements of this novel framework.

Our main contributions are three. First, we develop a framework linking different types of motives to trademark suggested by the three perspectives. Second, we complement existing reviews of trademark research which have focused on economic studies (Schautschick and Greenhalgh 2016) or on management studies only (Castaldi 2019) and present an interdisciplinary review focusing on the important question of why firms trademark. Third, we offer an interdisciplinary agenda for future trademark research from the perspectives of IO, innovation and entrepreneurship research. This agenda fits well with the aims and scope of *Industry and Innovation* which is an interdisciplinary journal and has developed into one of the premier outlets for trademark research.

2. A conceptual framework linking trademarking motives to firm and innovation lifecycle

To connect the different perspectives and offer a conceptual framework for further research, we discuss the motives to file trademarks according to where the firm and its products are located in the firm and innovation lifecycle. We thereby integrate trademark research from the three perspectives introduced above as well as the studies from this special issue. The entrepreneurship domain has of course focused mostly on the specific challenges of young firms, while the IO domain has looked at how trademarks are used by mature firms, often the incumbents in a given industry, to protect and exploit their respective market positions. The innovation domain can be placed at the intersection: innovation can either emerge in young entrepreneurial firms or in the more routinised settings of established firms.

2.1. Securing market positions as a motive (IO perspective)

A rational motive to file trademarks is that they bring significant private returns to firms (Schautschick and Greenhalgh 2016). de Rassenfosse (2019) in this special issue provides original evidence that trademarks bear value to firms by showing that the price elasticity for their demand is low: higher fees hardly dampen demand. The strategic motives of mature firms to trademark appear strongest in markets where competition is driven by product differentiation (WIPO 2013). Most often these are B2C markets (Reitzig 2004) and key examples include pharma, electronics and consumer goods. Service firms in markets characterised by strong information asymmetries, like financial, information and digital services, have also clear incentives to use trademarks, since trademarks secure the protection of important reputational assets (Castaldi and Giarratana 2018; Castaldi 2019).

Some mature firms cash in on trademark assets through licencing, so that participation in 'markets for brands' is emerging as an additional motive to file and maintain trademarks (Graham *et al.* 2013; Frey *et al.* 2015). Ferrucci et al. (2019) in this issue offer a first in-depth overview of the trademark licencing agreements officially registered at the USPTO (building on data from Graham, Marco, and Myers 2018). A first insight is that licencing volumes and properties differ significantly across markets, suggesting that market-level analysis is the most fruitful direction for a further understanding of the phenomenon. A second insight is that applicant firm size, a proxy for maturity, and trademark age appear related to the probability of a trademark being licenced. This suggests that mature firms are better able to judge the value of their trademark assets and that the valuation process is easier for established trademarks.

2.2. Appropriation of rents as a motive (innovation perspective)

The innovation perspective highlights how trademarks are used in appropriation strategies of innovative firms, particularly in the later phases of the innovation life cycle. In this special issue, the study of Llerena and Millot (2019) looks at the relation between trademarks and patents in appropriation strategy. They confirm empirically that the complementarity between trademarks and patents depends on market characteristics, particularly on advertising spillovers and depreciation rates. They show that in case of high advertising spillovers and low advertising depreciation rates, as a consequence of long life cycles of technologies, the complementarity is strongest. In line with their findings, Thoma (2019), also in this special issue, shows with USPTO data that an appropriation strategy that pairs patents and trademarks almost doubles patent value. Not all industries show this patent-trademark complementarity. Strictly, trademarks cannot substitute patents, since trademark law and patent law are inherently different. Yet, innovators sometimes use them as such, for reasons of limited financial resources or lifecycle characteristics of new technologies (Flikkema et al. 2019). In these cases, innovators often try to combine lead time advantage and trademark protection to build and maintain brand loyalty even when fast second movers enter the market soon.

Increasingly, companies skilfully combine trademarks with other intellectual property rights (Seip et al. 2019) and blend them with informal appropriation mechanisms (Miric, Boudreau, and Jeppesen 2019). Trademarks allow companies to prolong market dominance after patent expiry, in case of science or technology based markets (Reitzig 2004) and copyright expiry in case of creative industries (Calboli 2014). These strategies are almost exclusively leveraged by large, asset-intensive companies that can handle the legal complexities that come with them.

Interestingly, the ownership of trademarks might also play a role in the very early phase of the innovation lifecycle, in an indirect way. Bei (2019) shows that owning valuable trademarks correlates with the success of technology sourcing strategies and Sebrek (2019) finds a relation between the breadth of the trademark portfolios of firms and the geographic scope of their external search activities. At the same time, mature firms may only see the need for filing a trademark after the product has proven to be a success (Fink, Hall, and Helmers 2018). Dinlersoz et al. (2018) found that the propensity to file trademarks significantly increases with firm size, while there is only a significant relation with firm age in the first 10 to 15 years, depending on the sector. Their result seems to suggest that trademark filing is driven more by resources and stakes than by experience.

A final consideration is that firms might not trademark their innovation at all. Castaldi (2018) proposed that firms might have both myopic and rational motives not to trademark. Myopic motives include unawareness of the possibility and/or the benefits of trademark registration because of a lack of knowledge or resources. This is a well-known issue that affect SMEs and startups most strongly (Block et al. 2015a) and also can be found with the filing of other IP rights (de Rassenfosse and van Pottelsberghe de la

Potterie 2013). Athreye and Fassio (2019) in this special issue investigated a broad set of innovative firms and suggested how two factors explain the decision not to trademark. On the one hand, innovators might already have protected their positions in other ways and will not file for a separate trademark for a new innovation project. On the other hand, the collaborative nature of an innovation project can lead firms not to claim property of rights for fear of endangering goodwill in the collaboration.

2.3. Resource attraction as a motive (entrepreneurship perspective)

When it comes to trademarks, one insight is that startups tend to have stronger incentives to file trademarks earlier in the innovation lifecycle than mature firms (Seip et al. 2018). As startups suffer from liabilities of newness and smallness, they use trademarks as a means to attract resources. This motive to file trademarks relates to the signalling function of trademarks and targets different actors: VCs and other specialised investors in a very early phase for the case of innovative startups, all other investors in the R&D phase and customers and competitors in the commercialisation phase (Block et al. 2014, Zhou *et al.* 2016; De Vries et al. 2017). Block et al. (2014) showed that the number and breadth of trademark applications have a positive effect on VCs' valuations of startups. This positive valuation effect, however, seems to decrease when the startup progresses into a more advanced development stage (Block et al. 2014). The paper by Lyalkov et al. (2019) in this special issue confirms the notion that entrepreneurship activities at the country level are positively linked to trademarking. Although the motivation to trademark was not explicitly investigated in their study, some aspects of their results are in line with the signalling value of trademarks for startups. For example, they find that opportunity entrepreneurship relates positively to trademark registrations whereas no such effect was found for necessity entrepreneurship or entrepreneurship without employees, which are typically unambitious forms of entrepreneurship (Block et al. 2015b; Poschke 2013). deGrazia, Myers, and Toole (2019), also in this special issue, use aggregated data about trademark filings for product and service offerings and show that such data can help to predict business cycles. Whether these trademark filings are from established firms or from Schumpeterian-like innovative new firms remains a question of further research.

Table 1 summarises the trademarking motives and their contingencies; Table 2 aligns these motives in a firm and innovation lifecycle framework.

3. Conclusions

This editorial has connected three different trademark research streams into a comprehensive framework that both integrates existing studies (including the ones in the special issues) and guides further efforts. We wish to conclude by outlining specific directions for further research.

Both entrepreneurship and innovation studies have suggested a strong link between trademarks and innovation. In startups trademarks often mark the start of a business (De Vries et al. 2017). Research on trademarks in entrepreneurship has focused on the signalling function of trademarks to attract financial resources. Further research might go beyond this particular form of resource and broaden the scope towards non-financial resources that are needed to successfully build and grow a venture. For example, it would

Table 2. A conceptual framework linking firm and innovation lifecycle to the different trademarking motives (TM = trademarks).

		Innovation lifecycle		
		Idea phase	R&D phase	Commercialisation phase
Firm lifecycle	Young firm	TM not high priority due to lack of resources and little knowledge about TMs.;	TM filed as a signal to attract resources for funding R&D.	TM as a signal to attract resources for funding market entry; TM as a signal for attracting customers and flagging market introduction of new product; TM as a complementary asset to appropriate innovation rents; TM to differentiate own products from products by competitors and protect brand investments.
	Mature firm	New TM not necessarily needed; rational not to trademark as it is unclear how the product will fit to existing firm products; TM as specialised complementary assets driving technology sourcing.	TM not necessarily needed.	TM as a strategic tool to differentiate own products from products by competitors; TM as a complementary asset to appropriate innovation rents; TM as asset in markets for brands; TM to prolong protection after patent or copyright expiration. No TM if collaborative innovation or existing TM is available.

be interesting to learn how trademarks and their related brands help to attract co-founders and early employees (Coad, Nielsen, and Timmermans 2017), which are of crucial importance for high-growth firms. This question is of high practical importance as innovative startups compete fiercely with established firms on the labour market and typically are not able to offer as highly paid jobs as established firms do (Block, Fisch, and van Praag 2018; Burton, Dahl, and Sorenson 2018).

So far, we know little about the relatedness of trademarks to innovation in mature firms. For product and service innovation, micro-level studies that also encompass branding strategies, as Flikkema et al. (2019) propose, bear potential for establishing the trademark-innovation link. Aaker's (2007) 'Innovation, brand it or lose it' nearly speaks for itself. Studying branding strategies (for innovation) in depth may help to better understand when and why new trademarks are filed. Most empirical studies into the relatedness of trademarks and innovation pursued a cross-sectional approach and mea-sured the firm-level use of trademarks with dichotomies: 'yes' or 'no'. There is an evident need for case studies that try to match innovation portfolios and trademark portfolios at the firm-level, to understand trademark propensities for various types and modes of open and closed innovation (see also Zobel, Lokshin, and Hagedoorn 2017; Athreye and Fassio 2019; Morales et al. 2019).

While the motives for firms to trademark might be quite clear and strengthened by the evidence of substantial private returns (Schautschick and Greenhalgh 2016), it remains unclear whether the societal benefits of trademarks are as strong as the private ones. The early IO studies stressed how the higher prices that consumers pay for trademark-protected products are compensated by the decrease in search and transaction costs (Landes and Posner 1987) and/or the increase in availability of new products (Besen and Raskind 1991). Greenhalgh and Rogers (2012) showed that trademark activity positively correlated with dynamic competition confirming arguments from the innovation per-spective on motives to trademark. Other authors have been more critical and argued that trademarks might be associated with monopolistic practices with negative outcomes for consumers and society enlarge (Lunney 1999, Beebe and Hemphill 2017). Emerging evidence on practices that one could call 'strategic trademarking' also casts doubts on the welfare efficiency of current trademark systems. Large incumbent firms resort to 'sub-marine trademarks' (Fink et al. 2018) by filing trademarks at obscure trademark offices to avoid revealing their market strategies while being able to claim priority. Other practices are 'trademark cluttering', i.e. multiple trademark filing to claim priority without an intention to market (von Graevenitz 2013) and 'trademark squatting', i.e. filing of trademarks by someone other than the brand owner (Fink, Helmers, and Ponce 2018). All these strategic motives to trademark potentially endanger the informational value of trademarks and the very functioning of trademark systems. Research, both theoretical and empirical is dramatically lacking on these issues, hence the social returns of trade-marks represent an important avenue for further research.

Herein one promising line of research stemming from the entrepreneurship domain would be to assess the link between trademarks and impactful entrepreneurship: one would investigate not only whether trademarking is beneficial for the firms themselves but whether those new firms also create jobs or spur dynamic competition in markets. Detecting (high-impact) entrepreneurship in populations, regions and industries is however difficult as entrepreneurship as a concept is vague, elusive and sometimes ill-defined (Guzman and Stern 2015; Block, Fisch, and van Praag 2017; Henrekson and Sanandaji 2019). Trademark-based measures in combination with other firm measures could be a solution. A recent joint report of the European Patent Office (EPO) and the European Union Intellectual Property Office (EUIPO) finds, for example, that SMEs which have filed trademarks are significantly more likely to experience a growth period afterwards (EPO-EUIPO 2019). Two papers in this special issue (Lyalkov et al. 2019; deGrazia, Myers, and Toole 2019) show that macro-level trademark data can be used to predict aggregate level entrepreneurship. Whether this is Kirznerian, Schumpeterian or none of the two forms of entrepreneurship remains a question for further research. Most likely, the answer to this question will involve accounting for environmental conditions such as the appropriation and IPR regimes and the state of country development. Several opportunities for cross-industry and cross-country comparisons lie ahead. Our frame-work could be extended by taking into account the contingencies of specific industries and markets. Such extensions seem particularly useful in light of the policy questions around trademark practices and their effects on industrial dynamics and market competition.

Disclosure statement

No potential conflict of interest was reported by the authors.

ORCID

Carolina Castaldi http://orcid.org/0000-0001-5747-6788

References

Aaker, D. 2007. "Innovation: Brand It or Lose It." *California Management Review* 50 (1): 8–24. doi:10.2307/41166414.

Appelt, S. 2009. Early Entry and Trademark Protection: An Empirical Examination of Barriers to Generic Entry. Paper Presented at the DRUID Summer Conference 2009.

Athreye, S., and C. Fassio. 2019. "Why Do Innovators Not Apply for Trademarks? The Role of Information Asymmetries and Collaborative Innovation." *Industry and Innovation* 1–21. this issue. doi:10.1080/13662716.2019.1616533.

Beebe, B., and C. S. Hemphill. 2017. "The Scope of Strong Marks: Should Trademark Law Protect The Strong More than The Weak." *NYUL Rev.*, 92: 1339.

Bei, X. 2019. "Trademarks, Specialized Complementary Assets, and the External Sourcing of Innovation." *Research Policy* 48: 103709. doi:10.1016/j.respol.2018.11.003.

Besen, S. M., and L. J. Raskind. 1991. "An Introduction to the Law and Economics of Intellectual Property." *Journal of Economic Perspectives* 5 (1): 3–27. doi:10.1257/jep.5.1.3.

Block, J., C. Fisch, and M. van Praag. 2017. "The Schumpeterian Entrepreneur: A Review of the Empirical Evidence on the Antecedents, Behavior, and Consequences of Innovative Entrepreneurship." *Industry and Innovation* 24 (1): 61–95. doi:10.1080/13662716.2016.1216397.

Block, J., C. Fisch, and M. van Praag. 2018. "Quantity and Quality of Jobs by Entrepreneurial Firms." *Oxford Review of Economic Policy* 34 (4): 565–583. doi:10.1093/oxrep/gry016.

Block, J. H., C. O. Fisch, A. Hahn, and P. G. Sandner. 2015a. "Why Do SMEs File Trademarks? Insights from Firms in Innovative Industries." *Research Policy* 44 (10): 1915–1930. doi:10.1016/j.respol.2015.06.007.

Block, J. H., G. De Vries, J. H. Schumann, and P. Sandner. 2014. "Trademarks and Venture Capital Valuation." *Journal of Business Venturing* 29 (4): 525–542. doi:10.1016/j.jbusvent.2013.07.006.

Block, J. H., K. Kohn, D. Miller, and K. Ullrich. 2015b. "Necessity Entrepreneurship and Competitive Strategy." *Small Business Economics* 44 (1): 37–54. doi:10.1007/s11187-014-9589-x.

Burton, M. D., M. S. Dahl, O. Sorenson. 2018. "Do Start-s Pay Less?." *Industrial and Labor Relations Review* 17 (5): 1179–1200.

Calboli, I. 2014. "Overlapping rights: the negative effects of trademarking creative works." In *The Evolution and Equilibrium of Copyright in the Digital Age*, edited by S. Frankel and D. Gervais, Vol. 26, 52–78. Cambridge University Press.

Castaldi, C. 2018. "To Trademark or Not to Trademark: The Case of the Creative and Cultural Industries." *Research Policy* 47 (3): 606–616. doi:10.1016/j.respol.2018.01.006.

Castaldi, C. 2019. "All the Great Things You Can Do with Trademark Data: Taking Stock and Looking Ahead." *Strategic Organization.* doi:10.1177/1476127019847835.

Castaldi, C., and M. S. Giarratana. 2018. "Diversification, Branding, and Performance of Professional Service Firms." *Journal of Service Research* 21 (3): 353–364. doi:10.1177/1094670518755315.

Coad, A., K. Nielsen, and B. Timmermans. 2017. "My First Employee: An Empirical Investigation." *Small Business Economics* 48 (1): 25–45. doi:10.1007/s11187-016-9748-3.

de Rassenfosse, G. 2019. "On the Price Elasticity of Demand for Trademarks." *Industry and Innovation* 1–14. this special issue. doi:10.1080/13662716.2019.1591939.

de Rassenfosse, G., and B. van Pottelsberghe de la Potterie. 2013. "The Role of Fees in Patent Systems: Theory and Evidence." *Journal of Economic Surveys* 27 (4): 696–716. doi:10.1111/joes.2013.27.issue-4.

De Vries, G., E. Pennings, J. H. Block, and C. Fisch. 2017. "Trademark or Patent? The Effects of Market Concentration, Customer Type and Venture Capital Financing on Start-ups' Initial IP Applications." *Industry and Innovation* 24 (4): 325–345. doi:10.1080/13662716.2016.1231607.

deGrazia, C. A., A. Myers, and A. A. Toole. 2019. "Innovation Activities and Business Cycles: Are Trademarks a Leading Indicator?" *Industry and Innovation* 1–20. this special issue. doi:10.1080/13662716.2019.1650252.

Dinlersoz, E. M., N. Goldschlag, A. Myers, and N. Zolas. 2018. *"An Anatomy of US Firms Seeking Trademark Registration."* (No. w25038). National Bureau of Economic Research.

Dosso, M., and A. Vezzani. 2017. "Firm Market Valuation and Intellectual Property Assets." JRC Working Papers on Corporate R&D and Innovation 2017-07.

Economides. 1988. "The Economics of Trademarks." *Trademark Reporter* 78: 523–539.

EPO-EUIPO. 2019. "High-growth Firms and Intellectual Property Rights: IPR Profile of High-potential SMEs in Europe." May 2019. http://documents.epo.org/projects/babylon/eponet. nsf/0/F59459A1E64B62F3C12583FC002FBD93/$FILE/high_growth_firms_study_en.pdf

Ferrucci, E., M. I. Leone, M. Romagnoli, and A. Toros. 2019. "From a Distinctive Sign to an Exchangeable Asset: Exploring the U.S. Market for Trademark Licensing." *Industry and Innovation.* doi:10.1080/13662716.2019.1661225.

Fink, C., A. Fosfuri, C. Helmers, and A. F. Myers. 2018. *Submarine Trademarks.* Geneva: working paper nr 51.

Fink, C., B. H. Hall, and C. Helmers. 2018. "*Intellectual Property Use in Middle Income Countries: The Case of Chile.*" (No. w24348). National Bureau of Economic Research.

Fink, C., C. Helmers, and C. J. Ponce. 2018. "Trademark Squatters: Theory and Evidence from Chile." *International Journal of Industrial Organization* 59: 340–371. doi:10.1016/j. ijindorg.2018.04.004.

Flikkema, M. J., A. P. de Man, and C. Castaldi. 2014. "Are Trademark Counts a Valid Indicator of Innovation? Results of an In-depth Study of New Benelux Trademarks Filed by SMEs." *Industry and Innovation* 21 (4): 310–331. doi:10.1080/13662716.2014.934547.

Flikkema, M. J., C. Castaldi, A. P. de Man, and M. Seip. 2019. "Trademarks' Relatedness to Product and Service Innovation: A Branding Strategy Approach." *Research Policy* 48 (6): 1340–1353. doi:10.1016/j.respol.2019.01.018.

Forti, E., F. Munari, and C. Zhang. 2019. "Does VC Backing Affect Brand Strategy in Technology Ventures?" *Strategic Entrepreneurship Journal,* no. forthcoming. doi:10.1002/sej.1318.

Fosfuri, A., and M. S. Giarratana. 2009. "Masters of War: Rivals' Product Innovation and New Advertising in Mature Product Markets." *Management Science* 55 (2): 181–191. doi:10.1287/ mnsc.1080.0939.

Frey, C. B., A. Ansar, S. Wunsch-Vincent. 2015. "Defining and Measuring the "Market for Brands": Are Emerging Economies Catching Up?." *The Journal of World Intellectual Property* 18 (5): 217–244.

Graham, S. J., A. C. Marco, and A. F. Myers. 2018. "Monetizing Marks: Insights from the USPTO Trademark Assignment Dataset." *Journal of Economics & Management Strategy* 27 (3): 403–432. doi:10.1111/jems.12261.

Graham, S. J., G. Hancock, A. C. Marco, and A. F. Myers. 2013. "The USPTO Trademark Case Files Dataset: Descriptions, Lessons, and Insights." *Journal of Economics & Management Strategy* 22 (4): 669–705. doi:10.1111/jems.12035.

Grazzi, M., C. Piccardo, and C. Vergari. 2019. *Concordance and Complementarity in IP Instruments.* Milan, Italy: Università Cattolica del Sacro Cuore, Dipartimenti e Istituti di Scienze Economiche (DISCE) Working paper dipe0003.

Greenhalgh, C., and M. Rogers. 2012. "Trade Marks and Performance in Services and Manufacturing Firms: Evidence of Schumpeterian Competition through Innovation." *The Australian Economic Review* 45 (1): 50–76. doi:10.1111/j.1467-8462.2011.00665.x.

Gruber, M. 2004. "Marketing in New Ventures: Theory and Empirical Evidence." *Schmalenbach Business Review* 56 (2): 164–199. doi:10.1007/BF03396691.

Guzman, J., and S. Stern. 2015. "Where Is Silicon Valley?." *Science* 347 (6222): 606–609.

Henrekson, M., and T. Sanandaji. 2019. "Measuring Entrepreneurship: Do Established Metrics Capture High-Impact Schumpeterian Entrepreneurship?" *Entrepreneurship Theory and Practice, Forthcoming* 104225871984450. doi:10.1177/1042258719844500.

Hoffman, R. C., J. Munemo, and S. Watson. 2016. "International Franchise Expansion: The Role of Institutions and Transaction Costs." *Journal of International Management* 22 (2): 101–114. doi:10.1016/j.intman.2016.01.003.

Landes, W. M., and R. Posner. 1987. "Trademark Law: An Economic Perspective." *Journal of Law and Economics* 30: 265. doi:10.1086/467138.

Llerena and Millot. 2019. "Two Better than One?: Modelling the Complementary or Substitute Relationship between Patents and Trademarks." *Industry and Innovation.* doi:10.1080/13662716.2019.1688137.

Lunney Jr, G. S. 1999. "Trademark Monopolies." *Emory LJ* 48: 367.

Lyalkov, S., M. Carmona, E. Congregado, A. Millán, and J. M. Millán. 2019. "Trademarks and Their Association with Kirznerian Entrepreneurs." *Industry and Innovation* this special issue. doi:10.1080/13662716.2019.1586523.

Mendonça, S., T. S. Pereira, and M. M. Godinho. 2004. "Trademarks as an Indicator of Innovation and Industrial Change." *Research Policy* 33 (9): 1385–1404. doi:10.1016/j.respol.2004.09.005.

Milgrom, P., and J. Roberts. 1986. "Relying on the Information Of Interested Parties." *The RAND Journal of Economics* 18–32.

Miric, M., K. J. Boudreau, and L. B. Jeppesen. 2019. "Protecting Their Digital Assets: The Use of Formal & Informal Appropriability Strategies by App Developers." *Research Policy* 48 (forthcoming): 103738. doi:10.1016/j.respol.2019.01.012.

Morales, P., M. J. Flikkema, C. Castaldi, and A. P. de Man. 2019. "The Propensity to Trademark Innovation." *Academy of Management Proceedings* 2019. doi:10.5465/AMBPP.2019.12393abstract.

Poschke, M. 2013. "Entrepreneurs Out of Necessity: A Snapshot." *Applied Economics Letters* 20 (7): 658–663. doi:10.1080/13504851.2012.727968.

Ramello, G. B. 2006. "What's in a Sign? Trademark Law and Economic Theory." *Journal of Economic Surveys* 20 (4): 547–565. doi:10.1111/joes.2006.20.issue-4.

Reitzig, M. 2004. "Strategic Management of Intellectual Property." *MIT Sloan Management Review* 45 (3): 35–40.

Saiz, P., and R. Castro. 2018. "Trademarks in Branding: Legal Issues and Commercial Practices." *Business History* 60: 1105–1126. doi:10.1080/00076791.2018.1497765.

Sandner, P. G., and J. Block. 2011. "The Market Value of R&D, Patents, and Trademarks." *Research Policy* 40 (7): 969–985. doi:10.1016/j.respol.2011.04.004.

Schautschick, P., and C. Greenhalgh. 2016. "Empirical Studies of Trade Marks–The Existing Economic Literature." *Economics of Innovation and New Technology* 25 (4): 358–390. doi:10.1080/10438599.2015.1064598.

Sebrek, S. S. 2019. "Overlap in External Technology Search Locations and the Breadth of IPR Assets: Lessons from the Security Software Industry." *Industry and Innovation* 1–29. doi:10.1080/13662716.2019.1588710.

Seip, M., C. Castaldi, M. J. Flikkema, and A. P. de Man. 2019. "A Taxonomy of Firm-Level IPR Application Practices to Inform Policy Debates." LEM working paper, Sant'Anna School of Advanced Studies, Pisa.

Seip, M., C. Castaldi, M. J. Flikkema, and A. P. De Man. 2018. "The Timing of Trademark Application in Innovation Processes." *Technovation* 72: 34–45. doi:10.1016/j.technovation.2018.02.001.

Teece, D. J. 1986. "Profiting from Technological Innovation: Implications for Integration, Collaboration, Licensing and Public Policy." *Research Policy* 15 (6): 285–305.

Thoma, G. 2019. "The Valuation of Patent-trademark Pairing as IP Strategy: Evidence from the USPTO." *Industry and Innovation* 1–25. this special issue. doi:10.1080/13662716.2019.1633281.

von Graevenitz, G. 2013. "Trade Mark Cluttering–Evidence from EU Enlargement." *Oxford Economic Papers* 65 (3): 721–745. doi:10.1093/oep/gpt022.

WIPO. 2013. *Brands – reputation and image in the global marketplace.* Geneva: World intellectual property organization.

Zhou, H., P. G. Sandner, S. L. Martinelli, J. H. Block. 2016. "Patents, Trademarks, and their Complementarity in Venture Capital Funding." *Technovation* 47: 14–22.

Zobel, A. K., B. Lokshin, and J. Hagedoorn. 2017. "Formal and Informal Appropriation Mechanisms: The Role of Openness and Innovativeness." *Technovation* 59: 44–54. doi:10.1016/j.technovation.2016.10.001.

Which firms use trademarks? Firm-level evidence from Germany on the role of distance, product quality and innovation

Dirk Crass

ABSTRACT

Trademarking firms are more productive, generate higher profits, and have a better survival rate. Trademarking firms are in one word more successful, which might motivate non-trademarking firms to adopt a trademark strategy. But this does not seem to be the case. The proportion of trademarking firms in the German business sector amounts to just 18%. This figure is quite low, given that nearly each firm has reputation to protect. But why does the vast majority of firms not have registered trademarks? Using a representative sample of German firms, the present paper links certain firm characteristics to a firm's propensity to register trademarks. The empirical results point to circumstances under which trademarks are significantly more often used: this is the case where a large distance between a firm and its customers exists, a firm's product quality is difficult to assess, a firm's products are characterised by a limited (but not strong) substitutability, and where a firm is engaged in R&D and introduces innovative products. Trademarks are considerably less frequently used if none of this is the case.

1. Introduction

Brands and trademarks have a ubiquitous presence throughout the economy and in our everyday life. This has its advantages. They enable us to identify and memorise products, to determine their origin, and to distinguish products of different providers from each other. The identifiability of a product is an essential requirement for customers to draw on previous experiences with a product while making purchasing decisions. The experiences with a product, even those of others, may prove useful to assess otherwise unobservable product characteristics. Positive experiences are likely to lead to repeated purchases, while disappointed customers are more likely to avoid the product. This constitutes an incentive for firms to build a reputation to deliver products and services of a reliable quality, leading to the quality guarantee, implicitly indicated by trademarks. In turn, producers are able to differentiate their products against those of competitors and to establish brand reputation, leading, at best, to brand loyalty.

A brand is of economic value only if the respective firm has the right to use this reputational asset exclusively. In Germany, as in most European countries, the protection of marks might arise due to use of a sign in trade (§4(2) German Trademark Law). Protection is awarded if the mark is used intensively in commerce and a significant proportion of the relevant public has knowledge of the mark. A formal registration does not take place; trademarks acquired by use are therefore not observable by the researcher. There are good reasons for firms not to rely solely on the protection acquired by use and to choose an official registration: A trademark is protected once it is registered[1]; knowledge of the relevant public is not necessary. The scope of protection includes the selected product as well as service classes and applies to the whole territory of Germany; protection is not limited to the region in which the relevant public has knowledge of the mark. Registration takes place at reasonable cost: the registration fee at the German trade mark office (DPMA) amounts to 290 Euro and at the European Union Intellectual Property Office (EUIPO) to 900 Euro, possibly augmented by attorneys fees.

The registration of a brand as a trademark or through a bundle of trademarks protects the reputation of a brand. The registration defines the firm's rights against counterfeiting and fraud. The owner of this right is given a legal monopoly over the protected word, sign, symbol or other graphical representation in connection with the attached commodity. It has the exclusive right to commercially use the protected trademark and is exclusively protected against infringement (Economides 1998; Baroncelli, Fink, and Javorcik 2004). The protection from misuse does not happen automatically; the trademarking firm has to proactively police for trademark violations and enforce its rights against infringement. Internationally well-known and thus valuable brands are particularly affected (Fink, Helmers, and Ponce 2018). Von Graevenitz (2007) emphasises that trademark owners need the 'reputation of being tough on imitators'.

Empirical studies show positive associations between the use of registered trademarks and firm success. A trademarking firm exhibits on average a higher productivity (Greenhalgh and Longland 2005; Greenhalgh and Rogers 2012; Crass and Peters 2014), is more profitable (Ailawadi, Neslin, and Lehmann 2003; Griffiths, Jensen, and Webster 2011; Crass, Czarnitzki, and Toole 2019), yields higher market valuation (Bosworth and Rogers 2001; Krasnikov, Mishra, and Orozco 2009; Sandner and Block 2011; Greenhalgh and Rogers 2012), and has a better propensity to survive in the market (Jensen, Webster, and Buddelmeyer 2008; Buddelmeyer, Jensen, and Webster 2010; Helmers and Rogers 2010). Schautschick and Greenhalgh (2016) provide a detailed overview.

The empirical studies provide evidence of a positive contribution of trademarking to firm performance. This implies that a non-trademarking firm could benefit from adopting a trademark strategy. Hall et al. (2014) expect trademarks to be 'the most widely used' intellectual property right that is "available to essentially any firm". Graham et al. (2013) state that 'almost every firm, regardless of size, market, or business strategy, has goodwill to protect'. From this perspective, perhaps not every firm but the vast majority of firms can be expected to register trademarks. But contrary to expectations, why does a vast majority of firms not register trademarks at all? In Germany, the majority of firms do not register trademarks and just 18% of the firms are trademarking firms.

---

[1] The term *trademark* refers to the legal right that belongs to the wider family of intellectual property rights.

The group of trademarking firms seems to be special – or to be more precise, the group of firms registering trademarks. Flikkema, De Man, and Castaldi (2014) provide a compelling overview over the different motives for firms to register trademarks: increasing the distinctiveness of products, signalling important changes, appropriate the rents from innovation, build brand equity and hence customer loyalty, and gain a competitive advantage. For some firms trademarks are not indispensable. Athreye and Fassio (2020) study motives for innovators not to trademark such as the non-existing danger of infringement, the unsuitability of trademarks for specific innovations or just alternative distribution channels.

The empirical literature has stressed that larger firms use trademarks more frequently and that the proportion of trademarking firms is highest for manufacturing and especially for high-tech manufacturing firms (Greenhalgh et al. 2011; Millot 2011; Crass and Peters 2014). Dinlersoz et al. (2018) present a firm-trademark linked dataset that allows for the tracking of trademark filing activity over the life-cycle of a firm in the US. They find that first-time trademark filing is concentrated in young and relatively large firms and confirm empirical evidence that the likelihood of a trademark filing increases with firm size.

But are there any other reasons as to why relatively few firms register trademarks? Do certain firm characteristics make a company unsuitable for adopting a trademark strategy?

The purpose of this study is to describe relevant circumstances under which trademarks might be powerful instruments for a firm and to shed more light on firm and product characteristics that influence a firm's decision to trademark.

The empirical analysis relies on 5,335 firm-level observations from the 2011 survey of the Mannheim Innovation Panel (MIP). The 2011 survey provides information on each firm's trademark activity, its branding policy, as well as its competitive environment. The stratified random sample also allows for extrapolations to the total of German firms with at least five employees in the business sector. The data confirms large heterogeneity by size. While 73.9% of large firms with 1,000 employees and more, rely on trademarks, it turns out that the proportion of small firms with 5 to 49 employees is quite low at about 13.6%. As already mentioned, the extrapolated proportion of trademarking firms amounts to 17.8%.

The existing literature is extended in the following ways: Firstly, using a representative sample of German firms, the study provides extrapolated figures about the use of trademarks for the German business sector in total as well as for single industries. Secondly, it provides large-scale empirical evidence on the drivers of trademark decisions. Results show that firms use trademarks to overcome the distance to their customers, make product quality more assessable, differentiate their products against a limited (not large) number of competitors, and that especially R&D activities and product innovations induce the registration of trademarks.

2. The role of trademarks

2.1. The reputation of trademarks

A trademark is a sign which is designed to distinguish the firm's product(s) from those of its competitors. It is intended to identify the origin of a product, but the information content of the actual sign is quite restricted – unless it is charged with meaning. Economides (1998) highlights that a meaningful and thereby valuable trademark 'will be created with its identification with the product.' The identification can be accomplished in several ways. Borden (1944) argued that consumers associate the product with a trademark through recommendation, through use, or through advertisement. The association with a trademark makes former experiences with the product recognisable; own experiences, or even those of other people, can be assigned to the trademark to assess a product's quality.

2.1.1. Distance to customers

Trademarks are certainly not a recent invention. Moore and Reid (2008) emphasise that trademarks 'have existed for as long as it has been possible to trace artefacts of human existence.' But they underline, that trademarks have become 'more complex through time'. Borden (1944) described the point at which trademarks, which served (just) as a guarantee of origin, reached the next level of complexity and became a valuable asset for a company: He stresses the relevance of a 'close contact' between 'the maker and the buyer'. Their 'close contact', in an environment where everyone knows each other, provides a basis for a (often long-standing) personal relationship. The 'maker' is able to build a reputation in the course of the relationship and 'the buyer' in turn is enabled to assess the quality of the goods and services. The reputation of the 'maker' might not guarantee the best quality of the goods and services for 'the buyer' – but it limits the degree of uncertainty about the product. Borden (1944) dated the loss of a 'close contact' to the Middle Ages, where goods were traded over long distances. Trademarks took the place of the crucial personal relationship and became more and more 'guides of quality to buyers'.

The times when people ('the maker and the buyer') knew each other, which Borden (1944) referred to as village economy, are gone; though not completely. Many firms offer their goods and services solely in the immediate vicinity of where the company is located. This is often true in the case of handicraft businesses, law firms, or restaurants. These firms are able to maintain long standing customer relationships – even in our highly specialised economy. The personal relationship is here of primary importance and trademarks play only a subordinate role.

Geographical proximity of 'the maker and the buyer' might not be the only way to establish a personal relationship. A firm might be able to maintain very close contacts with its customers for example through regular meetings and client visits. The larger the distance that separates a firm from its customers, the larger the costs to overcome the distance. The costs of labour and travel-related expenses limit the number of customers with which a 'close contact' is worthwhile. Overall, this leads to the expectation that trademarks are of minor importance for regional providers and firms with comparatively few customers.

2.1.2. Product quality and the role of trademarks

Consumers do not often possess full knowledge of the quality characteristics of the products and services offered. Imperfectly informed customers are not able to price at the moment of the purchase unobservable quality features. Consumers would, consequently, not pay for unobservable and from their perspective at best uncertain quality features. For the maker of the product, however, these features are costly. It would not be profitable for a firm 'to incur higher costs for unobservable quality improvements if these could not be signalled to the prospective buyers to justify a higher sales price' (Baroncelli, Fink, and Javorcik 2004). Unobservable quality improvements would be crowded out from the market.

A trademark is an instrument designed to avoid this kind of market failure induced by information asymmetries. Akerlof (1970) refers already to trademarks as 'an institution which counteracts the effects of quality uncertainty'. A trademarked product is identifiable and recognisable so that customers are able to rely on former consumption experiences. After experiencing a product, they are better able to assess "how functional or effective the product is; how reliable it is; how long it lasts; how easy it is to use; how it tastes, sounds or smells; and what side effects it may have" (WIPO 2013, p.81). Especially the quality of services is difficult to assess without experiencing the service. The lack of any tangible attributes increases the uncertainty of consumers. A brand with its attached meaning acts here as a decision anchor (Castaldi and Giarratana 2018).

The information role of trademarks allows firms to build reputation for reliability and a certain consistent quality (Economides 1998; Landes and Posner 1987). The consistent quality is not to be confused with high quality. The reputation of the trademark of McDonalds illustrates the difference. While the worldwide operating fast food restaurants are not known for being gourmet restaurants, the trademark has the reputation to deliver a consistent quality everywhere in the world. A consumer can rely on her former culinary experience. She knows exactly what she will get and how the burger will taste. This leads to the expectation that trademarks are especially useful if the characteristics of a product are not directly observable.

2.1.3. Product substitutability

Identical products from different companies can generally be easily substituted. The more the products differ, the less substitutable they become. Otherwise identical products become less substitutable, for instance, if they are not available at the same location. This is due to transport costs and delivery times. Switching from one supplier to another can also cause additional costs. Physical product differentiation as well as differences in services bundled with products corresponds to individual consumer preferences. These real or perceived differences can also reduce substitutability.

Branding and advertising are one of the most effective instruments to establish lasting customer loyalty. Consumers might perceive physically substitutable products as being less interchangeable. Brands are legally protected by trademarks and incorporate durable symbols, words, and signs that consumers are likely to remember and help to avoid confusion among customers. Srinivasan, Hsu, and Fournier (2011) called the unique and memorable aspects of a brand the symbol system that firms use as the public face of the brand. The symbol system enables customers to identify the goods and services they prefer – for whatever reasons. A strong regime of brand-identification trademarks positively affects consumers preferences (Krasnikov, Mishra, and Orozco 2009). Apart from the quality information, brands convey also an image of the product. Sáiz and Fernández (2009) point out that 'the intangible prestige of brands is often much more difficult to imitate than the technological information contained in patents.' Over time a trademark can develop qualities that exist above and beyond the objective product or service such as customer awareness, perception of desirable overall quality, and favourable associations (Keller and Lehmann 2006). The development of a trademark takes time, but once a brand becomes familiar, people will select those products or services over an unknown brand (Aaker 1991).

The more this effect increases brand loyalty, the more effective the product differentiation strategy, which is likely to result in a weaker price competition. Especially firms with products that are easily substitutable would benefit from a high degree of product differentiation, since this could lead to a less elastic demand (Bagwell 2007).

2.2. The link between innovation and trademarks

New trademarks are correlated with the introduction of new product innovations, which qualifies trademarks as proxies for innovation (Schmoch 2003; Mendonca, Pereira, and Godinho 2004; Jensen and Webster 2009; Gotsch and Hipp 2014; Flikkema, De Man, and Castaldi 2014). But what causes this correlation?

The first explanation is a timing argument: A new product might come with a new name, perhaps a new logo. As part of the preparations for the market introduction, the new signs are registered as a trademark. The immediate registration is not compelling, but advisable: the desired sign might be in conflict with already registered ones and later changes of the sign can become expensive. The sign belonging to the new product is immediately protected as registered trademark. The achieved protection acts against imitations of new products and services from competitors. At least for the knowledge-intensive business services industries, the protection against competitors is the primary reason for registering a new trademark (Gotsch and Hipp 2014).

Once customers associate the trademark with the product, it becomes much more difficult for competitors to imitate the product. In this way, a trademark registration enhances a firm's ability to appropriate the economic returns of an innovation (Mendonca, Pereira, and Godinho 2004). In this respect, trademarks might be complementary or even substitutable to patents (Llerena and Millot 2013; Amara, Landry, and Traoré 2008). The resulting coincidence in time of trademark registration and market introduction qualifies trademark applications as proxy for innovations (Greenhalgh and Rogers 2012). The correlation between trademarks and product innovation may also be explained by the information argument. The introduction of a product innovation is per definition the introduction of a good or service that is 'new' for a firm's customers. Potential customers have no experience with the new product to judge the product quality against former purchases. Is the new product sold under a trademark, the reputation of the trademark might balance out a consumer's lack of experience with the new product. In this sense, trademarks have the potential to reduce uncertainty about the quality of product innovations. This might be especially relevant for product innovations to explain why innovative firms pursue more often a trademark strategy.

An alternative explanation for the correlation between trademarks and innovation reverses the direction of causality: The reputation for a brand encourages a firm to improve the quality of its products (Ramello 2006; Greenhalgh and Rogers 2012). In this case, trademarks might serve as a proxy for innovation.

This implies that innovative firms can be expected to use trademarks more frequently.

3. Empirical implementation

3.1. Data sets

Firm-level data is obtained from the 2011 survey of the Mannheim Innovation Panel (MIP), which is a stratified random sample (stratified by sector, size and region) of German firms. The MIP is the German contribution to the European-wide harmonised Community Innovation Surveys (CIS). It is based on the concepts and definitions of the Oslo Manual (2005) for collecting data on innovation processes. It targets legally independent firms with at least five employees. The MIP sample is disproportionally drawn. Higher drawing probabilities are applied to larger size classes, cells from Eastern Germany and cells with a high variation of innovation activities. For a more detailed description of the dataset, the survey, and the methodology in general, see Peters and Rammer (2013) as well as Aschhoff et al. (2013) for the 2011 survey.

The MIP, started in 1993, is conducted annually. Though it is designed as a panel, the 2011 survey is the only wave which includes information on the distance between firms and customers, product quality, and product substitutability. The 2011 questionnaires had been returned by nearly 7,000 firms in manufacturing and services, which constituted a 20% response rate. The firms provide information on their innovation activities and general firm information such as sales, employment, exports, and other major control variables. Surveyed MIP firms have been linked with information on firm's trademark activity at the German Patent and Trademark Office (DPMA) and at the European Union Intellectual Property Office (EUIPO).[2]

3.2. Trademarking firms

There are three options for a firm to obtain trademark protection in Germany through registration: Firms can choose between a registration of a national (German) trademark at the German Patent and Trademark Office (DPMA), the registration of a European Community Trademark at the European Union Intellectual Property Office (EUIPO), or the registration of an International Trademark at the Bureau of the World Intellectual Property Organisation (WIPO). A trademark registration at all three offices has the same protective effect for Germany; a Community trademark or an International Trademark completely replaces the need for a German Trademark – and vice versa (with respect to the territory of Germany). At all offices, the initial term of trademark protection is 10 years and can be indefinitely renewed for further 10-year periods. International Trademarks are not explicitly considered in the empirical analysis, which should not affect the results: An international registration must be based on a registration of the same mark in one of the member states of the Madrid Agreement for the International Registration of Marks. For the sample of German firms in question, an International Trademark is almost certainly based on a Community Trademark or a (national) German Trademark.

---

[2]Firm-specific trademark information were collected by matching the name of the firms participating in the innovation survey with the names of applicants at the EUIPO and the DPMA using a special software developed at ZEW, and including an extensive manual double-check.

The aim of this paper is to explain the firm's trademarking status, regardless of the trademark office chosen. The binary dependent variable *trademarks* indicates whether a firm has at least one valid trademark in 2010. A trademark is considered as valid, if it has been registered at either trademark office and if its protection period has not expired. This is the case for 31% of the firms in the sample (Table 2).

The sample is, as already pointed out, disproportionally drawn. Firm responses and information from the trademark register are weighted to represent the total firm population covered by the Mannheim Innovation Panel (MIP). Disproportional sampling by sector, size class and region as well as differences in response rates are taken into account. Table 1 provides the extrapolated absolute number and the proportion of trademarking firms by sector and size classes.

A total of roughly 48,000 firms with more than five employees in the German business sector have at least one valid trademark in 2010. This corresponds to a proportion of 17.8% of the total firm population surveyed. This figure would probably be considerably smaller if the high number of very small firms with less than five employees were also included. The proportion of trademarking firms in the US, including also very small firms, amounts to roughly five percent (Dinlersoz et al. 2018).

Table 1. Absolute number and proportion of trademarking firms in Germany.

Sector	WZ 2008	Trademarking Firms	
		absolute	in %
Food/Beverage/Tobacco	10–12	1,793	10.1
Textile/Clothes/Leather	13–15	767	32.0
Wood/Paper	16–17	644	13.6
Chemicals/Pharmaceuticals	20–21	1,368	57.1
Rubber-/Plastics products	22	1,475	30.3
Glass/Clay/Stone	23	869	24.2
Metal	24–25	3,250	15.6
Electronics	26–27	2,750	36.2
Machinery	28	3,562	34.8
Motor vehicles	29–30	855	38.4
Furnit./Toys/Medick. instr./Repair	31–33	2,393	16.6
Energy/Mining/Petroleum	5–9, 19, 35	607	22.6
Water/Waste disposal/Recycling	36–39	322	7.2
Wholesale	46	7,483	19.6
Transportation/Postal services	49–53, 79	1,865	6.0
Media services	18, 58–60	2,191	26.5
IT/Telecommunication	61–63	4,996	37.9
Financial services	64–66	1,432	20.7
Technical/R&D services	71–72	2,205	13.6
Consultancy/Advertising	69, 70.2, 73	3,470	11.1
Corporate services	74, 78, 80–82	3,663	14.1
Research-intensive manufacturing	20–21, 26–30	8,535	38.0
Other manufacturing	5–19, 22–25, 31–39	12,512	15.7
Knowledge-intensive services	58–66, 69, 70.2, 73	13,902	19.4
Other services	46, 49–53, 74, 78–82	13,011	13.6
Size Class (# employees)		31,247	13.6
50–249		12,272	38.8
250–999		3,457	58.8
1000 and more		984	73.9
Total		**47,960**	**17.8**

Firms in Germany having at least 5 employees in German Classification of Economic Activities, 2008 edition (WZ 2008) 5–39, 46, 49–53, 58–66, 69–74 (not 70.1), 78–82. All figures are extrapolated to the total firm population in Germany.
Source: ZEW: Mannheim Innovation Panel, survey 2011.

Table 2. Descriptive statistics of main variables (not weighted).

| | (1) | | (2) | | (3) | |
| | Full Sample | | TM-Firms | | Difference | |
	Mean	SE	Mean	SE	Diff	SE
Trademark Activity						
Trademarks (D)	0.31	(0.01)	1.00	(0.01)	1.00	(0.00)
Personal Distance						
Few Customers (D)	0.15	(0.00)	0.10	(0.00)	−0.07***	(0.01)
Many Customers (D)	0.45	(0.01)	0.51	(0.01)	0.09***	(0.01)
Geographical Distance						
Regional Market (D)	0.63	(0.01)	0.52	(0.01)	−0.16***	(0.01)
National Market (D)	0.71	(0.01)	0.88	(0.01)	0.24***	(0.01)
International Market (D)	0.47	(0.01)	0.71	(0.01)	0.35***	(0.01)
Product Quality						
Quality Assessable (D)	0.22	(0.01)	0.21	(0.01)	−0.02	(0.01)
Substitutability						
Products Substitutable (D)	0.21	(0.01)	0.16	(0.01)	−0.07***	(0.01)
Few Competitors (D)	0.42	(0.01)	0.47	(0.01)	0.07***	(0.01)
Many Competitors (D)	0.19	(0.01)	0.12	(0.01)	−0.10***	(0.01)
Innovation						
Continuous R&D (D)	0.22	(0.01)	0.40	(0.01)	0.27***	(0.01)
EPO Patent (D)	0.12	(0.00)	0.30	(0.00)	0.26***	(0.01)
Process Innovation (D)	0.32	(0.01)	0.44	(0.01)	0.16***	(0.01)
Product Innovation (D)	0.44	(0.01)	0.65	(0.01)	0.30***	(0.01)
Basic Characteristics						
Firm Size (# of employees)	203.15	(21.07)	457.59	(21.07)	370.40***	(29.27)
Group (D)	0.29	(0.01)	0.44	(0.01)	0.22***	(0.01)
East Germany (D)	0.32	(0.01)	0.23	(0.01)	−0.13***	(0.01)
Firm Age (in years)	32.96	(0.50)	37.50	(0.50)	6.61***	(1.05)

The first column provides mean and standard error of the main variables for the full sample, the second column for the subsample of trademarking firms, and the third column provides the difference between trademarking and non-trademarking firms. D indicates a dummy variable.
Source: ZEW: Mannheim Innovation Panel, survey 2011.

Trademarks are used by firms in all sectors. The proportion of trademarking firms differs considerably between the various sectors, ranging from 6% to 57%; less between manufacturing (20.6%) and service industries (16.1%). Sectors with high absolute numbers of trademarking firms are wholesale, IT and telecommunication, corporate services, machinery, consultancy and advertising, and metal. The highest share of trademarking firms can be found in the chemicals and pharmaceutical sector (57.1% of all firms), followed by motor vehicles (38.4%), IT and telecommunication (37.9%), electronics (36.2%), and machinery (34.8%). The lowest share of trademarking firms can be seen in transportation and postal services (6%), water, waste disposal, and recycling (7.2%), and food, beverage, and tobacco (10.1%). The largest proportion of firms using trademarks is research-intensive manufacturing (38%). The proportion of trademarking firms is much smaller in knowledge-intensive services (19.4%), other manufacturing (15.7%), and other services (13.6%). The extrapolated figures also suggest that there is a link between *firm size* (measured by the number of employees in 2010) and a firm's tendency to trademark. The larger a firm the more likely its tendency to register trademarks. A break down by size classes illustrates this relationship: The proportion of trademarking firms is quite low for small firms (less than 50 employees) making up 13.6% of the total figure. The proportion rises already to 38.8% for medium-sized firms (50–249 employees) and to 58.8% for large firms (250–999 employees). The proportion of trademarking firms increases up to 73.9% for very large firms (1000 and more employees).

3.3. Explanatory variables

Based on the expectations developed above, four broad categories of explanatory variables are of special interest in the empirical analyses: distance to customers, product quality, product substitutability, and a firm's innovation activity. They will be explained in the following subsections together with basic firm characteristics which are used as control variables in the regression. Table 2 provides the sample mean and standard errors for the full sample in Column (1) and for the subsample of trademarking firms in Column (2). The difference between trademarking and non-trademarking firms shows Column (3). More detailed descriptive statistics are provided in Table 5 in the Appendix.

3.3.1. Distance between firm and customer

The distance between the firm and its customers is captured through two different dimensions: the geographical distance and the personal distance.

The geographical distance is measured through the geographic markets in which a firm is active. Three dummy variables account for a firm's activity in the local market (the firm sells goods or services within a radius of 50 km), the national market (Germany), and/or the international market. A firm is able to serve all or only some geographical markets. The local market allows, from the geographical perspective, the closest contact between a firm and its customers and is served by 63% of the sample firms. As a logical corollary, this means, that the local market is not relevant for the remaining 37% and that those firms have to deal more often with geographical distance. The same is true for 71% that serve the national market, and nearly half of the firms (47%) that serve the international market. Firms could use trademarks to deal with geographical distance. Table 2 supports this view: trademarking firms are more frequently active at the national or international level and less at the regional market.

The second distance dimension, the personal distance, captures the ability of a firm to build a personal relationship between its staff members and its customers. It is reasonable to assume that the more customers a firm has, the less able it is to establish a close relationship with all of its customers. The number of customers would be a good measure of the personal distance but is, unfortunately, not available from the survey and often unknown to the firm as well. The survey, instead, provides information on the share of turnover with the three most important customers. This measure is able to proxy the number of customers quite well: A firm that reports a share of turnover of 100 percent for its three most important customers, has not more than three customers. The lower the reported share, the larger in general the number of customers. Based on this survey information, the two binary variables, *few customers* and *many customers* account for personal distance. A close contact seems to be reachable for 15% of the sample firms with only few customers, while 45% are characterised as having many customers, associated with larger personal distance. Again, firms might deal with personal distance by using trademarks. The descriptive statistics (Table 2) are in line with this argument since the proportion of trademarking firms is larger with many customers and smaller with few customers.

3.3.2. Substitutability of products and services

Firms might be more likely to pursue a product differentiation strategy if operating in product markets in which product-substitutability is high. Whether or not a firm operates in a market in which *products are substitutable* is direct information from the questionnaire and is based on the assessment of the firms. Product substitutability applies fully for 21% of the sample firms but only for 16% of the trademarking firms.

The number of (main) competitors serves additionally as a measure of product substitutability and is again direct information from the survey. A firm with no or just few competitors sells goods and services which are, due to the lack of alternative suppliers, less easily substituted. The larger the number of competitors, the higher the number of potential providers, indicating that barriers to entry are low and that the firm is rather in polypolistic competition. Consequently, the degree of substitutability is relatively high. A small number of competitors (up to five, *'few competitors'*) is considered as less substitutable products and a large number (more than 50 competitors, *'many competitors'*) as easily substitutable products. Any number of competitors in between these two serves as the reference category. It turns out from the descriptive statistics that trademarking firms are less often faced by many competitors (12% in contrast to 22% of non-trademarking firms) and operate more often in a competition environment with few competitors (47% in contrast to 40%).

3.3.3. Product quality

An important aspect of product quality is the customer's assessability of quality prior to the purchase. The firms were asked to assess, on a four-point Likert scale (ranging from 'applies not' to 'applies fully') whether it is difficult for customers to assess the quality in a firm's product market. The binary variable *quality assessable* equals one, if customers have no difficulties to assess the product quality. Overall, that is the case for 22% of the firms. The proportion of suppliers with assessable quality is not smaller for trademarking firms (see Table 2).

3.3.4. Innovative activity of firms

Innovative firms are supposed to benefit particularly from the use of trademarks. A firm's technological capability and its innovative capability are used to identify innovative firms. Two dummy variables serve as indicators for a firm's technological capability: continuous internal R&D activities and at least one patent application at the European Patent Office (EPO). *Continuous R&D* is again direct information from the survey. Descriptive statistics reveal large differences between trademarking and non-trademarking firms: 40% of the trademarking firms conduct R&D continuously but just 13% of non-trademarking firms. The results for an *EPO patent* are similar: 30% of the trademarking and just 4% of the non-trademarking firms have a patent application at the EPO. Research oriented firms seem to be also trademarkoriented ones.

The innovative capability of a firm is captured by the current level of innovative activity, proxied by a set of dummy variables indicating *product innovation* and *process innovation* during the period 2008 to 2010. Again, trademarking firms are more often innovative: 44% introduced a process innovation (in contrast to 28% of non-trademarking firms) and 65% a product innovation (in contrast to 35% of non-trademarking firms). The current level of innovation seems to proxy the general innovativeness of a firm quite well, since innovation is shown to be persistent within firms (Peters 2009).

3.3.5. Basic firm characteristics

The group of basic firm characteristics includes besides firm size also *firm age* (measured in years), the type of ownership, the region of a firm's location, and its sector affiliation. The type of ownership distinguishes between unaffiliated firms (reference group) and those that belong to a *group*. The region distinguishes between firms located in West- (reference group) and *East* Germany and the sector affiliation between 21 aggregated sector groupings.

4. Empirical findings

4.1. The propensity to trademark

The dependent variable indicates whether a firm uses trademarks. Due to the binary character of the dependent variable, a probit model for the econometric analysis is used. The cross-sectional data allows no interpretation of the results as causal effects; the results should thus be taken as associations rather than as causal relationships. The main estimation results of gradually enriched probit models are presented in Table 3.[3] Each of the four columns contains two sub-columns, where the first provides the coefficients and standard errors from the regression and the second sub-column provides the more informative average marginal effects. Column (1) presents the estimates for a specification which only accounts for basic firm characteristics. The specification is gradually enriched by including components of personal and geographical distance, product quality, and product substitutability in Column (2). Alternatively, model (3) accounts for basic firm characteristics and innovation activity. The complete set of explanatory variables is used for estimation in Column (4).

A randomly drawn sample firm uses at least one trademark with a propensity of 31.3%. The regression results provide some more differentiated insights into the propensity to trademark in Column (1), solely based on basic firm characteristics. Firms are characterised by size, group status, location, firm age, and sector affiliation. As the results show, the size of a firm has a highly significant impact: the larger the firm, the higher the propensity to trademark. A one unit increase of *firm size* (the logarithm of the number of employees) increases the probability of using trademarks by 9.1 percentage points. The estimated marginal effect is lowered to 6.2 percentage points, after controlling for all additional variables in Column (4).

This indicates that firm size is positively correlated to these variables and captures them partly.

The single number of 6.2 percentage points represents the average marginal effect of firm size – but the effect might vary across the range from small to large firms. Williams (2012) recommends to choose ranges of values for one or more independent variables (in this case firm size) and to calculate marginal effects for this range of representative values. Figure 1 provides average adjusted predictions (AAPs) and average marginal effects

---

[3]The results of a weighted estimation are provided in Table 7 in the Appendix. The results differ only slightly.

Table 3. Firm characteristics and the propensity to trademark.

	(1) Trademarks(D)		(2) Trademarks(D)		(3) Trademarks(D)		(4) Trademarks(D)	
	β/SE	ME	β/SE	ME	β/SE	ME	β/SE	ME
Basic Characteristics								
Firm Size	0.316*** (0.016)	0.091***	0.282*** (0.016)	0.076***	0.263*** (0.016)	0.070***	0.243*** (0.017)	0.062***
Group	0.120** (0.048)	0.035**	0.074 (0.049)	0.020	0.065 (0.050)	0.018	0.036 (0.051)	0.009
East Germany	-0.248*** (0.044)	-0.070***	-0.195*** (0.046)	-0.053***	-0.223*** (0.045)	-0.059***	-0.180*** (0.047)	-0.046***
Firm Age	-0.001 (0.024)	-0.000	0.009 (0.025)	0.002	0.013 (0.025)	0.004	0.013 (0.026)	0.003
Personal Distance								
Few Customers			-0.153** (0.065)	-0.040**			-0.159** (0.066)	-0.039**
Many Customers			0.147*** (0.045)	0.040***			0.146*** (0.046)	0.038***
Geographical Distance								
Regional Market			-0.204*** (0.043)	-0.056***			-0.177*** (0.044)	-0.046***
National Market			0.418*** (0.059)	0.111***			0.401*** (0.059)	0.101***
International Market			0.450*** (0.048)	0.127***			0.353*** (0.049)	0.094***
Product Quality								
Quality Assessable			-0.139*** (0.050)	-0.037***			-0.138*** (0.051)	-0.035***
Substitutability								
Products Substitutable			-0.080 (0.053)	-0.022			-0.036 (0.054)	-0.009
Few Competitors			0.140*** (0.045)	0.039***			0.093** (0.046)	0.024**
Many Competitors			-0.206*** (0.060)	-0.053***			-0.173*** (0.060)	-0.043***
Innovator								
Continuous R&D					0.242*** (0.061)	0.068***	0.208*** (0.062)	0.056***

(*Continued*)

Table 3. (Continued).

	(1) Trademarks(D)		(2) Trademarks(D)		(3) Trademarks(D)		(4) Trademarks(D)	
	β/SE	ME	β/SE	ME	β/SE	ME	β/SE	ME
EPO Patent					0.866***	0.275***	0.800***	0.240***
					(0.067)		(0.069)	
Process Innovation					−0.019	−0.005	−0.042	−0.011
					(0.046)		(0.047)	
Product Innovation					0.292***	0.081***	0.203***	0.053***
					(0.051)		(0.052)	
W_Industry	0.000		0.000		0.000		0.000	
McFadden's R2	0.181		0.228		0.231		0.263	
McFadden's Adj R2	0.172		0.215		0.219		0.247	
Correctly Classified (%)	71.230		73.170		75.092		75.275	
Correctly Classified 1 (%)	72.063		76.096		70.836		74.342	
Correctly Classified 0 (%)	70.850		71.836		77.032		75.699	
Observations	5464		5464		5464		5464	

Source: ZEW: Mannheim Innovation Panel, survey 2011.

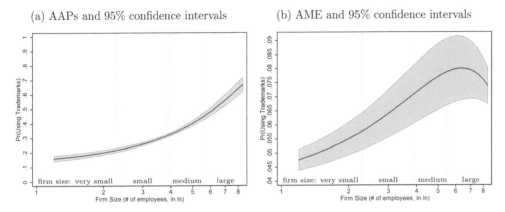

Figure 1. Firm size: a) Average adjusted predictions (AAPs), b) Average marginal effects (AMEs).

(AMEs) for a plausible range of firm size. The AAPs in Figure 1a illustrate the relevance of firm size after controlling for all other variables: a firm with 10 employees, which is at the border of being classified as very small to small (in logarithm at 2.3, the first dotted line), has a 22.3% predicted probability of using trademarks. A firm with 50 employees, which is on the border of being medium sized, has a 32.4% predicted probability and one with 250 employees on the border of being large, has a predicted probability of 44.1% to use trademarks. The average marginal effects (AMEs) are presented in Figure 1b for exactly the same range of firm size. The graph shows that an increase in firm size leads to an increase of the marginal effect of trademarking up to a firm size of 600 employees (about 6.4 in logarithm). This is the case for slightly less than 95% of all firms in the sample. An additional increase in firm size above 600 employees produces smaller but still positive increases in the likelihood to register trademarks.

A firm is, apart from its size, also characterised by its group status, its location in East or West Germany, and its sector affiliation. After controlling for all additional variables in Column (4), the propensity to register trademarks is reduced by 4.6 percentage points for a firm located in *East Germany*. Neither the fact that a firm is part of a *group* nor the *age* of a firm have a significant effect.

4.2. Distance, product quality and substitutability matter

Results for the first set of additional firm characteristics are given in Column (2). The results provide evidence that both dimensions of distance between a firm and its customers are significantly correlated to the use of trademarks: Trademarks are on average 4.0 percentage points less likely used in the case of short *personal distance* (few customers), while long personal distance (many customers) induce a 4.0 percentage points increase in the propensity to trademark. Furthermore, firms propensity to use trademarks is about 5.6 percentage points smaller in the case of a short *geographical distance* (regional market) and significantly higher in the case of a long distance; 11.1 percentage points larger for firms that serve the national market and 12.7 percentage points for those that serve the international market. The marginal effects are just slightly smaller after controlling for the full set of variables in Column (4).

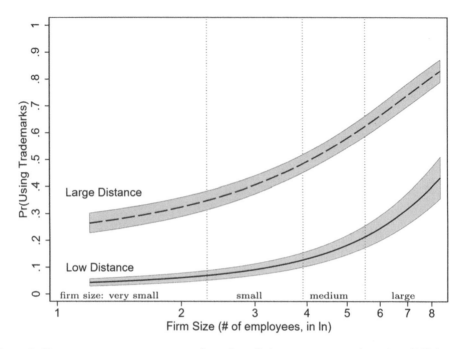

Figure 2. Distance to customers matters, adjusted predictions at representative values (APRs).

Notes: Long distance is defined as serving the national and international market as well as having many customers. Short distance firms serve just the regional market and have few customers.

To illustrate the relevance of distance in more detail, Figure 2 shows adjusted predictions for the same range of firm size as above, but distinguished by distance to customers. Short distance is defined as having a limited personal distance (few customers) and as having a limited geographical distance (being active just at the local market). Long distance firms are those with many customers, which are also active at the national and international market. Figure 2 tellingly reveals along the firm size distribution that the probability of trademarking is significantly larger for firms with a long distance, compared to those with a short distance to their customers – even after controlling for all other variables. A firm with a long distance to customers and 250 employees (in logarithm at 5.5, the third dotted line) has a three times higher predicted probability of trademarking (63% compared to 19.4%) than an equally sized firm with short distance to its customers. A small firm with 10 employees (in logarithm at 2.3, the first dotted line) and a long distance has actually a six times higher predicted propensity to trademark.

This implies that trademarks are frequently used as an instrument to overcome distance, which is otherwise preventing a close relationship to customers. A short distance on the other hand limits the need for trademarks, since it enables firms to establish a close relationship with its customers.

Trademarks are also less often needed, if the quality of a firm's products is easy to assess: Firms in a product market in which products are of *assessable quality* have a 3.4 percentage points lower probability of using trademarks. This confirms that a trademark is a useful instrument to signal those product quality features that are otherwise not obvious.

The number of competitors is used to proxy product substitutability. A low number of competitors (*few competitors*), is correlated with a 3.9 percentage points larger probability to use trademarks. A large number of competitors (*many competitors*) is correlated with a 5.3 percentage points lower propensity to trademark. This indicates that trademarks are used to differentiate a firm's product especially in the case of a small number of main competitors, when a firm operates in an oligopolistic market. Figure 3 compares adjusted predictions for firms with few and many competitors. The largest differences arise for small to medium sized firms with about 50 employees. The overlapping areas of the confidence intervals reveal that the difference is not significant for large firms.

The results can also be interpreted as indication for the competition-reducing effect of brands. The presence of strong brands might establish barriers to entry for potential competitors. Market entry is prevented because of the high fixed costs for a firm that enters the market and has to establish competitive brands.

4.3. Innovation matters

Innovative firms have a larger probability of using trademarks. Firm's conducting *continuous R&D* have a 6.8 percentage points higher propensity to trademark, whereas those with a *patent* application at the European Patent Office (EPO) have on average a 27.4 percentage points higher one. Both indicators capture a firm's technological capability and point to research intensive firms. The innovative capability captures the ability of a firm to introduce new products and processes into the market. Firms with product innovations have an 8.1 percentage points larger probability of using trademarks, while process innovations have no significant influence. The highly significant

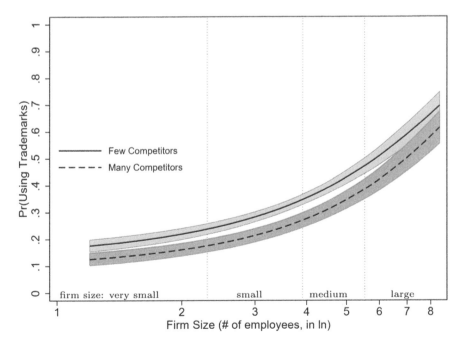

Figure 3. Substitutability matters, average adjusted predictions (AAPs).

correlation of a firm's innovation activities and its use of trademarks confirms related studies (Mendonca, Pereira, and Godinho 2004; Greenhalgh and Rogers 2012). Whether innovation activities lead to trademark registrations or the reverse, namely that a firm's brands lead to innovation activities is not clear.

Adjusted predictions are also chosen to illustrate the difference between innovative and non-innovative firms in Figure 4. Innovative firms are defined as firms that undertake R&D continuously, having a patent application at the EPO, and having introduced a product innovation. Non-innovative firms conduct no R&D, and have neither a patent registered nor a product innovation introduced. The introduction of process innovations has no significant effect and is therefore not taken into account. The probability of using trademarks differs significantly for the whole range of size classes. An innovative firm with 250 employees (on the border of being between medium and large sized) is more than twice as likely to trademark. After controlling for all other variables, the propensity to trademark is 77.0% for an innovative firm, compared to 36.4% for a non-innovative firm. The probability of trademarking of a small innovative firm with 10 employees (in logarithm at 2.3, the first dotted line) is more than three times greater (51.5% instead of 14.6%), compared to a non-innovative firm of the same size.

5. Conclusion

This paper provides empirical evidence of the proportion of firms that have registered trademarks in 2010 and analyses the role of several firm characteristics that are related to

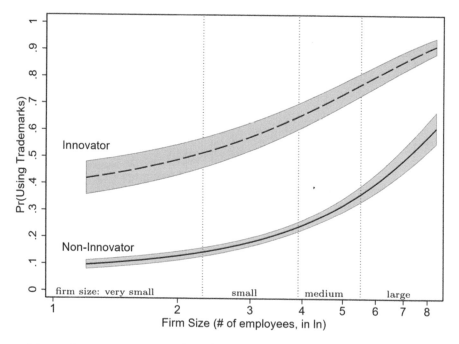

Figure 4. Innovation matters, average adjusted predictions (AAPs).

Notes: An innovator is defined as follows: she conducts R&D continuously, has an EPO patent application, and introduced a product innovation. The opposite is true for the definition of non-innovators.

a firm's decision to register trademarks. The empirical analysis relies on a large sample of about 5,400 German firms from many different industries in the business sector. The extrapolated proportion of 18% of firms with at least one registered and still valid trademark is representative for all firms with more than five employees in the corresponding sectors.

The empirical analysis investigates to what extent firm and product characteristics matter for the firms decision to use trademarks. The results cannot be taken as indicating causality because of potential endogeneity. But the results provide evidence that the decision of a firm to register trademarks is related to several firm characteristics: the distance between a firm and its customers, the assessability of product quality, the degree of substitutability, and innovative activities of a firm. Firms with a low level of personal as well as geographical *distance* use trademarks less often, while firms with longer distances use trademarks more frequently. This result suggests that trademarks are an appropriate instrument to overcome distance and are not needed in circumstances under which a firm and its customers are able to maintain a close relationship. The quality features of products offered are sometimes obvious, but more often not straightforward *assessable* at the time of the purchase. The results show that firms with products, whose quality is difficult to assess, use significantly more often trademarks. This might be interpreted as meaning that trademarks can help to solve the problem of asymmetric information: The reputation of a trademark helps to assess those products. Previous experiences with the product or even with similar products of the same brand, can be transferred to the current purchase decision. The results further indicate that trademarks are also more frequently used, if a firm's products are characterised by a limited (but not strong) *substitutability*. Pursuing a trademark strategy seems to be more promising, if a firm has to distinguish its products amongst few competitors. In fact, strong brands are typically found in oligopolistic markets such as smartphones, cars, telecommunications, soft drinks or credit cards. In the case of many competitors and thus easy substitutability, trademarks are significantly less used. Another important finding is that a firm that conducts continuous R&D is engaged in patenting and the introduction of innovative products has a significantly higher propensity to register trademarks. This confirms that product innovations and the registration of trademarks are correlated.

In the end to conclude, what are the circumstances under which trademarks are important for a firm? Overall, the results show that firms are more likely to register trademarks and pursue a trademarking strategy, provided that the distance to their customers is far, the product quality is not assessable, the number of competitors is small, or firms undertake R&D activities and introduce product innovations.

Some limitations need to be acknowledged. This study focuses on the investigation of firms with and without trademarks. The trademark data have been reduced to this key information and further interesting aspects were suppressed. This is to be mentioned as limitation, since trademark data allow more than the generation of an indicator variable. One can (i) count the registered trademarks and create trademark stocks (Krasnikov, Mishra, and Orozco 2009; Sandner and Block 2011), (ii) use the flow of trademark applications over time (Crass, Czarnitzki, and Toole 2019), (iii) differentiate between service, manufacturing and mixed trademarks (Schmoch and Gauch 2009), (iv) or analyse the portfolio of each firm to distinguish between corporate brands, umbrella brands, family brands, and individual product brands (Keller and Lehmann 2006).

Future research could build upon this study and try to validate the findings while investigating alternative representations of firms' trademark use.

Another limitation is the lack of information about the motives of firms for using trademarks (Flikkema, De Man, and Castaldi 2014; Castaldi 2018). Future research should complement the firm characteristics described with the motives to trademark. It could be examined whether the success of a trademark strategy relies on the described firm characteristics.

The results confirm the link between a firm's innovation and its trademark activity. Trademark data are an appropriate innovation indicator (Mendonca, Pereira, and Godinho 2004). This is especially relevant for innovation statistics in the services sector, where traditional innovation indicators like R&D expenses and patent applications are less frequently used (Schmoch and Gauch 2009). Trademark data fill this gap at least partially. The results presented show that a considerable number of firms do not use trademarks because of firm characteristics like a close contact to their customers. A certain amount of innovative firms which meet these characteristics will not appear in innovation statistics based on trademarks. Innovation indicators relying on trademark statistics might underestimate innovation.

The empirical evidence is unambiguous: Trademarking firms are more successful. The findings of this study suggest that many firms do not adopt a trademark strategy and have rational reasons for doing so. The characteristics of these firms or of their products and services do not match the problem that trademarks solve. The use of trademarks would not make this group of firms more successful. Policy-makers should keep this in mind if they want to encourage firms to adopt a trademark strategy.

Acknowledgments

I would like to thank Pierre Mohnen (MERIT), Bettina Peters (ZEW and University of Luxembourg), Georg von Graevenitz (Queen Mary), Alan Marco (USPTO and Georgia Tech), Stuart Graham (Georgia Tech) and participants at the Workshop on Empirical Studies of Trademark Data (USPTO, Alexandria, 2013) for valuable comments. Any errors remain those of the author.

Disclosure Statement

In this study I use the Mannheim Innovation Panel (MIP). The sponsor is the German Federal Ministry of Education and Research (BMBF). The survey is carried out in co-operation with infas (Institute of Applied Social Science) and Fraunhofer Institute for System and Innovation Research (ISI)

References

Aaker, D. A. 1991. *Managing Brand Equity: Capitalizing on the Value of a Brand Name.* New York: Free Press.

Ailawadi, K. L., S. A. Neslin, and D. R. Lehmann. 2003. "Revenue Premium as an Outcome Measure of Brand Equity." *Journal of Marketing* 67 (4): 1–17.

Akerlof, G. A. 1970. "The Market for 'Lemons': Quality Uncertainty and the Market Mechanism." *The Quarterly Journal of Economics* 84 (3): 488–500. doi:10.2307/1879431.

Amara, N., R. Landry, and N. Traoré. 2008. "Managing the Protection of Innovations in Knowledge-Intensive Business Services." *Research Policy* 37 (9): 1530–1547. doi:10.1016/j.respol.2008.07.001.

Aschhoff, B., E. Baier, D. Crass, M. Hud, P. Hünermund, C. Köhler, B. Peters, et al. 2013. Innovation in Germany - Results of the German CIS 2006 to 2010. Background report on the Innovation Surveys 2007, 2009 and 2011 of the Mannheim Innovation Panel. Mannheim: ZEW-Dokumentation 13–01.

Athreye, S., and C. Fassio. 2020. "Why Do Innovators Not Apply for Trademarks? The Role of Information Asymmetries and Collaborative Innovation." *Industry and Innovation* 27 (1–2): 134–154.

Bagwell, K. 2007. *The Economic Analysis of Advertising, Handbook of Industrial Organization*, Vol. 3, chapter 28, 1701–1844. Amsterdam: Elsevier.

Baroncelli, E., C. Fink, and B. K. S. Javorcik. 2004. *The Global Distribution of Trademarks: Some Stylized Facts*. Washington D.C: World Bank Publications.

Borden, N. H. 1944. *The Economic Effects of Advertising*. 3rd ed. Chicago: Richard D. Irwin.

Bosworth, D., and M. Rogers. 2001. "Market Value, R&D and Intellectual Property: An Empirical Analysis of Large Australian Firms." *The Economic Record* 77 (239): 323–337. doi:10.1111/1475-4932.t01-1-00026.

Buddelmeyer, H., P. H. Jensen, and E. Webster. 2010. "Innovation and the Determinants of Company Survival." *Oxford Economic Papers* 62 (2): 261–285.

Castaldi, C. 2018. "To Trademark or Not to Trademark: The Case of the Creative and Cultural Industries." *Research Policy* 47 (3): 606–616. doi:10.1016/j.respol.2018.01.006.

Castaldi, C., and M. S. Giarratana. 2018. "Diversification, Branding, and Performance of Professional Service Firms." *Journal of Service Research* 21 (3): 353–364. doi:10.1177/1094670518755315.

Crass, D., and B. Peters. 2014. "Intangible Assets and Firm-level Productivity." ZEW Discussion Papers 14–120. ZEW - Zentrum für Europäische Wirtschaftsforschung/Center for European Economic Research.

Crass, D., D. Czarnitzki, and A. A. Toole. 2019. "The Dynamic Relationship between Investments in Brand Equity and Firm Profitability: Evidence Using Trademark Registrations." *International Journal of the Economics of Business* 26 (1): 157–176. doi:10.1080/13571516.2019.1553292.

Dinlersoz, E. M., N. Goldschlag, A. Myers, and N. Zolas. 2018. "An Anatomy of US Firms Seeking Trademark Registration." Working Paper 25038. National Bureau of Economic Research.

Economides, N. 1998. "Trademarks." In *The New Palgrave Dictionary of Economics and the Law*, edited by P. Newman, 601–603. London: Macmillan Reference Limited.

Fink, C., C. Helmers, and J. C. Ponce. 2018. "Trademark Squatters: Theory and Evidence from Chile." *International Journal of Industrial Organization* 59 (2018): 340–371.

Flikkema, M., A.-P. De Man, and C. Castaldi. 2014. "Are Trademark Counts a Valid Indicator of Innovation? Results of an In-Depth Study of New Benelux Trademarks Filed by SMEs." *Industry and Innovation* 21 (4): 310–331. doi:10.1080/13662716.2014.934547.

Gotsch, M., and C. Hipp. 2014. "Using Trademarks to Measure Innovation in Knowledge-Intensive Business Services." *Technology Innovation Management Review* 4: 5. doi:10.22215/timreview/790.

Graham, S. J., G. Hancock, A. C. Marco, and A. F. Myers. 2013. "The USPTO Trademark Case Files Dataset: Descriptions, Lessons, and Insights." *Journal of Economics & Management Strategy* 22 (4): 669–705. doi:10.1111/jems.12035.

Greenhalgh, C., and M. Longland. 2005. "Running to Stand Still? - the Value of R&D, Patents and Trade Marks in Innovating Manufacturing Firms." *International Journal of the Economics of Business* 12 (3): 307–328. doi:10.1080/13571510500299326.

Greenhalgh, C., and M. Rogers. 2012. "Trade Marks and Performance in Services and Manufacturing Firms: Evidence of Schumpeterian Competition through Innovation." *Australian Economic Review* 45 (1): 50–76. doi:10.1111/j.1467-8462.2011.00665.x.

Greenhalgh, C., M. Rogers, P. Schautschick, and V. Sena. 2011. Trade Mark Incentives, Report for the UK Intellectual Property Office.

Griffiths, W., P. H. Jensen, and E. Webster. 2011. "What Creates Abnormal Profits?." *Scottish Journal of Political Economy* 58 (3): 323–346. doi:10.1111/sjpe.2011.58.issue-3.

Hall, B., C. Helmers, M. Rogers, and V. Sena. 2014. "The Choice between Formal and Informal Intellectual Property: A Literature Review." *Journal of Economic Literature* 52 (2): 375–423. doi:10.1257/jel.52.2.375.

Helmers, C., and M. Rogers. 2010. "Innovation and the Survival of New Firms in the UK." *Review of Industrial Organization* 36 (3): 227–248. doi:10.1007/s11151-010-9247-7.

Jensen, P. H., and E. Webster. 2009. "Another Look at the Relationship between Innovation Proxies." *Australian Economic Papers* 48 (3): 252–269. doi:10.1111/aepa.2009.48.issue-3.

Jensen, P. H., E. Webster, and H. Buddelmeyer. 2008. "Innovation, Technological Conditions and New Firm Survival." *The Economic Record* 84 (267): 434–448. doi:10.1111/ecor.2008.84.issue-267.

Keller, K. L., and D. R. Lehmann. 2006. "Brands and Branding: Research Findings and Future Priorities." *Marketing Science* 25 (6): 740–759. doi:10.1287/mksc.1050.0153.

Krasnikov, A., S. Mishra, and D. Orozco. 2009. "Evaluating the Financial Impact of Branding Using Trademarks: A Framework and Empirical Evidence." *Journal of Marketing* 73 (6): 154–166. doi:10.1509/jmkg.73.6.154.

Landes, W. M., and R. A. Posner. 1987. "Trademark Law: An Economic Perspective." *Journal of Law and Economics* 30 (2): 265–309. doi:10.1086/467138.

Llerena, P., and V. Millot. 2013. "Are Trade Marks and Patents Complementary or Substitute Protections for Innovation." Working Papers of BETA 2013-01. UDS, Strasbourg: Bureau d'Economie Théorique et Appliquée.

Mendonca, S., T. S. Pereira, and M. M. Godinho. 2004. "Trademarks as an Indicator of Innovation and Industrial Change." *Research Policy* 33 (9): 1385–1404. doi:10.1016/j.respol.2004.09.005.

Millot, V. 2011. "Firms' Intangible Assets: Who Relies on Trademarks? Analysis of French and German Firms' Trademarking Behaviour." Paper Presented at the DRUID Society Conference, Copenhagen, Denmark.

Moore, K., and S. Reid. 2008. "The Birth of Brand: 4000 Years of Branding." *Business History* 50 (4): 419–432. doi:10.1080/00076790802106299.

OECD, Eurostat. 2005. *Oslo Manual: Guidelines for Collecting and Interpreting Innovation Data.* 3rd ed. Paris.

Peters, B. 2009. "Persistence of Innovation: Stylised Facts and Panel Data Evidence." *The Journal of Technology Transfer* 34 (2): 226–243. doi:10.1007/s10961-007-9072-9.

Peters, B., and C. Rammer. 2013. "Innovation Panel Surveys in Germany." In *Handbook of Innovation Indicators and Measurement*, F. Gault edited by, 135–177. Cheltenham, UK and Northampton, MA, USA: Edward Elgar Publishing. chapter 6.

Ramello, G. B. 2006. "What's in a Sign? Trademark Law and Economic Theory." *Journal of Economic Surveys* 20 (4): 547–565. doi:10.1111/joes.2006.20.issue-4.

Sáiz, P., and P. Fernández. 2009. "Intangible Assets and Competitiveness in Spain: An Approach Based on Trademark Registration Data in Catalonia (1850–1946)." Working Papers in Economic History, No 2009/01. Universidad Autónoma de Madrid (Spain), Department of Economic Analysis (Economic Theory and Economic History).

Sandner, P. G., and J. Block. 2011. "The Market Value of R&D, Patents, and Trademarks." *Research Policy* 40 (7): 969–985. doi:10.1016/j.respol.2011.04.004.

Schautschick, P., and C. Greenhalgh. 2016. "Empirical Studies of Trade Marks the Existing Economic Literature." *Economics of Innovation and New Technology* 25 (4): 358–390. doi:10.1080/10438599.2015.1064598.

Schmoch, U. 2003. "Service Marks as Novel Innovation Indicator." *Research Evaluation* 12 (2): 149–156. doi:10.3152/147154403781776708.

Schmoch, U., and S. Gauch. 2009. "Service Marks as Indicators for Innovation in Knowledge-Based Services." *Research Evaluation* 18 (4): 323–335. doi:10.3152/095820209X451023.

Srinivasan, S., L. Hsu, and S. Fournier. 2011. "Branding and Firm Value." In *Handbook of Marketing and Finance*, edited by S. Ganesan and S. Bharadwaj, 155–203. Northampton: Edward Elgar Publishing.

von Graevenitz, G. 2007. Which Reputations Does a Brand Owner Need? Evidence from Trade Mark Opposition, Discussion Paper Series of SFB/TR 15 Governance and the Efficiency of Economic Systems 215, Free University of Berlin, Humboldt University of Berlin, University of Bonn, University of Mannheim, University of Munich. doi:10.1094/PDIS-91-4-0467B.

Williams, R. 2012. "Using the Margins Command to Estimate and Interpret Adjusted Predictions and Marginal Effects." *Stata Journal* 12 (2): 308–331. doi:10.1177/1536867X1201200209.

WIPO. 2013. "World Intellectual Property Report: Brands – Reputation and Image in the Global Marketplace." Wipo Economics & Statistics Series. Geneva.

Appendix

Definition of Variables

Table 4. Variable Definitions.

Variable	Definition
Trademarks	Dummy variable taking value 1, if firm has at least one registered trademark in 2010.
Firm Size	Log of the number of employees (in 2010).
Group	Dummy variable taking value 1, if firm reports to be part of an enterprise group in 2010.
East	Dummy variable taking value 1, if firm is located in East Germany (the former territory of the GDR and West-Berlin).
Firm Age	Log of the number of years (in 2010) since the enterprise was founded.
Few Customers	Dummy variable taking value 1, if a firms' reported share of sales in 2010 with the largest 3 customers is among the highest 15 percent of all sample firms.
Many Customers	Dummy variable taking value 1, if a firms' reported share of sales in 2010 with the largest 3 customers is below the median value of all sample firms.
Regional Market	Dummy variable taking value 1, if firm reports to be active on the regional market, defined as the area within a radius of 50 km.
National Market	Dummy variable taking value 1, if firm reports to be active on the national market (Germany).
International Market	Dummy variable taking value 1, if firm reports to be active on the international market.
Quality Assessable	Dummy variable taking value 1, if firm reports that its market is characterised by the fact that customers have no difficulties to assess the quality of products.
Products Substitutable	Dummy variable taking value 1, if firm states it applies fully that it operates in a market in which products are substitutable.
Few Competitors	Dummy variable taking value 1, if firm reports to have up to 5 competitors on its main product market in 2010.
Many Competitors	Dummy variable taking value 1, if firm reports to have more than 50 competitors on its main product market in 2010.
Continuous R&D	Dummy variable taking value 1, if firm reports to have continuous R&D activities during 2008–2010.
EPO Patent	Dummy variable taking value 1, if firm has at least one patent application.
Process Innovation	Dummy variable taking value 1, if firm introduced a process innovation during 2008–2010.
Product Innovation	Dummy variable taking value 1, if firm introduced a product innovation during 2008–2010.

Table 5. Descriptive Statistics of Main Variables.

	Mean	SD	Min	Max
Basic Characteristics				
Firm Size	3.58	1.62	−0.13	10.22
Group (D)	0.29	0.45	0.00	1.00
East Germany (D)	0.32	0.47	0.00	1.00
Firm Age	3.11	0.86	0.00	6.52
Sector Affiliation Food/Beverage/Tobacco	0.04	0.20	0.00	1.00
Textile/Clothes/Leather	0.03	0.17	0.00	1.00
Wood/Paper	0.03	0.17	0.00	1.00
Chemicals/Pharmaceuticals	0.04	0.18	0.00	1.00
Rubber-/Plastics products	0.03	0.17	0.00	1.00
Glass/Clay/Stone	0.02	0.15	0.00	1.00
Metal	0.07	0.25	0.00	1.00
Machinery	0.07	0.26	0.00	1.00
Electronics	0.07	0.26	0.00	1.00
Motor vehicles	0.03	0.16	0.00	1.00
Furnit./Toys/Medick. instr./Repair	0.03	0.18	0.00	1.00
Water/Waste disposal/Recycling	0.05	0.22	0.00	1.00
Energy/Mining/Petroleum	0.04	0.19	0.00	1.00
Wholesale	0.04	0.19	0.00	1.00
Transportation/Postal services	0.07	0.25	0.00	1.00
Media services	0.04	0.20	0.00	1.00
IT/Telecommunication	0.05	0.22	0.00	1.00
Financial services	0.03	0.17	0.00	1.00
Consultancy/Advertising	0.05	0.22	0.00	1.00
Technical/R&D services	0.07	0.26	0.00	1.00
Corporate services	0.06	0.23	0.00	1.00
Personal Distance	0.15	0.36	0.00	1.00
Few Customers (D)				
Many Customers (D)	0.45	0.50	0.00	1.00
Geographical Distance	0.63	0.48	0.00	1.00
Regional Market (D)				
National Market (D)	0.71	0.45	0.00	1.00
International Market (D)	0.47	0.50	0.00	1.00
Product Quality	0.22	0.42	0.00	1.00
Quality Assessable (D)				
Substitutability	0.21	0.41	0.00	1.00
Products Substitutable (D)				
Few Competitors (D)	0.42	0.49	0.00	1.00
Many Competitors (D)	0.19	0.39	0.00	1.00
Innovation	0.22	0.41	0.00	1.00
Continuous R&D (D)				
EPO Patent (D)	0.12	0.33	0.00	1.00
Process Innovation (D)	0.32	0.47	0.00	1.00
Product Innovation (D)	0.44	0.50	0.00	1.00

Source: ZEW: Mannheim Innovation Panel, survey 2011.

Correlation Matrix

Table 6. Correlation Matrix.

	1	2	3	4	5	6	7	8	9	10	11	12	13	14	15	16	17
(1) Trademarks (D)	1.00																
(2) Firm Size (# of employees)	0.16***	1.00															
(3) Group (D)	0.24***	0.20***	1.00														
(4) East Germany (D)	-0.13***	-0.07***	-0.09***	1.00													
(5) Firm Age (in years)	0.09***	0.09***	0.05***	-0.23***	1.00												
(6) Few Customers (D)	-0.08***	-0.03*	0.04**	0.05***	-0.09***	1.00											
(7) Many Customers (D)	0.08***	0.08***	0.03*	-0.08***	0.15***	-0.31***	1.00										
(8) Regional Market (D)	-0.15***	0.00	-0.10***	0.06***	0.07***	-0.06***	0.11***	1.00									
(9) National Market (D)	0.25***	0.06***	0.12***	-0.01	-0.06***	-0.05***	-0.12***	-0.37***	1.00								
(10) International Market (D)	0.32***	0.08***	0.19***	-0.11***	0.02	-0.08***	-0.05***	-0.20***	0.46***	1.00							
(11) Quality Assessable (D)	-0.02	0.01	0.06***	0.00	0.02	0.08***	-0.02	-0.01	-0.04***	0.00	1.00						
(12) Few Competitors (D)	0.05***	0.00	0.04***	0.01	0.02	0.08***	-0.01	0.03*	-0.08***	0.03**	0.09***	1.00					
(13) Many Competitors (D)	-0.11***	-0.03*	-0.08***	0.02	-0.03**	0.01	-0.03*	-0.01	-0.01	-0.12***	-0.01	-0.45***	1.00				
(14) Continuous R&D (D)	0.31***	0.15***	0.19***	-0.02	-0.02*	-0.02	-0.02	-0.13***	0.24***	0.35***	-0.02	0.06***	-0.12***	1.00			
(15) EPO Patent (D)	0.37***	0.14***	0.24***	-0.10***	0.07***	-0.02	0.01	-0.12***	0.19***	0.31***	0.02	0.09***	-0.09***	0.37***	1.00		
(16) Process Innovation (D)	0.17***	0.14***	0.18***	-0.05***	0.02	-0.04**	0.01	-0.06***	0.17***	0.20***	-0.02	0.03**	-0.08***	0.33***	0.16***	1.00	
(17) Product Innovation (D)	0.27***	0.11***	0.15***	-0.04***	-0.02	-0.07***	0.02	-0.15***	0.24***	0.30***	-0.05***	0.06***	-0.14***	0.61***	0.24***	0.39***	1.00

Notes: Significance levels: *** $p < 0.01$, ** $p < 0.05$, * $p < 0.1$.

Weighted Regression

Table 7. Weighted Regression: The Propensity to Trademark.

	(1) Trademarks (D)		(2) Trademarks (D)	
	β/SE	ME	β/SE	ME
Basic Characteristics				
Firm Size	0.243***	0.062***	0.345***	0.067***
	(0.017)		(0.041)	
Group	0.036	0.009	0.055	0.011
	(0.051)		(0.114)	
East Germany	−0.180***	−0.046***	−0.082	−0.016
	(0.047)		(0.090)	
Firm Age	0.013	0.003	−0.048	−0.009
	(0.026)		(0.047)	
Personal Distance				
Few Customers	−0.159**	−0.039**	−0.262**	−0.045**
	(0.066)		(0.123)	
Many Customers	0.146***	0.038***	0.107	0.021
	(0.046)		(0.090)	
Geographical Distance				
Regional Market	−0.177***	−0.046***	−0.229***	−0.046***
	(0.044)		(0.086)	
National Market	0.401***	0.101***	0.553***	0.101***
	(0.059)		(0.120)	
International Market	0.353***	0.094***	0.337***	0.069***
	(0.049)		(0.093)	
Product Quality				
Quality Assessable	−0.138***	−0.035***	−0.192*	−0.036*
	(0.051)		(0.104)	
Substitutability				
Products Substitutable	−0.036	−0.009	0.016	0.003
	(0.054)		(0.105)	
Few Competitors	0.093**	0.024**	0.270***	0.057***
	(0.046)		(0.088)	
Many Competitors	−0.173***	−0.043***	−0.221**	−0.038**
	(0.060)		(0.112)	
Innovator				
Continuous R&D	0.208***	0.056***	0.235**	0.049**
	(0.062)		(0.111)	
EPO Patent	0.800***	0.240***	0.705***	0.173***
	(0.069)		(0.119)	
Process Innovation	−0.042	−0.011	−0.035	−0.007
	(0.047)		(0.083)	
Product Innovation	0.203***	0.053***	0.016	0.003
	(0.052)		(0.087)	
W_Industry	0.000		0.000	
McFadden's R2	0.263		0.247	
McFadden's Adj R2	0.247		0.247	
Correctly Classified (%)	75.275			
Correctly Classified 1 (%)	74.342			
Correctly Classified 0 (%)	75.699			
Observations	5.464		5.464	

Column (1) provides results of an unweighted regression and Column 2 of a weighted regression.
Source: ZEW: Mannheim Innovation Panel, survey 2011.

Are Trademark Counts a Valid Indicator of Innovation? Results of an In-Depth Study of New Benelux Trademarks Filed by SMEs

MEINDERT J. FLIKKEMA, ARD-PIETER DE MAN and CAROLINA CASTALDI

ABSTRACT   This paper extends the emerging literature on the value of trademarks for innovation studies and policy-making with the first empirical study at the trademark level. It gives a view on how companies use trademarks and interpret trademark activities. A sample of 660 new Benelux trademarks registered by small- and medium-sized enterprises reveals that 60 per cent of recently registered Benelux trademarks refer to innovation activity, predominantly to product or service innovation. The reference to innovation co-varies with various applicant and trademark characteristics unknown from previous studies. Finally, the sample reveals that most of the trademarks used to signal innovative offers are filed close to its market introduction without combining them with other intellectual property rights. This holds especially for trademarks related to service innovation.

1. Introduction

The innovative performance of companies, industries and countries has been studied extensively and for a long time. The results of these studies, however, have not yet led to a generally accepted indicator of innovative performance or a common set of indicators (Kleinknecht, 2000; Hagedoorn and Cloodt, 2003). Recent studies argue that trademark analysis can contribute to capturing relevant aspects of innovation phenomena (Mendonça et al., 2004; Stoneman, 2010), in particular in service and low-tech industries, and in small- and medium-sized enterprises (SMEs) (Schmoch, 2003; Hipp and Grupp, 2005; Flikkema et al., 2007; Heidenreich, 2009; Schmoch and Gauch, 2009; Semadeni and Anderson, 2010). Empirical tests have yielded promising, but preliminary results: R&D statistics and trademark statistics correlate positively (Allegrezza and Guarda-Rauchs, 1999; Daizadeh, 2009) and innovative firms consistently use more trademarks than non-innovative firms (Mendonça et al., 2004; Millot, 2008). This supports the view that trademarks may be relevant for measuring innovation. However, to draw a definite conclusion about the value of trademark data for research and policy-making around innovation, we need to understand the relationship between individual trademarks and innovation activity.

Previous papers all investigated the *firm-level* propensity to apply for trademarks (Schmoch, 2003; Graham, 2004; Malmberg, 2005; Heidenreich, 2009). We expand upon that research by studying 660 trademarks and the extent to which they refer to innovation. Our study is the first one to present results of an extensive survey investigating *trademark- level* decisions. This begins to reveal the link between trademarks and innovation, which is called "an intriguing and unsolved puzzle of the IP community" (Smith, 2011: 18). We chose SMEs as our empirical setting because existing indicators do not adequately measure innovation in SMEs (Kleinknecht, 2000), among others because in general the propensity to patent is lower in SMEs (Blind et al., 2006; Leiponen and Byma, 2007; Thomä and Bizer, 2013). We explore the link between trademarks and innovation by studying (a) the motives for trademark registration, (b) the reference of trademarks to innovation and its covariates and (c) the timing of trademark filing in the innovation process.

First, the registration motives may be explicitly related to protecting IP despite the legal constraints of trademarks. However, trademarks may also be used to signal geographic diversification, build and capitalize on brand equity or for mimetic purposes. If this is true, trademarks may be less valuable for innovation research and policy-making. Second, we explore the reference of trademarks to various types of innovation. Existing indicators of innovation do not capture service, marketing and organizational innovation very well. As trademarks may be used for these "softer" types of innovation, to make them more tangible, they may capture non-technological innovation quite well. Third, existing indicators of innovation mostly focus on invention or other activities early in the innovation process. Indicators that measure innovation activity close to the market introduction stage are scarce or have important limitations. For example, the often used measure of the sales share of innovations is a rough estimate and is sensitive to business cycles (Kleinknecht, 2000). Trademarks may not suffer from these problems and hence we study the timing of trademark filing against the various stages of the innovation process to determine whether trademarks indicate innovations close to market introduction.

The main objective of our research is to establish to what extent trademarks can remedy the problems with existing innovation indicators. This is also relevant for practice. Our contribution could help policy-makers to identify new opportunities for innovation policy, in particular for SMEs and service sectors. Some more advanced policy instruments do consider trademarks, such as in the EU Innovation Scoreboard. Our study will enhance the relevance of this by clarifying under which circumstances trademarks are a good indicator of innovation.

This article will first discuss the theoretical background behind the research questions in more detail in Section 2. In Section 3, the research population, sample and the survey method will be described. Section 4.1 shows—for SMEs—the importance of the various motives for trademark registration. Section 4.1.1 studies the types of innovation trademarks refer to and its covariates. Section 4.1.2 takes a closer look at the service sector, because the literature suggests trademarks are particularly relevant there. Section 4.2 reveals patterns in the timing of registration. The final section contains the conclusions, limitations, suggestions for future research and implications for policy-making.

2. Theoretical Background

2.1 Approaches to Innovation

The conceptualization of innovation as well as the types and patterns of innovation have been discussed widely since the publication of Schumpeter's Theory of Economic Development (Schumpeter, 1934). Many academics have argued for a broad conceptualization of innovation, including soft aspects such as organizing, business modelling and branding (Den Hertog et al., 1997; Gallouj, 2000). Others, however, consider including the soft side of innovation as an overstretch of the Schumpeterian innovation notion. They hold that focusing on technological progress and its dissemination should be at the core of innovation research (Drejer, 2004).

To be able to meet the requirements of the various sides in this debate, we define innovation broadly (Coombs and Miles, 2000) and use several classifications developed in the recent literature. First, we make use of the common distinction among product, process and service innovation, used for instance in the Community Innovation Survey. Second, we take stock of more recent research distinguishing technological from non-technological innovation, in particular organizational or marketing innovation (Millot, 2008; Fosfuri and Giarratana, 2009). These two classifications of innovation are not mutually exclusive (Den Hertog, 2000). Our analysis aims to establish empirically to what extent they coincide in the context of trademark application.

2.2 Motives for Trademark Registration

We review here part of the literature on trademarks and discuss six groups of motives for trademark registration stemming from different strands of economic, marketing and management research. The economic literature has identified a number of motives companies may have to register trademarks. A first set of motives relates to increasing the distinctiveness of products or services. Trademarks signal the quality of products and services to customers and help to differentiate products from other products, which discourages the introduction of lower-quality imitations (Economides, 1998). Because a trademark conveys this information to buyers and sellers (Ramello, 2006; Ramello and Silva, 2006), firms can charge higher prices (Shaked and Sutton, 1982) and safeguard revenues, because they avoid customers switching to lower-quality alternatives marketed at a lower price.

Mendonça et al. (2004) emphasize another signalling motive, namely that trademarks may be used for signalling important changes in corporate strategy or corporate identity. For instance, they signal the strategic importance of entry in new markets, a geographic expansion strategy (Giarratana and Torrisi, 2010) or product and service differentiation (Semadeni, 2006). Ultimately, in this way, firms aim to attract new customers, distributors or investors, to gain information from competitors (Heil and Robertson, 1991) or to ward them off (Davis, 2009).

Other economic motives can be distilled from the Industrial Organization literature on IPRs and barriers to entry (Greenhalgh and Rogers, 2010). Here filing trademarks is seen as one of the formal tools to appropriate the rents from innovation. By means of trademarks, firms erect barriers to entry that enable them to protect their IP. Although trademarks do not protect inventions or new knowledge, as patents do, they may help to capitalize on first mover advantage, for example through brand identification and loyalty (Schmalensee, 1978; McClure, 1996; Rao, 2005; Aaker, 2007; Fosfuri et al., 2008; Davis, 2009). This seems to hold in particular for extensions of strong corporate brands (Wernerfelt, 1988; Aaker and Keller, 1990; Keller and Lehmann, 2006) or powerful series of trademarks (e.g., iPad, iBook, iTunes, iMac). In addition, trademarks may help to prolong other IPRs. In the pharmaceutical industry, for example, strong trademarks enable companies to benefit from their inventions long after patents have expired (Rujas, 1999). Others have also suggested or shown that trademarks may be a complementary means to appropriate the rents from innovation (Teece, 1986; Rujas, 1999; Miles et al., 2000; Amara et al., 2008). Likewise Miles et al. (2000) found combinations of trademarks, patents and copyrights to protect innovations in service industries, whereas Amara et al. (2008) show that patents, design rights and trademarks are used together for that purpose in knowledge-intensive business services (KIBS).

Yet another set of motives stems from the marketing literature and research on branding. Here firms apply for trademarks to be able to build brand equity and hence customer loyalty (Keller and Lehmann, 2006; Krasnikov et al., 2009). As Reitzig (2004) explains, firms may also use brand equity to increase their bargaining power with suppliers or with corporate clients. In the latter case, firms use trademarks for ingredient branding in end markets (Norris, 1992). The Intel Inside trademark is a case in point. Brand identification and hence the loyalty of customers in end markets has improved Intel's bargaining position with hardware vendors significantly. According to Mendonça et al. (2004) new trademarks filed by mature firms may also leverage the equity of corporate brands. This helps to support marketing efforts or to save on marketing expenditures. For example, the trademark symbol may signal innovation, which enhances a company's image concerning innovation (Aaker, 2007). This may be relevant in particular for start-up companies (Hsu and Ziedonis, 2007).

The next set of motives for trademarks derives from the strategy literature. The resource-based theory of the firm stresses the need to leverage and combine resources to gain a competitive advantage (Hamel and Prahalad, 1993; Hall, 2006). Trademarks are intangible resources that can be leveraged and that companies can capitalize on (Aaker, 2004; Srivastava et al., 2001). For example, Fosfuri et al. (2008) describe how hardware trademarks are used to benefit from Open Source software initiatives. Another way of capitalizing on brand equity lies in licensing and franchising purposes (Ramello, 2006) in national markets and for the low-risk market entry in foreign markets (Giarratana and Torrisi, 2010). In franchising relationships, the franchisor and franchisees share a common trademark, which is the manifestation of the franchise relationship (Spinelli and Birley, 1996). The franchisee is obligated to carry out the services for which the trademark is known to secure the service quality and experience. Basically, this motive is closely related to the registration argument put forward by Mendonça et al. (2004), who argue that trademark registration allows one to operate on the market for trademarks, including selling and licensing of marks.

A final, mimetic motive stems from institutional theory (DiMaggio and Powell, 1983). When organizations face uncertainty they may model themselves on organizations in their field that they perceive to be more legitimate or successful. Mimetic forces explain the widespread adoption of, for example, management fashions for which there is little empirical evidence of performance benefits (Abrahamson, 1996). Registration of trademarks might be higher in sectors where leading companies have traditionally applied for trademarks frequently.

Summarizing, different motives for trademark registration can be found in different schools of theory, but obviously companies may have combinations of these motives when they register trademarks. Empirical research into the dominant motives and whether they occur in combination or not is lacking. The extent to which these motives are innovation related is the prime focus of our study.

2.3 Reference of Trademarks to Innovation

The variety of registration motives discussed above raises the question of how relevant trademarks are for measuring innovation. Novelty and technological progress are no requirements for registering trademarks and trademark law was not designed to elevate discourse or disseminate knowledge the way copyright law does or to promote innovation, as patent law does (Barnes, 2006). "A trademark holder signals that no other company or invention can bear the same distinguishing mark, but not that the product itself is innovative" (Davis, 2009: 8). For instance, Fosfuri and Giarratana (2009) argue that in mature product markets new trademarks may serve best as an indicator of new advertising. Therefore, the relevant question is: to what extent do new trademarks refer to innovation and does this reference relate to applicant and trademark characteristics?

In this paper we will study this in depth for SMEs. We expect that trademarks refer to different types of innovation and that some of the new trademarks refer to multiple types of innovation, because new firm offerings increasingly contain complex product–service systems (Morelli, 2003; Pawar *et al.*, 2009). Similarly, service innovations may combine new processes with new technological options and new organizational arrangements (Den Hertog, 2000; Van der Aa and Elfring, 2002).

3. Survey and Sample

To answer the research questions of our study, we have approached all Benelux applicants of Benelux trademarks (BTMs) registered in the database of the Benelux Office for Intellectual Property (BOIP) between January 2007 and March 2008, whose email addresses were available. We invited 4430 applicants to fill out an online questionnaire: the Trademark Innovation Survey (TIS). TIS-1 contains several questions, ranging from structural characteristics of the respondent (firm size, sector) to the process of trademark registration (motives, timing, strategies of bundling with other IPRs), to the reference of trademarks to innovation. To improve the face validity of the survey, we asked a team of entrepreneurs, IP experts from the BOIP, the Dutch Ministry of Economic Affairs and the multinationals Philips and ING, to make suggestions for survey improvement. Their comments were gratefully incorporated.

The questionnaire was linked electronically with the BOIP trademark database (http://register.boip.int), which means that respondents could complete the online survey and inspect the details of their BTM filing in another window. In case of Benelux applicants with multiple BTM filings, we selected one of these filings randomly and asked the applicants to fill out the questionnaire for this BTM only.

We received 660 responses on our requests to fill out the TIS questionnaire. This implies a response rate of 15 per cent. A large majority (95 per cent) of the sample are firms with less than 50 employees. Very small firms (2 employees) and one-person firms together constitute roughly half of the sample; 3 per cent of the applicants represent medium-sized firms (51–250 employees), whereas large firms account for less than 2 per cent of the BTM filings. This distribution fits with an estimate of the European Union's Office for the Harmonization in the Internal Market (OHIM) that in recent years the SME share of trademarks has increased to well over 90 per cent (OHIM, 2011). The composition of our data-set makes it difficult to compare large with small firms. It does however enable us to answer our research questions for SMEs.

Each applicant indicated up to four NACE (Nomenclature generale des Activites economiques dans les Communautes Europeenes) sectors of significant economic activity (i.e. accounting for at least 25 per cent of total revenues), with about 60 per cent of the firms simply declaring one sector of activity. About 16 per cent firms reported both manufacturing and service sector activities, meaning that we can still reasonably classify firms into either manufacturing or services. The service sector (87 per cent) is better represented than manufacturing industries (25 per cent). These proportions, however, show important parallels with the sector contributions to the GDP and the labour force in the Benelux. To test if the sample is representative, we also compared the country distribution (Belgium, the Netherlands and Luxembourg), the trademark type distribution (verbal-figurative) and the volumes in the trademark NICE[1] classes in both the sample and the research population. The results indicate that our sample does not differ significantly from the overall population. Dutch applicants dominate both the sample (72.3 per cent) and the population (72.2 per cent). The number of applicants from Luxembourg is smallest (0.5 per cent vs. 2.5 per cent). We found no country effects in our analyses. There are as many verbal as figurative marks in the sample, which fits pretty well with that same proportion in the overall population (52.9 per cent:47.1 per cent). The distribution of the BTMs over the NICE classes is nearly the same in the sample and the research population, except for BTM counts in NICE class 42 (see Figure 1). Hence, the sample may not be completely representative for 1 of 45 NICE classes. Further analysis showed that this did not lead to an overestimation of the reference to service innovation.

4. Results

4.1 Motives for Trademark Registration

We compiled a list of registration motives based on the ones reviewed in Section 2.2. For each motive, the respondent could indicate its relevance for the registration of that specific trademark on a five-point Likert scale. In Table 1, we present the importance of the various motives for trademark registration included in our literature review. It is not surprising that

---

[1] The NICE classification established by the Nice Agreement (1957) is an international classification of goods and services, applied to the registration of trademarks.

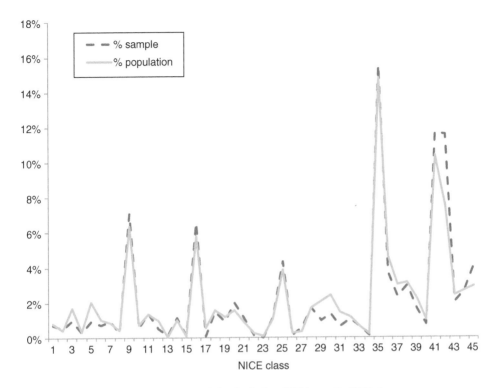

Figure 1. Sample and population distribution of BTMs over the NICE classes

avoiding imitation is ranked first, with 93 per cent of the companies ranking it with a four or five on our five-point scale. That is probably the first association most applicants have with trademark registration. The relatively low standard deviation expresses that this can be seen as an overarching motive. To support marketing processes is the second most important motive for trademark registration and protecting IP ranks third: more than 50 per cent of the respondents pinpoint the protection of IP as "important" or "very important". Note that also nearly a fourth of the trademark applicants indicated the importance of trademarks for the prolongation of other IP rights. This holds in particular for frequent users of CTMs[2] ($p = 0.04$), but also for BTMs ($p = 0.07$). Finally, improving the corporate image is in the top five as well as the monetary motive of safeguarding revenues.

From Table 1 we can also learn that signalling strategic change is of moderate importance for most of the respondents. This holds in particular for signalling geographic expansion and new market entry. Capitalizing on brand equity is of limited importance as well, although still more than 25 per cent of the respondents qualified it as relevant. Finally, just 1 of 10 applicants reported mimetic motives.

---

[2] We measured whether companies were frequent users or not by asking whether they had registered a CTM or BTM previously. A CTM is a community trademark registered at the OHIM.

Table 1. The importance of motives for trademark registration

Motives	Operationalization	Rank	Average importance (1–5)	Standard deviation	Importance 4 or 5 (per cent)	Not applicable (per cent)
To increase distinctiveness	To avoid imitation	1	4.74	0.67	93	1
	To charge higher prices	13	2.14	1.22	12	16
	To safeguard revenues	5	3.17	1.43	39	11
To signal strategic change	New market entry	12	2.23	1.30	17	15
	Geographic expansion	14	2.01	1.20	11	17
	Product or service differentiation	11	2.56	1.40	26	15
To formally protect IP	To protect IP	3	3.76	1.30	55	9
	To prolong other IPRs	9	2.68	1.38	23	19
To build brand equity	To improve customer loyalty	6	2.87	1.41	31	12
	To enhance the supply chain position	10	2.66	1.40	27	13
	To support marketing processes	2	3.88	1.26	66	4
	To improve the corporate image	4	3.52	1.39	56	6
To capitalize on brand equity	To enter markets for trademarks	7	2.80	1.44	31	13
	To support licensing or franchising activities	8	2.73	1.45	27	16
To deal with uncertainty	To imitate competitors	15	1.95	1.19	10	17

To identify the motives that explain most of the variance in the sample and to explore the theoretical rigour of the grouping of motives in Table 1, we performed a principal component analysis (PCA). We applied varimax rotation after transforming the "not applicable" scores into missing values. Subsequently, we proceeded stepwise and took into account two criteria, as suggested by Bose (2009). First, the communalities of all items had to exceed 0.5, meaning that more than half of the items' variance had to be explained by the extracted components. Second, cross-loadings had to be lower than 0.4, meaning that items loading substantially on more than one extracted component were dropped. Table 2 reports the results of PCA after two iterations. It reveals three principal components, which lend strong support for three of the six groups of motives discussed in Section 2.2. The value of the Kaiser–Meyer–Olkin (KMO) statistic, the outcome of Bartlett's test of sphericity and the Total Variance Explained (TVE) (75 per cent) confirm the appropriateness of the three-component model.

Four surveyed motives had to be dropped as a consequence of low communalities: (a) to avoid imitation, (b) to imitate competitors, (c) to safeguard revenues and (d) to enter markets for trademarks. This implies that the PCA solution did not explain sufficient variance for any of them, despite some of them being important according to our respondents. The latter holds in particular for "to avoid imitation". Three other surveyed motives had to be dropped as a consequence of high cross-loadings: (a) to charge higher prices, (b) to support licensing or franchising activities and (c) to enhance the supply chain position. This may

Table 2. Principal component analysis of trademark registration motives

Survey items	Component		
	To signal strategic change	To build brand equity	To formally protect IP
To signal new market entry	**0.907**	0.189	0.117
To signal geographic expansion	**0.886**	0.171	0.157
To signal product or service differentiation	**0.761**	0.295	0.096
To improve the corporate image	0.217	**0.829**	0.086
To support marketing processes	0.098	**0.794**	0.029
To improve customer loyalty	0.347	**0.776**	0.144
To protect IP	0.008	0.009	**0.904**
To prolong other IPRs	0.328	0.195	**0.715**
Share of explained variance	30.8 per cent	26.4 per cent	17.6 per cent

Notes: Results of principal components analysis with varimax rotation; pairwise deletion of missing values; communalities > 0.5, cross-loadings < 0.4. Eigen values > 1, TVE $= 74.8$ per cent, KMO $= 0.794$, Bartlett's test of sphericity, $p = 0.000$. In bold we highlight the motives with highest loadings that we use for the interpretation of the components.

refer to a measurement bias. However, the exclusion of several items from the final solution of our exploratory PCA prompts us to consider the possibility that a hierarchical structure connecting all motives exists, around a core of three sufficiently independent groups of motives exemplified by the extracted orthogonal components. In this structure, "to avoid imitation" can be seen as an overarching motive. The three principal components function as underlying motives, whereas the monetary motives, namely to charge higher prices, to safeguard revenues, but also to enter markets for trademarks, might well be ultimate motives for the applicants, although the average importance of these ultimate motives is relatively low. However, these motives may be latent for some of the applicants, others may be reluctant to admit them, or they may be blurred by post hoc evaluations of the trademarks' value. For the purpose of this paper, these are simply interpretations and of course further research aimed at developing a theoretical framework of the relations between motives can shed light on our speculations.

For the purpose of our investigation into the relevance of trademarks for measuring innovation, we can conclude that formally protecting IP plays an important role in decision-making about trademark registration. Although the view of Davis (2009) that trademarks provide exclusive rights but no incentive for innovation per se is largely correct, trademarks may help to protect IP indirectly, as a complementary asset (Teece, 1986) or as the primary way to protect IP. However, to test the robustness of the conclusion that trademarks are registered in many cases for innovation related reasons, it is necessary to study the relationship between trademarks and innovation activity in more detail.

4.1.1 Reference of Trademarks to Innovation. As discussed in Section 2.1, we define innovation broadly and distinguish among six types of innovation: product, process, service, technological, organizational and marketing innovation. Figure 2 shows the reference of BTMs to innovation activity graphically. We asked the respondents to indicate whether the

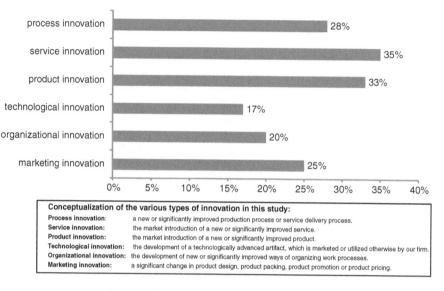

Figure 2. Trademark reference to innovation activity

trademark they registered referred to any of the types of innovation mentioned in Figure 2. We used the term "reference" because it is derived from *referre* (Latin), which basically means "point, place or source of origin". Products and services are by definition the sources of origin for trademarks (Landes and Posner, 2003).

Overall, 58 per cent of the BTMs in the sample refer to at least one of the innovation types. The reference of BTMs to product innovation (33 per cent) and service innovation (35 per cent) is highest, followed by the reference to process innovation (28 per cent). So even though, as Hipp and Grupp (2005) state and we empirically confirm, protecting technological progress may not be the principal motive for trademarking, this does not lead to the conclusion that trademarks are of limited use for measuring innovation. In fact, in our data nearly 60 per cent of the trademarks refer to innovation activity.

In line with previous studies (Graham, 2004; Malmberg, 2005), an initial exploration of our data also shows that the reference to innovation varies significantly across sectors. Here we wish to make full use of our data-set and investigate the key covariates of the reference to innovation in a multivariate setting. The first set of covariates includes the motives for trademark registration uncovered in section 4.1. We calculate the factor scores resulting from the PCA and use them as independent variables in the regression models. We have only included the three principal components as regressors because other motives lack variance ("to avoid imitation") or importance ("to imitate competitors"), or cross load with two principal components ("to support licensing or franchising activities"). Including the latter in regression analyses causes multicollinearity problems.

Second, we consider firm-level characteristics. Firm size is measured by the reported number of employees. Each firm also indicated one or more sectors of activity so that the number of different sectors can be used as a rough proxy for sectoral diversification. We asked respondents whether they had already registered other trademarks, either BTMs or CTMs. Whether companies are frequent users of trademarks, together with their branding

Table 3. Principal component analysis of the trademark reference to innovation

Survey items	Component		
	F1: Reference to service delivery innovation	F2: Reference to technological product innovation	F3: Reference to non-technological innovation
Reference to process innovation	**0.827**	−0.062	0.106
Reference to service innovation	**0.809**	0.222	0.089
Reference to product innovation	−0.086	**0.825**	0.159
Reference to technological innovation	0.332	**0.738**	−0.144
Reference to organizational innovation	−0.014	0.295	**0.801**
Reference to marketing innovation	0.244	−0.255	**0.754**
Share of explained variance	25.3 per cent	23.9 per cent	21.3 per cent

Notes: Results of principal components analysis with varimax rotation; list-wise deletion of missing values; communalities > 0.5, cross-loadings < 0.4. Eigen values > 1, TVE = 70.5 per cent, KMO = 0.570, Bartlett's test of sphericity, $p = 0.000$. In bold we highlight the motives with highest loadings that we use for the interpretation of the components.

strategy, may determine whether a given trademark refers to innovation or not. Davis (2009) emphasizes that a strong trademark position might lull managers into a false sense of security, decreasing their incentives to undertake new investments in R&D, and thereby their ability to continue to innovate. We also define the variable "manufacturing" ("services") for trademark applicants active in at least one manufacturing (service) sector of activity.[3]

Finally, we control for trademark-level characteristics. We distinguish between verbal and figurative marks (type = 1 if the trademark is verbal, type = 2 if the trademark is figurative) and we use the information on the NICE classes. Each trademark covers up to eight NICE classes, with more classes implying higher registration costs. The breadth of trademarks, defined as the number of NICE classes covered, can be seen as a proxy for the value of trademarks (Sandner and Block, 2011). It could also be related to different branding strategies: marks covering more NICE classes could be associated to "branded house" type of strategies, where the same symbol is used for all the products and services of a diversified company. The NICE classes can also be grouped into goods versus service categories, but a given trademark can of course cover both. We also included dummies for the NICE classes with the most trademarks in our data, namely NICE classes 9 (instruments and computers), 16 (paper and printed products), 25 (clothing and footwear) for goods and NICE classes 35 (advertising and management), 41 (education), 42 (scientific services) for services as suggested by Malmberg (2005). Finally, we asked the respondents whether the object covered in the given trademark is or will also be protected with other IPRs (patents, design rights, growers rights, copyrights).

---

[3] We also defined dummies for manufacturing/services by considering whether applicants were *only* active in manufacturing/service sectors: the model results remain qualitatively the same, which we take as a robustness check.

As for the dependent variable in our regressions, instead of repeating the analysis for each of the six types of innovation, which in fact are often reported in combination by our respondents, we first investigate whether the different types can be reduced to fewer categories using a PCA. The results, reported in Table 3, show that there are in fact three different categories of innovation types that can be distinguished meaningfully from our data. We interpret this result as being in line with the complexity to conceptually and operationally distinguish between different manifestations of innovation.

A first component is made out of observations combining references to process and service innovation. We label this component "reference to service delivery innovation" in keeping with conceptualization of service innovation by Den Hertog (2000). This states that service innovation often consists of new processes of delivering services, often derived from new technologies (which seems to be confirmed by the lower but still relevant 0.332 loading of the fourth survey item listed in Table 3). Notice also that the reference to process innovation only loads significantly on this first component, which further supports our interpretation of this component (F1) as "reference to service delivery innovation". The second component fits the definition of technological product innovation. The item referring to product innovation specifically loads on this component and not on the other two. Our data also indicate that technological innovation plays a role both in product and in service innovation, but this component is clearly about advanced technologies embedded in new products. The last component brings together marketing and organizational innovation, two types that seem quite different but apparently easily fall together in an "other" category of "non-technological innovation".

Table 4 summarizes the main descriptive statistics of all variables used and Table 5A and 5B report the standardized coefficients of three linear regression models estimated on our data; Table 5A for all cases and 5B for trademarks filed by service firms. We immediately see that the model explaining the reference to non-technological innovation has a very low goodness of fit ($R^2 = 0.042$) and only one clearly significant effect (see Table 5A). This result can be related to the fact that this last factor is in fact more of an "other" category that demands further specification. For now, we focus on the first two models.

Overall, the motives for trademark registration are strongly linked to the reference to innovation, but service and product innovation show different results. Trademarks registered to signal strategic change and build brand equity refer significantly more often to service delivery innovation, whereas formally protecting IP does not play a role. This could indicate that applicants do not believe that trademarks are effective protection tools, whereas they value much more their signalling role. Instead the IP protection motive is significantly related to a reference to technological product innovation, together with the motive of signalling strategic change.

Whether the applicant is a first or frequent user of trademarks does not seem to play a role, except for non-technological innovation and only for the frequent use of CTMs, which require a larger effort than BTMs. Apparently, frequent and advanced users of trademarks are more likely to register trademarks referring to organizational or marketing innovation. The NICE class of the trademark is somewhat informative, as trademarks registered in the class covering instruments and computers are more often associated with technological product innovation, whereas trademarks registered in the class covering advertising and management refer to service delivery innovation to a somewhat larger extent than the other NICE service classes considered.

Table 4. Descriptive statistics of all variables used in the regressions

				Descriptive statistics		
		N	Minimum	Maximum	Mean	Standard Deviation
Dependent variables	F1: Reference to service delivery innovation	447	−1.57	1.91	0.00	1.00
	F2: Reference to technological product innovation	447	−1.57	2.08	0.00	1.00
	F3: Reference to non-technological innovation	447	−1.38	2.08	0.00	1.00
Motives	To signal strategic change	335	−1.76	2.78	0.00	1.00
	To build brand equity	335	−2.09	1.99	0.00	1.00
	To formally protect IP	335	−2.50	2.04	0.00	1.00
Firm controls	Size	468	1.00	6.00	1.80	0.97
	Sectoral diversification	468	1.00	4.00	1.66	0.97
	First user BTM (1 = frequent user, 2 = first user)	660	1.00	2.00	1.61	0.49
	First user CTM (1 = frequent user, 2 = first user)	660	1.00	2.00	1.89	0.32
	Services	468	0.00	1.00	0.87	0.33
	Manufacturing	468	0.00	1.00	0.25	0.43
	Supplier-dominated services	468	0.00	1.00	0.17	0.37
	Physical networks	468	0.00	1.00	0.27	0.44
	Information networks	468	0.00	1.00	0.06	0.24
	Knowledge-intensive business services	468	0.00	1.00	0.47	0.50
TM controls	Figurative (2) versus verbal (1)	604	1.00	2.00	1.50	0.50
	Combined with other IPR	660	0.00	1.00	0.20	0.40
	NICE breadth	660	0.00	8.00	2.05	1.54
	Goods mark	660	0.00	1.00	0.50	0.50
	Service mark	660	0.00	1.00	0.50	0.50
NICE classes	9: instruments and computers	660	0.00	1.00	0.15	0.36
	16: paper and printed products	660	0.00	1.00	0.14	0.35
	25: clothing and footwear	660	0.00	1.00	0.09	0.29
	35: advertising and management	660	0.00	1.00	0.33	0.47
	41: education	660	0.00	1.00	0.25	0.43
	42: scientific services	660	0.00	1.00	0.25	0.43

From Table 5A and 5B we can also learn that the bundling of trademarks with other IPRs is significantly related to the reference of both service delivery and technological product innovation. Bundling can be seen as an additional effort showing the value of an object at hand (Sandner and Block, 2011), which makes the object more likely in turn to be a valuable innovation for the company. The effect of bundling is much stronger for technological product innovation, where the technological component of the innovation (captured in our factor) naturally links to a patent application.

Table 5A. Covariates of the trademark reference to innovation

		All cases					
		F1: Reference to service delivery innovation		F2: Reference to technological product innovation		F3: Reference to non-technological innovation	
		Standard coefficient	p-Value	Standard coefficient	p-Value	Standard coefficient	p-Value
	(Constant)		0.337		0.128		0.126
Motives	To signal strategic change	0.122**	0.035	0.153***	0.005	0.076	0.207
	To build brand equity	0.109*	0.063	0.074	0.173	0.064	0.286
	To formally protect IP	0.063	0.269	0.132**	0.014	0.077	0.194
Firm-level controls	Size	−0.002	0.967	−0.046	0.409	0.006	0.928
	Sectoral diversification	0.153**	0.011	−0.001	0.990	−0.043	0.485
	First-user BTM	−0.093	0.133	−0.073	0.206	−0.015	0.813
	First-user CTM	0.063	0.299	−0.033	0.562	−0.124**	0.049
	Service sector	0197***	0.001				
	Manufacturing sector			0.248***	0.000	0.078	0.201
TM-level controls	Figurative versus verbal	−0.106*	0.071	−0.088	0.107	−0.029	0.634
	Combined with other IPR	−0.111*	0.056	0.227***	0.000	0.029	0.630
	NICE breadth	0.005	0.937	−0.078	0.150	0.108*	0.072
	Service mark	0.026	0.657	−0.014	0.792	−0.012	0.839
	Goods mark			−0.014	0.792	−0.012	0.839
	N	290		290		290	
	R^2	0.120		0.244		0.042	

Note: $*p < 0.1$; $**p < 0.05$; $***p < 0.01$.

If a trademark refers to a new product in our sample, then in 25 per cent of the cases that product is protected by a patent as well. If however a trademark refers to a new service, then the trademark applicant has applied for a patent in only 3 per cent of the cases. This indicates that patents cover product innovation in 25 per cent of the trademarked cases but neglect service innovation almost completely.

Taking into account that some innovations are protected by more than two IPRs, including copyrights, growers rights and design rights, the overall bundling figures are 44 per cent for product innovations and 27 per cent for service innovations. Hence, bundling of trademarks with other IPRs is done 40−45 per cent more frequently in case of product innovation; the vast majority of service innovations will only be covered by trademarks. We can therefore conclude that the use of trademark data for SMEs seems most interesting for measuring service innovation. We will analyse whether this holds for all service sectors in Section 4.1.2.

4.1.2 A Closer Look at the Service Sector. Going back to the regression results, the strong significance of the manufacturing and service variables warrants a further analysis of cross-

Table 5B. Covariates of the trademark reference to innovation for service firms

		Service firms only			
		F1: Reference to service delivery innovation		F2: Reference to technological product innovation	
		Standard coefficient	p-Value	Standard Coefficient	p-Value
	(Constant)		0.888		0.101
Motives	To signal strategic change	0.176***	0.006	0.077	0.183
	To build brand equity	0.115*	0.072	0.075	0.194
	To formally protect IP	0.052	0.405	0.147***	0.010
Firm-level controls	Size	0.039	0.542	−0.086	0.151
	Sectoral diversification	0.131*	0.078	0.090	0.183
	First-user BTM	−0.068	0.313	−0.082	0.178
	First-user CTM	0.070	0.288	−0.054	0.372
	Supplier-dominated services	−0.059	0.420	0.024	0.723
	Physical networks	−0.160*	0.060	0.129*	0.085
	Information networks	0.046	0.476	0.015	0.801
	Knowledge-intensive business services	0.122	0.147	−0.210***	0.006
TM-level controls	Figurative vs verbal	−0.098	0.122	−0.068	0.245
	Combined with other IPR	−0.026	0.686	0.205***	0.001
	NICE breadth	−0.049	0.475	−0.058	0.335
NICE classes	Advertising and management	0.072	0.300		
	Education	0.005	0.936		
	Scientific services	−0.042	0.518		
	Instruments and computers			0.236***	0.000
	Paper and printed products			−0.033	0.576
	Clothing and footwear			−0.009	0.872
	N	251		251	
	R^2	0.148		0.283	

Note: *$p < 0.1$; **$p < 0.05$; ***$p < 0.01$.

sectoral variation. We focus on the broad service category given that this represents the largest share of our data and that previous studies have shown that the value added of trademarks as innovation indicators lies mostly within service sectors. We use the taxonomy originally proposed by Miozzo and Soete (2001) to distinguish four groups of service sectors sharing similar characteristics as regards to innovation: supplier-dominated services (SDS), physical networks (PN), information networks (IN) and science-based and specialized suppliers, often called KIBS.[4] Research on the validity of trademarks as innovation indicators has mostly focused on KIBS. As discussed also in Castaldi (2009), KIBS and IN

---

[4] We classified service sectors into four categories based upon the classification used in Castaldi (2009).

Table 6. Percentage of trademarks with reference to innovation in different service sectors

	Service	Product	Process	Technological	Organizational	Marketing	Any	n
Supplier-dominated services	49.4	44.3	39.2	24.1	27.8	34.2	82	79
Physical networks	38.4	56.8	36	30.4	24	47.2	83.2	125
Information networks	79.3	37.9	58.6	34.5	27.6	34.5	89.7	29
Knowledge-intensive business services	60.6	35.3	43.1	23.4	32.1	28	78	218

services are seen as advanced knowledge providers, whereas PN services are responsible for the physical infrastructure of the economy and SDS services play a marginal role when it comes to innovation generation.

To gauge the extent to which trademarks registered by companies across the four groups of sectors do refer to innovation in our data, we preliminarily look at the simple percentages reported in Table 6. What is interesting is that trademarks referring to innovation are widespread across all service sectors, if we consider all different innovation types. Indeed the reference to service innovation as such is highest for IN and KIBS, but PN and SDS firms in our data also register many trademarks referring to other forms of innovation, mainly product innovation for PN and a broad range of innovation types for SDS. To evaluate sectoral differences in a multivariate setting, we estimate similar regression models to the ones discussed in Section 4.1.1, but for the sub-sample of firms active in service sectors. We also include dummies for the four service categories and present the results for the models explaining the factor reference to service delivery innovation and the factor reference to technological product innovation in Table 5B. The difference in motives between the two models appears even stronger than what we found for the complete sample. Trademarks referring to service delivery innovation are registered by firms motivated to signal strategic change and build brand equity, whereas trademarks referring to technology-based product innovation are registered by applicants motivated by a quest for IP rents.

In terms of sectoral differences, the only significant effects we find indicate that trademarks registered by PN firms refer significantly less than average to service delivery innovation and trademarks registered by KIBS firms refer significantly less than average to technological product innovation. Otherwise, reference to the two innovation factors appears not to be affected by the sector of economic activity. As regards the information on the NICE classes, only trademarks registered under instruments and computers are more likely to refer to technological product innovation, a result already found for all firms and confirmed for service firms as well.

4.2 Timing of Trademark Registration

To compare the timing of BTM filing with the process of innovation, we used new product development model of Cooper (1983) as a reference model. This model comprises a linear sequence of seven stages: idea generation, research, development, testing, marketing, market introduction and commercialization.

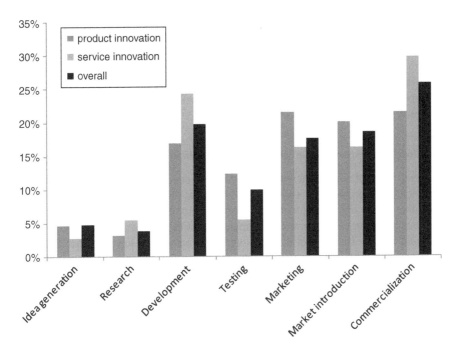

Figure 3. Trademark registration related to the stages of the innovation process

"It can be assumed that brands are registered just shortly before the launch of the product or service on the market, so they indicate a later phase as patents in the innovation process" (Hipp and Grupp, 2005: 526). Because no empirical material was available, Hipp and Grupp (2005) had to work with this assumption. Figure 3 shows that their assumption is largely correct, albeit some qualifications are in place. Figure 3 depicts the timing of the BTM filings referring to new products or services set against the stages of the innovation process (Cooper, 1983). Trademarks registered in the last three stages of the innovation process account for 62 per cent of the trademarks registered for innovative offers. However, 26 per cent of the trademarks were actually filed after the market introduction, so not before the launch of the product, but afterwards. The number of trademarks filed in the early phases of the innovation process is very limited. Only 5 per cent of trademarks was filed in the idea generation phase and only 4 per cent in the research phase. An interesting peak, however, occurs in the development process. One of five trademarks referring to new products or services is filed during development, which is relatively early.

The parallels between trademark registration in the case of product and service innovation are relatively strong. Nevertheless, trademarks referring to service innovation are registered relatively frequently in the development stage or after the market introduction and less frequently in the testing and marketing stage. These differences may be rooted in differences between product and service innovation processes. Customers play a relatively important role in the service innovation process (Johne and Storey, 1998) and often innovation emerges on the service job (Den Hertog, 2000). In such cases, service firms try to commoditize new work practices, methods and tools. Trademark registration may support commoditization. This may explain partly that 30 per cent of service innovations is trademarked in the stage of commercialization. In addition, services are intangible. This might imply an early need for new service marks not only to symbolize service innovation, but also to foster effective communication. However, the early need for service marks does not necessarily imply an early need for trademark filing. Therefore, an alternative explanation of the early trademark filing may be a lack of service testing in practice or an iterative way of developing and testing services.

5. Conclusion, Research Agenda and Policy Implications

Our in-depth study of new BTMs registered by SMEs revealed the importance of innovation-related registration motives as well as a high reference to innovation. The study therefore confirms the validity of trademark counts as an indicator of innovation for SMEs. Protecting IP is an important registration motive for about half of the trademark applicants and about 60 per cent of new trademarks refer to innovation activities. However, the reference to different types of innovation co-varies with trademark and applicant characteristics. It is, therefore, inappropriate to use raw counts of new trademark filings for innovation studies and policy-making for all SMEs.

Trademarks are particularly valuable as measures of service innovation. Most trademarks are not combined with other IPRs in these cases, whereas we found the combination with patents to be an important one in the case of technology-based product innovations. However, we also found that a substantial proportion of the trademarks referring to product innovation was not combined with patents. Regarding timing, trademarks referring to new products and services indicate innovations in the later stages of the innovation process. Consequently, trademark counts appear to solve two important drawbacks of other indicators for innovation as identified by Kleinknecht (2000). They allow a better measurement of service innovation and also of innovations in later stages. Moreover, our evidence shows that trademarks still provide information when measuring technology-based product innovation and that they reveal multiple types of innovation, including non-technological innovation.

A number of limitations need to be acknowledged and addressed regarding this study. The first limitation concerns the coverage of our sample. For practical reasons, we did not invite applicants from outside the Benelux to participate in our study. About 6 per cent of the BTM applicants in the research population reside in countries outside the Benelux. As Giarratana and Torrisi (2010) suggest, these applicants may use the BTMs predominantly for licensing and franchising purposes, as a low-risk entry strategy in foreign markets. If this can be confirmed, then it is unlikely that many of the trademarks owned by non-Benelux applicants refer to innovation activities in the Benelux. This implies that the reference of BTMs to innovation is probably slightly lower than reported in this paper.

The second limitation is that we have asked the trademark applicants to rate the importance of various registration motives ex post, even though within a relatively short time frame of 1 year. Basically, they have reconstructed their motives for trademark registration or they may have ex post rationalized their motivation with the perceived value of the trademark filing in mind. An alternative research design, which could be used in future research, would ask respondents to declare their motives at the very moment when they file their trademark application.

The third limitation concerns the fact that we have operationalized the use of trademarks as a dichotomy: first users versus frequent users of BTMs or CTMs. In line with the work of Davis (2009), one could measure trademark stocks more precisely and test hypotheses such as the "trademark trap". This refers to the hypothesized tendency of firms to become less innovative when a lot of resources are allocated to building and capitalizing on strong brands. Anonymity of the respondents made it impossible for us to test this with the current sample. Further research in this direction could also tackle the issue of whether excessive use of branding could lead to negative social returns of trademarks by inhibiting dynamic competition (Greenhalgh and Rogers, 2012)

More generally, our empirical results need to be confirmed in larger, cross-country samples and also for large firms. Although the vast majority of trademarks are registered by SMEs, large firms register them as well and their motives and IP strategies may be quite different. Finally, a replication of this study for CTMs is an important further research topic, because CTMs guarantee trademark protection at the EU level. One may assume that trademarks used to signal radical innovations are more frequently registered at the OHIM in Alicante. Radical innovations usually require high and high-risk investments. If a firm succeeds in developing a radical innovation, then it may (need to) exploit it internationally.

The results of this study are particularly relevant for policy-makers. Policy-makers have mainly used R&D expenses and patent data as indicators of innovation and have started to begin looking at trademarks. By including trademarks as an indicator of innovation, policy-makers may do more justice to the differences between industries and to the servitization of society. As our research has identified the contours of when and how trademark data should be used, policy-makers may build on our findings for more specific guidance. This holds in particular for measuring service innovation in SMEs.

Trademarks may also play a role in policy evaluation. If more trademarks get registered as a consequence of a new policy, this may show the policy worked. However, governments must keep in mind that applying for a trademark is easy and low cost. Organizations that receive an innovation subsidy may, therefore, apply for a trademark only to show the policy-makers that they have used the subsidy well, even though in reality no innovation was developed. It is easier to "cheat" in this way with trademarks, than with patents.

A final consideration regards the quality and availability of trademark data, both for scientific research and policy-making. Our analysis shows that a valid use of trademarks relies on additional information about applicants, such as company size but also the sector (s) of economic activity, bundling of IP rights and the timing of filing against the innovation process. Additional information could be included at trademark offices or further efforts could be made to link trademark data with firm-level data available from national business registers and also with patent and other IPR data. We envision much potential for the conceptual but also practical integration of trademark data into innovation research.

Acknowledgements

We thank the editor Francesco Lissoni and two anonymous reviewers for their constructive comments, which helped us to improve the manuscript significantly. We also thank Paula White for editing our manuscript. The usual disclaimer applies: any remaining errors are ours.

References

Aaker, D. (2004) Leveraging the corporate brand, *California Management Review*, 46(3), pp. 6–18.

Aaker, D. (2007) Innovation: brand it or lose it, *California Management Review*, 50(1), pp. 8–24.

Aaker, D. and Keller, K. L. (1990) Consumer evaluations of brand extensions, *Journal of Marketing*, 54(1), pp. 27–41.

Abrahamson, E. (1996) Management fashion, *Academy of Management Review*, 21, pp. 254–285.

Allegrezza, S. and Guarda-Rauchs, A. (1999) The determinants of trademarks deposits: an econometric investigation (a case study of the Benelux), *Economie Appliquée*, 52(2), pp. 51–68.

Amara, N., Landry, R. and Traoré, N. (2008) Managing the protection of innovations in knowledge-intensive business services, *Research Policy*, 37, pp. 1530–1547.

Barnes, J. W. (2006) A new economics of trademarks, *Northwestern Journal of Technology and Intellectual Property*, 22, p. 49.

Blind, K., Edler, E., Frietsch, R. and Schmoch, U. (2006) Motives to patent, *Research Policy*, 35, pp. 655–672.

Bose, A. (2009) *Principal Components Analysis* (Greater Noida, Uttar Pradesh: Bimtech).

Castaldi, C. (2009) The relative weight of manufacturing and services in Europe: an innovation perspective, *Technological Forecasting and Social Change*, 76, pp. 709–722.

Coombs, R. and Miles, I. (2000) Innovation, measurement and services: the new problematique, in: J. S. Metcalfe & I. Miles (Eds), *Innovation Systems in the Service Economy, Measurement and Case Study Analysis*, pp. 85–105 (Dordrecht: Kluwer Academic Publishers).

Cooper, R. G. (1983) A process model for industrial new product development, *IEEE Transactions on Engineering Management*, 30, pp. 2–11.

Daizadeh, I. (2009) An intellectual property-based corporate strategy: an R&D spend, patent, trademark, media communication, and market price innovation agenda, *Scientometrics*, 80(3), pp. 731–746.

Davis, L. N. (2009) Leveraging trademarks to capture innovation returns, paper presented at the *Druid Summer Conference 2009 on Strategy, Innovation and Knowledge*, Copenhagen, Denmark, 9–16 June.

Den Hertog, P. (2000) Knowledge-intensive business services as co-producers of innovation, *International Journal of Innovation Management*, 4, pp. 491–528.

Den Hertog, P., Bilderbeek, R. and Maltha, S. (1997) Intangibles—the soft side of innovation, *Futures*, 29(1), pp. 33–45.

DiMaggio, P. J. and Powell, W. W. (1983) The iron cage revisited: institutional isomorphism and collective rationality in organizational fields, *American Sociological Review*, 48(2), pp. 147–160.

Drejer, I. (2004) Identifying innovation in surveys of services: a Schumpeterian perspective, *Research Policy*, 33, pp. 551–562.

Economides, N. (1998) Trademarks, in: P. Newman (Ed.), *The New Palgrave Dictionary of Economics and Law* (London: Macmillan).

Flikkema, M. J., Jansen, P. G. W. and Van der Sluis, E. C. (2007) Identifying neo-Schumpeterian innovation in service firms: a conceptual essay with a novel classification, *Economics of Innovation and New Technology*, 16(7), pp. 541–558.

Fosfuri, A. and Giarratana, M. S. (2009) Masters of war: rivals' product innovation and new advertising in mature product markets, *Management Science*, 55(2), pp. 181–191.

Fosfuri, M. S., Giarratana, M. S. and Luzzi, A. (2008) The penguin has entered the building: the commercialization of open source software products, *Organization Science*, 19(2), pp. 292–305.

Gallouj, F. (2000) Beyond technological innovation: trajectories and varieties of services innovation, in: M. Boden & I. Miles (Eds), *Services and the Knowledge-based Economy*, pp. 129–145 (London: Continuum).

Giarratana, M. S. and Torrisi, S. (2010) Foreign entry and survival in a knowledge-intensive market: emerging economy countries' international linkages, technology competences, and firm experience, *Strategic Entrepreneurship Journal*, 4(1), pp. 85–104.

Graham, S. J. H. (2004) Complementary use of patents, copyrights and trademarks by software firms: evidence from litigation, paper presented at the *DRUID Summer Conference on Industrial dynamics, Innovation and Development*, Copenhagen, Denmark, 14–16 June.

Greenhalgh, C. and Rogers, M. (2010) *Innovation, Intellectual Property and Economic Growth* (Princeton, NJ: Princeton University Press).

Greenhalgh, C. and Rogers, M. (2012) Trademarks and performance in services and manufacturing firms: evidence of Schumpeterian competition through Innovation, *The Australian Economic Review*, 45, pp. 50–76.

Hagedoorn, J. and Cloodt, M. (2003) Measuring innovative performance: is there an advantage in using multiple indicators? *Research Policy*, 32, pp. 1365–1379.

Hall, R. (2006) A framework linking intangible resources and capabilities to sustainable competitive advantage, *Strategic Management Journal*, 14(8), pp. 607–618.

Hamel, G. and Prahalad, C. K. (1993) Strategy as stretch and leverage, *Harvard Business Review*, 71(2), pp. 75–84.

Heidenreich, E. (2009) Innovation patterns and location of European low- and medium-technology industries, *Research Policy*, 38, pp. 483–494.

Heil, O. and Robertson, T. S. (1991) Toward a theory of competitive market signaling: a research agenda, *Strategic Management Journal*, 12(6), pp. 403–418.

Hipp, C. and Grupp, H. (2005) Innovation in the service sector: the demand for service-specific innovation measurement concepts and typologies, *Research Policy*, 34, pp. 517–535.

Hsu, D. and Ziedonis, R. H. (2007) Patent as quality signal of entrepreneurial ventures. Working Paper (University of Pennsylvania).

Johne, A. and Storey, C. (1998) New service development: a review of the literature and annotated bibliography, *European Journal of Marketing*, 32(3–4), pp. 184–231.

Keller, K. L. and Lehmann, D. R. (2006) Brands and branding: research findings and future priorities, *Marketing Science*, 25(6), pp. 740–759.

Kleinknecht, A. H. (2000) Indicators of manufacturing and service innovation: their strengths and weaknesses, in: J. S. Metcalfe & I. Miles (Eds), *Innovation Systems in the Service Economy, Measurement and Case Study Analysis* (Dordrecht: Kluwer Academic Publishers).

Krasnikov, A., Mishra, S. and Orozco, D. (2009) Evaluating the financial impact of branding using trademarks: a framework and empirical evidence, *Journal of Marketing*, 73(6), pp. 154–166.

Landes, W. M. and Posner, R. A. (2003) Trademark law: an economic perspective, *The Journal of Law and Economics*, 30, pp. 265–309.

Leiponen, A. and Byma, J. (2007) If you cannot block, you better run: small firms, cooperative innovation and appropriation strategies, *Research Policy*, 38, pp. 1478–1488.

Malmberg, C. (2005) Trademark statistics as innovation indicator?: A micro study. Working Paper 2005/17 (Lund University: Circle Electronic).

McClure, D. M. (1996) Trademarks and competition: a recent history, *Law and Contemporary Problems*, 59(2), pp. 13–43.

Mendonça, S., Pereira, T. S. and Godinho, M. M. (2004) Trademarks as an indicator of innovation and industrial change, *Research Policy*, 33, pp. 1385–1404.

Miles, I., Andersen, B., Boden, M. and Howells, J. (2000) Service production and intellectual property, *International Journal of Technology Management*, 20(1/2), pp. 95–115.

Millot, V. (2008) *Trademarks as an indicator of product and marketing innovation*. OECD-DSTI/EAS/IND/WPIA(2008)10 (Paris: OECD Publishers).

Miozzo, M. and Soete, L. (2001) Internationalisation of services: a technology perspective, *Technological Forecasting and Social Change*, 67, pp. 159–185.

Morelli, N. (2003) Product-service systems, a perspective shift for designers: a case study: the design of a telecentre, *Design Studies*, 24 (1), pp. 73–99.

Norris, D. G. (1992) Ingredient branding: a strategy option with multiple beneficiaries, *Journal of Consumer Marketing*, 9(3), pp. 19–31.

OHIM (2011) *OHIM Strategic Plan 2011/2015*. Office for Harmonization in the Internal Market.

Pawar, K. S., Beltagui, A. and Riedel, J. C. K. H. (2009) The PSO triangle: designing product, service and organisation to create value, *International Journal of Operations & Production Management*, 29(5), pp. 468–493.

Ramello, G. B. (2006) What's in a sign? Trademark law and economic theory, *Journal of Economic Surveys*, 20(4), pp. 547–565.

Ramello, G. B. and Silva, F. (2006) Appropriating signs and meaning: the elusive economics of trademark, *Industrial and Corporate Change*, 15(6), pp. 937–963.

Rao, A. R. (2005) The quality of price as a quality cue, *Journal of Marketing Research*, 42(4), pp. 401–405.

Reitzig, M. (2004) Strategic management of intellectual property, *Sloan Management Review Spring*, 2004, pp. 35–40.

Rujas, J. (1999) Trade marks: complementary to patents, *World Patent Information*, 21, pp. 35–39.

Sandner, P. G. and Block, J. (2011) The market value of R&D, patents, and trademarks, *Research Policy*, 40(7), pp. 969–985.

Schmalensee, R. (1978) Entry deterrence in the ready to-eat breakfast cereal industry, *Bell Journal of Economics*, 9(2), pp. 305–327.

Schmoch, U. (2003) Service marks as novel innovation indicator, *Research Evaluation*, 12, pp. 149–156.

Schmoch, U. and Gauch, S. (2009) Service marks as indicators for innovation in knowledge-based services, *Research Evaluation*, 18(4), pp. 323–335.

Schumpeter, J. A. (1934) *The Theory of Economic Development: An Inquiry into Profits, Capital, Credit, Interest and the Business Cycle* (Cambridge, MA: Harvard University Press).

Semadeni, M. (2006) Minding your distance: how management consulting firms use service marks to position competitively, *Strategic Management Journal*, 27(2), pp. 169–187.

Semadeni, M. and Anderson, B. S. (2010) The follower's dilemma: innovation and imitation in the professional services industry, *Academy of Management Journal*, 53(5), pp. 1175–1194.

Shaked, A. and Sutton, J. (1982) Relaxing price competition through product differentiation, *The Review of Economic Studies*, 49(1), pp. 3–13.

Smith, A. (2011) Locating the missing link between trademarks and innovation, *World Trademark Review*, 30, pp. 16–22.

Spinelli, S. and Birley, S. (1996) Toward a theory of conflict in the franchise system, *Journal of Business Venturing*, 11(5), pp. 329–342.

Srivastava, R. K., Fahey, L. and Christensen, H. K. (2001) The resource-based view and marketing: The role of market-based assets in gaining competitive advantage, *Journal of Management*, 27, pp. 777–801.

Stoneman, P. (2010) *Soft Innovation: Economics, Design and the Creative Industries* (New York: Oxford University Press).

Teece, D. (1986) Profiting from technological innovation: implications for integration, licensing and public policy, *Research Policy*, 15(1), pp. 285–305.

Thomä, J. and Bizer, K. (2013) To protect or not to protect? Modes of appropriability in the small enterprises sector, *Research Policy*, 42, pp. 35–49.

Van der Aa, W. and Elfring, T. (2002) Realizing innovation in services, *Scandinavian Journal of Management*, 18(2), pp. 155–171.

Wernerfelt, B. (1988) Umbrella branding as a signal of new product quality, *Rand Journal of Economics*, 19, pp. 458–466.

Innovation activities and business cycles: are trademarks a leading indicator?

Charles A. W. deGrazia, Amanda Myers and Andrew A. Toole

ABSTRACT

Despite the widespread use of economic information to anticipate changes in business conditions, innovation metrics are not considered to be leading indicators. We argue that aggregate trademark data reflect firm-level choices that can help predict business cycles. In addition to establishing the conceptual basis for considering trademarks, our statistical evaluations, using turning point analysis and a novel machine learning method, find that trademark filings for product and service offerings in commercial use outperform many of the conventional leading indicators. Our work suggests that including trademark metrics in composite indexes could improve recession forecasting performance.

1. Introduction

Business leaders and policy makers consult a variety of leading indicators to help them understand how the business climate is likely to change over time. The custodian of the official U.S. leading index, The Conference Board (TCB), selects economic variables such as consumer expectations, unemployment claims, and manufacturing orders to construct a widely-used index called the Leading Economic Index (LEI).[1] Surprisingly, no economic variables capturing innovation are included among the ten separate indicators used by TCB to construct the LEI.[2]

In this paper, we argue that an indicator of firm-level innovative activities can reveal valuable information about emerging business conditions. In particular, we draw on a growing body of economic research that links firm-level trademark filing behaviour to product market innovation. Business managers and innovators across a wide variety of markets are creating and discontinuing trademarks as specific products and services are introduced and withdrawn from the market place. Trademarks reflect, at least to some

---

This article has been republished with minor changes. These changes do not impact the academic content of the article.

[1]The Bureau of Economic Analysis of the Department of Commerce decided in 1995 to seek a private organization to produce and disseminate its monthly cyclical indicators – including the leading economic indicators and the widely publicised composite leading index. After a bidding process, The Conference Board was selected to become the custodian of the official composite leading, coincident, and lagging indexes. See https://www.conference-board.org/data/bci/index.cfm?id=2157.

[2]At least since Schumpeter (1942), economists have recognized the possibility that innovation may cause business cycles through the process of creative destruction.

degree, the underlying product- and market-specific knowledge driving those decisions. In aggregate, this knowledge may help anticipate business cycles and be useful to business leaders and policy makers.

To statistically evaluate the relative performance of trademark-based indicators, we implement two complementary methods: turning point analysis and Bayesian Structural Time Series (BSTS). The two methods provide for a holistic approach to forecast performance by generating rankings for candidate indicators in isolation and as part of a composite index. Turning point analysis uses a standard probability modelling framework, such as a probit model, to rank alternative leading indicators based on forecast error. Our second approach, BSTS, is a novel application for the leading indicator literature to the best of our knowledge. It is a machine learning technique that allows for sophisticated variable selection. BSTS explicitly tests whether the inclusion of a particular trademark indicator improves upon the performance of a prediction model (Scott and Varian 2014).

Our results show that innovation indicators related to firm-level decisions to file for trademark protection on marketed products and services, called *tm_filing_use*, outperform most of the conventional leading indicators. It ranked sixth in the turning point analysis beating more traditional indicators, such as building permits, manufacturing orders for capital, and the yield curve. This indicator performed even better in the BSTS context, ranking third and fourth at different specified model sizes. Our results show that innovation indicators contain valuable information for anticipating business cycles and that including use-based trademark metrics in composite indexes may improve recession forecasting performance.

The rest of the paper is structured as follows. Section 2 lays out the case for trademark-based indicators, referencing relevant prior empirical research on trademarks. In Section 3, we provide a detailed description of the data. Section 4 discusses the methods we adopt to evaluate the predictive power of trademark indicators in forecasting recessions. Section 5 presents the evaluation results and Section 6 concludes.

2. Trademark-based leading indicators

For economists who study innovation, it is quite surprising that the variables most widely used as leading indicators of economic activity do not include any metrics related to innovative activities. Within the forecasting literature, there is broad and longstanding agreement regarding the characteristics of a good leading indicator (see Marcellino 2006 for an overview). In this section, we briefly summarize how well trademark-based metrics satisfy these properties.

The first two properties require a leading indicator to systematically anticipate the peaks and troughs of a target variable, preferably with stable lead-time, and to have good forecasting properties outside these turning points. Figure 1 shows trends in the growth of trademark application filings with the USPTO relative to real GDP growth for the 1990–2016 period. While trademark filings tend to be more volatile, we generally see similar growth patterns over time, particularly after the 2001 recession. Figure 1 provides some visual evidence that aggregate trademark filings satisfy the first two established properties of a leading indicator. Turning point analysis (see Section 4) provides a formal means to assess whether candidate leading indicators satisfy these properties.

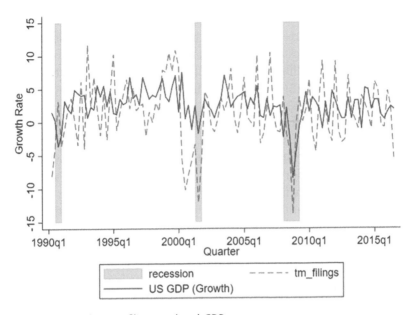

Figure 1. Trademark application filings and real GDP.

Note: The grey shaded areas represent recessionary periods (quarters) in the U.S. economy according to the National Bureau of Economic Research (NBER). The U.S. GDP growth rate data were obtained from the Federal Reserve Economic Data (FRED) database, maintained by the Federal Reserve Board of St. Louis. The trademark variable, tm_filings, represents the growth rate of aggregate trademark filings, the data for which were provided by the USPTO.

The third established property of a leading indicator is economic significance. Namely, does economic theory provides support that the indicator causes business cycles or, more crucially, quickly reacts to negative and positive shocks? While economic significance cannot be formally evaluated, there is conceptual and empirical evidence linking trademark statistics to business cycle fluctuations through innovative activities related to the introduction of new products and methods as well as changes in expected demand.

Dating back to Schumpeter (1934, 1939), several theoretical papers have established a link between innovative activity and business cycles. Schumpeter attributes business cycles almost exclusively to innovative activity within firms. Through the process of 'creative destruction', firms' introduction of new product varieties, expansion into new markets, and adoption of new methods of production drives fluctuations across the entire economy (Schumpeter 1942).

Correspondingly, a growing body of research associates firm-level decisions to register a trademark with the market introduction of products, services, and new varieties of existing goods and services. Mendonça, Pereira, and Godinho (2004) makes a strong case that trademarks reflect firm-level innovative output based on European Union data for Community Trade Marks. However, the empirical literature on trademarks is much broader in its industrial and geographic scope, linking trademark use to innovation in both products (Allegrezza and Guarda-Rauchs 1999; Mendonça, Pereira, and Godinho 2004; Jensen and Webster 2008; Millot 2009; Seip et al. 2018; Flikkema et al. Forthcoming) and services (Schmoch 2003; Hipp and Grupp 2005; Semadeni 2006; Schmoch and Gauche 2009; Gotsch and Hipp 2012; Greenhalgh and Rogers 2012; Flikkema, de Man, and Castaldi 2014; Crass and Schwiebacher 2016; Seip et al. 2018) in other parts of the world. The use of trademarks in this fashion seems to reflect firm-level strategies for horizontal product differentiation between rival firms (Semadeni 2006), vertical differentiation resulting from process or technological innovation (Gao and Hitt 2012) and quality differentiation (Aribarg and Arora 2008; Greenhalgh and Rogers 2012). Additionally, trademarks have been shown to complement other strategies for protecting product and technology innovations (Somaya and Graham 2006; Sandner 2009; Ceccagnoli et al. 2010; Llerena and Millot 2013; Hall et al. 2014; Zhou et al. 2016; Bei forthcoming) as well as innovations in knowledge-intensive service sectors (Amara, Landry, and Traore 2008; Fosfuri, Giarratana, and Luzzi 2008).

Using trademarks as part of firm-level innovation strategies appears to be successful. There is mounting evidence of a positive relationship between trademark-based metrics – applications, stock of registrations, and trademark intensity – and firm survival (Jensen and Webster 2008; Buddelmeyer, Jensen, and Webster 2010; Helmers and Rogers 2010; Schautschick 2015); firm productivity (Greenhalgh and Longland 2005); firm profitability (Griffiths, Jensen, and Webster 2011; Crass, Czarnitzki, and Toole 2019); firm employment and revenue growth (Dinlersoz et al. forthcoming); firm-level brand equity (Krasnikov, Mishra, and Orozco 2009; de Rassenfosse 2017); and firm market value (Seethamraju 2003; Greenhalgh and Rogers 2006, 2012; Griffiths and Webster 2006; Krasnikov, Mishra, and Orozco 2009; Sandner and Block 2011).

Taken as a whole, the prior literature provides ample evidence to support the economic significance of trademark-derived indicators to business cycles. By capturing innovative activity, particularly the creation of new product varieties as well as future demand expectations, trademark data is clearly linked to business cycle fluctuations.

The remaining three properties of a good leading indicator concern statistical reliability, prompt availability without major revisions, and relatively smooth monthly or quarterly fluctuations (Marcellino 2006). For these properties, trademark data performs well, particularly when compared to traditional indicators which tend to suffer from delayed reporting and substantial revisions. Trademark metrics provide exact measurability of trademark activity by individuals and firms and, particularly in the case of those derived from trademark filings or registrations, are promptly available and generally lack revisions.[3] The final property of smooth quarterly fluctuations is satisfied by considering multiple variable transformations. Trademark-based metrics are typically non-stationary and exhibit seasonality, requiring variable transformation and seasonal adjustment (see Section 3).

Overall trademark-based metrics satisfy the formal properties of a leading indicator. A primary advantage is the ability of trademark data to capture innovative activity and future demand expectations for a relatively large and diverse number of economic actors. We contend that trademark-based indicators are a valuable addition to the established set of economic and financial indicators used by scholars, forecasters, and policy analysts. We now more formally evaluate this contention using traditional and novel forecasting evaluation techniques.

---

[3]The USPTO provides daily-updated XML files containing pending and registered trademark applications via https://bulkdata.uspto.gov/data/trademark/dailyxml/applications/.

3. Data

Our analysis combines data from three sources. First, we obtained data on the various types and disposition of U.S. trademarks from the Trademark Case Files dataset from the U.S. Patent and Trademark Office (USPTO). Second, we downloaded time series data on the Leading Economic Index and its current components from The Conference Board (TCB). Lastly, we obtained official indicators of U.S. recessions from the National Bureau of Economic Research (NBER).

The Trademark Case Files dataset contains detailed information on applications filed with the USPTO for federal trademark registration (Graham et al. 2013). We use the 2016 update to the dataset, which includes roughly 8.6 million U.S. trademark applications and registrations for the 1870 through 2016 period.[4] Coverage, however, varies over time, and left-censoring limits data coverage for older applications and registrations. Due to substantive changes to the U.S. federal trademark system in late 1989, we focus our analysis on the 1990 to 2016 period.

We construct a set of ten trademark-based indicators using trademark filings, registrations, and abandonments in aggregate and for subsets using the 'legal basis' at filing. To file for a U.S. trademark registration with the USPTO, an applicant must specify a legal basis for each product or service class included in the application. The main bases are called 'use' and 'intent to use'. A use trademark filing indicates the mark is currently being used in commerce on the specified goods or services whereas an intent-to-use filing is done to secure a trademark for use in the future. We expect use filings to measure the introduction of new product varieties, while intent-to-use filings will be more forward-looking and may capture expectations regarding future demand or competitive conditions.

Applicants can also file for a U.S. trademark registration based on an application or registrations in a foreign jurisdiction under the Paris Convention or based on an international registration under the Madrid Protocol (Graham et al. 2013). Such filings reflect foreign firms seeking trademark registration before entering the United States and capture the introduction of new product varieties from abroad as well as expectations of foreign firms regarding U.S. demand. However, because international trademark filings are more sensitive to global industrial production levels (de Rassenfosse 2019) and legal changes abroad, applications filed under the Paris Convention or Madrid Protocol may also measure aspects of the interplay between global economic, political conditions, and U.S. business cycles.

One noteworthy limitation of metrics derived from intent-to-use trademark applications is the unavailability of data prior to 1990 Q2. The intent-to-use application was introduced as part of the substantive changes to the U.S. federal trademark system implemented in late 1989. While we observe the full series of intent-to-use filings during our sample period, the disposal of such applications is not fully observed until after the second quarter of 1990. Consequently, we do not consider disposal metrics (abandonment or registration) for intent-to-use applications. Definitions for the trademark-based indicators are provided in Table 1, and summary statistics appear in the Appendix.

---

[4]The USPTO Trademark Case Files dataset is available at https://www.uspto.gov/learning-and-resources/electronic-data-products/trademark-case-files-dataset-0.

Table 1. Trademark indicators.

Indicator	Definition
tm_filings_all	Number of applications filed during the period
tm_filings_itu	Number of applications filed based on an intent to use during the period
tm_filings_paris_madrid*	Number of applications filed under Paris Convention or Madrid Protocol during the period
tm_filings_use	Number of applications filed based on use during the period
tm_abandonments_all	Number of applications abandoned during the period
tm_abandonments_paris_madrid*	Number of applications originally filed under Paris Convention or Madrid Protocol that were abandoned during the period
tm_abandonments_use	Number of applications originally filed based on use that were abandoned during the period
tm_registrations_all	Number of registrations issued during the period
tm_registrations_paris_madrid*	Number of registrations resulting from applications originally filed under Paris Convention or Madrid Protocol that issued during the period
tm_registrations_use	Number of registrations resulting from applications originally filed based on use that issued during the period

Note: All trademark indicators calculated at the class-level.
* The Madrid Protocol went into effect in the United States on 2 November 2003. Data prior to that date reflects only applications filed based on a foreign application or registration under the Paris Convention.
Source: Trademark indicators calculated from USPTO Trademark Case Files Dataset, 2016 update.

We obtained data for the LEI and its components from TCB. None of the components reflect innovation per se, but they do capture various aspects of economic activity (new orders, building permits, etc.) and expectations or sentiment (consumer expectations, stock market prices, etc.).[5] We include all components of the LEI in our analysis with the exception of the ISM® index of new orders, which we were unable to access. Definitions for LEI and its components are provided in Table 2, and summary statistics appear in the Appendix.

To identify recessionary periods, we use the NBER quarterly recession indicator. Rather than define a recession as two consecutive quarters of negative real GDP growth, NBER incorporates additional economy-wide indicators, capturing the magnitude of decline, and more targeted indicators to identify recessionary events.[6] Between 1990Q1 and 2016Q3, the U.S. economy was in a recession for twelve quarters or three distinct recessions (early 1990's, 2001, and the Great Recession of 2007 to 2009).

4. Methodology

We use two approaches to evaluate the value of trademark-based indicators in predicting downturns in the business cycle: turning point analysis and Bayesian Structural Time-Series (BSTS). Turning point analysis assesses how well each trademark indicator anticipates the peaks and troughs in real GDP growth (Diebold and Rudebusch 1989; Dueker 1997; Levanon 2009; Levanon, et al. 2011a, 2011b; Levanon et al. 2015; Lahiri and Yang 2015). We use this analysis to assess which indicator performs best among the entire set of

---

[5]The ten components of the LEI for the United States (as of March 2019) include: average weekly hours, manufacturing; average weekly initial claims for unemployment insurance; manufacturers' new orders, consumer goods and materials; ISM® index of new orders; manufacturers' new orders, nondefense capital goods excluding aircraft orders; building permits, new private housing units; stock prices, 500 common stocks; Leading Credit Index; interest rate spread, 10-year Treasury bonds less federal funds; and average consumer expectations for business conditions.
[6]See http://www.nber.org/cycles/recessions.html for more information on the NBER recession dating procedure.

Table 2. LEI and LEI components.

Indicator	Definition
building_permits	The number of residential building permits issued is an indicator of construction activity, which typically leads most other types of economic production. (SAAR, Thous.)
common_stock_500_index	Stock prices, 500 common stocks. The stock price index reflects the price movements of a broad selection of common stocks traded on the New York Stock Exchange. Increases (decreases) of the stock index can reflect both the general sentiments of investors and the movements of interest rates, which is usually another good indicator for future economic activity.
consumer_exp_bus_conditions	Average Consumer Expectations for Business and Economic Conditions. This index reflects changes in consumer attitudes concerning future economic conditions and, therefore, is the only indicator in the LEI that is completely expectations-based. It is an equally weighted average of consumer expectations of business and economic conditions using two questions, Consumer Expectations for Economic Conditions 12-months ahead from Survey of Consumers conducted by Reuters/University of Michigan, and Consumer Expectations for Business Conditions 6-months ahead from Consumer Confidence Survey conducted by The Conference Board. Responses to the questions concerning various business and economic conditions are classified as positive, negative, or unchanged.
Leading Credit Index (LCI)	The Conference Board's Leading Credit Index (std. dev.). This index consists of six financial indicators: 2-year Swap Spread (real time), LIBOR 3 month less 3 month Treasury-Bill yield spread (real time), Debit balances at margin account at broker dealer (monthly), AAII Investors Sentiment Bullish (%) less Bearish (%) (weekly), Senior Loan Officers C&I loan survey – Bank tightening Credit to Large and Medium Firms (quarterly), and Security Repurchases (quarterly) from the Total Finance-Liabilities section of Federal Reserve's flow of fund report. Because of these financial indicators' forward-looking content, LCI leads economic activities.
Leading Economic Index (LEI)	The Conference Board's Leading Economic Index (LEI) is a commonly-used forecasting tool that aims to predict changes in the direction of aggregate economic activity and business cycle turning points. The LEI is comprised of ten components intended to measure various aspects of economic activity and expectations or sentiment. The index summarises the cyclical movements of its various components. The contributions of the individual components vary over time, depending on the character of each cycle.
mfg_orders_capital	Manufacturers' New Orders: Nondefense Capital Goods excluding Aircraft (SA, Mil. Chn. 1982$). This index, combined with orders from aircraft (in inflation-adjusted dollars) are the producers' counterpart to mfg_orders_consumer.
mfg_orders_consumer	Manufacturers' New Orders: Consumer Goods & Materials (SA, Mil. 1982$). These goods are primarily used by consumers. The inflation-adjusted value of new orders leads actual production because new orders directly affect the level of both unfilled orders and inventories that firms monitor when making production decisions. The Conference Board deflates the current dollar orders data using price indexes constructed from various sources at the industry level and a chain-weighted aggregate price index formula.
weekly_hours_worked_mfg	Average Weekly Hours: Manufacturing (SA, Hours). The average hours worked per week by production workers in manufacturing industries tend to lead the business cycle because employers usually adjust work hours before increasing or decreasing their workforce.
weekly_unemploy_insurance_claims	Average Weekly Initial Claims Unemployment Insurance (SA, Thous.). The number of new claims filed for unemployment insurance are typically more sensitive than either total employment or unemployment to overall business conditions, and this series tends to lead the business cycle. It is inverted when included in the leading index; the signs of the month-to-month changes are reversed, because initial claims increase when employment conditions worsen (i.e. layoffs rise and new hiring fall).
yield_curve	Interest Rate Spread: 10-Year Treasury Bonds Less Federal Funds (%). The spread or difference between long and short rates is often called the yield curve. This series is constructed using the 10-year Treasury bond rate and the federal funds rate, an overnight interbank borrowing rate. It is felt to be an indicator of the stance of monetary policy and general financial conditions because it rises (falls) when short rates are relatively low (high). When it becomes negative (i.e. short rates are higher than long rates and the yield curve inverts) its record as an indicator of recessions is particularly strong.

Source: The Conference Board.

candidate trademark indicators. Our second method, the BSTS model (Scott and Varian 2014), utilizes a machine learning variable selection approach for time series forecasting.

4.1. Turning point analysis

For our turning point analysis, we first model the NBER recession indicator as a function of each economic indicator variable individually. Using the binary nature of the NBER recession data, we specify a probit model using maximum likelihood estimation:

$$\ln L(\beta) = \sum_{t=1}^{T} (y_t \ln \Phi(x_t'\beta) + (1 - y_t) \ln(1 - \Phi(x_t'\beta))) \tag{1}$$

where y_t takes a value of one for each quarter t in a recession and zero otherwise, and x_i represents a vector of one and two lagged periods of each indicator.

We estimate the parameters specified in (1) for each indicator and use these parameters to generate in-sample predicted probabilities ($\widehat{y}_{ti}$). We then calculate the quadratic probability score (QPS_i) for each economic indicator as:

$$QPS_i = \frac{2}{T} \sum_{t=1}^{T} (y_{ti} - \widehat{y}_{ti})^2 \tag{2}$$

The difference in per period predicted probabilities and NBER recession indicator ($y_{ti} - \widehat{y}_{ti}$) demonstrates how close the predicted outcome is to the realised outcome. Thus, the QPS is the binary outcome counterpart of the mean squared forecast error. A low QPS results when the difference between the actual and predicted values is small, indicating that the economic indicator i could be a good predictor of the likelihood of recession.

Although estimating the QPS statistic allows researchers to rank candidate indicators by their ability to forecast recessions, the statistic does not provide information on the performance of each indicator relative to the frequency of the event itself. That is, the QPS of the best performing indicator does not convey any information about the absolute performance of the indicator, especially for rare events. The Brier's Skill Score (BSS), a modification of the QPS metric (Brier 1950; Lahiri and Wang 2013; Lahiri and Yang 2015), accounts for the relative frequency of the event (in this case, recessions in the U.S. economy) and provides a reference point using an 'unskilled' baseline forecast (Lahiri and Wang 2013). The BSS is defined as:

$$BSS_i(f, x) = 1 - \left[\frac{QPS_i(f, x)}{QPS(\mu_x, x)}\right] \tag{3}$$

Where $QPS_i(f, x)$ is the QPS for variable i and $QPS(\mu_x, x)$ is the QPS using the average number of recession periods in the sample as the predicted outcome for each period (*i.e.* the 'unskilled' baseline forecast), where μ_x is roughly 11 percent. The BSS provides a benchmark for the QPS, resulting in a positive BSS if the QPS for variable i is lower than the QPS using the average number of recessionary periods as the predicted probability. A negative BSS implies that predicting a recessionary period using the historical average outperforms the model with variable i, indicating a poor predictor.

4.2. Bayesian structural time series

Unlike turning point analysis, BSTS incorporates all the potential leading indicators thereby allowing us to evaluate the forecasting performance of trademark indicators relative to those currently used by The Conference Board. BSTS uses a machine learning approach for variable selection (Scott and Varian 2015). It considers a model for every possible combination of indicators and calculates a posterior model inclusion probability based on the probability that the coefficient on any given variable is non-zero. Ranking the posterior inclusion probabilities provides a clear metric to evaluate whether candidate indicators should be included (or not) in the recession forecasting model. A primary advantage of BSTS is that it evaluates candidate indicators simultaneously, estimating the relative importance of each candidate to the model. Moreover, while we cannot directly create and evaluate the forecast performance of a modified Leading Economic Index that includes trademark variables, the BSTS model provides an alternative method for assessing the contribution of trademark indicators to such an index.

As described by Scott and Varian (2015), BSTS combines three separate methodologies: a 'basic structural model'[7]; variable selection using a spike and slab regression; and Bayesian model averaging. The basic structural model generalises the constant linear trend model and may consist of several equations.[8] In our application, the structural component is a system of two equations, namely the observation and transition equations. As with latent index models such as probit and logit, the observation equation indexes the latent state. Equation 4 combines a dynamic binary outcome model (logit) with local level and regression components. The transition equation (5) specifies how the latent state changes over time. We apply the model to a binary response variable, specifically a recessionary period indicator:

$$logit(p_t) = \mu_t + \beta^T x_t \qquad (4)$$

$$\mu_{t+1} = \mu_t + \eta_t \qquad (5)$$

Where p_t is the probability of a recessionary period at time t, μ_t is the trend component, x_t is the set of potential leading indicators, and η_t is the error term associated with the trend.[9]

Spike-and-slab variable selection is a model selection approach (Mitchell and Beauchamp 1988; Madigan and Raftery 1994; George and McCulloch 1997; Ishwaran and Rao 2005). For each subset of potential leading indicators, the spike-and-slab method specifies two prior distributions. The 'spike' prior refers to the probability that the coefficient for a given potential leading indicator is zero ($p(\gamma_i)$ – where γ_i is a binary variable representing model inclusion for variable i). For this, we assume the standard prior distribution of an independent Bernoulli, leading to a positive probability mass at zero.[10]

---

[7] The BSTS model applies the Kalman filter (Kalman 1960; Harvey 1989; Scott and Varian 2015), which recursively calculates the predictive distribution of the state in t + 1 by the predictive distribution of the state in t using the time-series of y_t from t = 1, …, t-1 combined with the observed value of y_t. This process uses 'a standard set of formulas that is logically equivalent to linear regression,' (Scott and Varian 2014). An in-depth discussion of the Kalman filter is beyond the scope of this paper.

[8] The classic constant-trend model can be written as $y_t = \mu + bt + \beta x_t + \varepsilon_t$.

[9] Steven L. Scott first suggested this BSTS model specification in a blog post, see http://www.unofficialgoogledatascience.com/2017/07/fitting-bayesian-structural-time-series.html.

[10] The prior probability of inclusion (π_i) for each variable i is set to 1/K, where K is equal to the total number of potential leading indicators in our sample. This corresponds to the total number of relevant variables expected in our model.

The 'slab' component specifies a prior distribution for the regression coefficients conditional on inclusion in the model. We use Bayesian model averaging to calculate the posterior distribution of y_{t+1} by repeatedly drawing posterior parameters and estimating y_{t+1} for each model. By repeating the estimation of y_{t+1} numerous times, we can calculate the posterior distribution of y_{t+1}. For each candidate indicator, this process yields a posterior inclusion probability, which ranks how much the data supports inclusion of the variable in the recession forecast regression (Tsangarides 2004).

5. Results

5.1. Turning point analysis results

Using turning point analysis, we ran a univariate probit model for each trademark indicator and calculated the QPS and BSS based on the model's predicted probability of recession.[11] Table 3 reports the QPS and BSS for each indicator from the probit models with a two-quarter forecast lag. Figure 2 additionally presents the QPS and BSS results for trademark and LEI indicators graphically. Recall that an indicator with a lower QPS is considered a better predictor because the difference between actual and predicted

Table 3. Probit model QPS and BSS.

Variable	TM Indicator	(1) QPS	(2) BSS
LEI		0.0569	0.7142
LCI		0.0579	0.7091
weekly_unemploy_insurance_claims		0.1041	0.4775
consumer_exp_bus_conditions		0.1118	0.4388
mfg_orders_consumer		0.1168	0.4135
tm_filings_use	X	0.1367	0.3133
build_permits		0.1389	0.3025
mfg_orders_capital		0.1402	0.2961
common_stock_500_ind		0.1439	0.2776
tm_filings_all	X	0.1478	0.2580
tm_filings_itu	X	0.1492	0.2506
yield_curve		0.1561	0.2163
weekly_hours_worked_mfg		0.1576	0.2084
tm_filings_paris_madrid	X	0.1622	0.1854
tm_abandonments_paris_madrid	X	0.1738	0.1272
tm_registrations_use	X	0.1951	0.0204
tm_abandonments_all	X	0.1957	0.0171
tm_registrations_all	X	0.1972	0.0096
tm_abandonments_use	X	0.1983	0.0043
tm_registrations_paris_madrid	X	0.1990	0.0010
recession		0.1991	0.0000

Note: The quadratic probability score (QPS) is calculated using quarterly data from 1990–2016, where

$$QPS_i = \frac{2}{T}\sum_{t=1}^{T}(y_{ti} - \hat{y}_{ti})^2 .$$ A low QPS results when the difference between the actual and predicted values is small, indicating that the respective economic indicator may be a good predictor of the likelihood of recession. Brier's Skill Score (BSS), where $BSS(f,x) = 1 - \left[\frac{QPS_i(f,x)}{QPS(\mu_x,x)}\right]$, modifies the QPS statistic and accounts for the rarity of recessions in the U.S. economy.

---

[11]We consider multiple transformations of the trademark indicators included in Table 1, but we only report QPS and BSS results for the seasonally-adjusted growth rates as they were predominantly the best performing transformation.

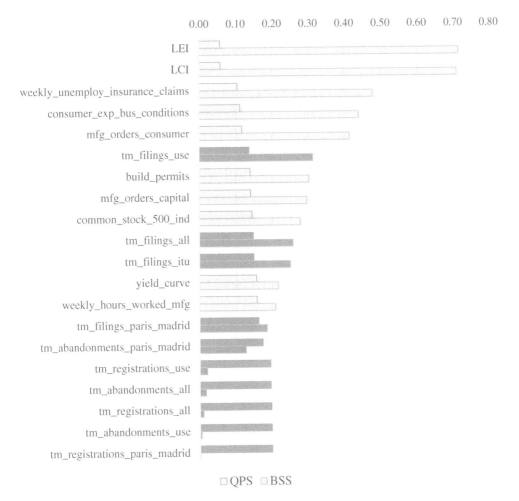

Figure 2. Probit model QPS and BSS.

Note: The quadratic probability score (QPS) is calculated using quarterly data from 1990–2016, where $QPS_i = \frac{2}{T} \sum_{t=1}^{T} (y_{ti} - \hat{y}_{ti})^2$. A low QPS results when the difference between the actual and predicted values is small, indicating that the respective economic indicator may be a good predictor of the likelihood of recession. Brier's Skill Score (BSS), where $BSS(f, x) = 1 - \left[\frac{QPS_i(f,x)}{QPS(\mu_x, x)} \right]$, modifies the QPS statistic and accounts for the rarity of recessions in the U.S. economy. Solid bars indicate trademark indicators.

values is small. A higher BSS, conversely, indicates how well a recession prediction based on the indicator performs relative to the unconditional probability of recession.

The best performing trademark indicator is applications filed based on prior use of the mark (tm_filing_use), which produces the lowest (highest) QPS (BSS) among the trademark measures and outperforms half of the LEI components. All filings (tm_filings_all) and intent-to-using filings (tm_filings_itu) also show relatively low (high) QPS (BSS) and outperform a couple of the LEI components.

Among the trademark-based measures, the filing indicators perform better than the disposal metrics – abandonments and registrations – whether aggregated or for a legal basis subset. Predictions based on a couple of the disposal metrics – registration derived from filings through the Paris or Madrid systems (tm_registrations_paris_madrid) and abandonments of applications filed based on prior use (tm_abandonments) – are only slightly better than the average number of recessionary periods over the sample period as evidenced by BSS estimates near zero. Additionally, the recession forecast error for the trademark abandonment and registration indicators, as measured by the QPS, is higher than that for all LEI components. Consequently, we conclude that the trademark disposal measures are not appropriate leading indicators for forecasting recessions and focus our remaining analysis only on the trademark filing measures.

QPS and BSS metrics provide an indication of how well each indicator predicts recessions over the entire sample period. To assess the performance of the trademark filing measures in predicting specific recessions and not falsely signalling recessions during periods of expansion, we plot each indicator's in-sample predicted probabilities of recession against actual recession periods in Figure 3. For comparison purposes, we also plot the predicted probabilities of recession based on the LCI (panel e) and the average weekly hours worked by manufacturing workers (weekly_hours_worked_mfg, panel f) as they are the best- and worst-performing LEI components, respectively, based on our QPS and BSS results (see Table 3).

Trademark applications filed based on prior use of the mark (tm_filings_use, panel a) shows reasonable discriminatory power, forecasting a high probability of recession for the early 1990s recession, though seeming to pre-empt the 2001 recession and failing to predict the Great Recession until the later years of that downturn. It also performs well in terms of avoiding false signals by generating small probabilities of recession during expansionary periods. We see similar patterns in the predicted probabilities of recession based on aggregate filings (tm_filings_all, panel b), intent-to-use filings (tm_filings_itu, panel c), and filings from abroad (tm_filings_paris_madrid, panel d). However, compared to use-based filings, each of the other three trademark filing indicators produces a lower probability of recession for the first downturn and some are more prone to false recession signals.

The risk of an indicator providing a false signal is contingent on the threshold at which we classify a predicted probability as indicating a recession. A higher (lower) threshold reduces (increases) the risk of false signals but increases (decreases) the risk of failing to detect a true recession. In Figure 4, we use receiver operating characteristic (ROC) curves to assess the false positive and true positive rates for predictions based on trademark filing indicators at different thresholds.[12] The closer the ROC curve is to the upper left corner, the better the model, and thereby the indicator, is at classifying each time period as a recession or not, even at lower probability thresholds. The diagonal line represents the result of a model with no discriminatory power, meaning a random classifier that is equally likely to predict a recession or not for any given period. Again, we include the LCI and average weekly hours worked by manufacturing workers (weekly_hours_worked_mfg) in Figure 4 for comparison purposes only.

As the ROC curves in Figure 4 show, the LCI has considerable discriminatory power and does not falsely signal recessions even at low thresholds. By contrast, the trademark

---

[12]The ROC curve effectively classifies whether the probit model predicted recession accurately or generated a false signal at the probability threshold w. The ROC curve plots the true positive rate ($\Pr(p_t > w | Z_t = 1)$) against the false positive rate ($\Pr(p_t > w | Z_t = 0)$) at different values of w (Lahiri and Yang 2015).

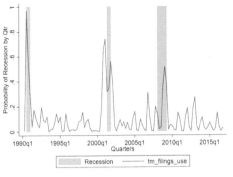

(a) trademark filings based on prior mark use

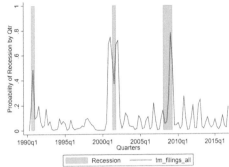

(b) trademark filings aggregated

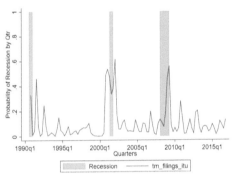

(c) trademark filings based on intent to use

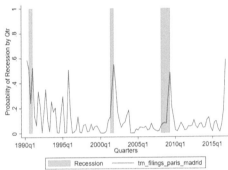
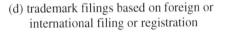

(d) trademark filings based on foreign or international filing or registration

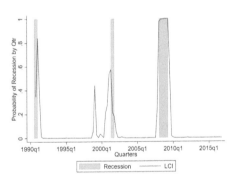

(e) LCI

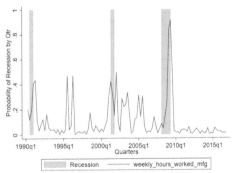

(f) average weekly hours worked by manufacturing workers

Figure 3. In-sample probit model forecasts.

Note: The grey shaded areas represent recessionary periods (quarters) in the U.S. economy according to the National Bureau of Economic Research (NBER). The trademark filing variables (panels a through d) represent the growth rate of trademark use (a), aggregate (b), intent-to-use (c), and foreign or international (d) filings, the data for which were calculated from USPTO Trademark Case Files Dataset, 2016 update. Data for the LEI component variables, LCI (e) and average weekly hours worked by manufacturing workers (f), were provided by The Conference Board.

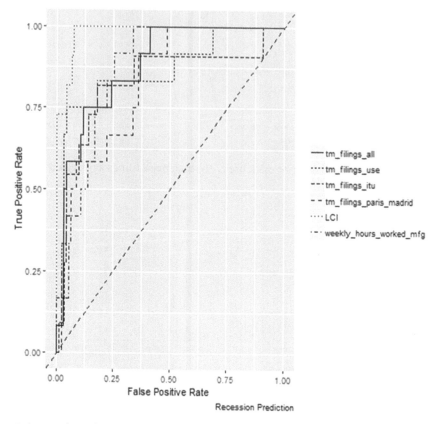

Figure 4. In-sample probit model ROC Curves.

Note: The Receiver Operating Characteristic (ROC) curve above, plots the true positive rate (recall) against the false positive rate (1-specificity). The trademark filing variables represent the growth rate of, aggregate (tm_filings_all), use (tm_filings_use), intent-to-use (tm_filings_itu), and foreign or international (tm_filings_paris_madrid) filings, the data for which were calculated from USPTO Trademark Case Files Dataset, 2016 update. Data for the LEI component variables, LCI and average weekly hours worked by manufacturing workers (weekly_hours_worked_mfg), were provided by The Conference Board.

filing indicators are somewhat more sensitive to the threshold. At lower probability thresholds, the probit models based on trademark indicators have higher false positive rates, though comparable to those of the average weekly hours worked by manufacturing workers.

5.2. Bayesian structural time series

Next we use the BSTS approach to evaluate whether trademark filing indicators should be included (or not) in the model forecasting recessions. Figure 5 shows the inclusion probabilities, which indicate the proportion of the iterations that selected the indicator for inclusion in the model, of the top performing BSTS indicators. We initially restrict BSTS to select ten variables in each iteration (panel a). Then, we re-run the BSTS allowing for the best five variables (panel b). The former replicates the LEI, which

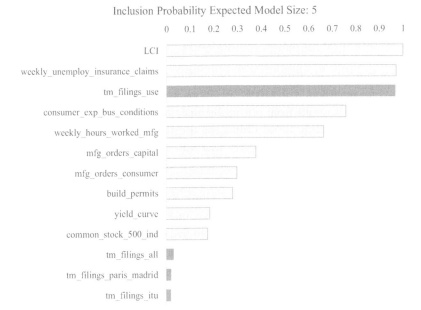

(a) BSTS expected model size: 10 variables

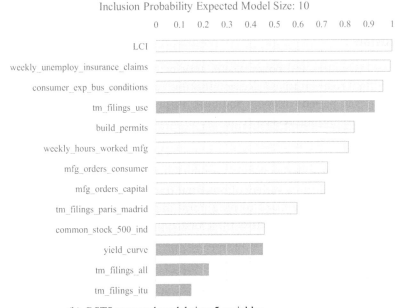

(b) BSTS expected model size: 5 variables

Figure 5. BSTS inclusion probabilities.

Note: The BSTS graph above shows the results from the BSTS model described in Section 4. In both models (a and b), the prior probability of inclusion for each variable is set to 1/K, where K is equal to the number of relevant variables expected in our model, specifically (a) 10 and (b) 5. Models include each component of the LEI (except the LEI itself) and each of the trademark filing variables (tm_filings_all, tm_filings_use, tm_filings_itu, tm_filings_paris_madrid). Solid bars indicate trademark indicators.

consists of ten components. The latter is more restrictive and, thus, provides more compelling support for inclusion of the selected indicators.

We see consistent results across both panels of Figure 5. In each panel, the inclusion probabilities for the same two LEI components are the highest. The LCI is the most informative indicator for predicting recessions, with an inclusion probability of 1.00, meaning it was selected for inclusion in all (100%) iterations whether limited to ten or five variables. This is consistent with results from our probit analysis as well as prior literature (Levanon et al. 2015). Average weekly initial claims for unemployment insurance (weekly_unemploy_insurance_claims) also performs very well with an inclusion probability of 0.99 when ten variables are selected and roughly 0.97 when we restrict BSTS to five variables.

The best performing trademark indicator is also consistent across panels in Figure 5. Trademark filings based on prior use (tm_filings_use) outperform the other trademark indicators and most LEI components with an inclusion probability of 0.93 when ten variables are selected and 0.97 when restricted to five variables. We note that the inclusion probability for the use-based trademark filing increases when we restrict the BSTS model to fewer variables, indicating that the measure conveys novel information beyond that captured by the existing LEI components. While Figure 5 shows that the trademark filings based on a prior foreign filing or registration (tm_filings_paris_madrid) indicator is included in 60% of BSTS models with ten variables, neither it nor the other trademark indicators have an inclusion probability more than 0.05 in the restricted BSTS model.

6. Conclusion

By helping stakeholders and policymakers anticipate business cycles, leading indicators play an important role in business decision making, economic forecasting and government policy responses to periods of boom and bust. Surprisingly, official leading indicators do not include any innovation related economic variables. In this paper, we consider several trademark-based indicators as candidates for leading indicators. A sizeable literature supports the linkage between firm-level decisions to use or abandon trademarks and innovative activity, particularly related to product and service introductions.

We statistically evaluate a variety of potential trademark-based candidates as leading indicators using both a standard turning point approach and an innovative machine learning approach. The results across these two approaches were consistent and identified one standout trademark-based indicator – trademark filings based on current use, called *tm_filings_use* – for possible inclusion in a leading economic indicator index. This metric performs quite well and surpasses many of the current and conventional leading indicators. Our work suggests that including trademark metrics in composite indexes can provide real improvements to recession forecasting performance and forecasters should adopt this novel source of information.

Disclaimer

The views expressed are those of the individual authors and do not necessarily reflect the official positions of the Office of the Chief Economist or the U.S. Patent and Trademark Office.

Acknowledgements

The authors would like to thank Mary Denison, the USPTO Commissioner for Trademarks, for suggesting the possibility that trademarks may help anticipate economic activity.

Disclosure statement

No potential conflict of interest was reported by the authors.

References

Allegrezza, S., and A. Guarda-Rauchs. 1999. "The Determinants of Trademark Deposits: An Econometric Investigation." *Economie Appliquée: Archives de l'Institut de Sciences Mathématiques et Economiques Appliquées* 52 (2): 51–68.

Amara, N., R. Landry, and N. Traore. 2008. "Managing the Protection of Innovations in Knowledge-intensive Business Services." *Research Policy* 37 (9): 1530–1547. doi:10.1016/j.respol.2008.07.001.

Aribarg, A., and N. Arora. 2008. "Interbrand Variant Overlap: Impact on Brand Preference and Portfolio Profit." *Marketing Science* 27 (3): 474–491. doi:10.1287/mksc.1060.0262.

Bei, X. Forthcoming. "Trademarks, Specialized Complementary Assets, and the External Sourcing of Innovation." *Research Policy.* doi:10.1016/j.respol.2018.11.003.

Brier, G. W. 1950. "Verification of Forecasts Expressed in Terms of Probability." *Monthly Weather Review* 78 (1): 1–3. doi:10.1175/1520-0493(1950)078<0001:VOFEIT>2.0.CO;2.

Buddelmeyer, H., P. H. Jensen, and E. Webster. 2010. "Innovation and the Determinants of Company Survival." *Oxford Economic Papers* 62 (2): 261–285. doi:10.1093/oep/gpp012.

Ceccagnoli, M., S. Graham, M. Higgins, and J. Lee. 2010. "Productivity and the Role of Complementary Assets in Firms' Demand for Technology Innovations." *Industrial and Corporate Change* 19 (3): 839–869. doi:10.1093/icc/dtq033.

Crass, D., D. Czarnitzki, and A. A. Toole. 2019. "The Dynamic Relationship between Investments in Brand Equity and Firm Profitability: Evidence Using Trademark Registrations." *International Journal of the Economics of Business* 26 (1): 157–176. doi:10.1080/13571516.2019.1553292.

Crass, D., and F. Schwiebacher. 2016. "The Importance of Trademark Protection for Product Differentiation and Innovation." *Economia E Politica Industriale* 44 (2). doi:10.1007/s40812-016-0058-1.

de Rassenfosse, G. 2017. "An Assessment of How Well We Account for Intangibles." *Industrial and Corporate Change* 26 (3): 517–534. doi:10.1093/icc/dtw034.

de Rassenfosse, G. 2019. "On the Price Elasticity of Demand for Trademarks." *Industry and Innovation* 1–14. doi:10.1080/13662716.2019.1591939.

Diebold, F. X., and G. D. Rudebusch. 1989. "Scoring the Leading Indicators." *The Journal of Business* 62 (3): 369–391. doi:10.1086/296467.

Dinlersoz, E., N. Goldschlag, A. Myers, and N. Zolas. Forthcoming. "An Anatomy of U.S. Firms Seeking Trademark Registration." In *Measuring and Accounting for Innovation in the 21st Century*, edited by C. Corrado, J. Miranda, J. Haskel, and D. Sichel, 1–31. Chicago: University of Chicago Press. NBER Working Paper No. 13891.

Dueker, M. 1997. "Strengthening the Case for the Yield Curve as a Predictor of US Recessions." *Federal Reserve Bank of St. Louis Review* 79 (2): 41–51.

Flikkema, M., C. Castaldi, A. de Man, and M. Seip. Forthcoming. "Trademarks' Relatedness to Product and Service Innovation: A Branding Strategy Approach." *Research Policy.* doi:10.1016/j.respol.2019.01.018.

Flikkema, M. J., A. P. de Man, and C. Castaldi. 2014. "Are Trademarks Counts a Valid Indicator of Innovation? Results from an In-Depth Study of New Benelux Trademarks Filed by SMEs." *Industry and Innovation* 21 (4): 310–331. doi:10.1080/13662716.2014.934547.

Fosfuri, A., M. Giarratana, and A. Luzzi. 2008. "The Penguin Has Entered the Building: The Commercialization of Open Source Software Products." *Organization Science* 19 (2): 292–305. doi:10.1287/orsc.1070.0321.

Gao, G., and L. Hitt. 2012. "Information Technology and Trademarks: Implications for Product Variety." *Management Science* 58: 6. doi:10.1287/mnsc.1110.1480.

George, E., and R. McCulloch. 1997. "Approaches for Bayesian Variable Selection." *Statistica Sinica* 7 (2): 339–373.

Gotsch, M., and C. Hipp. 2012. "Measurement of Innovation Activities in the Knowledge-intensive Services Industry: A Trademark Approach." *The Service Industries Journal* 32 (13): 2167–2184. doi:10.1080/02642069.2011.574275.

Graham, S. J. H., G. Hancock, A. C. Marco, and A. Myers. 2013. "The USPTO Trademark Case Files Dataset: Descriptions, Lessons, and Insights." *Journal of Economics & Management Strategy* 22 (4): 669–705. doi:10.1111/jems.12035.

Greenhalgh, C., and M. Rogers. 2006. "Market Valuation of UK Intellectual Property: Manufacturing, Utility and Financial Services Firms." In *The Management of Intellectual Property*, edited by D. Bosworth and E. Webster, 132–145. Cheltenham: Edward Elgar Publishing.

Greenhalgh, C., and M. Longland. 2005. "Running to Stand Still? – The Value of R&D, Patents and Trade Marks in Innovating Manufacturing Firms." *International Journal of the Economics of Business* 12 (3): 307–328. doi:10.1080/13571510500299326.

Greenhalgh, C., and M. Rogers. 2012. "Trade Marks and Performance in Services and Manufacturing Firms: Evidence of Schumpeterian Competition through Innovation." *Australian Economic Review* 45 (1): 50–76. doi:10.1111/j.1467–8462.2011.00665.x.

Griffiths, W., and E. Webster. 2006. "Trends in the Market Valuation of Australian Intellectual Property." In *The Management of Intellectual Property*, edited by D. Bosworth and E. Webster, 146–158. Cheltenham: Edward Elgar Publishing.

Griffiths, W., P. H. Jensen, and E. Webster. 2011. "What Creates Abnormal Profits?" *Scottish Journal of Political Economy* 58 (3): 323–346. doi:10.1111/j.1467-9485.2011.00549.x.

Hall, B., C. Helmers, M. Rogers, and V. Sena. 2014. "The Choice between Formal and Informal Intellectual Property: A Review." *Journal of Economic Literature* 52 (2): 375–423. doi:10.1257/jel.52.2.375.

Harvey, A. C. 1989. *Forecasting, Structural Time Series Models and the Kalman Filter*. Cambridge: Cambridge University Press.

Helmers, C., and M. Rogers. 2010. "Innovation and the Survival of New Firms in the UK." *Review of Industrial Organization* 36 (3): 227–248. doi:10.1007/s11151-010-9247-7.

Hipp, C., and H. Grupp. 2005. "Innovation in the Service Sector: The Demand for Service-specific Innovation Measurement Concepts and Typologies." *Research Policy* 34 (4): 517–535. doi:10.1016/j.respol.2005.03.002.

Ishwaran, H., and J. S. Rao. 2005. "Spike and Slab Variable Selection: Frequentist and Bayesian Strategies." *The Annals of Statistics* 33 (2): 730–773. doi:10.1214/009053604000001147.

Jensen, P. H., and E. Webster. 2008. "Labelling Characteristics and Demand for Retail Grocery Products in Australia." *Australian Economic Papers* 47 (2): 129–140. doi:10.1111/j.1467-8454.2008.00336.x.

Kalman, R. E. 1960. "A New Approach to Linear Filtering and Prediction Problems." *Journal of Basic Engineering* 82 (1): 35–45. doi:10.1115/1.3662552.

Krasnikov, A., S. Mishra, and D. Orozco. 2009. "Evaluating the Financial Impact of Branding Using Trademarks: A Framework and Empirical Evidence." *Journal of Marketing* 73 (6): 154–166. doi:10.1509/jmkg.73.6.154.

Lahiri, K., and J. G. Wang. 2013. "Evaluating Probability Forecasts for GDP Declines Using Alternative Methodologies." *International Journal of Forecasting* 29 (1): 175–190. doi:10.1016/j.ijforecast.2012.07.004.

Lahiri, K., and L. Yang. 2015. "A Further Analysis of the Conference Board's New Leading Economic Index." *International Journal of Forecasting* 31 (2): 446–453. doi:10.1016/j.ijforecast.2014.12.006.

Levanon, G. 2009. "Evaluating and Comparing Leading and Coincident Economic Indicators." *Business Economics* 45 (1): 16–27. doi:10.1057/be.2009.29.

Levanon, G., A. Ozyildirim, B. Schaitkin, and J. Zabinska. 2011b. *"Comprehensive Benchmark Revisions of the Conference Board Leading Economic Index® for the United States."* The Conference Board Economics Program Working Paper Series, EPWP 1106.

Levanon, G., J. Manini, A. Ozyildirim, B. Schaitkin, and J. Tanchua. 2015. "Using Financial Indicators to Predict Turning Points in the Business Cycle: The Case of the Leading Economic Index for the United States." *International Journal of Forecasting* 31 (2): 426–445. doi:10.1016/j.ijforecast.2014.11.004.

Levanon, G., J. C. Manini, A. Ozyildirim, B. Schaitkin, and J. Tanchua. 2011a. "Using a Leading Credit Index to Predict Turning Points in the U.S. Business Cycle." *Economics Program Working Papers 11-05*. The Conference Board.

Llerena, P., and V. Millot. 2013. "Are Trade Marks and Patents Complementary or Substitute Protections for Innovation?" Paper presented at the Druid 2012 Conference, Copenhagen, Denmark, June 19-21.

Madigan, D., and A. Raftery. 1994. "Model Selection and Accounting for Model Uncertainty in Graphical Models Using Occam's Window." *Journal of the American Statistical Association* 89 (428): 1535–1546. doi:10.1080/01621459.1994.10476894.

Marcellino, M. 2006. "Leading Indicators." In *Chapter 16 in Handbook of Economic Forecasting*, edited by G. Elliott, C. W. J. Granger, and A. Timmermann, 879–960. Amsterdam: North-Holland Publishing Company.

Mendonça, S., T. S. Pereira, and M. M. Godinho. 2004. "Trademarks as an Indicator of Innovation and Industrial Change." *Research Policy* 33 (9): 1385–1404. doi:10.1016/j.respol.2004.09.005.

Millot, V. 2009. "Trademarks as an Indicator of Product and Marketing Innovations." *STI Working Paper 2009/6*, April 8. OECD.

Mitchell, T. J., and J. J. Beauchamp. 1988. "Bayesian Variable Selection in Linear Regression." *Journal of the American Statistical Association* 83 (404): 1023–1032. doi:10.1080/01621459.1988.10478694.

Sandner, P. G. 2009. "The Identification of Trademark Filing Strategies: Creating, Hedging, Modernizing, and Extending Brands." *The Trademark Reporter* 99 (5): 1257–1298.

Sandner, P. G., and J. Block. 2011. "The Market Value of R&D, Patents, and Trademarks." *Research Policy* 40 (7): 969–985. doi:10.1016/j.respol.2011.04.004.

Schautschick, P. 2015. "An Economic Investigation of the Use and Impact of Patents and Trade Marks in Germany." Ph.D. diss., Ludwig Maximilian University.

Schmoch, U. 2003. "Service Marks as Novel Innovation Indicator." *Research Evaluation* 12 (2): 149–156. doi:10.3152/147154403781776708.

Schmoch, U., and S. Gauche. 2009. "Service Marks as Indicators for Innovation in Knowledge-Based Services." *Research Evaluation* 18 (4): 323–335. doi:10.3152/095820209X451023.

Schumpeter, J. A. 1934. *The theory of economic development: an inquiry into profits, capital, credit, interest, and the business cycle.* Translated from the German by Redvers Opie (1961) New York.

Schumpeter, J. A. 1939. *Business Cycles: A Theoretical, Historical, and Statistical Analysis of the Capitalist Process.* New York: McGraw-Hill.

Schumpeter, J. A. 1942. *Capitalism, Socialism and Democracy.* New York: Harper and Brothers.

Scott, S., and H. R. Varian. 2015. "Bayesian Variable Selection for Nowcasting Economic Time Series." In *Economic Analysis of the Digital Economy*, edited by A. Goldfarb, S. M. Greenstein, and C. E. Tucker, 119–135. Chicago: University of Chicago Press.

Scott, S., and H. R. Varian. 2014. "Predicting the Present with Bayesian Structural Time Series." *International Journal of Mathematical Modelling and Numerical Optimisation* 5: 1/2. doi:10.1504/IJMMNO.2014.059942.

Seethamraju, C. 2003. "The Value Relevance of Trademarks." In *Intangible Assets: Values, Measures, and Risks*, edited by J. Hand and B. Lev, 228–247. Oxford: Oxford University Press. Chapter 9.

Seip, M., C. Castaldi, M. Flikkema, and A. De Man. 2018. "The Timing of Trademark Application in Innovation Processes." *Technovation* 72–73 (April–May): 34–45. doi:10.1016/j.technovation.2018.02.001.

Semadeni, M. 2006. "Minding Your Distance: How Management Consulting Firms Use Service Marks to Position Competitively." *Strategic Management Journal* 27 (2): 169–187. doi:10.1002/(ISSN)1097-0266.

Somaya, D., and S. Graham. 2006. *Vermeers and Rembrandts in the Same Attic: Complementarity between Copyright and Trademark Leveraging Strategies in Software*. Georgia Institute of Technology. TIGER Working Paper. Georgia Institute of Technology. Available on SSRN. https://papers.ssrn.com/sol3/papers.cfm?abstract_id=887484

Tsangarides, C. 2004. "A Bayesian Approach to Model Uncertainty." *IMF Working Paper 04/68*. International Monetary Fund, April. doi:10.5089/9781451849028.001.

Zhou, H., P. G. Sandner, S. L. Martinelli, and J. H. Block. 2016. "Patents, Trademarks, and Their Complementarity in Venture Capital Funding." *Technovation* 47 (January): 14–22. doi:10.1016/j.technovation.2015.11.005.

Part II

Trademarks as Assets

On the price elasticity of demand for trademarks

Gaétan de Rassenfosse

ABSTRACT

One underexplored factor directly affecting firms' use of trademarks relates to the fees associated with obtaining a mark. This paper provides econometric estimates of the fee elasticity of demand for trademark applications. Using a panel of monthly international trademark applications, I find that a 10-percent increase in fees leads to a 2.5–4.0-percent decrease in applications. The econometric analysis also highlights that trademark filings react strongly to economic activity. The results bear implications for literature on the value of trademarks and for the use of trademarks as innovation indicator. Specifically, low elasticity estimates suggest that trademarks provide significant economic value to their owners relative to their costs. However, one must exercise caution when comparing trademark numbers across countries to the extent that fees might differ substantially.

1. Introduction

This paper contributes to trademark research by providing estimates of the fee elasticity of demand for trademark protection. Such estimates matter for at least three reasons. First, they offer us a window on the value of trademarks. The price elasticity of demand for a good depends on the economic value it brings to its owner relative to its cost. Thus, low fee elasticity estimates would suggest that trademarks provide significant economic value to their owners. Second, understanding which features of the trademark system affect trademark usage provides a better understanding of the use of trademark data as innovation indicator. If fees are found to matter, scholars and policy analysts would need to exercise caution when comparing trademark activity across countries. Third, sound price elasticity estimates would also contribute to evidence-based policymaking. Changes in the schedule of fees always raise budget concerns and price elasticity estimates would help Intellectual Property (IP) offices to forecast potential revenue changes.

Because trademark filing fees are inexpensive relative to standard marketing budgets, it would be tempting to assume that these fees are of secondary importance in the filing decision. This assumption is misguided. Lessons learned from patents, another type of IP right, suggest that application fees have significant effects on firm behavior (e. g. de Rassenfosse and Jaffe 2018). So far, we have little knowledge of this subject with respect to trademarks.

The empirical analysis focuses on trademark applications filed through the Madrid system, which is the primary international system for facilitating the registration of trademarks in multiple jurisdictions (so-called international trademarks). A key feature of the Madrid system is that the application fee must be paid in Swiss francs to the World Intellectual Property Organization (WIPO), which is based in Geneva. Hence, the effective fee paid by applicants from the various member states of the Madrid protocol fluctuates based on the exchange rate relative to the Swiss franc. The empirical analysis in this paper exploits this source of heterogeneity to estimate price elasticity. It relies on a panel of monthly applications filed from 2004 to 2013 in 42 countries, which adds up to approximately 340,000 trademark applications.

To briefly summarize the results, estimates of the fee elasticity of demand for trademarks range from −0.25 to −0.40. In other words, a 10-percent increase in fees led to a 2.5 to 4.0 percent decrease in the demand for trademarks. These estimates are substantially lower than those presented in Herz and Mejer (2016) for national trademarks.

The remainder of this paper is organized as follows. Section 2 provides background information on the trademark filing process and discusses elements likely to affect the fee elasticity of demand for trademarks. Section 3 introduces the econometric model. Section 4 presents the data, and section 5 discusses the results. Section 6 concludes with implications for trademark research.

2. Background

2.1. The international trademark system

The Madrid System for the International Registration of Marks was established by the 1891 Madrid Agreement with the aim of facilitating the registration of marks world-wide. The Madrid System makes it possible to protect a mark in about 100 countries by obtaining an international registration that takes effect in each of the designated contracting nation-parties. A firm files a trademark application in one of three official languages (English, French, Spanish) with any participating trademark office, usually its national office. The office then forwards the application to WIPO. The payment of fees occurs at the time of filing and must be made in Swiss francs directly to WIPO.

Once WIPO receives the application, it conducts a formal examination of the international application, which, if approved, is recorded in the International Register. WIPO then notifies the IP offices in all the territories in which the firm wishes to have its mark protected. It is then the responsibility of each national IP office to perform a substantive examination and decide on issuance in accordance with its legislation.

2.2. Insights from economic theory

To the best of my knowledge, Herz and Mejer (2016) is the only study looking at the fee elasticity of demand for trademarks. These authors use quarterly fee and filing data from 20 European offices from 1993 to 2011 to estimate the sensitivity of national filings to fees. In this manner, they find a fee elasticity of −1.05, meaning that a 10-percent increase in fees leads to a 10.5-percent reduction in trademark filings. Thus, existing evidence would suggest that trademarks are very sensitive to fees. This section uses insights from economic theory to reflect on the price elasticity of demand for trademarks.

First, the price elasticity of demand for a good depends on the availability of substitutes. There are no clear substitutes for protecting brand names and brand marks, which would suggest a low elasticity.[1] However, when filing a trademark application, firms have a variety of choices. They can seek protection at the national IP office, at the regional (European Union) level by filing a 'Community Trade Mark' at the Office for Harmonization in the Internal Market (OHIM), or at the global level through the Madrid System at the WIPO.

Second, the price elasticity of demand for a good also depends on the economic value it provides to its owner. Regarding patents, scholars have long demonstrated the existence of a causal premium associated with patenting (Arora, Ceccagnoli, and Cohen 2008; Jensen, Thomson, and Yong 2011). By contrast, trademark research is still in an early stage and the majority of studies have documented a positive correlation between trademark protection and various indicators of firm performance (Buddelmeyer, Jensen, and Webster 2010; Flikkema, De Man, and Castaldi 2014; Greenhalgh and Rogers 2006; Krasnikov, Mishra, and Orozco 2009; Mendonça, Santos Pereira and Mira Godinho 2004; Sandner and Block 2011). Because the present paper focuses on the most valuable trademarks – those for which firms seek international coverage – elasticity is likely to be low relative to the estimates obtained by Herz and Mejer (2016) for national trademarks.

Third, the price elasticity of a good depends on its actual price level and, in particular, on how much of the firm's overall budget it represents. There is a general sense that the trademark application process is inexpensive. As one practitioner puts it: 'Not only is trademarking your intellectual property easy, it's also extremely inexpensive in the grand scheme of things. Many trademarks can be had for a few hundred dollars, and they never expire.'[2] And indeed, the cost of trademark protection is quite low compared to market research and marketing expenditures. It is limited to drafting and filing fees, which should suggest a low elasticity.[3] The basic fee for filing a trademark in 2018 is 653 CHF at WIPO, 850 EUR at OHIM, 400 USD at the U.S. Patent and Trademark Office, and 250 AUD at IP Australia.

To sum up, the lack of substitutes, the economic benefits that trademarks confer and the low price level suggest that the demand for trademark filing should be fairly inelastic. However, previous estimates point to a highly elastic demand function.

3. Econometric model

As opposed to research on patent filings, research on the aggregate determinants of trademark filings remains in its early stages. Herz and Mejer (2016) use a country's gross domestic product (GDP) as the main covariate to capture both demand and

---

[1] In common law jurisdictions, a substitution exists in the form of unregistered trademarks (usually denoted with the symbol ™). However, registered trademarks (denoted with the symbol ®) afford a number of benefits.

[2] Bert Seither, 'Why Trademarking Makes Business Sense', *Forbes Community Voice*, 27 September 2018. Available at: https://bit.ly/2RcVlW2.

[3] Anecdotal evidence suggests that the cost of a trademark attorney for filing an application is in the range $1000–$2000.

supply side factors. de Rassenfosse (2017) uses GDP to capture demand side and 'brand equity' investment to capture supply side. The brand equity investment series is computed using data on advertising expenditures (collected from surveys or from input-output tables) and costs of market research (collected from input-output tables).[4] Unfortunately, this series is available for only a limited number of countries.

The main covariates used in the present empirical analysis are GDP and trademark filing fees, explained in greater detail in Section 4 below. A feature of trademark fees at WIPO is that applicants must pay them in Swiss francs. Exogenous variations in the effective fees paid by applicants in country i stem from variations in the exchange rate of country i's currency to the Swiss franc.

Both Hertz and Mejer (2016) and de Rassenfosse (2017) model the demand for trademarks using a partial adjustment model à la Nerlove (1958), following de Rassenfosse and van Pottelsberghe de la Potterie (2012) for patents. This model captures a great deal of cross-country heterogeneity in the number of trademark filings by including the lagged number of trademark applications. The basic model of trademark filings by applicants from country i in month t is given by

$$T_{it}^* = f(Y_{it},\ F_{it})e^{v_{it}}$$

where T_{it}^* denotes the steady-state level of trademark applications, Y_{it} is the GDP, F_{it} is the filing fee, and v_{it} is the error term. This model uses a dynamic process to allow for the possibility that the number of trademark filings does not immediately adjust to its steady-state level. The 'distance' between T_{it}^* and the actual T_{it} closes partially in each period as firms adjust to the new level of fees and other changes in economic conditions:

$$\frac{T_{it}}{T_{it-1}} = \left(\frac{T_{it}^*}{T_{it-1}}\right)^{\lambda}$$

with $0 < \lambda \le 1$ as the speed of adjustment. Combining these two equations and taking natural logs yields

$$\ln T_{it} = \lambda \ln f(Y_{it},\ F_{it}) + (1 - \lambda)\ln T_{it-1} + \epsilon_{it}$$

where ϵ_{it} is a rescaling of v_{it} by a factor λ. The parameterization of the trademark production function $f(Y_{it}, F_{it})$ is a Cobb-Douglas utility function of the form $\phi_i Y_{it}^{\alpha_1} F_{it}^{\alpha_2}$ where α_1 and α_2 capture long-term elasticities. The regression model is

$$\ln T_{it} = \beta_{0i} + \beta_i \ln Y_{it} + \beta_2 \ln F_{it} + (1 - \lambda)\ln T_{it-1} + \epsilon_{it} \qquad (1)$$

where $\beta_2 = \lambda \alpha_2$ is the short-term fee elasticity and β_{0i} is the country fixed effect.

One should take note of three econometric issues. The first relates to the possibility of spurious results when the series are not stationary (Yule 1926). The next section assesses the presence of unit roots using a Fisher-type test. This test is well suited to an unbalanced panel with a large time dimension. Anticipating the results, I find evidence that the trademark filing series are stationary.

---

[4]Input-output tables are produced by national statistical agencies and provide detailed information about the supply and use of products in the economy, and the structure of and inter-relationships between industries.

Second, the presence of the lagged dependent variable is a source of endogeneity when the series exhibit serial correlation (Nickell 1981). Although the problem is especially acute when the time dimensionality is small, I nevertheless correct for the possibility of dynamic panel bias using the bias approximation in Bun and Kiviet (2003) that is extended to unbalanced panels by Bruno (2005).

Another potential pitfall is the simultaneity bias typically associated with price elasticity estimates (*i.e.* price affects demand and vice-versa). A valuable feature of the current set-up is that it presents no such concern: the application fee at WIPO has not been adjusted over a 10-year period, although the worldwide demand for international trademarks grew at an annual rate of 4.75 percent during the study period. Fee changes come from variations in the exchange rate, which are exogenous to the change in trademark filing numbers. However, the identification strategy opens the door to a confounding factor, namely changes in economic conditions, that may affect both the exchange rate and the demand for trademarks. Although the GDP variable accounts for long-term economic changes, a more finely grained indicator of economic activity is needed. Thus, the empirical analysis includes the monthly level of the country's industrial production as a control variable.

4. Data

The dependent variable is the number of international trademark applications filed at WIPO by applicants from country i in month t (T_{it}). The sample includes 42 countries with an average of more than five applications per month during the 01/2004–12/2013 period.[5]

The key independent variable is the filing fee (F_{it}). The basic fee for filing a trademark is 653 CHF. The fee is to be paid in CHF, has not changed since 1996, and is converted into nominal local currency using monthly exchange rate series obtained from the foreign exchange trading platform Oanda.com. The fee values are then converted into 2011 constant international dollars using the GDP deflators from the IMF World Economic Outlook (WEO) database.

The main control variable is yearly GDP (Y_{it}), obtained from the IMF WEO database. Monthly series were obtained by linear interpolation of the yearly series. The variable Y_{it} is reported in 2011 constant international dollars.

As discussed above, the model includes monthly industrial production (I_{it}), which is obtained from the OECD Key Short Term Indicators database. The variable is available for 28 countries and is therefore not included in the baseline specification; it is expressed as an index that takes the value of 1 in January 2006. Table 1 provides descriptive statistics for the month of December 2010. The number of trademark applications ranges from 2 for Iceland to 440 for Germany, with a mean of 68. The fee ranges from USD PPP 454 for Australia to USD PPP 15,616 for Estonia, with a mean of USD PPP 1260. In terms of GDP, the smallest country in the sample is Iceland and the largest is the United States. Appendix Table A1 provides the list of 42

---

[5]The Benelux countries have a common trademark office and individual country figures on trademark filings are not available. Country figures have been estimated on a pro rata basis using each country's GDP. The results are robust to the exclusion of Benelux countries from the sample.

Table 1. Overview of a data slice, December 2010.

	N	Min	Mean	Max	Std. Dev.
Applications (T_{it})	41	2	68	440	102
Fees (F_{it})	42	454.40	1259.54	15,616.51	2301.52
GDP (Y_{it})	42	12.47	1379.86	15,273.22	3009.15
Industrial production (I_{it})	28	0.97	1.03	1.11	0.03

There are 120 time periods. GDP is expressed in billions. There are 41 observations for the variable T_{it} because one country (New Zealand) entered the Madrid system in 12/2012.

countries included in the sample together with the country-specific means and standard deviations of the variables T_{it} and F_{it}.

Table 2 presents the results of a Fisher-type panel unit root test. This test is well suited to the data because there are many time periods and the panel is unbalanced. The null hypothesis is that all individual series contain a unit root, and the alternative is that at least one series is stationary. The table reports the p-values associated with the inverse normal Z statistic. The test strongly rejects the null hypothesis regarding trademark applications (with 1 or 3 lags) and GDP (with 3 lags only). The null hypothesis cannot be rejected in the case of the fees series, suggesting the presence of a unit root. However, given that the dependent variable is stationary, there is no risk of spurious results.

5. Results

5.1. Cross-section estimates

Figure 1 provides a graphical illustration of 120 monthly cross-section estimates of the price elasticity of demand for trademarks (one for each time period) to provide a sense of the data. Ninety-five percent of the estimates are in the range of −0.24 and −0.88, and the mean is −0.52. Coincidentally, this figure is remarkably similar to cross sectional estimates obtained for patent data in de Rassenfosse and van Pottelsberghe de la Potterie (2007).

The elasticity appears to be higher in the post-2008 period than in the pre-2008 period. The estimates average −0.41 in the 2004–2007 period and −0.60 in the 2008–2013 period. This sharp increase in the elasticity parameter may be a consequence of the global financial crisis (GFC): the worsening of economic conditions could have lowered the returns from new products, which could make trademarks more sensitive to fees.

5.2. Dynamic panel estimates

Table 3 presents baseline panel estimates for the sample of all 42 countries. The results shown in column (1) suggest that the short-term fee elasticity is −0.290, meaning that

Table 2. Fisher-type panel unit root tests (p-values).

	Applications (T_{it})	GDP (Y_{it})	Fees (F_{it})
Augmented Dickey-Fuller, 1 lag	0.000	0.1709	0.2423
Augmented Dickey-Fuller, 3 lags	0.000	0.1678	0.2515
Phillips-Perron, 1 lag	0.000	0.000	0.2809
Phillips-Perron, 3 lags	0.000	0.000	0.2553

p-values associated with the inverse normal Z statistic. Panel-specific autoregressive parameter and panel means included. There is no time trend.

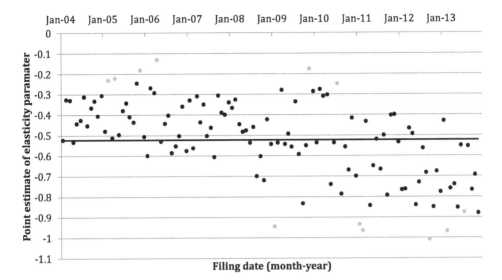

Figure 1. Monthly cross-section estimates.

Notes: grey dots are the 5 percent extreme values on each side.

Table 3. Estimates of Equation (1).

	(1)	(2)	(3)	(4)	(5)
Estimator:	F.E.	LSDVB	LSDVB	LSDVB	LSDVB
ln T_{it-1}	0.132***	0.139***	0.134***	0.133***	0.133***
	(0.013)	(0.008)	(0.010)	(0.010)	(0.010)
ln Y_{it}	0.982***	0.970***	0.831***	0.813***	0.794***
	(0.082)	(0.077)	(0.154)	(0.129)	(0.149)
ln F_{it}	−0.290***	−0.287***	−0.267*	−0.268**	−0.266**
	(0.057)	(0.090)	(0.142)	(0.117)	(0.114)
$GFC_t * \ln F_{it}$					0.023
					(0.059)
Country effect	Yes	Yes	Yes	Yes	Yes
Time effect	No	No	Yes	Yes	Yes
Month effect	No	No	No	Yes	Yes
N countries	42	42	42	42	42
N obs.	4694	4694	4694	4694	4694
R^2	0.64	0.64	0.66	0.66	0.62

The dependent variable is the log number of trademark applications.
T_{it}: Applications; Y_{it}: GDP; F_{it}: Fees; Y_{it}: GDP; *GFC*: Global Financial Crisis.
F.E.: fixed effect estimator with robust standard errors; and LSDVB: least square dummy variable correcting for
  dynamic panel bias estimator with bootstrapped standard errors in parentheses (Bruno 2005).
***: p-value < 0.01; **: p-value < 0.05; *: p-value < 0.10.
Constant term included but not reported.
R^2 estimated as the square of the correlation coefficient between the actual and the predicted values.

a 10 percent increase in the fee leads to a 2.90 percent decrease in trademark applications. The corresponding long-term elasticity is reported in column (1) of Table 4 and reaches −0.334. The two values are close to one another because the speed of adjustment is close to 1 ($\lambda = 1-0.132 = 0.868$). In other words, firms adjust almost contemporaneously to the change in fees.

Correcting for the dynamic bias in column (2) has virtually no impact on both the short- and long-term elasticity estimates. The regression models presented in columns (3)–(4) of

Table 4. Long-term fee elasticities (recovered from Table 3).

	(1)	(2)	(3)	(4)	(5 pre-GFC)
a_2	−0.334***	−0.334***	−0.309*	−0.310**	−0.307**

***: p-value < 0.01; **: p-value < 0.05; *: p-value < 0.10.

Table 3 control for time effects. The model in column (3) includes dummies for each individual month to capture global time effects that may affect all countries simultaneously. An F-test of joint statistical significance leads to the rejection of the null hypothesis of no time effect (p-value of 0.013). The model in column (4) additionally includes twelve monthly dummies to capture, for instance, the effect of measurement errors arising from the linear interpolation of yearly GDP series into monthly series. The dummies are jointly significantly different from zero (there seem to be more applications in the May–July period), but the coefficients associated with the fee variable remain largely unchanged.

The model in the last column tests whether the fee elasticity changed in the post-GFC period as suggested by the cross-section estimates presented in Figure 1. The dummy variable GFC takes the value of 1 on or after January 2008 and 0 before. The point estimate of the parameter associated with the variable $GFC_t * \ln F_{it}$ is not statistically significantly different from zero, suggesting no change in the elasticity. This finding further indicates that the time effects and the GDP variable pick up changes in the economic environment in a satisfactory manner.

Table 4 presents estimates of the long-term price elasticity that is recovered from the parameters in Table 3. The elasticity ranges between −0.307 and −0.334, which is, as expected, substantially lower than the cross-section estimates presented in Figure 1.

Table 5 presents estimates performed on a subsample of countries for which industrial production data are available. As discussed above, we must control for the possibility that a change in economic conditions affects both the exchange rate and the demand for trademarks. The regression model presented in column (1) adopts the same specifications as the model in column (4) of Table 3 and serves to assess the sensitivity of the results to the use of a different sample. The estimate of the elasticity parameter is quantitatively similar but it is less precisely estimated.

The model presented in column (2) controls for industrial production at home. First, the considerable increase in model fit compared to column (1) is notable, suggesting that industrial production accounts for a non-trivial proportion of heterogeneity in trademark filings. The variable has a large and statistically significant effect on the demand for trademarks: a one-percent increase in industrial production leads to a 0.25-percent increase in trademark filings. The price elasticity in column (2) is sensibly higher than in column (1), with a point estimate for the short-term elasticity at −0.338 and for the long-term elasticity at −0.392 (column 2 of Table 6).

The specification presented in column (3) enables an investigation of the effects of the global industrial production level (G_{it}), as measured by the GDP-weighted sum of production levels in each country except country i. The effect of global industrial production is imprecisely estimated, and the point estimate of the coefficient associated with the national production remains unchanged.

Table 5. Estimates of Equation (1).

	(1)	(2)	(3)
Estimator:	LSDVB	LSDVB	LSDVB
ln T_{it-1}	0.140***	0.139***	0.139***
	(0.010)	(0.010)	(0.010)
ln Y_{it}	0.923***	0.545	0.571
	(0.289)	(0.381)	(0.404)
ln F_{it}	−0.215	−0.338*	−0.342*
	(0.159)	(0.187)	(0.181)
ln I_{it}		0.249*	0.251*
		(0.143)	(0.136)
ln G_{it}			0.658
			(0.875)
Country effect	Yes	Yes	Yes
Time effect	Yes	Yes	Yes
Month effect	Yes	Yes	Yes
N countries	28	28	28
N obs.	3148	3148	3148
R^2	0.64	0.73	0.73

The dependent variable is the log number of trademark applications.
T_{it}: Applications; Y_{it}: GDP; F_{it}: Fees; Y_{it}: GDP; I_{it}: Industrial production at home; G_{it}: Global Industrial production.
LSDVB: least square dummy variable correcting for dynamic panel bias estimator with bootstrapped standard errors in parentheses (Bruno 2005).
***: p-value < 0.01; **: p-value < 0.05; *: p-value < 0.10.
The constant term is included but not reported.
R^2 is estimated as the square of the correlation coefficient between the actual and the predicted values.

Table 6. Long-term fee elasticities (recovered from Table 5).

	(1)	(2)	(3)
α_2	−0.250	−0.392*	−0.397*

***: p-value < 0.01; **: p-value < 0.05; *: p-value < 0.10.

The long-term elasticities, which are presented in Table 6, are slightly higher than those in Table 4 but are in the same general range.

5.3. Additional considerations

The present paper studies firms' reactions at the extensive margin (whether or not to file a trademark application) and omits firms' reactions at the intensive margin. Firms can alter the fees associated with a trademark application by changing the number of Nice classes it covers. Nice classes describe the 45 categories of goods and services in which the trademark is to be used. While firms have the option to file multiple single-class trademarks across different classes, they typically list different Nice classes in a multi-class trademark application. Thus, reactions at the intensive margin are unlikely to affect the results substantially. This conclusion is particularly true for international trademark applications, as the basic fee already covers three classes. In 2016, the average number of Nice classes per application was 1.40, well below 3.[6]

---

[6]Source: 2017 'World Intellectual Property Indicators' Report by WIPO, page 98.

In a similar vein, the fee indicator does not consider designation fees. These fees, which are jurisdiction-specific, depend on where applicants want to protect their marks. They can be paid either at the time of filing or subsequently to international registration. Total designation fees vary from one trademark application to another; they are endogenous to the applicant's budget and the trademark's value. Accounting for the effect of designation fees would require detailed trademark-level data, which is outside the scope of the present study. That said, the role of designation fees on the *demand* for trademarks is likely to be negligible; most of the effect would logically occur at the intensive margin. Indeed, similar evidence on patent validation fees at the European Patent Office, which are due once a patent is granted, suggests an effect on applicant's validation behavior (Harhoff et al. 2009).

The present analysis also omits agent fees, which can account for a substantial share of the overall trademark budget. The omission of agent fees is common to all studies on the price elasticity of demand for IP rights due to the difficulty of assembling panel data for a large number of countries (let alone a single country). Moreover, one can expect great heterogeneity in agent fees. In the context of this study, changes in official fees are orthogonal to changes in agent fees such that elasticity estimates are unbiased.

Finally, this paper estimates the own-price elasticity of international trademarks. It would also be interesting to study the cross-price elasticity, particularly with respect to European Community trademarks. This research question is outside the scope of the present paper, but it is worth emphasizing that the estimates are not affected by the omission of substitutes. Indeed, variations in the prices of substitutes are exogenous to variations in the prices of international trademarks. Another interesting avenue for future research involves estimating the fee elasticity for different groups of applicants (*e.g.* first-time applicants, startups and SMEs).

6. Conclusion

The importance of trademarks to marketing and innovation practices should encourage scholars to study how the design of the trademark system affects firm behavior. This paper takes a step in this direction by studying the price elasticity of demand for international trademark applications. The long-term price elasticity of demand for trademarks is between −0.25 and −0.40, depending on model specification and sample composition.

Another notable finding relates to the fact that economic conditions strongly affect the number of trademark filings, as witnessed by the positive impact of the variable capturing industrial production. While trademark data are being used as an innovation indicator, this finding suggests that they are also an indicator of economic activity.

The fee elasticity estimates provide a window onto the economic returns of trademarks, a question that is receiving increasing attention in the literature (Schautschick and Greenhalgh 2016). The stream of income associated with a trademark drives a firm's filing decision, and low elasticity estimates are suggestive of high returns from trademark protection, *ceteris paribus*. Thus, the results can be taken as an indication that international trademarks provide economic value to their owners (relative to their costs).

Interestingly, my estimates are substantially lower than those obtained by Herz and Mejer (2016). One key difference between the two studies is that the present study focuses on trademarks that target the international market, whereas Herz and Mejer (2016) focus on trademarks filed in national offices in Europe. The difference in elasticity estimates between the two studies could signal the fragility of the national trademark systems. First, the average fee for filing a national trademark application process in European countries is around 300 USD (Herz and Mejer 2016, 1045), which is substantially lower than the application fees at WIPO. Yet, the fee elasticity is substantially higher. Second, national trademark offices in Europe compete with the office for harmonization of internal market (OHIM). Applicants may find it more profitable to go directly to OHIM should national filing fees increase. And indeed, the number of applications at OHIM grew from about 50,000 in the early 2000s to about 150,000 today.

More generally, this paper also contributes to advancing knowledge on the use of trademark in scholarly research. It illustrates that factors unrelated to innovation and marketing activities affect the volume of trademark filings. Scholars sometimes employ the number of trademark applications as a measure of a firm's brand equity (e.g. Krasnikov, Mishra, and Orozco 2009; Bahadir, DeKinder, and Kohli 2015). Nonetheless, this paper is a reminder that differences in the number of trademark filings across firms should be interpreted cautiously because they are affected by factors not directly related to brand equity. Although this paper uncovers macro-level determinants, micro-level determinants such as credit constraints, international exposure, or strategic considerations (e.g. Fink et al. 2014; Block et al. 2015; De Vries, Enrico Pennings, and Fisch 2017) also merit further research. At a more aggregate level, such estimates are important if we are to better understand the relevance of the use of trademark data for cross-country comparisons of innovative output. Trademark data are increasingly considered a worthy innovation output measure (Flikkema, De Man, and Castaldi 2014; Mendonça, Santos Pereira, and Mira Godinho 2004; Millot 2009), but the empirical analysis suggests that both the level of fees and economic activity significantly affect the number of trademark filings. A clear takeaway regarding the use of trademark data for cross-country comparison of innovation performance is that differences in the level of fees should be accounted for if there are large variations across countries. Conversely, they can be neglected if variations are small.

The results also bear implications for policy. A first implication concerns subsidies for trademark applications. Subsidies can come from national governments to domestic companies or in the form of rebates that WIPO grants to groups of applicants such as SMEs. The small fee elasticity combined with low level of filing fees would suggest a limited effectiveness of subsidies overall – although I acknowledge that applicants in some countries or certain groups of applicants may be highly sensitive to fees. Second, regarding budgeting, trademark offices can use the results and apply the method to assess the potential impact of a planned fee reform. Third, this paper serves as a reminder that we know little about what the 'optimal' level of fees should be. Fees should be set to maximize social welfare, but the literature offers no clear practical guidelines regarding the setting of fees.

Acknowledgments

WIPO provided funding for this study. The author is grateful to Carsten Fink, Georg Licht, Julio Raffo and two anonymous referees for helpful suggestions.

Disclosure statement

No potential conflict of interest was reported by the author.

References

Arora, A., M. Ceccagnoli, and W. M. Cohen. 2008. "R&D and the Patent Premium." *International Journal of Industrial Organization* 26 (5): 1153–1179. doi:10.1016/j.ijindorg.2007.11.004.

Block, J. H., C. O. Fisch, A. Hahn, and P. G. Sandner. 2015. "Why Do SMEs File Trademarks? Insights from Firms in Innovative Industries." *Research Policy* 44 (10): 1915–1930. doi:10.1016/j.respol.2015.06.007.

Bruno, G. S. F. 2005. "Approximating the Bias of the LSDV Estimator for Dynamic Unbalanced Panel Data Models." *Economic Letters* 87 (3): 361–366. doi:10.1016/j.econlet.2005.01.005.

Buddelmeyer, H., P. H. Jensen, and E. Webster. 2010. "Innovation and the Determinants of Company Survival." *Oxford Economic Papers* 62 (2): 261–285. doi:10.1093/oep/gpp012.

Bun, M. J. G., and J. F. Kiviet. 2003. "On the Diminishing Returns of Higher-Order Terms in Asymptotic Expansions of Bias." *Economics Letters* 79 (2): 145–152. doi:10.1016/S0165-1765(02)00299-9.

de Rassenfosse, G. 2017. "An Assessment of How Well We Account for Intangibles." *Industrial and Corporate Change* 26 (3): 517–534.

de Rassenfosse, G., and A. Jaffe. 2018. "Are Patent Fees Effective at Weeding Out Low-Quality Patents?" *Journal of Economics & Management Strategy* 27: 134–148. doi:10.1111/jems.12219.

de Rassenfosse, G., and B. van Pottelsberghe de la Potterie. 2007. "Per Un Pugno Di Dollari: A First Look at the Price Elasticity of Patents." *Oxford Review of Economic Policy* 23 (4): 588–604. doi:10.1093/oxrep/grm032.

de Rassenfosse, G., and B. van Pottelsberghe de la Potterie. 2012. "On the Price Elasticity of Demand for Patents." *Oxford Bulletin of Economics and Statistics* 74 (1): 58–77. doi:10.1111/j.1468-0084.2011.00638.x.

De Vries, G., J. H. B. Enrico Pennings, and C. Fisch. 2017. "Trademark or Patent? the Effects of Market Concentration, Customer Type and Venture Capital Financing on Start-Ups' Initial IP Applications." *Industry and Innovation* 24 (4): 325–345. doi:10.1080/13662716.2016.1231607.

Fink, C., C. Helmers, and C. Ponce. 2014. "Trademarks Squatters: Evidence from Chile." *WIPO Economic Research Working paper* No. 22. Geneva: World Intellectual Property Organization.

Flikkema, M., A.-P. De Man, and C. Castaldi. 2014. "Are Trademark Counts a Valid Indicator of Innovation? Results of an In-Depth Study of New Benelux Trademarks Filed by SMEs." *Industry and Innovation* 21 (4): 310–331. doi:10.1080/13662716.2014.934547.

Greenhalgh, C., and M. Rogers. 2006. "The Value of Innovation: The Interaction of Competition, R&D and IP." *Research Policy* 35 (4): 562–580. doi:10.1016/j.respol.2006.02.002.

Harhoff, D., K. Hoisl, B. Reichl, and B. van Pottelsberghe de la Potterie. 2009. "Patent Validation at the Country Level—The Role of Fees and Translation Costs." *Research Policy* 38 (9): 1423–1437. doi:10.1016/j.respol.2009.06.014.

Herz, B., and M. Mejer. 2016. "On the Fee Elasticity of the Demand for Trademarks in Europe." *Oxford Economic Papers* 68 (4): 1039–1061. doi:10.1093/oep/gpw035.

Jensen, P. H., R. Thomson, and J. Yong. 2011. "Estimating the Patent Premium: Evidence from the Australian Inventor Survey." *Strategic Management Journal* 32 (10): 1128–1138. doi:10.1002/smj.925.

Krasnikov, A., S. Mishra, and D. Orozco. 2009. "Evaluating the Financial Impact of Branding Using Trademarks: A Framework and Empirical Evidence." *Journal of Marketing* 73 (6): 154–166. doi:10.1509/jmkg.73.6.154.

Mendonça, S., T. Santos Pereira, and M. Mira Godinho. 2004. "Trademarks as an Indicator of Innovation and Industrial Change." *Research Policy* 33 (9): 1385–1404. doi:10.1016/j.respol.2004.09.005.

Millot, V. 2009. "Trademarks as an Indicator of Product and Marketing Innovations." *OECD Science, Technology and Industry Working Papers 2009/06*. Paris, France: Organisation for Economic Co-operation and Development.

Nerlove, M. 1958. "Distributed Lags and Estimation of Long-Run Supply and Demand Elasticities: Theoretical Considerations." *Journal of Farm Economics* 40 (2): 301–311. doi:10.2307/1234920.

Nickell, S. 1981. "Biases in Dynamic Models with Fixed Effects." *Econometrica* 49 (6): 1417–1426. doi:10.2307/1911408.

S. Cem, B., J. S. DeKinder, and A. K. Kohli. 2015. "Marketing an IPO Issuer in Early Stages of the IPO Process." *Journal of the Academy of Marketing Science* 43 (1): 14–31. doi:10.1007/s11747-014-0393-6.

Sandner, P. G., and J. Block. 2011. "The Market Value of R&D, Patents, and Trademarks." *Research Policy* 40 (7): 969–985. doi:10.1016/j.respol.2011.04.004.

Schautschick, P., and C. Greenhalgh. 2016. "Empirical Studies of Trade Marks–The Existing Economic Literature." *Economics of Innovation and New Technology* 25 (4): 358–390. doi:10.1080/10438599.2015.1064598.

Yule, G. U. 1926. "Why Do We Sometimes Get Nonsense-Correlations between Time-Series? A Study in Sampling and the Nature of Time-Series." *Journal of the Royal Statistical Society* 89 (1): 1–63. doi:10.2307/2341482.

Appendix

Table A1. Monthly number of applications and fees, 2004–2014.

	Applications		Fees	
	Mean	Std. Dev.	Mean	Std. Dev.
Australia	85.73	25.49	515.56	62.31
Austria	86.89	25.76	596.02	48.54
Belarus	9.87	10.62	1'822.40	393.31
Belgium	65.99	15.42	591.96	46.50
Bulgaria	27.96	11.23	1'565.05	169.20
China	137.61	75.07	1'441.74	202.27
Croatia	13.97	11.66	977.44	82.69
Czech Republic	40.34	14.64	978.13	100.91
Denmark	38.53	12.67	481.20	34.41
Estonia	5.33	3.94	15'398.77	2'002.23
Finland	18.76	7.65	529.89	40.36
France	310.42	69.39	562.46	50.39
Germany	440.82	75.99	624.52	56.47
Greece	6.10	4.80	722.90	51.06
Hungary	19.96	21.70	1'109.45	115.06
Iceland	5.88	8.31	536.78	131.91
Israel	13.85	7.04	639.50	33.46
Italy	205.09	80.41	645.72	53.89
Japan	108.51	43.84	532.43	52.00
Latvia	9.36	4.99	758.90	121.06
Lithuania	7.15	4.69	1'127.45	108.14
Luxembourg	6.63	1.49	558.38	41.53
Morocco	6.17	5.22	1'450.63	114.84
Netherlands	112.41	26.34	567.31	52.16
New Zealand	25.38	5.68	618.43	46.11
Norway	27.32	10.60	472.46	49.93
Poland	28.03	8.98	1'120.15	137.89
Portugal	18.77	9.07	780.69	72.48
Republic of Korea	25.63	15.55	828.88	113.27
Romania	7.25	5.80	1'431.22	254.84
Russian Federation	89.33	43.26	1'496.87	364.04
Serbia	15.95	10.99	1'517.61	197.01
Singapore	14.87	7.73	1'017.88	63.48
Slovakia	14.25	8.03	1'006.96	80.58
Slovenia	17.47	11.07	773.56	74.79
Spain	65.83	22.46	691.88	67.63
Sweden	29.30	13.40	533.25	32.78
Switzerland	221.96	38.49	492.33	14.76
Turkey	72.98	27.52	1'154.90	125.11
Ukraine	20.91	15.60	1'849.90	406.55
United Kingdom	98.02	26.83	576.29	85.18
United States of America	323.21	110.65	640.18	56.88

Application fees are in constant USD PPP.
The conversion of nominal fees into constant international dollars explains the variation in the fees paid by applicants in Switzerland.

From a distinctive sign to an exchangeable asset: exploring the U.S. market for trademark licensing

Edoardo Ferrucci, Maria Isabella Leone, Manuel Romagnoli and Andrea Toros

ABSTRACT

A remarkable growth in the value of trademark licencing has been recently recorded. Our paper contributes to the understanding of this under-explored phenomenon using a dataset newly released by the USPTO. Our study analyses the evolution of licencing activities in the U.S. during the 2003–2017 period, the characteristics of these trademarks and agreements, and certain features of the licencing parties involved. We found that licencing activities varied considerably during these years. They were usually signed between two parties only, and, on average, they involved more than one trademark. Excluding under-reporting effect, the analyses reveal that a large portion of heterogeneity in licencing activity is due to the NICE international classes associated with each trademark. Indeed, trademark licencing agreements appear to be unevenly distributed across these classes, suggesting that this activity and the way it is carried out is correlated with the market to which the licenced trademark refers.

1. Introduction

An estimated 9.11 million trademark applications were filed worldwide in 2017 (WIPO 2018), with trademarks as Intellectual Property (IP) right being the most widely used by firms worldwide. Indeed, unlike patents, trademark use is not simply limited to innovative companies facing competitive pressures to build and consolidate their technological leadership (Graham, Marco, and Myers 2018; WIPO 2013). Almost all types of organisations of any size, across all economic sectors, including institutions and governmental and non-governmental bodies, use trademarks to develop, support, promote, and consolidate the recognition and reputational value of their brands in the product and service markets (Castaldi 2018a, 2019b; Graham, Marco, and Myers 2018; Frey, Ansar, and Wunsch-Vincent 2015; WIPO 2013).

Albeit the two terms are highly intertwined (Frey, Ansar, and Wunsch-Vincent 2015; Landes and Posner 1987; Castaldi 2018b), *trademark* and *brand* don't fully overlay. Not all the brands are trademarks and brands can encompass more than one trademark. Indeed, besides the legal rights, a variety of both tangible and intangible corporate assets (e.g. technology, know-how, product design, human capital, distribution channels) contribute to the development of the brand and its value (Frey, Ansar, and Wunsch-Vincent 2015; WIPO 2013). Hence trademarks represent 'the legal incarnation of brands' (WIPO 2013: 3) and create a series of legally operable property rights that can be exchanged among organisations (WIPO, 2013)[1].

The widespread and increased use of trademarks worldwide has fostered a progressive process of disembodiment – also called 'unbundling' (Ramello 2006) – of the value of the sign (the trademark itself) from that of the product/service involved. Regardless of who manufactures/offers the product/service, what makes the difference is having and exploiting the associated trademarks. Consequently, we are witnessing an increasing number of trademarks being licenced, bought and sold between different entities, both at the national and international level (Frey, Ansar, and Wunsch-Vincent 2015), which shows that this sign has become more and more an asset that can be autonomously traded (Beebe 2004; Ramello 2006; Ramello and Silva 2006). The massive volume of trademark transactions resulted in the unveiling of the economic relevance of the markets for trademarks (Castaldi 2019b; Graham, Marco, and Myers 2018; Frey, Ansar, and Wunsch-Vincent 2015; WIPO 2013).

Albeit only recently, several authors (e.g. Millot 2009; Colucci, Montaguti, and Lago 2008; De Vries et al. 2017; Castaldi 2019b; Block et al. 2014; Flikkema, De Man, and Castaldi 2014) have contributed towards enriching the discussion of the role of the trademark as a 'sophisticated business tool' rather than as a 'humble identifier of origin' (WIPO 2013, 4) or as a legal right characterised by high symbolic power (Brown 1948; Landes and Posner 1987; Carter 1990; Beebe 2004; Katz 2010). However, the market for trademarks remains a relatively unexplored territory compared to markets for technology/patents, which have received a great deal of attention so far in the academic literature (i.e. Arora, Fosfuri, and Gambardella 2001; Gambardella, Giuri and Luzzi, 2007; Arora and Gambardella 2010). In addition, to the best of our knowledge, this new research still lacks an empirical understanding of the phenomenon, due to the scarce data on transactions available, until recently (Frey, Ansar, and Wunsch-Vincent 2015; Graham, Marco, and Myers 2018). Therefore, there is a clear opportunity to contribute both from a conceptual and a methodological perspective to this topic (Castaldi 2019a). Accordingly, we have embraced the call raised by Castaldi (2019a) and Graham et al. (2013, 669), to open 'new streams of research on trademarks and what they indicate about their users, [and] the strategies for employing them', by providing fresh and original evidence on the market for trademarks. We decided to dig into the licencing share of this market[2], as it has been

---

[1] Albeit we acknowledge that the concept of 'markets for brands' (Frey, Ansar, and Wunsch-Vincent 2015; Castaldi 2019a) is in assonance with that of 'markets for technologies' (Arora, Fosfuri, and Gambardella 2001), we prefer to adhere to the more recent contributions in the patent-based literature that explicitly refer to 'the market for patents' (Gambardella, Giuri, and Luzzi 2007) as they specifically look at patent licencing as we do with trademark licencing. Hence in the present paper, we decided to narrow down our perspective and focus on trademarks transactions, which represent a subset of the so-called 'market for brands' (Frey, Ansar, and Wunsch-Vincent 2015; Castaldi 2019a), as they are often an integral part of brands transactions (WIPO 2013: 62).

[2] Under a licencing contract, the licensor grants the right of use of the property for a certain period, in a specific field within a specified geographical area, under binding conditions (e.g. exclusive terms), to the licensee who agrees to use the trademark right in full compliance with these conditions in exchange for monetary and/or non-monetary compensation.

overlooked so far, despite the fact that the economic importance of this type of transactions is soaring year after year. According to the Global Licensing Industry Survey[3] (2018) the aggregate value of the trademark-licencing transactions amounted to $14.5 billion in royalty revenues on $271.6 billion in retail sales in 2017, up 2.6% and 3.3%, respectively, compared to 2016. If we turn our attention to the Top Licensor of the year in 2017, the Walt Disney Company, which 'ranks steadily first with $53 billion in retail sales of licensed merchandise' (Top 150 Global Licensor 2018[4], 6), we can further appreciate the vast potential of this phenomenon.

Inspired by these numbers, we carried out an empirical study based on a novel long-itudinal database of U.S. trademark licencing agreements signed over the period 2003–2017 which had been drawn from the USPTO Trademark Assignment dataset (see Graham, Marco, and Myers 2018 for a full reference). The aim of our research is to provide some of the first empirical evidence on the phenomenon of trademark licencing by looking at the characteristics of the trademarks that are licenced. Besides offering a full picture of the phenomenon in terms of volume, industry and types of trademarks involved, we are particularly interested in understanding whether there are some features (e.g. trademark classes) linked to licenced trademarks that are more often associated with the licencing phenomenon. Whilst our empirical results do not provide any cause-and-effect evidence, we think they bring to light some interesting correlations that can pave the way for future research in this area.

In more detail, the analysis of the data reveals that in the US, the development of the market for trademark licences has been fostered by the soaring number of trademarks that have been registered since the beginning of the new millennium. This market, however, is not evenly distributed across all goods and services. In fact, the analysis of the distribution by international classification reveals that licenced trademarks are more frequent in some classes than in others. This evidence, together with the fact that the average amount of time between registration and the licencing agreement also varies across classes, suggests that the trademark licencing phenomenon is strictly connected to the characteristics of the markets and niches where trademarked goods and services are exchanged[5]. At the firm level, our results show that licencing activity bears more weight for organisations with a smaller trademark portfolio, both in the licensor's and licensee's shoes. All together this evidence may suggest that this practice is used to enter specific markets (for the licensor) with a visible sign (for the licensee).

The findings of this explorative study, albeit limited by the scant availability and incompleteness of the data[6], reveal at least three contributions to the extant literature. First, they add to the 'Market for Trademarks' literature (Frey, Ansar, and Wunsch-Vincent 2015; Graham, Marco, and Myers 2018) through a granular description of one relevant

---

[3]Global Licencing Industry Survey 2018, available at: https://www.licensingitalia.it/en/2018-lima-global-licencing-industry-survey/, accessed on June 2019.

[4]'Top 150 Global Licensor', LICENCE GLOBAL. The Licencing Industry's Thought Leader, available at: https://www.licenseglobal.com/resource/top-150-global-licensors-2018, accessed on June 2019.

[5]We also try to provide stronger evidence than mere descriptive statistics on the role of trademark classes for the licencing process by running two econometric exercises. The main purpose of these exercises is to show the persistence of heterogeneity across classes even when controlling for other structural aspects. All in all, we find robust evidence that trademark classes capture a significant degree of variation both in the probability of licencing and in the speed of trademark licencing. For full references, see the Empirical Analysis section.

[6]See Frey, Ansar, and Wunsch-Vincent (2015) and WIPO (2013); Graham et al. (2013) and Graham, Marco, and Myers (2018) for a full-fledged analysis of the reasons for the lack of complete data on the licencing phenomenon.

portion of this market – the licencing phenomenon – shedding light on its main features from different angles and hence fostering our understanding of its importance. Second, our findings contribute to the 'Marketing and Innovation' literature (De Vries et al. 2017; Castaldi 2016; Block et al. 2014; Flikkema, De Man, and Castaldi 2014) by affording the reader a novel grasp of the practice of trademark trade, which is fast becoming a viable mean for firms both to access a third party's trademark in order to flag their innovation efforts while augmenting the value perception of their offerings (demand side) and to reap new opportunities for increasing revenues and sustaining profits (supply side). Finally, our research discloses new lines of research focused on trademark development and deployment in accordance with a broader Intellectual Property (IP) management strategy, which has traditionally centred on 'high-value patents' (Graham, Marco, and Myers 2018, 403; Fosfuri 2006; Arora and Gambardella 2010; Leone and Reichstein 2012).

The remainder of this paper includes a section that provides a broad overview of the extant literature on trademark roles and markets, with specific emphasis on licencing transactions, followed by a section that encompasses a detailed description of the data collection process and a full-fledged analysis and discussion of the findings of the empirical study. Finally, the paper closes with concluding remarks and suggestions for future research.

2. Theoretical background

2.1. The evolving role of trademarks: from a distinctive sign to an exchangeable asset

Traditionally, trademarks involve a *distinctive function* (WIPO 2013) as they signal and convey to the market relevant information about the product/service sold and the company itself (Economides 1988; Landes and Posner 1987; Ramello 2006; Ramello and Silva 2006; WIPO 2013). This allows consumers to draw a connection between certain goods and the information collected from past consumer experiences (Economides 1988; Landes and Posner 1987), either through advertising and other forms of marketing activity (Wilkins 1992; WIPO 2013) or indirectly through third parties (Landes and Posner 1987; WIPO 2013), and to then repeat purchases accordingly (Mangàni 2006). Put differently, trademarks are symbols which have the power to influence the desirability of the commodity upon which they appear (Brown 1948), and hence to mould consumers' expectations of the quality, functionality, reliability and other attributes of the product or service (Economides 1988; Landes and Posner 1987; WIPO 2013). These 'packets of information' (Carter 1990, 759) allow consumers to reduce search costs (Landes and Posner 1987), to mitigate the riskiness of the purchase (Lane 1988), and essentially to make informed purchasing decisions[7] (Economides 1988; Landes and Posner 1987; WIPO 2013). In addition, this virtuous circle provides companies with an incentive to avoid opportunistic behaviour and meet the qualitative standards of their offerings (Landes and Posner 1987; Mangàni 2006;

---

[7]In other words, trademarks are the remedy introduced to mitigate a failure of the market – namely, information asymmetry (Akerlof 1970)– which characterises the relations between producers and consumers in terms of their knowledge of the characteristics and quality of goods and services (Landes and Posner 1987; Ramello 2006; Ramello and Silva 2006; WIPO 2013). In modern markets, especially those of consumer goods, the neoclassical assumption of perfect information – where buyers have full knowledge of the quality and characteristics of all the products and services offered – is not fulfiled in practice (WIPO 2013).

Ramello 2006; Ramello and Silva 2006), in turn allowing them to build trusting and long-lasting relationships with their customer base (so-called *brand loyalty*) while attracting potential new ones (Landes and Posner 1987; Mangàni 2006; Wilkins 1992; WIPO 2013). Definitively, companies also use trademarks to reap reputational benefits (Economides 1988; Landes and Posner 1987; Ramello 2006).

Recently, some authors (Castaldi 2019b; Flikkema, De Man, and Castaldi 2014; Greenhalgh et al. 2011; Greenhalgh and Rogers 2012; Millot 2009; Block et al. 2014) have investigated the role of trademarks as an indicator of the innovative performance of the attached product/service/companies. Although novelty and technological progress are not requirements for registering a trademark (Flikkema, De Man, and Castaldi 2014), these authors demonstrate that the registration of a new one is usually linked to the launch of an improved version of a product (i.e. quality upgrades or new varieties) (Greenhalgh and Rogers 2012; Millot 2009). In this vein, trademarks may entail some comparative advantages over the more frequently-used innovation indicators (Castaldi 2016; Greenhalgh et al. 2011; Mendonça, Pereira, and Godinho 2004; Millot 2009; Potepa and Welch 2017): while patents refer more to inventions and R&D investments (*input* indicators), trademarks are very often filed in proximity to the launch of the product/service on the market (*output* indicators) (Castaldi 2016; Flikkema, De Man, and Castaldi 2014; Greenhalgh et al. 2011; Millot 2009). Furthermore, trademarks can encapsulate a broader range of innovations (Potepa and Welch 2017) that may encompass, among others, non-technological (e.g. marketing) innovations (OECD/Eurostat 2005; Millot 2009) and those that do not quite achieve the 'inventive step' necessary to benefit from patent protection (e.g. incremental innovations, Millot 2009). Additionally, trademarks capture innovation activities in low-tech sectors and the service sector – where patents are not frequently used – as well as innovation activities carried out by small and medium enterprises (SMEs), which mostly prefer trademarks to patents because their registration is less costly, and the registration requirements are more easily met (Castaldi 2018; De Vries et al. 2017)[8].

More recently, with the increasing recognition of their economic importance and given the soaring number of trademark filings and transaction trends, scholars have started evaluating the progressive evolution of the role played by trademarks in market dynamics. From an instrument originally designed to facilitate product purchases (i.e. 'mental shortcuts when making purchasing decisions', Katz 2010, 1; Ramello and Silva 2006), the trademark seems to have assumed the traits of an autonomous economic entity, which produces its own utility and turns it into a specific willingness of the market to potentially pay for it (Ramello 2006). In other words, the meaning (and the value) of trademarks is, to a lesser extent, attached to purely informative content (Economides 1988; WIPO 2013), but more and more often it falls within the sphere of pure semiotics, which is not necessarily underpinned by any of the concrete features of goods themselves (Ramello and Silva 2006). The process of disembodiment or 'unbundling' (Ramello 2006) of the value of the sign from that of the associated product/service determines the transformation of the trademark into

---

[8]For a further analysis of trademark functions and impacts, refer to the article 'Empirical studies of trade marks – the existing economic literature' by Schautschick and Greenhalgh (2016), which offers a wider review of trademark-related literature.

a commodity (Beebe 2004; Lemley 1999; Ramello 2006; Ramello and Silva 2006), which can then be transferred from one product/company to another and freely traded on the market (Ramello 2006; Ramello and Silva 2006).

2.2. The rise of markets for trademarks: exploring the potential of trademark licencing

Markets for trademarks 'allow companies to diversify their business and to expand into additional product categories [...] [and] to access competences outside their own core strategic assets, and to generate new revenues without substantial investments into building or acquiring additional knowhow or manufacturing capability' (WIPO 2013, 12). They include both the 'temporary transfer of the right to use an IP' (trademark licencing and franchising) and the 'sale or purchase of IP ownership rights' (trademark acquisition) (Frey, Ansar, and Wunsch-Vincent 2015).

Recently, scholars have started appraising the rise and economic relevance of the market for trademarks (Graham, Marco, and Myers 2018; Frey, Ansar, and Wunsch-Vincent 2015; WIPO, 2013), partly thanks to the opportunity for data access that has only recently become available (Castaldi 2018; Castaldi 2019a, 2019b). As a matter of fact, the obstacles in reporting systematic data on each type of transfer mechanism and the lack of granular knowledge – mainly due to the sensitive nature of this information (Frey, Ansar, and Wunsch-Vincent 2015) – have so far not allowed a deeper investigation of the phenomenon. This is why the United States Patent and Trademark Office (USPTO) has recently tackled the challenge of data unavailability by releasing the USPTO Trademark Assignment Dataset (Graham, Marco, and Myers 2018), thus offering detailed data on all the transactions affecting title or pertaining to mark ownership (assignments, security interest agreements and licences) that have been registered by the Office since 1952[9].

Despite these attempts, the lack of empirical understanding of markets for trademarks is more evident if we turn our attention to the licencing phenomenon, which is systematically underreported in the public record (e.g. 'licences' comprise less than 2% of all transactions, Graham, Marco, and Myers 2018, 410). We nevertheless decided to take the opportunity to delve deeper into the exploration of licencing transactions, firstly because there is a need for a better understanding of the phenomenon in practical terms, given its increasing financial weight in the overall value of trademark transactions (WIPO 2013; Global Licencing Industry Survey 2018); secondly, we did so because there is an original academic interest in trademark licencing, traced back to the 1980s, when economic scholars theoretically debated the motives for and barriers to this mechanism for trade (for instance, Meyer, Tinney, and Tinney 1985; and more recently:; Jiang and Menguc 2012; Jayachandran et al. 2013); thirdly, another reason was that our analysis would

---

[9]The USPTO Trademark Assignment Dataset is publicly available for download at: https://www.uspto.gov/learning-and-resources/electronic-data-products/trademark-assignment-dataset. We used the 2017 version, which is the most recently updated. A complete description of this dataset is provided by Graham, Marco, and Myers (2018).

complement the corresponding patent-based literature, which has provided several insights on the market for patent licencing (among others: Fosfuri 2006; Arora and Gambardella 2010; Leone and Reichstein 2012).

Trademark licencing, indeed, entails several strategic opportunities for both the licensor and the licensees. First of all, it opens up new opportunities for increasing revenues and sustaining profits[10] (Frey, Ansar, and Wunsch-Vincent 2015; Meyer, Tinney, and Tinney 1985; WIPO 2003, 2010) from the licensor's perspective; namely, the additional financial inflows from the commercial exploitation of the trademark make it possible to recover the investment incurred during construction of brand value and image and while gathering new resources to develop long-term company projects, such as innovation and growth (Quelch 1985). Trademark licencing can also be a valid option for the owner to monetise the value of dismissed or non-strategic trademarks, as an alternative to their outright sale (WIPO 2010). From the licensee's perspective, trademark licencing provides substantial cost savings by avoiding the complexities and the time and effort required for the creation of a valuable new brand from scratch (Frey, Ansar, and Wunsch-Vincent 2015). In addition, in the specific case of a well-established trademark, the licensee may be better equipped to augment the value perception of his or her offering, which justifies the payment of a premium price (Meyer, Tinney, and Tinney 1985; WIPO 2010, 2013).

Besides the direct economic returns, trademark licencing can also bring indirect economic effects. First, as underscored by Meyer, Tinney, and Tinney (1985), the licence can contribute to the pursuit of many key marketing objectives, such as brand and product awareness, customer recognition, image building, and customer loyalty (Albanese 2001; Meyer, Tinney, and Tinney 1985). Secondly, trademark licencing affords the opportunity to not only enter new sectors but also new geographic and product markets that might otherwise be inaccessible or difficult to reach internally[11] (Clegg and Cross 2000; WIPO 2003), thus supporting the process of international growth and business diversification (Frey, Ansar, and Wunsch-Vincent 2015; Tomar 2009; WIPO 2003, 2010). By so doing, licensors can exploit synergies between their intangible assets and licensees' productive and commercial assets (Calboli 2007; Colucci, Montaguti, and Lago 2008; U.S. FTC 2017; Jiang and Menguc 2012; WIPO 2003). This is particularly evident in cases of internationalisation, where partnering with foreign partners ameliorates the presence and the international reputation of the brand (Jayachandran et al. 2013) and, at the same time, ensures the safeguarding of a given licensor's trademark rights in those markets, where the original company could not or does not wish to operate directly[12] (Frey, Ansar, and Wunsch-Vincent 2015; Jayachandran et al. 2013). In addition, licensees can leverage a licensor's

---

[10]According to the 2013 WIPO report, the analysis of available deals shows that, across sectors, average royalty rates in trademark licencing agreements vary from less than 5% to more than 25% of (gross or net) sales. The highest average rates are found within the Celebrity and Character category, while the lowest average royalty rates relate to Corporate/Product and Fashion trademarks.

[11]Trademark licencing is one of the few strategies that companies can use to gain access to markets in which commercial, regulatory or cultural barriers preclude – or strongly discourage – the use of autonomous entry methods such as exports and direct investments (Clegg and Cross 2000; WIPO 2003).

[12]In almost any jurisdiction, trademark protection is linked to its effective use; therefore, businesses need to show stable commercial use of a trademark in order to preserve the rights they have over it. Since the licensee's use of the brand is to the benefit of the licensor, the licence allows him/her to defend his/her rights in all countries and for all product categories for which the trademark has been regularly registered but not directly used by the original owner (Frey, Ansar, and Wunsch-Vincent 2015).

brand reputation and visibility and combine his or her trademarks with their own technology portfolio (WIPO 2003), thus allowing them to introduce new products and services to the market more quickly and effectively (Albanese 2001; Frey, Ansar, and Wunsch-Vincent 2015; WIPO 2003).

We therefore identify the need to further explore the trends and characteristics of the licencing transactions so as to uncover the potential of this ever-increasing IP strategy. We will achieve this through an exploratory analysis, as explained in the following section.

3. Empirical analysis

3.1. Data sources and sample construction

The study is based on a dataset consisting of primary data relating to trademark licencing agreements signed for the U.S. market. The data were gathered from the Trademark Assignment Dataset – provided by the USPTO – which includes more than 970,000 trademark transactions (assignments, security interest agreements, licences and other types of agreement) that have been registered between 1952 and 2018.

For the aim of our analysis we selected only those transcriptions referring to trademark licencing operations. We therefore used the brief description available in the original registration (termed 'conveyance text' in the original file[13]) to exclude all those records not dealing with newly signed licencing agreements (i.e. termination, cancellation, releases, corrective registrations[14] and the like). We also decided to exclude sub-licencing agreements, cross-licencing agreements and licences operating in the context of settlement agreements, due to the peculiarities of those transactions.

To build the final database we restricted our focus to the most recent years, namely trademark licencing agreements whose execution dates ranged from 2003 to 2017.[15] For these transactions, we retrieved the basic information on the date of the event,[16] the names of the licensors and the licensees, and the licenced trademark serial numbers. This process led us to define a final set of 995 licences, corresponding to a sample of 1732 unique companies: 895 contracted as licensors, 810 contracted as licensees and 27 operating both as licensor and licensee in different agreements. All told, 4534 licenced trademarks were involved. Finally, we used the USPTO Trademark Case Files Dataset[17]

---

[13]Conveyance text captures non-standardised information from the coversheet describing the interest conveyed or transaction recorded (Graham, Marco, and Myers 2018).

[14]We identified corrective registrations as corrections, re-recordations or amendments (and the like), and manually corrected them by linking these registrations, when possible, to the original recordations (through the unique licence code).

[15]Since the data gathered so far for 2018 might underestimate the extent of the phenomenon – due to the lag between execution and recordation date of the most recent agreements (Graham, Marco, and Myers 2018) – we have opted to omit this year.

[16]As suggested by Graham, Marco, and Myers (2018), we used a given contract's execution date (or the acknowledgement date if the execution date field was not populated) – not the recordation date – to be the reference starting date of the agreement. Since transactions are recorded on a per-assignor basis and multiple execution dates are possible for a single transaction, we used the most recent execution date under the assumption that it denoted the moment the transaction was complete.

[17]The Trademark Case Files Dataset contains detailed information on approximately 9.1 million trademark applications filed with, or registrations issued by, the USPTO between 1870 and 2018 (https://www.uspto.gov/learning-and-resources/electronic-data-products/trademark-case-files-dataset-0). A complete description of this dataset is provided by Graham et al. (2013).

to link each agreement to the corresponding licenced trademarks (retrieving information on dates for key events, trademark status,[18] classification and the like) and then to
determine the breadth of their registered trademark portfolio (number of classes) and
the modal primary class of the company trademarks included in our database.
Throughout the dataset, the same company may have been registered with different
names due to misspelling or changes in the corporate structure and therefore to
denomination and the like. There is a vast literature on how to disambiguate individuals
(Pezzoni, Lissoni, and Tarasconi 2014) and companies (Morrison, Riccaboni, and
Pammolli 2017). We applied similar principles, although in a less sophisticated fashion,
as this went well beyond the scope of this research. We compared the similarity of
company names and reduced the number of firms that engaged in licencing activities
by 2.5%.

3.2. Findings

3.2.1. General trends in trademark and trademark licencing activities in the US
During the last two decades US markets have been witnessing a blossoming of new
trademarks. Indeed, starting in 2003 the sheer number of newly registered trademarks

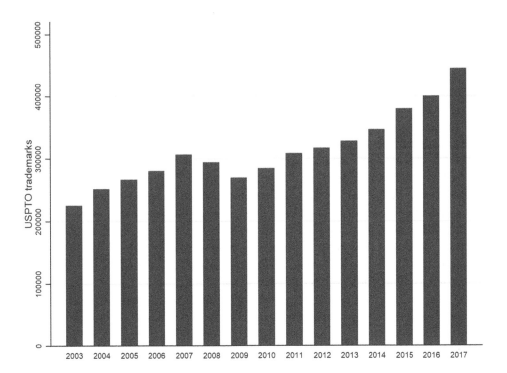

Figure 1. Number of newly registered trademarks per year.
Note: The height of the bars represents the whole number of newly registered trademarks in each year. Source: authors'
elaboration on USPTO dataset.

---

[18]Status was captured using a three-digit code indicating whether an application was abandoned or pending or
whether a registration was live, cancelled or expired (Graham et al. 2013).

Table 1. Trademarks classes (nice classification).

Code	Trademark Class	Code	Trademark Class
1	Chemicals	24	Fabrics
2	Paints	25	Clothing
3	Cosmetics and cleaning preparations	26	Fancy goods
4	Lubricants & fuels	27	Floor coverings
5	Pharmaceuticals	28	Toys and sporting goods
6	Metal goods	29	Meats and processed foods
7	Machinery	30	Staple foods
8	Hand tools	31	Natural agricultural products
9	Electrical & scientific apparatus	32	Light beverages
10	Medical apparatus	33	Wine and spirits
11	Environmental control apparatus	34	Smokers' articles
12	Vehicles	35	Advertising and business
13	Firearms	36	Insurance and financial
14	Jewellery	37	Building construction and repair
15	Musical Instruments	38	Telecommunications
16	Paper goods and printed matter	39	Transportation and storage
17	Rubber goods	40	Treatment of materials
18	Leather goods	41	Education and entertainment
19	Non-metallic building materials	42	Computer, scientific & legal
20	Furniture and articles not otherwise classified	43	Hotels and Restaurants
21	Housewares and glass	44	Medical, beauty & agricultural
22	Cordage and fibres	45	Personal
23	Yarns and threads		

has steadily exceeded 200,000 units and, despite a mild reduction in the aftermath of the crisis, it almost reached 445,000 units in 2017 (Figure 1).

Yet the protection of one's own product via trademark is not an evenly distributed practice across markets (Table 1).

By looking at the distribution of trademarks by international NICE classes[19] (Figure 2) it is possible to observe some heterogeneity. Trademarks seem to be more concentrated in some categories of goods and services than in others. For example, class 15 ('musical instruments') contains 8,000 trademarks, which constitutes less than the 1% of the size of the two top classes combined (9 'electrical and scientific apparatuses' and 25 'clothing'). These differences seem to be correlated with the extent of a market which, in return, is associated with the type of demand and the number and nature of market niches. This evidence could be the outcome of different dynamics. On the one hand, it may be driven by structural differences since the need for firms to distinguish their own products/services from those offered by their rivals is stronger in some sectors than in others. On the other hand, it may be bound to technological factors deriving from the fact that the rate of product/service innovations varies from one sector to the other.

Given the fact that trademarks may be assigned to multiple classes, we computed the total number of trademarks by international class in two different ways. In the first one (Figure 2, blue bars), when a trademark presented more than one class, we assigned an equal share of the trademark to each one of those classes. For instance, if a trademark fell within four classes, we assigned 0.25 of that trademark to each one of these classes. This technique labelled 'fractional count' (De Rassenfosse et al. 2013), is used in order

---

[19]The NICE classification, named after the 'Nice Agreement' (1957), is an international standard to classify goods and services on the basis of their trademarks. It is made of 45 classes: the first 34 refer to goods while the remaining 11 refer to services. https://www.wipo.int/classifications/nice/en/.

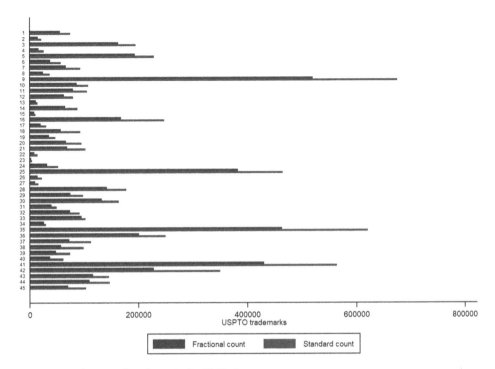

Figure 2. Distribution of trademarks by NICE class.

Note: the length of each bar represents the number of trademarks falling within the corresponding NICE class. Blue bars report the distribution computed with the 'fractional count technique' (De Rassenfosse et al. 2013) while maroon bars report the distribution with standard count. By means of 'fractional count', when a trademark was associated with more than one class, an equal share of it was allocated among these classes. By means of standard count, when a trademark was associated with more than one class, it was counted once in each one of them. The numbers on the y-axis correspond to the NICE classes: 001 'Chemicals', 002 'Paints', 003 'Cosmetics and cleaning preparations', 004 'Lubricants & fuels', 005 'Pharmaceuticals', 006 'Metal goods', 007 'Machinery', 008 'Hand tools', 009 'Electrical & scientific apparatus', 010 'Medical apparatus', 011 'Environmental control apparatus', 012 'Vehicles', 013 'Firearms', 014 'Jewellery', 015 'Musical Instruments', 016 'Paper goods and printed matter', 017 'Rubber goods', 018 'Leather goods', 019 'Non-metallic building materials', 020 'Furniture and articles not otherwise classified', 021 'Housewares and glass', 022 'Cordage and fibres', 023 'Yarns and threads', 024 'Fabrics', 025 'Clothing', 026 'Fancy goods', 027 'Floor coverings', 028 'Toys and sporting goods', 029 'Meats and processed foods', 030 'Staple foods', 031 'Natural agricultural products', 032 'Light beverages', 033 'Wine and spirits', 034 'Smokers' articles', 035 'Advertising and business', 036 'Insurance and financial', 037 'Building construction and repair', 038 'Telecommunications', 039 'Transportation and storage', 040 'Treatment of materials', 041 'Education and entertainment', 042 'Computer, scientific & legal', 043 'Hotels and Restaurants', 044 'Medical, beauty & agricultural', 045 'Personal'. Source: authors' elaboration on USPTO data.

to avoid multiple allocations of the same trademark to different classes. Without this correction, the size of classes whose trademarks belong to multiple classes might be overestimated. For the sake of completeness, though, in Figure 2 (maroon bars) we report the same distribution by allocating the different trademarks without fractional counting. Although the two distributions seem to be similar, the relative importance of classes changes. For example, in the case of a fractional count, the ratio between the number of trademarks belonging to class 25 and the number of trademarks belonging to class 9 equals 0.74, whereas, without a fractional count, this statistic comes to 0.69.

The pattern of expansion described above has also paved the way for the rise and development of an ad-hoc market where these property rights could be exchanged via

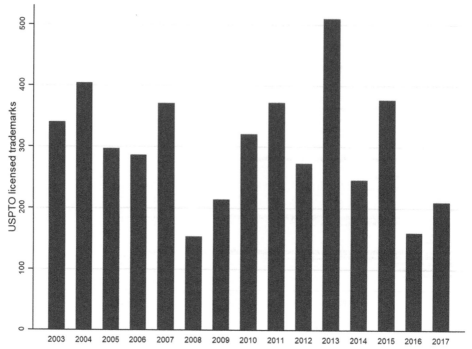

Figure 3. Number of newly licenced trademarks per year.

Note: The height of the bars represents the whole number of newly licenced trademarks in a specific year. Source: authors' elaboration on USPTO dataset.

licences. In particular, the USPTO data show that, from 2003 to 2017 the overall number of trademarks licenced in the US totalled about 4,534 units (Figure 3).

It is important to stress that these data may suffer from an underestimation problem. As underlined by Graham et al. (2018, 411), the 'executed assignments that have yet to be recorded will be (increasingly) missing for the most recent years'. Nonetheless, the presence of truncation problems does not seem to affect the representativeness of the sample of licenced trademarks for the most recent years. As a matter of fact, by comparing the distribution of licenced trademarks by class over the whole sample with the distribution of licenced trademarks by class over a shorter time span, regarded as less likely to suffer from truncation issues (2003–2011), we do not observe any substantial difference (see Figure A1 in the Appendix).

Providing we exclude 2008 and 2009 (the epicentre of the financial crisis), up until 2011 the yearly number of newly licenced trademarks was, on average, 333. If we also include the most recent years within this computation, this number drops to 302, while its standard deviation more than doubles. Although the aforementioned truncation issue makes it impossible to assess the exact volume of licenced trademarks, we can conclude that, if a reduction in this activity occurred it did not dramatically change the size of this market.

3.2.2. The agreements and the players of licencing activity

The picture drawn so far has focused on trademarks. Although, at this stage, this is the most relevant level of analysis to tackle the trademark licencing phenomenon, a broader

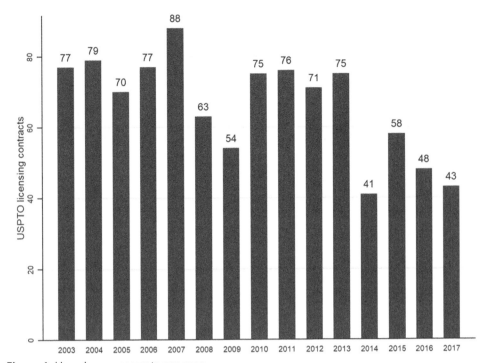

Figure 4. Licensing agreements per year.

Note: The height of the bars (and the corresponding numbers) represents the whole number of licensing agreements newly stipulated in each year. Source: authors' elaboration on USPTO dataset.

framework is needed to better understand how this activity unfolds. In particular, two aspects are important: the licencing agreements and the players stipulating these agreements. Indeed, the trend of licences outlined in the previous section is the outcome of licencing activity that exchanges trademarks by means of an agreement (i.e. the licence) between two parties (i.e. licensors and licensees). An understanding of how these agreements have been designed and of how many parties are involved in these agreements complements an analysis of the evolution of trademark licencing.

To begin with, the 4,534 trademarks licenced during the period 2003–2017 were exchanged through almost 1,000 (995) licencing agreements, which implies, on average, 4.6 trademarks per licence. Although the picture appears to be far from steady due to its fluctuating trend, the yearly number of agreements fluctuated around 66 over the whole period, increasing to 73 if we consider only the 2003–2011 subperiod (Figure 4). The major discrepancies in these averages can be observed during two periods: the first is between 2008 and 2009 and the second from 2014 to the most recent years. In the former it is reasonable to assume that the drop in the number of licences can be correlated with the outbreak of the financial crisis. The considerable reduction in the number of licencing agreements that occurred in the most recent years may be partly due to an underestimate deriving from the truncation problem discussed in the previous pages.

In the large majority of these cases, the licences were stipulated between two firms, i. e. one licensor (henceforth LOR) and one licensee (henceforth LEE), with each firm undersigning one licencing contract per year only (Figure 5). Indeed, if we look at the

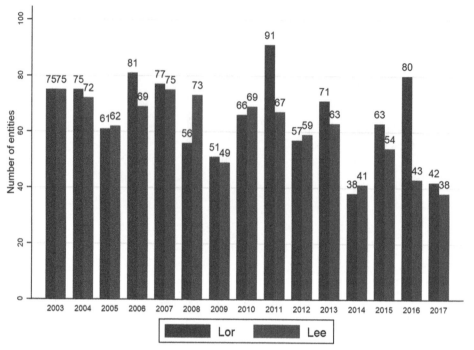

Figure 5. Number of licensors and licensees per year.
Note: The height of the blue bars (and the corresponding numbers) represents the whole number of licensors (Lor) in each year. The height of the maroon bars (and the corresponding numbers) represents the whole number of licensees (Lee) in each year. **Source**: authors' elaboration on USPTO dataset.

numbers of LORs and LEEs rather than at the number of contracts, the order of magnitude remains the same as that of Figure 5. The differences that emerge between Figures 4 and 5 are driven either by a few firms that stipulated multiple licencing contracts in the same year or by a few trademark licences that involved more than one LOR/LEE at a time.

If we focus on these firms' characteristics, we can observe two main results. First of all, over 60% of licensors tend to licence a trademark falling within the same class of its trademark portfolio mode. This percentage drops to 50% for licensees. This may suggest that licensees use trademark licences as a way to enrich the variety of trademarks in their portfolio. Second, the importance of licencing activity varies across firms of different size. Figure 6 reports the average share of trademarks given/taken as licences by firms by dividing organisations into three classes, identified on the basis of the size of their trademark portfolio. Specifically:

- the first group (i.e. *small*) includes all the firms (LORs and LEEs) with a trademark portfolio whose size falls within the 33rd percentile of the distribution (equal to 6 trademarks);
- the second group (i.e. *medium*) includes all the firms (LORs and LEEs) with a trademark portfolio whose size falls between the 33rd and the 66th percentile of the distribution (equal to 28 trademarks);

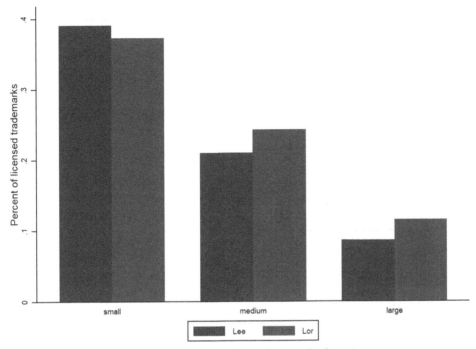

Figure 6. Average share of trademarks given/taken as licences by firm size.

Note: The height of the blue bars represents the average share of licensed trademarks over the whole portfolio of trademarks among licensors (Lor). The height of the maroon bars represents the average share of licensed trademarks over the whole portfolio of trademarks among licensees (Lee). The numbers on the x-axis correspond to the three size classes: class 'small' includes all the entities with a trademark portfolio whose size is smaller than the 33rd percentile (included) of the trademark portfolio size distribution; class 'medium' includes all the entities with a trademark portfolio whose size falls within the 33rd percentile (excluded) and the 66th percentile (included) of the trademark portfolio size distribution; class 'large' includes all the entities with a trademark portfolio whose size is larger than the 66rd percentile (excluded) of the trademark portfolio size distribution **Source**: authors' elaboration on USPTO dataset.

- the third group (i.e. *large*) includes all the firms (LORs and LEEs) whose trade-mark portfolio is larger than the 66th percentile of the distribution.

These data suggest that licencing activity has a greater bearing on smaller than on larger firms. Indeed, as the size of the trademark portfolio increases, the average share of licenced trademarks decreases. To an extent, it is thus possible to hypothesise that licencing activity is a significant policy option, especially for smaller organisations.

3.2.3. Characteristics of licenced trademarks

In the previous sections we sought to shed some light on the phenomenon of trademark licencing in the US by providing some figures on its extent in terms of licenced trademarks, classes, agreements (licences) and players (LORs and LEEs) involved. In this section we go a step further and provide some evidence useful in understanding whether there are structural characteristics of a trademark which are most correlated with the licencing process.

In interpreting the following statistics, however, it is important to bear a major caveat in mind: our evidence can only provide some indications on the mechanisms underlying the dynamics of interest and, if any relationship is mentioned, it is only a

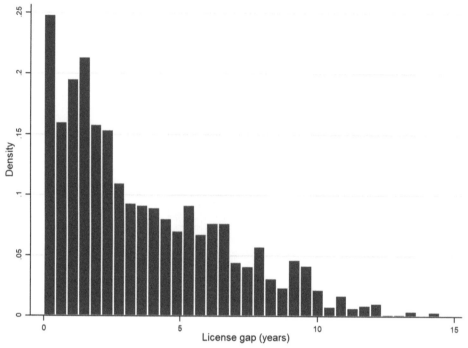

Figure 7. Distribution of the time before a trademark is licensed.

Note: The graph reports the distribution of the time before a trademark is licensed, computed as the difference (in days terms) between the filing date of the trademark and the execution date of the license. The data have been rescaled to provide the information in years' term. **Source**: authors' elaboration on USPTO dataset.

matter of speculation based on our results. To put it in another way, we interpret the following analyses as a starting point for future work investigating the correlations emerging from our data.

The first aspect relates to the breadth of a trademark, which is interpreted as the number of classes it belongs to (that is, quoting Block et al. 2014 'the number of distinct industries in which the trademark is filed and granted protection'). As shown in section 3.2.1., a significant degree of heterogeneity displayed by trademarks (both licenced and non-licenced) depends on the classes with which each trademark is associated. If one considers that different classes are connected to different markets, the larger the number of classes to which a trademark belongs, the wider its applicability on different markets. As a result, the breadth of a trademark can be connected to its future uses and also to its likelihood of being licenced.

To delve into this issue, we compared the average number of classes assigned to licenced trademarks with the average number of classes assigned to non-licenced trademarks for the 2003–2017 period. Table 2 reports the results of a series of t-tests in which we compared the average breadth of licenced vs non-licenced trademarks. We relaxed the classic t-test assumption of equal variances by using the Welch approximation (Welch 1947). Results indicate that the average breadth lies between 1 and 2, implying that multi-class trademarks are rather uncommon. At the same time, we did not find any statistically significant difference between the two groups, suggesting that the number of classes is not a pivotal aspect in the licencing process.

Table 2. T test: Average scope by trademark.

Year	Licenced trademarks	Non licenced trademarks	Difference	p-value
2003	1,35	1,25	0,09	0,28
2004	1,28	1,27	0,01	0,90
2005	1,42	1,29	0,13	0,04
2006	1,32	1,31	0,01	0,90
2007	1,26	1,33	−0,07	0,27
2008	1,32	1,33	0,00	0,98
2009	1,21	1,31	−0,10	0,05
2010	1,34	1,32	0,02	0,82
2011	1,45	1,33	0,12	0,34
2012	1,47	1,33	0,13	0,37
2013	1,31	1,34	−0,04	0,61
2014	1,59	1,35	0,24	0,09
2015	1,42	1,36	0,06	0,67
2016	1,62	1,37	0,24	0,11
2017	2,00	1,36	0,64	0,38

In addition to the above, the low degree of variability in the average breadth leads us to believe that the heterogeneity highlighted above does not stem from the number of classes associated with each trademark. If this is the case, then, these differences are linked first and foremost to the specific characteristics of the market where each trademark is used.

The choice of whether to grant a trademark licence or not may occur at different stages of maturity of a trademark. Therefore, a second important element is represented by the time occurring between the filing date of the trademark and the execution date of the licencing contract. Figure 7 reports the distribution of these time spans. According to our results, about 70% of trademarks are licenced within 5 years of their filing date while only 3% of them are licenced after 10 or more years. These results may be due to different strategies adopted by firms, ranging from the use of trademark licencing as a vehicle to scan the potential profitability of unexplored geographical markets (Park and Lippoldt 2005) to the attempt to further exploit trademarks during a declining phase of their lifecycle.

If we split this distribution by trademark classes (Figure 9) we observe a substantial degree of variability. This implies that, despite the aforementioned contingent strategies implemented by firms, there are structural differences across markets. For example, on average, trademarks falling within classes 2 ('Paints') and 26 ('Fancy goods') take between 7 and 8 years to be licenced whereas trademarks falling within classes 1 ('Chemicals'), 15 ('Musical instruments') and 39 ('Transportation and storage') only take 2 to 3 years.

All in all, then, these results seem to point to the prominent role played by the markets bound to each trademark class. This implies that licencing activities and strategies are at least to some extent influenced by the context in which the firms operate. In order to bolster this purely descriptive evidence we decided to perform two exploratory econometric exercises.

First, we inspected the factors associated with the probability of a trademark being licenced. We fit a simple linear probability model in which we regressed the licencing status (a variable that takes value 1 for licenced trademarks and 0 for non-licenced ones) on a set of filing year dummies, a set of class dummies and a variable that measures trademark breadth. Given that licenced trademarks account only for 0.04% of the overall trademarks registered in the US between 2003 and 2017, we extracted a subsample of observations that closely resemble the pool of licenced ones from the sample of non-licenced trademarks, by means of

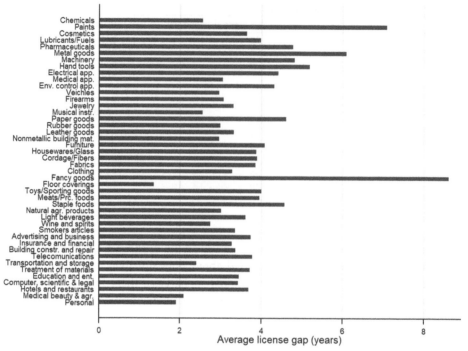

Figure 8. Average number of days before a trademark is licensed in each class.

Note: The length of each bar represents the average number of years (computed as the number of days divided by 365) between the filing date of the trademark and the execution date of the licence in each NICE class. **Source**: authors' elaboration on USPTO dataset.

a propensity score technique (Rosenbaum and Rubin 1983; Dehejia and Wahba 2002). The variables that were entered into the matching process were the same as those used in the regression. In the Appendix (see Figure A2) we report the values of the propensity score before and after the matching process. We can observe a substantial reduction in the imbalance between the characteristics of licenced and non-licenced trademarks. Nevertheless, some differences remain, as shown in Figure 10, where we plot the coefficients relative to the trademark class dummies; the probability of incurring in a licencing event differs across classes. The class in which a trademark is registered emerges as a discriminant dimension within licencing activities.

The second econometric exercise delves into the pool of licenced trademarks only. We try to highlight some of the factors that are associated with the heterogeneity observed in the time span that occurs between the trademark filing date and the licencing contract execution date. Specifically, such differences (expressed in years) were regressed on the same set of covariates that we used in our first econometric specification (that is, filing year dummies, trademark class dummies and trademark breadth). Results indicate that trademarks falling within specific classes such as 2 (Paints), 5 (Pharmaceuticals) and 26 (Fancy goods) are, on average, licenced at a slower pace compared with trademarks that belong to, for instance, class 12 (Vehicles), 13 (Firearms) and 15 (Musical instruments). It is reasonable to hypothesise that the time spans between the filing date of a trademark and the execution of the licencing contract depend on the intrinsic characteristics of the

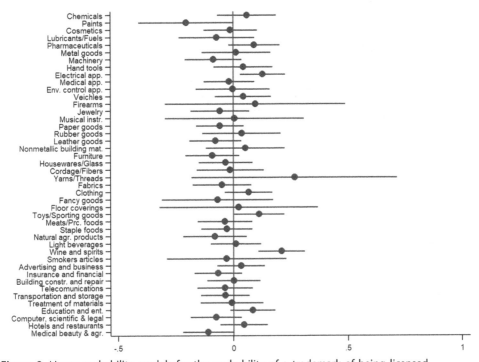

Figure 9. Linear probability models for the probability of a trademark of being licensed.

Note: Regression coefficients of trademarks NICE class dummies. Results refer to a linear probability model in which the dependent variable is a dummy that takes value 1 if the trademark has been licensed, zero otherwise. Controls include: filing year dummies and the scope of the trademark. Bootstrapped standard errors (1000 reps).

trademarked goods/services which are, in turn, related to the structure of the market and the nature of the technology behind them (Figure 10).

4. Conclusion

This paper is the first attempt to provide an original representation of the trademark licencing market based on a recently released USPTO trademark transactions dataset (Graham, Marco, and Myers 2018). We decided to focus on trademark licencing because, despite its remarkable growth in terms of volume and value (WIPO 2013), little is known about the features of trademark transactions. The lack of empirical investigation and understanding of this market is also surprising given the fact economics and marketing scholars have already debated the motives for and barriers to this mechanism of trade (for instance, Meyer, Tinney, and Tinney 1985; and more recently; Jiang and Menguc 2012; Jayachandran et al. 2013), and given the great consideration paid to the corresponding patent-based market (among others, Fosfuri 2006; Arora and Gambardella 2010; Leone and Reichstein 2012).

We therefore aimed to further our understanding of the relevance of trademarks in current market dynamics by focusing on their new role – that of an exchangeable asset. Our reasoning and empirical investigation are therefore rooted in a recognition of the progressive process of disembodiment or 'unbundling' (Ramello 2006) of the value of the sign (the trademark itself) from that of the associated product/service. This

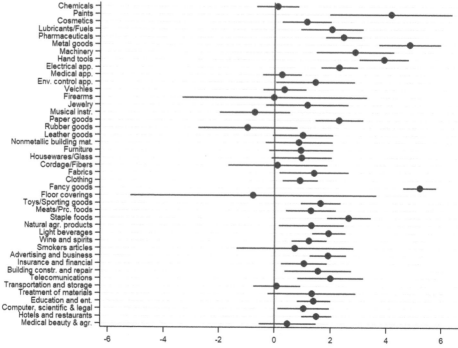

Figure 10. Regression on the speed of licensing

Note: Regression coefficients of trademarks NICE class dummies. Results refer to an OLS model in which the dependent variable is the number of years (computed as the number of days divided by 365) between the filing date and the license registration date. Controls include: filing year dummies, scope of the trademark. Bootstrapped standard errors (1000 reps).

unbundling process has driven the transformation of the trademark into an autonomous economic entity, which produces its own utility and subsequently cultivates a specific willingness of the market to potentially pay for it (Ramello 2006).

Building on a theoretical investigation of the transformative evolution of trademarks from a distinctive sign to an exchangeable asset, as well as an exploration of the potential of markets for trademarks, we proposed a novel investigation into the trademark-licencing field. We studied the growth of licencing activities in the U.S. during the 2003–2017 period, the characteristics of the trademarks, the agreements, and, finally, some features of the licencing parties involved (i.e. licensors and licensees).

The findings reveal that licencing activities varied in these years, even though the reduction recorded during the latest period may not entirely reflect a reduction in this market but rather could be due to truncation issues resulting from the dataset (Graham, Marco, and Myers 2018). At the same time, a large majority of these contracts were stipulated by two parties only, i.e. one licensor and one licensee, but, on average, they contain more than one trademark each. This means that, usually, firms trade bundles of marks rather than single marks. The analyses reveal, however, that a large amount of heterogeneity in licencing activity is due to the classes associated with each trademark. Indeed, trademark licencing turns out to be unevenly distributed across these international classes, suggesting that trademark licencing activity and the way it is carried out both depend on the product/service market to which the licenced trademark refers. Additionally, the findings suggest that this practice works more for firms with smaller trademark portfolios.

Our results call for a deeper investigation of the trademark licencing phenomenon at least along five lines of research. On a broad level the evidence provided in the document highlights a high degree of heterogeneity across trademark classes: whether this is due to the underpinning product/service markets or to some specific characteristics of the firms, or to both these factors is an open issue. Thus, future research may dig deeper, on the one hand, (i) into the relationship between trademark licencing and the corresponding product/service market and, on the other hand, (ii) into the relationship between a firm's structure and its trademark licencing activity. The first line of research could focus on sector specificities in conducting trademark licencing while the second one could place more attention to the analysis of possible strategies of trademark development and deployment through either internal growth or external acquisition, and in relation to other IP strategies, which are mainly patent based, in order to understand the factors underpinning licensors and licensees' behaviours.

Another open issue, which could be very interesting to investigate, relates to the impact of licencing on a firm's economic and financial performance, as the literature so far has dwelt only either on the link between trademarks and the innovation of the underlying product/service and companies (e.g. Millot 2009; Colucci, Montaguti, and Lago 2008; De Vries et al. 2017; Castaldi 2016; Block et al. 2014; Flikkema, De Man, and Castaldi 2014) or on the link between trademark and the market value of the firm (Bosworth and Rogers 2001; Feeny and Rogers 2003; Greenhalgh and Rogers 2006). This last strand of literature has recently provided evidence of how different characteristics of the trademark are associated to different probabilities of its renewal, which is an indirect measure for its value (Nasirov 2019). Yet, no distinction has been hitherto made between licenced and non-licenced trademarks. Since our evidence has shown how some of the characteristics affecting trademark values – such as age and breadth – are also corelated with the licencing activity, it would be interesting to study how these phenomena cope together by seeking answering questions such as 'under what conditions licensed trademarks increase the value of a firm?', 'Are these conditions the same for licensed and non-licensed trademarks?' and alike.

A fourth issue that would be interesting to investigate relates to licencing activity and the access to external finance. Indeed, trademarks represent a very important type of intangible investment (de Rassenfosse, 2017) which can foster firms' market value. However, not all the firms that possess trademarks are publicly traded and it is important to understand how other sources of external finance (such as bank or trade credits) relate to trademarks. Having said that, licencing activities constitute a way of generating new cash flow without resorting to external financing partners. Thus, it would be interesting to understand under what circumstances trademark licencing activity can substitute credit for licensors. In a specular way, scholars could focus on whether and how the acquisition of a trademark licence by a licensee relaxes or increases financial constraints. All these arguments are of paramount importance, given that, as our data show, trademark licencing is particularly relevant for smaller organisations, which are more likely to face financial constraints.

Finally, we more generally advocate further evidence on the trademark licencing activity across different institutional environments. As a matter of fact, to the best of our knowledge, the main works on this issue have focused mainly on USPTO data which refer to a very specific institutional setting. However, new evidence from other countries, possibly with different industrial and economic structures, would help corroborating our hypotheses and results.

This study is not immune to limitations. To begin with, we are aware that transactions are recorded with minimal verification by the USPTO (Graham, Marco, and Myers 2018). While we endeavoured to find and resolve these flaws, recording errors and redundancies may still have partially affected our dataset. Furthermore, 'censoring' due to non-recorded transactions ('a substantial underreporting in the original data'), and 'truncation' due to the lag between execution and recordation date of the most recent agreements, may have caused lower estimates in our statistics (Graham, Marco, and Myers 2018). Notwithstanding this, we believe and hope that our paper can be a catalyst for future research on this topic in terms of marketing, innovation and IP management, and that it can stimulate further and better investigations of the underlying mechanisms driving the choices of licensor and licensees.

Disclosure statement

No potential conflict of interest was reported by the authors.

References

Akerlof, G. 1970. "The Market for 'Lemons': Quality Uncertainty and the Market Mechanism." *The Quarterly Journal of Economics* 84 (3): 488–500. doi:10.2307/1879431.
Albanese, F. 2001. "Merchandising and Licensing to Improve Brand Equity. The Coca-Cola Case." *Symphonia. Emerging Issues in Management* 1: 51–65.
Arora, A., A. Fosfuri, and A. Gambardella. 2001. "Markets for Technology and Their Implications for Corporate Strategy." *Industrial and Corporate Change* 10 (2): 419–451. doi:10.1093/icc/10.2.419.
Arora, A., and A. Gambardella. 2010. "Ideas for Rent: An Overview of Markets for Technology." *Industrial and Corporate Change* 19 (3): 775–803. doi:10.1093/icc/dtq022.
Beebe, B. 2004. "The Semiotic Analysis of Trademark Law." *UCLA Law Review* 51 (3): 621–704.
Block, J. H., G. De Vries, J. H. Schumann, and P. Sandner. 2014. "Trademarks and Venture Capital Valuation." *Journal of Business Venturing* 29 (4): 525–542. doi:10.1016/j.jbusvent.2013.07.006.
Bosworth, D., and M. Rogers. 2001. "Market Value, R&D and Intellectual Property: An Empirical Analysis of Large Australian Firms." *Economic Record* 77 (239): 323–337. doi:10.1111/1475-4932.t01-1-00026.
Brown, R. 1948. "Advertising and the Public Interest: Legal Protection of Trade Symbols." *Yale Law Journal* 57 (7): 1165–1206. doi:10.2307/793310.
Calboli, I. 2007. "The Sunset of Quality Control in Modern Trademark Licensing." *American University Law Review* 57 (2): 341–407.
Carter, S. L. 1990. "The Trouble with Trademark." *Yale Law Journal* 99 (4): 759–800. doi:10.2307/796637.
Castaldi, C. 2018a. "The Economics and Management of Non-Traditional Trademarks: Why, How Much, What, and Who." Chap. 3 in *The Protection of Non-traditional Trademarks: Critical Perspectives*, edited by Irene Calboli and Martin Senftleben. Oxford: University Press.
Castaldi, C. 2018b. "To Trademark or Not to Trademark: The Case of the Creative and Cultural Industries." *Research Policy* 47 (3): 606–616. doi:10.1016/j.respol.2018.01.006.

Castaldi, C. 2019a. "All the Great Things You Can Do with Trademark Data: Taking Stock and Looking Ahead." *Strategic Organization.* doi:10.1177/1476127019847835.

Castaldi, C. 2019b. "On the Market: Using Trademarks to Reveal Organizational Assets, Strategies and Capabilities." doi:10.2139/ssrn.3255864.

Clegg, J., and A. R. Cross. 2000. "Affiliate and Non-Affiliate Intellectual Property Transactions in International Business: An Empirical Overview of the UK and USA." *International Business Review* 9 (4): 407–430. doi:10.1016/S0969-5931(00)00011-1.

Colucci, M., E. Montaguti, and U. Lago. 2008. "Managing Brand Extension via Licensing: An Investigation into the High-End Fashion Industry." *International Journal of Research in Marketing* 25 (2): 129–137. doi:10.1016/j.ijresmar.2008.01.002.

de Rassenfosse, G. 2017. "An Assessment of How Well We Account for Intangibles." *Industrial and Corporate Change* 26 (3): 517–534. doi:10.2139/ssrn.2807079.

De Rassenfosse, G., H. Dernis, D. Guellec, L. Picci, and B. V. P. De la Potterie. 2013. "The Worldwide Count of Priority Patents: A New Indicator of Inventive Activity." *Research Policy* 42 (3): 720–737. doi:10.1016/j.respol.2012.11.002.

De Vries, G., E. Pennings, J. H. Block, and C. Fisch. 2017. "Trademark or Patent? the Effects of Market Concentration, Customer Type and Venture Capital Financing on Start-ups' Initial IP Applications." *Industry and Innovation* 24 (4): 325–345. doi:10.1080/13662716.2016.1231607.

Dehejia, R. H., and S. Wahba. 2002. "Propensity Score-Matching Methods for Nonexperimental Causal Studies." *Review of Economics and Statistics* 84 (1): 151–161. doi:10.1162/003465302317331982.

Economides, N. S. 1988. "The Economics of Trademarks." *The Trademark Reporter* 78 (4): 523–539.

Feeny, S., and M. Rogers. 2003. "Innovation and Performance: Benchmarking Australian Firms." *Australian Economic Review* 36 (3): 253–264. doi:10.1111/1467-8462.00285.

Flikkema, M., A. P. De Man, and C. Castaldi. 2014. "Are Trademark Counts a Valid Indicator of Innovation? Results of an In-Depth Study of New Benelux Trademarks Filed by SMEs." *Industry and Innovation* 21 (4): 310–331. doi:10.1080/13662716.2014.934547.

Fosfuri, A. 2006. "The Licensing Dilemma: Understanding the Determinants of the Rate of Technology Licensing." *Strategic Management Journal* 27 (12): 1141–1158. doi:10.1002/(ISSN)1097-0266.

Frey, C. B., A. Ansar, and S. Wunsch-Vincent. 2015. "Defining and Measuring the 'Market for Brands': Are Emerging Economies Catching Up?" *The Journal of World Intellectual Property* 18 (5): 217–244. doi:10.1111/jwip.v18.5.

Gambardella, A., P. Giuri, and A. Luzzi. 2007. "The Market for Patents in Europe." *Research Policy* 36 (8): 1163–1183. doi:10.1016/j.respol.2007.07.006.

Global Licensing Industry Survey. 2018. https://licensinginternational.org/.

Graham, S. J., A. C. Marco, and A. F. Myers. 2018. "Monetizing Marks: Insights from the USPTO Trademark Assignment Dataset." *Journal of Economics & Management Strategy* 27 (3): 403–432. doi:10.1111/jems.12261.

Graham, S. J., G. Hancock, A. C. Marco, and A. F. Myers. 2013. "The USPTO Trademark Case Files Dataset: Descriptions, Lessons, and Insights." *Journal of Economics & Management Strategy* 22 (4): 669–705. doi:10.1111/jems.12035.

Greenhalgh, C., and M. Rogers. 2006. "Market Value of UK Intellectual Property: Manufacturing, Utility and Financial Service Firms." In *The Management of Intellectual Property*, edited by D. Bosworth and E. Webster, 132–145. Cheltenham, UK: Edward Elgar.

Greenhalgh, C., and M. Rogers. 2012. "Trademarks and Performance in Services and Manufacturing Firms: Evidence of Schumpeterian Competition through Innovation." *Australian Economic Review* 45 (1): 50–76. doi:10.1111/j.1467-8462.2011.00665.x.

Greenhalgh, C., M. Rogers, P. Schautschick, and V. Sena. 2011. "Trade Mark Incentives." *Intellectual Property Office Research Paper No. 2011/1.*doi:10.2139/ssrn.2710619.

Jayachandran, S., P. Kaufman, V. Kumar, and K. Hewett. 2013. "Brand Licensing: What Drives Royalty Rates?" *Journal of Marketing* 77 (5): 108–122. doi:10.1509/jm.11.0145.

Jiang, M. S., and B. Menguc. 2012. "Brand as Credible Commitment in Embedded Licensing: A Transaction Cost Perspective." *International Marketing Review* 29 (2): 134–150. doi:10.1108/02651331211216952.

Katz, A. 2010. "Beyond Search Costs: The Linguistic and Trust Functions of Trademarks." *Brigham Young University Law Review* 2010 (5): 1555–1608.

Landes, W. M., and R. A. Posner. 1987. "Trademark Law: An Economic Perspective." *The Journal of Law and Economics* 30 (2): 265–309. doi:10.1086/467138.

Lane, W. 1988. "Compulsory Trademark Licensing." *Southern Economic Journal* 54 (3): 643–655. doi:10.2307/1059008.

Lemley, M. A. 1999. "The Modern Lanham Act and the Death of Common Sense." *Yale Law Journal* 108 (7): 1687–1716. doi:10.2307/797447.

Leone, M. I., and T. Reichstein. 2012. "Licensing-in Fosters Rapid Invention! the Effect of the Grant-Back Clause and Technological Unfamiliarity." *Strategic Management Journal* 33 (8): 965–985. doi:10.1002/smj.v33.8.

Mangàni, A. 2006. "An Economic Analysis of Rise of Service Marks." *Journal of Intellectual Property Rights* 11 (4): 249–259.

Mendonça, S., T. S. Pereira, and M. M. Godinho. 2004. "Trademarks as an Indicator of Innovation and Industrial Change." *Research Policy* 33 (9): 1385–1404. doi:10.1016/j.respol.2004.09.005.

Meyer, T. A., C. H. Tinney, and T. J. Tinney. 1985. "Guidelines for Corporate Trademark Licensing." *Journal of Product Innovation Management* 2 (3): 196–204. doi:10.1111/1540-5885.230196.

Millot, V. 2009. "Trademarks as an Indicator of Product and Marketing Innovations." *OECD Science, Technology and Industry Working Papers No. 2009/06.* Paris: OECD Publishing. doi:10.1787/224428874418.

Morrison, G., M. Riccaboni, and F. Pammolli. 2017. "Disambiguation of Patent Inventors and Assignees Using High-Resolution Geolocation Data." *Scientific Data* 2017 (4): 170064. doi:10.1038/sdata.2017.64.

Nasirov, S. 2019. "The Value of Trademarks: A Study of the Trademark (protection) Lifecycle in the US Pharmaceutical Industry". doi:10.2139/ssrn.3326972.

OECD/Eurostat (Organization for Economic Cooperation and Development). 2005. *Oslo Manual: Guidelines for Collecting and Interpreting Innovation Data.* 3rd ed. Paris: OECD Publishing. doi: 10.1787/9789264013100-en.

Park, W. G., and D. Lippoldt. 2005. "International Licensing and the Strengthening of Intellectual Property Rights in Developing Countries during the 1990s." *OECD Economic Studies* 2005 (1): 7–48. doi:10.1787/eco_studies-v2005-art2-en.

Pezzoni, M., F. Lissoni, and G. Tarasconi. 2014. "How to Kill Inventors: Testing the Massacrator© Algorithm for Inventor Disambiguation." *Scientometrics* 101 (1): 477–504. doi:10.1007/s11192-014-1375-7.

Potepa, J., and K. T. Welch. 2017. "Innovation Worth Buying: The Fair-Value of Innovation Benchmarks and Proxies." *Working paper, The George Washington University.* https://goo.gl/kD8vVw

Quelch, J. A. 1985. "How to Build a Product Licensing Program." *Harvard Business Review* 63 (3): 186–197.

Ramello, G. B. 2006. "What's in a Sign? Trademark Law and Economic Theory." *Journal of Economic Surveys* 20 (4): 547–565. doi:10.1111/joes.2006.20.issue-4.

Ramello, G. B., and F. Silva. 2006. "Appropriating Signs and Meaning: The Elusive Economics of Trademark." *Industrial and Corporate Change* 15 (6): 937–963. doi:10.1093/icc/dtl027.

Rosenbaum, P. R., and D. B. Rubin. 1983. "The Central Role of the Propensity Score in Observational Studies for Causal Effects." *Biometrika* 70 (1): 41–55. doi:10.1093/biomet/70.1.41.

Schautschick, P., and C. Greenhalgh. 2016. "Empirical Studies of Trade Marks - the Existing Economic Literature." *Economics of Innovation and New Technology* 25 (4): 358–390. doi:10.1080/10438599.2015.1064598.

Tomar, V. 2009. "Trademark Licensing & Franchising: Trends in Transfer of Rights." *Journal of Intellectual Property Rights* 14 (5): 397–404.

U.S. FTC (US Department of Justice & Federal Trade Commission). 2017. "Antitrust Guidelines for the Licensing of Intellectual Property." https://bit.ly/2kaelst

Welch, B. L. 1947. "The Generalization of Student's' Problem When Several Different Population Variances are Involved." *Biometrika* 34 (1/2): 28–35. doi:10.1093/biomet/34.1-2.28.

Wilkins, M. 1992. "The Neglected Intangible Asset: The Influence of the Trade Mark on the Rise of the Modern Corporation." *Business History* 34 (1): 66–95. doi:10.1080/00076799200000004.

WIPO (World Intellectual Property Organization). 2003. "Licensing of Intellectual Property Assets: Advantages and Disadvantages." https://goo.gl/GsYNZN

WIPO (World Intellectual Property Organization). 2010. "IP Panorama Module 12: Trademark Licensing." https://goo.gl/2X8jtG

WIPO (World Intellectual Property Organization). 2013. *World Intellectual Property Report 2013 – Brands – Reputation and Image in the Global Marketplace.* https://goo.gl/zcp67x

WIPO (World Intellectual Property Organization). 2018. "World Intellectual Property Indicators 2018." https://bit.ly/2AJXVS9

Appendix

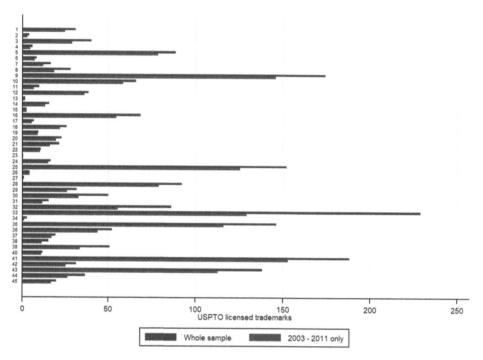

Figure A1. Distribution of licenced trademarks by nice class.

Note: the length of each bar represents the number of trademarks falling within the corresponding NICE class. Blue bars report the distribution relative to the whole-time span, while maroon bars report the distribution relative to the 2003–2011 period. The numbers on the y-axis correspond to the NICE classes: 001 'Chemicals', 002 'Paints', 003 'Cosmetics and cleaning preparations', 004 'Lubricants & fuels', 005 'Pharmaceuticals', 006 'Metal goods', 007 'Machinery', 008 'Hand tools', 009 'Electrical & scientific apparatus', 010 'Medical apparatus', 011 'Environmental control apparatus', 012 'Vehicles', 013 'Firearms', 014 'Jewellery', 015 'Musical Instruments', 016 'Paper goods and printed matter', 017 'Rubber goods', 018 'Leather goods', 019 'Non-metallic building materials', 020 'Furniture and articles not otherwise classified', 021 'Housewares and glass', 022 'Cordage and fibres', 023 'Yarns and threads', 024 'Fabrics', 025 'Clothing', 026 'Fancy goods', 027 'Floor coverings', 028 'Toys and sporting goods', 029 'Meats and processed foods', 030 'Staple foods', 031 'Natural agricultural products', 032 'Light beverages', 033 'Wine and spirits', 034 'Smokers' articles', 035 'Advertising and business', 036 'Insurance and financial', 037 'Building construction and repair', 038 'Telecommunications', 039 'Transportation and storage', 040 'Treatment of materials', 041 'Education and entertainment', 042 'Computer, scientific & legal', 043 'Hotels and Restaurants', 044 'Medical, beauty & agricultural', 045 'Personal'. Source: authors' elaboration on USPTO data.

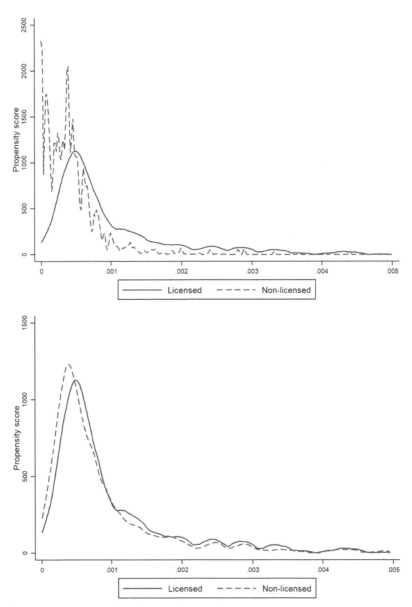

Figure A2. Propensity score values before the matching process.

Firm market valuation and intellectual property assets

Mafini Dosso ⓘ and Antonio Vezzani ⓘ

ABSTRACT

This paper investigates the relationship between the innovative activity of the top corporate R&D investors worldwide and their market valuation. The analysis exploits a sample of more than 1,250 publicly listed Multinational Corporations (MNCs) and their intellectual property rights (IPR) – patents and trademarks – filed between 2005 and 2012. The study contributes to the literature on the IPR-market value link by examining the premium resulting from the interactive use of different IPR. Moreover, the empirical setting allows differentiating the effects of an increase in market value derived from additional IPR (within-effects) with respect to the premium received for holding more IPR than the competitors (between-effects). The findings suggest that investors value the simultaneous use of the two IPRs and form their expectations by benchmarking firms. Finally, significant industrial specificities are observed in the individual effects of patents, trademarks and their interactions on the market value of firms.

1. Introduction

The transition from industrial to knowledge-based economies came with large investments into the development and protection of intangible assets. Indeed, intangibles – computerised information, innovative property and economic competences – are now considered to be equally or even more strategically important for the performances of firms than tangible assets (Corrado, Haltiwanger, and Sichel 2005; OECD 2013; WIPO 2017). This shift has important implications at macro- and micro-economic levels because intangible capital investments are growing faster than tangible investments in several countries (Corrado, Hulten, and Sichel 2009; Dal Borgo et al. 2012) and the management of intellectual property has become central for the economic and financial performance of companies, that is for their survival (Schautschick and Greenhalgh 2016).

On the financial markets, these trends are reflected in the increasing importance that investors place on intellectual property rights (IPR) and, more in general, the importance given to the strategies pursued by companies in appropriating and securing the returns from their innovations. The IPR strategies of companies influence the perceptions and valuations of investors and industry analysts, which in turn are translated into potential premiums on the financial markets (Sandner and Block 2011). Indeed, the market valuation of corporate tangible and intangible assets depends on the actual performance of firms and on investor' expectations of their future performance. Moreover, a higher market valuation can also constitute a relevant leverage for obtaining cheaper and/or larger funds (Hottenrott, Hall, and Czarnitzki 2016).

There is a flourishing literature in line with this perspective which has looked at the effects of firms' IPR on stock market valuation, confirming the importance of IPR for the valuation of companies on financial markets (e.g. Hall, Jaffe, and Trajtenberg 2005; Sandner and Block 2011). However until recently, the majority of studies have mainly investigated this relationship by focusing on R&D and/or patents as the main proxies for the technological intangibles of firms (Montresor and Vezzani 2016).

Only a limited number of studies have considered those intangibles which may capture the non-technological capabilities of firms. A few country-specific market value studies have extended their empirical assessment through the integration of alternative IPR such as trademarks (see Schautschick and Greenhalgh 2016 for a summary). Nevertheless, few scholars have assessed the market valuation of trademarks and patents together (e.g. Greenhalgh and Rogers 2006, 2012). Trademarks are *distinctive symbols, pictures or words that identify specific product and services*[1], whose purpose is to legally protect marketing assets, as brands, against imitation or detrimental activities of competitors (Sandner and Block 2011). Differently from patents, they are not subject to novelty requirement but confer a renewable right for exclusive use of the brands. Given their informational role for customers, trademarks may also provide incentives for firms to differentiate and improve the quality of their offer (Economides 1988; Cabral 2000). Hence, they may carry valuable information for investors (de Vries et al. 2017) and so influence the valuations of companies on financial markets, depending on the branding strategies of firms (Block, Fisch, and Sandner 2014). In addition, trademarks may enable the firms to extend the 'monopoly' rents of patented innovations beyond the patent term (Statman and Tyebjee 1981; Reitzig 2004) by steering potential customers through the brand and symbols protected by the trademark(s) (Rujas 1999).

Following these arguments, the study presented in this paper exploits a sample of the top R&D investors worldwide in order to assess the contribution of their patents and trademarks portfolios on their valuation on financial markets. First, it adds to the existing economic literature by considering the simultaneous and interactive use of different IPR (patents and trademarks) on a large sample of R&D-investing firms from different countries and industries. Second, we argue that investors do not form their opinions and projections only using information about the target firm exclusively (Ramnath 2002). Indeed, they also benchmark firms within the same market sector, thus considering the overall sector performance. Translating this practice into an econometric setting requires the correct accounting of between-firms effects in addition to the within-firm effects commonly investigated in the literature. Indeed, the results presented in this paper suggest that differences across firms are more important in explaining the intangibles premiums. Finally, a finer investigation at the industry level brings additional evidence on the industry-specific features of the effects of patents, trademarks and their interactions on the market valuation of companies.

---

[1]Definition from the American Marketing Association accessed online on November 29th, 2018, https://www.ama.org/resources/Pages/Dictionary.aspx?dLetter=T .

The remainder of the paper is organised as follows. Section 2 outlines the theoretical background. Then, Section 3 presents the data and the methodological framework. Section 4 discusses the results, and lastly, Section 5 presents the conclusions.

2. Theoretical background

As emphasised by Griliches (1981) and more recently by Hall (2000) and Hall, Thoma, and Torrisi (2007), the valuation of firms in public financial markets constitutes a relevant indicator of the expected success of their innovation activities.[2] In addition, market valuation measures can allow the early effects of firms' innovations to be captured and can be seen as a forward-looking indicator of the performances of firms, relevant to investors who assess future profitability (Griffiths et al. 2011). This is because longer and uncertain time lags can be expected between the innovation investments and the realisation of their effects on productivity and on the market *via* products sales and profit. These delayed effects, known as the problem of timing and costs revenues (Hall 2000), may narrow the scope of impact studies exploiting measures related to the profits, sales and productivity during a given period of time (e.g. Geroski, Machin, and Van Reenan 1993).

The increasing competition in the markets for technologies reduces the possibility for firms to realise long-term returns from their innovative activities. According to Schumpeter (1942), the growth process is largely driven by the so-called creative destruction, a conflict between incumbents and new innovators. In this framework, the rents deriving from innovation activities are constantly threatened by new innovations that make the dominant products and technologies on the market obsolete (Aghion & Howitt 1990). A temporary monopoly power may help firms to recover their R&D investments. Firms in these cases may have greater incentives to invest further, which in turn would reduce the overall under-investments that may derive from the differences between the social and private returns from innovations (Arrow 1962; Bloom, Schankerman, and Van Reenen 2013).

In order to extend the rent extraction from their innovations, firms have developed sophisticated innovative strategies, which often bring together technological and non-technological forms of innovations, such as new business methods, and organisational and marketing innovations (Frenz and Lambert 2009; Evangelista and Vezzani 2010). Indeed, evidence on these mixed modes of innovation show that this shift concerns both large and small firms as well as manufacturing and services sectors (OECD 2011). These dynamics were originally pointed out by Hall (1993), who showed the increasing importance of advertising-related expenditures compared to R&D expenditures in the stock market valuation of companies. This finding supports further the importance to account for broader sets of intangible assets in order to explain the performance of firms on financial markets.

2.1. The importance of patents and trademarks for the valuation of firms on financial markets

The increasing use of intangible assets for the purposes of appropriation and rent-extraction by firms has resulted in a rich literature, which examines their effects on the

---

[2]See Hall (2000) for a detailed earlier review.

financial performances of companies (for example, see Hall 2000; Neuhäusler et al. 2011, and the reviews by; Hall and Harhoff 2012; Schautschick and Greenhalgh 2016). However, while research on the link between patents and market value is well established, only a few studies have accounted for the impact of a broader set of IPRs. Earlier studies from the economic literature exploited R&D- and patents-based[3] indicators in order to assess the market value of corporate knowledge assets (Griliches 1981; Griliches, Hall, and Pakes 1991; Toivanen, Stoneman, and Bosworth 2002; Hall, Jaffe, and Trajtenberg 2005). A similar emphasis on patents-related measures was also underlined for the IPRs studies in the innovation management tradition (Candelin-Palmqvist, Sandberg, and Mylly 2012). Thanks to the availability of R&D and patent data at the firm level, the market value studies have been able to further confirm the importance of R&D, as well as to identify additional effects of patents indicators on the market valuation of companies: patents embed information about the market value of firms over and above the information R&D is able to convey (Hall and Harhoff 2012). This significant association may present different patterns across jurisdictions (Hall, Thoma, and Torrisi 2007; Belenzon and Patacconi 2013). Moreover, besides their conventional protective and incentive functions, patents can also constitute a signal to investors that reduce the information asymmetries and mitigates their financial constraints, thus revealing somehow the ability of firms to leverage funds on the markets (Hottenrott, Hall, and Czarnitzki 2016).

However, if it is true that patents do carry additional information about the value of firms for financial markets, they may not be as relevant in industries where patents are not so important, and also in the cases where the inventions or innovations are hardly or not patentable. Furthermore, on the one hand, in opting for patent protection of their new processes, firms can disclose 'too much' information, which in turn can be more easily used by competitors (Hall et al. 2014).[4] On the other hand, partly due to the inherent characteristics of patents,[5] some innovations may not be patentable. Indeed, some innovations such as new varieties or incremental quality changes may not pass the novelty requirements of patents (Greenhalgh and Rogers 2012). In these cases, firms may make recourse to alternative means of protecting their innovations such as trademarks.[6]

Trademark is the term for the legal protection of brands and other marketing assets (American Marketing Association). Trademarks were originally conceived to attenuate the information asymmetries between buyers and sellers[7] (informational role of trademarks) by enabling the identification (and differentiation) of the origin of a good and by acting as an incentive for quality improvements of the offers (Ramello and Silva 2006). As such, they can carry valuable information for investors and enable firms to extend the 'monopoly' rents of patented innovations beyond the patent term (Statman and Tyebjee 1981; Reitzig 2004) by steering potential customers through the brand and symbols protected with the trademark(s) (Rujas 1999). Together with brands, trademarks

---

[3]See Kleinknecht, Van Montfort, and Brouwer (2002) and Hagedoorn and Cloodt (2003) for detailed discussions on the use of these indicators to assess the innovative performances of firms.

[4]Hall et al. (2014) give a conceptual framework to improve the understanding of the drivers behind the choice firms make regarding informal (e.g. secrecy) versus formal protection (e.g. patents).

[5]See Acs and Audretsch (1989), Griliches (1990), de Rassenfosse et al. (2013) for discussions on the use of patent as an indicator of innovative activities.

[6]See Mendonça, Pereira, and Godinho (2004); Flikkema, de Man, and Castaldi (2014) for evidence on the links between trademarks and innovation.

[7]See Akerlof (1970) for a seminal illustration of these information asymmetries on the 'market for lemons'.

constitute key drivers in the ability to command higher prices. Therefore, they play an important role across different market segments and can account for significant shares of the market value of firms (Corrado and Hulten 2010; Block, Fisch, and Sandner 2014; Schautschick and Greenhalgh 2016; World Intellectual Property Organization, WIPO 2017). The market value effects of individual trademarks will differ depending on the type of trademarks and their relationship to the branding strategy of firms (Krasnikov, Mishra, and Orozco 2009; Block, Fisch, and Sandner 2014).

Moreover, firms often rely on bundles of IPR to protect different facets of the same innovation. Such IPR strategies, referred to as the IPR bundles, may allow innovators to delay the imitation and to benefit from greater innovation returns (Greenhalgh and Longland 2005). The use of IPR combinations is increasingly documented at the country, sectoral and firm-levels (OECD 2011; Millot 2012; and see; Dernis et al. 2015 for detailed statistics about the industry-specific patterns of IPR combination in the sample of companies used in this paper). In addition, these combinations can significantly increase the probability of receiving larger amounts of venture capital, compared to situations where firms only resort to a single intellectual property (Zhou et al. 2016). These empirical observations are consistent with Rujas's conceptual framework on the complementarity of patents and trademarks. Similarly, it can be argued that different IPR may convey different signals to investors: while patents carry information on the technological capabilities of the firms and serve forward-looking purposes more, trademarks would convey information on the actual commercial and marketing capabilities of the firms (Rujas 1999; de Vries et al. 2017).

Only a few studies have attempted to assess the effects of patents and trademarks together on the stock market performances of the firms, framing the analysis within the Tobin-q approach. The market value of a given company in the Tobin-q framework is derived from the bundle of its tangible (total) and intangible (IPR) assets (see, for example, Griliches 1981 or Greenhalgh and Rogers 2006). Table 1 presents the firm-level studies that are close to the conceptual framework and questions of this paper. Accordingly, only those empirical works that have investigated the role of both patents and trademarks in the valuation of firms on financial markets are considered.

Most of the works considered focused on a sample of firms from a specific country (the UK, France and Australia). To the best of our knowledge, the analysis of Sandner and Block (2011) is the only one to consider a multi-country and multi-sector perspective. This makes any comparisons between countries difficult, but the overall results suggest that trademarks and patents may simultaneously account for a significant share of the valuation of companies on the financial markets. Furthermore, what these studies underline further are the different effects of patents-trademarks combinations across sectoral groups or industries. However, none of the market value studies has investigated the potential impacts of the interactions between patent and trademark portfolios. Yet, such explorations are able to unveil significant patterns on the combined use of patents and trademarks, as emphasised by Llerena and Millot (2013) for a sample of French listed companies.[8]

---

[8] For close conceptual discussions on other protection means, see also the study on trademarks and copyrights by Somaya and Graham (2006).

Table 1. Market value studies considering both patents and trademarks.

Author/year	Sample	Estimation Method (fixed/random)	Variable for Market Value	Main results: (sign) and/or sig	IPIP Interaction	Sectors analysis	How IPs enter in the estimation
Bosworth and Rogers (2001)	1994–1996 averaged 60 Australian listed firms	LSDV and fixed effects	Tobin's Q (sum of market valuation and book value of debt)	PAT/Tangibles assets: (+) significant; TM/tangibles assets: non significant	NO	NO (Industries dummies)	Flows (averaged)
Greenhalgh and Rogers (2006)	1989–2002 4367 UK companies	OLS (industry & year dummies)	log(market value) = outstanding shares (average in year) × price (end accounting period) + creditors and debt – current assets.	UK PAT/Total assets: non-sign (negative only in suppliers-dominated); EPO PAT/Total assets: (+) significant (only in production intensive & science-based); TM/Total assets: non-significant; (+) significant all sectors but (-) significant in information intensive	NO	YES 6 Pavitt macro-sectors (suppliers-dominated; production intensive; science-based; information intensive; software firms)	Flows
Sandner and Block (2011)	1996–2002 1216 companies from different countries	Non-linear least squares	ln of Tobin's Q (Market value of comp/Book value of assets)	R&D stocks/assets: (+) significant; PAT stock/R&D stock: non-significant; Citations stock/R&D stock: (+) significant; TM stocks/Marketing assets: (+) significant	NO	YES for Trademark intensity (large coefficients in Machinery & computer eq, Transport equipment and Biotech & Pharma)	Stocks
Greenhalgh and Rogers (2012)	1996–2000 1600 UK companies	OLS with industry & year dummies	log(MV/Tangible assets)	CTM/TA: (+) significant in manuf. & services; UK TM/TA: non-significant; EPO PAT/TA: (+) significant in manufacturing; UK PAT/TA: non-significant in manufacturing; Included also Interaction terms (Trend*IP/TA)	NO	YES Manufacturing (Pat & TM) and Services (TM only)	Flows + Dummies

(Continued)

Table 1. (Continued).

Author/year	Sample	Estimation Method (fixed/random)	Variable for Market Value	Main results: (sign) and/or sig	IPIP Interaction	Sectors analysis	How IPs enter in the estimation
Llerena and Millot (2013)	2007 French listed companies	Supermodularity tests	log(Market value):	Only PAT: not significant Only TM: (+) significant PAT & TM: (+) significant	YES (dummies)	YES Pharma & Chemicals (complementarity) Computer & Electronics (substituability)	Dummies
Korkeamäki and Takalo (2013)	1999–2009 Case study (Apple, introduction of different versions of iPhone)	OLS + testing average returns on days close to patent/trademark publication	Stock returns at day t (ln of Trading volume/Market capitalisation)	Patent application/grants: stronger effects on Apple's abnormal returns with patent application Trademark filing: non-significant reaction	NO	One firm – one product	Patent Trademark publication
This study	2005–2012 1,273 listed Multinational Corporations from different countries	Panel estimation – Decomposition of within and between effects	Market capitalisation = market price × outstanding shares + long term debts and current liabilities	Within effects: not significant for PAT, TM, PAT & TM Between effects: (+) significant for PAT, TM, PAT & TM	YES	YES Pharma: within PAT & TM (+) sign. between TM (+) sign. Auto: between PAT (+) sign. Computer & Elect.: between PAT, TM, PAT&TM (+) sign	Flows

The contribution made in this paper provides complementary evidence on this issue and provides an assessment of the effects of patents, trademarks and their combined use on the market value of companies. Furthermore, the present study exploits a sample of leading R&D-investing companies worldwide and so also contributes to the still under-documented features of IPR complementarities in large firms (Zhou et al. 2016).

2.2. Why are the links between IPRs and market valuation industry-specific?

The well-known taxonomy of Pavitt (1984) and the subsequent literature (e.g. Malerba and Orsenigo 1997; Marsili 2001; Castellacci 2008) have greatly advanced the knowledge on the industry-specific nature and processes of innovation. They illustrate how different industries are characterised, for instance, by different dominant types of innovation, sources of technology, the requirements of users, and appropriability conditions. The specific pattern of innovative activity that emerges in a given industry therefore depends on the technological regime or the combination of specific technological opportunities, the conditions for the appropriability of innovations, the patterns of cumulativeness of technical advances and the properties of the knowledge base (Breschi, Malerba, and Orsenigo 2000). Industrial specificities in the innovation process are associated with differentiated marketing and IPR strategies implemented by firms across industries (Cohen, Nelson, and Walsh 2000; Krasnikov, Mishra, and Orozco 2009; Gallié and Legros 2012). In other words, appropriability conditions are likely to influence the relationship between the innovation and their market performances of companies; and they are likely to do so differently across industries and depending on the IPR considered (Greenhalgh and Rogers 2006; Castaldi and Dosso 2018).

Focusing on the recourse to patents and/or trademarks, Dernis et al. (2015) confirm that strong industrial specificities can also be observed among large R&D-investing companies. For instance, companies operating in the Computers and electronics, Pharmaceuticals and Transport equipment sectors tend to rely more often on IPR portfolios made of patents and trademarks than on single IPR strategies – only patents or only trademarks – (Dernis et al. 2015). These distinctive patterns partly reflect the relative importance of each IPR, their combination, and their eventual relevance as means of appropriation of innovation returns across different industries. The use of patents (and trademarks) as indicators of innovation activities has been extensively discussed in the literature (Acs and Audretsch 1989; Griliches 1990; de Rassenfosse et al. 2013 on patents and; Mendonça, Pereira, and Godinho 2004; Malmberg 2005; Flikkema, de Man, and Castaldi 2014 for evidence on trademarks). With respect to patents, Hall et al. (2014) drew attention to a dichotomic picture, distinguishing between *discrete product industries* – such as pharmaceuticals, metals, and metal products – where patents are still the preferred means to secure the returns to innovation, and *complex product industries* – such as computers, software, electrical equipment and transportation equipment – where they serve more strategic purposes (Hall et al. 2014). Using evidence at the trademark level in the automobile industry, Malmberg (2005) suggested that automobiles companies would opt for models number rather than trademarks for their new products. The author concludes: '*The negative conclusion regarding the use of trademark in these companies must therefore be considered valid also today.*' (Malmberg 2005, 35). These arguments are accounted for in the present study and the paper provides an updated, yet partial, assessment of the relevance of patents, trademarks and their combination across different industries, namely Computers, Pharmaceuticals and Automobiles.

These three IPR-intensive sectors feature very distinct patterns of innovation behaviours and marketing strategies. These differences should translate into specific combinations of patents and trademarks that help sustain the IPR-based competitive advantages of firms (Reitzig 2004). Patents and trademarks in the pharmaceutical industry are more likely to be used as complements to protect the new molecules and to extend the rent extraction beyond the patent term through strong brand- and reputation-building strategies (Reitzig 2004; Millot 2012); one patent and trademark pair in this industry can indeed have a high valuation (Thoma 2015). In more complex industries such as computers and transport equipment, characterised by fast product depreciation rates, and where single-branded products are commonly based on many patents (Hall et al. 2014, Reitzig 2014), investors are likely to grant relatively much higher value to patents than to trademarks (Llerena and Millot 2013). Nevertheless, companies such as Apple (Computers industry) or Toyota, (Automobiles industry) feature in the most valuable trademarks-protected brands of the world.[9] This questions Malmberg's earlier finding on the low importance of trademarks in the Automobiles sector where trademarks-protected brands are used to differentiate products and services, as well as for reputational purposes (Hoeffler and Keller 2003). However, traditional carmakers are facing a greater technological competition on the parts and components segment, a growing standardisation shifting the power from automobile brands to suppliers, and the recent opening up of patent portfolios in key technologies such as electric vehicles, batteries and fuels life cells[10] These dynamics have speeded the patent race, shortened the technology cycles, and may have favoured the increased use of alternative or complementary means of protection (Alcácer, Beukel, and Cassiman 2017). At the same time, one or a few valuable patents may actually grant a great market power and provide the basis to build up strong trademark-protected brands on technological reputation. Similarly, technological competition in the computers industry is particularly strong and firms rely heavily on patents (Daiko et al. 2017). However, the decrease of production prices and of the margins derived from technological advances has led some companies to develop strong trademark-based differentiation strategies. This hints at the importance of combining technological and non-technological intangibles in this industry.

As shown in Table 1, the relationship between IPR and market value is indeed industry-specific. However, empirical research is still needed to improve the understanding of the effects of patents and trademarks and their combined use in distinct industrial contexts. Consequently, this study contributes to the literature on the IPR-market value link and examines how patents-trademarks combinations yield different pay-offs for leading R&D-investing firms operating in the computers, pharmaceuticals and automobiles industries.

---

[9]See the Forbes's 2018 ranking of the World's most valuable brands at https://www.forbes.com/powerful-brands/list/#tab:rank.

[10]See Tesla Motors and Toyota companies' announcements to open their patents portfolios related to hybrid and electric vehicles technologies: https://www.forbes.com/sites/briansolomon/2014/06/12/tesla-goes-open-source-elon-musk-releases-patents-to-good-faith-use/#73b5853c3c63 and https://techcrunch.com/2019/04/03/toyota-is-giving-automakers-free-access-to-nearly-24000-hybrid-car-related-patents/..

3. Data and methodology

3.1. Data

The original sample is based on the 2013 EU Industrial and R&D Investment Scoreboard,[11] which provides annual data on the top 2000 corporate R&D investors worldwide. These companies account for about 80% of business investment in R&D in the world (European Commission 2013). The patents and trademarks filed by these companies at the United States Patent and Trademark Office (USPTO) have been retrieved from the EPO's PATSTAT and the OECD internal databases in the framework of a joint JRC-OECD project. The matching was carried out on a country-by-country basis using a series of string matching algorithms contained in the Imalinker system (Idener Multi Algorithm Linker) developed for the OECD by IDENER.[12] The matching exercise uses information on the subsidiary structure of the Scoreboard companies (about 500,000 subsidiaries) as reported in the Bureau van Dijk's ORBIS[13] database. Subsidiaries located in a different country than the headquarters of a company were included for the matching of patents and trademarks to company-level data. Their patent and trademark applications were consolidated into the relevant parent company. A detailed description of the approach used to perform the matching can be found in Dernis et al. (2015).

The initial dataset includes information on patents and trademarks filed at the USPTO by more than 1,500 Multinational Corporations (MNCs) in the period 2005–2012.

The advantage of using USPTO data lies in the importance of US markets for both the technologies and the end-products. Besides, these companies show a relatively greater IPR activity in the US market, with the average number of patents and trademarks being the largest at the USPTO for more than half of the industries. Data on market value were obtained from the ORBIS database and market value is calculated by multiplying the share price by the number of outstanding shares. Additional company-level data are taken from the EU Industrial and R&D Investment Scoreboard's dataset. The availability of the different data used in the analysis reduces the estimation sample to 1273 companies.

Most of the companies in our estimation sample are headquartered in the US (38.6%), in a European country (24.7%) or in Japan (24.4%); the remaining 12.4% of companies are headquartered in the Rest of the World (Table 2). In terms of sectors, the sample is largely composed of companies operating in the Computer & Electronics one (25%).

In accordance with the extant literature, separate sector regressions were run on the companies operating in Computer & Electronics (Computer), Pharmaceuticals (Pharma, 7%) and Transport Equipment (Auto, 8%).On the other hand, other sectors largely represented in the sample such as Chemicals (8%) and Machinery (9%) are not discussed. However, separate regressions were also run for these two sectors, which show similar

---

[11]For more information on the sample of companies included in the EU Industrial and R&D Investment Scoreboard, see at http://iri.jrc.ec.europa.eu/scoreboard.html.

[12]IDENER is a private research SME company composed of a team of researchers with a scientific background in different disciplines related to systems engineering (electronics and computer, systems integration and control, and process engineering).

[13]The ORBIS database provides economic and financial information on over 280 million of public and private companies in the world. More details about the contents and the uses of ORBIS can be found at https://www.bvdinfo.com/en-gb /our-products/data/international/orbis .

Table 2. Distribution of companies across world regions.

Region	# of companies	Frequency (%)
USA	491	38.6
EU	314	24.7
(Germany	70	5.5)
(France	57	4.5)
(UK	51	4.0)
Japan	310	24.4
Rest of the world	158	12.4
(Taiwan	54	4.2)
(China	35	2.8)
Total	1,273	100

regression results to those obtained for the Automobiles industry. It should be noted that, by construction, the sample does not need to be representative of the population of firms across countries and sectors as it is explicitly compiled to represent the top R&D investors in the world. Moreover, the availability of stock market data and the various propensities of firms to file patents and trademarks at the USPTO tend to favour US companies and the Computer & Electronic sector. All in all, compared to similar studies, the sample used in the study presented in this paper covers more countries and seems to be better suited to analysing the links between IPRs and market value for multinational companies.

3.2. Econometric strategy

In the empirical application, we model the (natural logarithm of) market value of a given company upon a series of indicators influencing the market perception of its actual worth and potential future performances. Similarly to prior contributions (e.g. Greenhalgh and Rogers 2012), the market capitalisation is computed as the market price multiplied by the outstanding shares plus the long-term debts and current liabilities.

To estimate the relationship between IPRs and the market value of a given company, the following equation was estimated:

$$mcap_{i,t} = \alpha + \beta_j IPR_{ji,t-1} + \gamma X_{i,t} + \vartheta Z_{i,t-1} + \delta_1 year + \delta_2 industry + \delta_3 market + \mu_i + \varepsilon_{it}$$

$$(1)$$

where IPR_{jit} represents the intellectual property rights (j = Patents; Trademarks; their interaction) filed by company i in year t; in particular, we consider the number of patents applications and registered trademarks. X_{it} stands for a series of explanatory variables that enter into the estimation equation without a lag. In particular, we control for the total assets of a company, its one-year sales growth and the sales growth of the sector in which a company operates. The inclusion of total assets is crucial to align the estimation framework to the Tobin-q theory and to estimate the coefficients attached to the IPR variables correctly. Z_{it-1} represents the lagged values of the labour productivity of a company (proxied by the ratio of sales over employees). A set of binary variables is also introduced as controls for year, industry (using the ISIC rev.4 classification) and the financial market on which a company i is listed. Finally, μ_i in equation (1) represents the unobserved company-specific factors, and ε_{it} the error term; both parameters are assumed to be normally distributed.

To estimate equation (1), this study uses a correlated panel random effects approach initially proposed by Mundlak (1978), modified by Neuhaus and Kalbfleisch (1998) and recently discussed by Schunck (2013) and Bell and Jones (2015). The choice of the estimation strategy is driven by two considerations. First, the greatest share of the variation in the dependent variable is cross-sectional: more than 95% of the market value variation in our data is due to differences between firms (see Table 3), while changes in market value of individual firms (within) explain less than 5%.[14] Given the nature of the data a standard fixed effects specification, focusing on within company variations, does not appear to be the best approach to estimating the impact of IPR on a company's market value.[15]

Second, the correlated panel random effect approach allows different context-specific heterogeneity to be considered through the inclusion of time-invariant covariates (for instance the industrial sector in which a company operates or the market in which it is listed) and estimating the within and between effects into a single specification. This approach reflects, in a more realistic manner, the behaviour of investors as they do not only consider specific company's performances, but also benchmark them against the performance of other companies. Indeed, as pointed out by King (1966), stocks are often seen by investors as falling into groups with 'similar' performance. Firms in the same group share similar costs of capital and correlated results. More recently, Piotroski and Roulstone (2004) consider three types of investors and argue that market analysts have more restricted access to idiosyncratic information about firms than other investors (management or institutional investors with a large ownership stake) and tend to incorporate market- and industry-level information in their stock price formation. This is supported by the evidence on a positive relationship between the analysts' accuracy and the industry specialisation and on the fact that they tend to adjust their firm-specific earnings forecasts in response to announcements by other firms in the same industry (Ramnath 2002).

The within (fixed) effect can be incorporated into a random-effects model by decomposing the variables of interest into a between $\left(\overline{IPR}_i = \frac{1}{n_i} * \sum_{t=1}^{n_i} IPR_{it}\right)^{16}$ and a within $\left(IPR_{it} - \overline{IPR}_i\right)$ component. Therefore, following Allison (2009), the *hybrid* estimation equation can be written as:

Table 3. Descriptive statistics of the market value.

Market Capitalisation (log)	Mean	Std. Dev.	Min	Max	Observations (Companies)	Share of within variation	Share of between variation
All sample	14.69	1.78	9.44	20.25	6856 (1273)	2.4	97.6
Computers & electronics	14.07	1.67	9.44	19.78	1756 (322)	3.5	96.5
Pharma	14.07	2.23	9.52	18.84	468 (91)	2.4	97.6
Auto	15.20	1.74	10.24	19.15	833 (102)	2.0	98.0

[14]Please note that these numbers are computed on the whole market capitalisation figures and are not limited to the estimation sample.
[15]Moreover, a fixed effect framework only looking at deviations around firms' averages may be largely influenced by short-run fluctuations, subject to measurement framework and other transitory influences (Griliches 1990).
[16]Where n_i stands for the number of years for which we observe a company in the sample.

$$\text{mcap}_{it} = \alpha + \beta_{wj}\left(\text{IPR}_{jit-1} - \overline{\text{IPR}}_{ji}\right) + \beta_{bj}\overline{\text{IPR}}_{ji} + \gamma X_{it} + \delta \text{controls} + \mu_i + \varepsilon_{it} \qquad (2)$$

The coefficients β_w and β_b in equation (2) represent the within and the between effects of the intellectual property assets of a company, respectively. This formulation, by company mean centring the intellectual property assets $\left(\text{IPR}_{jit-1} - \overline{\text{IPR}}_{ji}\right)$, solves the collinearity problems that may arise from the correlation between IPR_{ji} and $\overline{\text{IPR}}_{ji}$ as in the Mundlak approach. Therefore, it leads to more stable and precise estimates.

3.3. Discussion of the variables used for the empirical analyses

The main variables of interest are the natural logarithm (Ln) of patents and trademarks counts and the interaction between these two and then transformed as explained with the paragraph above. In addition, the (logarithm of) total assets of a company is controlled for, a standard approach in market value studies.

We also control for the impact of the sales growth of the company and the influence of sector sales growth on its market value. The former captures the prospects for future growth of a particular company that is not directly linked to its current innovative activities while the latter reflects the tendency of investors to prefer companies operating in sectors with higher future growth prospects and the eventual premium for related companies (see also Hall 1993).

Furthermore, firms with higher labour productivity, a signal of efficiency and greater potential returns, are expected to obtain higher rewards on the financial markets. This effect should translate into a positive coefficient on the labour productivity variable, here defined by the ratio of sales over employees.

Finally, the possibility that markets may penalise firms with very high R&D expenditures as compared to physical investment is accounted for by introducing the ratio between R&D and capital investment flows. It should be noted that once controlling for the intangible assets considered (patents and trademarks), this variable captures the proportion of knowledge inputs not materialised in terms of IPR compared to tangible and more tradable investments. The IPR enter with a lag in the model in order to account for the time delay in the identification and treatment of the information they may convey to the (potential) investors. Because yearly data are used, the eventual immediate reaction of markets to a patent (trademark) filing cannot be discerned as in Korkeamäki and Takalo (2013) and the IPR variables should be lagged so as to be able to identify their effect. Moreover, given the theoretical arguments, we do not think that longer lags would provide useful information as in productivity or profit studies. Descriptive statistics of the variables and correlations among them are reported in Table A1 and Table A2, respectively (see the Appendix).

As a robustness check, the model is also estimated by integrating the 'quality' of the IPR in accordance with the insight of Scherer (1965) that the quality of patented inventions varies across patents, firms and industries. Among the proxies for IPR quality (see Squicciarini, Dernis, and Criscuolo 2013) a slightly modified measure of scope, originally proposed by Lerner (1994) was used in this study.[17]

The scope (s_{IP}) of a patent (trademark) is the number of distinct technology (product) classes contained in the IPR document (ip). Technologies feature intrinsic characteristics that can confer them a broader or narrower scope; the same holds true for products.[18] Therefore, the scope of a patent (trademark) is weighted according to the $IPC4$ (Nice) classes it refers to.[19] In particular, the average scope of all the patents and trademarks containing that specific class in a given year (s_c) was computed for each IPC4 and Nice class. The scope of an IPR is then normalised by the average scope of the classes contained in it:

$$wscope_{IP} = \frac{s_{IP}}{\frac{1}{s_{IP}} \sum_c s_c}$$

Accordingly, the within- and between-effects of patents and trademarks on the market valuation of firms are addressed by considering together their volume and using quality adjusted measures.

4. Results

4.1. Estimates for the whole sample

Table 4 reports the results of the estimations for the whole sample of companies. The industry-specific results are discussed in the next section.

The first two columns report the estimates using the volumes of patent and trademark activities, while the last columns present the results for the regressions using quality adjusted volumes. For each of the two models, a specification (spec. 1) is presented first where the interaction between patents and trademarks is not included, and then the results from a specification including the interactions (spec. 2) are reported. Although the correlations of our explanatory variables show acceptable levels (see Table A2 in the appendix), we also run two additional specifications (3 and 4) with only total assets and the IPR explanatory variables. The coefficients of these specifications do not differ significantly from the estimates obtained when the full set of explanatory variables are included (see Table 4).

The estimations confirm that markets grant a premium for holding a larger sets of IPRs than the competitors (between-effects) rather than to the additional innovation assets of a company (within-effects). In contrast to the previous literature, by looking only at within-effects (see Table 1), the approach taken in this study allows us to highlight a key feature of the investors' endeavours on the financial markets: they mainly form

[17]The most common way of accounting for patent quality is by weighting patents by forward citations. However this paper uses the scope, because it is the only measure that can be built on both patents and trademarks. Moreover, it should be noted that forward citations are an ex-post measure (normally considering between 3 and 7 years lags) of the goodness of a patented technology. Considering both market and technology uncertainty it seems hard to assume that market operators are able to effectively discount the potential of a patented invention. The authors think that it is a more plausible hypothesis to assume that the market operator considers the product/technology breadth.

[18]Think about comparing a car engine with a medical pill.

[19]Trademarks are filed in accordance with the International Classification of Goods and Services, also known as the Nice Classification, while the International Patent Classification (IPC) is used to allocate patents to technological fields.

Table 4. Market value regressions – Whole sample.

	Counts		Quality adjusted		Counts without controls	
	Spec. 1	Spec. 2	Spec. 1	Spec. 2	Spec. 3	Spec. 4
IP – Within effect						
Log Patents (t-1)	0.001	0.001	0.001	0.002	-0.001	-0.001
	(0.008)	(0.008)	(0.008)	(0.008)	(0.008)	(0.008)
Log Trademarks (t-1)	0.003	0.003	0.000	0.001	-0.003	-0.003
	(0.006)	(0.006)	(0.006)	(0.006)	(0.006)	(0.006)
Patents*Trademarks (t-1)		-0.002		-0.018		0.000
		(0.014)		(0.015)		(0.014)
IP – Between effect						
Log Patents (t-1)	0.128***	0.077***	0.132***	0.090***	0.119***	0.073***
	(0.013)	(0.018)	(0.013)	(0.018)	(0.013)	(0.018)
Log Trademarks (t-1)	0.169***	0.062**	0.195***	0.096***	0.167***	0.069**
	(0.018)	(0.031)	(0.020)	(0.034)	(0.018)	(0.031)
Patents*Trademarks (t-1)		0.030***		0.028***		0.027***
		(0.007)		(0.008)		(0.007)
Other variables						
Total assets (t)	0.661***	0.657***	0.658***	0.655***	0.691***	0.688***
	(0.011)	(0.011)	(0.011)	(0.011)	(0.011)	(0.011)
Sales growth (t)	0.260***	0.259***	0.259***	0.258***		
	(0.014)	(0.014)	(0.014)	(0.014)		
Sector sales growth (t)	0.026**	0.026**	0.026**	0.026**		
	(0.012)	(0.012)	(0.012)	(0.012)		
R&D-Capital expenditure ratio (t-1)	-0.064***	-0.065***	-0.065***	-0.066***		
	(0.007)	(0.007)	(0.007)	(0.007)		
Log labour productivity (t-1)	0.162***	0.163***	0.162***	0.162***		
	(0.012)	(0.012)	(0.012)	(0.012)		
Sector fixed effect	Included	Included	Included	Included	Included	Included
Time fixed effect	Included	Included	Included	Included	Included	Included
Market fixed effect	Included	Included	Included	Included	Included	Included
Constant	4.479***	4.622***	4.538***	4.644***	3.801***	3.922***
	(0.406)	(0.406)	(0.406)	(0.406)	(0.412)	(0.413)
Observations	6,856	6,856	6,856	6,856	6,856	6,856
Number of bvd_panel	1,273	1,273	1,273	1,273	1,273	1,273
R-squared (overall)	0.891	0.891	0.891	0.892	0.884	0.884
R-squared (between)	0.901	0.902	0.901	0.902	0.896	0.896
R-squared (within)	0.300	0.300	0.300	0.300	0.249	0.250
Rho	0.800	0.800	0.800	0.800	0.795	0.794
RMSE	0.262	0.262	0.262	0.261	0.273	0.272

Standard errors in parentheses, clustered at the company level – *** $p < 0.01$, ** $p < 0.05$, * $p < 0.1$

their expectations by benchmarking firms and award a premium for holding more innovation assets than the competitors.

In other words, when jointly considering the within and between effects the within elasticity of market value – the increase in the market value of a company derived from additional IPR – is not significant, either for patents or for trademarks. Market valuation responds significantly to differences in the overall IPR of companies (the between effect); the estimated between elasticities (spec. 1) are of 12.8% for patents and above 16% for trademarks when the interaction term is excluded (spec. 1, Table 4).

These findings suggest that investors tend to value the long term and overall innovative capabilities of companies more by benchmarking them against other companies. This may also reflect some degree of uncertainty in the evaluation of the market potentialities of the latest intangible assets developed by a specific company. Indeed, one specific patent or trademark may have a huge immediate impact on the market valuation, as illustrated in several case studies (e.g. the Apple's iPhone, see Table 1). Nevertheless, the initial uncertainty about the future success of new technological solutions and products – especially when technological alternatives are being developed by different companies – and the highly skewed distribution of IPR value (Gambardella, Harhoff, and Verspagen 2008) suggest that on average (and ex-ante) the probability that a single IPR has a significant impact are small. In other words the innovative track record of firms and the market context matter. An intuition of this finding can be illustrated by the story of the Google glasses. Google glasses were launched at the beginning of 2013 and perceived by many as a potential game changer in the consumer good market. In 2015, Google announced that they were considering closing the project, which was later continued in enterprises versions. During this period, Google launched many other innovative projects and its innovative leadership has hardly been questioned so far.

Overall, the results show that financial markets do value the technical and commercial capabilities conveyed by corporate patents and trademarks. Moreover and in contrast to the full model estimations of Greenhalgh and Rogers (2006, 2012) suggesting a non-significant impact of trademarks flows on market valuation, a positive and strong relation between trademarks and market valuation is found.[20] Despite the different specifications, the results for the trademarks variable are in line with the findings of Sandner and Block (2011). Twenty years after Hall (1993), who showed the increasing importance of advertising related expenditures during the 1980s, we find that product differentiation through trademarks pay off (in terms of market valuation), besides the effects of new technological developments.

The inclusion of a proxy for the combined use of patents and trademarks brings further findings. The coefficients associated with each individual IPR do not differ much but a positive and significant impact is found for their interaction. This latter result suggests that having a larger patent portfolio pay off more for those companies which also own trademarks, and *vice versa*. In other words, investors seem to award a premium to those companies mastering a wider and possibly interrelated range of technical and commercial capabilities. Moreover, this result also holds true in the model integrating

---

[20]It should be noted that the estimation of Greenhalgh and Rogers (2006, 2012) relies on fixed effect specification. Therefore, the non-significant effects of trademarks are in line with those found for the within variation.

quality-adjusted volumes, while the between coefficients of patents and trademarks slightly increase.

Consistent results emerge for the remaining control variables across the different models and specifications. Larger firms, or more accurately, firms that *ceteris paribus* have greater total assets would obtain a higher valuation on the market. Firms with higher sales growth are also more likely to yield a higher value on the markets, confirming the positive valuation that investors to the growth performances of companies. Moreover, investors tend to place a positive premium on companies operating in sectors with above-average growth, as suggested by the positive and significant coefficients on the sector sales growth. In other words, companies also benefit from operating in sectors with overall potential for sales increase. Once the intangible assets (in terms of patents and trademarks) have been accounted for, the results indicate that the investors would rather penalise companies with a higher ratio of R&D over capital expenditures. As expected, firms with a higher productivity also benefit from a market premium, as shown by the persistent positive sign on the coefficient associated with the ratio of sales per employee.

4.2. Estimates by industry

Table 5 provides the estimations results for the regressions focusing on Computers and electronics, Pharmaceuticals and Automobiles, three industrial sectors with a large number of companies in the sample.

In line with the aggregate results, the industry-specific regressions confirm that markets are more likely to reward the companies for being more innovative than their competitors (between-effects) rather than for their additional intangible assets as individual companies (non-significant within-effects of single IPR). Nevertheless, the within-elasticity of market valuation of pharma companies to the interaction term is significant which suggests that, in this sector, specific combinations of patents and trademarks can be a relevant signal to investors. By pairing patents and trademarks pharmaceutical companies can yield high rewards, 'independently' of the performances of their competitors. This finding is consistent with the empirical analysis of Thoma (2015) who found that patents-trademarks pairs stand out due to higher valuations in the pharmaceuticals industry. Besides, the non-significance of the within coefficients on single IPR confirms the intuition of Reitzig (2004) according to which (exclusively) patents-based competitive advantage is fading away in many industries. The study even suggests that pharmaceuticals companies are not an exception anymore. However, developing an effective combination of IPR can indeed mitigate this trend in the pharmaceutical sector, especially if new technological developments are combined with 'strong, trademark-protected brands' (Reitzig 2004, 39). The non-significance of patents in the within estimation for the Computers and Automobiles industries could be due to the 'dense web of overlapping IPRs that a company must hack its way through in order to actually commercialize new technology' (Shapiro 2001, 120), which is known as the patent thicket. The existence of these thickets makes the evaluation of individual IPR difficult in these complex products industries (Heeley, Matusik, and Jain 2007), where patents are also likely to be used for strategic purposes (Hall et al. 2014).

Table 5. Market value regressions by industry.

	Spec. 1 – Counts			Spec. 2 – Counts			Spec. 3 – Counts		
	Computer	Pharma	Auto	Computer	Pharma	Auto	Computer	Pharma	Auto
IP – Within effect									
Log Patents (t-1)	-0.006 (0.017)	0.058 (0.040)	0.000 (0.025)	-0.006 (0.017)	0.062 (0.040)	0.000 (0.025)	-0.011 (0.018)	0.059* (0.035)	0.007 (0.026)
Log Trademarks (t-1)	0.006 (0.013)	0.013 (0.030)	0.015 (0.017)	0.005 (0.013)	0.008 (0.030)	0.015 (0.017)	0.005 (0.013)	0.006 (0.030)	0.025 (0.018)
Patents*Trademarks (t-1)				0.023 (0.028)	0.215*** (0.083)	0.025 (0.047)			
IP – Between effect									
Log Patents (t-1)	0.153*** (0.025)	0.005 (0.078)	0.082** (0.037)	0.120*** (0.031)	0.017 (0.090)	0.082* (0.048)	0.166*** (0.027)	-0.003 (0.080)	0.084** (0.040)
Log Trademarks (t-1)	0.267*** (0.037)	0.462*** (0.088)	0.024 (0.047)	0.150* (0.077)	0.487*** (0.144)	0.02 (0.102)	0.266*** (0.041)	0.464*** (0.090)	0.033 (0.052)
Patents*Trademarks (t-1)				0.025* (0.015)	-0.008 (0.030)	0.001 (0.022)			
Other variables									
Total assets (t)	0.617*** (0.024)	0.590*** (0.048)	0.835*** (0.031)	0.613*** (0.024)	0.599*** (0.049)	0.833*** (0.032)	0.617*** (0.025)	0.622*** (0.048)	0.834*** (0.030)
Sales growth (t)	0.489*** (0.039)	0.03 (0.030)	0.646*** (0.070)	0.487*** (0.039)	0.024 (0.030)	0.644*** (0.070)			
R&D-Capital expenditure ratio (t-1)	-0.099*** (0.015)	-0.056** (0.026)	-0.025 (0.027)	-0.101*** (0.015)	-0.060** (0.026)	-0.024 (0.027)			
Log labour productivity (t-1)	0.155*** (0.029)	0.094*** (0.034)	0.131** (0.052)	0.156*** (0.029)	0.085** (0.034)	0.131** (0.052)			
Time & market fixed effect	Included	Included	Included	Included	Included	Included	Included	Included	Included
Constant	5.241*** (0.30)	5.180*** (0.612)	2.554*** (0.485)	5.442*** (0.322)	5.014*** (0.645)	2.586*** (0.530)	4.938*** (0.298)	4.528*** (0.585)	2.435*** (0.432)
Observations	1,756	468	550	1,756	468	550	1,756	468	550
Number of bvd_panel	322	91	102	322	91	102	322	91	102
R-squared (overall)	0.867	0.906	0.938	0.868	0.908	0.938	0.841	0.901	0.926
R-squared (between)	0.886	0.908	0.946	0.886	0.91	0.946	0.863	0.903	0.935
R-squared (within)	0.324	0.281	0.429	0.325	0.292	0.429	0.241	0.267	0.342
Rho	0.752	0.772	0.759	0.751	0.768	0.763	0.768	0.781	0.775
RMSE	0.293	0.336	0.214	0.293	0.335	0.214	0.31	0.337	0.229

Standard errors in parentheses, clustered at the company level – *** p <0.01, ** p <0.05, * p <0.1

Looking at the between-effects row in Table 5, it can be seen that patents and/or trademarks have significant effects on the market valuation in the selected industries. Again, this result highlights the importance to investors of benchmarking corporate IPR portfolios when making the investment decisions. In fact, in the Computer and Automobile industries, only the between differences seems to matter. In other words, in these industries, the markets seem to grant higher premiums to the companies that seem relatively more innovative than their competitors (between-effects), rather than rewarding a premium to any additional innovation assets from a company (within-effects). Nevertheless, significant differences emerge across the industries and depending on the IPR or their combination: *i)* in the Computer industry, both patents and trademarks are significantly valued by the markets; *ii)* only patents are effective for Automobile companies[21] and; *iii)* for Pharmaceutical companies, only trademarks show significant between-effects. For the Automobiles companies, the results of this study would thus not contradict the earlier work of Malmberg who suggests that these companies may still not prefer trademarks (only) to protect their new products (Malmberg 2005). Regarding the pharmaceuticals industry, where the within variations matter, the results suggest a lesser importance of benchmarking the patenting activity of companies. The fast development of generic or alternative drugs have certainly influenced the trend in this industry, making the implementation of strong differentiation strategies even more fundamental, for instance through massive investments in trademarks-protected brands and other marketing assets.

The results for the remaining control variables are similar to the ones observed for the aggregate regression. However, two main differences arise. First, there is no significant effect of sales growth in the Pharmaceuticals sector as compared to the other two industries. Consistently with the within estimates, IPRs, here trademarks, may incorporate a much clearer signal of economic performances for investors. Second, the negative effect of a higher ratio of R&D over capital expenditures is statistically significant for the Computer and Pharmaceutical industries. This ratio in the former industry is much higher (also due to lower capital expenditures), while the pharmaceuticals companies are the subject of research and drugs development costs that are rising quickly (and requiring longer periods).[22]

5. Conclusion

The study presented in this paper provides evidence on the strategic role of IPRs in the valuation of firms on the financial markets. Investors do account for and confer a premium on the technical, functional, commercial and marketing information conveyed by corporate patents and trademarks. The empirical application on a large sample of R&D-investing firms from different countries and industries shows that investors value the simultaneous use of patents and trademarks, hinting at a premium for their complementary use. Moreover, the findings presented in this paper indicate that the expectations of investors are made (more) by benchmarking firms, rather than only by using information on the

---

[21] As mentioned in section 3, separate regressions for the Chemicals and Machinery provide results similar to those obtained for Auto companies.
[22] See https://www.mckinsey.com/industries/pharmaceuticals-and-medical-products/our-insights/the-road-to-positive-r-and-38d-returns and https://www.ncbi.nlm.nih.gov/pmc/articles/PMC3146086/.

target firm. From a company perspective, a key implication is that during the development of new technologies and product, IPR should be identified and managed by considering the strategies of relevant competitors. Failure to do so might limit the ability of companies to effectively communicate their capacity to appropriate and secure their innovation returns to the markets.

The analysis also confirms the relevance of industrial specificities in the IPR-market valuation relationship and does so by considering a finer inspection at the industry level, compared to the previous literature. The relationship observed between the innovative outputs of companies and their stock market performances is, for instance, influenced by the patterns of the dominant technologies in use, and more generally by the current technological regime – technological opportunities, conditions for the appropriability of innovations, patterns of cumulativeness in technical advances and properties of the knowledge base – that prevail in a given industry (Breschi, Malerba, and Orsenigo 2000; Mazzucato 2006). Besides, the differences observed between the Computer, Pharmaceutical and Automobile industries point to specific structural features such as the degree of complexity and modularity of the products as well as differences in the strategic and competitive behaviours of companies. Unfortunately, our data do not allow us to investigate further into the industry-specific features of technological regimes and their impact on the IPR-market valuation relationships. Significantly, the findings on the Pharmaceuticals industry confirm the intuition of Reitzig (2004) concerning the declining importance of only patents-based commercial successes. In fact, the analysis actually suggests that pharmaceuticals companies do not seem to be an exception anymore. From a corporate point of view, this underlines the need to devote more careful attention to trademark management, not only to protect brands and marketing assets but also to send signals to the financial markets.

Moreover, the estimations suggest that the effect of IPR strategies on the market value of firms mainly operates through the cross-sectional dimension (the between effects prevail). What really seem to matter are the relative superior abilities of firms to develop new technological and commercial capabilities. When interpreting the overwhelming importance of the between effects as compared to the within effects, it should also be noted that the sample covers the top corporate R&D investors worldwide and consequently does not include high innovative start-ups which have recently come onto the market. For these companies, which often rely upon narrow and specialised IPR portfolios, the within effect may be substantially significant.

Furthermore, some additional research avenues can be identified in relation to the caveats of the analysis and dataset. First, the use of alternative IPR quality indexes, for example, based on the number and content of claims, oppositions or renewals, may facilitate a finer assessment of the importance of specific IPR in the competitiveness of firms. Second, characterising the trademarks families and the associated branding strategies – creation, modernisation, and/or extension of brands – of large firms will also contribute to the identification of the trademarks filing strategies that feature higher premiums on the financial markets. Finally, richer qualitative analyses of patents and trademarks combinations at firms and products levels may contribute to solving the puzzle of strategic IPR versus IPR always leading to or supporting news products and services.

Disclaimer

The analyses presented in this paper do not necessarily represent the views of the European Commission. Neither the European Commission nor anyone acting on its behalf can be held responsible for any use made thereof.

ORCID

Mafini Dosso ⓘD http://orcid.org/0000-0003-4132-2914
Antonio Vezzani ⓘD http://orcid.org/0000-0001-8077-2489

References

Acs, Z. J., and D. B. Audretsch. 1989. "Patents as a Measure of Innovative Activity." *Kyklos* 42 (2): 171–180. doi:10.1111/kykl.1989.42.issue-2.

Aghion, P., and P. Howitt, 1990. "A Model of Growth through Creative Destruction (No. w3223)". National Bureau of Economic Research. doi: 10.1099/00221287-136-2-327

Akerlof, G. 1970. "The Market for "Lemons": Quality Uncertainty and the Market Mechanism." *Quarterly Journal of Economics* 84: 488–500. doi:10.2307/1879431.

Alcácer, J., K. Beukel, and B. Cassiman. 2017. "Capturing Value from Intellectual Property (IP) in a Global Environment." In *Geography, Location, and Strategy*, edited by J. Alcácer, B. Kogut, C. Thomas, and B. Y. Yeung, Vol. 36, 163–228. Bingley: Emerald Group Publishing, Advances in Strategic Management. doi:10.1108/S0742-332220170000036006.

Allison, P. D. 2009. *Fixed Effects Regression Models*. Thousand Oaks, CA: Sage.

Arrow, K. 1962. "Economic Welfare and the Allocation of Resources for Invention." In *The Rate and Direction of Inventive Activity: Economic and Social Factors*, 609–626. Cambridge, MA: Princeton University Press.

Belenzon, S., and A. Patacconi. 2013. "Innovation and Firm Value: An Investigation of the Changing Role of Patents, 1985–2007." *Research Policy* 42 (8): 1496–1510. doi:10.1016/j. respol.2013.05.001.

Bell, A. J. D., and K. Jones. 2015. "Explaining Fixed Effects: Random Effects Modelling of Time-Series Cross-Sectional and Panel Data." *Political Science Research and Methods* 3: 133–153. doi:10.1017/psrm.2014.7.

Block, J. H., C. Fisch, and P. G. Sandner. 2014. "Trademark Families: Characteristics and Market Values." *Journal of Brand Management* 21 (2): 150–170. doi:10.1057/bm.2013.27.

Bloom, N., M. Schankerman, and J. Van Reenen. 2013. "Identifying Technology Spillovers and Product Market Rivalry." *Econometrica* 81 (4): 1347–1393.

Bosworth, D. 2001. "Market Value, R&D and Intellectual Property: An Empirical Analysis of Large Australian Firms." *The Economic Record* 77 (239): 323–337.

Breschi, S., F. Malerba, and L. Orsenigo. 2000. "Technological Regimes and Schumpeterian Patterns of Innovation." *The Economic Journal* 110 (463): 388–410. doi:10.1111/1468-0297.00530.

Cabral, L. M. B. 2000. "Stretching Firm and Brand Reputation." *RAND Journal of Economics* 31 (4): 658–673. doi:10.2307/2696353.

Candelin-Palmqvist, H., B. Sandberg, and U.-M. Mylly. 2012. "Intellectual Property Rights in Innovation Management Research: A Review." *Technovation* 32 (9–10): 505–512. doi:10.1016/j. technovation.2012.01.005.

Castaldi, C., and M. Dosso (2018). "From R&D to Market: Using Trademarks to Capture the Market Capability of Top R&D Investors, JRC Working Papers on Corporate R&D and Innovation No 01/2018, JRC110520." Joint Research Centre.

Castellacci, F. 2008. "Technological Paradigms, Regimes and Trajectories: Manufacturing and Service Industries in a New Taxonomy of Sectoral Patterns of Innovation." *Research Policy* 37 (6–7): 978–994. doi:10.1016/j.respol.2008.03.011.

Cohen, W. M., R. R. Nelson, and J. P. Walsh (2000). "Protecting Their Intellectual Assets: Appropriability Conditions and Why US Manufacturing Firms Patent (Or not) (No. w7552)." National Bureau of Economic Research.

Corrado, C., J. Haltiwanger, and D. Sichel. 2005. "Measuring Capital and Technology: An Expanded Framework." In *Measuring Capital in the New Economy*, edited by C. Corrado, J. Haltiwanger, and D. Sichel, 11–46. Chicago: University of Chicago Press.

Corrado, C., C. Hulten, and D. Sichel. September 2009. "Intangible Capital and U.S. Economic Growth." *Review of Income and Wealth* (3). doi: 10.1111/j.1475-4991.2009.00343.x.

Corrado, C. A., and C. R. Hulten. 2010. "How Do You Measure a" Technological revolution"." *The American Economic Review* 100 (2): 99–104. doi:10.1257/aer.100.2.99.

Daiko, T., H. Dernis, M. Dosso, P. Gkotsis, M. Squicciarini, and A. Vezzani (2017), "*World Corporate Top R&D Investors: Industrial Property Strategies in the Digital Economy.*" A JRC and OECD common report. Luxembourg: Publications Office of the European Union.

Dal Borgo, M., P. Goodridge, J. Haskel, and A. Pesole. 2012. "Productivity and Growth in UK Industries: An Intangible Investment Approach." *Oxford Bulletin of Economics and Statistics* 76 (6): 806–834.

de Rassenfosse, G., H. Dernis, D. Guellec, L. Picci, and B. V. P. de la Potterie. 2013. "The Worldwide Count of Priority Patents: A New Indicator of Inventive Activity." *Research Policy* 42 (3): 720–737. doi:10.1016/j.respol.2012.11.002.

de Vries, G., E. Pennings, J. H. Block, and C. Fisch. 2017. "Trademark or Patent? the Effects of Market Concentration, Customer Type and Venture Capital Financing on Start-ups' Initial IP Applications." *Industry and Innovation* 24 (4): 325–345. doi:10.1080/13662716.2016.1231607.

Dernis, H., M. Dosso, F. Hervas, V. Millot, M. Squicciarini, and A. Vezzani (2015). "*World Corporate Top R&D Investors: Innovation and IP Bundles.*" A JRC and OECD common report. Luxembourg: Publications Office of the European Union.

Economides. 1988. "The Economics of Trademarks." *Trademark Reporter* 78: 523–539.

European Commission. 2013. *The 2013 EU Industrial R&D Investment Scoreboard.* Luxembourg: Publications Office of the European Union.

Evangelista, R., and A. Vezzani. 2010. "The Economic Impact of Technological and Organizational Innovations. A Firm-level Analysis." *Research Policy* 39 (1): 1253–1263. doi:10.1016/j.respol.2010.08.004.

Flikkema, M. J., A. P. de Man, and C. Castaldi. 2014. "Are Trademark Counts a Valid Indicator of Innovation? Results of an In-depth Study of New Benelux Trademarks Filed by SMEs." *Industry and Innovation* 21 (4): 310–331. doi:10.1080/13662716.2014.934547.

Frenz, M., and R. Lambert. 2009. "Exploring Non-technological and Mixed Modes of Innovation across Countries." In *Innovation in Firms: A Microeconomic Perspective*, 69–109. Paris: OECD Publications. https://doi.org/10.1787/9789264056213-4-en.

Gallié, E.-P., and D. Legros. 2012. "French Firms' Strategies for Protecting Their Intellectual Property." *Research Policy* 41 (4): 780–794. doi:10.1016/j.respol.2011.12.008.

Gambardella, A., D. Harhoff, and B. Verspagen. 2008. "The Value of European Patents." *European Management Review* 5: 69–84. doi:10.1057/emr.2008.10.

Geroski, P. A., S. Machin, and J. Van Reenan. 1993. "The Profitability of Innovating Firms." *RAND Journal of Economics* 24: 198–221. doi:10.2307/2555757.

Greenhalgh, C., and M. Longland. 2005. "Running to Stand Still? – The Value of R&D, Patents and Trade Marks in Innovating Manufacturing Firms." *International Journal of the Economics of Business* 12 (3, November): 307–328. doi:10.1080/13571510500299326.

Greenhalgh, C., and M. Rogers. 2006. "The Value of Innovation: The Interaction of Competition, R&D and IP." *Research Policy* 35 (4): 562–580. doi:10.1016/j.respol.2006.02.002.

Greenhalgh, C., and M. Rogers. 2012. "Trade Marks and Performance in Services and Manufacturing Firms: Evidence of Schumpeterian Competition through Innovation." *The Australian Economic Review* 45 (1): 50–76. doi:10.1111/j.1467-8462.2011.00665.x.

Griffiths, W., P. H. Jensen, and E. Webster. 2011. "What Creates Abnormal Profits?." *Scottish Journal of Political Economy* 58: 323–346. doi:10.1111/sjpe.2011.58.issue-3.

Griliches, Z. 1981. "Market Value, R&D and Patents." *Economics Letters* 7: 183–187. doi:10.1016/0165-1765(87)90114-5.

Griliches, Z. 1990. "Patent Statistics as Economic Indicators: A Survey." *Journal of Economic Literature* 28: 1661–1707.

Griliches, Z., B. Hall, and A. Pakes. 1991. "R&D, Patents and Market Value Revisited: Is There a Second (Technological opportunity) Factor." *Economic of Innovation and New Technology* 1: 183–202. doi:10.1080/10438599100000001.

Hagedoorn, J., and M. Cloodt. 2003. "Measuring Innovative Performance: Is There an Advantage in Using Multiple Indicators?" *Research Policy* 32: 1365–1379. doi:10.1016/S0048-7333(02)00137-3.

Hall, B., C. Helmers, M. Rogers, and V. Sena. 2014. "The Choice between Formal and Informal Intellectual Property: A Review." *Journal of Economic Literature* 52 (2): 375–423. doi:10.1257/jel.52.2.375.

Hall, B. H. 1993. "The Stock Market's Valuation of R&D Investment during the 1980's." *American Economic Review* 83: 259–264.

Hall, B. H. 2000. "Innovation and Market Value." In *Productivity, Innovation and Economic Performance*, edited by R. Barrell, G. Mason, and M. O'Mahoney. Cambridge: Cambridge University Press. https://catalogue.nla.gov.au/Record/512308.

Hall, B. H., A. Jaffe, and M. Trajtenberg. 2005. "Market Value and Patent Citations." *Rand Journal of Economics* 36: 16–38.

Hall, B. H., G. Thoma, and S. Torrisi (2007). "The Market Value of Patents and R&D: Evidence from European Firms."*NBER Working Paper* No. 13428, Cambridge, MA. doi: 10.1094/PDIS-91-4-0467B

Hall, H., and D. Harhoff. 2012. "Recent Research on the Economics of Patents, Annual Review of Economics." *Annual Reviews* 4 (1): 541–565.

Heeley, M., S. Matusik, and N. Jain. 2007. "Innovation, Appropriability, and the Underpricing of Initial Public Offerings." *The Academy of Management Journal* 50 (1): 209–225. doi:10.5465/amj.2007.24162388.

Hoeffler, S., and K. Keller. 2003. "The Marketing Advantages of Strong Brands." *Journal of Brand Management* 10 (6): 421–445. doi:10.1057/palgrave.bm.2540139.

Hottenrott, H., B. H. Hall, and D. Czarnitzki. 2016. "Patents as Quality Signals? the Implications for Financing Constraints on R&D." *Economics of Innovation and New Technology*, Special Issue " Financing constraints R&D investments and innovation performances 25 (3): 197–217. doi:10.1080/10438599.2015.1076200

King, B. F. 1966. "Market and Industry Factors in Stock Price Behavior." *Journal of Business* 39 (1): 139–190. doi:10.1086/294847.

Kleinknecht, A., K. Van Montfort, and E. Brouwer. 2002. "The Non-trivial Choice between Innovation Indicators." *Economics of Innovation and New Technologies* 11: 109–121. doi:10.1080/10438590210899.

Korkeamäki, T., and T. Takalo. 2013. "Valuation of Innovation and Intellectual Property: The Case of Iphone." *European Management Review* 10: 197–210.

Krasnikov, A., S. Mishra, and D. Orozco. 2009. "Evaluating the Financial Impact of Branding Using Trademarks: A Framework and Empirical Evidence." *Journal of Marketing* 73 (6): 154–166. doi:10.1509/jmkg.73.6.154.

Lerner, J. 1994. "The Importance of Patent Scope: An Empirical Analysis." *RAND Journal of Economics* 25 (2): 319–333. doi:10.2307/2555833.

Llerena, P., and V. Millot (2013). "Are Trade Marks and Patents Complementary or Substitute Protections for Innovation." *BETA Document de Travail*, 1.

Malerba, F., and L. Orsenigo. 1997. "Technological Regimes and Sectoral Patterns of Innovative Activities." *Industrial and Corporate Change* 6: 83–117. doi:10.1093/icc/6.1.83.

Malmberg, C. 2005. Trademarks Statistics as Innovation Indicator? - A Micro Study, No 2005/17, Papers in Innovation Studies. Lund University, CIRCLE - Center for Innovation, Research and Competences in the Learning Economy. https://EconPapers.repec.org/RePEc:hhs:lucirc:2005_017.

Marsili, O. 2001. *The Anatomy and Evolution of Industries: Technological Change and Industrial Dynamics.* Cheltenham, UK and Northampton, MA: Edward Elgar.

Mazzucato, M. 2006. "Innovation and Stock Prices: A Review of Some Recent Work." *Revue De L'ofce* 5: 159–179. https://doi.org/10.3917/reof.073.0159.

Mendonça, S., T. S. Pereira, and M. M. Godinho. 2004. "Trademarks as an Indicator of Innovation and Industrial Change." *Research Policy* 33: 1385–1404. doi:10.1016/j.respol.2004.09.005.

Millot, V. (2012). *"Trademark Strategies and Innovative Activities."* PhD. thesis, Université de Strasbourg. doi: 10.1094/PDIS-11-11-0999-PDN

Montresor, S., and A. Vezzani. 2016. "Intangible Investments and Innovation Propensity: Evidence from the Innobarometer 2013." *Industry and Innovation* 23 (4): 331–352. doi:10.1080/13662716.2016.1151770.

Mundlak, Y. 1978. "On the Pooling of Time Series and Cross Section Data." *Econometrica* 46 (1): 69–85. doi:10.2307/1913646.

Neuhaus, J. M., and J. D. Kalbfleisch. 1998. "Between- and Within-cluster Covariate Effects in the Analysis of Clustered Data." *Biometrics* 54: 638–645. doi:10.2307/3109770.

Neuhäusler, P., R. Frietsch, T. Schubert, and K. Blind (2011). "Patents and the Financial Performance of Firms - an Analysis Based on Stock Market Data." *Fraunhofer ISI discussion papers*, 28, Fraunhofer: Karlsruhe. http://nbn-resolving.de/urn:nbn:de:0011-n-1582128

OECD. 2011. "Mixed Modes of Innovation." In *OECD Science, Technology and Industry Scoreboard 2011*, 140–141. Paris: OECD Publishing. https://doi.org/10.1787/sti_scoreboard-2011-44-en.

OECD. 2013. *Supporting Investment in Knowledge Capital, Growth and Innovation.* Paris: OECD Publishing.

Pavitt, K. 1984. "Sectoral Patterns of Technical Change: Towards a Taxonomy and a Theory." *Research Policy* 13 (6): 343–373. doi:10.1016/0048-7333(84)90018-0.

Piotroski, J. D., and D. T. Roulstone. 2004. "The Influence of Analysts, Institutional Investors, and Insiders on the Incorporation of Market, Industry, and Firm-Specific Information into Stock Prices." *The Accounting Review* 79 (4): 1119–1151. doi:10.2308/accr.2004.79.4.1119.

Ramello, G. B., and F. Silva. 2006. "Appropriating Signs and Meaning: The Elusive Economics of Trademark." *Industrial and Corporate Change* 15 (6): 937–963. doi:10.1093/icc/dtl027.

Ramnath, S. 2002. "Investor and Analyst Reactions to Earnings Announcements of Related Firms: An Empirical Analysis." *Journal of Accounting Research* 40 (5): 1351–1376. doi:10.1111/joar.2002.40.issue-5.

Reitzig, M. 2004. "Strategic Management of Intellectual Property." *MIT Sloan Management Review* 45 (3, Spring): 35–40.

Rujas, J. 1999. "Trademarks: Complementary to Patents." *World Patent Information* 21: 35–39. doi:10.1016/S0172-2190(99)00023-X.

Sandner, P. G., and J. Block. 2011. "The Market Value of R&D, Patents, and Trademarks." *Research Policy* 40 (7): 969–985. doi:10.1016/j.respol.2011.04.004.

Schautschick, P., and C. Greenhalgh. 2016. "Empirical Studies of Trade Marks–The Existing Economic Literature." *Economics of Innovation and New Technology* 25 (4): 358–390. doi:10.1080/10438599.2015.1064598.

Scherer, F. M. 1965. "Firm Size, Market Structure, Opportunity, and the Output of Patented Inventions." *American Economic Review* 55 (5): 1097–1125.

Schumpeter, J. 1942. *Capitalism, Socialism, and Democracy.* New York: Harper & Bros.

Schunck, R. 2013. "Within and between Estimates in Random-Effects Models: Advantages and Drawbacks of Correlated Random Effects and Hybrid Models." *Stata Journal*, StataCorp LP 13 (1): 65–76. doi:10.1177/1536867X1301300105

Shapiro, C. 2001. "Navigating the Patent Thicket: Cross Licenses, Patent Pools, and Standard-setting." *Innovation Policy and the Economy* 1: 119–150.

Somaya, D., and S. J. Graham (2006). "Vermeers and Rembrandts in the Same Attic: Complementarity between Copyright and Trademark Leveraging Strategies in Software." *Georgia Institute of Technology TIGER Working Paper.*

Squicciarini, M., H. Dernis, and C. Criscuolo (2013). "Measuring Patent Quality." *OECD Science, Technology and Industry Working Papers 2013/03.*

Statman, M., and T. T. Tyebjee. 1981. "Trademarks, Patents, and Innovation in the Ethical Drug Industry." *The Journal of Marketing* 71–81. doi:10.1177/002224298104500306.

Thoma, G. 2015. "Trademarks and the Patent Premium Value: Evidence from Medical and Cosmetic Products." *World Patent Information* 41: 23–30. doi:10.1016/j.wpi.2015.02.003.

Toivanen, O., P. Stoneman, and D. Bosworth. 2002. "Innovation and the Market Value of UK Firms, 1989–1995." *Oxford Bulletin of Economics and Statistics* 64: 39–61. doi:10.1111/obes.2002.64.issue-1.

World Intellectual Property Organization, WIPO. (2017). "World Intellectual Property Report 2017: Intangible Capital in Global Value Chains." Geneva: WIPO. https://www.wipo.int/edocs/pubdocs/en/wipo_pub_944_2017.pdf

Zhou, H., P. G. Sandner, S. L. Martinelli, and J. H. Block. 2016. "Patents, Trademarks, and Their Complementarity in Venture Capital Funding." *Technovation* 47: 14–22. doi:10.1016/j.technovation.2015.11.005.

Table A1. Descriptive statistics.

	Whole sample		Computer		Pharma		Auto	
	Mean	Standard Deviation	Mean	Standard Deviation	Mean	Standard Deviation	Mean	Standard Deviation
Market Capitalisation (ln)	14.69	1.8	14.07	1.7	14.07	2.2	15.20	1.7
Total Assets (ln)	14.84	1.73	14.19	1.55	14.24	2.11	15.50	1.68
Patents (ln)	3.06	1.75	3.70	1.75	2.70	1.66	3.41	1.74
Trademarks (ln)	1.60	1.34	1.39	1.21	1.79	1.75	1.46	1.29
Sales growth	0.06	0.29	0.05	0.24	0.07	0.69	0.05	0.19
Sector sales growth	0.43	0.50	1.02	0.57	0.32	0.19	0.40	0.36
R&D-Capital expenditure ratio (ln)	0.02	1.56	0.83	1.18	1.45	1.44	−0.16	0.81
Log labour productivity (ln)	−1.37	0.79	−1.53	0.61	−1.48	1.10	−1.38	0.63

Table A2. Correlation across variables.

	1.	2.	3.	4.	5.	6.	7.	8.	9.
1. Market value (ln)	1.000								
2. Total assets (ln)	0.888	1.000							
3. Patents within (ln)	−0.002	−0.009	1.000						
4. Trademarks within (ln)	0.006	0.005	0.074	1.000					
5. Patents between (ln)	0.446	0.487	−0.015	−0.006	1.000				
6. Trademarks between (ln)	0.551	0.462	−0.024	−0.001	0.492	1.000			
7. Sales growth	0.011	−0.106	−0.004	0.008	−0.087	−0.014	1.000		
8. Sales growth (sector)	−0.170	−0.205	−0.002	0.011	0.162	−0.064	0.074	1.000	
9. R&D-Capital expenditure ratio	−0.470	−0.563	0.006	−0.007	0.037	−0.038	−0.010	0.262	1.000
10.Llabour productivity (ln)	0.294	0.350	0.000	0.002	0.133	0.096	−0.187	−0.108	−0.224

Part III

Trademarks and IP strategies of Innovative Firms

Concordance and complementarity in IP instruments

Marco Grazzi ⓘ, Chiara Piccardo and Cecilia Vergari

ABSTRACT
This work investigates the relationship between proxies of innovation activities, such as patents and trademarks, and firm performance in terms of revenues, growth, and profitability. By resorting to the virtual universe of Italian manufacturing and service firms, this work provides a rather complete picture of the Intellectual Property (IP) strategies pursued by Italian firms, in terms of patents and trademarks, and studies whether the two instruments for protecting IP exhibit complementarity or substitutability. In addition, and to our knowledge novel, we propose a measure of concordance (or proximity) between the patents and trademarks owned by the same firm and we then investigate whether such concordance exerts any effect on performance. The results suggest that while patents and trademarks independently exert a relevant impact on firm performance, there is no convincing evidence in favour of a complementary role of IP.

1. Introduction and related literature

This work investigates the effect of patents and trademarks on firm performance. To do this, we employ the virtual universe of Italian limited liability manufacturing companies and we analyse their Intellectual Property (IP) strategies. We then study whether the joint use of patents and trademarks exhibits complementarity or substitutability and, finally, we propose a novel measure to assess the concordance between the two instruments, when firms employ both.

The question of how innovation activity affects firms' performance has a long tradition in economics, with many recent contributions focusing on the analysis of *R&D* and patents, especially for large and medium firms. In particular, starting with Griliches (1981), many authors investigated the relationship between firm's market value and its *R&D* expenditures and number of patents, often focusing on large-quoted companies (see, e.g. Hall 2000; Toivanen, Stoneman, and Bosworth 2002). Others, in addition to *R&D*, analyse the impact of product and process innovation based on survey data (see, e.g. among the many others, Hall, Lotti, and Mairesse 2009).

A recent wave of studies, starting with Mendonça, Pereira, and Godinho (2004), has suggested that, on top of patents, trademarks provide a useful proxy for firms' innovation activity. This is even more true for small and medium enterprises, SMEs henceforth, and for 'softer' types of (non-patentable, non-technological) innovation like service, marketing, and organisational innovations as well as innovation activities closer to the market introduction stage (see, e.g. Flikkema, De Man, and Castaldi 2014; Helmers and Rogers 2010; Flikkema et al. 2019). Indeed, for instance, SMEs may not be in the position of affording other protection mechanisms, see for instance Block et al. (2015). Moreover, while patents have a finite duration, trademarks do not expire as long as all post-registration maintenance documents are timely filed. A trademark can thus, in a sense, prolong the protection of a product (or service) when a similarly aged patent would expire.[1] Schautschick and Greenhalgh (2016) provide a detailed survey of the empirical works revealing significant correlations between innovation, patents, and trademarks and testing for the suitability of trademarks as proxy for innovation.

In line with this recent strand of literature, we study how and to what extent, innovation activities, as proxied by patents and trademarks, affect firms' performance in terms of revenues, growth, and profitability. We consider balance-sheet data matched with IP activity of the (virtual) universe of Italian manufacturing limited liability firms, independently of their size. This feature of the dataset allows us to contribute to the literature in several directions. First, we can provide a complete picture of patent and trademark activities of Italian firms and assess whether, for instance, there exists a size or sector-specific pattern. Second, we can dig into the effects of these innovation proxies, not only on large firms (as investigated, among others, by Castaldi and Dosso 2018) but also on small and medium firms. Note that this is quite relevant as SMEs, which represent the vast majority of Italian firms, are more likely to resort to trademarks over patents, relative to large firms. Moreover, we investigate whether there is some complementarity or substitutability among the two IP instruments. Finally, and to our knowledge completely novel, for firms reporting both patents and trademarks, we employ the available information to build a measure of concordance (or proximity) between the stocks of patents and trademarks owned by the same firm and we then investigate whether such concordance may have an impact on performance. Notice that our approach, although different, bears some complementarity with that proposed in Flikkema et al. (2019) where trademarks are shown to be related to product innovation and, even more so, for manufacturing firms.

The direction we start to explore here is made available by the contemporaneous availability of firm-level IP data and recent developments in Algorithmic Links with Probabilities (ALP) (see, among the others, Lybbert and Zolas 2014). Although not perfect, the linkages established between patents and trademarks thanks to ALP enables to investigate a number of issues. In this respect, with the limitations just recalled, our work provides an analytical tool to relate trademarks to innovation, in our case proxied by patents. The framework we propose also allows us to assess the relative timing in the activities of patenting and trademarking and the impact of the concordance measure on firm performance. In this respect, our prior, in line with the capability view of the firm, is that a higher concordance or overlap between the pool of knowledge, as proxied by patents, and the set of products sold, as proxied by trademarks, should be associated with

---

[1]Specifically, a trademark is a sign that identifies a firm's product or service, so that it allows consumers to distinguish between different goods (see, e.g. Mendonça, Pereira, and Godinho 2004; Ramello 2006).

better firm performance (see among the many others Teece et al. 1994; Markides and Williamson 1996; Bryce and Winter 2009).

Our findings reveal that both patents and trademarks do have a role in explaining firm performance, in terms of revenues, growth, and profitability. In particular, firms' with both IP rights enjoy a higher premium than firms only owning either patents or trademarks. Moreover, our findings suggest that the positive impact of having only trademarks is somewhat larger than the positive impact of owning patents alone. Due to the lack of more qualitative data, it is not easy to provide a clear interpretation to such finding, however, we conjecture that this is related to the very nature of trademarks as 'recognisable designations and symbols for goods and services' (Mendonça, Pereira, and Godinho 2004) hence playing a more crucial role in the process of marketing innovation *vis à vis* patents. Further, trademarks are the most diffused instrument of IP protection for Italian firms. We have to notice however that when focusing on the degree of concordance between the stock of patents and trademarks, one faces the constraint, particularly binding for the Italian case, of restricting the sample to firms owning both IP instruments.

As said, following the seminal work of Mendonça, Pereira, and Godinho (2004), a number of contributions has focused on trademarks as an appropriate indicator of innovation output, in addition to the more standard proxy traditionally provided by patents. Due to data constraints, most of these works focus on large and medium firms that are publicly traded and find evidence of a positive effect of trademarks on firms' stock market value (see, e.g. Greenhalgh and Rogers 2006, 2012).

Interestingly, Llerena and Millot (2013) examine the separate and combined effects of patents and trademarks on the market value of a sample of French-quoted companies. They develop a theoretical model and, based on super-modularity theory, they test whether the two types of IP are complementary or substitute. In line with their theoretical predictions, they find that results differ across sectors. In chemical and pharmaceutical industries, patents, and trademarks tend to be complementary whereas, in high-tech business sectors, where the crucial asset to be protected is the technology rather than the brand, they are found to be substitutes.

In general, there are few contributions encompassing also small and medium firms. An exception is Rogers, Helmers, and Greenhalgh (2007) that cover the UK small and medium firms over the period 2001–2004. They study the effect of the registration of a new trademark over the following years and find that, because of the investment needed to launch an innovation, the profits may initially decrease even when the new product is ultimately successful. In comparison with the other companies, trademark active firms are more concentrated in the lowest and highest quartiles of the profits distribution.

The rest of the paper is organised as follows. The description of the data and the definition of the variables of interest are reported in Section 2. We next present some non-parametric evidence based on univariate kernel density estimations and on the Fligner-Policello test of stochastic equality in Section 4. Section 5 illustrates our empirical strategy and discusses the empirical results. Section 6 concludes.

2. Data and variables of interest

The empirical analysis is based on AIDA (Analisi Informatizzata delle Aziende) and AMADEUS data, two datasets provided by Bureau van Dijk (BvD).

The AIDA dataset provides detailed information on Italian limited liability companies operating in both the manufacturing and service sectors which, in accordance to the law, have to deposit their balance sheets to the Chamber of Commerce. The data provide financial and economic information for Italian firms, as well as a wide set of relevant indicators, including a number of employees, incorporation year and sector of activity, among others.[2]

The AIDA dataset, due to its nature, covers virtually the universe of Italian limited liability firms independently of their size or age, thus representing an ideal set of data to study the dynamics of firms and industries. This is a noteworthy feature with respect to many previous works (see Fang, Palmatier, and Grewal (2011), Chang, Chen, and Huang (2012), Dernis et al. (2015), Daiko et al. (2017) and Dosso and Vezzani (2017), among others) that, due to data constraints, could only focus on top corporate R&D investors or on firms operating in high-tech industries. The time period covered by our empirical analysis spans from 2006 to 2014 and we focus primarily on manufacturing firms, although we verify whether similar results also hold for service firms.[3]

We integrate AIDA data with information on the stock of applied patents[4] and registered trademarks owned by firms in each relevant year. As for patents, AMADEUS provides some relevant information, including international patent classification (IPC), the application date and whether a patent has been granted or not, among others; while, for filed trademarks, one can resort to NICE classification code, the filing date, and information on their registration. In particular, information on the patents and trademarks classifications (IPC and NICE, respectively) are crucial in order to define a measure of economic concordance between the technological fields of the two measures of IP rights.

Before proceeding with some descriptive statistics on the dataset, we illustrate the strategy adopted to characterise firms' innovation activity and the degree of concordance between the domains of knowledge incorporated in the firms' stocks of patents and trademarks, respectively.

2.1. Patents, trademarks, and a measure of IP instruments concordance

In order to obtain a suitable measure of firms' innovation activities as proxied by patents, we consider data on applied patents, irrespectively of the outcome of the application, that have been applied at the United States Patent and Trademark Office (USPTO), at the European Patent Office (EPO), and/or at the Italian Patent and Trademark Office (IPTO).[5] The stock of patents for each firm, in each year, does not include patents

---

[2]We use two AIDA 'historic' disks in the release version of December 2015 and December 2016, respectively. For a detailed description of the procedures followed in building the dataset, refer to Grazzi, Piccardo, and Vergari (2018).
[3]As suggested by the previous literature, see OHIM (2015); Schautschick and Greenhalgh (2016); Graham et al. (2018) among others, patenting activity is mainly observed within manufacturing sectors, while trademarks are of more widespread use independently of the sector of activity. Consistent evidence emerges using the AIDA-AMADEUS dataset in this work. However, in Section 5.2, we replicate our main analysis for firms in service sector, in order to check for potential differences.
[4]We have opted to focus on applied, rather than granted patents, to enlarge as much as possible the sample of observations, given the very small percentage of Italian firms with patents. Results on the smaller sample (granted patents) are also available upon request.
[5]Patents could be owned by more than one firm; in these cases, we associated the patents to each owner, as suggested by the existing literature.

applied more than 20 years before the year of interest. That is, if a patent was applied in 1991 by a firm, we include it in the patent count from 2006 to 2010, but not from 2011 onward. This choice allows us to forego patents which are too 'old' to adequately represent a valuable proxy of firms' technological capabilities.[6] Note that the range of information on patents accessible through BvD is only a subset of what available through PATSTAT, see for instance De Rassenfosse, Dernis, and Boedt (2014). Also note that, as shown in Table 1, only a very small fraction of Italian firms, around 7%, holds patents, see also Malerba and Orsenigo (1999), Cefis and Orsenigo (2001) and the more recent Dosi, Grazzi, and Moschella (2015). One known issue of the literature on IP is the matching to firm-level data. In this respect, note that we are employing patents and trademarks linked to firms as originally provided in BvD AMADEUS.[7]

With regard to trademarks, we focus on registered trademarks that have been filed at the United States Patent and Trademark Office (USPTO) or at the European Union Intellectual Property Office (EUIPO), formerly known as Office for Harmonisation in the Internal Market (OHIM).[8] We identify the stock of registered trademarks for each firm, in each year, by considering trademarks applied before or in the year of interest and expiring after the year of analysis. Unfortunately, differently from patents, AMADEUS does not provide information for registered trademarks also at the national level.[9]

Before proceeding let us also notice that the results that we present in the following are robust to marginal adjustments such as considering a shorter lifetime for both patents and trademarks or applying some discounting factor to patents.

We next define, at the firm level, a variable to measure the degree of concordance between the two classes of IP instruments, patents, and trademarks. For this purpose, we need information on IPC codes associated to each patent and NICE code linked to each trademark.[10] In the AMADEUS dataset, a single patent can be associated with more than one IPC code, while for trademarks only a single NICE code is provided.

---

[6]Czarnitzki and Kraft (2004), Xu and Chiang (2005), Belderbos et al. (2014) and de Rassenfosse and Jaffe (2018), among others, have highlighted the importance to account for the decline in patents' value during the life of patented inventions. Our choice to censor the stock of patents for each firm, in each year, at 20 years is in line with the application of a constant 15% depreciation rate (that is commonly used in the literature in order to discount R&D, patent, and trademark values).

[7]An alternative attempt is provided, still on Italian firms, by Lotti and Marin (2013) on EPO applications which the authors match to a restricted sample of AIDA firms (the so-called, BvD AIDA TOP). In the end, their effort results in 5485 patenting firms over the period 2000–2007. It is however not possible to directly compare the two final datasets. It is true that our displays a higher number of firms with patents (8616 in 2006, see Table 1), but this is most likely due to employing the 'full' AIDA version and, although to a lesser extent, to counting USPTO and IPTO patent applications.

[8]As for patents, also trademarks can be jointly owned by more than one firm; in these cases, we associated the trademarks to each owner, as suggested by the existing literature. Note however that the phenomenon of joint trademark ownership is much more limited with respect to patents.

[9]The lack of applications for trademarks at the national level is of course expected to reduce both the overall stock of trademarks in the country as well as the share of firms holding trademarks. It is however very difficult to find a reference to assess how large is the actual impact on our dataset. To the best of our knowledge, OHIM (2015) provides some guidance in terms of aggregate statistics even if it is at the EU level with no possibility to distinguish among countries. According to OHIM (2015), Table 8 (page 40), '38.1 per cent of all large companies and 8.6 per cent of all SMEs own trademarks', either at national or EU. In our dataset, which includes USPTO and EUIPO trademarks, the corresponding percentages are, respectively (see Table 2) $57.9 \approx (679/1172)$ and $12.4 \approx (3805 + 2653)/(44148+8016)$. Hence, it would not appear that the lack of national trademarks greatly compromises the sample that we employ.

[10]The IPC is a classification for patents and utility models according to the different areas of technology to which they pertain. We use it at the 3-digit level. NICE is a 2-digit international classification of goods (codes from 1 to 34) and services (codes from 35 to 45) applied for the registration of trademarks that has been adopted with the Nice Agreement concluded in 1957 (a summary of the Nice Agreement is available at: https://www.wipo.int/treaties/en/classification/nice/summary_nice.html).

In order to build such concordance measure, we rely on a series of crosswalks linking different classifications of industries, products, IPC and NICE codes, for which we refer to the works of Lybbert and Zolas (2014), Zolas, Lybbert, and Bhattacharyya (2017) and Goldschlag, Lybbert, and Zolas (2016). As a preliminary step, we need to convert the IPC codes and the NICE codes to a common code. In particular, we associate the International Standard Industrial Classification (ISIC) to each IPC and to each NICE code, respectively, relying on the probabilistic algorithms developed by Lybbert and Zolas (2014) and Zolas, Lybbert, and Bhattacharyya (2017). These algorithms provide a concordance of each IPC and NICE code to ISIC codes. Namely, for each 3-digit IPC code several 2-digit ISIC codes may be associated, each with a weight that identifies the likelihood (or strength) of the linkage between that particular IPC code and that particular ISIC code. The sum of these weights is one. Similarly, each 2-digit NICE code is associated to several 2-digit ISIC codes, each with a weight that represents the probability of concordance between that particular NICE code and that particular ISIC code. The sum of these weights is then one.

We obtain the concordance measure between patents and trademarks following a three-step procedure. Note that this measure is provided for any firm with patents and trademarks and it might vary over time. *First*, for each firm (i) and year (t), we identify the sets of 3-digit IPC and 2-digit NICE codes associated to the stock of patents and trademarks, respectively, and we label $N_L^{i,t}$ ($N_K^{i,t}$) the number of IPC (NICE) codes associated to these sets.[11] In the *second* step, considering the ISIC codes and their probability weights,[12] we compute the overlapping coefficient, $overlap_{L-K}$, for each pair (L, K) of IPC and NICE codes.[13] Formally:

$$overlap_{L-K} = \sum_{j=1}^{N_{LK}} min\{p_L(isic_j), p_K(isic_j)\}, \quad (1)$$

where N_{LK} is the number of ISIC codes associated to each pair of 3-digit IPC and 2-digit NICE codes, $p_L(isic_j)$ is the probability weight that identifies the likelihood of the linkage between IPC code L and ISIC code j, and $p_K(isic_j)$ is the likelihood of the linkage between NICE code K and ISIC code j. The overlapping coefficient is higher than zero only when both the IPC and NICE codes are linked to at least one common ISIC code. Indeed, the probability weights in Equation (1) are both positive only when an ISIC code is associated to both IPC and NICE codes. Contrarily, if an ISIC code is not linked to either IPC or NICE code, the probability weight is set equal to zero.[14] In the *third* and final step, we

---

[11]Clearly, we do not account for patents and trademarks without information on the IPC and NICE codes.

[12]For the methodology and weights refer to works of Lybbert and Zolas (2014), Zolas, Lybbert, and Bhattacharyya (2017) and Goldschlag, Lybbert, and Zolas (2016).

[13]The overlapping coefficient is a measure of agreement (or similarity) which refers to the area under two probability density functions simultaneously. Notice that the overlapping coefficient between an IPC and a NICE code is not firm or time specific.

[14]Note that this overlapping measure is quite intuitive. Indeed, for each pair of IPC and NICE codes we end up with a number of common ISIC codes, and for each common ISIC code we have two weights: one representing the probability of concordance between that particular IPC code and that particular ISIC code, the other representing the probability of concordance between that particular NICE code and that same particular ISIC code. The probability of concordance can be calculated as the minimum of the pairwise likelihood of the match between those IPC and NICE codes. This is in line with the proximity measure proposed by Hidalgo et al. (2007) to analyse the role of the existing production structure on the regions pattern of specialisation as well as with the technology proximity measure developed by Colombelli, Krafft, and Quatraro (2014) that study the path-dependent emergence of new technological fields focusing on the nanotechnology sector, in the EU 15 countries in the period 1986–2006.

compute, for each firm and year, the degree of concordance between (the stock of IPC and NICE codes associated to) the stock of patents and trademarks. In particular, as shown in Equation (2), for each firm (i) in each year (t), we sum all the overlapping coefficients identified for each pair of IPC (L) and NICE (K) codes ($overlap_{L-K}$). Moreover, we normalise our measure dividing it by the product between the number of elements in the set of 3-digit IPC codes ($N_L^{i,t}$) and the number of elements in the set of 2-digit NICE codes ($N_K^{i,t}$).

$$conc_{i,t} = (\sum_{L=1}^{N_L^{i,t}} \sum_{K=1}^{N_K^{i,t}} overlap_{L-K})/(N_L^{i,t} * N_K^{i,t}) \tag{2}$$

The degree of concordance takes value zero if there are no common ISIC codes associated to the two sets of IPC and NICE codes, while strictly positive and higher values of $conc_{i,t}$ suggest higher concordance between the stocks of patents and trademarks. Notice that the measure we are proposing captures the degree of concordance between the stock of unique IPC and NICE codes associated to the stock of patents and trademarks of the firm. Accounting for unique IPC codes enables us to insulate against the existence of patents related to the same innovation (patent families) that cannot be identified in our data. As a robustness check, we also verify that the measure of concordance and its effect on firms' performance do not significantly change when considering, in building the measure, the number of patents and trademarks, as well as the number of times the IPC/NICE classifications appear in each patent and trademark.

Let us describe in a nutshell how the procedure actually works. Consider as an example a firm with one patent and one trademark. We exploit the crosswalk from IPC to ISIC codes (and we get a set, say A, of ISIC codes associated to the set of IPC codes of the unique patent). Analogously, we map NICE to ISIC codes (and we get a set, say B of ISIC codes associated to the set of NICE codes of its unique trademark), and then we analyse to which extent these two sets of ISIC codes (A and B) overlap. Suppose that these two IP rights are characterised by IPC and NICE codes that map in the same ISIC codes (suppose also with the same weights), so that sets A and B perfectly overlap and we would get a measure of concordance equal to one ($conc_{i,t} = 1$).[15] For illustrative purposes, in Appendix A, we provide an example from our database on how to construct this measure.[16]

3. Descriptive statistics

We next present some of the main highlights of the dataset that will be employed in the empirical analysis.

---

[15]Alternative procedures such as mapping IPC to ISIC codes and then ISIC to NICE codes of the firm (or, vice versa going from NICE to ISIC codes and then from ISIC to IPC codes) would of course be possible, but they would complicate the analysis and would underestimate the concordance measure as they would imply going through double weighting.

[16]Note that, as common to empirical investigations with firm-level data, our measure is potentially sensitive to relevant events affecting the life-cycle of a firm such as mergers and acquisitions. Consider two firms characterised by the maximal degree of concordance: each of them has only patents in technological fields perfectly related to its products (trademarks). Clearly, if these two firms merge, and their sets of IPC and NICE codes do not coincide, the degree of concordance of the new firm decreases. Of course, this issue is related to the impossibility to appropriately deal with such events in standard firm-level data.

3.1. Distribution of patents and trademarks

Table 1 reports the distribution of trademarks and patents for firms in the manufacturing sector. As expected on the basis of prior literature, the fraction of Italian firms owning IP instruments is very small and it displays different trends for patents and trademarks. Note indeed that the proportion of firms owning at least one registered European trademark increases during the period of investigation (from 4.062% of firms in 2006 to 6.857% in 2014); while it is not the same for the fraction of firms owning at least one patent (it is around 7% in each year).[17] Quite interestingly, in more recent years, the number of firms with European trademarks exceeds the number of firms with patents. This points to the increasing importance of trademarks as an instrument to protect IP, at least among Italian firms. However, also note, as shown by the last two columns of Table 1, that the total number of patents of Italian firms, even if decreasing in more recent years, is still bigger than the number of trademarks.[18] Thus, we can conclude that, at least in Italy, ownership of patents, differently from trademarks, is concentrated in a narrower set of companies and that trademarks are becoming more diffused as an instrument of IP protection. As suggested in Hall et al. (2013), the concentration of patent ownership might be related to the fact that '(a) some firms do not automatically patent all of their patentable inventions, (b) some firms avoid the patent system altogether, either because of its cost or because patenting is perceived to yield no additional benefit, and (c) some

Table 1. Number of firms, trademarks, and patents.

Year	Firms	Firms with tm (%) *	Firms with pat (%)*	Firms with tm and pat (%) *	Firms with $conc_{i,t} > 0$ (%) * *	Num of tm	Num of pat
2006	116507	4732 (4.062)	8616 (7.359)	1798 (1.543)	1623 (90.267)	13190	77312
2007	123007	5340 (4.341)	8884 (7.222)	2018 (1.641)	1822 (90.287)	15582	82797
2008	129334	6040 (4.670)	9100 (7.036)	2237 (1.730)	2013 (89.987)	18508	87536
2009	135091	6679 (4.944)	9261 (6.855)	2389 (1.768)	2147 (89.870)	21243	91482
2010	141070	7396 (5.243)	9506 (6.738)	2601 (1.844)	2347 (90.235)	24442	95635
2011	138641	8011 (5.778)	9591 (6.918)	2772 (1.999)	2499 (90.152)	27485	99510
2012	135299	8616 (6.368)	9419 (6.962)	2891 (2.137)	2606 (90.142)	30384	101552
2013	132731	9070 (6.833)	9062 (6.827)	2927 (2.205)	2644 (90.331)	32612	98872
2014	129253	8863 (6.857)	8608 (6.660)	2830 (2.190)	2556 (90.318)	31740	93229

We only consider firms operating in manufacturing sectors (we exclude firms operating in the following 2-digit ATECO 2007 code: 12 and 33).
* In brackets, percentage of total firms.
* * In brackets, as a percentage of firms with trademarks and patents.

---

[17] Such similar percentages of firms with patents and firms with trademarks might also be related to the absence of IPTO trademarks.

[18] A similar trend in the number of patents has been reported also by the Italian Observatory for patents, *Osservatorio Italiano Brevetti*, Osservatorio Italiano Brevetti (2014). Considering patents applied at the Italian Patent and Trademark Office (IPTO) from both Italian and foreign firms, the Observatory highlights a reduction in the number of applied patents starting from 2011.

innovations involve inventions that are not patentable.' Further, it also exists a size threshold below which firms find it more difficult to afford the cost related to the functioning of a formal R&D laboratory. To complete the picture, also notice that around 7% of firms with patents are involved in co-ownership (*co-patents*) and the number of the co-owned patents has increased over the years (the share of patents with more than one owner rises from 2.694% in 2006 to 3.145% in 2014).[19]

Note that due to the small number of firms owning IP rights in general, when we restrict to the sub-sample of firms with *both* patents *and* trademarks, we are left only with around 2% of the firms making up the original dataset, column (5) of Table 1. The share of firms owning both patents and trademarks slightly increases over time, from 1.543% in 2006 to 2.190% in 2014. Focusing on the concordance between IP instruments, around 90% of firms reporting both patents and trademarks, column (6) of Table 1, displays a strictly positive value for the degree of concordance, $conc_{i,t}$, as defined in Equation (2). Among these firms, the average degree of concordance is around 0.18. The whole distribution is plotted in Figure 1 and it does not vary much over time because, at the firm level, the value of the concordance measure is quite stable over the years. In turn, this is due to the poor dynamics in patenting and trademarking, that is, very few firms are registering or applying for new trademarks or patents over the time span covered by the database; hence also the measure does not change much over time. Unfortunately, the co-occurrence of a very low number of firms with both IP and a poor underlying dynamics do not make the 'Italian case' the ideal test-bed for the measure we are proposing here.

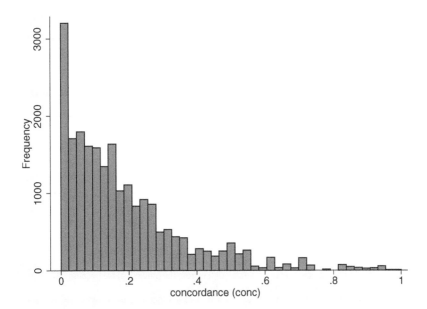

Figure 1. Distribution of the measure of IP concordance.

---

[19]In the interest of space, we do not show descriptive statistics considering co-ownership of patents. They are available upon request.

Finally, note that the proposed concordance measure, at least for the sample under investigation, appears to be independent from the size of the firm. The correlation coefficients between firm size and the concordance measure is around -0.001 in the manufacturing and -0.03 in the service sector.

3.2. Distribution of patents and trademarks according to firm size and sector

Table 2 shows the distribution of patents and trademarks across firms according to their size in 2014. The size classes are defined conforming to the Eurostat definition.[20] We consider four size classes: 'micro' firms with less than 10 workers; 'small' with workers ranging between 10 and 49; 'medium' between 50 and 249 and 'large' with more than 250 workers.[21]

Consistently with the actual population of Italian firms, also in our dataset the highest share of firms is represented by micro-firms (around 58%). The share of small firms is around 35%, while large firms are only less than 1%. Due to the shape of the firm size distribution, in absolute numbers, the two categories of SMEs are those more represented in terms of IP's holders, and represent the highest share of firms with concordant patents and trademarks (around 32% and 43% of firms with concordant IP rights, respectively). Note however that, in relative terms, while around 55% (645/1172) of large firms are patent holders, the relative share shrinks, respectively, to 30% for medium and to 8.6% for small firms.

Looking at the number of patents and trademarks we note that the largest number of trademarks falls in the medium class (around 35% of the total number of trademarks), while the highest share of patents is owned by large firms (around 42% of the total). In this respect, the descriptive evidence for Italy confirms the findings from previous studies

Table 2. Number of firms, trademarks, and patents for micro, small, medium, and large firms. Year 2014.

Size	Firms (%) *	Firms with tm(%) *	Firms with pat (%)*	Firms with tm and pat(%) *	Firms with $conc_{i,t} > 0$ (%) * *	Num of tm (%) * *	Num of pat (%) * *
0–9	73641	1668	1673	223	187	3076	5910
	(57.996)	(18.944)	(19.556)	(7.911)	(7.345)	(9.736)	(6.366)
10–49	44148	3805	3805	933	805	9356	20141
	(34.769)	(43.214)	(44.477)	(33.097)	(31.618)	(29.612)	(21.695)
50–249	8016	2653	2432	1208	1114	11246	27599
	(6.313)	(30.131)	(28.428)	(42.852)	(43.755)	(35.594)	(29.728)
250 and more	1172	679	645	455	440	7917	39187
	(0.923)	(7.712)	(7.539)	(16.140)	(17.282)	(25.058)	(42.211)

We only consider firms operating in manufacturing sectors (we exclude firms operating in the following 2-digit ATECO 2007 code: 12 and 33). The number of firms in this Table differs from the previous Table because 2276 firms do not have information on their size, measured in terms of workers, in 2014.
* In brackets, percentage of total firms, total firms with trademarks, patents, trademarks, and patents, concordant trademarks and patents, respectively.
* * In brackets, percentage of total number of trademarks and patents, respectively.

---

[20]The classification is available at: http://ec.europa.eu/eurostat/statistics-explained/index.php/Glossary:Enterprise_size
[21]Eurostat classification refers to the number of workers, thus including also the entrepreneur(s). AIDA dataset originally reports the number of employees and, as obvious, many SMEs report no employees. Hence, to make the two figures comparable, we approximate the number of workers as the number of employees plus one.

highlighting a higher propensity to patent for large firms and identify trademarks as the main IP instrument for small and medium firms (see Mendonça, Pereira, and Godinho (2004), Blind et al. (2006), Leiponen and Byma (2009) and Flikkema, De Man, and Castaldi (2014) among others).

Finally, focusing on the manufacturing sector, Table B1, in Appendix B, reports the distribution of patents and trademarks according to the sector of economic activity. Trademarks are mostly concentrated in food products (ATECO 10, with around 14% of total number of trademarks), manufacture of machinery and equipment n.e.c. (ATECO 28, with around 11% of total number of trademarks), chemical products, and wearing apparel (ATECO 20 and 14, both with around 8% of total number of trademarks). Sectors reporting the highest number of patents are manufacture of machinery and equipment n. e.c. (ATECO 28, with around 29% of total number of patents), manufacture of computer, electronic and optical products (ATECO 26, with around 13% of total number of patents) and manufacture of fabricated metal products, except machinery and equipment (ATECO 25, with around 11% of total number of patents).

3.3. The timing of applications

In addition to the analysis of IP bundles of firms and of their internal concordance, it is also much relevant to investigate if any regularity emerges in terms of the timing of applications for patents *vis à vis* trademarks. In this respect, our prior would be that in a given process of innovation, moving from the original concept, to the technological development of the product and finally to market introduction, the patent application, being more technology related, pre-dates the trademark application, which is more related to bringing the innovation to the market (see also the contribution of Mendonça, Pereira, and Godinho 2004; Aaker 2007; Helmers and Rogers 2010; Llerena and Millot 2013; Flikkema, De Man, and Castaldi 2014). In our dataset, as in most to date, we cannot directly observe: (a) which IP is related to a given product or line of business and, as a consequence, (b) the timing with which firms resort to patents and trademarks along the innovation process. We can only indirectly infer the existence of such a sequential timing by exploiting positive occurrences of our concordance measure to identify innovation processes that we can expect to be related to the same product (or line of business). In particular, we consider, in each year and for each firm, the pairs of 3-digit IPC and 2-digit NICE codes associated to the stock of patents and trademarks, for which the overlapping coefficient is higher than zero, that is, when we are inclined to expect that the patent and the trademark are related to the same line of product. Moreover, for each pair of IPC and NICE codes, for each firm and year, we account for the least recent patent and trademark in the firm portfolio. Our descriptive evidence provides only mild support to our hypothesis on the relative timing: depending on the year of analysis, in 50% to 55% of such IPC-NICE pairs the patent pre-dates the trademark.[22] Moreover, focusing on young firms, that is, considering only firms with age lower than 5 years (or alternatively 10 years) our data reveal that the percentage of IPC-NICE pairs for which patent pre-

---

[22]Dinlersoz et al. (forthcoming) perform a similar exercise on the relative timing for R&D, patents and trademark filings and report mild evidence in the opposite direction for US firms. Notice however that they do not employ any concordance measure.

dates trademark is even smaller and ranges between 53% and 43% (49% and 44% focusing on firms with age lower than 10 years) depending on the year of analysis. This is in line with the trademark literature revealing that many start-ups file trademarks very early on in order to attract venture capital (e.g. Zhou et al. 2016; Seip et al. 2018).

4. Non-parametric evidence

4.1. Comparison of the empirical distributions of firms' performance

Before proceeding with more standard econometric analysis we report evidence from univariate kernel density estimations, which allows us to graphically compare the performance of different groups of firms.

We compare the empirical distributions of firms' performance across four groups of firms: without IP instruments, owning only trademarks, owning only patents and firms with both patents and trademarks. In the following, we will refer to the firms of the first group as *non-innovative* and to the rest as *innovative* firms. We warn the reader that this distinction is made for the sake of the exposition only, firms might well opt for other modes to appropriate the returns from innovation. We proxy firms' performance by, alternatively, firms' total revenues in log ($ln(totrev_{i,t})$), yearly growth rate ($growth_{i,t}$), measured as the logarithmic difference between firms total revenues in two consecutive years,[23] and profitability ($ebitda\_sales_{i,t}$). We measure profitability as the ratio between EBITDA and sales (multiplied by 100), where EBITDA stands for earnings before interest, taxes, depreciation, and amortisation.[24] For the sake of completeness, we estimate kernel densities focusing on the first (2006) and last (2014) available years in the dataset, note however that there is not much intertemporal variation.

4.2. Innovative vs. non-innovative firms

Graphically, we identify relevant differences between groups of firms in terms of total revenues. As reported in Figure 2, firms without any IP instrument underperform firms with patents and/or trademarks in terms of revenues. Among innovative firms, those with both patents and trademarks tend to show higher values in terms of total revenues; while firms owning only trademarks or only patents display similar distributions. In terms of profitability, the graphical comparison displays that firms with IP rights outperform firms without patents and trademarks. On the contrary, these groups of firms do not seem to differ much in terms of growth rates. The only feature that is possible to appreciate for growth is the higher concentration around the mean for firms with both patents and trademarks, which might of course be related to the larger size (and smaller variance of growth rates) of firms with both IP.[25]

---

[23]As a robustness check, we alternatively compute firms' growth rates following the methodology suggested by Davis, Haltiwanger, and Schuh (1998), that allows us to account for firms' entry and exit. The use of this alternative specification for the growth rate does not change our conclusions on the relationship between firms' growth and their use of IP instruments. Results are available upon request.

[24]In order to mitigate problems related to measurement errors, we do not account for values of the profitability larger than 100 and lower than −300, the latter corresponding roughly to the bottom percentile of the distribution. In this way, over a total number of 1,180,933 observations for ebitda_sales, we remove around 15,000 observations.

[25]In the interest of space, we do not show graphical comparisons for growth and profitability, but they are available upon request.

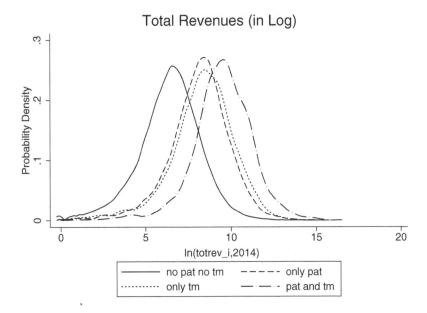

Figure 2. Empirical distribution of Total Revenues (in log) in 2014, *innovative* vs *non-innovative* firms.

The descriptive evidence on Italian firms is in line with the existing empirical literature, which reports higher performance for firms with IP instruments, even employing different measures of firm performance. In particular, given limited data availability on the universe, many contributions focus on market values of quoted companies or on specific sectors of the economy. Greenhalgh and Rogers (2012) and Sandner and Block (2011), among others, report a positive impact of both measures of IP on the markets' valuation of firms. Dosso and Vezzani (2017) and Llerena and Millot (2013) analyse and identify a positive influence of the combined use of patents and trademarks on firms' market value only for some industrial sectors. Graham, and Somaya (2004), focusing on the software industry, also report evidence in favour of the complementarity hypothesis. Moreover, Zhou et al. (2016) identify a positive impact of the joint use of patents and trademarks on the start-up amount of venture capital funding. Other studies investigate the effect of patent and trademark activity on firms' survival and identify a positive correlation between these two measures of IP and a higher increase in the expected life span of firms (e.g. Jensen, Webster, and Buddelmeyer 2008; Buddelmeyer, Jensen, and Webster 2010; Helmers and Rogers 2010; Wagner and Cockburn 2010).

4.3. Innovative firms: concordant vs. non-concordant IP rights

We now focus our attention on the restricted sample of firms with both patents and trademarks, and we divide these firms into two groups according to whether their degree of concordance, $conc_{i,t}$ as defined in Equation (2), is strictly positive (firms with concordant patents and trademarks) or nil. We graphically compare the distributions of these two groups. As exhibited in Figure 3, firms with concordant patents and trademarks

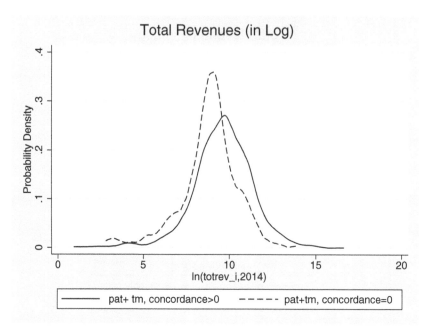

Figure 3. Empirical distribution of Total Revenues (in log) in 2014, concordant patents and trademarks vs. non-concordant.

mildly outperform those without concordant IP instruments in terms of total revenues.[26] Contrarily, kernel density estimations do not show any difference in terms of growth and profitability for the two groups of firms.[27]

4.4. Fligner-policello test of stochastic equality

To confer statistical accuracy to the graphical analysis reported above, we perform non-parametric Fligner-Policello (FP henceforth) test of stochastic equality, proposed by Fligner and Policello (1981) to compare *innovative* and *non-innovative* firms. As FP test allows to compare two groups at a time, we gather together firms with any proxy of innovative activity (firms owning only trademarks, only patents and both). The test is defined as follows. Let F_I and F_{NI} be the distributions of the relevant variables of *innovative* and *non-innovative* firms, respectively. Denote with $X_I \sim F_I$ and $X_{NI} \sim F_{NI}$ the associated random variables, and with X_I and X_{NI} two respective realisations. The distribution F_I is said to stochastically dominate F_{NI} if $Prob\{X_I > X_{NI}\} > 1/2$, where

$$Prob\{X_I > X_{NI}\} = \int dF_I(X) F_{NI}(X).$$ The null hypothesis in the FP test implies equality

of median among the compared distributions.

For each relevant variable (total revenues, growth, and profitability) we compare, *innovative* with *non-innovative* firms in years 2006 and 2014, respectively. A positive sign

---

[26]The graphical comparison between the two groups of firms in terms of growth and profitability is available upon request.
[27]Note that the non-parametric analysis only provides descriptive evidence. In order to take into consideration the size affect, we control for size in all the specifications included in the parametric analysis below.

of the FP statistic means that *innovative* firms have a higher likelihood to take on larger values of a given relevant variable (i.e. the distribution of *innovative* firms stochastically dominates the distribution of *non-innovative* firms), and the opposite holds if the statistic takes a negative sign.[28]

FP statistics show that *innovative* firms perform better with respect to *non-innovative* firms in terms of total revenues and profitability, while they do not appear to differ in terms of growth, in both years considered. FP statistics are thus confirming the descriptive evidence of the plots above.

Focusing on firms with both patents and trademarks, we perform the FP test in order to compare performance between the two groups of firms with concordant IP instruments and firms without such concordance. Similarly to the graphical comparisons, firms with concordant IP instruments result to be characterised by higher total revenues. However, no relevant difference is found for growth and profitability.

5. Parametric analysis of firms' performance

In this section, we investigate the effects of patents and trademarks on firms' performance resorting to parametric analysis. The dependent variable, $Y_{i,t}$, is firms' performance proxied by, alternatively (the log of) firms' total revenues ($ln(totrev_{i,t})$), yearly growth rate ($growth_{i,t}$), and profitability ($ebitda\_sales_{i,t}$).

We relate $Y_{i,t}$ to the innovation indicators and other controls through the following baseline specification:

$$Y_{i,t} = \beta_1 nopattm_{i,t-1} + \beta_2 tm_{i,t-1} + \beta_3 pat_{i,t-1} + \beta_4 both_{i,t-1}$$
$$+ \beta_5 ln(workers_{i,t-1}) + \beta_6 ln(LP_{i,t-1}) + X'_{i,t}\alpha + u_{i,t} \qquad (3)$$

where i denotes firms and t years. The explanatory variables that we are mostly interested in consist of four dummy variables $nopattm_{i,t-1}$, $tm_{i,t-1}$, $pat_{i,t-1}$ and $both_{i,t-1}$ equal to 1 if firms, respectively, do not own any IP right, own at least one registered trademark (but not patents), at least one (applied) patent (but not trademarks), both trademarks and patents. Resorting to a patent (and trademark) status is quite standard in the literature (see, e.g. Zhou et al. 2016; Guzman and Stern 2015; Llerena and Millot 2013; Hall et al. 2013; Cassiman and Veugelers 2006). This is true both for countries with very few patenting firms, see for instance Dosi, Grazzi, and Moschella (2015) on a similar dataset of Italian firms, and also in making international comparison of the propensity of firms to resort to IP, as in Lin and Lincoln (2017). Further motivation for the use of dummy variables for trademark and patent activities (also in line with Zhou et al. 2016) is that, in our sample, the majority of firms does not have any patent or trademark; among firms with IP instruments, the distribution of patents is much more heterogeneous than that of trademarks.[29] Finally, it is worth noting that the use of these dummy variables insulate us against potential bias related to employing patents and trademarks counts, if, as in our case, one cannot take into account their quality (as proxied by indicators such as forward citations, patent oppositions, and the size of patent families), see, e.g. Sandner and Block

---

[28]In the interest of space, we do not show the FP tests, but they are available upon request.
[29]The median number of patents and trademarks (excluding firms without such instruments) is, respectively, 3 and 2. Patents vary in the range 1–7174 while trademarks take values between 1 and 100.

(2011), Blind, Cremers, and Mueller (2009). As put forth in previous works (see, e.g. among others, Llerena and Millot 2013; Cassiman and Veugelers 2006), to ease the interpretation of coefficients and to allow us to test for complementarity between patents and trademarks, we include all the four exclusive IP strategy dummy indicators in the regressions, thus without the constant term.[30] These dummy variables are mutually exclusive so that we can better identify the different IP strategies of the firms; at the same time, we avoid problems of multicollinearity due to the high correlation between firms' trademarks and patents. Moreover, we include among independent variables firms' size, measured by the logarithmic transformation of the number of workers $(ln(workers_{i,t-1}))$ and the logarithmic transformation of labour productivity $(ln(LP_{i,t-1}))$.[31] In order to reduce the potential endogeneity of our regressors, these variables are lagged one period with respect to the dependent variable.[32] In the regression, we account for a vector of controls, $X'_{i,t}$, which includes: a set of 2-digit ATECO industry dummy variables; three geographical area dummy variables which identify firms operating in the North, Centre or South of Italy, respectively; and nine year dummies (2006–2014). These binary variables allow us to control for time-invariant sectoral effects, for the omission of geographical specific time-invariant characteristics which might bias our parameter estimates and, for the economic cycle and common macro-economic factors, respectively.[33]

In order to assess whether the concordance between firms' stocks of patents and trademarks positively impact on firms' performance, in an extended specification, we also include the degree of concordance between IP rights, $conc_{i,t-1}$, as defined in Equation (2), with a reporting lag of 1 year. Clearly, this specification only includes firms with both patents and trademarks. For these firms the dummy variable $both_{i,t-1}$ is equal to one, while all the other dummy variables for IP strategies ($nopattm_{i,t-1}$, $tm_{i,t-1}$ and $pat_{i,t-1}$) are equal to zero, thus we remove the four binary indicators for IP instruments among the regressors. Moving from the baseline specification to this extended one, the number of observations significantly decreases (from more than 600,000 to less than 18,000). In order to verify if results are driven by the lower number of observations, we also re-estimate the baseline specification on the sub-sample of firms with both patents and trademarks.[34]

We resort to Pooled OLS models for two reasons. First, given the rather poor dynamics in the patenting (trademarking) activities of Italian firms (i.e. firms are not registering or applying for many new trademarks or patents every year), for many

---

[30]We build the four dummy variables based on the yearly number of patents and registered trademarks owned by firms. For more details on the construction of patents and trademarks stocks refer to Section 2.1.

[31]Labour productivity is computed as the ratio between added value and number of workers.

[32]In order to account for the potential endogeneity between labour productivity and the indicators for innovation activities, we have also estimated a structural model following the methodology originally proposed in Crepon, Duguet, and Mairesse (1998). The results, which are quite reassuring, are not shown here in the interest of space, but are available upon request.

[33]Focusing on firms' growth as a measure of performance, our regression model is in line with specifications suggested by the applied literature which empirically tests the validity of Gibrat's law (see Santarelli, Klomp, and Thurik (2006) for an exhaustive survey of empirical studies testing Gibrat's law). In this literature, firms' growth is modelled as a function of the initial size. Moreover, this baseline specification has been extended in order to account for several major control variables in level, such as productivity, export, external finance, and R&D activity as well as others. We refer to, within the very vast literature that investigates the growth of firms, Gibrat (1931); Penrose (1959); Evans (1987a, 1987b); Doms, Dunne, and Roberts (1995); Del Monte and Papagni (2003); Garca-Manjón and Romero-Merino (2012).

[34]Correlation tables for the variables included in our specifications are available upon request.

companies the number of patents (trademarks) does not change over the period of observation, hence, for these firms, the effect of IP would get confounded with the firm fixed effect. Secondly, as shown by Angrist and Pischke (2008), estimating fully saturated dummy variables models with OLS is fully general, regardless of the distribution of the dependent variable. However, as robustness check we verify that, using similar specifications and accounting for firm-fixed effects our results do not vary.[35]

Results, shown in Table 3, suggest that firms' innovative capacity is positively associated with performance. In particular, coherently with the non-parametric results, estimates show that patents and trademarks exert a positive impact on firms' total revenues, growth, and profitability. More in detail, let β_1, β_2, β_3 and β_4 denote the coefficients of firms without IP rights, firms owning only trademarks, firms owning only patents and firms owning both patents and trademarks, respectively. The estimates report coefficients that are larger for the group of firms owning both IP instruments rather than either patents or trademarks. Our results suggest that having both patents and trademarks results in around a 32.2% increase in total revenues, a 7.5% increase in firms' growth and a 3.08% increase in profitability compared with not having both IP instruments,[36] while having only trademarks or only patents have a lower effect.

In order to confer statistical precision to the results above, we verify the order of the coefficients for the IP binary variables performing a series of one-sided Wald-tests. A first set of tests (that we label H1_a, H1_b, and H1_c in Table 3) reveals that, independently of the measure of performance considered, firms show higher performance if they own any IP right. We find that coefficients β_2, β_3 and β_4 are statistically larger than β_1.[37] Moreover, in a second set of tests (that we label H1_d and H1_e), we compare, on one hand, the magnitude of the coefficients of firms owning either only trademarks or patents (that is β_2, and β_3, respectively), and, on the other hand, the magnitude of the coefficients for the group of firms owning both patents and trademarks (that is β_4). Tests show that owning both IP rights has a higher impact than owning only one of the two IP instruments on all measures of performance (that is, $\beta_4 > \beta_2$ and $\beta_4 > \beta_3$).[38] Note, however, that this result is not sufficient to conclude for the existence of complementarity effects on the performance of the joint ownership of patents and trademarks.

In order to assess the potential complementarity in performance of these two IP rights, we rely on the theory of super-modularity (Milgrom and Roberts 1990, 1995) according to which two activities are complementary if adding one (e.g. trademarks) while the other is already being performed (e.g. patents) has a higher incremental effect on performance than adding this activity (e.g. trademarks) in isolation. Thus, we can assert that patents and trademarks display complementarity if the following inequality holds[39]

---

[35]Results accounting for firms fixed effects are available upon request.

[36]The effect of having both IP on firms' performance is computed as follows: $(\beta_4-\beta_1)*100$ when we consider total revenues and growth as a measure of performance and $(\beta_4-\beta_1)$ when use profitability as a proxy for performance. Similarly, it is possible to identify the effect of having either only trademarks or patents on firms' performances, using the estimated coefficients β_2 and β_3, respectively. Our results suggest that having only trademarks results in around a 31% increase in total revenues, a 5% increase in firms' growth and a 0.75% increase in profitability compared with not having both IP instruments. Moreover, having only patents results in around a 17% increase in total revenues, a 3% increase in firms' growth and a 0.74% increase in profitability compared with not having IP instruments.

[37]In Table 3 (columns 1,4 and 7) we reject the following null hypotheses: H0_a: $\beta_2 \leq \beta_1$, H0_b: $\beta_3 \leq \beta_1$ and H0_c: $\beta_4 \leq \beta_1$.

[38]The null hypotheses are H0_d: $\beta_4 \leq \beta_2$ and H0_e: $\beta_4 \leq \beta_3$.

[39]The same condition can be expressed as follows: $\beta_4 - \beta_2 > \beta_3 - \beta_1$.:

Table 3. POOLED OLS estimates. Dummy variables for IP strategies. MANUFACTURING SECTOR.

	(1)	(2)	(3)	(4)	(5)	(6)	(7)	(8)	(9)
	ln(totrev_i,t)	ln(totrev_i,t)	ln(totrev_i,t)	growth_i,t	growth_i,t	growth_i,t	ebitda_sales_i,t	ebitda_sales_i,t	ebitda_sales_i,t
nopattm_i,t-1	2.772***			0.286***			0.897***		
	(0.00873)			(0.00584)			(0.200)		
tm_i,t-1	3.078***			0.338***			1.654***		
	(0.0102)			(0.00677)			(0.238)		
pat_i,t-1	2.941***			0.321***			1.638***		
	(0.00998)			(0.00664)			(0.235)		
both_i,t-1	3.094***			0.361***			3.980***		
	(0.0109)			(0.00731)			(0.251)		
ln(workers_i,t-1)	0.898***	0.965***	0.965***	-0.0183***	-0.00521*	-0.00523*	-1.505***	0.363***	0.362***
	(0.000920)	(0.00437)	(0.00437)	(0.000616)	(0.00310)	(0.00310)	(0.0236)	(0.101)	(0.101)
ln(LP_i,t-1)	0.742***	0.782***	0.782***	-0.0538***	-0.0110	-0.0110	3.595***	7.189***	7.186***
	(0.00166)	(0.0138)	(0.0138)	(0.00123)	(0.00960)	(0.00958)	(0.0420)	(0.331)	(0.331)
conc_i,t-1			-0.0210			-0.0153			-0.610
			(0.0275)			(0.0185)			(0.591)
_cons		2.599***	2.605***		0.123**	0.127**		-19.20***	-19.03***
		(0.0797)	(0.0789)		(0.0572)	(0.0552)		(1.722)	(1.715)
N	686252	17929	17929	684323	17917	17917	680718	17869	17869
r2	0.987	0.877	0.877	0.0261	0.0444	0.0445	0.116	0.141	0.141
F	2183334.0.6	2069.7	2008.3	456.9	28.30	27.45	3425.6	29.07	28.28
H1_a: $\beta_2 > \beta_1$	4961.41***			431.35***			50.84***		
H1_b: $\beta_3 > \beta_1$	2123.85***			235.19***			58.62***		
H1_c: $\beta_4 > \beta_1$	4518.83***			625.97***			777.25***		
H1_d: $\beta_4 > \beta_2$	8.27***			45.53***			291.18***		
H1_e: $\beta_4 > \beta_3$	821.28***			142.73***			327.36***		
H1_f: $\beta_4 - \beta_3 > \beta_2 - \beta_1$	528.54			9.62			95.48***		

Robust standard errors in parentheses.

$* p < 0.10$, $** p < 0.05$, $*** p < 0.01$.

In each specification, we include ATECO 2 digit sectors, geographical areas and years dummy variables.

All tests are one-tailed since the hypotheses are directional.

$$\beta_4 - \beta_3 > \beta_2 - \beta_1 \qquad (4)$$

The one-sided Wald test reported in Table 3 (H1_f), column 7, suggests that we can reject the null hypothesis of absence of complementarity between patents and trademarks only for profitability. Thus, there is statistical evidence that having both patents and trademarks is a superior IP strategy with respect to having only one of the two IP rights in order to increase firms' profitability. On the contrary, we do not find evidence of complementarity on revenues and growth (we refer to the tests reported in columns 1 and 4, respectively).

It is not obvious to compare our results to the extant literature as, to our knowledge, we are the first to investigate the role of patents and trademarks on the entire population of firms, hence including also SMEs and micro ones. To the extent that such comparison is possible, our results are coherent with Zhou et al. (2016) who find that start-ups with both patents and trademarks obtain higher amount of venture capital funding than firms with only one of the two IP instruments. As for the combined effect of IP rights on firms' performance, our results on the absence of complementarity between patents and trademarks, when we consider revenues and growth as measures of performance, are in line with Llerena and Millot (2013). Considering firms' market value, the authors do not find any evidence of complementarity between patenting and trademarking activities on the whole sample of publicly-traded French firms. They find however that complementarity (substitutability) between IP strategies varies across sectors. In particular, they identify a positive-combined effect for firms operating in chemical and pharmaceutical industries (they find a negative-combined effect for firms operating in high-tech sectors). Also, Dosso and Vezzani (2017) show that having both patents and trademarks implies higher firms' market value only for the automobile sector.

As far as the comparison between the two IP instruments is concerned, our estimates suggest that firms owning only trademarks show higher revenues and growth than firms with only patents. On the contrary, the impact of having only trademarks and the effect of having only patents do not differ when we consider profitability as proxy of firms' performance.[40] These results differ from Guzman and Stern (2015) and Castaldi and Dosso (2018) that focus on firms' growth as a measure of performance. In particular, Guzman and Stern (2015) identify a higher effect of patents, compared to the effect of trademarks, on the start-up probability of achieving a meaningful growth outcome. Conversely, focusing on top R&D investors, Castaldi and Dosso (2018) find only an indirect impact of trademarks on growth, with trademarks only mitigating the negative effect of patents on firm growth.

Focusing on the degree of concordance between the stock of patents and trademarks, as proxied by our proposed measure, parametric estimates do not suggest a significant relationship between the concordance of firms' IP rights and performance. Indeed, the degree of concordance never shows up as significant. We are cautious in interpreting this as suggesting the irrelevance of such measure, but rather consider this as the consequence of the very small number of Italian firms for which it is possible to compute the measure,

---

[40]More precisely, the one-sided Wald-tests comparing the magnitude of coefficients β_2 and β_3 of Table 3 (not shown in the interest of space), support this evidence: in columns 1 and 4, coefficients β_2 are bigger than coefficients β_3 (they are 3.078 and 2.941 in column 1 and 0.338 and 0.321 in column 4, respectively); whereas, coefficients β_2 and β_3 in column 7 do not statistically differ (they are 1.654 and 1.638, respectively). These tests are available upon request.

that is, less than 2% of the complete sample.[41] The same constraint was also affecting the analysis of the diversification patterns in knowledge (as proxied by patents) of Italian firms reported in Dosi, Grazzi, and Moschella (2017). A certainly more appropriate context to assess its relevance would be provided by larger firms owning patents and trademarks, and also pursuing some – more or less deliberate – pattern of diversification in their technological knowledge.

In considering the other control variables of Table 3, we find that firms' size has a positive impact on firms' total revenues and a negative effect on growth.[42] Focusing on profitability as a measure of performance, size displays a negative and significant impact on firms' profitability when considering the whole sample (column 7), whereas it turns out as positive on the restricted sample (columns 8 and 9). This result might be explained by the larger size of firms with both IP rights. As shown by Crass, Czarnitzki, and Toole (2019), firms' profit margin falls as size increases and rises after a certain threshold. Focusing on productivity, our findings suggest a positive and significant impact on firms' total revenues and profitability, regardless of the sample considered (whole sample in columns 1 and 7, and sub-sample of firms with both IP rights in columns 2 and 3 and in columns 8 and 9). When considering growth as a dependent variable, productivity displays a negative and significant impact on the whole sample (column 4), whereas it turns out as not significant on the restricted one (columns 5 and 6). The lack of the (expected) positive relation between productivity and growth is not much surprising, at least for the Italian case, see Bottazzi, Grazzi, and Secchi (2005), (2008).

5.1. Accounting for patent and trademark counts

While the previous regression analysis only considered dummy variables to account for patents and trademarks, in this section we extend our analysis to include the count of patents and trademarks. Although this certainly enables to extract a richer amount of information from IP data, it also comes at the cost of some possible bias. Indeed, as we are not able to identify patents belonging to a common family, for some firms we might overestimate the true number of patents. Moreover, we recall that our dataset might under-estimate the number of registered trademarks as AMADEUS provides information about trademarks filed at the United States Patent and Trademark Office (USPTO) or at the European Union Intellectual Property Office (EUIPO), but not at national level.

To account for patent and trademark counts, we modify our baseline specification as follows:

$$Y_{i,t} = c + \beta_1 ln(tm\_i, t-1) + \beta_2 ln(pat\_i, t-1) + \beta_3 ln(pat\_i, t-1) * ln(tm\_i, t-1)$$
$$+ \beta_4 ln(workers_{i,t-1}) + \beta_5 ln(LP_{i,t-1}) + X'_{i,t}\alpha + u_{i,t} \tag{5}$$

where $ln(tm\_i, t-1)$ and $ln(pat\_i, t-1)$ are the number, in log, of patents and trademarks owned by each firm i in each year $t-1$, respectively, and $ln(pat\_i, t-1) * ln(tm\_i, t-1)$ is their interaction.[43] To estimate the baseline and the extended

---

[41]Also, note that the lack of significance of the concordance coefficients might also be related to the nature of the innovation itself and specifically product versus process innovations. Unfortunately, for the time being, we cannot distinguish patents (or trademark) as related to product or process innovation.
[42]The negative impact of initial firms' size on their growth is a common result in the literature, also known as a violation of Gibrat's (see, e.g. Mazzucato and Parris 2015; Castaldi and Dosso 2018; Grazzi and Moschella 2018).
[43]We refer to Section 2.1 for more details on the construction of patent and trademark stocks.

specification, for both the whole sample and the restricted sample of firms with both IP rights, we build the number of patents and trademarks as the count of instruments in the stock of patents and trademarks plus one, this enables to include in the analysis also firms without IP instruments. In the extended specification, we include the degree of concordance between IP rights, $conc_{i,t-1}$, its interaction with both the IP indicators $(ln(tm\_i, t-1) * conc\_i, t-1$ and $ln(pat\_i, t-1) * conc\_i, t-1)$ and the triple interaction $(ln(pat\_i, t-1) * ln(tm\_i, t-1) * conc\_i, t-1)$ in order to verify whether IP rights with higher concordance benefit the firm more.

Results for these specifications are shown in Table 4. This further analysis confirms the positive impact of patents and trademarks on performance for the whole sample of firms (see columns 1, 4 and 7 in Table 4); indeed, independently of the measure considered, firms' performance increases as the number of patents and trademarks rises. Moreover, the interaction terms between patents and trademarks, reported in columns 1 and 4, suggest that having a larger patent (trademark) stock pay less, in terms of revenues and growth, for those firms which also own trademarks (patents). These results are in line with the evidence of a lack of complementarity between patenting and trademarking activity in enhancing firms' total revenues and growth already shown in Table 3. Further, when considering patents and trademarks counts we do not find evidence of complementarity for profitability either. A possible explanation for this different result (as compared with column 7 of Table 3) is related to the potential bias of patent counts in measuring the value of patents.[44] Moreover, there is evidence of a possible trade-off between the quantity and quality of patent applications (see, De Rassenfosse 2013) which could further explain the presence of synergies between patenting and trademarking activities detected in Table 3 column 7, but the absence of complementarity between the number of patents and trademarks on profitability.

Notice that since our concordance measure takes real values (between 0 and 1) only for firms owing both IP instruments, the specification that includes concordance can only be performed on the restricted sample, as it was the case when IP was measured by dummy variables (Table 3). Hence, in the regressions on the restricted sample one is estimating the impact of having an additional IP instruments among the subset of firms with both patents and trademarks. This and the restricted sample size contribute to explain the lack of significance or the change in sign with respect to full sample (Columns 1, 4 and 7 vers3 USD, 6 and 9 of Table 4). More precisely, the change in the significance of patents and trademarks coefficients between columns 4 and 5 reveals that firms having IP instruments grow more than firms without patents and trademarks, but among firms with both patents and trademarks, the number of IP instruments in their stocks does not matter. The same reasoning applies for the non-significant effect of trademarks on profitability (column 7 versus column 8). In contrast, the negative sign of the patents coefficient for the subsample of firms having both IP instruments (column 8 of Table 4) suggests a negative effect on profitability related with having a larger patent portfolio. While at first sight counterintuitive, this result might be reconciled with the existence of a trade-off between the quantity and the quality of patent applications: the effect of the

---

[44]This is pointed out in, among others, Sandner and Block (2011). Further evidence (see, e.g. Levin et al. 1987; Cohen, Nelson, and Walsh 2000) shows that in many cases firms rely on patents for strategic reasons rather than for appropriating the returns from their innovations; and Blind, Cremers, and Mueller (2009) suggests that patents filed for traditional motives (i.e. protect their inventions) are associated with higher quality.

Table 4. POOLED OLS ESTIMATES. Patents and trademarks counts.

	(1) ln(totrev_i,t)	(2) ln(totrev_i,t)	(3) ln(totrev_i,t)	(4) growth_i,t	(5) growth_i,t	(6) growth_i,t	(7) ebitda_sales_i,t	(8) ebitda_sales_i,t	(9) ebitda_sales_i,t
ln(tm_i,t-1)	0.233***	0.0843***	0.108***	0.0422***	0.00892	0.0114	1.086***	-0.0147	-0.228
	(0.00315)	(0.0148)	(0.0224)	(0.00184)	(0.00753)	(0.0106)	(0.0721)	(0.274)	(0.377)
ln(pat_i,t-1)	0.0913***	0.0188***	0.0189	0.0212***	-0.00225	0.00142	0.654***	-0.439***	0.0895
	(0.00188)	(0.00730)	(0.0115)	(0.00119)	(0.00396)	(0.00635)	(0.0493)	(0.163)	(0.246)
ln(pat_i,t-1)*ln(tm_i,t-1)	-0.0520***	-0.00873**	-0.0117*	-0.00735***	0.00270	0.00107	0.0558	-0.0199	-0.0778
	(0.00150)	(0.00399)	(0.00701)	(0.000851)	(0.00197)	(0.00324)	(0.0396)	(0.0982)	(0.149)
ln(workers_i,t-1)	0.897***	0.951***	0.951***	-0.0187***	-0.00908**	-0.00896**	-1.544***	0.535***	0.553***
	(0.000933)	(0.00550)	(0.00554)	(0.000625)	(0.00398)	(0.00405)	(0.0239)	(0.128)	(0.130)
ln(LP_i,t-1)	0.742***	0.770***	0.770***	-0.0538***	-0.0142	-0.0142	3.581***	7.312***	7.317***
	(0.00166)	(0.0142)	(0.0142)	(0.00123)	(0.0100)	(0.0100)	(0.0419)	(0.342)	(0.342)
conc_i,t-1			0.127			0.0315			1.964
			(0.115)			(0.0680)			(2.284)
ln(tm_i,t-1)*conc_i,t-1			-0.134			-0.0181			1.493
			(0.0847)			(0.0421)			(1.570)
ln(pat_i,t-1)*conc_i,t-1			0.00541			-0.0243			-3.123***
			(0.0557)			(0.0328)			(1.187)
ln(pat_i,t-1)*ln(tm_i,t-1)*conc_i,t-1			0.0155			0.0111			0.173
			(0.0380)			(0.0203)			(0.760)
_cons	2.776***	2.570***	2.556***	0.287***	0.135**	0.130**	1.004***	-19.80***	-20.36***
	(0.00875)	(0.0326)	(0.0817)	(0.00585)	(0.0598)	(0.0563)	(0.200)	(1.821)	(1.859)
N	686252	17929	17929	684323	17917	17917	680718	17869	17869
r2	0.781	0.878	0.878	0.0248	0.0455	0.0455	0.0361	0.142	0.144
F	57273.4	2323.0	2106.5	358.0	26.10	24.07	452.5	27.25	25.14

Robust standard errors in parentheses.

* $p < 0.10$, ** $p < 0.05$, *** $p < 0.01$.

In each specification, we include ATECO 2 digit sectors, geographical areas and years dummy variables.

counts might mix a quantity and a quality effect that can go in opposite directions. We conjecture that this effect arises only for profitability as this performance measure takes into account the firms' costs that reasonably increase with the patent portfolio because of increasing maintaining patent protection costs (patent maintenance fees and other potential costs related with, for instance, litigation). This explanation is also in line with the evidence in Harhoff et al. (2009) on the EPO system.[45]

5.2. A focus on the service sector

We have so far focused only on firms from manufacturing sectors, as out of doubt they account for the largest share of IP instruments in the economy. However, not only the service sector has become much more relevant in terms of GDP share, but the propensity to resort to IP has much increased as well. Hence, in this section, we replicate our main analysis on the sub-sample of service firms.

Table 5 reports the distribution of trademarks and patents for firms in the service sector. In line with the literature, most service firms do not use any IP and the fraction of firms owning IP instruments is smaller than in the manufacturing sector. Taking as a reference the last year of observation (2014), 1.15% of firms own at least one trademark, around 0.68% at least one patent and only around 0.10% both IP instruments. Focusing on firms with both patents and trademarks, the degree of concordance, as defined in Equation (2), is on average 0.18, much similar to the manufacturing sector.

We estimate Equation (3) on the sub-sample of service firms. Results, reported in Table 6, are much similar to manufacturing. Independently of the measure of performance considered, firms with any IP right display a superior performance *vis à vis* firms

Table 5. Number of firms, trademarks, and patents. SERVICE SECTOR.

Year	Firms	Firms with tm (%) *	Firms with pat (%)*	Firms with tm and pat(%) *	Firms with $conc_{i,t} > 0$ (%) * *	Num of tm	Num of pat
2006	476903	2556 (0.536)	4157 (0.872)	310 (0.065)	244 (78.710)	6396	21146
2007	525751	3094 (0.588)	4401 (0.837)	358 (0.068)	287 (80.168)	7930	22586
2008	575973	3690 (0.641)	4606 (0.800)	406 (0.070)	325 (80.049)	9752	24002
2009	627089	4378 (0.698)	4784 (0.763)	440 (0.070)	350 (79.545)	11691	25129
2010	684923	5219 (0.762)	5035 (0.735)	522 (0.076)	414 (79.310)	14017	26999
2011	684039	6044 (0.884)	5093 (0.745)	581 (0.085)	472 (81.239)	16165	27853
2012	673793	6884 (1.022)	5007 (0.743)	635 (0.094)	515 (81.102)	18430	27808
2013	663075	7640 (1.152)	4730 (0.713)	666 (0.100)	543 (81.532)	20397	26300
2014	644237	7381 (1.146)	4354 (0.676)	625 (0.097)	509 (81.440)	19741	24502

We only consider firms operating in service sectors (we exclude firms operating in the following 2-digit ATECO 2007 code: 64, 65, 66, and 68)
* In brackets, percentage of total firms.
* * In brackets, as a percentage of firms with trademarks and patents.

---

[45]Results in Table 4 are robust to the use, for patent and trademark counts, of inverse hyperbolic sine transformation rather than logarithmic transformation.

without IP rights (tests H1_a, H1_b, and H1_c in Table 6); owning both IP rights has a higher impact than owning only one for all measures of performance considered (tests H1_d and H1_e in Table 6) and complementarity between patents and trademarks holds only with respect to profitability (tests H1_f in Table 6). Moreover, estimated coefficients (having only trademarks, only patents or both of them) are slightly higher in the service sector than in the manufacturing, independently of the measure of performance. Further, having both IP rights is associated to an increase in total revenues by 37.2% (by 32.2% for firms in the manufacturing sector), growth by 9.6% (by 7.5% for firms in the manufacturing sector) and profitability by 4,4% (by 3.08% for manufacturing firms). These results are quite in line with evidence from Hall and Sena (2017) and Greenhalgh and Rogers (2012).

As far as the comparison between the two IP instruments is concerned, our estimates for the service sector are in line with those shown for manufacturing firms. The impact of owning only trademarks is larger for revenues and growth as compared to owning only patents.

In concluding, despite the different propensity to use IP rights for manufacturing and service firms (Tables 1 vs 5), the evidence from regression analysis suggests that the impact of IP strategies on firms' performance in both macro-sectors is significantly positive and similar.[46]

6. Conclusion

We have analysed the relationship between innovation activities and firms' performance in terms of revenues, growth, and profitability.

Our contribution is threefold. First, differently from most empirical works, which focus on large and medium firms, on top corporate R&D investors or on firms operating in high-tech industries (see, e.g. Greenhalgh and Rogers 2006; Fang, Palmatier, and Grewal 2011; Chang, Chen, and Huang 2012; Greenhalgh and Rogers 2012; Dernis et al. 2015; Daiko et al. 2017; Dosso and Vezzani 2017; Castaldi and Dosso 2018), we have performed our analysis on IP taking into account the virtual universe of Italian limited liability manufacturing firms. Second, we have investigated whether there is a complementary or substitute relationship between the two instruments of IP. To the best of our knowledge, only a few studies examine the combined impact of patents and trademarks on firms' performance (see, e.g. Greenhalgh and Rogers 2012; Sandner and Block 2011; Dosso and Vezzani 2017; Llerena and Millot 2013; Jensen, Webster, and Buddelmeyer 2008; Buddelmeyer, Jensen, and Webster 2010; Helmers and Rogers 2010; Wagner and Cockburn 2010). Finally and completely novel, for firms owning both IP instruments, we have proposed a measure of concordance between a firm's stock of patents and trademarks, investigating the effect of this concordance on firms' performance.

---

[46]Estimates of the baseline specification on more disaggregated sub-samples of firms according to their sector of activity (2-digit ATECO sectors for manufacturing firms, and ATECO Sections for firms operating in the service sector), show that the relationship between firms' IP strategies and their performances are rather homogeneous across sectors, with the noteworthy exception of the regression on profitability, which exhibits clear sectoral patterns. Conversely, we do not find relevant differences on the relationship between IP instruments and firms' performances across small, medium, and large firms, operating in both the manufacturing and the service sectors. Results are available upon request.

Table 6. POOLED OLS estimates. Dummy variables for IP strategies. SERVICE SECTOR.

	(1)	(2)	(3)	(4)	(5)	(6)	(7)	(8)	(9)
	ln(totrev$_{i,t}$)	ln(totrev$_{i,t}$)	ln(totrev$_{i,t}$)	growth$_{i,t}$	growth$_{i,t}$	growth$_{i,t}$	ebitda_sales$_{i,t}$	ebitda_sales$_{i,t}$	ebitda_sales$_{i,t}$
nopattm$_{i,t-1}$	2.799***			0.561***			18.74***		
	(0.0117)			(0.00699)			(0.330)		
tm$_{i,t-1}$	3.136***			0.638***			19.96***		
	(0.0135)			(0.00794)			(0.373)		
pat$_{i,t-1}$	3.040***			0.625***			19.96***		
	(0.0135)			(0.00814)			(0.368)		
both$_{i,t-1}$	3.171***			0.657***			23.15***		
	(0.0189)			(0.0113)			(0.542)		
ln(workers$_{i,t-1}$)	0.855***	0.954***	0.954***	-0.0130***	0.00108	0.00107	-2.841***	-0.314	-0.320
	(0.000558)	(0.00989)	(0.00989)	(0.000386)	(0.00683)	(0.00684)	(0.0143)	(0.271)	(0.270)
ln(LP$_{i,t-1}$)	0.624***	0.756***	0.755***	-0.0907***	-0.0129	-0.0129	3.677***	5.957***	5.942***
	(0.000748)	(0.0249)	(0.0250)	(0.000580)	(0.0136)	(0.0136)	(0.0199)	(0.912)	(0.911)
conc$_{i,t-1}$			-0.186**			-0.00238			-3.293
			(0.0772)			(0.0364)			(2.113)
_cons		3.002***	3.058***		0.104	0.104		12.40	13.41
		(0.331)	(0.332)		(0.160)	(0.163)		(8.631)	(8.796)
N	2641117	3256	3256	2606283	3247	3247	2593930	3203	3203
r2	0.972	0.874	0.875	0.0243	0.0293	0.0293	0.127	0.112	0.112
F	1937606.7	1697.9	1688.1	729.1	5.313	5.257	5235.5	29.32	28.89
H1_a: $\beta_2 > \beta_1$	3029.22***			496.55***			51.70***		
H1_b: $\beta_3 > \beta_1$	1390.60***			255.15***			60.13***		
H1_c: $\beta_4 > \beta_1$	641.66***			121.64***			107.61****		
H1_d: $\beta_4 > \beta_2$	5.08**			4.02*			49.50***		
H1_e: $\beta_4 > \beta_3$	68.35***			11.41***			49.84***		
H1_f: $\beta_4 - \beta_3 > \beta_2 - \beta_1$	144.51			20.22			16.87***		

Robust standard errors in parentheses.

* $p < 0.10$, ** $p < 0.05$, *** $p < 0.01$.

In each specification, we include ATECO 2 digit sectors, geographical areas and years dummy variables.

All tests are one-tailed since the hypotheses are directional.

Overall, our results indicate that IP rights exert a positive impact on firms' performance. When we focus on our preferred specification, having patent and trademark (irrespectively from their number) display a complementary effect when performance is measured by profitability.

Although Italian firms do not represent the ideal testbed due to the very low share of firms with both patents and trademarks, we believe that the measure of concordance we propose can contribute to better understand how business firms engage in innovation activities and how this affects their performance. Establishing a linkage between patents and trademarks can shed some new light on the deliberate choice of the relative timing for the two activities. Do firms start with seeking protection for their technological innovation, or they rather decide to apply for a patent only when the introduction of a certain line of business, possibly protected by a trademark, has already proved to be successful? Further, the concordance measure or in other terms, the extent to which a given trademark (and the related product) is 'backed up' by a patent, provides a more detailed perspective on the complementarity existing between IP instruments as it focuses on a specific product or line of business. Is the existence of patent-to-trademark linkage evidence of a 'stronger' innovation, which is expected to generate higher profits?

We are of course aware of some limitations of our work. We remind the reader that for the construction of the measure of concordance we have extensively resorted to 'Algorithmic Links with Probabilities (ALP)' which have themselves some limitations in terms of lack of precision. On a brighter side, also note that the public availability and use of such (and similar) ALP is also likely to generate some improvement over time. Second, and as apparent from this work even more relevant, the returns from employing the concordance measure largely depend on the characteristic of firms and in particular on their propensity to apply for patents and trademarks. Finally, and related to the latter point, we acknowledge that, focusing on patents and trademarks, we focus only on a subset of the instruments available to firms to appropriate the returns from formal and informal innovation activities (see among the others, Griliches 1990; Dosi, Marengo, and Pasquali 2006; Cohen, Nelson, and Walsh 2000).

Acknowledgments

We thank the participants to the Department of Economics Unibo internal seminar (June 2018), the European Commission Joint Research Center seminar (JRC-Seville, June 2018), the European Association for Evolutionary Political Economy (EAEPE) conference (September 2018), the IP Statistics for Decision Makers (IPSDM) conference in Alicante (October 2018) and the Sant'Anna Institute of Economics seminar (October 2018). We are grateful to Roberto Susanna (Infocamere press office) and to Bureau van Dijk for their technical assistance at various stages. We are also indebted to Caterina Giannetti, Hanna Hottenrott, Laura Magazzini, Arianna Martinelli, Daniele Moschella, Gabriele Pellegrino, Emanuele Pugliese, Enrico Santarelli, Antonio Vezzani, and Nikolas J. Zolas for insightful comments. All remaining errors are our own. This work received fundings by the Fondazione Cassa di Risparmio of Forlì, project ORGANIMPRE. This work has been partly supported by the European Commission under the H2020, GROWINPRO, Grant Agreement 822781.

Disclosure Statement

No potential conflict of interest was reported by the authors.

Funding

This work was supported by the European Commission H2020, project name: GROWINPRO [822781]; Fondazione Cassa di Risparmio of Forlì, project ORGANIMPRE [ORGANIMPRE];

ORCID

Marco Grazzi ⓘ http://orcid.org/0000-0002-4196-6122

References

Aaker, D. 2007. "Innovation: Brand It or Lose It." *California Management Review* 50: 8–24. doi:10.2307/41166414.

Angrist, J. D., and J.-S. Pischke. 2008. *Mostly Harmless Econometrics: An Empiricist's Companion.* Princeton, NJ: Princeton university press.

Belderbos, R., B. Cassiman, D. Faems, B. Leten, and B. V. Looy. 2014. "Co-ownership of Intellectual Property: Exploring the Value-appropriation and Value-creation Implications of Co-patenting with Different Partners." *Research Policy* 43: 841–852. doi:10.1016/j.respol.2013.08.013.

Blind, K., J. Edler, R. Frietsch, and U. Schmoch. 2006. "Motives to Patent: Empirical Evidence from Germany." *Research Policy* 35: 655–672. doi:10.1016/j.respol.2006.03.002.

Blind, K., K. Cremers, and E. Mueller. 2009. "The Influence of Strategic Patenting on Companies Patent Portfolios." *Research Policy* 38: 428–436. doi:10.1016/j.respol.2008.12.003.

Block, J. H., C. O. Fisch, A. Hahn, and P. G. Sandner. 2015. "Why Do SMEs File Trademarks? Insights from Firms in Innovative Industries." *Research Policy* 44: 1915–1930. doi:10.1016/j. respol.2015.06.007.

Bottazzi, G., A. Secchi, and F. Tamagni. 2008. "Productivity, Profitability and Financial Performance." *Industrial and Corporate Change* 17: 711–751. doi:10.1093/icc/dtn027.

Bottazzi, G., M. Grazzi, and A. Secchi. 2005. "Input Output Scaling Relations in Italian Manufacturing Firms." *Physica A* 355: 95–102. doi:10.1016/j.physa.2005.02.070.

Bryce, D. J., and S. G. Winter. 2009. "A General Interindustry Relatedness Index." *Management Science* 55: 1570–1585. doi:10.1287/mnsc.1090.1040.

Buddelmeyer, H., P. H. Jensen, and E. Webster. 2010. "Innovation and the Determinants of Company Survival." *Oxford Economic Papers* 62: 261–285. doi:10.1093/oep/gpp012.

Cassiman, B., and R. Veugelers. 2006. "In Search of Complementarity in Innovation Strategy: Internal R&D and External Knowledge Acquisition." *Management Science* 52: 68–82. doi:10.1287/mnsc.1050.0470.

Castaldi, C., and M. Dosso 2018. "From R&D to Market: Using Trademarks to Capture the Market Capability of Top R&D Investors." Tech. rep., Joint Research Centre (Seville site).

Cefis, E., and L. Orsenigo. 2001. "The Persistence of Innovative Activities: A Cross-countries and Cross-sectors Comparative Analysis." *Research Policy* 30: 1139–1158. doi:10.1016/S0048-7333(00)00139-6.

Chang, K.-C., D.-Z. Chen, and M.-H. Huang. 2012. "The Relationships between the Patent Performance and Corporation Performance." *Journal of Informetrics* 6: 131–139. doi:10.1016/j.joi.2011.09.001.

Cohen, W. M., R. R. Nelson, and J. P. Walsh 2000. "Protecting Their Intellectual Assets: Appropriability Conditions and Why U.S. Manufacturing Firms Patent (Or Not)." Working Paper 7552. National Bureau of Economic Research.

Colombelli, A., J. Krafft, and F. Quatraro. 2014. "The Emergence of New Technology-based Sectors in European Regions: A Proximity-based Analysis of Nanotechnology." *Research Policy* 43: 1681–1696. doi:10.1016/j.respol.2014.07.008.

Crass, D., D. Czarnitzki, and A. A. Toole. 2019. "The Dynamic Relationship between Investments in Brand Equity and Firm Profitability: Evidence Using Trademark Registrations." *International Journal of the Economics of Business* 26: 157–176. doi:10.1080/13571516.2019.1553292.

Crepon, B., E. Duguet, and J. Mairesse. 1998. "Research, Innovation And Productivity: An Econometric Analysis At The Firm Level." *Economics of Innovation and New Technology* 7: 115–158. doi:10.1080/10438599800000031.

Czarnitzki, D., and K. Kraft. 2004. "Innovation Indicators and Corporate Credit Ratings: Evidence from German Firms." *Economics Letters* 82: 377–384. doi:10.1016/j.econlet.2003.09.016.

Daiko, T., H. Dernis, M. Dosso, P. Gkotsis, M. Squicciarini, A. Tuebke, and A. Vezzani 2017. "World Top R&D Investors: Industrial Property Strategies in the Digital Economy." JRC Working Papers JRC107015. Joint Research Centre (Seville site).

Davis, S., J. Haltiwanger, and S. Schuh. 1998. *Job Creation and Destruction*. Vol. 1. 1 ed. Cambridge, Massachusetts: MIT Press.

De Rassenfosse, G. 2013. "Do Firms Face a Trade-off between the Quantity and the Quality of Their Inventions?" *Research Policy* 42: 1072–1079. doi:10.1016/j.respol.2013.02.005.

de Rassenfosse, G., and A. B. Jaffe. 2018. "Econometric Evidence on the Depreciation of Innovations." *European Economic Review* 101: 625–642. doi:10.1016/j.euroecorev.2017.11.005.

De Rassenfosse, G., H. Dernis, and G. Boedt. 2014. "An Introduction to the Patstat Database with Example Queries." *Australian Economic Review* 47: 395–408. doi:10.1111/aere.v47.3.

Del Monte, A., and E. Papagni. 2003. "R&D and the Growth of Firms: Empirical Analysis of a Panel of Italian Firms." *Research Policy* 32: 1003–1014. doi:10.1016/S0048-7333(02)00107-5.

Dernis, H., M. Dosso, F. Hervas, V. Millot, M. Squicciarini, and A. Vezzani 2015. "World Corporate Top R&D Investors: Innovation and IP Bundles." JRC Working Papers JRC94932. Joint Research Centre (Seville site).

Dinlersoz, E., N. Goldschlag, A. Myers, and N. Zolas. forthcoming. "An Anatomy of U.S. Firms Seeking Trademark Registration." In *Measuring and Accounting for Innovation in the 21st Century,* edited by C. Corrado, J. Haskel, J. Miranda and D. Sichel. Chicago, IL: University of Chicago Press.

Doms, M., T. Dunne, and M. J. Roberts. 1995. "The Role of Technology Use in the Survival and Growth of Manufacturing Plants." *International Journal of Industrial Organization* 13: 523–542. doi:10.1016/0167-7187(95)00503-X.

Dosi, G., L. Marengo, and C. Pasquali. 2006. "How Much Should Society Fuel the Greed of Innovators?: On the Relations between Appropriability, Opportunities and Rates of Innovation." *Research Policy* 35: 1110–1121. doi:10.1016/j.respol.2006.09.003.

Dosi, G., M. Grazzi, and D. Moschella. 2015. "Technology and Costs in International Competitiveness: From Countries and Sectors to Firms." *Research Policy* 44: 1795–1814. doi:10.1016/j.respol.2015.05.012.

Dosi, G., M. Grazzi, and D. Moschella. 2017. "What Do Firms Know? What Do They Produce? A New Look at the Relationship between Patenting Profiles and Patterns of Product Diversification." *Small Business Economics* 48: 413–429. doi:10.1007/s11187-016-9783-0.

Dosso, M., and A. Vezzani 2017. "Firm Market Valuation and Intellectual Property Assets." Tech. rep., Joint Research Centre (Seville site).

Evans, D. S. 1987a. "The Relationship between Firm Growth, Size, and Age: Estimates for 100 Manufacturing Industries." *Journal of Industrial Economics* 35: 567–581. doi:10.2307/2098588.

Evans, D. S. 1987b. "Tests of Alternative Theories of Firm Growth." *The Journal of Political Economy* 95: 657–674. doi:10.1086/261480.

Fang, E., R. W. Palmatier, and R. Grewal. 2011. "Effects of Customer and Innovation Asset Configuration Strategies on Firm Performance." *Journal of Marketing Research* 48: 587–602. doi:10.1509/jmkr.48.3.587.

Fligner, M., and G. Policello. 1981. "Robust Rank Procedures for the BehrensFisher Problem." *Journal of the American Statistical Association* 76: 141–206. doi:10.1080/01621459.1981.10477623.

Flikkema, M., A.-P. De Man, and C. Castaldi. 2014. "Are Trademark Counts a Valid Indicator of Innovation? Results of an In-Depth Study of New Benelux Trademarks Filed by SMEs." *Industry and Innovation* 21: 310–331. doi:10.1080/13662716.2014.934547.

Flikkema, M., C. Castaldi, A.-P. de Man, and M. Seip. 2019. "Trademarks' Relatedness to Product and Service Innovation: A Branding Strategy Approach." *Research Policy* 48: 1340–1353. doi:10.1016/j.respol.2019.01.018.

Garca-Manjón, J. V., and M. E. Romero-Merino. 2012. "Research, Development, and Firm Growth. Empirical Evidence from European Top R&D Spending Firms." *Research Policy* 41: 1084–1092. doi:10.1016/j.respol.2012.03.017.

Gibrat, R. 1931. *Les Inègalitès Èconomiques*. Paris: Librairie du Recuil Sirey.

Goldschlag, N., T. J. Lybbert, and N. J. Zolas 2016. "An Algorithmic Links with Probabilities Crosswalk for USPC and CPC Patent Classifications with an Application Towards Industrial Technology Composition." Working Papers 16–15. Center for Economic Studies, U.S. Census Bureau.

Graham, S., and D. Somaya. 2004. "The Use of Patents, Copyrights, and Trademarks in Software: Evidence from Litigation." In *Patents, Innovation and Economic Performance*, edited by D. Guellec, 265–288. Paris: OECD.

Graham, S. J., C. Grim, T. Islam, A. C. Marco, and J. Miranda. 2018. "Business Dynamics of Innovating Firms: Linking U.S. Patents with Administrative Data on Workers and Firms." *Journal of Economics & Management Strategy* 27: 372–402. doi:10.1111/jems.12260.

Grazzi, M., C. Piccardo, and C. Vergari. 2018. "Building a Firm Level Dataset for the Analyses of Industrial Dynamics and Demography." *Journal of Economic and Social Measurement* 43: 169–197. doi:10.3233/JEM-180456.

Grazzi, M., and D. Moschella. 2018. "Small, Young, and Exporters: New Evidence on the Determinants of Firm Growth." *Journal of Evolutionary Economics* 28: 125–152. doi:10.1007/s00191-017-0523-7.

Greenhalgh, C., and M. Rogers. 2006. "Market Valuation of UK Intellectual Property: Manufacturing, Utility and Financial Services Firms." In *The Management of Intellectual Property*, edited by D. Bosworth and E. Webster, 132–145, Vols. Chapters, chap. 7. Cheltenham, UK: Edward Elgar Publishing.

Greenhalgh, C., and M. Rogers. 2012. "Trade Marks and Performance in Services and Manufacturing Firms: Evidence of Schumpeterian Competition through Innovation." *Australian Economic Review* 45: 50–76. doi:10.1111/j.1467-8462.2011.00665.x.

Griliches, Z. 1981. "Market Value, R & D, and Patents." *Economics Letters* 7: 183–187. doi:10.1016/0165-1765(87)90114-5.

Griliches, Z. 1990. "Patent Statistics as Economic Indicators: A Survey." *Journal of Economic Literature* 28: 1661–1707.

Guzman, J., and S. Stern. 2015. "Where Is Silicon Valley?" *Science* 347: 606–609. doi:10.1126/science.aaa0201.

Hall, B. H. 2000. "Innovation and Market Value." In *Productivity, Innovation and Economic Performance*, edited by R. Barrell, G. Mason, and M. OMahony, 13–33. Vol. 33. Cambridge: Cambridge University Press.

Hall, B. H., C. Helmers, M. Rogers, and V. Sena. 2013. "The Importance (Or Not) of Patents to UK Firms." *Oxford Economic Papers* 65: 603–629. doi:10.1093/oep/gpt012.

Hall, B. H., F. Lotti, and J. Mairesse. 2009. "Innovation and Productivity in SMEs: Empirical Evidence for Italy." *Small Business Economics* 33: 13–33. doi:10.1007/s11187-009-9184-8.

Hall, B. H., and V. Sena. 2017. "Appropriability Mechanisms, Innovation, and Productivity: Evidence from the UK." *Economics of Innovation and New Technology* 26: 42–62. doi:10.1080/10438599.2016.1202513.

Harhoff, D., K. Hoisl, B. Reichl, and B. van Pottelsberghe de la Potterie. 2009. "Patent Validation at the Country Level. The Role of Fees and Translation Costs." *Research Policy* 38: 1423–1437. doi:10.1016/j.respol.2009.06.014.

Helmers, C., and M. Rogers. 2010. "Innovation and the Survival of Sew Firms in the UK." *Review of Industrial Organization* 36: 227–248. doi:10.1007/s11151-010-9247-7.

Hidalgo, C. A., B. Klinger, A.-L. Barabási, and R. Hausmann. 2007. "The Product Space Conditions the Development of Nations." *Science* 317: 482–487. doi:10.1126/science.1144581.

Jensen, P. H., E. Webster, and H. Buddelmeyer. 2008. "Innovation, Technological Conditions and New Firm Survival." *Economic Record* 84: 434–448. doi:10.1111/ecor.2008.84.issue-267.

Leiponen, A., and J. Byma. 2009. "If You Cannot Block, You Better Run: Small Firms, Cooperative Innovation, and Appropriation Strategies." *Research Policy* 38: 1478–1488. doi:10.1016/j.respol.2009.06.003.

Levin, R. C., A. K. Klevorick, R. R. Nelson, S. G. Winter, R. Gilbert, and Z. Griliches. 1987. "Appropriating the Returns from Industrial Research and Development." *Brookings Papers on Economic Activity* 1987: 783–831. doi:10.2307/2534454.

Lin, J. X., and W. F. Lincoln. 2017. "Pirate's Treasure." *Journal of International Economics* 109: 235–245. doi:10.1016/j.jinteco.2017.05.008.

Llerena, P., and V. Millot 2013. "Are Trade Marks and Patents Complementary or Substitute Protections for Innovation." Working Papers of BETA 2013-01. Strasbourg: Bureau d'Economie Thèorique et Appliquèe, UDS.

Lotti, F., and G. Marin 2013. "Matching of PATSTAT Applications to AIDA Firms: Discussion of the Methodology and Results." Questioni di Economia e Finanza (Occasional Papers) 166. Bank of Italy, Economic Research and International Relations Area.

Lybbert, T. J., and N. J. Zolas. 2014. "Getting Patents and Economic Data to Speak to Each Other: An Algorithmic Links with Probabilities Approach for Joint Analyses of Patenting and Economic Activity." *Research Policy* 43: 530–542. doi:10.1016/j.respol.2013.09.001.

Malerba, F., and L. Orsenigo. 1999. "Technological Entry, Exit and Survival: An Empirical Analysis of Patent Data." *Research Policy* 28: 643–660. doi:10.1016/S0048-7333(99)00005-0.

Markides, C. C., and P. J. Williamson. 1996. "Corporate Diversification And Organizational Structure: A Resource-Based View." *Academy of Management Journal* 39: 340–367.

Mazzucato, M., and S. Parris. 2015. "High-growth Firms in Changing Competitive Environments: The US Pharmaceutical Industry (1963 to 2002)." *Small Business Economics* 44: 145–170. doi:10.1007/s11187-014-9583-3.

Mendonça, S., T. S. Pereira and M. M. Godinho. 2004. "Trademarks as an Indicator of Innovation and Industrial Change." *Research Policy* 33: 1385–1404. doi:10.1016/j.respol.2004.09.005.

Milgrom, P., and J. Roberts. 1990. "The Economics of Modern Manufacturing: Technology, Strategy, and Organization." *American Economic Review* 80: 511–528.

Milgrom, P., and J. Roberts. 1995. "Complementarities and Fit: Strategy, Structure, and Organizational Change in Manufacturing." *Journal of Accounting and Economics* 19: 179–208. doi:10.1016/0165-4101(94)00382-F.

OHIM. 2015. "Intellectual Property Rights and Firm Performance in Europe: An Economic Analysis." Tech. rep., Office for Harmonization in the Internal Market (OHIM).

Osservatorio Italiano Brevetti. 2014. "Analisi del brevetto italiano. Dati sttistici e trends degli ultimi anni." Technical report. OIB.

Penrose, E. T. 1959. *The Theory of the Growth of the Firm*. 3rd ed. Oxford: Blackwell.

Ramello, G. B. 2006. "What's in a Sign? Trademark Law and Economic Theory." *Journal of Economic Surveys* 20: 547–565. doi:10.1111/joes.2006.20.issue-4.

Rogers, M., C. Helmers, and C. Greenhalgh 2007. "An Analysis of the Characteristics of Small and Medium Enterprises that Use Intellectual Property." Tech. rep., London: Report for the UK Intellectual Property Office. doi: 10.1094/PDIS-91-4-0467B.

Sandner, P. G., and J. Block. 2011. "The Market Value of R&D, Patents, and Trademarks." *Research Policy* 40: 969–985. doi:10.1016/j.respol.2011.04.004.

Santarelli, E., L. Klomp, and A. R. Thurik. 2006. "Gibrats Law: An Overview of the Empirical Literature." In *Entrepreneurship, Growth, and Innovation*, edited by E. Santarelli, 41–73. Boston, MA: Springer.

Schautschick, P., and C. Greenhalgh. 2016. "Empirical Studies of Trade Marks–the Existing Economic Literature." *Economics of Innovation and New Technology* 25: 358–390. doi:10.1080/10438599.2015.1064598.

Seip, M., C. Castaldi, M. Flikkema, and A.-P. De Man. 2018. "The Timing of Trademark Application in Innovation Processes." *Technovation* 72: 34–45. doi:10.1016/j.technovation.2018.02.001.

Teece, D. J., R. Rumelt, G. Dosi, and S. Winter. 1994. "Understanding Corporate Coherence: Theory and Evidence." *Journal of Economic Behavior & Organization* 23: 1–30. doi:10.1016/0167-2681(94)90094-9.

Toivanen, O., P. Stoneman, and D. Bosworth. 2002. "Innovation and the Market Value of UK Firms, 1989–1995." *Oxford Bulletin of Economics and Statistics* 64: 39–61. doi:10.1111/obes.2002.64.issue-1.

Wagner, S., and I. Cockburn. 2010. "Patents and the Survival of Internet-related IPOs." *Research Policy* 39: 214–228. doi:10.1016/j.respol.2009.12.003.

Xu, B., and E. P. Chiang. 2005. "Trade, Patents and International Technology Diffusion." *The Journal of International Trade & Economic Development* 14: 115–135. doi:10.1080/0963819042000333270.

Zhou, H., P. G. Sandner, S. L. Martinelli, and J. H. Block. 2016. "Patents, Trademarks, and Their Complementarity in Venture Capital Funding." *Technovation* 47: 14–22. doi:10.1016/j.technovation.2015.11.005.

Zolas, N., T. J. Lybbert, and P. Bhattacharyya. 2017. "An Algorithmic Links with Probabilities Concordance for Trademarks with an Application Towards Bilateral IP Flows." *The World Economy* 40: 1184–1213. doi:10.1111/twec.2017.40.issue-6.

Appendices

Appendix A. Appendix: Example of concordance measure construction

For illustrative purposes, consider the following example taken from our database for a firm (labelled 1) with four patents and nine trademarks in year 2006. As we can see from Table A1, the first patent (patent 1) has two IPC codes (A61 and H02), the second patent has one IPC code (C09) and both the third and fourth patents have one IPC code (A61). Thus, for firm 1 in year 2006, the set of 3-digit IPC codes includes the following three codes: A61, H02, and C09. Looking at the stock of trademarks, the first eight trademarks have the 2-digit NICE code 2, while the ninth trademark has the NICE code 35. Hence, for firm 1 in the year 2006, the set of NICE codes includes the following two codes: 2 and 35. So that $N_L^{1,2006} = 3$ and $N_K^{1,2006} = 2$. Based on the probabilistic algorithms by Lybbert and Zolas (2014) and Zolas, Lybbert, and Bhattacharyya (2017), in Table A2 each IPC and NICE code is associated to the corresponding ISIC sectors (it can be more than one) with the relative probability weights. For example, we link the 3-digit IPC code A61 to the following ISIC codes 10, 20, 21, 32, and 36. For each ISIC code, the algorithm provides a probability weight which identifies the likelihood of the linkage between the IPC code and each ISIC code. Similarly, for NICE code 2, we consider the following ISIC codes 2, 20, 25 and 41, each of them linked to a given probability weight.

In order to compute $conc_{1,2006}$, we first determine the overlapping coefficient for each of the six pairs of IPC and NICE codes (A61-2, A61-35, C09-2, C09-35, H02-2 and H02-35). For instance, $overlap_{A61-2} = 0.0505$, with $N_{A61,2} = 8$, that is the number of ISIC codes associated to the pair (A61,2).[47] Hence, the degree of concordance between the two IP instruments is given by:

$$conc_{1,2006} = (0.0505005 + 0 + 0.1203539 + 0 + 0 + 0)/(3*2) = 0.028475733. \qquad (6)$$

[47]A common 2-digit ISIC code is identified only for the pairs of IPC and NICE codes A61-2 and C09-2. In particular, both the IPC code A61 and the NICE code 2 are linked to the ISIC code 20; while, both the IPC code C09 and the NICE code 2 are linked to the ISIC code 20. Thus, the overlapping coefficients are different from zero only for these pairs on IPC and NICE codes (0. 0505005 and 0.1203539 for pairs A61-2 and C09-2, respectively).

Table A1. Number of elements in the set of 3-digit IPC and 2-digit NICE codes.

D	PAT	IPC
1	1	A61
1	1	H02
1	2	C09
1	3	A61
1	4	A61

ID	TM	NICE
1	1	2
1	2	2
1	3	2
1	4	2
1	5	2
1	6	2
1	7	2
1	8	2
1	9	35

Table A2. Moving from IPC and NICE to ISIC codes.

IPC	ISIC	$P_{IPC}(ISIC)$
A61	10	0.0361579
A61	20	0.0505005
A61	21	0.8616829
A61	32	0.0302412
A61	36	0.0214176
C09	20	0.9659607
C09	23	0.0340393
H02	24	0.0637551
H02	26	0.0888389
H02	27	0.8212442
H02	28	0.0261618

NICE	ISIC	$P_{NICE}(ISIC)$
2	2	0.0491944
2	20	0.1203539
2	25	0.8065651
2	41	0.0238867
35	46	0.1524157
35	63	0.0744019
35	69	0.0240318
35	70	0.0710176
35	73	0.4864157
35	78	0.0490504
35	82	0.0307544
35	90	0.0424586
35	94	0.0694538

Appendix B. Appendix – Sectoral statistics

Table B1. Number of firms, trademarks, and patents for 2 digit ATECO manufacturing sectors. Year 2014.

ATECO	Firms (%) *	Firms with tm(%) *	Firms with pat (%)*	Firms with tm and pat(%) *	Firms with concordance (%) * *	Num of tm (%) * *	Num of pat (%) * *
10	11560	954	210	97	79	4431	1505
	(8.944)	(10.764)	(2.440)	(3.428)	(3.091)	(13.960)	(1.614)
11	1754	335	29	15	10	2203	99
	(1.357)	(3.780)	(0.337)	(0.530)	(0.391)	(6.941)	(0.106)
13	5012	336	218	62	48	1087	1028
	(3.878)	(3.791)	(2.533)	(2.191)	(1.878)	(3.425)	(1.103)
14	7414	721	117	48	38	2545	684
	(5.736)	(8.135)	(1.359)	(1.696)	(1.487)	(8.018)	(0.734)
15	5262	467	156	72	60	1646	1081
	(4.071)	(5.269)	(1.812)	(2.544)	(2.347)	(5.186)	(1.160)
16	4529	102	117	34	32	240	441
	(3.504)	(1.151)	(1.359)	(1.201)	(1.252)	(0.756)	(0.473)
17	2229	105	147	32	27	528	896
	(1.725)	(1.185)	(1.708)	(1.131)	(1.056)	(1.664)	(0.961)
18	4671	67	75	10	9	108	315
	(3.614)	(0.756)	(0.871)	(0.353)	(0.352)	(0.340)	(0.338)
19	289	17	16	7	7	74	46
	(0.224)	(0.192)	(0.186)	(0.247)	(0.274)	(0.233)	(0.049)
20	3579	510	345	157	148	2777	3763
	(2.769)	(5.754)	(4.008)	(5.548)	(5.790)	(8.749)	(4.036)
21	586	146	164	89	88	1355	5252
	(0.453)	(1.647)	(1.905)	(3.145)	(3.443)	(4.269)	(5.633)
22	5921	459	708	222	187	1514	6299
	(4.581)	(5.179)	(8.225)	(7.845)	(7.316)	(4.770)	(6.756)
23	7430	282	292	86	81	914	1576
	(5.748)	(3.182)	(3.392)	(3.039)	(3.169)	(2.880)	(1.690)
24	2039	106	163	52	48	257	1085
	(1.578)	(1.196)	(1.894)	(1.837)	(1.878)	(0.810)	(1.164)
25	26951	799	1463	347	308	1888	10301
	(20.851)	(9.015)	(16.996)	(12.261)	(12.050)	(5.948)	(11.049)
26	4749	409	532	171	154	1228	12125
	(3.674)	(4.615)	(6.180)	(6.042)	(6.025)	(3.869)	(13.006)
27	5576	478	573	208	189	1752	8211
	(4.314)	(5.393)	(6.657)	(7.350)	(7.394)	(5.520)	(8.807)
28	15075	1376	2311	758	721	3557	27394
	(11.663)	(15.525)	(26.847)	(26.784)	(28.208)	(11.207)	(29.384)
29	1687	172	200	70	64	619	3513
	(1.305)	(1.941)	(2.323)	(2.473)	(2.504)	(1.950)	(3.768)
30	2081	148	114	43	38	616	2285
	(1.610)	(1.670)	(1.324)	(1.519)	(1.487)	(1.941)	(2.451)
31	5858	389	295	103	93	945	1953
	(4.532)	(4.389)	(3.4227)	(3.640)	(3.638)	(2.977)	(2.095)
32	5001	485	363	147	127	1456	3377
	(3.869)	(5.472)	(4.217)	(5.194)	(4.969)	(4.587)	(3.622)

We only consider firms operating in manufacturing sectors (we exclude firms operating in the following 2-digit ATECO 2007 code: 12 and 33).

* % is the share of total firms, total firms with trademarks, patents, trademarks and patents, concordant trademarks and patents, respectively.

* * % is the share of total number of trademarks and patents, respectively.

Are two better than one? Modelling the complementarity between patents and trademarks across industries

Patrick Llerena and Valentine Millot

ABSTRACT

Intellectual property (IP) rights are a major component of firms' strategies to appropriate the benefits of their innovations. This paper aims at assessing the interactions between two types of IP rights, namely patents and trademarks. We first model the effect of these two types of IP rights on the returns of innovations for firms. Based on a supermodularity analysis, we then show that the complementarity between trademarks and patents varies according to the characteristics of the market. Depending on the levels of advertising's spillovers and depreciation rate, trademarks are found to be complementary or not to patents. Finally, based on a data set encompassing the IP activity of a sample of publicly traded firms among the top corporate R&D investors worldwide, we find that patents and trademarks are complementary in chemical and pharmaceutical sectors, but not in Information and Communication Technologies (ICT) sectors.

1. Introduction

The benefits of product innovations for firms strongly depend on their ability to develop various appropriability means (Teece 1986; Levin et al. 1987; Cohen, Nelson, and Walsh 2000; Fischer and Henkel 2013; Thomä and Bizer 2013). Intellectual property (IP) rights, such as patents and trademarks, are a major factor of firms' appropriability strategies. Both patents and trademarks are important to appropriate the benefits of innovation, one protecting mainly upstream assets and the other one protecting mainly market-oriented capabilities. Indeed patents alone do not guarantee that the firm will benefit from innovation, which also requires the development of market-based assets to ensure the success of the commercialisation of the innovation (Rogers 1998; Jennewein, Durand and Gerybadze, 2010; Aaker, 2007). In this respect, trademarks are likely to constitute an important protection, complementary to patents.

The creation of a new trademark may enhance consumers' perception of innovative products and may constitute a basis for advertising (Athreye and Fassio 2019). Moreover, if a firm launches an innovative product under a certain brand name, consumers are likely to remain loyal to this pioneer brand even after competitors enter the market

(Davis 2009). Statman and Tyebjee (1981), for example, observe that due to brand loyalty, the expiration of patents for ethical drugs has only a minor effect on their market dominance, as the patent period is used to transfer the value of the patent into the trademark. Jennewein, Durand, and Gerybadze (2010) analyse the phenomena in the longitudinal case of Bayer Aspirin. The Aspirin case is particularly inspiring because, according to the countries (US vs Germany) patenting was possible or not; and trademarks were used differently and sequentially. A number of studies have documented the complementarity between technological investments and advertising or marketing investments (Hirschey 1982; Snyder and King 2007; Brekke and Straume 2008; Askenazy, Breda, and Irac 2010). There are also evidences in the existing literature of interactions between different types of IP rights, especially patents and trademarks, often considered as proxies for technological and marketing investments (Graevenitz and Sandner 2009; Schwiebacher and Müller 2009). However, a number of research questions remain unaddressed in the literature so far. A first question relatively unexplored is what the factors underlying the interaction effects between patents and trademarks are, and how to explain that these effects vary across markets and industries. A second question is to know whether the effect of combined use of patents and trademarks comes from the IP rights themselves or rather reflects interactions between the different types of assets that these IP rights are meant to protect. No study has tried to model the relationship between patents and trademarks based on their core function of legal protection devices. This implies modelling beforehand the impact of protecting an innovation by a trademark, which to our knowledge has never been done in the previous literature. Finally, while previous studies have documented the existence of a premium of combined use of patents and trademarks compared to their separate use, there are to our knowledge no comparisons of the size of this premium compared to the premium of using only one type of IP right. This question is important given the non-negligible costs of both patents and trademark filings (Rassenfosse 2019; Herz and Mejer 2016), which imply that the premium corresponding to combined use may not always compensate the costs of seeking these two types of protection.

The present paper aims to contribute to answering the above questions. Through a formal approach, we analyse the interaction effects that occur between trademarks and patents as legal devices that enable the protection of a certain brand and a certain technology. We consider fully fledged firms introducing technological innovations and with capabilities and resources in both upstream and downstream activities. We build a model that encompasses the separate and combined effects on the profits of an innovating firm of using both IP rights and we analyse the conditions in which they can be considered as substitutable or complementary. We rely on the concept of supermodularity, which defines complementarity between two inputs as the fact that using one input while also using the other input has a higher incremental effect on performance than using one input alone (Milgrom and Roberts 1990, 1995). Substitutability, on the contrary, corresponds to the case where using one input alone has as a higher incremental effect on performance than using the input while also using the other input, and vice versa. This implies comparing the size of the premium associated to using both types of IP rights with the size of the premium associated to using only one type of IP right. We then analyse how this effect is likely to vary across industries and characteristics of the market. Finally, we illustrate our findings by an empirical analysis of the complementary or substitute relationship (following the supermodularity approach) of patents and trademarks in different innovative sectors.

The theoretical model consists of a duopoly in which one firm innovates (leader) and another imitates (follower). Each firm may choose to incur advertising expenditure, which enables them to build their goodwill stock, in a dynamic framework. Advertising expenditure is not entirely appropriable: competitors can benefit from the effects of advertising spillovers. Filing a patent grants the right to prevent competitors from using the patented technology. Although patents do not always make it possible to exclude other firms from the market, they tend to decrease competition. Schematically, we assume that if the firm files a patent, it benefits from a monopoly power for a limited period. As for trademarks, there is a lack of conceptual framework in the literature explaining their relation to innovation. We stick to the legal definition and consider that trademarks grant the right to prevent other parties from benefiting from the trademark-ing firm's reputation by creating confusion on the origin of the product. Without trade-mark, advertising has the characteristics of a public good and benefits equally all firms in the market. Filing a trademark enables the firm to appropriate part of its advertising expenditure. Besides, if the firm registers a trademark, the reputation built during the monopoly period entirely benefits the monopoly firm. Hence, the competitor does not benefit from any spillover of advertising expenditure incurred during the patent period. The interaction between patents and trademarks is then characterised by two counter-balancing effects. The first one is a substitutability effect, as the trademark has no impact on the firm's profit during the patent period, given our assumption of perfect appro-priability. This implies a substitutability effect (in the sense of the supermodularity theory), as this makes the incremental benefit of filing a trademark comparatively lower when the firm files a patent than when it does not. The second effect is a complementarity effect, as the reputation built in the monopoly period has an ex post impact on the trademark benefits after the patent has expired, which makes the incremental benefit of filing a trademark comparatively higher when the firm files a patent than when it does not. The main prediction of our theoretical model is that the predominance of the complementarity or the substitutability effect is not straightfor-ward. We show that, for example, by changing the level of two selected parameters of the model, namely advertising spillovers and depreciation rate, patents and trademarks can be either substitutes, or complements.

Using a firm-level database that encompasses the trademarking and patenting activity of a sample of more than 1500 publicly listed firms among the top 2000 corporate R&D investors worldwide – relying on the JRC-OECD, COR&DIP© database (Daiko et al. 2017) –, we test the complementary or substitute relationship between patents and trademarks across firms. To get a sense of how this relationship varies according to advertising and depreciation rate (which are not directly observable in our data), we test this relationship across different sectors, where these markets characteristics tend to be different. We find that in chemical and pharmaceutical industries, where the depreciation rate of advertising is likely to be low and advertising spillovers are likely to be high, the two IP rights tend to be complementary. In contrast, in Information and Communication Technologies (ICT) sectors, which are likely characterised by high advertising depreciation rates and low advertising spillovers, the two IP rights tend to be substitutes. These results tend to confirm our theoretical predictions.

The remainder of this paper is organised as follows. Section 2 presents an overview of the literature on IP rights as means to appropriate the benefits of innovation and in particular papers looking at the possible interactions between different types of IP rights. Section 3 lays out our theoretical model of the interacting effects of trademark and patent protections, from which we analytically derive some predictions on their complementary or substitute relationship. Section 4 presents our empirical strategy with which we test the model predictions and our main empirical results. Section 5 concludes with the implications of the model.

2. Patents and trademarks as interacting means to profit from innovation: previous literature and existing evidence

Over the past decades, a long strand of literature has been exploring firms' strategies to appropriate the benefits from their innovations (Teece 1986; Levin et al. 1987; Cohen, Nelson, and Walsh 2000). According to Teece (1986), the ability of firms to profit from their innovations depends on the 'appropriability regime' in which they operate (i.e. the technical and legal conditions which make the innovation easily imitable by competitors or not), and on the complementary assets that the firm has developed to support the successful commercialisation and marketing of its innovation. Firms may use different appropriation and protection mechanisms, which may interact with each other and may be either complementary or substitute. Indeed, the literature on innovation management shows that the effectiveness of various appropriability mechanisms may be affected by interactions between them (Milgrom and Roberts 1990; Fischer and Henkel 2013).

2.1. Patents and trademarks as appropriability means of innovation

IP rights play a crucial role in the ability of firms to appropriate the benefits from their innovations, as they may influence both the strength of the knowledge 'appropriability regime' and the ability of the firm to build strong complementary assets. The use of patents may for example increase the cost and time of imitation of a technology by competitors (Hurmelinna and Jauhiainen 2004; Pisano 2006), while filing a trademark often constitutes a first step to branding and building strong marketing assets (Athreye and Fassio 2019). A vast literature has documented the links between patents and innovation (Griliches 1991; Mazzoleni and Nelson 1998; Sampat 2018), starting from the premise that the original role of patents is to incentivise innovation: by allowing inventors to exclude others from using a technology, patents generate profits associated with market power, which allow firms to appropriate the benefits from their innovation investments. Although the relationship between innovation investments and patents differs widely across markets and industries, patents remain one of the most obvious source of information to study technical change (Griliches 1991). A more recent literature mentions that trademarks can be used in relation to innovative activity (Schmoch 2003; Mendonça, Pereira, and Godinho 2004; Greenhalgh and Rogers 2007; Millot 2009; Flikkema, De Man, and Castaldi 2014; Block et al. 2015; Schautschick and Greenhalgh 2016; De Vries et al. 2017). Trademarks can be used to capture the benefits induced by reputational assets and market-oriented capabilities (Mendonça, Pereira, and Godinho 2004; Castaldi and Dosso 2018; Castaldi 2019). Researchers have even developed innovation measures using trademarks data (EC 2015; OECD 2015), which are particularly relevant in the case of low-tech or non-technological innovations (marketing or organisational innovation, innovation in services …) which are not well reflected in patent data (Millot 2009).

It is also well documented that trademarks, as well as patents, contribute to economic performance. For example, in the UK case, Greenhalgh and Rogers (2012) find a convincingly significant relation between market value of firms and the existence of a trademark (Sandner and Block 2011; Castaldi and Dosso 2018). Guzman and Stern (2015) show that both patent and trademark activities positively affect growth of a sample of start-ups in the Silicon Valley. Greenhalgh and Rogers (2012) and Sandner and Block (2011), among others, report a positive impact of both measures of IP on the markets' valuation of firms. Other studies investigate the effect of patent and trademark activity on firms' survival and identify a positive correlation between these two measures of IP and a higher increase in the expected life span of firms (e.g. Jensen et al., 2008; Buddelmeyer et al., 2010; Helmers and Rogers, 2010; Wagner and Cockburn, 2010). However, these studies do not focus on the interactions between patents and trademarks, i.e. the specific effect of combined use of patents and trademarks compared to the separate use of either one or the other type of IP right.

2.2. Combined use and interacting effects of patents and trademarks

Innovations are not all associated with a patent, neither are they all associated with a trademark (Flikkema et al. 2015; Seip et al., 2019). The fact that there is no one-to-one relationship between innovation and patents or innovation and trademarks raises the question whether these two types of protections act as substitutes or complements in the appropriation of the benefits of innovation.

A few papers have empirically tested the complementarity between patents and trademarks at the firm level. In similar ways, but on different sets of firms, the existence of complementarity effects have been found between these two types of IP rights (Schwiebacher and Müller 2009; von Graevenitz and Sandner 2009; Zhou et al. 2016; Dosso and Vezzani 2017; Castaldi and Dosso 2018; Grazzi, Piccardo, and Vergari 2019). One interpretation of these results is that the observed complementarity between patents and trademarks reflects the complementarity between their respective underlying investments, i.e. technological and marketing investments (Schwiebacher and Müller 2009; von Graevenitz and Sandner 2009). Another possible interpretation has been put forward Somaya and Graham (2006), who find complementarity effects in the joint use of copyrights and trademarks in software industries, and interpret this as the existence of scale economies in deploying organisational resources for IP management.

2.3. Differences across industries and potential factors influencing the complementarity between patents and trademarks

In Dosso and Vezzani (2017), on more than 1 500 top publicly listed Multinational Corporations (MNCs) performing R&D worldwide (the same data source as the data used in this paper), patents and trademarks exhibit a positive relation with market valuation, and the combined use of patent and trademarks is found to bring a significant market premium. However, this combined effect is found to differ across industries, and little is known on the factors explaining these differences.

To contribute to answering this question, we also investigate in the present paper how the level of complementarity between patents and trademarks differs across sectors, and we try to identify which market characteristics could shape the relationship between patents and trademarks and explain these differences. Among these market characteristics, we focus in particular on two parameters that allow us to model the effect of trademarks: the level of advertising spillovers and the depreciation rate of advertising. These two parameters are likely to vary across sectors, independently of the level of innovativeness of the sector (see Ben Elhadj, Lahmandi-Ayed, and Laussel 2014, for a discussion of how advertising spillovers differ across market structures and sectors (Bilir 2014), for a detailed analysis of product life cycle lengths across sectors, which is likely correlated with advertising depreciation rate). Moreover, as shown in the theoretical model detailed in the next session, they may play an important role in the relationship between patents and trademarks.

3. Modelling the interacting effects of trademark and patent protections

This section presents a theoretical model of the effect of trademarks and patents on firms' innovation returns. We first present the general framework of the model and the effect of patent and trademark protection, and then we examine the outcomes of various IP strategies (patent and trademark, patent only, trademark only, or no IP right). Finally, we study the conditions under which patents and trademarks can be considered as complementary or substitute. The general theoretical framework used to model the effects is consistent with the variable used in the empirical approach used later in the paper, where we consider the effects of the IP strategies on the market value of the innovative firms, as similar empirical papers mentioned above.

3.1. General framework

The starting point of the model is a firm introducing an innovation, leading to the creation of a new market for a product. The innovating firm can choose to register a patent, a trademark, or both or neither of them.

3.1.1. The two-period game
If the innovating firm files a patent, the model has two distinct periods: a monopoly period under the patent protection and then a competition period, which is modelled as a standard homogeneous-good Cournot-type duopoly between the innovating firm (leader) and an imitating firm (follower). We make the simplifying assumption that the innovation is instantaneously imitable, so if the innovating firm files no patent, the competition starts in the first period, as soon as the innovation is introduced. Firms choose their production and advertising levels maximising their intertemporal profit in this framework.

3.1.2. Advertising and reputation
Firms incur advertising expenditure, which enables them to build their reputation (i.e. goodwill), which in turn positively affects the demand for the product. Following Nerlove

and Arrow (1962), we assume that advertising expenditure is cumulative: firm's goodwill is built with advertising expenditure incurred in each period, and depreciates at rate δ. In a two-period framework, this translates into an equation of evolution of the goodwill stock G_t from first period to second period:

$$G_2 - G_1 = a_2 - \delta G_1, \qquad (1)$$

where a_2 is the amount of second period advertising expenditure and δ is the depreciation rate of advertising between the two periods. The firms only start advertising expenditure when they enter the market, so in the first period the amount of goodwill is $G_1 = a_1$.

Besides, we assume that advertising expenditure is not entirely appropriable by firms (Friedman 1983) and is subject to spillovers. The interpretation of those spillovers is that part of the advertising launched by a firm corresponds to advertising for the product in general and not for its own brand, so that the competitor can also benefit from it. Advertising expenditure incurred by each firm therefore divides into two parts, one share benefiting all firms in the market and the other share benefiting only the firm that has incurred the advertising expenditure.

3.1.3. Effect of trademark with or without patent

To model the effect of trademarks, we stick to the legal definition and consider that trademarks prevent other parties from infringing on the firm's reputation by creating confusion on the origin of the product. We assume that in the absence of trademark, competitors can imitate not only the functional features of the product but also its appearance and the signs referring to the brand image (e.g. the brand name). In that case, no part of advertising expenditure can be appropriated by the firm. Advertising expenditure and goodwill have therefore the characteristics of a public good: they benefit equally all the firms present in the market. If the leader files a trademark, the total amount of second period advertising expenditure benefiting the follower is $\overline{a_2} + s a_2$, where a_2 (resp. $\overline{a_2}$) is the amount of advertising expenditure incurred by the leader (resp. the follower) in period 2, and s is the level of advertising spillovers benefiting the follower (with $0 < s < 1$). If the leader does not file a trademark, the total amount of second period advertising expenditure benefiting the follower is $\overline{a_2} + a_2$.

One key assumption of our model is that if the leader files both a trademark and a patent, all the advertising expenditure incurred during the patent period corresponds to advertising for the brand and benefits only the leader's goodwill. Indeed, during the patent period, the reputation of the product coincides with the reputation of the monopoly brand, so that the brand entirely captures the reputation of the product. This means that the follower will benefit from no spillover of advertising expenditure incurred during the monopoly period. To benefit from spillovers, since the respective brand images of the leader and the follower are not confusable, the follower needs first to start to advertise its product so that the customers realise that the products are identical. Advertising spillovers are then only effective in the second period when the follower enters the market. By contrast, if no trademark is filed, the competitor can play on confusion on the appearance of the product and thus benefit from advertising spillovers of all periods, including the monopoly period, as customers will mistakenly attribute the goodwill of the leader to the product sold by the competitor.

Lastly, if no patent is filed, the follower benefits from a share s of the leader's advertising expenditure in each period in case a trademark is filed, and from the totality of the leader's advertising expenditure if no trademark is filed.

Table 1 summarises the amount of goodwill benefiting the leader and the follower in the second period, depending on the IP strategy adopted by the leader, where: a_2 and $\overline{a_2}$ are the advertising expenditure incurred in the second period by the leader and by the follower, respectively; a_1 and $\overline{a_1}$ are the levels of advertising expenditure in the first period; δ is the depreciation rate of advertising over the two periods; $\overline{s}$ is the level of advertising spillovers benefiting the leader; and s is the level of advertising spillovers benefiting the follower if the leader files a trademark.

The amount of goodwill benefiting the leader and the follower in the first period, depending on the IP strategy adopted is shown in Table 2.

3.1.4. Inverse demand function

Following Dixit (1979), we assume that the inverse demand function facing each firm in the market is negatively related to the total amount of quantities sold. Assuming a quadratic utility function of customers, the relationship between price and quantities is linear (Dixit 1979). We then assume that advertising increases customers' willingness to pay for the product (Brady 2009), so that the goodwill stock has a positive impact on the price for a given quantity sold. The effect of goodwill stock is assumed to have decreasing marginal returns. The inverse demand function facing the leader is:

$$P_t = \propto -\beta(Q_t + \overline{Q_t}) + \tau\sqrt{G_t}, \qquad (2)$$

where Q_t and $\overline{Q_t}$ are the quantities sold by the firm and its competitor in t and G_t represents the goodwill stock of the firm, with α, β and τ strictly positive parameters. The inverse demand function facing the follower is symmetrical.

3.1.5. Supermodularity analysis

Based on this framework, we compare the inter-temporal profits resulting from the various IP strategies to investigate the complementarity relationship between the various protection means, relying on the concept of supermodularity (Milgrom and Roberts 1990, 1995). This framework makes it possible to analyse complementarity in the context of discrete choices (in which pay-offs are not continuous); this is appropriate here since we focus on a single innovation so that the firm registers at most one trademark and one patent.[1] The supermodularity theory states that two inputs are complements only if using one input while also using the other input has a higher incremental effect on performance

Table 1. Amount of goodwill benefiting the leader and the follower in the second period, depending on the IP strategy adopted by the leader.

		TM	No TM
PAT	Leader	$(1-\delta)a_1 + a_2 + \overline{s}a_2$	
	Follower	$\overline{a_2} + sa_2$	$\overline{a_2} + (1-\delta)a_1 + a_2$
No PAT	Leader	$a_2 + (1-\delta)a_1 + \overline{s}(\overline{a_2} + (1-\delta)\overline{a_1})$	
	Follower	$\overline{a_2} + (1-\delta)\overline{a_1} + s(a_2 + (1-\delta)a_1)$	$\overline{a_2} + (1-\delta)\overline{a_1} + a_2 + (1-\delta)a_1$

[1]This constitutes a simplifying assumption as, in practice, firms in some industries may protect their innovation with several patents or several trademarks..

Table 2. Amount of goodwill benefiting the leader and the follower in the first period, depending on the IP strategy adopted by the leader.

		TM	No TM
PAT	Leader		a_1
	Follower		-
No PAT	Leader		$a_1 + \overline{s a_1}$
	Follower	$\overline{a_1} + s a_1$	$\overline{a_1} + a_1$

than using one input alone, following the intuitive idea that 'the whole is more than the sum of its parts' (see Guidetti, Mancinelli, and Mazzanti 2009; Cassiman and Veugelers 2006; Cavaco and Crifo 2014; Ballot et al. 2015; Fares, Raza, and Thomas 2018 for other applications of the supermodularity concept[2]).

We test the validity of the following fundamental inequality, where V is the intertemporal profit gained from innovation and the exponents indicate the presence or not of a trademark (TM) or a patent (PAT):

$$V^{TM,PAT} + V^{0,0} > V^{TM,0} + V^{0,PAT}. \tag{3}$$

If this inequality is verified, patents and trademarks are complementary, whereas if the reverse inequality is verified, they are substitutes.

3.2. Outcome of the various intellectual property strategies

Based on the above framework, we derive the outcome of the various IP strategies on the profit of the innovating firm.[3]

The intertemporal profit of the firm is:

$$V = [P(Q_1, G_1) - c]Q_1 - a_1 + r[P(Q_2, G_2) - c]Q_2 - ra_2 - 1_{PAT=1} * C_{PAT} - 1_{TM=1} * C_{TM}$$

where c is the cost of production, assumed linear, r is the discount rate between the two periods (with $r > 0$, decreasing with the duration of the patent), and C_{PAT} and C_{TM} correspond to the costs of filing a trademark and a patent, respectively.[4]

3.2.1. Case of patent protection
a. If the innovating firm files a trademark:

If the leader registers both a patent and a trademark, its inter-temporal profit is, from (2) and replacing G_1 and G_2 by their expressions in Tables 1 and 2:

---

[2]Cassiman and Veugelers (2006) use the supermodularity framework for the analysis of the complementarity between internal R&D and external knowledge acquisition; Guidetti, Mancinelli, and Mazzanti (2009) for the complementarity in training practices; Cavaco and Crifo (2014) for the complementarity between various dimensions of corporate social responsibility and financial performance; Ballot et al. (2015) for complementarities in performance between product, process and organisational innovation; and Fares, Raza, and Thomas (2018) for the complementarity between labels and brands.

[3]For the sake of readability, we do not report all the calculation steps here. The full demonstration with detailed calculation steps is available from the authors on request.

[4]The cost associated to filing a trademark or a patent are not negligible. Indeed recent research shows that patent and trademark fees have significant effect on the demand for patent and trademark applications (Rassenfosse 2019; Herz and Mejer 2016). Moreover, firms often use other services such as legal advice for IP filings which are likely to generate additional costs..

$$V = [\propto -\beta Q_1 + \tau\sqrt{a_1} - c]Q_1 - a_1$$
$$+ r\left[\propto -\beta(Q_2 + \overline{Q_2}) + \tau\sqrt{(1-\delta)a_1 + a_2 + \overline{sa_2}} - c\right]Q_2 - ra_2 - C_{PAT} - C_{TM},$$

$$(4)$$

The inter-temporal profit of the follower is:

$$\overline{V} = r\left[\propto -\beta(\overline{Q_2} + Q_2) + \tau\sqrt{\overline{a_2} + sa_2} - c\right]\overline{Q_2} - r\overline{a_2}$$

$$(5)$$

The model is solved through backward induction: the firms first determine their optimal levels of advertising expenditure and quantities sold in the second period considering the stock of advertising expenditure of the leader in the first period given, then the leader maximises its inter-temporal profit on the choice variables of the first period.

First step: maximisation of the second period profits on $Q_2, \overline{Q_2}, a_2,$ and $\overline{a_2}$ considering a_1 given

The respective programmes of the leader and the follower are:

$$\max_{Q_2, a_2}\left(r\left[\propto -\beta(Q_2 + \overline{Q_2}) + \tau\sqrt{(1-\delta)a_1 + a_2 + \overline{sa_2}} - c\right]Q_2 - ra_2\right)$$

and

$$\max_{\overline{Q_2}, \overline{a_2}}\left(r\left[\propto -\beta(\overline{Q_2} + Q_2) + \tau\sqrt{\overline{a_2} + sa_2} - c\right]\overline{Q_2} - r\overline{a_2}\right).$$

The system of first order conditions yields the following Nash-Cournot equilibrium:

$$\begin{cases} Q_2^* = \overline{Q_2^*} = \frac{2(\propto-c)}{6\beta-\tau^2} \\ a_2^* = \frac{1-\overline{s}}{1-\overline{s}s}\left(\frac{\tau(\propto-c)}{6\beta-\tau^2}\right)^2 - \frac{1-\delta}{1-\overline{s}s}a_1 \\ \overline{a_2^*} = \frac{1-s}{1-\overline{s}s}\left(\frac{\tau(\propto-c)}{6\beta-\tau^2}\right)^2 + s\frac{1-\delta}{1-\overline{s}s}a_1 \end{cases}$$

$$(6)$$

The optimal quantities in second period are equal for both firms. Considering $\overline{s} = s$, the optimal amount of advertising expenditure in period 2 is higher for the follower. Indeed, since the follower does not benefit from advertising expenditure incurred in period 1, it has to catch up with the leader in order to sell at the same price (in a Cournot competition framework[5]).

From first order condition on Q_2, and the previous expression of Q_2^* and a_2^* in (6), (4) becomes:

$$V = [\propto -\beta Q_1 + \tau\sqrt{a_1} - c]Q_1 - a_1 + r\beta\left(\frac{2(\propto-c)}{6\beta-\tau^2}\right)^2 - r\frac{1-\overline{s}}{1-\overline{s}s}\left(\frac{\tau(\propto-c)}{6\beta-\tau^2}\right)^2$$
$$+ r\frac{1-\delta}{1-\overline{s}s}a_1 - C_{PAT} - C_{TM}.$$

Second step: maximisation of the leader inter-temporal profit on a_1, Q_1:

The leader then maximises the above intertemporal profit on the choice variables of the first period. The system of first order conditions on Q_1, a_1 yields:

---

[5]In other competition frameworks, we might observe that followers have lower advertising expenditure than leaders, and compensate by a significantly lower selling price of the same product, which corresponds for example to the situation of firms selling generic drugs.

$$\begin{cases} Q_1^* = \frac{2\left(1 - r\frac{1-\delta}{1-\bar{s}s}\right)(\alpha - c)}{4\beta\left(1 - r\frac{1-\delta}{1-\bar{s}s}\right) - \tau^2} \\ a_1^* = \left(\frac{\tau(\alpha - c)}{4\beta\left(1 - r\frac{1-\delta}{1-\bar{s}s}\right) - \tau^2}\right)^2 \end{cases}.$$

The model has an interior solution if $4\beta\left(1 - r\frac{1-\delta}{1-\bar{s}s}\right) - \tau^2 > 0$ (guaranteeing that Q_2^*, $\overline{Q_2^*}$,

Q_1^*, $\overline{a_2^*}$, and a_1^* are positive) and $\left(\frac{4\beta\left(1 - r\frac{1-\delta}{1-\bar{s}s}\right) - \tau^2}{6\beta - \tau^2}\right)^2 > \frac{1-\delta}{1-\bar{s}}$ (guaranteeing that a_2^* is positive),

i.e. if β, the negative impact of quantities on demand is large enough compared to the impact of advertising τ, and the depreciation rate of advertising δ is large enough.

Rewriting (4) with the equilibrium values of Q_2^*, $\overline{Q_2^*}$, a_2^*, $\overline{a_2^*}$, Q_1^* and a_1^*, the final profit of the innovating firm in case it files both a patent and a trademark is then equal to:

$$V^{TM,PAT} = (\alpha - c)^2 \left(\frac{1 - r\frac{1-\delta}{1-\bar{s}s}}{4\beta\left(1 - r\frac{1-\delta}{1-\bar{s}s}\right) - \tau^2} + r\beta\left(\frac{2}{6\beta - \tau^2}\right)^2 - r\frac{1 - \bar{s}}{1 - \bar{s}s}\left(\frac{\tau}{6\beta - \tau^2}\right)^2\right)$$
$$- C_{PAT} - C_{TM}. \tag{7}$$

b. If the innovating firm does not register a trademark

In this case, the intertemporal profit expressions of the leader and the follower are:

$$V = [\alpha - \beta Q_1 + \tau\sqrt{a_1} - c]Q_1 - a_1$$
$$+ r\left[\alpha - \beta(Q_2 + \overline{Q_2}) + \tau\sqrt{(1 - \delta)a_1 + a_2 + \overline{a_2}} - c\right]Q_2 - ra_2 - C_{PAT}$$

$$\overline{V} = r\left[\alpha - \beta(\overline{Q_2} + Q_2) + \tau\sqrt{\overline{a_2} + (1 - \delta)a_1 + a_2} - c\right]\overline{Q_2} - r\overline{a_2}$$

Maximising V on Q_2, $\overline{Q_2}$, a_2, and $\overline{a_2}$ considering a_1 given yields the following Nash-equilibrium:

$$\begin{cases} Q_2^* = \overline{Q_2^*} = \frac{2(\alpha - c)}{6\beta - \tau^2} \\ a_2^* = \left(\frac{\tau(\alpha - c)}{6\beta - \tau^2}\right)^2 - (1 - \delta)a_1 \\ \overline{a_2^*} = 0 \end{cases}$$

If the leader files no trademark, the follower relies entirely on advertising spillovers, and does not incur any advertising expenditure in the second period.

The intertemporal profit of the leader is then:

$$V = [\alpha - \beta Q_1 + \tau\sqrt{a_1} - c]Q_1 - a_1 + r\beta\left(\frac{2(\alpha - c)}{6\beta - \tau^2}\right)^2 - r\left(\frac{\tau(\alpha - c)}{6\beta - \tau^2}\right)^2 + r(1 - \delta)a_1$$
$$- C_{PAT}$$

Maximising V on a_1, Q_1 yields:

$$\begin{cases} Q_1^* = \frac{2(1 - r(1-\delta))(\alpha - c)}{4\beta(1 - r(1-\delta)) - \tau^2} \\ a_1^* = \left(\frac{\tau(\alpha - c)}{4\beta(1 - r(1-\delta)) - \tau^2}\right)^2 \end{cases}$$

A solution exists on the condition that $4\beta(1 - r(1 - \delta)) - \tau^2 > 0$ (guaranteeing that $Q_2^*, \overline{Q_2^*}, Q_1^*$ and a_1 are positive) and $\left(\frac{4\beta(1-r(1-\delta))-\tau^2}{6\beta-\tau^2}\right)^2 > (1 - \delta)$ (guaranteeing that a_2^* is positive), i.e. if β, is large enough compared to τ, and δ is large enough.

The profit of the innovating firm in case it files a patent but no trademark is then equal to:

$$V^{0,PAT} = (\alpha - c)^2 \left(\frac{(1 - r(1 - \delta))}{4\beta(1 - r(1 - \delta)) - \tau^2} + r\beta \left(\frac{2}{6\beta - \tau^2} \right)^2 - r \left(\frac{\tau}{6\beta - \tau^2} \right)^2 \right) - C_{PAT}$$

$$(8)$$

3.2.2. Case without patent protection
If the innovative firm does not protect its innovation with a patent, the competition starts in the first period. Inter-temporal profits are:

$$V = \left[\alpha - \beta(Q_1 + \overline{Q_1}) + \tau\sqrt{a_1 + s\overline{a_1}} - c \right] Q_1 - a_1$$
$$+ r\left[\alpha - \beta(Q_2 + \overline{Q_2}) + \tau\sqrt{a_2 + (1 - \delta)a_1 + \overline{s}(\overline{a_2} + (1 - \delta)\overline{a_1})} - c \right] Q_2 - ra_2$$
$$- (1_{TM=1})C_{TM},$$

and

$$\overline{V} = \left[\alpha - \beta(Q_1 + \overline{Q_1}) + \tau\sqrt{\overline{a_1} + sa_1} - c \right] \overline{Q_1} - \overline{a_1}$$
$$+ r\left[\alpha - \beta(Q_2 + \overline{Q_2}) + \tau\sqrt{\overline{a_2} + (1 - \delta)\overline{a_1} + s(a_2 + (1 - \delta)a_1)} - c \right] \overline{Q_2} - r\overline{a_2}.$$

with $0 < s < 1$ in case a trademark is filed and $s = 1$ in case no trademark is filed. Maximising V on a_2, Q_2, and $\overline{V}$ on $\overline{Q_2}, \overline{a_2}$ considering a_1 and $\overline{a_1}$ given yields the following symmetrical Nash-equilibrium:

$$\begin{cases} Q_2^* = \overline{Q_2^*} = \frac{2(\alpha-c)}{6\beta-\tau^2} \\ a_2^* = \frac{1-\overline{s}}{1-\overline{s}s} \left(\frac{\tau(\alpha-c)}{6\beta-\tau^2} \right)^2 - (1 - \delta)a_1 . \\ \overline{a_2^*} = \frac{1-s}{1-\overline{s}s} \left(\frac{\tau(\alpha-c)}{6\beta-\tau^2} \right)^2 - (1 - \delta)\overline{a_1} \end{cases}$$

The intertemporal profits of the leader and the follower then are:

$$V = \left[\alpha - \beta(Q_1 + \overline{Q_1}) + \tau\sqrt{a_1 + s\overline{a_1}} - c \right] Q_1 - a_1 + r\beta \left(\frac{2(\alpha-c)}{6\beta - \tau^2} \right)^2$$
$$- r\frac{1-\overline{s}}{1-\overline{s}s} \left(\frac{\tau(\alpha-c)}{6\beta - \tau^2} \right)^2 + r(1 - \delta)a_1,$$

and

$$\bar{V} = \left[\alpha - \beta(Q_1 + \overline{Q_1}) + \tau\sqrt{\overline{a_1} + s a_1} - c\right]\overline{Q_1} - \overline{a_1} + r\beta\left(\frac{2(\alpha - c)}{6\beta - \tau^2}\right)^2$$
$$- r\frac{1-s}{1-\bar{s}s}\left(\frac{\tau(\alpha - c)}{6\beta - \tau^2}\right)^2 + r(1-\delta)\overline{a_1}.$$

Maximising V on a_1, Q_1 and $\bar{V}$ on $\overline{a_1}$, $\overline{Q_1}$ yields:

$$\begin{cases} Q_1^* = \overline{Q_1^*} = \frac{2(1-r(1-\delta))(\alpha-c)}{6\beta(1-r(1-\delta))-\tau^2} \\ a_1^* = \frac{1-\bar{s}}{1-\bar{s}s}\left(\frac{\tau(\alpha-c)}{6\beta(1-r(1-\delta))-\tau^2}\right)^2 \\ \overline{a_1^*} = \frac{1-s}{1-\bar{s}s}\left(\frac{\tau(\alpha-c)}{6\beta(1-r(1-\delta))-\tau^2}\right)^2 \end{cases}$$

An interior solution exists on the condition that $6\beta(1 - r(1 - \delta)) - \tau^2 > 0$ (guaranteeing that $Q_2^*, \overline{Q_2^*}, Q_1^*, \overline{Q_1^*}, a_1^*$ and $\overline{a_1^*}$ are positive) and $\left(\frac{6\beta(1-r(1-\delta))-\tau^2}{6\beta-\tau^2}\right)^2 > (1 - \delta)$ (guaranteeing that a_2^* and $\overline{a_2^*}$ are positive), i.e. if β is large enough compared to τ, and δ is large enough. The leader's inter-temporal profit in case it files a trademark but no patent equals:

$$V^{TM,0} = (\alpha - c)^2 \left((1 - r(1-\delta))\left(\frac{4\beta(1-r(1-\delta)) - \frac{1-\bar{s}}{1-\bar{s}s}\tau^2}{(6\beta(1-r(1-\delta)) - \tau^2)^2}\right) + r\beta\left(\frac{2}{6\beta - \tau^2}\right)^2\right.$$
$$\left. - r\frac{1-\bar{s}}{1-\bar{s}s}\left(\frac{\tau}{6\beta - \tau^2}\right)^2\right) - C_{TM} \tag{9}$$

In case neither a patent nor a trademark is filed, the expression of the intertemporal profit is the same as above, with $s = 1$ and no filing cost:

$$V^{0,0} = (\alpha - c)^2 \left((1 - r(1-\delta))\left(\frac{4\beta(1-r(1-\delta)) - \tau^2}{(6\beta(1-r(1-\delta)) - \tau^2)^2}\right) + r\beta\left(\frac{2}{6\beta - \tau^2}\right)^2\right.$$
$$\left. - r\left(\frac{\tau}{6\beta - \tau^2}\right)^2\right). \tag{10}$$

3.3. Comparison of outcomes and complementarity analysis

Based on the previous results, we seek to determine the optimal IP right strategies for innovating firms, by comparing the intertemporal profits resulting from the different IP right combinations. We then examine the conditions under which patents and trademarks can be considered as complementary or substitute, according to the supermodularity approach.

3.3.1. Determination of the optimal IP right strategy

From (7) and (8), we get:

$$V^{TM,PAT} - V^{0,PAT} = (\propto -c)^2 \left(\frac{\tau^2 r(1-\delta)\left(\frac{\bar{s}s}{1-\bar{s}s}\right)}{\left(4\beta\left(1 - r\frac{1-\delta}{1-\bar{s}s}\right) - \tau^2\right)\left(4\beta(1 - r(1-\delta)) - \tau^2\right)} \right. $$

$$\left. +r\bar{s}\left(\frac{\tau}{6\beta - \tau^2}\right)^2 \frac{1-s}{1-\bar{s}s} \right) - C_{TM} = K_1 - C_{TM} \qquad (11)$$

with $K_1 > 0$

From (9) and (10):

$$V^{TM,0} - V^{0,0} = (\propto -c)^2 \left((1 - r(1-\delta)) \frac{\left(\tau^2 \bar{s}\frac{1-s}{1-\bar{s}s}\right)}{(6\beta(1 - r(1-\delta)) - \tau^2)^2} \right.$$

$$\left. +r\bar{s}\left(\frac{\tau}{6\beta - \tau^2}\right)^2 \frac{1-s}{1-\bar{s}s} \right) - C_{TM} = K_2 - C_{TM} \qquad (12)$$

with $K_2 > 0$. Considering sufficiently low filing costs, it is always beneficial for firms to file a trademark.

Besides, from (7) and (9), we get

$$V^{TM,PAT} - V^{TM,0} = (\propto -c)^2 \left(1 - r\frac{1-\delta}{1-\bar{s}s} \right) *$$

$$\frac{(6\beta(1 - r(1-\delta)) - \tau^2)^2 - \left(4\beta(1 - r(1-\delta)) - \frac{1-\bar{s}}{1-\bar{s}s}\tau^2\right)\left(4\beta(1 - r(1-\delta)) - \tau^2\left(1 + \frac{\bar{s}sr(1-\delta)}{1-\bar{s}s-r(1-\delta)}\right)\right)}{\left(4\beta\left(1 - r\frac{1-\delta}{1-\bar{s}s}\right) - \tau^2\right)(6\beta(1 - r(1-\delta)) - \tau^2)^2} - C_{PAT}$$

$$= K_3 - C_{PAT},$$

with $K_3 > 0$.

From (8) and (10):

$$V^{0,PAT} - V^{0,0} = (\propto -c)^2$$

$$* \left((1 - r(1-\delta)) \left(\frac{(6\beta(1 - r(1-\delta)) - \tau^2)^2 - (4\beta(1 - r(1-\delta)) - \tau^2)^2}{(4\beta(1 - r(1-\delta)) - \tau^2)(6\beta(1 - r(1-\delta)) - \tau^2)^2} \right) \right)$$

$$-C_{PAT} = K_4 - C_{PAT}$$

with $K_4 > 0$.

As well as for trademarks, the benefit of filing a patent is positive if the filing costs are sufficiently low. This may not always be the case as the registration of a patent – more than a trademark – is a relatively complex procedure and requires some human and financial resources. Therefore, the costs of filing a patent may outweigh the benefits gained from the patent protection.

Considering sufficiently low levels of filing costs, we have:

$$V^{TM,PAT} > \left\{ V^{TM,0}, V^{0,PAT} \right\} > V^{0,0}.$$

The optimal IP right strategy for the innovating firm is thus always to register both a patent and a trademark when considering negligible filing costs. Besides, the trademark benefit differs depending on whether a patent is also filed or not. We then seek to analyse this difference in order to conclude about the complementary or substitute relationship between the two IP rights.

3.3.2. Supermodularity analysis: determining the conditions of complementarity or substitutability between patents and trademarks

In the following, we investigate in which conditions the supermodularity inequality (3) is verified, i.e. where the difference $\left(V^{TM,PAT} - V^{0,PAT}\right) - \left(V^{TM,0} - V^{0,0}\right)$ is positive. This amounts to comparing the benefit of filing a trademark in case of patent protection and in case of no patent. From (11) and (12) we deduce that:

$$\left(V^{TM,PAT} - V^{0,PAT}\right) - \left(V^{TM,0} - V^{0,0}\right) = (\propto -c)^2 \left(\frac{\tau^2 r(1-\delta)\left(\frac{s\bar{s}}{1-\bar{s}s}\right)}{\left(4\beta\left(1-r\frac{1-\delta}{1-\bar{s}s}\right) - \tau^2\right)\left(4\beta(1-r(1-\delta)) - \tau^2\right)} \right.$$

$$\left. -(1-r(1-\delta))\frac{\tau^2\bar{s}\frac{1-s}{1-\bar{s}s}}{\left(6\beta(1-r(1-\delta)) - \tau^2\right)^2} \right).$$

The sign of this expression is dependent on market contexts. To illustrate this, we focus in the following on two selected parameters of the model, s and δ.

We have

$$\frac{\partial\left[\left(V^{TM,PAT} - V^{0,PAT}\right) - \left(V^{TM,0} - V^{0,0}\right)\right]}{\partial s} = (\propto -c)^2 \left(\frac{(1-r(1-\delta))\tau^2(1-\bar{s})\bar{s}}{\left(6\beta(1-r(1-\delta)) - \tau^2\right)^2(1-\bar{s}s)^2} \right.$$

$$\left. + \frac{(1-\delta)r\tau^2\bar{s}}{\left(4\beta\left(1-r\frac{1-\delta}{1-\bar{s}s}\right) - \tau^2\right)^2(1-\bar{s}s)^2} \right)$$

This expression is always positive if $1 - r(1-\delta) > 0$, which is always true under the conditions of existence of an equilibrium. The level of complementarity between trademarks and patents is thus increasing with the level of advertising spillovers.

For s approaching 0, we have:

$$\left(V^{TM,PAT} - V^{0,PAT}\right) - \left(V^{TM,0} - V^{0,0}\right) \to (\propto -c)^2 \left(-(1-r(1-\delta))\frac{\tau^2\bar{s}\frac{1-s}{1-\bar{s}s}}{\left(6\beta(1-r(1-\delta)) - \tau^2\right)^2} \right),$$

which is always negative under the conditions of existence of an equilibrium, so trademarks and patents are substitute. For s approaching 1, we have:

$$\left(V^{TM,PAT} - V^{0,PAT}\right) - \left(V^{TM,0} - V^{0,0}\right) \to (\propto -c)^2 \left(\frac{\tau^2 r(1-\delta)\frac{\bar{s}}{1-\bar{s}}}{\left(4\beta\left(1-r\frac{1-\delta}{1-\bar{s}}\right) - \tau^2\right)\left(4\beta(1-r(1-\delta)) - \tau^2\right)} \right),$$

which is positive under the conditions of existence of an equilibrium. Therefore, for high values of s, trademarks and patents are complementary. Indeed, in the first period, trademarks provide full protection of the goodwill in case of patent protection, whereas in case of no patent protection, trademarks still allow a non-null level of advertising spillovers s. The higher those advertising spillovers are, the more beneficial it is to reinforce the trademark with a patent.

Besides, we have:

$$\frac{\partial\left[\left(V^{TM,PAT}-V^{0,PAT}\right)-\left(V^{TM,0}-V^{0,0}\right)\right]}{\partial\delta}$$

$$= (\propto-c)^2 r\tau^2\left(\frac{1}{(4\beta(1-r(1-\delta))-\tau^2)^2}+\bar{s}\frac{1-s}{1-\bar{s}s}\frac{6\beta(1-r(1-\delta))+\tau^2}{(6\beta(1-r(1-\delta))-\tau^2)^3}\right.$$

$$\left.-\frac{1}{1-\bar{s}s}\frac{1}{\left(4\beta\left(1-r\frac{1-\delta}{1-\bar{s}s}\right)-\tau^2\right)^2}\right).$$

This expression is negative for sufficiently high values of s, so above a certain threshold of advertising spillovers, the complementarity tends to decrease with the depreciation rate of advertising. Indeed, with high depreciation rates, only a small proportion of the goodwill accumulated in the monopoly period is transferred to the second period, which tends to decrease the complementarity effect.

For δ approaching its minimum value, for which $(4\beta(1-r(1-\delta))-\tau^2) = 0$, we have:

$$\left(V^{TM,PAT}-V^{0,PAT}\right)-\left(V^{TM,0}-V^{0,0}\right)\rightarrow+\infty$$

and for δ approaching 1, we have:

$$\left(V^{TM,PAT}-V^{0,PAT}\right)-\left(V^{TM,0}-V^{0,0}\right)\rightarrow-(\propto-c)^2\frac{\tau^2\bar{s}\left(\frac{1-s}{1-\bar{s}s}\right)}{(6\beta-\tau^2)^2}<0.$$

So for high levels of depreciation rate of advertising, patents and trademarks tend to be

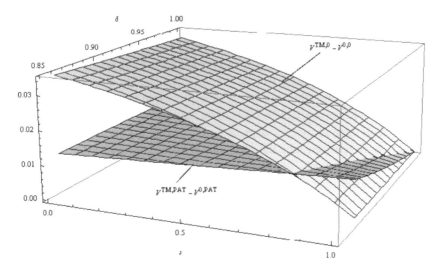

Figure 1. Benefits of trademark filing in case of patent protection and no patent protection.

substitutes.

In the following, we consider the parameters of the inverse demand function β and τ given, as well as $\bar{s}$, the amount of spillovers benefiting the leader: $\beta = \tau = 1$, and $\bar{s} = 1/2$,

and we attribute a definite value to the discount rate between the two periods r. A reasonable value for r is 0.6[6] Lastly, we attribute a value of 1 to the common scaling parameter $(\alpha - c)^2$. We can then represent the level of trademark benefits in case of patent and of no patent according to s and δ, considering negligible costs of IP rights (Figure 1)
[7]

$$\beta = \tau = 1, r = 0.6, \bar{s} = \frac{1}{2}, (\alpha - c)^2$$

$$= 1. \text{ Values of } s \text{ and } \delta \text{ verifying } \left(\frac{4\beta\left(1 - r\frac{1-\delta}{1-\bar{s}s}\right) - \tau^2}{6\beta - \tau^2} \right)^2 > \frac{1-\delta}{1-\bar{s}}$$

Under the assumptions of the model, depending on the level of advertising spillovers s and on the level of depreciation of advertising expenditure, patents and trademarks can be found to be either complementary or substitute. The interpretation of the results is the following. The interaction between patents and trademarks is characterised by two counterbalancing effects. There is, on the one hand, a substitutability effect (as defined in the supermodularity theory). Indeed, the trademark benefits the firm only when it faces competition. As we assume that patent leads to a non-competition period, trademarks are comparatively less advantageous for the pioneer firm when there is also a patent filed. In the extreme, if the protection offered by patent was infinite in time, the benefit of trademark would be null, as the firm would not need to protect its brand from confusion with other firms. On the other hand, we find a complementarity effect: the trademark makes it possible to capture entirely the goodwill built during the monopoly period. The trademark benefits in the second period will be even more important if the firm has benefited from a monopoly period, so that trademarks in the second period are comparatively more advantageous if the firm had a patent filed in the first period.

Depending on the levels of advertising spillovers and advertising depreciation rate, either the first effect or the second effect can be predominant. For sufficiently high values of advertising spillovers and low values of advertising depreciation rate, patents and trademarks are found to be complementary. This is likely to be the case for example in pharmaceutical industries. Indeed, in these sectors, the depreciation of advertising are likely to be low, as the products tend to have relatively long life cycles and remain stable over time. In addition, in these sectors technology is well codified, which implies that innovations can be perfectly duplicated, so that advertising performed by firms is very likely to benefit the product in general. The level of advertising spillovers in those sectors is then relatively high (Ben Elhadj, Lahmandi-Ayed, and Laussel 2014; Szegedy-Maszak 2004).[8] In contrast, in other high-tech sectors such as computer and electronic products, the depreciation rate of advertising tends to

---

[6]Assuming an annual interest rate of r_0, and a patent period of T years, the discount rate between the two periods in the model can be approximated by $r \equiv \frac{\sum_{t=0}^{T} \left(\frac{1}{1+r_0}\right)^t}{\sum_{t=T+1}^{\infty} \left(\frac{1}{1+r_0}\right)^t} = 1 - \left(\frac{1}{1+r_0}\right)^T$. Taking $r_0 = 0.05$, and considering that the patent period lasts twenty years, we obtain a value of $\cong 0.6$.

[7]The conditions of the model require that $\left(\frac{4\beta\left(1 - r\frac{1-\delta}{1-\bar{s}}\right) - \tau^2}{6\beta - \tau^2}\right)^2 > \frac{1-\delta}{1-\bar{s}}$, so that with $\beta = \tau = 1$ and $\bar{s} = 1/2$, the model does not admit an equilibrium for $\delta < 0.85$.

[8]Szegedy-Maszak (2004) for example found that the advertising for a new drug for adult attention deficit disorder, Strattera, increased demand for all drugs targeted to this disorder.

be high (as the product life cycle is short[9]) and advertising spillovers tend to be low[10] (as the technology is not entirely codified and the products are less substitutable). In these sectors, the substitutability effect tends to outweigh the complementarity effect. This does not necessarily imply that firms use only one type of IP right, as in the case of negligible registration costs the optimal strategy is always to file both a patent and a trademark. However, in those cases, the incremental benefit of using both types of IP rights instead of one is lower.

4. Empirical investigation

This section presents some preliminary empirical evidence aiming at illustrating the theoretical model presented above. The general purpose is to test the complementarity or substitutability between the use of trademarks and the use of patents by firms as tools to protect their assets, depending on the characteristics of the market.

4.1. Tested hypotheses and methodology

The theoretical model considers the link between patents and trademarks at the product level. Since IP right data are generally not available at the product level, in the following, we shift the framework of analysis from product-level to firm-level. Although those frameworks are not equivalent (as firms are likely to sell several products on the market), we may assume that the IP strategies observed at the firm-level are representative of the strategy adopted by the firm at each product launch (a number of companies registering systematically new trademarks, or patents, or both each time they introduce a new product on the market). Our general empirical strategy then consists in estimating and comparing the firms' performance resulting from various IP right strategies. We use the market value of the firm as a measure of firm performance, which enables an intertemporal analysis of the effects of IP rights: assuming efficient stock markets, the firm's market value is equal to the sum of its discounted future profits, which is the target variable in our previous theoretical model. Another measure of performance, such as the present profit margin at time t, would be inadequate as the context of the model is dynamic, with inter-temporal effects of IP strategy choices.

We follow the market value approach, which combines accounting data with the valuation on the stock market. This approach has been used in particular to assess returns to innovation (Griliches 1981; Hall, Jaffe, and Trajtenberg 2000; Greenhalgh and Rogers 2007; Sandner 2009). The general idea of those models is that investors estimate a firm's value according to the returns that they expect from its assets (either tangible or intangible). The purpose of those models is generally to disentangle the contribution of tangible and intangible assets, intangible assets being proxied by measures of R&D, the number of patents or the number of trademarks. In our model, by contrast, the intangible assets of the firm are considered as given, and IP rights are used to appropriate the benefits of those assets. We thus seek to analyse how the IP strategy affects the value of the firm, considering everything else equal, notably their levels of R&D and innovative activity, as reflected in intangible assets.

---

[9]According to Bilir (2014), electronics products and computers have some of the shortest product life cycle length.
[10]As noted by Ben Elhadj, Lahmandi-Ayed, and Laussel (2014), advertising spillovers can even be negative in some cases, as for example in the mobile phone market.

We consider the market value V of an innovating firm as a function of its total (tangible and intangible) assets A and a coefficient q:

$$V = qA$$

We then focus on the evolution of the firm's market value over time, depending on the evolution of the firm's assets.[11]

$$\frac{V_{t2}}{V_{t1}} = q\frac{A_{t2}}{A_{t1}}$$

We assume that the coefficient q depends on the IP strategy of the innovating firm over the period: use of no patent and no trademark ($q_{0,0}$), of trademarks but no patents ($q_{TM,0}$), of patents but no trademarks ($q_{0,PAT}$), and of both patents and trademarks ($q_{TM,PAT}$). The growth in market value depends on the IP strategy specifically associated to the assets acquired between both periods.

Following the supermodularity approach (see Mohnen and Röller 2003 for deeper methodological explanations on empirical tests of supermodularity), our estimation strategy consists in regressing the ratio of the firm's market value to its total assets (in log) in time 2 on the same ratio in time 1 and the four dummies associated to the potential IP right strategies. All dummies are included in the regression, which is thus 'without constant'. This is necessary in order to get all the estimates of coefficients and variance/covariance. We estimate the following model:

$$ln\left(\frac{V_{t2}}{A_{t2}}\right) = ln\left(\frac{V_{t1}}{A_{t1}}\right) + \beta_1(1_{0,0}) + \beta_2(1_{TM,0}) + \beta_3(1_{0,PAT}) + \beta_4(1_{TM,PAT}) + \gamma X$$

where the dummy variables correspond to the use of the corresponding IP right between t = 1 and t = 2, and X is a set of control variables at the firm level.

From the previous theoretical section, we derive that complementarity holds if $\beta_1 + \beta_4 > \beta_2 + \beta_3$. To investigate this, we apply a one-sided t-test of complementarity, also used in Cassiman and Veugelers (2006), with null hypothesis:

$$H_0 : \beta_1 + \beta_4 - \beta_2 - \beta_3 > 0.$$

The one-sided t-test rejects the null hypothesis of complementarity at 5% level if the value of the t statistic is lower than −1.645 (then – non strict – substitutability holds). If the value of the t statistic is higher than 1.645, then strict complementarity holds at 5% level.[12]

According to the theoretical model prediction, the result depends on market characteristics and is thus likely to vary across sectors. After estimating the effects and testing the complementarity on the whole sample, we therefore estimate the results separately on specific sectors. We focus on pharma and chemicals and on ICT, for which we expect to obtain different results on complementarity, based on extrapolations from our theoretical model (see Section 3.2.2).

---

[11]The fact that we look at the evolution of the ratio of market value to assets over a limited period of time reduces the possibility that our empirical model captures the effect of innate differences in the nature of the firms, in addition to the effect of IP strategy choices.

[12]The previous threshold is ± 1.282 at 10% level, and ± 2.326 at 1% level.

Table 3. Descriptive statistics for the final sample.

Variable	Obs	Mean	Std.Dev	Min	Max
Valuation and asset variables (bil. Eur)					
Market Value 2014	1584	13.521	32.655	0.004	487.559
Market value 2011	1584	9.510	25.151	0.000	431.273
Total assets 2014	1584	14.008	36.203	0.002	532.903
Total assets 2011	1584	12.017	32.254	0.000	555.058
IP strategy distribution					
TM, PAT	1219				
TM,0	127				
0,PAT	162				
0,0	76				
Country distribution					
United States	541				
EU28	337				
Other countries	706				

Sector specific descriptive statistics

	Obs	Average R&D spending (million Eur)	Patenting rate	Trademarking
Chemical and Phama. (Nace Rev. 2 20 and 21)	272 (17%)	412.151	93.0%	90.8%
CT-related sectors (Nace Rev. 2 26, 58–63)	546 (34%)	318.624	83.3%	87.5%
Other sectors	766 (49%)	254.032	83.3%	85.6%

Average R&D spending is based on the average R&D spending of firms over the period 2011 to 2014. IP strategies as well as patenting and trademarking rates are observed on the period 2012 to 2014.

4.2. Data sources

The various tests described in the previous paragraph are performed on a firm-level database encompassing the trademarking and patenting activity of the top 2000 corporate R&D investor, the JRC-OECD, COR&DIP© database v.1, 2017 (Daiko et al. 2017). This database links several data sources. General and financial information about the R&D investors comes from the 2015 EU Industrial R&D Investment Scoreboard, relying on data collected by Bureau van Dijk Electronic Publishing GmbH. By nature, firms covered in this dataset tend to be fully fledged firms operating in high-tech sectors, highly innovative and with capabilities and resources in both upstream and downstream activities, which is in line with our theoretical framework (see Table 3 for descriptive statistics on these firms). These data are then matched to IP related information from various sources, including the European Patent Office (EPO)'s Worldwide Patent Statistical Database (PATSTAT, Autumn 2016) for patents, and United States Patent and Trademark Office (USPTO) and European Union Intellectual Property Office (EUIPO) trademark data. IP data are linked to enterprise data using the names of the top corporate R&D investors and of their subsidiaries (as of 2014) and matching them to the applicants' names provided in IP documents, based on a series of algorithms contained in the Imalinker system (Idener Multi Algorithm Linker) developed for the OECD by IDENER, Seville[13] Since firm data are based on the corporate group structure in 2014 and this structure is likely to evolve over time, the history of the IP filings to which the firm data are matched is restricted to 3 years, so the final database covers the period 2012 to 2014 (Daiko et al. 2017). We further extended the COR&DIP© database by matching it with additional financial data

---

[13]A number of other initiatives have aimed at linking firm-level data and IP data, notably the NBER patent data project, linking USPTO patents to the Standard and Poor's Compustat database on US firms (Hall et al., 2000) and the Oxford Firm-Level Intellectual Property (OFLIP) database, linking UK firm data from the FAME database and UKIPO patents and trade marks data (Helmers, Rogers and Schautschick, 2011). For an overview of other initiatives, see for example Helmers, Rogers and Schautschick (2011)..

(market value and total assets) retrieved from the ORBIS© database available at the OECD (version March 2016). Since market value is used as one component of the dependent variable in the regression, we restrict the sample to publicly traded firms. Restricted to firms for which financial and accounting data are available throughout the sample period, the final sample counts 1584 observations[14]

The dependent variable used in the regressions is the natural logarithm of the ratio of firm's market value to total assets (q ratio), market value and total assets being retrieved directly from ORBIS©. The variable 'total assets' is defined as the sum of tangible and intangible assets. Although IP rights are sometimes qualified as 'intangible assets', patents and trademarks applied for by the firm are not accounted in the intangible assets. The latter are recorded on balance sheets at cost, so IP rights are only included in intangible assets if they have been acquired from an external source (see International Accounting Standards Board, 2007). For IP rights acquired internally, what is recorded is their corresponding investments (R&D or brand equity investments), and not the IP right itself whose financial value is not possible to assess. This avoids the presence of an endogeneity issue in the joint inclusion of IP rights dummies and intangible assets in the set of explanatory variables in the regressions. The variable 'intangible assets' in ORBIS© contains R&D, advertising and organisational expenses (see Giannetti 2003). Thus, what the model captures is the respective effects of intangible investments and of the use of IP rights to protect those investments, which is in line with the theoretical framework used in Section 3.

The model focuses on the difference in q ratio at the beginning (end of 2011) and at the end of the period (end of 2014) and looks at the impact of different IP right strategies using dummy variables indicating whether the firm applied for at least one patent and/or at least one trademark during the period 2012 to 2014[15]

Since the propensity of firms to apply for IP rights at the EPO, EUIPO and the USPTO is likely to depend across countries (given that IP filings are subject to home bias), the regression also includes country fixed effects.

Moreover, we control for the age of the firm (calculated based on the incorporation date) since the IP right strategy is likely to be dependent on the life cycle of the firm: firms tend to file more IP right applications in their early lifetime (protecting the name of the firm or their core technology).

4.3. Descriptive statistics

Table 3 gives descriptive statistics for the final dataset. The different IP strategies are not equally represented in the sample. A large majority of firms in the sample use IP rights: 95% applied for at least one patent or one trademark at the USPTO, the EUIPO or the

---

[14]To be consistent with the theoretical model, the sample should ideally be restricted to innovative firms. Otherwise, we cannot know if firms have no IP right activity because they do not innovate (which would have a negative impact on market value compared to other firms) or because they innovate but do not protect their innovations with IP rights. One possibility to have information on innovating behaviour would be to match the dataset with innovation survey data. However, because of the small size of innovation survey samples, this would reduce our sample size drastically. Moreover our sample, which focuses on the top corporate R&D investors worldwide, is by nature likely to be composed of innovative firms..

[15]This corresponds to our theoretical framework, where the IP choice is considered as discrete: the firm either files a trademark or not, and either files a patent or not..

EPO during 2011–2014. Those high shares can be explained by the fact that the sample contains only publicly listed among the top R&D investors worldwide, which tend to be more active in IP than the whole population of firms. The use of trademarks is slightly less frequent than the use of patents (85% of firms used trademarks, 87% used patents). The proportion of firms using both types of IP rights represents the large majority of our sample (77%).

The majority (51%) of the firms in our sample operate in two groups of sectors: chemical and pharmaceutical sectors (Nace Rev.2 sectors 20 and 21, 17% of the sample) and ICT-related sectors (manufacture of computers, electronic and optical products and information and communication services, Nace Rev.2 sectors 26, 58–63, 34% of the sample). We perform the regressions on the whole sample as well as separately on these two groups of sectors in order to investigate if the complementary or substitute relationship between patents and trademarks varies depending on the market considered.

4.4. Results

Table 4 presents the results of the regressions based on the above specification. Column 1 presents results of the regressions performed on the whole sample, whereas Column 2 (resp. Column 3) presents results for the Pharmaceutical and Chemical sectors (resp. ICT-related sectors). Results on the full sample tend to be in line with the theoretical model predictions. The order of the coefficients for IP right variables are consistent with the expectations: $1_{0,0} < 1_{0,PAT}, 1_{TM,0} < 1_{TM,PAT}$. To investigate if the complementarity hypothesis holds, we apply a one-sided t-test on the obtained coefficients, with null hypothesis: $H_0: \beta_1 + \beta_4 - \beta_2 - \beta_3 > 0$ (see Section 4.1 for more details on the test). The complementarity test does not give any significant result on the total sample. This could

Table 4. Market value regressions and one-sided t-tests.

VARIABLES	(1) All sectors	(2) Pharma. and Chemical	(3) ICT
Dependent variable: ln(mv/total assets i,2014)			
ln(mv/total assetsi,2011)	0.62050***	0.61742***	0.52440***
	−0.01696	−0.0558	−0.0273
Age	−0.00093**	−0.00141	−0.00156
	−0.00038	−0.00088	−0.00102
10,0	0.14871	0.98625**	−0.22835
	−0.20516	−0.49399	−0.3297
10,PAT	0.17851	0.2445	0.09463
	−0.198	−0.41918	−0.3049
1TM, 0	0.15747	0.33149	−0.07001
	−0.19664	−0.4289	−0.30799
1TM, PAT	0.20133	0.29486	−0.0638
	−0.19368	−0.39636	−0.30125
Country fixed effects	yes	yes	yes
Observations	1,584	272	546
R-squared	0.616	0.671	0.602
AdjR2	0.606	0.633	0.576
F	57.55	17.76	22.78
Complementarity test: H0: 1TM, PAT-10,PAT>1TM,0-10,0			
t-stat	0.16	2.08**	−1.93*
Conclusion	−	Complementary	Substitute

Standard errors in parentheses
*** p < 0.01, ** p < 0.05, * p < 0.1

be expected since the theoretical model indicates that the results are likely to vary across sectors, which is confirmed by the results shown in Column 3 and 4.

In pharmaceutical and chemical sectors, the test tends to be in favour of the complementarity hypothesis. In ICT-related sectors, by contrast, the supermodularity test tends to be in favour of substitutability.[16] Although various factors are likely to drive these results, one interpretation can be made in the light of our theoretical framework and the two model parameters chosen to test the sensitivity of the complementarity or substitutability relationship between patents and trademarks to market contexts. In pharmaceutical sectors, innovation often consists in launching new drugs or chemical products based on new molecules, and competitors are generally able to launch perfect substitutes on the market. In this situation, advertising is for a large part likely to be advertising for the product in general, so that it is not easily appropriable by the firm even if the latter registers a trademark. Besides, drugs and chemical products tend to have relatively long life cycles, so that the advertising depreciation rate over time is likely to be relatively low. In those types of sectors, the theoretical model predicts that the complementarity effect tends to outweigh the substitutability effect so that it is in the firms' interest to use patents jointly with trademarks in order to build goodwill during the monopoly period and continue to benefit from it after the expiration of the patent. Our result are also in line with the case study on Bayer Aspirin detailed in Jennewein, Durand, and Gerybadze (2010).

In contrast, in ICT sectors relying on cutting-edge technology, the depreciation rate of products and therefore of advertising is likely to be very high. The patent period might then cover the major part of the life cycle of the technology, so that products are less likely to be imitated and trademark protection is less needed. In that case, the substitutability effect tends to outweigh the complementarity effect.

5. Conclusion

In the paper by Amara and Traoré (2008), which shows complementarities between various IP protection mechanisms for firms in knowledge-intensive business services (KIBS) sectors, the authors call for future research on the factors that could explain those complementarities. The main contribution of the present paper is to assess the interacting effects of patents and trademarks. We tackle this question both through a formal theoretical model and through an empirical analysis. Using a basic modelling approach, we compare the outcome of adopting various IP right strategies for innovating firms that commercialise their own innovation: patent or not and/or trademark or not, and then assess the complementarity or substitutability relationship between the two IP rights based on the supermodularity approach.

The main finding of our model is that the complementary or substitutable relationship between trademarks and patents is not straightforward. We find that the interaction between the two IP rights is characterised by two counterbalancing effects: a temporal substitutability effect – as the patent period reduces the time during which the firm faces competition and needs a trademark to protect its reputation against other firms – and

---

[16]These results are robust to including additional controls on the firm characteristics such as detailed information on the sector of activity and information on size based on the number of employees. The corresponding results are available upon request.

a complementarity effect – as the trademark enables the firm to extend the reputational benefits of the monopoly period beyond the expiration of the patent. We show that the predominance of one or the other effect depends on exogenous parameters, such as the levels of advertising depreciation rate and spillovers. If spillovers are low and the depreciation rate is high, as for example in ICT-related sectors, then the benefits of registering a trademark will be more important if the firm cannot register a patent, so patents and trademarks are likely to be substitutes, as defined in the supermodularity approach. This does not imply that a patent can substitute a trademark or vice versa, but the incremental benefit of using one type of IP right is higher when this type of IP right is used alone than when the other type of IP right is also used. In contrast, if advertising spillovers are high and the advertising depreciation rate is low, as for example in pharmaceutical or chemical sectors, then trademarks and patents are likely to be complementary, i.e. the incremental benefit of filing a trademark is comparatively higher when the firm files a patent than when it does not, and vice versa. These two parameters are admittedly not the only determinants of the choice of IP right strategy. IP right bundling strategies may depend on a wide range of factors, such as the position of the firm – upstream or downstream – in the value chain, the maturity of the firm (Flikkema et al. 2019), the type of technologies and innovation capabilities developed, or the extent to which the firm takes part in collaborative innovation (Athreye and Fassio 2019). Further research would be needed to analyse the extent to which these factors also influence the level of complementarity between patents and trademarks. Our model could serve as a starting point for this type of analyses.

Despite the assumptions made, this model highlights some of the complexities of IP bundling choices. The main implication of the model is that the optimal IP right strategy for firms to appropriate the benefits of innovation may vary from one firm to another and depend on the characteristics of the market. Following the conclusion of Teece (1986) stating that the profit gained from innovation depends on the appropriability regime and on the possibility of the firm to use complementary assets, our model states that complementarities may exist between IP rights, contributing to the strength of the appropriability regime. We show that these complementarities are themselves dependent on the context in which the firms operate. This tends to corroborate empirical results from the previous literature showing that the level of complementarity between patents and trademarks differs across sectors (Dosso and Vezzani 2017).

Our findings also speak more generally to the literature on trademarks and innovation. By modelling the impact of protecting an innovation by a trademark, we provide a possible theoretical underpinning for the relationship between trademarks and innovative activity of firms. Our model also suggest that it is not always beneficial to protect innovations by trademarks, as the benefits may in some case be reduced by the presence of other types of IP rights, and these benefits have to be weighed against the cost of trademark filings.

The practical implications of our analysis are twofold. First, the model has implications for empirical economic analyses. Whenever investigating firms' IP activity, for example, as a proxy for other intangible assets, one should bear in mind the existence of context-dependent interaction effects between the various types of protection. It means that using patents as well as trademarks as indicators for innovation requires some caution, in particular for industries where a combined usage of IP rights is possible.

Secondly, there are implications for IP right management within firms. We show that beyond the question of the eligibility of the innovation to the various types of IP rights, the profitability of a diversified IP strategy depends on context elements, which need to be taken into account to determine the benefits and costs of the various combinations. Failure to identify complementarity (resp. substitutability) between some protection mechanisms may lead to underexploitation (resp. over-exploitation) of synergies, and underprotection (resp. overprotection) of innovations. In some market contexts, for example, when advertising spillovers are weak and product depreciation is rapid, the premium of combining patent and trademark protection may be too small to compensate the additional cost of filing two types of IP rights. On the contrary, innovators operating in a strong appropriability regime context may underestimate the potential synergies of developing strong complementary assets. In organisational terms, it implies also some changes. Trademarks are very often related to marketing or commercial departments and patents are usually the realm of innovation or R&D departments. The exploitation of interdependencies (and in particular of complementarities) requests a stronger coordination and at least to share a common IP strategy and joined knowledge appropriation mechanisms.

Acknowledgments

The opinions expressed in this paper are the sole responsibility of the authors and do not necessarily reflect those of the OECD or of the governments of its member countries. Authors are grateful to Tim Folta, Georg von Graevenitz, Mariagrazia Squicciarini, Hélène Dernis, Betrand Koebel, Isabelle Maret, Christian Martinez-Diaz, the editors and the referees for their helpful suggestions and valuable comments. All mistakes remain those of the authors alone.

Disclosure statement

No potential conflict of interest was reported by the authors.

References

Aaker, D. 2007. "Innovation: Brand It or Lose It." *California Management Review* 50 (1): 8–24. doi:10.2307/41166414.

Amara, N. L., and N. Traoré. 2008. "Managing the Protection of Innovations in Knowledge-intensive Business Services." *Research Policy* 37: 1530–1547. doi:10.1016/j.respol.2008.07.001.

Askenazy, P., T. Breda, and D. Irac. 2010. "Innovation and Advertising: Theory and Evidence." *Banque de France Working Paper No. 284.*

Athreye, S., and C. Fassio. 2019. "Why Do Innovators Not Apply for Trademarks? the Role of Information Asymmetries and Collaborative Innovation." *Papers in Innovation Studies No. 2019/2.* Lund University, CIRCLE - Center for Innovation, Research and Competences in the Learning Economy.

Ballot, G., F. Fakhfakh, F. Galia, and A. Salter. 2015. "The Fateful Triangle: Complementarities in Performance between Product, Process and Organizational Innovation in France and the UK." *Research Policy* 44 (1): 217–232. doi:10.1016/j.respol.2014.07.003.

Ben Elhadj, N., L. Lahmandi-Ayed, and D. Laussel. 2014. "Advertising Spillovers and Market Structure." *Recherches Économiques De Louvain* 80 (3): 51–98. doi:10.3917/rel.803.0051.

Bilir, K. L. 2014. "Patent Laws, Product Life-Cycle Lengths, and Multinational Activity." *American Economic Review* 104 (7): 1979–2013. doi:10.1257/aer.104.7.1979.

Block, J., C. Fisch, A. Hahn, and P. Sandner. 2015. "Why Do SMEs File Trademarks? Insights from Firms in Innovative Industries." *Research Policy* 44 (10): 1915–1930. doi:10.1016/j. respol.2015.06.007.

Brady, M. 2009. "Advertising Effectiveness and Spillover: Simulating Strategic Interaction Using Advertising." *System Dynamics Review* 25 (4): 281–307. doi:10.1002/sdr.426.

Brekke, K., and O. R. Straume. 2008. "Pharmaceutical Patents: Incentives for R&D or Marketing?" *CESifo Working Paper Series No. 2433*.

Buddelmeyer, H., P. Jensen, and E. Webster. 2010. "Innovation and The Determinants of Company Survival." *Oxford Economic Papers* 62 (2): 261–285. doi:10.1093/oep/gpp012.

Cassiman, B., and R. Veugelers. 2006. "In Search of Complementarity in Innovation Strategy: Internal R&D and External Knowledge Acquisition." *Management Science* 52 (1): 68–82. doi:10.1287/mnsc.1050.0470.

Castaldi, C. 2019. "All the Great Things You Can Do with Trademark Data: Taking Stock and Looking Ahead." *Strategic Organization*. doi:10.1177/1476127019847835.

Castaldi, C., and M. Dosso. 2018. "From R&D to Market: Using Trademarks to Capture the Market Capability of Top R&D Investors." *JRC Technical reports, JRC working papers on corporate R&D and Innovation* N°01/2018.

Cavaco, S., and P. Crifo. 2014. "CSR and Financial Performance: Complementarity between Environmental, Social and Business Behaviours." *Applied Economics* 46 (27): 3323–3338. doi:10.1080/00036846.2014.927572.

Cohen, W., R. Nelson, and J. Walsh. 2000. "Protecting Their Intellectual Assets: Appropriability Conditions and Why U.S. Manufacturing Firms Patent (Or not)." *NBER Working Papers No. 7552*. National Bureau of Economic Research.

Daiko, T., H. Dernis, M. Dosso, P. Gkotsis, M. Squicciarini, and A. Vezzani. 2017. *World Corporate Top R&D Investors: Industrial Property Strategies in the Digital Economy*. Luxembourg: JRC and OECD common report. Publications Office of the European Union.

Davis, L., 2009. "Leveraging Trade Marks to Capture Innovation Returns." Paper presented to the DRUID-DIME Academy Summer 2009 Conference, Copenhaguen Denmark, June 17–19.

De Vries, G., E. Pennings, J. Block, and C. Fisch. 2017. "Trademark or Patent? the Effects of Market Concentration, Customer Type and Venture Capital Financing on Start-ups' Initial IP Applications." *Industry and Innovation* 24 (4): 325–345. doi:10.1080/13662716.2016.1231607.

Dixit, A. 1979. "A Model of Duopoly Suggesting A Theory of Entry Barriers." *The Bell Journal of Economics* 10 (1): 20–32. doi:10.2307/3003317.

Dosso, M., and A. Vezzani. 2017. "Firm Market Valuation and Intellectual Property Assets." *JRC working papers on Corporate R&D and Innovation* N°07/2017

EC. 2015. *Innovation Union Scoreboard*. Brussels: European Commission.

Fares, M., S. Raza, and A. Thomas. 2018. "Is There Complementarity between Labels and Brands? Evidence from Small French Co-operatives." *TSE Working Paper No. 18-895*. Toulouse School of Economics (TSE).

Fischer, T., and J. Henkel. 2013. "Complements and Substitutes in Profiting from innovation—A Choice Experimental Approach." *Research Policy* 42 (2): 326–339. doi:10.1016/j. respol.2012.06.004.

Flikkema, M., A. P. De Man, and C. Castaldi. 2014. "Are Trademark Counts a Valid Indicator of Innovation? Results of an In-depth Study of New Benelux Trademarks Filed by SMEs." *Industry and Innovation* 21 (4): 310–331. doi:10.1080/13662716.2014.934547.

Flikkema, M., C. Castaldi, A. P. de Man, and M. Seip. 2015. "Explaining the Trademark-Innovation Linkage: The Role of Patents and Trademark Filing Strategies." *Academy of Management Proceedings* 2015 (1): 16624. doi:10.5465/ ambpp.2015.16624abstract.

Flikkema, M., C. Castaldi, A. P. De Man, and M. Seip. 2019. "Trademarks' Relatedness to Product and Service Innovation: A Branding Strategy Approach." *Research Policy* 48 (6): 1340–1353. doi:10.1016/j.respol.2019.01.018.

Friedman, J. W. 1983. "Advertising and Oligopolistic Equilibrium." *The Bell Journal of Economics* 14 (2): 464–473. doi:10.2307/3003647.

Giannetti, M. 2003. "Do Better Institutions Mitigate Agency Problems? Evidence from Corporate Finance Choices." *Journal of Financial and Quantitative Analysis* 38 (01): 185–212. doi:10.2307/4126769.

Grazzi, M., C. Piccardo, and C. Vergari. 2019. "Concordance and Complementarity in Intellectual Property Instruments." *LEM Working paper series No. 2019/19*. Scuola Superiore Sant'Anna Pisa: Institute of Economics.

Greenhalgh, C., and M. Rogers. 2007. "Trade Marks and Performance in UK Firms: Evidence of Schumpetarian Competition through Innovation." *Economic Series Working Paper No. 300.* University of Oxford, Department of Economics doi:10.1094/PDIS-91-4-0467B.

Greenhalgh, C., and M. Rogers. 2012. "Trademarks and Performance in Services and Manufacturing Firms: Evidence of Schumpeterian Competition through Innovation." *The Australian Economic Review* 45 (1): 50–76. doi:10.1111/j.1467-8462.2011.00665.x.

Griliches, Z. 1981. "Market Value, R&D, and Patents." *Economics Letters Elsevier* 7 (2): 183–187. doi:10.1016/0165-1765(87)90114-5.

Griliches, Z. 1991. "Patent Statistics as Economic Indicators: A Survey." *NBER Working Papers 3301.* National Bureau of Economic Research.

Guidetti, G., S. Mancinelli, and M. Mazzanti. 2009. "Complementarity in Training Practices Methodological Notes and Empirical Evidence for a Local Economic System." *The IUP Journal of Applied Economics* IUP Publications 8(1): 39–56.

Guzman, J., and S. Stern. 2015. "Where Is Silicon Valley?." *Science* 347 (6222): 606–609. doi:10.1126/science.aaa0201.

Hall, B., A. Jaffe, and M. Trajtenberg. 2000. "Market Value and Patent Citations: A First Look." *NBER Working Paper No. 7741.* National Bureau of Economic Research.

Helmers, C., and M. Rogers. 2010. "Innovation and the Survival of New Firms in the UK." *Review of Industrial Organization* 36 (3): 227–248. doi:10.1007/s11151-010-9247-7.

Herz, B., and M. Mejer. 2016. "On the Fee Elasticity of the Demand for Trademarks in Europe." *Oxford Economic Papers* 68 (4): 1039–1061. doi:10.1093/oep/gpw035.

Hirschey, M. 1982. "Intangible Aspects of Advertising and R&D Expenditures." *Journal of Industrial Economics* 30: 375–390. doi:10.2307/2097924.

Hurmelinna, P., and T. Jauhiainen. 2004. "IPR Strategies and Appropriability Regime – Protecting and Exploiting Innovations and Knowledge in ICT Companies." *International Journal of Business & Economics* 3: 76–79.

Jennewein, K., T. Durand, and A. Gerybadze. 2010. "When Brands Complement Patents in Securing the Returns from Technological Innovation: The Case of Bayer Aspirin." *Management International* 14 (3): 73–86. doi:10.7202/044294ar.

Jensen, P. H., E. Webster, and H. Buddelmeyer. 2008. "Innovation, Technological Conditions and New Firm Survival." *The Economic Record* 84 (267): 434–448. doi:10.1111/ecor.2008.84.issue-267.

Levin, R., A. Kevorick, R. R. Nelson, and S. Winter. 1987. "Appropriating the Returns from Industrial R&D." *Brookings Papers on Economic Activity Economic Studies Program* The Brookings Institution 18 : 783–832. doi:10.2307/2534454.

Mazzoleni, R., and R. R. Nelson. 1998. "Economic Theories about the Benefits and Costs of Patents." *Journal of Economic Issues* 32 (4): 1031–1052. doi:10.1080/00213624.1998.11506108.

Mendonça, S., T. S. Pereira, and M. Godinho. 2004. "Trade Marks as an Indicator of Innovation and Industrial Change." *Research Policy* 33: 1358–1404. doi:10.1016/j.respol.2004.09.005.

Milgrom, P., and J. Roberts. 1990. "The Economics of Modern Manufacturing: Technology, Strategy, and Organization." *American Economic Review* 80: 511–528.

Milgrom, P., and J. Roberts. 1995. "Complementarities and Fit: Strategy, Structure and Organizational Change in Manufacturing." *Journal of Accounting and Economics* 19: 179–208. doi:10.1016/0165-4101(94)00382-F.

Millot, V. 2009 "Trademarks as an Indicator of Product and Marketing Innovation." *OECD Science, Technology and Industry Working Paper No. 2009/6.* OECD publishing

Mohnen, P., and L. Röller 2003 "Complementarities in Innovation Policy." *CIRANO Working Papers 2003s-60*. Montréal: CIRANO.

Nerlove, M., and K. J. Arrow. 1962. "Optimal Advertising Policy under Dynamic Conditions." *Economica* 39: 129–142. doi:10.2307/2551549.

OECD. 2015. *OECD Science, Technology and Industry Scoreboard 2015: Innovation for Growth and Society*. Paris: OECD publishing.

Pisano, G. 2006. "Profiting from Innovation and the Intellectual Property Revolution." *Research Policy* 35 (8): 1122–1130. doi:10.1016/j.respol.2006.09.008.

Rassenfosse, G. 2019. "On the Price Elasticity of Demand for Trademarks". *Industry and Innovation*. Current issue.

Rogers, M. 1998 "The Definition and Measurement of Innovation." *Melbourne Institute Working Paper No. 10/98*.

Sampat, B. 2018. "A Survey of Empirical Evidence on Patents and Innovation." *NBER Working Papers No 25383*.

Sandner, P. 2009 "The Market Value of R&D, Patents, and Trade Marks." *SSRN Working Paper No. 1469705*.

Sandner, P., and J. H. Block. 2011. "The Market Value of R&D, Patents, and Trademarks." *Research Policy* 40 (7): 969–985. doi:10.1016/j.respol.2011.04.004.

Schautschick, P., and C. Greenhalgh. 2016. "Empirical Studies of Trade Marks–The Existing Economic Literature." *Economics of Innovation and New Technology* 25 (4): 358–390. doi:10.1080/10438599.2015.1064598.

Schmoch, U. 2003. "Service Marks as a Novel Innovation Indicator." *Research Evaluation* 12: 149–156. doi:10.3152/147154403781776708.

Schwiebacher, F., and E. Müller 2009. "How Companies Use Different Forms of IP Right Protection: Are Patents and Trade Marks Complements or Substitutes?" Paper presented to the DRUID-DIME Academy Winter 2010 PhD Conference, Aalborg Denmark, January 21–23.

Seip, M., C. Castaldi, M. Flikkema, and A. P. de Man. 2019. "A Taxonomy of Firm-level IPR Application Practices to Inform Policy Debates." *LEM Working paper series No. 2019/3*. Scuola Superiore Sant'Anna Pisa: Institute of Economics.

Snyder, S., and A. King 2007 "Joint Determination of Prices, R&D and Marketing Expenditure in the Pharmaceutical Enterprise: A Theoretical Model of Profit Maximizing Behavior." *Martindale Center Working Paper*, November. doi:10.1094/PDIS-91-4-0467B.

Somaya, D., and S. Graham. 2006. *Vermeers and Rembrandts in the Same Attic: Complementarity between Compyrights and Trademarks Leveraging Strategies in Software*. Georgia Institute of Technology TIGER Working Paper. doi:10.2139/ssrn.887484.

Statman, M., and T. Tyebjee. 1981. "Trade Marks, Patents, and Innovation in the Ethical Drug Industry." *The Journal of Marketing* 45 (3): 71–81. doi:10.1177/002224298104500306.

Szegedy-Maszak, M. 2004. "Driven to Distraction." *U.S. News and World Report, 26 April 2004*, 52–64.

Teece, D. 1986. "Profiting from Technological Innovation: Implications for Integration, Collaboration, Licensing, and Public Policy." *Research Policy* 15: 285–305. doi:10.1016/0048-7333(86)90027-2.

Thomä, J., and K. Bizer. 2013. "To Protect or Not to Protect? Modes of Appropriability in the Small Enterprise Sector." *Research Policy* 42 (1): 35–49. doi:10.1016/j.respol.2012.04.019.

von Graevenitz, G., and P. Sandner. 2009. "Are Advertising and R&D Complements?." Paper presented at the TIME Kolloquium, Technical University Munich and Ludwig-Maximilians-Universität Munich (Germany). doi: 10.2139/ssrn.1443415.

Wagner, S., and I. Cockburn. 2010. "Patents and the Survival of Internet-related IPOs." *Research Policy* 39 (2): 214–228. doi:10.1016/j.respol.2009.12.003.

Zhou, H., P. G. Sandner, S. L. Martinelli, and J. H. Block. 2016. "Patents, Trademarks and Their Complementarity in Venture Capital Funding." *Technovation* 47: 14–22. doi:10.1016/j.technovation.2015.11.005.

The valuation of patent-trademark pairing as IP strategy: evidence from the USPTO

Grid Thoma

ABSTRACT

The benefits of an IP strategy for an innovative project that combines both patenting and trademarking are compared to those of patenting alone. The results of the proposed econometric analysis of patents indicate that a strategy that pairs patenting and trademarking almost doubles patent value. The validity of this result was confirmed by examining several patentee demographic characteristics and an extensive set of patent value indicators regarding breadth and technology potential, prior art and patent background, filing and procedural aspects of a patent and IP usage mode. Quite interesting, when the holder of a utility patent also obtains a design patent, rather than opting for a trademark, there is no enhancement of the premium value.

1. Introduction

Even though in most cases patent protection conveys little or no value to innovators (Moore 2005; Lemley and Shapiro 2005),[1] many billions of dollars are spent annually for prosecuting patents at the U.S. Patent and Trademark Office (USPTO) alone (Lemley 2001).[2] Several methods for the appraisal of patent value have been outlined in the literature, based on estimates of cost, as well as analysis of the revenue and market value demanded for the inception and usage of the patent protection. More recently, several authors have proposed indicators for devising timely predictions of the value of patents (Nagaoka, Motohashi, and Goto 2010). Most of the indicators rely on information extracted from a patent's front-page (Contropia, Lemley, and Sampat 2013).

Even so, patent indicators are likely to account for a limited part of patent value (Gambardella, Harhoff, and Verspagen 2008). In fact, typical indicators are primarily explicative of the intrinsic value of an underlying technological invention (Gittelman 2008). Conversely, on the basis of market value econometric analyses, a number of

---

This article has been republished with minor changes. These changes do not impact the academic content of the article.

[1]Moore (2005) documents that at the USPTO about 16 percent of utility patents are never renewed after they have been granted, and only 46 percent of them provide full-term statutory protection.

[2]With respect to the prosecution costs at the USPTO from start until patent issue, in 2000 Lemley (2001) estimated a lower bound of \$ 10 thousand and upper bound \$ 30 thousand in current values, which in terms of 2015 prices amount to \$ 13 thousand and \$ 40 thousand respectively. In 2015, the USPTO issued about 300 thousand utility patents, which means an overall range in prosecution costs of between \$ 4 and 12 billion.

🅑 Supplemental data for this article can be accessed here.

authors have argued that the benefits the innovator can obtain from a patent depend drastically upon the complementary investment necessary for the commercial translation of that invention (McGahan and Silverman 2006). Furthermore, a patentee can actively pursue strategies to improve the conditions that directly enhance the value of a patented invention (Teece 1986; Gans and Stern 2003). With the exception of a few works, the previous literature has overlooked the role that the innovator's strategic behaviour and business model play in determining patent value (Crass, Czarnitzki, and Toole 2016; Gambardella, Harhoff, and Verspagen 2017; Gambardella and McGahan 2010). This paper aims to bridge this gap by offering an analysis of how trademarking affects patent value.

According to the findings of the entrepreneurial finance literature, the value of patents goes beyond the sole protection of intellectual property. Hsu and Ziedonis (2013) argued that firms with more patents receive relatively more venture funding, and Häussler, Harhoff, and Mueller (2014) claimed that external investors gauge the value of patents even before the patents are granted. Cockburn and McGarvie (2007) documented that patents are used in requests for external financing also in the case of an IPO or acquisition of a firm. When patents are combined with other IP strategies, external investors have a better understanding about the value of the patented inventions (Alvarez-Garrido and Dushnitsky 2013; Block et al. 2014; Zhou et al. 2016). Nevertheless, with the exceptions of the study by Block et al. (2014) and Zhou et al. (2016), the previous literature has seldom examined how marketing and commercialization activities affect patent valuation. In particular, there is a dearth of evidence on the determinants of patent value when two strategies are combined for the same innovative project (Derclaye 2017).

Building upon recent research on IP strategies as quality signals (Hall 2019; Hall and Harhoff 2012; Gambardella 2013), this paper is among the first attempts to analyse how trademarking impacts the value of a patented invention. More specifically, I claim that trademarks increase the value of the patented R&D, because they enhance the signaling function of patents and expand the relative breadth and length of protection. In this direction, the paper introduces a novel concept, the patent-trademark pair, which indicates a situation in which the output of the invention process is protected by a combined IP strategy constituted by patenting and trademarking. I report that patents combined with trademarks show on average almost twice higher valuations, and when compared to other combined IP strategies they account for a larger variability of the patent value distribution, which points to their stronger signaling function.

The paper proceeds as follows. Section 2 discusses the theoretical background and presents the testable hypotheses, while the following section introduces the patent valuation approach by sketching an optimal renewal model of the payment of patent fees. Section 4 elaborates a new method and dataset in order to appraise patent value by integrating several data sources: bibliographic information from patent and trademark records, patent renewal decisions and corresponding fee payments, patentee information from procedural filing records, and others. Section 5 provides econometric evidence in support of the testable hypotheses and assesses the robustness of the results, although it is inconclusive on the problem of causal inference. The final section discusses the managerial implications arising from the research findings.

2. Background and hypotheses

Recent studies have explored how patent and trademark strategies affect firm performance, and a number of authors have adopted the view that trademarks are a proxy of the brand equity,[3] marketing and commercialization ability, and unobserved quality of the innovative assets of the firm. Helmers and Rogers (2010) found that the impact on firm survival afforded by trademark stock is two percentage points higher than that provided by patents. Buddelmeyer, Jensen, and Webster (2010) argued that trademarks are positively associated with survival over both the short and the long term, while patent stocks positively affect survival only in the long run. Furthermore, Srinivasan, Lilien, and Rangaswamy (2008) and Pederzoli, Thoma, and Torricelli (2013) showed that the value of unweighted patent stock hastens the termination of the firm's activities, whereas trademarks have the converse effect on survival. Crass, Czarnitzki, and Toole (2016) and Barroso, Giarratana, and Pasquini (2019) argued that trademarking significantly affects firm profitability above and beyond the patenting strategy, while Bei (2019) analysed the market share increase generated by two IP strategies pursued by innovative startups. In a quite interesting observation, Crass, Czarnitzki, and Toole (2016) claimed that the benign effect of trademarking on firm performance is identified between the fourth and the nineteenth year after registration, which points to the fact that usually the trademark lifecycle is similar to that of patenting. The combination of patent and trademark strategies increases the likelihood that the patentee will be the target of external acquisitions (Srinivasan, Lilien, and Rangaswamy 2008). Helmers and Rogers (2011) reported that trademarks also impact asset growth, whereas the salience of patents is demonstrated solely in manufacturing and R&D intensive sectors, and when the most valuable filing strategies are taken into account, such as patents that have international breadth.

A complete sectoral investigation of the appraisal of patent and trademark strategies was conducted by Greenhalgh and Rogers (2006), who claimed that technological trajectories given by the so-called 'Pavitt's taxonomy' can disentangle the differential impact of the two IP strategies on the market valuation of a firm. Except in the software industry and for other high value-added services, trademark stock contributes positively and significantly to a firm's market value in addition to the investment in R&D and intangibles, whereas patents are positively appraised solely in the case of specialized suppliers and science based firms.

This framework was extended by Sandner and Block (2011) by considering indirect indicators for the valuation of trademarks in the same fashion as those used for patents, such as the breadth of protection and opposition decisions. They found that the size of the trademark portfolio is value enhancing above and beyond the effect of patent assets and the range of operative activities. Moreover, a firm's market capitalization is correlated with the extent of jurisdictions of the trademark protection and number of opposition actions undertaken by the focal firm but not the number of those received.

Korkeamäki and Takalo (2013) scrutinized how patents and trademarks concerning Apple's iPhone product platform affect the market capitalization of the firm and that of its network of suppliers, service providers, and competitors. The iPhone related

[3]In the marketing literature, brand equity encompasses not only its value but also the brand meaning and strength (For a fuller discussion on the concept of brand equity see the survey by Srinivasan, Hsu, and Fournier 2012).

capabilities and resources account for about fifteen percent of Apple's total market capitalization, and patents and trademarks constitute about one fourth of the iPhone's overall market value. There is also a positive effect on the suppliers' market capitalization, but no additional value gains can be traced with respect to the other players of Apple's value network.

Some other studies have analysed how R&D, patenting and investment in information technology affect trademark activity and value, after having conditioned for advertisement and marketing expenses. Gao and Hitt (2012) showed that investment in information technology significantly enhances the number of trademarks in terms of applications and active registrations, above and beyond the effect of R&D stock, but the relative coefficient is distant from R&D. Giarratana and Torrisi (2010) claimed that the patent stock has no effect on the decision to obtain the first trademark by foreign software firms in the US market, but the typical patenting firm has at least one active trademark registration. Quite interestingly, Melnyk, Giarratana, and Torres (2014) found that software security firms with patents tend on average to renew their trademarks less often than firms without patents, which is consistent with the view that the former firms face greater marketing risk.

Patenting and trademarking have also been analysed in the context of the pre-money valuation by venture capitalists. Block et al. (2014) argued that trademarks can constitute a quality signal between the inventor and the potential financier that is as suitable as patents, and thus reduce information asymmetries à la Spence (1973).[4] Having investigated a large sample of firms, they confirmed that the combination of the two IP strategies affects the pre-money valuation of startups, although the signaling effect decreases with the number of trademarks held by a firm and in the latter rounds of financing, when the financier could evaluate the economic potential of a startup through other means. Further, Zhou et al. (2016) confirmed these findings by analysing a richer albeit smaller dataset, which also encompassed information on other IP strategies followed by a startup, such as trade secrets.

More broadly, these findings are in line with several studies in the entrepreneurial finance literature that claim that the value of patenting goes beyond mere IP protection, because typically venture capitalists operationally analyse patent portfolios in order to appraise the quality of startups (see for instance Mann and Sager 2007; Häussler, Harhoff, and Mueller 2014; Hsu and Ziedonis 2013; Hall 2019).[5] Nonetheless, with the exception of Block et al. (2014) and Zhou et al. (2016), this stream of literature has seldom debated how the firm valuation is affected when a firm combines patent and trademark strategies.

More in general, the unit of analysis proposed by the current valuation literature is firm level. An understanding of how the use of complementary IP strategies affects the value of individual patents can only be arrived at indirectly (Murphy, Orcutt, and Remus 2012). In this context, Gambardella, Harhoff, and Verspagen (2017) advanced

---

[4]For recent surveys of the IP signaling theory in the context of entrepreneurial financing see Gambardella (2013), Hall (2019) and Hall and Harhoff (2012).

[5]Furthermore, it has been found that patenting attracts financing from prominent VCs who contribute with a larger share of non-financial capital (Hsu and Ziedonis 2013). Although patents are valuable signals for new investors but not old ones (Conti, Thursby, and Thursby 2013), only patents held by the inventor prior to the first round of financing have the biggest signaling value (Hoenen et al. 2014), and the intensity of the signal lessens with the number of patents (Mann and Sager 2007).

direct value appraisals of a patent depending on its market potential as represented by the number of complementary inventions within the same portfolio, while Odasso, Scellato, and Ughetto (2015) and Ashtor (2015) controlled for the business model of the patent owner. Nonetheless, previous literature has not analysed how the marketing and commercialization activities directly associated with a patented invention enhance its valuation, and there is limited quantitative evidence on the determinants of patent value when trademarking is combined with patenting for the same innovative project.

Since trademarking is sought in order to improve publicity for inventions and build brand awareness in the marketplace (Krasnikov, Mishra, and Orozco 2009), the commercial success of a patent is augmented in several ways when it is paired with a trademark filing. First, trademarks signal product quality not only during the sale and distribution phase but also in the advertisement and promotion process, and thus compared to the incumbent business model, in a situation in which complementary assets are enablers of market presence, the choice to pair trademarks with patents speeds the translation of the patented technology into commercial activities (Teece 1986; Gans and Stern 2003). In fact, an IP strategy articulated through a patent-trademark pair constitutes a signaling device of the market potential of an invention, and thus it is likely to correspond to high economic return and valuation (Crass, Czarnitzki, and Toole 2016).[6]

In addition, by facilitating communication and publicity, patent strategies combined with trademarking reduce uncertainty about product performance (Bao, Shao, and Rivers 2008; Castaldi 2018) and establish a trust relationship between technological producers and consumers (Rujas 1999; Block et al. 2015). Brand names play a fundamental role for the commercial success of new products, because consumers rely upon preconceived beliefs about the names of specific product types, and the importance of an appropriate name extends well beyond the consumer goods industries (Kohli and LaBahn 1997; Klink 2003).[7] In this direction, by increasing the information available to consumers about product categories, trademarks stimulate learning in the marketplace during the product launch (Ching 2010) and sustain consumer preference for a technological product (Arvidsson 2005; Bao, Shao, and Rivers 2008), thus improving the integration of the invention phase with commercialization.

Finally, trademarking extends the commercial success of a patented product beyond the statutory limit of the patent right, if the consumers still perceive a differential value of the branded product after patent expiration (Rujas 1999; Smith and Richey 2013). In fact, recent survey evidence at the level of single trademark registrations has indicated that up to one-fourth of the firms have trademarked in order to prolong the protection obtained by the means of other IP strategies (Flikkema, De Man, and Castaldi 2014). From a legal point of view, the validity of trademarks can be perpetuated endlessly, although the owner has to demonstrate that the mark is continuously used in commerce. Moreover, trademarks can provide IP protection for unpatentable complementary innovative activities by the patentee regarding market experimentation.

---

[6]An analyst claimed that *'it is no coincidence that many of the world's best known and most valuable brands have other IP traits in common: their reputation for quality, innovation, and consistency not only facilitates product sales and shareholder interest, but also enhances the value of their patents.'* (Berman 2008, interviewed in IP Close UP, 15 November 2012).

[7]See Landes and Posner (1987) and Beebe and Fromer (2018) for a discussion on different types of trademarks.

Complementary innovative products or ideas being tested in the market might be considered unpatentable because they are non-novel and obvious from a technical point of view, or because they are outside the scope of patentable subject matter, or because they were not yet ready to be protected by patenting when the prosecution of the underlying patent was begun (Abramowicz and Duffy 2008). During litigation, having a trademark can improve the position of the patent owner (Derclaye 2017), and in this direction, patentees who have combined patenting with trademarks have more and larger options when legal action is required to protect their invention (Marco 2005).

Thus, on the basis of these considerations regarding the ability of a trademark to signal quality and to enhance the inventor's conditions of profiting from the innovative product (appropriability), a first *ceteris paribus* testable hypothesis can be advanced:

HP 1: A patent-trademark pair is positively associated with the value of the underlying patented invention.

2.1. IP strategies and signaling

The theory of signaling suggests that signals (a patent or trademark or other evidence of quality) function properly when they are costly for the firms (the 'issuers') who send (or issue) them to 'receivers' (consumers or potential investors in the firm, for example) (Spence 1973). In order for the signaling to create a separating equilibrium for high and low quality issuers, the signal should be more costly at issuing for the low quality and less productive issuers. The cost could regard various aspects: investment or expenditure in the process of obtaining a patent or trademark or other 'signal' of quality, opportunity cost of the investment, and non-monetary and unquantifiable costs related to status or social networks.

Pursuing IP strategies at the USPTO could involve such costs as attorney fees, office fees and document drafting costs (Burstein 2016). Lemley (2001) provided an excellent review of the cost estimates for patent prosecution – arguing that a patent grant would require an expenditure of around twenty thousand dollars (see discussion in footnote 2) – and the costs of a trademark attorney and office fees could amount to one-fifth to one-fourth of this estimate (AIPLA 2015).[8] Furthermore, document drafting costs for trademark applications could be at least as high as the attorney and office fees, because this task is typically performed during the name branding process, which involves significant legal work with internal and external experts (Kohli and LaBahn 1997). A few analysts and scholars have claimed that trademark drafting costs have ballooned because name depletion, congestion and cluttering have caused increasing uneasiness about the name branding process (See for example Gabler 2015; Beebe and Fromer 2018; Von Graevenitz 2013).

---

[8]The AIPLA survey (2015) estimated that the attorney's fee for a typical trademark application in 2010 amounted to $ 3,050. Other costs involved in design search could increase this expenditure. In terms of office fees, the 2010 USPTO schedule included trademark application and statement of use fees of about $ 475 per international class, which means $ 665 for a typical trademark with 1.4 international classes. However, these are lower bound procedural fees at the PTO, and other costs would be incurred for 'intent-to-use in commerce' applications or more complex trademark filings. Hence, on average, trademark attorney and office fees could amount to $ 4,000–5,000.

Thus, signaling by means of patent-trademark pairing is more costly than a patenting strategy alone. Indeed, it also means that the underlying invention is somehow in an advanced stage and closer to the market. In fact, to obtain official registration of a trademark, some degree of intrinsic distinctiveness for consumers typically needs to be featured. In this case, the patentee could have spent a considerable sum on its commercialization or borne cumulative R&D costs along a technological trajectory, which is often associated with irreversible investments, and there is a commitment that the inventor will continue to invest along that trajectory in the future. In fact, Spence (1973) argued that strong signals should generate commitment in order to be credible as a sorting mechanism. The definition of the separating equilibrium implies some kind of strategic complementarity across issuers, because the development of signals demands time and often requires irreversible investments, and thus issuers are motivated to continue to use the signals in subsequent periods.

Moreover, the strength of the signal and the informational benefits obtained by the receiver vary not only because of the cost of the signaling and the commitment it entails, but also in function of the certifiability, visibility, clarity, and consistency the signal confers upon the firm that is marketing the innovative trademarked or patented product (Deb 2013). In practice, there is certifiability when an independent and neutral organization approves the patent or trademark in accordance to specific and predetermined guidelines. In the case of patent and trademark offices, expert reviewers verify though a substantive examination that IP applications comply with standard criteria of patentability/registration before approval. For example, at the USPTO, patents should be novel, not obvious to experts, and useful in practice. In the same vein, there are many registration requirements in the trademark approval process, and very often the most critical one is the distinctiveness from previously registered marks.[9]

The visibility of the signal to the receiver and other external parties is ensured by the publication of the examination results by the patent and trademark offices (Landes and Posner 1987). Typically, the granting process is finalized when the patent and trademark filing has entered the official register of authorised rights, which is visible and accessible to external parties in all aspects of the approved intellectual property. More recently, patent office procedures have been harmonised and now patent filings are published within 18 months of the earliest date of application or priority, after which search reports and patentability assessments by examiners are also made public. At the USPTO, trademarks are also published before registration, when third parties have a limited time to oppose the registration on the basis of substantive or procedural aspects of the trademark.

With respect to the clarity or measurability of strong signals, it is noteworthy that uncertainty and ambiguity exist as long as the IP application has not been officially approved (Gans, Hsu, and Stern 2008; Beebe 2017). During the patent prosecution, the examiner can ask for amendments to various aspects of the application, including the number and breadth of patent claims or the identification of goods and services covered

---

[9]Another criterion for approval of the registration of a mark is that the application should not be deceptive and contrary to law or morality.

THE ROLE OF TRADEMARKS

by the mark. If the application does not comply with the patentability or registration criteria, the examiner will not partially or fully approve the request for protection.

Lastly, Deb (2013) argued that in order to be credible for the receivers, signals should be consistent, meaning that they are stable and do not deteriorate over time when investors have subsequent interactions with the issuing firms. While patents can be maintained only until the statutory limit, trademarks can be renewed an endless number of times. Moreover, the protection deriving from trademarks can be transferred and extended in novel markets beyond those currently in existence (Ramello 2006; Ramello and Silva 2006), although firms typically request extensions in the case of multi-product umbrella branding, in presence of well-known and strong corporate brands (Völckner and Sattler 2006), and in later periods of the product lifecycles (DeGraba and Sullivan 1995). Further, when multiple trademarks are paired with one or multiple patents, these strategies are often associated with highly distinctive and identifiable words, and so there is consistency in the usage of the same wording across patent titles and wordmarks. Assuming these synergic signal characteristics, an additional *ceteris paribus* testable hypothesis can be posited regarding the strength of the signaling conveyed by the firm's combined IP strategies:

HP 2:   *A patent-trademark pair is a stronger predictor than sole patenting of the value of the underlying patented invention.*

3. Patent premium value

To assess the value of the patent-trademark pairs, I relied on renewal fee data, which ' … *captures the many forms of private value that may be conferred by a patent: defensive, deterrent, signaling, and revenue generation.*' (Moore 2005: 1526). In fact, for patents kept in force, renewal fees are considered as lower bound revenues that the patent yields to the owner, and more specifically, they concern the incremental premium value that the patent protection strategy generates as compared to a world without such IP protection (Barney 2002; Bessen 2008; Kim 2015). Furthermore, the payment of renewal fees to keep a patent active could function as a signaling device for the growth potential in the technological and market conditions faced by the patentee (Crampes and Langinier 1998; Langinier 2004). Therefore, the analysis of actual patent renewal data allows the computation of the premium value of patent rights, once some assumptions about the functional form of the patent value distribution have been made (Schankerman 1998; Barney 2002).

Models similar to that of Schankerman (1998) assume that the patenting agent maximises the benefits derived from the protection strategy by choosing how many years to keep a patent in force. In particular, the net benefits of a patent from cohort j in age t are represented as current benefits B_{tj} minus the costs of renewal fees C_{tj}. Thus the agent optimizes the discounted value on T

$$max_{T \in [1,2,...,\bar{T}]} V(T) = \sum_{t=1}^{T} (B_{tj} - C_{tj})(1+i)^{-t} \qquad (1)$$

where $\bar{T}$ is the statutory limit to patent protection and i is the discount rate, which is typically assumed at the level of ten percent. The optimal patent maintenance T^* is the first age when $B_{tj} - C_{tj} < 0$, otherwise it coincides with the statutory limit. Renewal fees, C, are non-decreasing in age, whereas benefits, B, are non-increasing in age, meaning that in each time t the benefits can be expressed as a function of initial benefits B_{0j}. Assuming that the benefits from patents decay with a time invariant rate d, then the patentee will renew the protection in time t solely when $B_{0j} \geq C_{tj} \prod_{\tau=1}^{t} (1 - d_\tau)^{-1}$.

If $F(B_{0j}, \theta_j)$ denotes the cumulative distribution of the initial benefits, where θ_j indicates a vector of parameters, then the proportion of patents from cohort j renewed in age t is $P_{tj} = 1 - F(B_{0j}, \theta_j)$, and the log of the initial benefits is distributed as $b_{0j} \sim N(\mu_j, \sigma_j)$ with mean μ_j and standard deviation σ_j. The owner will renew the patent protection if and only if

$$\frac{b_{0j} - \mu_j}{\sigma_j} \geq \frac{lnC_{tj} - t*\ln(1-d) - \mu_j}{\sigma_j} \tag{2}$$

which implies that the proportion of patents in cohort j that drops out by age t is given by $1 - P_{tj} = \Phi(z_{tj}, \theta_j)$ where $\Phi(.)$ is the standardized normal distribution function with $z_{tj} = lnC_{tj} - t*ln(1-d)$.[10]

To a large extent, previous studies have advanced estimates of the premium value of patents with respect to European countries, where renewal decisions must be made annually.[11] Conversely, at the USPTO, post-grant fees are paid 3.5, 7.5, and 11.5 years after issuance in order to keep a patent in force respectively in years 4, 8, and 12 (Barney 2002; Bessen 2008).[12] Hence, application of the condition expressed by Equation (1) to a dyadic context should take into the account not only the higher frequency of the renewal decisions, but also the differential timing when patent validity commences. The 1994 World Trade Organization agreement on trade-related aspects of intellectual property rights (TRIPS) harmonized the patent procedure between Europe and America, setting the statutory limit for patent protection to 20 years from filing. However, until 1995, the USPTO rule was that protection lasted 17 years from patent issuance.

For the computation of dollar estimates of the premium value imposed by Equation (1), I analysed the historical fee schedules for U.S. patents for the cohorts 1985–1995, and their EPC direct equivalents with designations in France, Germany, and the United Kingdom.[13] In particular, I tracked the U.S. renewal decisions for patents issued by year 1997, following them up to year 2010, whereas for Europe

[10]It is noteworthy that the assumption of monotonicity of non-increasing benefits R – given the non-decreasing fee costs C – is sufficient but not necessary for the validity of Equation (2), which is required to hold solely in the neighbourhood of the optimal renewal age. In particular, there is a time $\check{T}$ for which $R_{tj} - C_{tj} > 0$ for $t < \check{T}$ and $R_{tj} - C_{tj} < 0$ for $t > \check{T}$, where $\check{T}$ is the last age which the patentee pays the renewal fees. Hence, the net revenues may be increasing in some periods before $\check{T}$.

[11]See Lanjouw (1998) for Germany, Schankerman (1998) for France, Deng (2007) for Belgium and Austria, and Grönqvist (2009) for Finland.

[12]At the USPTO, the renewal fees for small patenting entities are halved, and under strict conditions patent expiration due to unpaid fees could be invalidated. For fuller details see Moore (2005).

[13]Limiting the analysis to these European economies does not hamper the sample coverage at the European level because they represent a sufficiently large market to attract the lion's share of the EPC designation and renewal decisions. With respect to the above cohorts, around 83.8%, 94.4%, and 87.3% of European patents have designations in France, Germany, and the United Kingdom respectively (PatStat 2016). Furthermore, patents are maintained for a statistically significant longer period in the largest European economies than in the other EPC member countries (PatStat 2016).

I examined the renewal decisions of the equivalents of those cohorts for the years 1986 to 2014.

Since the year 2010 is used as base year,[14] the renewal fees were deflated using a production index for services, because a deflator for business investment is not available for the overall period.[15] The decay rate was assumed to be fifteen percent,[16] and the central moments of the distribution were estimated parametrically. Next, I drew fifty thousand pseudo-random variables from a lognormal distribution, and calculated V for each of them using Equation (1). In the value computations, the granting fees were not included and the filing year constituted the starting time. Solely the patents held by U.S. business organizations at issuance were considered,[17] and in addition, their EPC equivalents with combined patent designations in France, Germany, and the United Kingdom were identified using direct priority links.[18] In conclusion, the mean, median, and interquartile range of patent value distributions of the dyadic dataset were estimated respectively to be about PPP $ 123 thousand, $ 34 thousand, and $ 62 thousand.

4. Dataset creation

The dataset used in the econometric analysis is the combination of several data sources with respect to patent information, trademark registrations, and design patents.

4.1. Patent information

The renewal decisions of the U.S. and EPC patent cohorts over the period 1985–1995 were observed, until the payment of the last post-grant fee or up to the end of the statutory period of patent protection. For the U.S. patents, procedural information on renewal decisions came from the Maintenance Fee Events File (Marco 2012),[19] whereas for Europe, the EPO Patent Register was the source (PatStat 2016). The payment date events were connected with the historical fee cost schedules extracted from archival sources and field interviews with patent office managers.[20]

From PatStat (2016) I also extracted information on priority links and patent citations, and then consolidated this information using the INPADOC patent family definition of priority links.[21] For detailed information on the fractional patent applications, I relied on the USPTO's PAIR dataset, whereas claim counts and number of

---

[14]This year is also the time reference for the exchange rate of European patent legislation fees in PPP U.S. dollars.
[15]The empirical investigation assessed the robustness of the results by considering a GDP deflator at the national level instead of for the service sector alone.
[16]As a robustness check, I relaxed this depreciation assumption and used higher levels of the depreciation rate.
[17]Given the importance of the United States as a locus of R&D activities, I do not think that limiting the analysis to the patented inventions owned by U.S. patentees is a serious drawback.
[18]The direct priority links were garnered from the PatStat (2016).
[19]The Maintenance Fee Events File is accessible at www.google.com/googlebooks/uspto-patents-maintenance-fees. html .
[20]A complete list of sources for the historical fee cost schedules is available upon request to the author.
[21]While strict equivalents are patent filings including exactly the same priorities or combination of priorities, an INPADOC patent family constitutes a self-contained and consolidated group of priority links including any direct or indirect priority link. For more information on the patent family definition see Martinez (2011).

words in each claim were garnered from the U.S. Patent Claims Research Dataset (both datasets available at www.uspto.gov/economics).

With regard to patentee information, the main source was the NBER patent project (available at sites.google.com/site/patentdataproject), which allows identification of the assigned entities and their addresses for the population of U.S. patents issued over the period 1969–2006. Furthermore, I integrated this data source with the PAIR dataset and Maintenance Fee Events File in order to build several demographic variables on patentee characteristics.

Appendix B of the Supplementary Material presents the measurement approach for the patentee level control variables and the construction of the patent indicators with regard to breadth and technology potential, prior art and background of the invention, filing and procedural aspects of the patent, and IP usage mode.

4.2. Trademark registrations

The registration requirements for obtaining trademark protection at the USPTO demand that the mark not be deceptive or contrary to law or morality, and that it be characterised by intrinsic distinctiveness from previously registered marks.[22] Typically, distinctiveness is demonstrated when the patentee has invested in the product's brand equity, and when the related marketing activities were underway in the marketplace before the filing date.[23] From the point of view of trademark prosecution, the legal basis for demonstrating a mark's commercial involvement is a so-called 'use in commerce' declaration by the patentee.[24] Since the U.S. Trademark Law Revision Act of 1988 entered into force on 16 November 1989, patentees also have had a second option at the filing stage, that of stating the intention of commercial use of the trademark, called 'intent-to-use in commerce'. Once the trademark application has been examined and approved, this option allows the patentee a delay of up to 36 months in the actual use of the trademark in commercial activities.[25]

It is worth noting that according to the Lanham Act, trademark protection in the U.S. can be sought even without registration at the USPTO, provided that the trademark is distinctive and used in commerce. However, formal registration of a mark at the USPTO offers significant benefits above and beyond those obtained without such registration. The patentee has nationwide priority of ownership and exclusive use of the mark since the filing date, and the mark can become incontestable after five years. Moreover, in case of infringement, there are enhanced remedies, and imported goods that infringe on the mark can be blocked. Furthermore, through the USPTO the patentee has an access route to international registration.[26]

---

[22]See Lanham Act § 2.
[23]See Lanham Act § 1(a).
[24]At the USPTO, a prior application or registration in a foreign jurisdiction or under the Madrid Protocol system could serve as the legal basis for filing a trademark application, without the requirement of declaration of 'use in commerce' as of the filing date. Foreign priorities used as legal basis at filing are a relatively rare event in the population of the U.S. trademark filing (For more information see Graham et al. 2013).
[25]See Lanham Act § 1(b, d).
[26]For a broader discussion of the differences between common law trademarks and federally registered trademarks in the U.S. see Graham et al. (2013).

The present analysis has limited the focus to U.S. federal trademark registrations, which I do not believe to be a serious limitation for a preliminary investigation of this kind. In fact, Dinlersoz et al. (2018) analysed the impact of trademarking on firm growth, using a census-wide dataset of the universe of firms in the U.S. during the period 1997–2013. They found that the potential selection and treatment effects of the trademarking decision on firm performance deriving from the common law trademarks are similar to the case of federal registered trademarks. In this direction, the inclusion of common law trademarks in the analysis would not tend to reduce the effects of the patent-trademark pairing strategy on patent valuation as predicted by HP 1.

Bibliographic information on the U.S. federal trade and service mark registrations was obtained from the Stata files of the USPTO's Trademark Reporting and Application Monitoring dataset (TRAM, available at www.uspto.gov/economics).[27] Furthermore, this data source was combined with the NBER's patentee dataset, by jointly matching entity names and their addresses in patent and trademark documents. In addition, the IP datasets were integrated through the matching of the textual content of an entity's legal documents. The next section briefly sketches the matching framework with regard to textual content, while Appendix A of the Supplementary Material provides a more detailed explanation of the method and the steps used.

4.2.1. Matching framework

I analysed the textual content of the underlying legal documents in order to gauge the combined IP strategies and identify a patent-trademark pair (Ceccagnoli et al. 2010).[28] For the matching of textual content, I developed a string similarity algorithm to account for differences due to the position of the same word between otherwise identical strings. In particular, I implemented the string similarity J^w index discussed in Thoma et al. (2010), which computes the percentage of common words after breaking up the strings into words at the blank spaces and weighting each word of a given string by its statistical frequency.[29] This weighted string similarity J^w index was executed for all the words appearing in patent titles as compared to wordmarks, which are typically made of very unique and distinctive words.[30] In fact, titles are succinct categorisations of a patent and report its most salient feature. On the other hand, wordmarks are carefully scrutinized by expert reviewers who approve their registration according to strict criteria: they must be distinctive, and must not be similar or identical to any earlier mark.

While it could be argued that this procedure measures only incidental text similarity across patent and trademark documents, and therefore the matching algorithm could generate false positives, a few caveats are worth mentioning. The matching of patent and trademark documents employs the weighted J^w index of

---

[27]This data source collects complete bibliographic information on the universe of U.S. federal mark registrations from 1978 up to 2015, including date of filing and priority, description of a mark in terms of goods and services, sectoral classification, and other procedural information (Graham et al. 2013).

[28]During the time period covered by the analysed dataset (1982–1998) 95.7% of the registrations include textual information and 68.3 relied only on text.

[29]An extensive discussion of the string similarity J^w index, matching methodology and related implementation in the case of patent and trademark documents is presented in Appendix A of the Supplementary Material.

[30]For a battery of examples see Appendix Table 3.

string similarity, which takes into account the statistical frequency of a token in the overall dataset, and thus avoids spurious matching of frequent and non-discriminating words. Moreover, given the intrinsic distinctiveness of the wording in trademarks, the potential false positives that emerge from matching patents with trademarks should be more limited than when other types of documents are analysed (such as the matching of patents with scientific publications).[31] Lastly, to reduce potential false positives of the matched patents and trademarks – and also to mitigate selection and treatment effects related to the timing of the decision to pursue an IP strategy – I restricted the matching procedure to a narrow time interval between the filing dates of the underlying IP documents. In particular, because the patenting and trademarking activities for the same innovative project are expected to be closely intertwined, a three-year time lag between the filing of the patent and the matched mark was allowed for the computation a patent-trademark pair.[32]

4.3. Design patents

To account for potential heterogeneity deriving from the combination of other patenting strategies that could affect patent valuation – as posited by the HP 2 – I considered design patent rights that protect purely decorative and ornamental products. A design patent is granted only after a substantive examination verifies that the design is novel and not obvious, as well as original and ornamental. U.S. design patent holders benefit from a statutory limit of protection of 14–15 years without any intercurrent renewal term.[33]

Patentees can obtain many overlapping intellectual property rights for the same innovative project in order to increase the number of remedies that can be requested in patent disputes (Heller and Eisenberg 1998; Lanjouw and Lerner 1998). In this case, it is not the patent-trademark pair strategy per se that affects the value of patents, but the ability of the patentee to obtain protection by combining several IP strategies. In fact, during litigation the IP overlap effect may be particularly favourable for the owner of a design patent because infringements must be remedied without apportionment of the total profit deriving from the infringing product (Burstein 2016).[34]

---

[31]Several visual inspections revealed that the textual similarity across the portfolio of patents and trademarks originated from: a) discriminating token(s) in the patent title and wordmark; b) combination of non-discriminating tokens from a patent title, that could appear in one single wordmark or in combination of wordmarks in distinct trademarks (within the same portfolio); c) one single and non-discriminating token from a patent title repeated in many trademarks from the same portfolio, which can be assimilated to umbrella branding.

[32]This assumption is broadly consistent with the time lag between a firm's first patent and its trademark, as shown in Appendix A of the Supplementary Material: seven out of ten of the firms that obtain patents and trademarks start both IP strategies within three years of each other, while half of them are contemporaneous first-time filers (within a year) of a patent or trademark.

[33]As the U.S. joined the Hague Agreement Concerning the International Deposit of Industrial Designs, the statutory limit of protection for design patents filed on or after 13 May 2015 is 15 years since the date of patent issuance, while applications filed before that date benefit from only 14 years of protection. For a discussion of the procedural aspects of the Hague system see Beebe (2017).

[34]This provision is unavailable in the case of a legal dispute over a utility patent or trademark (Burstein 2016; Lemley 2013).

Box 1. IP pairing strategies.

Patent-trademark pair	The weighted J^w index of string similarity (Thoma et al. 2010), computed over the tokens appearing in the title of a utility patent as compared to the wordmark of a mark. The index measures the percentage of common tokens over the total number of tokens, once each token has been inversely weighted by its statistical frequency (for a formal definition, see Appendix A of the Supplemental Material). The time lag between the filing dates of two IP strategies is within three years.
D (Patent-trademark pair)	A binary variable with positive outcome when the string similarity J^w index equals the top quartile of the relative similarity distribution, zero otherwise.
Patent-trademark pair – 'intent-to-use in commerce' legal basis at filing	As above, the weighted J^w index of string similarity (Thoma et al. 2010), computed over the tokens appearing in the title of a utility patent vis-à-vis the wordmark of a mark, which has been applied on the legal basis of a declaration of 'intent-to-use in commerce' at the date of filing.
Patent-trademark pair – 'use in commerce' legal basis at filing	As above, the weighted J^w index of string similarity (Thoma et al. 2010), computed over the tokens appearing in the title of a utility patent vis-à-vis the wordmark of a mark, which has not been applied on the legal basis of a declaration of 'intent-to-use in commerce' at the date of filing.
Patent-design pair	As above, the weighted J^w index of string similarity (Thoma et al. 2010), computed over the tokens appearing in the title of a utility patent vis-à-vis the title of a design patent. The time lag between the filing dates of two IP strategies is within three years.
D (Trade name)	A binary variable with positive outcome when the trade name of a patentee appears in the title of the focal patent, zero otherwise, which controls for other potential signaling effects (Kashmiri and Mahajan 2015).

Using data from the Patent Application Information Retrieval dataset (PAIR, available at www.uspto.gov/economics) I built IP pairs in which the design patent title is the same or similar to the utility patent title.[35] Once again, the weighted string similarity J^w index discussed in Thoma et al. (2010) was computed to determine this other type of IP pair and a maximum three year time lag was allowed for the filing dates of the two IP strategies.

Box 1 presents a detailed list of the main variables and a short description of the related measurement methodology.

5. The determinants of the patent premium value

The econometric analysis is based on a series of linear equations against the log premium value of utility patents of the proposed measures of the combined IP strategies, using a dataset constituted by the universe of U.S. patent cohorts from 1985 to 1995 issued by the end of 1997. Only U.S. business firms that obtained patents were considered, therefore I excluded foreign patentees, non-business organizations, sole inventors and non-assigned patents, in doing so reducing the sample size to about 410,780 patents, which is 39.9 percent of the overall dataset.[36] The regressions employed weights in order to tackle the selection bias arising from the fact of analysing

---

[35]In addition to the title of the design patent application, the patentee must provide drawings and/or photographs depicting the characteristics of the design in order to obtain patent protection.

[36]For 42 patents invented by the U.S. business patentees, I could not identify bibliographic information or patentee demographics.

the dataset with a reduced number of observations as compared to the universe of utility patents. Furthermore, in the computation of the patent premium value, I consolidated patent families with the EPC direct equivalents that designated France, Germany, or the United Kingdom.[37] Thus 15.7 percent of the patents have direct equivalents with validations in at least one of the three major European patent legislations. Table 1 depicts the descriptive statistics of the combined IP strategies, the controls for the patenting firm, and various types of patent indicators.

All the regressions analysed a complete set of patent indicators regarding patent breadth and technology potential, prior art and patent background, filing and procedural aspects of a patent, and the IP usage mode – such as patent reassignments, pledges in financing obligations, and inventions created with government involvement.[38] Additional controls concerned the demographic characteristics of the patent owner, such as experience, size and its changes during the patent lifecycle, listing in financial markets, growth of R&D personnel, and others (see Appendix B of the Supplementary Material for more details on the approach used to measure the control variables). Last but not least, the regressions were executed with dummies to condition for fixed effects with respect to cohort, two and three digit technological classifications, and year-technology interaction effects defined at the two digit classification level.[39]

In this section I discuss the econometric evidence in order to assess the proposed testable hypotheses, while the discussion of the results connected to the controls at the firm level and the value appraisal of the remaining control variables is presented in Appendix C of the Supplementary Material.

The valuation of the combined IP strategies is regressed in Model 1 of Table 2 in terms of the analysis of patent-trademark pairs, whereas Models 2 and 3 also scrutinize the pairing strategies with design patents and relative interaction term, respectively. Furthermore, Model 3 controls for other potential effects of signaling by the means of a binary variable with the positive outcome when the trade name of the patentee is shown in the title of the focal patent (Kashmiri and Mahajan 2015).[40] I find that the combination of patenting with trademarking on the same invention is positively and significantly associated with the premium value of patents, confirming HP 1 (a patent-trademark pair is positively associated with the value of the underlying patented invention).

In terms of signaling, this result suggests that the joint use of patents and trademarks constitutes a signal for competitors, investors, or commercial partners that the underlying

---

[37]In terms of the renewal fee payment, I computed the present value rule starting with the application year both for the U.S. and EPC patents and did not consider the application and grant fees in the value computations. See section 3 for a fuller presentation.

[38]The continuous indicators were detrended for time and technology effects, using the geometric mean method.

[39]Twelve dummies of the year-technology interaction effects computed at the two digit classification could not be identified, and hence they were aggregated to the left-out category in the regression analysis.

[40]Although according to the Trademark Manual of Examining Procedure (TMEP § 1202.01, available at tmep.uspto.gov) trade naming does not constitute a demonstration of the use requirement of the Lanham Act, it is suitable for trademark protection through the common law system, when it is also employed as a product or service name in the marketplace. Thus, a patent titled with the trade name could be indicative of a common law trademark owned by the patentee. In fact, this protection strategy could be sought by younger firms and those with a limited number of product lines (See discussion in Appendix A of the Supplementary Material).

The finding that a trade name shown in the patent title does not enhance patent valuation above and beyond the patent-trademark pairing obtained through the U.S. federal registration system does not contradict the assumption advanced by Dinlersoz et al. (2018), who claimed that the potential selection and treatment effects of the trademarking decision on firm performance arising from the common law trademarks are similar to the federal registered ones (For more details see section 4.2.).

Table 1. Descriptive statistics.

Variables	Mean	Median	S.D.	Min	Max
Dependent variable: Patent value (log)	10.109	10.440	1.742	5.899	16.639
Main indipendent variables					
Patent-trademark pair	0.016	0.000	0.061	0.000	1.000
D (Patent-trademark pair)	0.020	-	-	-	-
Patent-trademark pair – 'intent-to-use in commerce' legal basis	0.007	0.000	0.038	0.000	1.000
Patent-trademark pair – 'use in commerce' legal basis	0.011	0.000	0.052	0.000	1.000
Patent-design pair	0.050	0.000	0.126	0.000	1.000
D (Trade name)	0.019	-	-	-	-
Patentee characteristics					
D (Large patentee)	0.826	-	-	-	-
D (Patentee change – from small to large)	0.002	-	-	-	-
D (Patentee change – from large to small)	0.003	-	-	-	-
Ln (Patentee experience – age of the first patent)	2.782	2.996	0.710	0.000	4.174
D (Fortune 500 patentee: ranking 1–100)	0.323	-	-	-	-
D (Fortune 500 patentee: ranking 101–200)	0.065	-	-	-	-
D (Fortune 500 patentee: ranking 201–300)	0.036	-	-	-	-
D (Fortune 500 patentee: ranking 301–400)	0.019	-	-	-	-
D (Fortune 500 patentee: ranking 401–500)	0.013	-	-	-	-
D (Persistent Fortune 500 patentee)	0.392	-	-	-	-
D (Listed firm)	0.584	-	-	-	-
Growth of R&D personnel	0.179	0.114	0.179	−0.193	0.500
D (Patentee name change)	0.113	-	-	-	-
Patent usage					
D (Patent reassignment)	0.370	-	-	-	-
D (M&A patent reassignment)	0.076	-	-	-	-
D (Security interest)	0.195	-	-	-	-
D (Government interest)	0.010	-	-	-	-
D (Other R&D collaboration)	0.007	-	-	-	-
Patent breadth and technology potential					
Ln (Patent family)	0.628	0.493	0.558	0.148	6.727
Ln (Patent family weighted by the market size)	0.451	0.392	0.175	0.319	2.567
Ln (Independent claims)	0.585	0.511	0.291	0.000	3.403
Ln (Independent claim length)	1.208	1.056	0.795	0.000	37.952
Ln (Dependent claims)	0.790	0.773	0.437	0.000	4.595
D (Re-examined)	0.005	-	-	-	-
Ln (Forward citations)	0.807	0.676	0.603	0.000	5.550
Generality index	0.585	0.684	0.422	0.000	1.876
Share of self-citations	0.133	0.000	0.231	0.000	1.000
Patent prior art and background of the invention					
Ln (Inventors)	0.511	0.513	0.231	0.284	2.547
D (Law firm external attorney)	0.371	-	-	-	-
Ln (Backward citations)	0.745	0.659	0.478	0.000	6.040
Ln (Non patent references)	0.476	0.000	0.721	0.000	4.716
Originality index	0.596	0.667	0.289	0.000	1.000
Filing and procedural aspects of the patent					
Ln (Grant lag)	0.677	0.656	0.203	0.000	2.114
D (PCT route)	0.115	-	-	-	-
D (Continuation – Parent)	0.073	-	-	-	-
D (Continuation in Part – Parent)	0.056	-	-	-	-
D (Division – Parent)	0.080	-	-	-	-
D (Continuation – Child)	0.138	-	-	-	-
D (Continuation in Part – Child)	0.122	-	-	-	-
D (Division – Child)	0.097	-	-	-	-
D (Reissued)	0.004	-	-	-	-
Ln (Patent title length) †	3.860	3.892	0.535	0.000	5.628
Ln (Number of words in patent title) †	1.829	1.946	0.562	0.000	3.784
D (No forward citations)	0.029	-	-	-	-
D (No backward citations)	0.003	-	-	-	-

Notes: a) n = 410,780 US patents from the cohorts 1985–1995, corresponding to 47,316 distinct patentees. b) With the exeption of textual information variables †, all the continuous variables regarding the patent-level indicators have been detrended for time and technology effects using the geometric mean method.

Table 2. Patent premium value: Log linear regression results for patent cohorts during 1985–1995 (n = 410,780).

	OLS (1)	OLS (2)	OLS (3)	OLS (4)	OLS (5)	PANEL FE (6)	PANEL RE (7)
	Dependent variable: log value of patent rights based on historical renewal fee costs (US 2010 PPP $)						
Patent-trademark pair	0.510 [0.132]***						
D (Patent-trademark pair)[e]		0.491 [0.140]***	0.516 [0.133]***		0.125 [0.030]***	0.061 [0.018]***	0.072 [0.017]***
Patent-trademark pair – 'intent-to-use in commerce' legal basis				0.427 [0.233]*			
Patent-trademark pair – 'use in commerce' legal basis				0.409 [0.116]***			
Patent-design pair		0.088 [0.094]	0.097 [0.103]	0.088 [0.094]			
Patent-trademark-design pair[f]			−0.226 [0.358]				
D (Trade name)			0.027 [0.024]				
	Patentee characteristics and other controls at the patent level (See Appendices B-C in the Supplementary Material)						
Patentee characteristics (15)	Yes	Yes	Yes	Yes	Yes	Yes	Yes
Patent usage indicators (13)	Yes	Yes	Yes	Yes	Yes	Yes	Yes
Breadth & technology potential of patent (10)	Yes	Yes	Yes	Yes	Yes	Yes	Yes
Prior art & background of the invention (5)	Yes	Yes	Yes	Yes	Yes	Yes	Yes
Filing & procedural aspects of the patent (12)	Yes	Yes	Yes	Yes	Yes	Yes	Yes
Time dummies (11)	Yes	Yes	Yes	Yes	Yes	Yes	Yes
Patent class dummies (367)	Yes	Yes	Yes	Yes	Yes	Yes	Yes
Category dummies (36)	Yes	Yes	Yes	Yes	Yes	Yes	Yes
Time-category interaction dummies	Yes	Yes	Yes	Yes	Yes	Yes	Yes
Adjusted R^2	0.420	0.420	0.420	0.420	0.419	0.394	0.400

Notes: a) n = 410,780 US patents from the cohorts 1985–1995, corresponding to 47,316 distinct patentee. b) *** indicates statistically significant at 1% level; **5% level and * 10% level. c) Standard errors clustered at the patentee level. d) Weights have been computed because of the oversampling observations as compared to the universe of patents. e) It is computed as binary variable when the Patent-trademark pair equals the top quartile of the relative distribution. f) It is computed as interaction term between Patent-trademark pair and Patent-design pair.

focal invention is highly valuable from a commercial point of view. The finding is valid even when I take into the account design patents (Models 2 and 3), and hence does not falsify HP 2 on the heterogeneity of the strength of signals issued by combined IP strategies (a patent-trademark pair is a stronger predictor than sole patenting of the value of the underlying patented invention), supporting the claim that the valuation of an IP pair is greater when patenting is combined with trademarks rather than with the design patents.

In terms of appropriability, the patenting strategy combined with trademarks increases the value of patent rights by expanding the breadth and length of protection. In fact, trademarks can prolong the commercial success of a patented product beyond the statutory limit, provide IP protection for unpatentable complementary innovative activities regarding market experimentation and testing, and improve the plaintiffs' position during litigation. Heller and Eisenberg (1998) claimed that combined strategies of overlapping intellectual property rights could increase the number of remedies that can be requested in legal disputes. The present analysis shows that while trademarks are positively associated with patent valuation, design patents have an insignificant impact. These findings do not falsify the assumption that a design patent offers second-tier protection (Greenhalgh and Rogers 2010) and is no more useful than a utility patent for improving the appropriability conditions of the patentee.[41]

On the other hand, trademarks play an essential role in the branding and commercialization activities of the innovator, and thus they complement the protection obtained from utility patents. In this context, given its potential indefinite term of protection, trademarking could also surrogate the IP protection provided by design patents when the underlying design elements – through the continued use in commerce – have acquired distinctiveness of source of a product, which is an indication of the particular source where the product comes from (Beebe 2017). Since design patents do not slacken the coefficient of the former combined IP strategy, it can be concluded that the increase in the value of the patent premium, generated from pairing patents with trademarks, exceeds the effect of the mere combination of multiple IP strategies. More broadly, given the extent of controls conditioning the regressions, the validity of the patent-trademark pairs in predicting patent valuation is demonstrated above and beyond the typical patent indicators adopted in the literature (OECD 2009).

I conducted several robustness analyses of the results. First, I conditioned for the value heterogeneity of the trademark protection. Previous research has argued that the legal basis under which trademark protection is requested from the USPTO affects the associated premium value (Thoma 2019). In particular, the 1988 U.S. Trademark Law Revision Act widened the range of protection to those applications that previously could not obtain approval because of lack of commercial use as of filing date. This legislation allows patentees who file a trademark application through the 'intent-to-use in commerce' legal basis to delay the actual involvement in commercial activities of the mark to 36 months after the application has been examined and approved. Therefore, as the value of the trademark protection was lessened with the new legal basis, I expect that the patent strategy combined with trademarking incepted with an 'intent-to-use in

---

[41]For example, the patentability of a design could be mitigated by the functionality principle. See Beebe (2017) for a full discussion of the application and interpretation this principle in case of designs.

commerce' application would generate a smaller beneficial effect on patent premium value.

In fact, the findings of Model 4 do not contradict this view if a significance level of at least five percent is assumed. Pairing patents with trademarks obtained under 'intent-to-use in commerce' legal basis has a slightly significant effect on valuation, while on the contrary the trademarks obtained under the 'use in commerce' legal basis has a very significant positive bearing on the patent value regressions. Therefore, it can be concluded that when the two IP protection strategies are combined, the value heterogeneity of the trademark protection influences patent valuation.

Secondly, my calculations included a binary transformation of the patent-trademark pair string similarity measure to make it easier for managers to interpret the results. When the string similarity J^w index equals the top quartile of the related similarity distribution, I found that one additional patent-trademark pair generates an increase of 12.5 percentage points on the log premium value of patents, or in terms of an absolute number, PPP \$ 88 thousand average difference (Model 5).[42] In a regression analysis not reported in this article, I used different thresholds of the similarity distribution to define a patent-trademark pair, 'namely' the top decile or the median of the J^w index. The results of this analysis pointed to a comparable impact of the patent-trademark pairing strategy on patent valuation, that is a range between nine to twelve percentage points on the log premium value of patents, respectively.[43] This result further supports the validity of the J^w index in measuring the textual similarity across IP documents (Arts, Cassiman, and Gomez 2018).

An additional robustness analysis consisted in the execution of the value regressions by means of panel estimations: Model 6 computes the fixed effect estimator that accounts for the time invariant unobserved heterogeneity at the patentee level, while Model 7 presents the random effect estimator which deals with the problem of autocorrelation of the disturbances. Although the value impact of the patent-trademark pair strategy is half that of the pooled linear estimator, I still find a positive and statistically significant coefficient in both types of panel estimations. It is worth noting that while downward biased estimates are typically expected in the case of firm panel data (for a discussion see Kanwar and Hall 2017), I confirm that this bias is stronger for the fixed effects than for the random ones.

The last robustness assessment involved the computation of the initial benefits of the patent protection strategy by elaborating alternative indices to deflate the renewal fees and by considering higher levels of depreciation rate in the calculations. Although the usage of a GDP deflator at the national level was accompanied by a bigger mean and standard deviation of patent value, it indicated that the patent-trademark pair strategy has a similar magnitude impact on patent valuation. On the other hand, when a depreciation rate of 20 or 25 percent was assumed, it generated a proportional value increase of a patent-trademark pair.

---

[42]This average difference estimate is the mean of two alternative prediction methods relying on the normal distribution assumption and the so-called Duan's method. For a fuller presentation of the implementation of average difference prediction methods see Cameron and Trivedi (2010).

[43]Furthermore, I executed a pairwise correlation analysis of the patent-trademark pairs computed as binary variables at different thresholds of the similarity distribution of the J^w index with the log number of forward citations, and I confirm a positive Pearson's coefficient even at a one percent level of significance.

6. Conclusions

This paper is among the first studies to analyse how an IP strategy that pairs patenting with trademarking might affect patent premium value. I elaborate a novel method and dataset to identify patents combined with trademarks for the same innovative project. This approach contributes more generally to the research agenda in proposing timely indicators for innovative activities (OECD 2009). In particular, I define a new concept, namely, a patent-trademark pair, in which a firm's innovative activities are protected by both a patent and a trademark. Relying on previous research on quality signaling, I present a theoretical framework that argues that trademarks increase the value of the patented R&D, because they improve the signaling function of patents and expand their breadth and length of protection. Furthermore, the strength of the signaling afforded by the IP strategies is articulated according to their cost, commitment, certifiability, clarity, visibility, and consistency. In this context, signals issued by patent-trademark pairs are stronger than other types of combined IP strategies, which affect patent valuation in a different way.

I find striking evidence that the combined IP strategy based on a patent-trademark pair is associated with higher patent premium value – in absolute numbers, I estimated that adding a trademark to a patent creates an additional value of PPP $ 88 thousand. On the contrary, according to my analyses, when the IP strategy combines design patents with utility patenting, the value effect is absent. This finding is in line with the view that design patents constitute a second-tier protection mechanism for smaller and incremental inventions, and hence they do not conflate into bigger patent valuations.

It is worth noting that the results reported in this paper hold after controlling for an extensive set of other patent characteristics. First, I have accounted for the traditional patent value indicators proposed in the literature on patent valuation, namely, patent breadth and technology potential, prior art and patent background, filing and procedural aspects of a patent, and IP usage mode. Furthermore, I have controlled for several other characteristics of the patent owner, which are expected to correlate with patent value, such as the firm's size and experience, its listing in financial markets, the growth of R&D personnel, and other factors. Last but not least, the regression analysis, which conditioned for the value heterogeneity of the trademark protection strategy and advanced panel estimations, confirmed the robustness of the results regarding the proposed testable hypotheses, although it is not suited to solve the problem of causal inference (Castaldi and Giarratana 2018).

Given the increasing ease of access to and usage of IP information (Ouellette 2012), this research offers salient input for managerial decisions. Managers may benefit from monitoring the combined IP strategies of their competitors in order to anticipate the value creation and evolution in the marketplace. In particular, the strong market presence ensured by highly distinctive trademarks is predictive of a firm's greater potential for successfully translating inventions into commercially viable offerings, and therefore the time-to-market of new product launches is likely to be accelerated. Moreover, by combining patent and trademark strategies for the same innovative project, firms not only can prolong the period of protection of the inventive outcomes and provide protection to complementary market experimentation activities that are unpatentable, but also optimise the value creation of technologically important patents by strengthening the patent quality signals. In this direction, firms should ensure that the legal documents of their IP portfolio feature significant name consistency, which could be achieved, for instance, by using unique and highly identifiable words across patent titles and wordmarks.

Acknowledgments

I would thank for comments at various stages of this project Ashish Arora, Bronwyn H. Hall, Alan Marco, Amanda F. Myers, Mark Schankerman, Nathan Wajsman and all the participants at the European Policy for Intellectual Property Annual Conference in Oxford, U.K. (September 2016), Academy of Management Annual Conference in Atlanta (GA), U.S. (August 2017), and STATA Users' Conference in Florence, Italy (November 2017). Furthermore this study has benefitted significantly from comments by two anonymous reviewers and the special issue editorial team. The usual disclaimer applies.

Disclosure statement

No potential conflict of interest was reported by the author.

References

Abramowicz, M., and J. F. Duffy. 2008. "Intellectual Property for Market Experimentation." *New York University Law Review* 83: 337–410.

AIPLA. 2015. "Report of the Economic Survey." American Intellectual Property Law Association.

Alvarez-Garrido, E., and G. Dushnitsky. 2013. "Publications and Patents in Corporate Venture Backed Biotech." *Nature Biotechnology* 31 (6): 495–497. doi:10.1038/nbt.2595.

Arts, S., B. Cassiman, and J. C. Gomez. 2018. "Text Matching to Measure Patent Similarity." *Strategic Management Journal* 39 (1): 62–84. doi:10.1002/smj.2699.

Arvidsson, A. 2005. "Brands: A Critical Perspective." *Journal of Consumer Culture* 5: 235–258. doi:10.1177/1469540505053093.

Ashtor, J. H. 2015. "Redefining 'Valuable Patents': Analysis of the Enforcement Value of U.S. Patents." *Stanford Technology Law Review* 18: 497–545.

Bao, Y., A. T. Shao, and D. Rivers. 2008. "Creating New Brand Names: Effects of Relevance, Connotation, and Pronunciation." *Journal of Advertising Research* 48 (1): 148–162. doi:10.2501/S002184990808015X.

Barney, J. A. 2002. "A Study of Patent Mortality Rates: Using Statistical Survival Analysis to Rate and Value Patent Assets." *AIPLA Quarterly Journal* 30 (3): 317–352.

Barroso, A., M. S. Giarratana, and M. Pasquini. 2019. "Product Portfolio Performance in New Foreign Markets: The EU Trademark Dual System." *Research Policy* 48 (1): 11–21. doi:10.1016/j.respol.2018.07.013.

Beebe, B. 2017. "Design Protection Law Chap. 20." In *The Oxford Handbook of Intellectual Property Law*, edited by R. Dreyfuss and J. Pilla, 572–593. Oxford: Oxford University Press, Kindle Edition.

Beebe, B., and J. Fromer. 2018. "Are We Running Out of Trademarks? an Empirical Study of Trademark Depletion and Congestion." *Harvard Law Review* 131: 945–1045.

Bei, X. 2019. "Trademarks, Specialized Complementary Assets, and the External Sourcing of Innovation." *Research Policy*. doi:10.1016/j.respol.2018.11.003.

Berman, B. 2008. *From Assets to Profits: Competing for IP Value and Return*. Hoboken (NJ): John Wiley & Sons.

Bessen, J. 2008. "The Value of U.S. Patents by Owner and Patent Characteristics." *Research Policy* 37: 932–945. doi:10.1016/j.respol.2008.02.005.

Block, J. H., C. O. Fisch, A. Hahn, and P. G. Sandner. 2015. "Why Do SMEs File Trademarks? Insights from Firms in Innovative Industries." *Research Policy* 44 (10): 1915–1930. doi:10.1016/j.respol.2015.06.007.

Block, J. H., G. De Vries, J. H. Schumann, and P. Sandner. 2014. "Trademarks and Venture Capital Valuation." *Journal Business Venturing* 29: 525–542. doi:10.1016/j.jbusvent.2013.07.006.

Buddelmeyer, H., P. Jensen, and E. Webster. 2010. "Innovation and the Determinants of Company Survival." *Oxford Economic Papers* 62 (2): 261–285. doi:10.1093/oep/gpp012.

Burstein, S. 2016. "Costly Designs." *Ohio State Law Journal* 77 (1): 107–157.

Cameron, A. C., and P. K. Trivedi. 2010. *Microeconometrics Using Stata.* Revised Ebook ed. College Station (TX): Stata Press.

Castaldi, C. 2018. "To Trademark or Not to Trademark: The Case of the Creative and Cultural Industries." *Research Policy* 47 (3): 606–616. doi:10.1016/j.respol.2018.01.006.

Castaldi, C., and M. S. Giarratana. 2018. "Diversification, Branding, and Performance of Professional Service Firms." *Journal of Service Research* 21 (3): 353–364. doi:10.1177/1094670518755315.

Ceccagnoli, M., S. J. H. Graham, M. J. Higgins, and J. Lee. 2010. "Productivity and the Role of Complementary Assets in Firms' Demand for Technology Innovations." *Industrial and Corporate Change* 19 (3): 839–869. doi:10.1093/icc/dtq033.

Ching, A. T. 2010. "Consumer Learning and Heterogeneity: Dynamics of Demand for Prescription Drugs after Patent Expiration." *International Journal of Industrial Organization* 28: 619–638. doi:10.1016/j.ijindorg.2010.02.004.

Cockburn, I., and M. McGarvie. 2007. "Patents, Thickets and the Financing of Early-Stage Firms: Evidence from the Software Industry." *Journal of Economics and Management Strategy* 18 (3): 729–773. doi:10.1111/j.1530-9134.2009.00228.x.

Conti, A., M. Thursby, and J. Thursby. 2013. "Patents as Signals for Startup Financing." NBER Working Paper No. 19191, Cambridge, MA: National Bureau of Economic Research.

Contropia, C., M. A. Lemley, and B. Sampat. 2013. "Do Applicant Patent Citations Matter?" *Research Policy* 42: 844–854. doi:10.1016/j.respol.2013.01.003.

Crampes, C., and C. Langinier. 1998. "Informational Disclosure and the Renewal of Patents." *Annals of Economics and Statistics* 49/50: 265–288.

Crass, D., D. Czarnitzki, and A. A. Toole 2016. "The Dynamic Relationship between Investments in Brand Equity and Firm Profitability." *USPTO Economic Working Paper No. 2016-1,* Alexandria (VA): Office of the Chief Economist, United States Patent and Trademark Office.

Deb, P. 2013. "Signaling Type and Post-IPO Performance." *European Management Review* 10: 99–116. doi:10.1111/emre.2013.10.issue-2.

DeGraba, P., and M. W. Sullivan. 1995. "Spillover Effects, Cost Savings, R&D and the Use of Brand Extensions." *International Journal of Industrial Organization* 13: 229–248. doi:10.1016/0167-7187(94)00448-B.

Deng, Y. 2007. "Private Value of European Patents." *European Economic Review* 51: 1785–1812. doi:10.1016/j.euroecorev.2006.09.005.

Derclaye, E. 2017. "Overlapping Rights Chap. 22." In *The Oxford Handbook of Intellectual Property Law,* edited by R. Dreyfuss and J. Pilla, 618–651. Oxford: Oxford University Press, Kindle Edition.

Dinlersoz, E. M., N. Goldschlag, A. Myers, and N. Zolas 2018. "An Anatomy of US Firms Seeking TM Registration." *NBER Working Paper No. 25038,* Cambridge (MA): National Bureau of Economic Research.

Flikkema, M., A. P. De Man, and C. Castaldi. 2014. "Are Trademark Counts a Valid Indicator of Innovation? Results of an In-Depth Study of New Benelux Trademarks Filed by SMEs." *Industry and Innovation* 21 (4): 310–331. doi:10.1080/13662716.2014.934547.

Gabler, N. 2015. "The Weird Science of Naming New Products." *New York Times,* January 15.

Gambardella, A. 2013. "The Economic Value of Patented Inventions: Thoughts and Some Open Questions." *International Journal of Industrial Organization* 31: 626–633. doi:10.1016/j.ijindorg.2013.02.007.

Gambardella, A., and A. McGahan. 2010. "Business-Model Innovation: General Purpose Technologies and Their Implications for Industry Structure." *Long Range Planning* 43: 262–271. doi:10.1016/j.lrp.2009.07.009.

Gambardella, A., D. Harhoff, and B. Verspagen. 2008. "The Value of European Patents." *European Management Review* 5 (2): 69–84. doi:10.1057/emr.2008.10.

Gambardella, A., D. Harhoff, and B. Verspagen. 2017. "The Economic Value of Patent Portfolios." *Journal of Economics and Management Strategy* 26 (4): 735–756.

Gans, J. S., D. H. Hsu, and S. Stern. 2008. "The Impact of Uncertain Intellectual Property Rights on the Market for Ideas: Evidence from Patent Grant Delays." *Management Science* 54 (5): 982–997. doi:10.1287/mnsc.1070.0814.

Gans, J. S., and S. Stern. 2003. "The Product Market and the Market for Ideas: Commercialization Strategies for Technology Entrepreneurs." *Research Policy* 32: 333–350. doi:10.1016/S0048-7333(02)00103-8.

Gao, G., and L. M. Hitt. 2012. "Information Technology and Trademarks: Implications for Product Variety." *Management Science* 58 (6): 1211–1226. doi: 10.1287/mnsc.1110.1480.

Giarratana, M. S., and S. Torrisi. 2010. "Foreign Entry and Survival in a Knowledge-Intensive Market: Emerging Economy Countries' International Linkages, Technology Competences, and Firm Experience." *Strategic Entrepreneurship Journal* 4: 85–104. doi: 10.1002/sej.84.

Gittelman, M. 2008. "The Value of European Patents." *European Management Review* 5: 85–89. doi:10.1057/emr.2008.12.

Graham, S., G. Hancock, A. Marco, and A. F. Myers. 2013. "The USPTO Trademark CASE File Dataset: Descriptions, Lessons, and Insights." *Journal of Economics and Management Strategy* 22 (4): 669–705. doi:10.1111/jems.12035.

Greenhalgh, C., and M. Rogers. 2006. "The Value of Innovation: The Interaction of Competition, R&D and IP." *Research Policy* 35: 562–580. doi:10.1016/j.respol.2006.02.002.

Greenhalgh, C., and M. Rogers. 2010. *Innovation, Intellectual Property and Economic Growth.* Princeton (NJ): Princeton University Press.

Grönqvist, C. 2009. "The Private Value of Patents by Patent Characteristics: Evidence from Finland." *Journal of Technology Transfer* 34 (2): 159–168. doi:10.1007/s10961-007-9067-6.

Hall, B. H. 2019. "Is There a Role for Patents in the Financing of Innovative Firms?" *Industrial and Corporate Change* 28: 657–680. doi:10.1093/icc/dty074.

Hall, B. H., and D. Harhoff. 2012. "Recent Research on the Economics of Patents." *Annual Review of Economics* 4: 541–565. doi:10.1146/annurev-economics-080511-111008.

Häussler, C., D. Harhoff, and E. Mueller. 2014. "How Patenting Informs VC Investors – The Case of Biotechnology." *Research Policy* 43 (8): 1286–1298. doi:10.1016/j.respol.2014.03.012.

Heller, M. A., and R. S. Eisenberg. 1998. "Can Patents Deter Innovation? the Anticommons in Biomedical Research." *Science* 280: 698–700. doi:10.1126/science.280.5364.698.

Helmers, C., and M. Rogers. 2010. "Innovation and the Survival of New Firms in the UK." *Review of Industrial Organization* 36: 227–248. doi:10.1007/s11151-010-9247-7.

Helmers, C., and M. Rogers. 2011. "Does Patenting Help High-Tech Start-Ups?" *Research Policy* 40: 1016-27. doi:10.1016/j.respol.2011.05.003.

Hoenen, S., C. Kolympiris, W. Schoenmakers, and N. Kalaitzandonakes. 2014. "The Diminishing Signaling Value of Patents between Early Rounds of Venture Capital Financing." *Research Policy* 43: 956–989. doi:10.1016/j.respol.2014.01.006.

Hsu, D., and R. Ziedonis. 2013. "Resources as Dual Sources of Advantage: Implications for Valuing Entrepreneurial-Firm Patents." *Strategic Management Journal* 34: 761–781. doi:10.1002/smj.2013.34.issue-7.

IP CloseUp 2012. "Leading Brands Increasingly Have the Most Valuable Patents." *By Bruce Berman, Appeared on November 15.* Accessed ipcloseup.wordpress.com/2012/11/15/leading-brands-increasingly-have-the-most-valuable-patents/

Kanwar, S., and B. H. Hall. 2017. "The Market Value of R&D in Weak Innovation Regimes." *B E of Journal Economic Analysis and Policy* 17 (1): 1–22.

Kashmiri, S., and V. Mahajan. 2015. "The Name's the Game: Does Marketing Impact the Value of Corporate Name Changes?" *Journal of Business Research* 68: 281–290. doi:10.1016/j.jbusres.2014.07.007.

Kim, J. 2015. "Patent Portfolio Management of Sequential Inventions: Evidence from U.S. Patent Renewal Data." *Review of Industrial Organization* 47: 195–218. doi:10.1007/s11151-015-9468-x.

Klink, R. R. 2003. "Creating Meaningful Brands: The Relationship between Brand Name and Brand Mark." *Marketing Letters* 14 (3): 143–157. doi:10.1023/A:1027476132607.

Kohli, C., and D. W. LaBahn. 1997. "Creating Effective Brand Names: A Study of the Naming Process." *Journal of Advertising Research* 37: 67–75.

Korkeamäki, T., and T. Takalo. 2013. "Valuation of Innovation and Intellectual Property: The Case of iPhone." *European Management Review* 10: 197–210. doi:10.1111/emre.2013.10.issue-4.

Krasnikov, A., S. Mishra, and D. Orozco. 2009. "Evaluating the Financial Impact of Branding Using Trademarks: A Framework and Empirical Evidence." *Journal of Marketing* 73 (6): 154–166. doi:10.1509/jmkg.73.6.154.

Landes, W. M., and R. Posner. 1987. "Trademark Law: An Economic Perspective." *Journal of Law and Economics* 30: 265–309. doi:10.1086/467138.

Langinier, C. 2004. "Are Patents Strategic Barriers to Entry?" *Journal of Economics and Business* 56 (5): 349–361. doi:10.1016/j.jeconbus.2004.02.002.

Lanjouw, J. O. 1998. "Protection in the Shadow of Infringement: Simulation Estimations of Patent Value." *Review of Economic Studies* 65 (4): 671–710. doi:10.1111/1467-937X.00064.

Lanjouw, J. O., and J. Lerner. 1998. "The Enforcement of Intellectual Property Rights: A Survey of the Empirical Literature." *Annals of Economics and Statistics* 49/50: 223–246.

Lemley, M. 2013. "A Rational System of Design Patent Remedies." *Stanford Technology Law Review* 17: 221–240.

Lemley, M. A. 2001. "Rational Ignorance at the Patent Office." *Northwestern University Law Review* 95 (4): 1495–1529.

Lemley, M. A., and C. Shapiro. 2005. "Probabilistic Patents." *Journal of Economic Perspectives* 19 (2): 75–98. doi:10.1257/0895330054048650.

Mann, R. J., and T. W. Sager. 2007. "Patents, Venture Capital, and Software Startups." *Research Policy* 36: 193–208. doi:10.1016/j.respol.2006.10.002.

Marco, A. 2012. "Citations and Renewal: A Window into Public and Private Patent Value." Paper Presented at the Third Asian Pacific Innovation Conference, Seoul, October 13–14.

Marco, A. C. 2005. "The Option Value of Patent Litigation: Theory and Evidence." *Review of Financial Economics* 14 (3–4): 323–351. doi:10.1016/j.rfe.2004.09.003.

Martinez, C. 2011. "Patent Families: When Do Different Definitions Really Matter?" *Scientometrics* 86: 39–63. doi:10.1007/s11192-010-0251-3.

McGahan, A. M., and B. S. Silverman. 2006. "Profiting from Technological Innovation by Others: The Effect of Competitor Patenting on Firm Value." *Research Policy* 35 (8): 1222–1242. doi:10.1016/j.respol.2006.09.006.

Melnyk, V., M. Giarratana, and A. Torres. 2014. "Marking Your Trade: Cultural Factors in the Prolongation of Trademarks." *Journal of Business Research* 67: 478–485. doi:10.1016/j.jbusres.2013.06.003.

Moore, K. A. 2005. "Worthless Patents." *Berkeley Technology Law Journal* 20 (4): 1521–1552.

Murphy, W. J., J. L. Orcutt, and P. C. Remus. 2012. *Patent Valuation: Improving Decision Making.* Hoboken(NJ): John Wiley & Sons, Kindle edition.

Nagaoka, S., K. Motohashi, and A. Goto. 2010. "Patent Statistics as Innovation Indicators Chap. 25." In *Handbook of the Economics of Innovation*, edited by B. H. Hall and N. Rosenberg, 10973–12068. Amsterdam: Elsevier, Kindle Edition.

Odasso, C., G. Scellato, and E. Ughetto. 2015. "Selling Patents at Auction: An Empirical Analysis of Patent Value." *Industrial and Corporate Change* 24 (2): 417–438. doi:10.1093/icc/dtu015.

OECD. 2009. *OECD Patent Statistics Manual.* Paris: OECD.

Ouellette, L. L. 2012. "Do Patents Disclose Useful Information?" *Harvard Journal of Law and Technology* 25 (2): 531–545.

PatStat 2016. "European Patent Office (EPO) Worldwide Patent Statistical Database." It includes an upgrade to the EPO Patent Register, April Edition.

Pederzoli, C., G. Thoma, and C. Torricelli. 2013. "Modelling Credit Risk for Innovative Firms: The Role of Innovation Measures." *Journal of Financial Services Research* 44 (1): 111–129. doi:10.1007/s10693-012-0152-0.

Ramello, G. 2006. "What's in a Sign? Trademark Law and Economic Theory." *Journal of Economic Surveys* 20: 547–565. doi:10.1111/joes.2006.20.issue-4.

Ramello, G., and F. Silva. 2006. "Appropriating Signs and Meaning: The Elusive Economics of Trademark." *Industrial and Corporate Change* 15 (6): 937–963. doi:10.1093/icc/dtl027.

Rujas, J. 1999. "Trademarks: Complementary to Patents." *World Pat Inform* 21: 35–39. doi:10.1016/S0172-2190(99)00023-X.

Sandner, P., and J. Block. 2011. "The Market Value of R&D, Patents, and Trademarks." *Research Policy* 40: 969–985. doi:10.1016/j.respol.2011.04.004.

Schankerman, M. 1998. "How Valuable Is Patent Protection: Estimates by Technology Fields." *Rand Journal Economics* 29 (1): 77–107. doi:10.2307/2555817.

Smith, G., and S. Richey. 2013. *Trademark Valuation*. Hoboken (NJ): John Wiley & Sons, Kindle edition.

Spence, M. 1973. "Job Market Signaling." *Quarterly Journal of Economics* 87: 355–374. doi:10.2307/1882010.

Srinivasan, R., G. L. Lilien, and A. Rangaswamy. 2008. "Survival of High Tech Firms: The Effects of Diversity of Product–Market Portfolios, Patents, and Trademarks." *International Journal of Research in Marketing* 25: 119–1280. doi:10.1016/j.ijresmar.2007.12.005.

Srinivasan, S., L. Hsu, and S. Fournier. 2012. "Branding and Firm Value. Chap. 7." In *Handbook of Marketing and Finance*, edited by S. Ganesan, 155–203. Cheltenham: Edward Elgar.

Teece, D. 1986. "Profiting from Technological Innovation." *Research Policy* 15 (6): 285–305. doi:10.1016/0048-7333(86)90027-2.

Thoma, G. 2019. "Composite Value Index of Trademark Indicators." *World Patent Information* 56: 64–75. doi:10.1016/j.wpi.2019.01.004.

Thoma, G., S. Torrisi, A. Gambardella, D. Guellec, B. H. Hall, and D. Harhoff 2010. "Harmonizing and Combining Large Datasets – An Application to Firm-Level Patent and Accounting Data." *NBER Working Paper No. 15851*, Cambridge (MA): National Bureau of Economic Research.

Völckner, F., and H. Sattler. 2006. "Drivers of Brand Extension Success." *Journal of Marketing* 70: 18–34. doi:10.1509/jmkg.70.2.18.

Von Graevenitz, G. 2013. "Trade Mark Cluttering: Evidence from EU Enlargement." *Oxford Economic Papers* 65 (3): 721–745. doi:10.1093/oep/gpt022.

Zhou, H., P. G. Sandner, S. L. Martinelli, and J. H. Block. 2016. "Patents, Trademarks, and Their Complementarity in Venture Capital Funding." *Technovation* 47: 14–22. doi:10.1016/j.technovation.2015.11.005.

Why do innovators not apply for trademarks? The role of information asymmetries and collaborative innovation

Suma Athreye and Claudio Fassio

ABSTRACT
This paper analyses the underlying reasons why innovators do not apply for trademarks for all of their valuable inventions. Using a unique database of UK innovations linked to innovative firms, the empirical analysis highlights the many ways that firms can alleviate information asymmetries and the constraints imposed by collaborative innovation without taking recourse to trademarks. When information asymmetries are not at stake, i.e. when firms use an already existing trademark for their innovations or when they use intermediaries for its distribution, trademarks no longer serve their purpose, leading firms to avoid using it for their innovations. Open innovation also decreases the incentive to trademark, especially when the innovative process involves users, mainly because of property rights issues or because the innovator prefers to use the clients' own distribution channels.

1. Introduction

Trademarks are something (such as a word) that identifies a particular company's product and cannot be used by another company without permission. They can apply to a single product, groups of product and to goods or services. In the innovation literature trademarks have been often compared with patents, since they can be both used to protect the returns from innovation. However, while patents and trademarks share the characteristic of exclusivity, and are often administered by the same entity, trademarks protect a quite different market failure than do patents. Trademarks help consumers identify the product produced by a firm in a crowded marketplace and such become relevant when firms have a clearly identified a market for their innovation. The market failure they address is the presence of asymmetric information between buyers and sellers. In the case of patents and copyright, the market failure addressed arises from the public good nature of technology and the need to protect the returns to inventive and creative output.

WIPO (2013, 87) notes that trademarks are the most widely used form of Intellectual Property and are much more popular than patents. Consistent with the observation about the difference in the market failures corrected by patent and trademarks, in their empirical assessment they find trademark use is not limited to firms that operate at the technology frontier, or to sectors that witness rapid technological progress – instead firms in almost every sector of the economy employ trademarks to protect the exclusivity of their brands. Furthermore, they note that trademarks are far cheaper to apply for than patents and firms can use them forever, as long as they renew the trademark.

Although, trademarks *per se* do not require the company's product to be innovative or novel, a number of recent studies suggest that innovators do use trademarks more often than other kinds of firms (Mendonça, Pereira, and Godinho 2004; Jensen and Webster 2009; Götsch and Hipp 2012). What lies behind this widely observed correlation? The clearest rationale for this is provided by the work of Greenhalgh and Rogers (2012) who argue that when product innovations fall short of novelty but incorporate several small improvements in product characteristics, firms may use trademarks to protect such improvements. Similarly, innovations that cannot be protected by patents (such as services) may take recourse to protection by trademarks. Greenhalgh and Rogers (2012) find that trademark stocks influence value added and market value in a manner qualitatively similar to patents, thus strengthening the argument that trademarks may be used by innovating firms in a manner similar to patents in order to protect their incremental product innovations.

Since trademarks are used as a method to protect the market for incremental innovations and service innovations, it may be worth asking why every innovator does not use them as they are so much cheaper to obtain than patents and deliver the same advantages of exclusivity for a longer period of time. Put differently, why are innovations sometimes not associated with trademarks? This is the question we study in this paper drawing on unique and novel survey data from 2015.

Unlike, previous studies that have typically used trademark filings by a firm, the survey data we use elicits responses from innovators about the protection of their most commercially most valuable innovation and the reasons for not patenting or trademarking that innovation. This is useful for two reasons – first a very valuable innovation is the one a firm is most likely to protect with patent and/or trademarks. Second, it helps us disentangle the firm level and innovation level attributes that are associated with trademarking or not trademarking.

The reasons for not trademarking are less understood in the literature and we believe our paper is the first to provide any empirical estimates of them. We find the most important reason for not trademarking an innovation was because the innovator had already protected the market in other ways, such as through the use of alternative distribution channels, or through an existing trademark. Secondly, we find collaborative innovation with clients may be associated with much lower numbers of trademark applications – both because the innovation was too bespoke to be offered generally and because there may have been agreements in place to prevent the innovator from using trademarks.

The remainder of this paper is organised in the following way: Section 2 briefly reviews the literature on trademark protection and literature that finds a linkage between trademark application and innovativeness of firms. Section 3 describes the data and methods employed in our analysis. Section 4 describes the data and Section 5 reports on the results of the multivariate analysis. Section 6 concludes.

2. Innovators and trademark applications

The rationale for a trademark is believed to be information asymmetry between buyer and seller (Landes and Posner 1987) and as such trademarks secure customer loyalty for some perceived qualities associated with the products of the firm. This theory directly suggests that trademarks signal the distinctiveness of the production origins of a product. However, in their paper surveying developments in the economics and law of trademarks, Ramello and Silva (2006) note that in practice, trademarks had moved beyond signalling 'source distinctiveness' to offering 'differential distinctiveness'.

Differential distinctiveness refers to product differentiation in the market place that may be attributed to particular firms. This differentiation may involve completely new attributes of a product being developed as suggested by Fosfuri and Giarratana (2009) or it may involve an improvement of existing attributes and incremental innovation as studied by Greenhalgh and Rogers (2012). Thus, trademarks act as both an exclusionary device and a source of new advertising (and product information) in a contested marketplace, which in turn draws the attention of potential consumers to the new product innovation. In this sense, trademarks are a precursor to creating brands and goodwill – two important intangible assets that a firm may possess. These assets are of course, very complementary to other intangible assets possessed by innovative firms such as patents and reputation. Thus, it should come as no surprise that several empirical studies have found innovating firms to invest in trademarks.

As Greenhalgh and Rogers (2012) note, even the static 'signalling of asymmetric information model' contains the idea that trademarks may encourage firms to invest in improving the quality of their products. Thus, when exploring the reasons why firms may not trademark their innovations it may be useful to start with the information asymmetry lens as we do below. But we believe information asymmetry may not be enough of reason to explain why firms do not always trademark innovations. This is because a large proportion of modern day innovators are service firms who innovate through collaboration with suppliers and clients. While Miozzo et al. (2016) show that despite the low priority given to formal appropriation methods service firms do tend to use trademarks and patents much more during collaborative innovation, Desyllas et al. (2018) find that innovations from the service sector are heterogeneous and this heterogeneity has implications for the use of patents and trademarks. In particular, they find cost-oriented service firms may accord more importance to formal appropriability but product differentiation oriented service firms "may generate client-specific innovations which are sufficiently protected through resource immobility, causal ambiguity and/or competitors' lack of absorptive capacity to not require formal protection. We thus also explore the effect of openness on a innovators decision not to trademark for all valuable innovations.

2.1. Trademarks, information asymmetry and innovative products

The extent of information asymmetry between buyer and seller may be high when firms introduce new technological products or improve the characteristics associated with their product innovations. The nature of the technology may be unknown and the buyer may not always associate the firm with that product and so firms that desire the loyalty of their old customers may prefer to register a new trademark. Thus, if the technology product market is marked by information asymmetry between buyer and seller about the quality or reliability of the product, then we may expect firms to overcome this problem by using a trademark. Indeed, consistent with this reasoning Flikkema, de Man, and Castaldi (2014) find that most trademarks are applied for in the later (marketing) phases of the innovation process.

A wide range of empirical studies confirm this theoretical proposition between the information asymmetry caused by a new (technological) product and the use of trademarks. Thomä and Bizer (2013) show that trademarks are more frequently used in markets with competition based on product differentiation rather than price. Many studies find robust evidence of a positive association between trademarks and, respectively, R&D intensity (see Allegrezza and Guarda-Rauchs 1999) and innovation activities at the firm level (see Schmoch 2003; Greenhalgh and Rogers 2012; Götsch and Hipp 2012), strongly suggesting indeed that many innovative firms do make use of trademarks. The use of trademarks has also been pronounced for some types of innovation that cannot be patented, such as innovative activities in services. Knowledge Intensive Business Sectors, companies might rely on trademarks as a preferred way of protecting their intellectual property embedded in their products (Schmoch 2003; Amara, Landry, and Traoré 2008; Castaldi 2018).

In the same context of product innovation, looking at trademarking from the lens of information asymmetry between buyer and seller also suggests some reasons when trademarking may not be required. There are two distinct scenarios to consider here viz. when an information asymmetry problem between buyer and seller does not exist and when the information asymmetry issue is resolved in other ways.

Trademarks often refer to all the commercialised products of a firm. Hipp and Grupp (2005) point out that products or services containing no innovation at all (in terms of product characteristics) can be protected by a trademark, differently from what concerns patent application. Thus, Amazon and Walmart are important trademarks used by trading companies but which do not have any innovations associated to the trademark. This does not mean of course, the companies were not innovative but their innovation rested on having innovation in the field of business-related computer services which were not easy to protect through patents. Equally, some sorts of trademarks have no innovation associated with them (e.g. Wedgewood porcelain). Thus, while there is some kind of correlation between innovating firms and trademark application, it may not imply causation.

Flikkema et al. (2019) recognise that while trademarks can be of different types (brand extending, brand creation, brand modernising) and while in some cases they can be related to the introduction of a new product (innovation), in some other cases this might not be the case. Moreover, a firm can also choose to simply adopt an existing brand/trademark for a new product in order to benefit from the existing reputational factor associated with it. For example, Microsoft has been diversifying its product lines to include video game consoles, consumer electronics and digital services – but has not sought a new trademark. (It might however have applied for patents to protect its new technology). Thus, there are numerous examples which suggest that a firm's market for technological products may be protected by pre-existing trademarks and in such cases they may not apply for a new trademark for their innovations.

While large firms with several products may have less to gain by adding an additional trademark, as their product may already be covered by existing trademarks, as trademark are relatively cheap to obtain (for example, compared with the costs of filing for a patent) and in many cases can cover a number of products, we should expect innovative small firms to apply for trademarks in larger numbers. For the UK, there is compelling evidence in Rogers, Greenhalgh, and Helmers (2007) that shows that small firms are more likely to use trademarks than other kinds of firms. Helmers and Rogers (2011) also suggest many firms start by applying for trademarks and then go on to file for patents later in their life. Yet clear evidence about the propensity to trademark and firm size is lacking – as WIPO (2013) notes that despite the comparatively low costs of trademark filing only about half of all start-ups in technology sectors actually file trademarks.

An important reason why small firms may not trademark extensively or do so much later in their history may be related to the use of alternate channels of marketing. Trademarks are used when a firm directly markets to the end customer, as a means of identifying its own products. Yet, small firms may reach this point relatively late in their company's history. Very often products are marketed to end consumers through wholesalers, retailers and agents. He, Brouthers, and Filatotchev (2018) argue that the most popular channels of marketing the exports of SME are agents and distributors or partners in the host country, as the SME firm may itself lack the resources and market orientation to do so. These alternative channels are more likely to provide information about their client's product to the customer and also collect information about custo-mer reactions to feed back to the firm. In this case, the firm using them does not require trademarks as the problem of asymmetric product information vis-à-vis buyers is likely to be resolved through the choice of marketing channels.

On the basis of the above consideration, it seems likely then to observe a decreased propensity to trademark innovations by firms, when they can use existing and well-established trademarks for their new products, or when they use alternative marketing channels, such as intermediaries, selling agents or distributors.

2.2. Collaborative innovators and trademark applications

The propensity to trademark an important innovation can also be affected by the specific process through which the innovation has been developed. Openness of the innovative process is seen as a factor that is likely to affect this propensity and that has not been explored in the existing trademark literature. While many studies have investigated the relationship between open innovation and the propensity to patent (Laursen and Salter 2014; Arora, Athreye, and Huang 2016), few studies have explored the role of collaborative innovation on the propensity to trademark.

When collaboration for innovation is upstream with suppliers, it is likely that firms will use patents to protect the technology around the innovation, but the final markets they sell their products in may not come into play. Considering the role of trademarks as an activity that is performed in later stages of the invention process (i.e. marketing and commercialisation) it is particularly interesting to investigate what happens to trademark propensity when innovative collaboration are established by the innovating firms with its own users/customers.

When collaboration is downstream with clients, we may distinguish between two distinct situations. The first case is when the innovation is bespoke and responds to some client's need, but is unlikely to result in a market in the traditional sense (with many other buyers). Here there is no information asymmetry and the need to trademark does not arise. Second, when the market is general and the innovation is developed together with users, the innovators may have the incentive to use trademarks but may nevertheless face several constraints. One type of constraint is that the innovating firm might not own completely the property rights of the innovation developed and may be contractually prevented from applying for a trademark. Very large firms may be able to overcome this limitation through contracts. For example, ARM collaborates with its RISC chip clients but reserves the right to incorporate all the information gathered into improvements in its RISC chips without specific attribution to any particular client. Alternatively, the innovator's customers might be more able at appropriating the market rents from innovation, since they know the market better. The innovator may hence end up selling their innovation through the customer's distribution channels. This is common in the pharmaceutical sector: for many years Ranbaxy had a contract to sell its licensed generic drugs through Eli-Lilly's distribution channels in America (Bhandari 2005). Though the company had a trademark, it was not well recognised in the US and so it sought this way to overcome the problem of information asymmetry with the buyers.

Thus, our analysis suggests that collaborative innovation with clients may be associated with fewer opportunities for trademarking the innovative product. Furthermore, the reasons for not trademarking may be due to the bespoke nature of the innovation or for contractual reasons – both of which may mean that a trademark is not possible – or because the client has better distribution channels, which the innovators may also use.

3. Data and methods

The propensity to trademark, in the context of the present study, refers to the probability that a firm will trademark any given innovation. An important limitation of existing empirical studies on trademark propensity is that they use firm-level data, which typically indicates a positive correlation between innovativeness of companies and use of trademarks, but we cannot find evidence of a one-to-one relationship between the innovation of the company and trademark use. Recent studies (Flikkema, de Man, and Castaldi 2014) using trademark-level data allows a partial redress of this issue as they look directly at innovations that are protected by trademarks. However, since trademark application is extremely cheap and product novelty is not a prerequisite for trademark applications, also these studies have a hard time identifying trademarks that protect real and valuable innovations, from other less relevant (and less innovative) products.

We use a unique dataset, which directly asks innovative firms to identify their most valuable innovation and then asks them whether they have protected it with a trademark (or a patent) – thus directly correcting for many of the identified issues.[1] For those innovators who did not apply for a trademark the survey specifically asks

[1]Firms that reported a valuable innovation were asked 'Did you apply for a trademark for that innovation?', followed by 'Did you apply for a patent for that innovation?'. We found only 35 firms of 277 had applied for both.

them to indicate the reasons why they have not done so. This procedure allows a step forward with respect to existing studies on the propensity to use trademarks for innovations, as it provides data at the invention level and it also focuses on products and processes that have a high commercial value for the firm – those innovations where protection is most likely to be sought.

3.1. Data

The Survey of Innovation and Patent Use 2015 (henceforth SIPU 2015) was administered to all those respondents in the UKIS 2015 (CIS9) who consented to answer questions about their single most valuable innovation. This provided a total eligible sample of 886 businesses. 477 (54%) of these businesses had specifically indicated on the UKIS 2015 that they had engaged in product, process or business strategy forms of innovation activity in the period 1 January 2012 to 31 December 2014. The survey achieved a response rate of 72% with 277 innovators and 291 non-innovators.

Figures 1 and 2 below compare the sample achieved by SIPU2015 to the CIS2015. In Figure 1, we see that SIPU over-sampled the small firms but under-sampled medium and large firms in comparison to the UK CIS. Figure 2 shows that SIPU over-sampled innovative firms overall, but also oversampled product innovators vis-à-vis the CIS.

Table 1 reports the industry distribution in SIPU and CIS. SIPU over-sampled manufacturing of all types in comparison to CIS 2015 but it under-sampled construction hotels and restaurants and all types of services, generally, including professional services. To the extent that manufacturing firms are more likely to use patents and trademarks – this may influence our aggregate results.

4. Trademark propensity of different groups of firms

In order to understand why firms do not always use trademarks for their innovations, we start by identifying which are the factors that in our sample of firms are associated (or not) with the decision to apply for a trademark. We introduce a number of innovation-specific factors that we believe are likely to be correlated with the decision

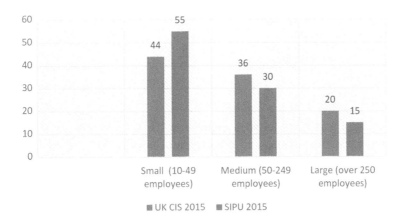

Figure 1. Size distribution of firms in the SIPU 2015 sample compared to CIS 2015.

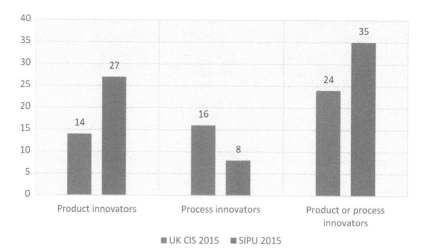

Figure 2. Distribution of innovators in SIPU and CIS.

Table 1. Sectoral distribution of sample in CIS and SIPU.

Industry sector	CIS	% of sample	SIPU	% of sample
05–09: Mining and Quarrying	137	0.91	3	0.47
10–18: Manufacture of food, clothing and wood	682	4.52	22	3.47
19–25: Manufacture of fuels, chemicals and plastics	755	5.00	40	6.31
26–28: Manufacture of electrical & optical equips	478	3.17	25	3.94
29–30: Manufacture of transport equipment	262	1.74	10	1.58
31–33: Manufacture not elsewhere classified	280	1.86	19	3.00
35–39: Electricity, gas and water supply	232	1.54	8	1.26
41–43: Construction	740	4.90	23	3.63
45–46: Wholesale trade (including cars and bikes)	4214	27.92	163	25.71
47: Retail Trade (excluding cars and bikes)	460	3.05	13	2.05
49–52: Transport	592	3.92	20	3.15
53: Post and courier activities	120	0.80	4	0.63
55–56: Hotels & restaurants	684	4.53	28	4.42
58, 62, 63: Computer and related activities	449	2.98	26	4.10
59–60: Motion picture, video and TV programmes	126	0.83	11	1.74
61: Telecommunications	166	1.10	9	1.42
64–66: Financial intermediation	668	4.43	22	3.47
68: Real estate activities	361	2.39	8	1.26
69,70,75,76,78–83: Other services	2208	14.63	102	16.09
71.1: Architectural & engineering activities	421	2.79		0.00
71.2: Clinical testing and analysis	113	0.75	25	3.94
72: Research and experimental development	399	2.64	37	5.84
73: Advertising and market research	186	1.23	4	0.63
74: Other professional, scientific activities	146	0.97	6	0.95
77: Renting of machinery and equipment	212	1.40	6	0.95

Based on SIC 2007 codes.

of the firm to use a trademark for such innovation. These include the type of innovation (product or process innovation) and the degree of novelty. We believe that firms will not have the same propensity to trademark different types of innovation, for example, process innovation may be less likely to be associated to a trademark. Also, the novelty of the innovation may have an impact, although we expect a somehow weaker (positive) relationship than in the case of patents as we think trademarks are preferred for incremental product innovations.

We control for the characteristics of the inventive process (open or closed innovation, the presence or not of external financing), as we think these might have important implications on the probability to use trademark or not. We are also able to control for the specific type of external partners involved (customers, suppliers, etc.) in developing the valuable innovation.

Lastly, we include a number of firm-level characteristics that, as noted in Section 2.1., have been found to influence the general propensity of a firm to trademark the innovation: these include the size of the firm, the presence of R&D expenditures, and the overall patent propensity.

4.1. Methodology and variables used

We start by examining how the descriptive statistics of the average propensity of firms to trademark changes across different characteristics, and checking whether firms that differ in some of these features display a different propensity to trademark their most valuable innovation. We then translate these initial descriptive results in a multivariate context, by employing a simple probit analysis on the probability that a firm applies for a patent. This allows us to obtain a conditional mean of the trademark propensity, net of all the above-mentioned factors that might influence the firms' decision.

In our probit analysis, the dependent variable is a dummy variable built on the basis of the answer to the SIPU2015 questionnaire, equal to 1 if firms applied for a trademark for its most valuable innovation and zero otherwise. The sample of firms for which we can perform our analysis corresponds to the 277 innovators who answered to the SIPU survey. The explanatory variables used in the analysis are based on the innovation specific answers of firms to the SIPU2015 questionnaire (where firms focused on their most valuable9 innovation), as well as on the firm-specific answers to the CIS9 data. This allows us to include both types of control variables in our model specification. The specific questions used in the SIPU questionnaire are attached as an appendix to this paper. These refer to the specific nature of innovation (product, process or business strategy), the presence of external financing for the specific innovation, the specific value of the innovation, and the level of openness of the innovative process, distinguishing between collaboration with suppliers, clients or other types of actors. Moreover, the use of the CIS frame to collect data on the most valuable innovation in SIPU allows us to match the two questionnaires and control for a rich variety of firm characteristics. These include: firm size, investments in Research and Development activities, industrial sector of affiliation, as well as the proportion of innovations protected by patents. Table 2 details the variables we constructed more fully.

Our methodology allows identification of the characteristics that are associated with the decision to apply for a trademark for the most important innovation of a company. However, since we do not implement an empirical strategy that allows for a causal interpretation of our results, we cannot rule out the possibility that omitted variables or reverse causality issues affect our estimates. In some cases, the decision to trademark (or not) an innovation might be co-determined at the moment in which the innovation process is started. For example, a firm may make the decision to adopt an open innovation strategy and to apply (or not) for a trademark simultaneously. Thus, our results should not be interpreted as a strong evidence of the existence of causal relationships.

Table 2. Dependent and independent variables created.

A. Dependent variables

Variable	Source of Data	Description of the variable
Trademark application (Table 4)	SIPU 2015	Dummy variable = 1 when respondent reports applying for a trademark to protect their most valuable innovation
Trademark not necessary (Table 6)	SIPU 2015	Dummy variable = 1, if firm said any of the following reasons prevented them from applying for a trademark: a) trademarks not considered important, b) no danger of infringement and c) use of alternative distribution channels
Trademark not possible (Table 6)	SIPU 2015	Dummy variable = 1, if firm said any of the following reasons prevented them from applying for a trademark: a) trademark was not possible and b) non-novel innovation
Existing trademarks (Table 6)	SIPU 2015	Dummy variable = 1, if firm said its reason for not seeking a trademark was because the innovation was already covered by existing trademarks

B. Associated characteristics

Firm-specific variables

	Source of Data	Description of the variable
Small firm	CIS 2015	Dummy variable = 1, if the firm employed less than 50 persons
Medium firm	CIS 2015	Dummy variable = 1, if the firm employed between 50 and 249 employees
Large firm	CIS 2015	Dummy variable = 1, if the firm employed more than 250 employees
Continuous R&D	CIS 2015	Dummy variable that takes value 1 if firms had undertaken internal R&D in 2012, 2013 & 2014
Overall patent propensity	CIS 2015	The proportion of innovations between 2012–2014 that was protected by patents
17 Industrial sectors	CIS 2015	Based on the 2-digit SIC and aggregated to get a minimum of 20 observations per group. See Table A1 for details

Innovation-specific variables (for the commercially most valuable innovation)

Openness	SIPU 2015	Dummy variable = 1 when respondent reports collaborative partner was involved in producing its most valuable innovation
Suppliers	SIPU 2015	Dummy variable = 1 when respondent reports collaboration with supplier was involved in producing its most valuable innovation
Clients	SIPU 2015	Dummy variable = 1 when respondent reports collaboration with client was involved in producing its most valuable innovation
Other types of collaboration	SIPU 2015	Dummy variable = 1 when respondent reports collaboration with public sector labs, consultants, competitors or HEI was involved in producing its most valuable innovation
Value of innovation	SIPU 2015	Value of turnover (%) in 2014 accounted for by the most valuable innovation
Product innovation	SIPU 2015	Dummy variable = 1, if the most valuable innovation was a product innovation
Process innovation	SIPU 2015	Dummy variable = 1, if the most valuable innovation was a process innovation
Business strategy innovation	SIPU 2015	Dummy variable = 1, if the most valuable innovation was a wider innovation
New to the market innovation	SIPU 2015	Dummy variable = 1, if the most valuable innovation was a new to the market
New to the firm innovation	SIPU 2015	Dummy variable = 1, if the most valuable innovation was new to the firm
Any external finance		Dummy variable = 1, if the firm used any external finance to finance its most valuable innovation

4.2. Results

Table 3 reports the frequency of firms applying for a trademark (or a patent) for their innovations in SIPU 2015 and in CIS9. The SIPU data are innovation specific, they only refer to the most significant innovation, while the CIS data are firm specific. The table also looks at different groups of firms to assess how this proportion varies. Although our interest is primarily in trademark usage, we also report the results for patenting as a benchmark and also in order to account for the correlation between both forms of innovation protection, stressed by many recent studies (Flikkema et al. 2019).

According to the CIS data, more firms apply for trademarks when compared to patents. Thus, about 3 in 10 innovators will apply for a trademark while only over a quarter of firms patent their most valuable innovation. Interestingly this pattern is different when we use SIPU data to look at the most valuable innovation of a firm. The proportion of firms patenting still stays a quarter but the proportion of firms applying for trademarks drops to about 23%. One reason for this could be that the same trademark could protect more than one innovation, as trademarks are granted to firms and are not necessarily innovation specific.

Looking across groups of firms we find that in the CIS data small firms are more likely to trademark but when we look at innovation specific data there is no such difference. Instead, consistent with the literature linking innovation and trademarking we find that firms that undertake regular R&D, or report a valuable product innovations or a valuable new to market innovation were more likely to trademark Götsch and Hipp (2012). These same characteristics also drive patenting behaviour.

In Table 4 we examine these differences in a multivariate context controlling for several other factors such as the industry affiliation of the firm (proxied by 17 industry dummies),[2] its level of openness to external technology and the firm's reported levels of imitative competition.

Table 3. Frequency of innovators applying for trademarks and patents in the CIS9 and in SIPU for their most valuable innovation.

	Trademarks all CIS innovators (1)		Trademarks SIPU (2)		Patents all CIS innovators (3)		Patents SIPU (4)	
	Num.	%	Num.	%	Num.	%	Num.	%
Total Innovating firms	2578		277		2641		277	
Total firms using trademarks/patents	761	29.52	63	22.7	666	25.22	71	25.63
Small firms (<49 employees)	248	25.1***	33	23.4	197	19.58***	35	24.8
Medium firms (50–249 employees)	326	30.96	22	23.9	285	26.46***	25	27.2
Large Firms (>250 employees)	187	34.82	8	18.2	184	32.97***	11	25
Product innovation	584	38.8***	50	29.1***	546	35.23***	57	33.1**
Process innovation	454	25.65	6	11.3	381	21.04	10	18.9
New to Market	379	43.87***	37	27.4**	397	43.77***	44	32.5**
New to Firm	436	31.43	9	12.8	328	23.4	10	14.3
Continuous R&D	438	38.9***	41	29.1***	451	38.06***	49	34.75***
No R&D or discontinuous R&D	323	22.25	22	16.2	215	14.77	22	16.18
Independent firms	–	–	35	24			30	20.6
Affiliated to a group	–	–	28	21.4			41	31.3**
Internally financed	–	–	47	22.6			46	22.1
Any external finance	–	–	14	24.5			23	40.4***

Source: Computations from UK CIS 2015 and SIPU 2015.
** for significance at 5%.
*** for significance at 1%.

Table 4. Trademark propensity.

	Trademark application		
	(1)	(2)	(3)
Innovation-specific variables			
Reference product innovation			
Process innovation	−0.142***	−0.122**	−0.15***
	(0.051)	(0.056)	(0.049)
Business strategy	−0.076	−0.059	−0.095
	(0.068)	(0.074)	(0.061)
New to the market innovation	0.063	0.048	0.072
	(0.054)	(0.055)	(0.053)
Openness measures			
Openness (dummy)	−0.121**		
	(0.053)		
Level of openness		0.108	
		(0.151)	
Suppliers			−0.053
			(0.054)
Clients			−0.18***
			(0.047)
Other types of collaborations			−0.076
			(0.063)
Value of invention	0.014	0.012	0.014
	(0.017)	(0.017)	(0.016)
Any external finance	−0.003	−0.018	−0.011
	(0.063)	(0.063)	(0.065)
Firm-specific variables			
Small firm (<49 employees)	0.020	0.007	0.033
	(0.057)	(0.058)	(0.057)
Continuous R&D	0.057	0.057	0.053
	(0.057)	(0.058)	(0.058)
Overall patent propensity	0.183**	0.191**	0.168*
	(0.084)	(0.086)	(0.086)
Reference no competition			
Competitors 1 to 5	−0.028	−0.030	−0.025
	(0.057)	(0.057)	(0.056)
Competitors more than 5	0.086	0.096	0.069
	(0.098)	(0.094)	(0.097)
17 industry dummies	yes	yes	yes
Observations	277	277	277
Pseudo R-squared	0.142	0.127	0.157
Log-likelihood	−127.4	−129.6	−125.2

The coefficients report the marginal effects from probit estimations. Robust standard errors in parentheses, *** $p <$ 0.01, ** $p < 0.05$, * $p < 0.1$.

We restrict our attention to SIPU innovators and estimate a probit model to explain the probability of trademark application, in order to protect the most valuable innovation. The results confirm all the descriptive findings of Table 3 with a few exceptions. We do not find a statistically significant impact of R&D activities and new-to-market innovation, once we control for industry-specific factors. This can probably be explained by the presence of the R&D variable: since in most cases doing R&D is a necessary precondition to be able to develop patentable brand new products, once we control for it the positive effect of new to the market innovation fades away. Also in this case firm size does not significantly affect trademark propensity.

---

[2] The results are robust to the use of less fine-grained industry dummies (we also ran our models with only 7 macro-industry dummies), in order to avoid the risk of over-fitting of the model.

Among the other control variables, we also include some new variables not included in Table 3. We check for the effect of openness, i.e. the fact that a firm develops its most important innovation with other external partners, and we find that it exerts a negative effect on trademarking. When we further investigate the effect of openness we find that it is not the degree of openness (the number of different types of different external actors involved in the innovative process) that matters for the decision to trademark or not. Rather, we find that it is mainly the collaboration with clients that decreases the willingness of firms to use trademarks. This is in line with our theoretical reasoning, according to which collaboration with downstream clients might present issues with respect to intellectual property or also may pre-dispose innovators to rely on the distribution channels of their clients.

We also investigate a possible linkage between trademarking and patenting activity. We want to check if the firms that patent a large share of their new products are also more likely to apply for a trademark for their most valuable innovation. This may indicate a higher firm awareness about the use of intellectual property appropriability tools, as well as a general indication of the innovativeness of the company. In Table 4, the overall propensity to patent for the firms' innovation portfolio (available from UK CIS 2015) is positive and significant suggesting that innovators with larger patent portfolios are also more likely to apply for trademark protection for their most valuable innovation. The effect of patent portfolios on trademark propensity suggests that indeed a higher share of patented new products also increases the likelihood that a firm will apply for a trademark for their most valuable innovation.

5. Reasons why innovators do not apply for trademark protection

An additional way by which we can understand the motives that lead innovators to not use trademarks is to ask them to explain the reasons why. In SIPU, innovators were also asked for the reasons why they did not apply for a trademark for their most valuable innovation. The list of reasons for not using trademarks that respondents could choose included a) the innovation was already protected by existing trademarks, b) there was no danger of infringement, c) the firm uses distribution channels to market our product. In addition, there was a free form field where firms could enter other reasons not included on the list. We examined each of these additional reasons and classified them in the three additional groups: d) trademarks were not perceived as important by the firm, e) trademarks were not possible for the specific type of innovation, f) the innovation was not novel enough to be eligible for trademark use.

In order to analyse the reasons for not trademarking within a regression framework, we reclassify the reasons provided by the firms for not trademarking their innovation into three main categories:

(i) *Trademark not necessary and alternative channels*, which includes the following reasons b) no danger of infringement, c) use of alternative distribution channels and d) trademarks not considered important,

(ii) *Trademark not possible*, which includes the reasons e) trademark was not possible and f) non-novel innovation

(iii) *Already existing trademarks*: when a) the innovation was already covered by existing trademarks

In Figure 3 we show through a Venn diagram the distribution of these three main reasons and the overlapping of these reasons. The figure shows that by regrouping the reasons in such a way around half of the firms are classified in the category 'trademark not necessary and alternative channels', while the other two categories 'already existing trademark' and "trademark not possible " include 28% and 17%, respectively, of SIPU innovators (who did not use trademarks). The limited overlap between these reasons suggests that they are not complementary reasons.

Due to the limited overlap across reasons, we estimate three separate probit models to account for the possible factors that might influence the selection of each one of the three reasons for not applying for trademark for the innovation.

$$y_i^s = a_0 + a_1 INN\_TYPE + a_2 OPEN + a_2'X + u_i \qquad (2)$$

where y stands for a set of s dummy variables (0/1) that denote whether the firm indicated a specific reason to explain the choice of not applying for a trademark for its most relevant innovation.

We include a number of independent variables that we believe might explain the reasons for not trademarking: INN_TYPE indicate the specific type of innovation (product, process or business strategy; OPEN, which indicates whether the firm engaged in collaborative open innovation for the development of the specific innovation, since we believe that especially interaction with customers might be correlated with the use of channels that are alternative to trademarks. Finally, X stands for other innovation-specific and firm-specific factors that are likely to be correlated with the reason chosen by the firm for not using trademarks. The innovation-specific factors include the degree of novelty of the innovation, the value of the innovation and the presence of financing that is external to the firm (grants, policy programmes, venture capital, etc.). The firm-level variables include firm size, the presence of investments in

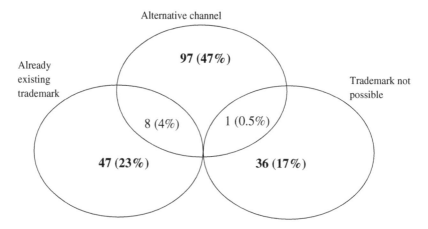

Figure 3. Venn diagram of reasons for not filing for trademark.
N = 203 (100%); in 14 cases (7%) none of the three reasons was specified as important (other reasons were specified as important).

Research and Development, the overall patent propensity and the industry affiliation. We run our probit analyses on 196 firm-innovation observations, that is the number of innovators in SIPU2015 who have not applied for a trademark for their most valuable innovation.[3]

6. Results

In Table 5 we present some data about the frequency of each of these different reasons for different groups of firms. The most common reason for not applying for a trademark is the presence of a pre-existing trademark (27% of cases), followed by no danger of infringement (24%). Respectively, 21% and 15% of the firms reported that trademarks were not important or that they were not possible for the specific innovation introduced. 11% percent of firms, instead, reported that they used alternative distribution channels and, hence, did not need to trademark their innovations.

Overall, the results highlight the fact that there is not a one-to-one correspondence between innovations and trademarks; firms might introduce new products and still use (extend) their old trademarks to also cover the new product. The second finding is that a number of innovators do not perceive trademarks to be a very effective way to protect their innovations, since they do not believe that there is significant danger of infringement, or they generally do not consider them as relevant tools for appropriating value (such as when innovation involved bespoke work). In some cases, then, the specific nature of the innovation did not allow for trademark application.

When looking at the impact of size on the different reasons indicated by firms who did not use trademarks, we find that small firms are generally more likely to say that trademarks were not important, while large firms are more likely to say that trademarks were not possible due to the specific nature of the innovation. This suggests that while large firms are more aware of which kind of products can be protected by trademarks and which cannot, small firms tend to underestimate the value of trademark protection, possibly also because of lower awareness of how to use them.

Among firms that collaborate with external partners (open innovators), we find that they are more likely to consider trademarks as not important (due to the bespoke nature of the work) and because open firms reported use of other distribution channels to market their products.

In Table 6 we report three probit estimates that explain the probability to indicate each of the three reasons identified above as relevant for the decision not to apply for a trademark for the most relevant innovation. These are: a) Trademark not necessary and alternative channels b) Trademark not possible c) Already existing trademarks. Looking at the results, all of which control for industry-specific factors, we find that few of the factors related to firm or innovation-specific features are able to explain the different reasons indicated by the respondents. Research and Development, and overall patent propensity are not significant, as well as the type of innovation (product, process or business strategy) and the degree of novelty of the innovation. Firms that obtained

---

[3]For 18 firms who innovate and did not apply for a trademark we could not perform our probit analyses. This is because some firms indicated different reasons for the decision not to apply for trademark (not included in our three categories), while a few firms did not answer to all of the questions of the survey, resulting in some missing values among our covariates.

Table 5. Reasons for forgoing trademark protection given by innovating firms (% of firms choosing each reason).

Reasons for no trademark	No Trademark firms (n = 203)		Small firms	Medium Firms	Large firms	Product innovators	Process innovators	No continuous R&D	Continuous R&D	Not Open	Open
Already existing trademark	55	27.1	29.2	25.4	23.3	25.2	25.5	28.4	25.5	25.7	27.8
No danger of infringement	49	24.1	20.8	28.4	26.7	24.3	31.9	**18.3**	**30.9**	28.6	21.8
Trademark not perceived important	44	21.7	**25.5**	17.9	16.7	20.0	21.3	25.7	17.0	**14.3**	**25.6**
Trademark not possible	32	15.8	11.3	17.9	**26.7**	19.1	10.6	14.7	17.0	**24.3**	**11.3**
Distribution channel to market product	24	11.8	12.3	13.4	6.7	13.9	6.4	11.0	12.8	**4.3**	**15.8**
Innovation without novelty	5	2.5	3.8	1.5	0.0	**0.9**	**6.4**	3.7	1.1	4.3	1.5
Other reasons	14	6.9	6.6	8.9	3.3	8.6	4.2	7.3	6.4	5.7	7.5

Source: SIPU2015.
Values in bold identify statistically significant differences.

Table 6. Reasons for not filing trademarks.

VARIABLES	Not necessary and alternative channels		Trademark not possible		Existing trademark	
	(1)	(2)	(3)	(4)	(5)	(6)
Innovation-specific variables						
Reference product innovation						
Process innovation	0.040	0.057	−0.009	−0.011	−0.011	−0.024
	(0.098)	(0.098)	(0.023)	(0.022)	(0.082)	(0.079)
Business strategy	0.002	0.012	−0.027	−0.027	0.102	0.065
	(0.113)	(0.115)	(0.020)	(0.020)	(0.104)	(0.102)
New to the market innovation	−0.095	−0.109	0.014	0.014	−0.069	−0.048
	(0.080)	(0.080)	(0.022)	(0.022)	(0.067)	(0.066)
Openness measures						
Openness (dummy)	0.152*		−0.065*		0.028	
	(0.079)		(0.034)		(0.067)	
Suppliers		0.057		−0.036*		0.123
		(0.099)		(0.019)		(0.092)
Clients		0.208**		−0.039**		−0.103
		(0.096)		(0.020)		(0.079)
Other types of collaborations		0.219**		−0.046***		0.057
		(0.110)		(0.017)		(0.111)
Value of invention	−0.004	−0.010	0.001	0.001	0.030	0.036*
	(0.024)	(0.024)	(0.006)	(0.006)	(0.021)	(0.021)
Any external finance	−0.171*	−0.178*	0.003	0.004	0.249***	0.240**
	(0.096)	(0.097)	(0.027)	(0.028)	(0.096)	(0.094)
Firm-specific variables						
Small firm (<49 employees)	0.065	0.058	−0.025	−0.023	−0.020	−0.013
	(0.090)	(0.091)	(0.025)	(0.026)	(0.079)	(0.079)
Continuous R&D	0.048	0.056	−0.006	−0.006	0.010	0.007
	(0.086)	(0.086)	(0.024)	(0.024)	(0.074)	(0.074)
Overall patent propensity	0.068	0.086	−0.012	−0.014	−0.002	−0.003
	(0.151)	(0.153)	(0.039)	(0.039)	(0.129)	(0.132)
17 industry dummies	YES	YES	YES	YES	YES	YES
Observations	196	196	198	198	196	196
Pseudo R-squared	0.0588	0.0685	0.168	0.173	0.0810	0.103
Log-likelihood	−127.7	−126.4	−80.51	−80.08	−106.0	−103.5

The coefficients report the marginal effects from probit estimations. Robust standard errors in parentheses, *** p < 0.01, ** p < 0.05, * p < 0.1.7

external financing were more likely to have an existing trademark, which probably worked as a quality signal also for the financiers.

In line with the results in Table 5 we find instead that adopting an open strategy for innovation increases the likelihood that trademarks were deemed not necessary or that alternative channels had been used. More specifically we find that when clients are involved the likelihood of using other channels to market the innovation increases. This is in line with our expectations about the involvement of clients in the collaborative process: having them collaborate in innovation also increases the likelihood of using the clients' distribution channels for the marketing of the innovation. On the contrary we find that open innovation and collaboration with clients is negatively related with the fact that trademark was not possible, confirming that it is not the nature of the innovation per se that prevents firms from trademarking when open innovation is at stake, but rather the fact that firms choose alternative channels when they collaborate with other actors (and especially with customers). The results in column (3) instead show that the value of the innovation is positively correlated with the decision to use an already existing trademark for the protection of the new product. This speaks in favour of the fact that especially when an innovation is valuable firms may resort to the use of already existing trademark rather than introducing a new one just for the specific innovation.

7. Summary and implications

In the marketing literature, trademark application is often seen as a precursor to branding, but in recent years trademark applications have attracted the attention of several scholars of technology management as a distinct IP strategy for innovators. Many empirical studies have found trademark applications to be associated with innovation (Mendonça, Pereira, and Godinho 2004; Flikkema, de Man, and Castaldi 2014; Block et al. 2014) and that innovative companies tend to trademark more than non-innovative ones.

Despite exclusivity advantages and the comparatively low costs of trademark filing, only about half of all start-ups in technology sectors actually file trademarks. In this paper, we ask why more innovators do not file for trademarks, even though they are so cheap to obtain? We investigate this question using a novel survey that obtains innovation specific data about the reasons for not trademarking and is built to link into the CIS. This data structure enables us to simultaneously look at innovation specific and firm-specific characteristics of innovations that make particular reasons for not trademarking more likely than others.

The theoretical literature sees trademarks as essentially solving an information asymmetry problem between the firm and its customers. For innovative firms, this may be information about the quality of their products and services (Block et al. 2014) or in the case of new innovators, trademarks can flag the market introduction of completely new products and services (Flikkema, de Man, and Castaldi 2014). Brands may also convey this information readily to customers for all products of a firm. New and existing innovators may also depend upon distributors and agents to reach the product and the information about the product to consumers. In both of these cases, firms would not need to trademark because the information problem is being sorted out using other means viz. brands, distribution channels. Where a firm has a trademark, the trademark may cover several types of goods supplied by the firm. Our results broadly support these arguments as important ones for not trademarking an innovation.

Service firms are heavy users of trademarks to protect their innovations which are often collaborative and not patentable. The literature on collaborative (open) innovation has highlighted the challenge that collaborative innovation may pose for the enforcement of formal IP rights. The discussion on this issue has tended to focus disproportionately on patents strategy with regard to patenting but our results suggest that open firms are less likely to apply for trademarks and those collaborating with clients are more likely to cite having alternative channels or agreements that prevent a trademark application from being made.

Thus, our empirical analysis finds that while there is an undeniable linkage between innovations and trademarking this is not a one-to-one relationship. Fewer innovations of value are trademarked than patented. Even though innovative products may be associated with higher information asymmetry than other kinds of goods, existing trademarks, alternative distribution channels and pre-existing agreements may protect a firm without having to take recourse to trademark applications.

Our analysis is not free of important limitations that should be taken into account when interpreting our results. First, our empirical methodology is not able to identify clear causal relationships, so our results should be interpreted rather as an indication that specific firm-level or innovation-specific factors are associated (or not) with the decision to apply for a trademark, as well as to the specific reasons behind the decision not to apply for it. Secondly, while we believe that the focus on 'significant innovations' represents an important novelty and adds to the overall contribution of our study, it is also important to acknowledge that the generalisability of the results is limited to this specific type of innovation. In other words, it could be for example that trademarks are especially important for innovations that are less relevant or central in the innovation portfolio of a company. If that is the case our results should be interpreted keeping this into account. Lastly, our results provide very detailed information about the reasons why firms do *not* apply for trademarks, but they do not provide the same level of detail about the reasons why firms instead use them. From our empirical analysis about the propensity to apply for a trademark we can identify the main factors that are associated with this decision, which provide a hint of which are types of innovations and the firm-level factors that are generally associated with the decision to apply for trademarks, but do not know the explicit motives behind it. This leaves room for future survey-based empirical studies who might explicitly ask firms who apply for trademarks the reasons behind it.

Despite these important limitations, this study allows us to draw some useful policy implications. Recent years have witnessed an increased interest in the analysis of trademarks as a possible indicator of firms' innovation, as opposed to other traditional indicators such as patents or innovation surveys. Typically this can lead to policies aimed at boosting the use of trademarks by firms, both because this would also mean that firms are more innovative, and because it may provide more incentives to firms' innovation, by increasing the appropriability of their innovation efforts. Our analysis shows that many innovating firms may decide not to trademark even very valuable innovations simply because they are not needed and a variety of scenarios correspond to this – for example, because of collaborative innovation with users gives innovators access to client distribution channels, because of the existence of previously established distribution channels, or because pre-existing trademarks covering also the new products. These specific cases may undermine the effectiveness of policies aimed at increasing trademark applications.

Acknowledgments

We are grateful to the UK IPO for allowing us use of their proprietary SIPU data and to David Humphries and Pippa Hall for comments on earlier draft versions of the paper. The views expressed in this paper are the authors' views and we remain responsible for any errors that remain.

Disclosure statement

No potential conflict of interest was reported by the authors.

References

Allegrezza, S., and A. Guarda-Rauchs. 1999. "The Determinants of Trademarks Deposits: An Econometric Investigation (A Case Study of the Benelux)." *Economie Appliquée* 52 (2): 51–68.

Amara, N., R. Landry, and N. Traoré. 2008. "Managing the Protection of Innovations in Knowledge-Intensive Business Services." *Research Policy* 37: 1530–1547. doi:10.1016/j.respol.2008.07.001.

Arora, A., S. Athreye, and C. Huang. 2016. "The Paradox of Openness Revisited." *Research Policy* 45 (7): 1352–1361. doi:10.1016/j.respol.2016.03.019.

Bhandari, B. 2005. *The Ranbaxy Story: The Rise of an Indian Multinational*. India: Penguin Global.

Block, H., G. De Vries, J. H. Schumann, and P. Sandner. 2014. "Trademarks and Venture Capital Valuation." *Journal of Business Venturing* 29 (4): 525–542. doi:10.1016/j.jbusvent.2013.07.006.

Castaldi, C. 2018. "To Trademark or Not to Trademark: The Case of the Creative and Cultural Industries." *Research Policy* 47 (3): 606–616. doi:10.1016/j.respol.2018.01.006.

Desyllas, P., M. M. Miozzo, H. F. Lee, and I. Miles. 2018. "Capturing Value from Innovation in Knowledge-Intensive Service Firms: The Role of Competitive Strategy." *British Journal of Management* 29 (4): 769–795. doi:10.1111/1467-8551.12273.

Flikkema, M. J., A. P. de Man, and C. Castaldi. 2014. "Are Trademark Counts a Valid Indicator of Innovation? Results of an In-Depth Study of New Benelux Trademarks Filed by SMEs." *Industry and Innovation* 21 (4): 310–331. doi:10.1080/13662716.2014.934547.

Flikkema, M. J., C. Castaldi, A.-P. De Man, and M. Seip. 2019. "Trademarks' Relatedness to Product and Service Innovation: A Branding Strategy Approach." *Research Policy* 48 (6): 1340–1353. doi:10.1016/j.respol.2019.01.018.

Fosfuri, A., and M. S. Giarratana. 2009. "Masters of War: Rivals' Product Innovation and New Advertising in Mature Product Markets." *Management Science* 55 (2): 181–191. doi:10.1287/mnsc.1080.0939.

Götsch, M., and C. Hipp. 2012. "Measurement of Innovation Activities in the Knowledge Intensive Services Industry: A Trademark Approach." *The Service Industries Journal* 32 (13): 2167–2184. doi:10.1080/02642069.2011.574275.

Greenhalgh, C., and M. Rogers. 2012. "Trade Marks and Performance in Services and Manufacturing Firms: Evidence of Schumpeterian Competition through Innovation." *Australian Economic Review* 45 (1): 50–76. doi:10.1111/j.1467-8462.2011.00665.x.

He, X., K. D. Brouthers, and I. Filatotchev. 2018. "Market Orientation and Export Performance: The Moderation of Channel and Institutional Distance." *International Marketing Review* 35 (2): 258–279. doi:10.1108/IMR-09-2015-0194.

Helmers, C., and M. Rogers. 2011. "Does Patenting Help High-Tech Start-Ups?" *Research Policy* 40 (7): 1016–1027. doi:10.1016/j.respol.2011.05.003.

Hipp, C., and H. Grupp. 2005. "Innovation in the Service Sector: The Demand for Service-Specific Innovation Measurement Concepts and Typologies." *Research Policy* 34: 517–535. doi:10.1016/j.respol.2005.03.002.

Jensen, P. H., and E. Webster. 2009. "Another Look at the Relationship between Innovation Proxies." *Australian Economic Papers* 48 (3): 252–269. doi:10.1111/aepa.2009.48.issue-3.

Landes, W., and R. Posner. 1987. "Trademark Law: An Economic Perspective." *Journal of Law and Economics* 30 (2): 265–309. doi:10.1086/467138.

Laursen, K., and A. J. Salter. 2014. "The Paradox of Openness: Appropriability, External Search and Collaboration." *Research Policy* 43 (5): 867–878. doi:10.1016/j.respol.2013.10.004.

Mendonça, S., T. S. Pereira, and M. M. Godinho. 2004. "Trademarks as an Indicator of Innovation and Industrial Change." *Research Policy* 33: 1385–1404. doi:10.1016/j.respol.2004.09.005.

Miozzo, M., P. Desyllas, H. Lee, and I. Miles. 2016. "Innovation Collaboration and Appropriability by Knowledge-Intensive Business Services Firms." *Research Policy* 45 (7): 1337–1351. doi:10.1016/j.respol.2016.03.018.

Ramello, G. B., and F. Silva. 2006. "Appropriating Signs and Meaning: The Elusive Economics of Trademark." *Industrial and Corporate Change* 15: 937–963. doi:10.1093/icc/dtl027.

Rogers, M., C. Greenhalgh, and C. Helmers. 2007. *The Association between the Use of IP by UK SMEs in 2001 and Subsequent Performance in 2002 to 2004.* mimeo. doi:10.1094/PDIS-91-4-0467B.

Schmoch, U. 2003. "Service Marks as Novel Innovation Indicator." *Research Evaluation* 12: 149–156. doi:10.3152/147154403781776708.

Thomä, J., and K. Bizer. 2013. "To Protect or Not to Protect? Modes of Appropriability in the Small Enterprise Sector." *Research Policy* 42 (1): 35–49. doi:10.1016/j.respol.2012.04.019.

WIPO. 2013. *World Intellectual Property Report 2013 – Brands – Reputation and Image in the Global Marketplace.*

Part IV
Trademarks and Entrepreneurship

Trademarks and their association with *Kirznerian* entrepreneurs

Serhiy Lyalkov(iD), Mónica Carmona(iD), Emilio Congregado(iD), Ana Millán(iD) and José María Millán(iD)

ABSTRACT

Although trademarks are the most widely used form of Intellectual Property Rights (IPRs) by firms across all economic sectors worldwide, this indicator is a much less exploited information resource in empirical analysis compared with patents. Our work addresses this gap by investigating the relationship between trademark registration and entrepreneurial activity using data for 33 European countries. Our empirical results show a positive and significant relationship between the share of the self-employed workforce in a given country that can be considered 'entrepreneurial' – which we associate with the share of *Kirznerian* entrepreneurs – and trademark registration at the country level. These results have important implications for scholars, practitioners and policymakers, which are discussed in this work.

1. Introduction

There is a large body of theoretical and empirical literature suggesting that Intellectual Property Rights (IPRs) make countries more innovative and consequently cause higher economic growth (Varsakelis 2001; Branstetter, Fishman, and Foley 2006; Kanwar 2006; Allred and Park 2007; Acs and Sanders 2012). The rationale is that, presumably, the protection provided to innovators by IPRs guarantees their economic rents, which stimulate investment in knowledge and innovation and, subsequently, economic growth.

Both patents and trademarks are IPR indicators which are positively correlated with innovation performance and provide an insight into ongoing processes of industrial change (Mendonça, Pereira, and Godinho 2004; Mendonça 2012). While patents are typically related to original, non-trivial and productive inventions (i.e. technological aspects of a firm's business model), trademarks such as brand names and logos are registered to distinguish and protect the reputation of goods, services and corporate identities (i.e. marketing aspects) (Mendonça, Pereira, and Godinho 2004; Srinivasan, Lilien, and Rangaswamy 2008; Mendonça 2012; De Vries et al. 2017). Hence, these indicators provide complementary

All authors contributed equally to the manuscript.

information on the industrial composition in a given region: patent counts are a pointer of technological expertise and trademark statistics are an indicator of commercial capability (Mendonça 2012).

Specifically, trademarks are of great interest for social science research, as they are not only an important aspect of contemporary culture worldwide (Mendonça, Pereira, and Godinho 2004) but also the most widely used form of IPRs by firms across all economic sectors worldwide (WIPO 2017). Figure 1 shows the evolution of both indicators for selected economies in the period 2000–16.[1]

In this line, the increasing importance of trademarks has recently spawned research investigating (i) the patterns of firms' usage of trademarks in relation to their innovation activities and new products, (ii) trademarks' relations to firms' economic performance and productivity and (iii) the interplay between social costs and value of trademarks (see Malmberg 2005; Schautschick and Greenhalgh 2016 for reviews). Furthermore, trademark-based indicators show promise for advancing research agendas concerned with (i) the rates and directions of product innovations in different industrial sectors, (ii) international patterns of specialisation, (iii) links between technological and marketing activities and (iv) the evolution of economic organisations and structures (Mendonça, Pereira, and Godinho 2004).

However, although both patents and trademarks allow for complementary readings, patents have been used for decades in empirical analysis, whereas trademark data is a much less exploited information resource (Mendonça 2012). Thus, patents are common-place in standard economic benchmarking publications (e.g. OECD or World Bank reports), whereas trademarks use as a country-level indicator has been very limited.[2] In particular, fundamental aspects of the function of trademark data as an additional indicator of innova-tive and entrepreneurial activity remain unexplored. Addressing this research gap is precisely the main aim of this work.

This work contributes to this scant literature by assessing the appropriateness of trademark data as a source of qualitative information about the self-employed workforce within a particular country or region. In this sense, there are some arguments for assuming certain properties of trademark data reveal hidden information about the self-employment

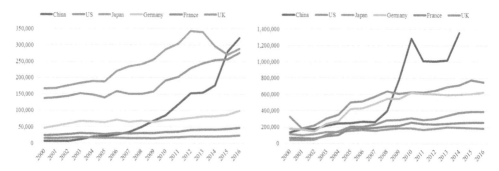

Figure 1. Total patent (*left panel*) and trademark (*right panel*) registrations for selected countries.
Source: WIPO IP Statistics Database.

---

[1]The observed differences in favour of trademark registration figures can be explained (at least) by (i) their compara-tively lower cost and (ii) the absence of novelty requirement for trademark registration.
[2]Some notable exceptions are presented in subsection 2.1 below.

population in a given economy. Thus, the majority of enterprises (between 70% and 95%) in all OECD countries are micro-businesses (i.e. enterprises with fewer than 10 employees) and the share of SMEs over the population of enterprises rises above 99% (OECD 2019a). Therefore, the proportion of individuals within the self-employment population running SMEs is very large. However, the propensity to patent is rather low in SMEs (Blind et al. 2006; Leiponen and Byma 2007; Thomä and Bizer 2013; Flikkema, De Man, and Castaldi 2014) and, hence, patents cannot adequately measure innovation in SMEs (Kleinknecht 2000). In contrast to patents, trademarks can be used to capture the 'softer' non-technological types of innovation, i.e. service, marketing and organizational innovation, which are more probable within the SME framework (Flikkema, De Man, and Castaldi 2014). Under a microeconomic theoretical framework, the *Schumpeterian* entrepreneur (1912, 1942) would be more likely linked with R&D efforts and patent registration activity in large firms, while the *Kirznerian* entrepreneur (1973) would be more likely associated with trademark registration practices within the SME and self-employment framework.[3] Therefore, irrespective of the (rather low) share of technologically innovative or Schumpeterian entrepreneurs in a given economy,[4] an association is expected between trademark data and the relative weight of Kirznerian entrepreneurial activities over total self-employment in a given economy.

More specifically, this paper explores whether registered trademarks at the country level can be linked to the existing heterogeneity within entrepreneurship in 33 European countries. To this aim, an *ad hoc* country-level dataset covering the periods 2010 and 2015 is generated and linear regression models are used. As dependent variables, we use information on registered patents and trademarks provided by the *World Intellectual Property Organization* (WIPO). To account for this entrepreneurial heterogeneity, and based on microdata drawn from the *European Working Conditions Survey*, we use as covariates different groups of self-employed workers, from more to less entrepreneurial in a Kirznerian sense. Our proxies for Kirznerian entrepreneurs are self-employed with employees and opportunity entrepreneurs. Conversely, our proxies for less entrepreneurial forms of self-employment are dependent self-employed workers (i.e. self-employed without employees who generally has only one client) and necessity entrepreneurs. For all countries in our sample, this micro-level information is turned into macro-level data by estimating the share of self-employed workers belonging to the different groups of self-employed workers. Our regressions also include information about expenditure on R&D activities provided by Eurostat. As regards the evidence obtained, we observe how both our proxies for Kirznerian entrepreneurs are positively and statistically associated with trademark registration at the country level. Conversely, none of our groups of self-employed workers, from more to less entrepreneurial in a Kirznerian sense, seems to be statistically associated with patent registration activities at the country level. Our results have important implications for academics, practitioners and policymakers.

The remainder of the paper is structured as follows: Section 2 provides background information from which our general hypothesis is derived. Section 3 describes our data

---

[3]There is also a growing body of empirical literature exploring the different impacts of entrepreneurship on regional economic growth depending on whether regional entrepreneurship is based on technological innovations (Schumpeterian type) or opportunity discoveries (Kirznerian type) (see e.g. Sundqvist et al. 2012; Aparicio, Urbano, and Audretsch 2016; Ferreira et al. 2017 as recent examples).

[4]Most entrepreneurs don't employ personnel, are home-based, and earn low incomes (Shane 2009).

and variables. Section 4 presents the descriptive analysis and multivariate results, and Section 5 concludes with a discussion of implications, limitations of this study and suggestions regarding possible directions for future research.

2. Background

Four elements are part of the background of this study. First, a small review of studies using trademarks as a country-level indicator is presented. Second, a brief review of Schumpeterian and Kirznerian views of entrepreneurship is provided. Next, we present the existing relationship between these two types of entrepreneurs and some particular IPR indicators such as patents and trademarks and derive our proposed relationship between Kirznerian entrepreneurship and trademarks (i.e. the general hypothesis to be tested in this work). Finally, possible operationalisations of Kirznerian entrepreneurship are discussed.

2.1. Trademarks as a country-level indicator

In contrast to patents, the use of trademark data as a country-level indicator in the economic literature has been scarce and sporadic. The more notable exceptions, to our knowledge, are presented below.

Thus, Fink, Javorcik, and Spatareanu (2005) use data on international trademark registrations as an indicator of both product quality and the extent of brand differentiation in order to examine an extension of Linder's (1961) hypothesis.[5] Similarly, Mangani (2007) proposes the use of registered trademarks to estimate the variety and quality of goods and services in an economy and, thus, describes the patterns of production and exports of about 120 countries. Baroncelli, Fink, and Javorcik (2005) use trademark registration data as an information source on how reputational assets are distributed and how they are exploited in international commerce. Baroncelli, Krivonos, and Olarreaga (2007) explore the extent to which discrimination against foreign applicants in the trademark registration is used as a *behind-the-border* barrier to imports, i.e. a protectionism indicator. Mendonça (2012) employs trademarks as an indicator for assessing dynamic competition and international competitiveness in the telecommunications equipment and services sector. De Rassenfosse (2016) observes the validity of an intangible investment, such as *brand equity*, as a powerful predictor of trademark applications.[6] Finally, Herz and Mejer (2016) suggest that the increase in trademark applications experienced over the last 20 years in Europe is not a sign of increased innovative performance but rather the result of (i) national trademark filings simply being price-sensitive, and (ii) a decrease and convergence of trademark filing fees across countries in Europe.

---

[5]Linder's (1961) hypothesis suggests the quality of products as being the main determining factor of the closeness of exporter supply structures and importer preferences, which in turn explains why richer countries trade more among themselves than with poorer countries.

[6]Brand equity investment series data were obtained from studies that have followed the Corrado-Hulten-Sichel (CHS) methodology (Corrado, Hulten, and Sichel 2005).

2.2. Schumpeterian and Kirznerian entrepreneurs in brief

The Schumpeterian (1912, 1942) view of innovation is an industry phenomenon where new products or practices spread among competing firms or drive out those firms that are unable to adapt. The result is change of industry practices. Hence, the *creativity* of Schumpeterian entrepreneurs *disrupts* what would otherwise have been a serene market. The creative genius of Schumpeterian entrepreneurs is thus scarce in nature.

In contrast, Kirzner's (1973) entrepreneurs are often viewed as merely speculative agents or arbitrageurs, i.e. individuals who are *alert* to price differentials which others had not yet noticed (Von Mises 1952). The discrepancies which the entrepreneur notices appear in the form of profit opportunities and, specifically, the prompt exploitation of such perceived opportunities by these entrepreneurs is what *drives the market towards the* (relevant new) *equilibrium* configurations.

Therefore, there is room for both views of the entrepreneurial process, and they are not at all mutually exclusive. Conversely, market dynamics can be seen as the outcome of two distinct kinds of entrepreneur-driven changes (Kirzner 2009). Furthermore, there are (at least) two arguments that support the existence of some overlapping (to a certain extent) between Schumpeterian and Kirznerian entrepreneurs. *First*, although the role of creator and innovator is commonly associated with Schumpeterian entrepreneurs, Kirzner's view is also linked to innovation in the sense that 'his entrepreneur' discovers that there is indeed an opportunity to make a profit by introducing an innovation to a market (Dahlqvist and Wiklund 2012). Thus, while Kirzner's (1973) earlier work might paint an image of the entrepreneur as an arbitrageur who *sees* the existing, but hitherto overlooked, opportunity, his more recent work (e.g. Kirzner 2009) suggests that the discovery of opportunity by what he refers to as *real-world entrepreneurs* takes creativity, imagination and even talent.[7] And *second*, as Kirzner (2009) argues, the bold, creative, innovative (Schumpeterian) entrepreneur is, at a higher level of abstraction, also engaged in arbitrage. In this regard, Prof. Kirzner claimed the following:

> What [a Schumpeterian entrepreneur] 'sees' is that, by assembling available resources in an innovative, hitherto undreamt of fashion, and thus perhaps converting them into new, hitherto undreamt of products, he may be able (in the future) to sell output at prices which exceed the cost of that output to himself. In 'all' its manifestations, entrepreneurship identifies arbitrage opportunities. (Kirzner 2009, 150)

All in all, Schumpeterian entrepreneurs can be viewed as decisive drivers of economic development and, simultaneously, a (small) *subset* of Kirznerian entrepreneurs.

2.3. The relationship between entrepreneurship and IPR indicators

The existing controversy between Schumpeterian and Kirznerian entrepreneurs and their respective innovation types runs parallel to other innovation indicators, i.e. the tandem patents and trademarks. Both types of IPRs allow the holder to protect his or her market power and, hence, guarantee economic rents. However, while patents are typically related to original, non-trivial and productive inventions (i.e. technological

---

[7]See Dahlqvist and Wiklund (2012) for an interesting discussion of this issue.

aspects of a firm's business model), trademarks can conversely be used to capture the 'softer' non-technological types of innovation (i.e. service, marketing and organisational innovation).

In industrial organisation terms, those (presumably large) firms which are active in R&D-intensive and technology-oriented industries would be more likely to register patents, whereas firms that are active in advertising-intensive, consumer-related and service-related industries would be more likely to register trademarks (Amara, Landry, and Traoré 2008; Block et al. 2015a). These 'softer' non-technological types of innovation, i.e. service, marketing and organisational innovation which can be better captured by trademarks, are, however, more probable within the SME framework (Flikkema, De Man, and Castaldi 2014). Hence, trademarks are also a useful resource to protect and appropriate the value of innovations in sectors or activities where patents are not a viable option (De Vries et al. 2017). As a result, start-ups are more likely to file trademarks than patents when entering the market (De Vries et al. 2017). In contrast, the likelihood of patent is rather low in SMEs (Blind et al. 2006; Leiponen and Byma 2007; Thomä and Bizer 2013; Flikkema, De Man, and Castaldi 2014) and, hence, trademarks are revealed as a more appropriate measure of innovation than patents in SMEs (Kleinknecht 2000). Therefore, since the share of individuals within the self-employment population running SMEs is broad (as argued in the introductory section), an important relationship between trademark filing behaviour and some innovative self-employed individuals is to be expected.

Stated under a microeconomic theoretical framework, two claims emerge from our previous discussion. *First*, the bold, disruptive, *Schumpeterian* entrepreneur would be more active in R&D exertion and patent registration activity in large firms, whereas the opportunity-alert *Kirznerian* entrepreneur would be more involved in trademark registration practices within the SME and self-employment framework. *Second*, patents and trademarks are related but distinct means of appropriating the benefits of innovation with a low degree of substitution. Indeed, both IPRs are only observed to successfully work as complementary assets in some highly innovative sectors (Srinivasan, Lilien, and Rangaswamy 2008; Llenera and Millot 2013).[8]

However, the causality of these relationships among entrepreneurship and different innovation types and their associated IPRs may go in both directions (Wennekers et al. 2010). Thus, since entrepreneurs are responsible for registering both patents and trademarks, *Schumpeterian* and *Kirznerian* entrepreneurial activities can thus naturally explain the occurrence of intellectual protection. However, the inverse relationship can also occur, i.e. IPR measures can also help explain levels of entrepreneurial activity.

As regards patents, since registration makes others pay for using some particular technological knowledge, this form of IPR becomes an important incentive for entrepreneurial R&D commitment. In addition, the patents a firm owns can also affect the prospects for follow-up funding (Audretsch, Bönte, and Mahagaonkar 2012; Hsu and Ziedonis 2013; Haeussler, Harhoff, and Mueller 2014), which can be used in later R&D investments. Furthermore, patents reveal that the firm was able to create an innovation

---

[8]Srinivasan, Lilien, and Rangaswamy (2008) find patents and trademarks to be complementary assets in the high-tech industry. Llenera and Millot (2013) find evidence of this complementarity in sectors such as pharmaceutical or chemical products.

and might do so again in the future (Farre-Mensa, Hegde, and Ljungqvist 2017); i.e. patents can be a proxy for future R&D efforts. Finally, by publishing these rights, i.e. in the form of patents, technological knowledge becomes accessible in the form of 'spillovers of R&D' which, in turn, raises business opportunities and new R&D efforts for the firms' neighbourhood (Jaffe 1986; Audretsch and Feldman 1996; Thumm 2004; Cassiman and Veugelers 2006).

When turning our attention to trademarks, analogous arguments can also be applied. Thus, filing trademarks demonstrates a start-up's degree of market and growth orientation and its willingness to protect its current and future marketing efforts from the impairment of others (Krasnikov, Mishra, and Orozco 2009; Sandner and Block 2011; Brahem, El Harbi, and Grolleau 2013). Like patents, trademarks have been found to be positively related to firm survival (Srinivasan, Lilien, and Rangaswamy 2008; Helmers and Rogers 2010), firm valuations (Sandner and Block 2011; Greenhalgh and Rogers 2012) and access to external funds (Block et al. 2014). Moreover, particularly for nascent entrepreneurs (whose businesses are, by definition, small), the impact of trademark registration on both firm valuation and external investors is even higher than that by filed patents (Block et al. 2014). Finally, important knowledge spillovers can also occur as a result of registering trademarks. *First*, brand loyalty might spill over across products of the same firm (Parchomovsky and Siegelman 2002). *Second*, advertising of the trademarked product may spill over to its generic competitors, so that some of the benefit to the trademark 'leaks' away to its rivals (Llenera and Millot 2013). *Last*, product improvements (in the form of registered trademarks) can also generate knowledge spillovers which, in turn, may act as an important source of new business opportunities not only for imitative entrepreneurship but also innovative entrepreneurship that wishes to build further on the earlier innovations made in other firms (Acs et al. 2009; Burke and Fraser 2012).

Once the bidirectional relationship between entrepreneurship and IPRs has been argued, previous claims can be presented in a more straightforward manner: (i) *Schumpeterian* entrepreneurship is more likely linked with R&D efforts and patenting in large firms, and (ii) *Kirznerian* entrepreneurship is more likely associated with trademarking activity by SMEs and self-employed workers. Therefore, irrespective of the (rather low) share of technologically innovative or Schumpeterian entrepreneurs in a given economy, an association is expected between trademark data and the relative weight of Kirznerian entrepreneurial activities over total self-employment in a given economy.

Previous discussion leads us to state our general hypothesis for this work as follows:

General Hypothesis. Trademarks present a stronger association with Kirznerian entrepreneurs' activity in a given economy than patents.

This work specifically aims to assess the appropriateness of using this trademark and patent information as a source of qualitative information on the self-employed workforce within a country. Given the exploratory nature of the current study, such relationships are expressed in terms of associations and, hence, a formal analysis of the presumably bidirectional causality between these variables is a topic for further research.

2.4. Operationalisation of *kirznerian* entrepreneurship

Due to data availability constraints, the production of statistical evidence in order to test our general hypothesis is, however, not straightforward. Hence, a proper selection of indicators for entrepreneurship from the pool of available empirical operationalisations is required. In particular, detailed information not only about the number of entrepreneurs in a particular geographical area but also about the way these entrepreneurs carry out their task is crucial.

In this sense, and based on the so-called 'revealed preference' principle, *economists* tend to classify entrepreneurs into different types from actual observed attributes and behaviours. Thus, self-employment is the more common labour economists' working definition for entrepreneurs (Parker 2018). Its wide implementation – both at the individual level within human population surveys and at the national level, via the *OECD Labour Force Statistics* database – is, undoubtedly, a practical advantage. In this sense, approximately 15.8 per cent of the workforces in the EU-28 are self-employed (OECD 2019b).

The self-employed are formally considered as individuals working for themselves (instead of working for an employer that pays a salary or a wage) who derive their income by exercising their profession or business on their own account and at their own risk. However, there is plenty of heterogeneity behind this indicator, as acknowledged by the OECD's own self-employment definition: '*self-employment may be seen either as a survival strategy for those who cannot find any other means of earning an income or as evidence of entrepreneurial spirit and a desire to be one's own boss*' (OECD 2019b).

Both the *number of employees* and the *number of clients* are immediate sources of self-employment heterogeneity based on their observed attributes. The *number of employees* leads to the distinction between *self-employed with employees* and *own-account workers*. The former type contributes to the job-generation process and, hence, works on a larger scale than own-account workers, which implies some degree of business success (Earle and Sakova 2000). Indeed, self-employed with employees are considered as more entrepreneurial forms of self-employment than own-account workers (Earle and Sakova 2000; Kuhn 2000; Román, Congregado, and J.M. Millán 2013; J. M. Millán, Congregado, and Román 2014a, 2014b). This larger scale, however, would probably still remain within the SME framework, as argued in the preceding sections. As a consequence, both self-employed with and without employees would rarely participate in (Schumpeterian) R&D intensive and technology-oriented activities and, hence, would seldom be involved in patent registration. Conversely, their SME scale is more appropriate to performing those aforementioned 'softer' non-technological types of innovation which can be registered in the form of trademarks (Flikkema, De Man, and Castaldi 2014). Thus, although trademark registration seems more likely for the outperforming group, i.e. self-employed with employees, there are no a-priori reasons to assume that own-account workers will not register trademarks to a certain extent.

When turning our attention to the *number of clients*, an interesting distinction emerges within the group of own-account workers. Thus, as opposed to the *independent own-account self-employed* who work for different clients-firms, *dependent self-employed workers* work exclusively (or mainly) for a specific firm. Hence, they are economically dependent in the sense that they generate their whole (or a substantial part of their) income from this business relationship and, obviously, take an entrepreneurial risk

(Muehlberger and Bertolini 2008). The OECD defines this particular group as 'own-account self-employed whose conditions of work are nonetheless similar to those of employees, in the sense that they work mainly or exclusively for a specific client-firm with limited autonomy and often closely integrated into its organizational structure' (OECD 2014). Dependent self-employment can be regarded as a sub-phenomenon of a general trend towards increasing labour market flexibility (Eichhorst et al. 2013), to which the growth of the *gig economy*, typified by online platforms and isolated independent workers, is seriously contributing (Stewart and Standord 2017). Unfortunately, these workers are usually beyond the scope of labour law (Muehlberger and Bertolini 2008; Román, Congregado, and Millán 2011; A. Millán and J.M. Millán 2017; A. Millán, J.M. Millán, and Román 2018), collective bargaining and trade union representation (Supiot 2001; ILO 2003). We will agree at any rate that there is nothing entrepreneurial about merely being a disguised employee and, therefore, trademark registration is expected to be anecdotal among this group.

All in all, based on the *economists'* view, three groups of self-employed workers emerge, from more to less entrepreneurial in a Kirznerian sense: (1) *self-employed with employees*; (2) *independent own-account self-employed*; and (3) *dependent self-employed workers*.

Business scholars propose an alternative classification for entrepreneurs where the source of heterogeneity concerns their *start-up motivation*. We refer here to the distinction between *opportunity* and *necessity* entrepreneurs, for which the more widely used operationalisation is that based on the Global Entrepreneurship Monitor (GEM) definition proposed by Reynolds et al. (2002). In the GEM Adult Population Survey, respondents indicating that they run a business are asked whether they started their business because they saw a business opportunity they wanted to pursue, or whether they had no alternatives to obtain paid work.[9] This approach allows the contrast between those *opportunity-alert* (Kirznerian) entrepreneurs on the one hand, and those who can be considered self-employed as a *last resort* (Alba-Ramirez 1994; Hyytinen and Rouvinen 2008) on the other.

In this sense, these *opportunity entrepreneurs* can be interested in defending their market share, differentiating their products or services by means of trademarks as a way to guarantee their ability to compete monopolistically and, thus, ensure a compensation for their marketing investments (Malmberg 2005). Their involvement, however, in (Schumpeterian) R&D-intensive projects or patent registration is hardly expected, due to the same scale arguments we previously used when presenting the *economists'* approach; i.e. the proportion of self-employed individuals running large firms, in which registering patents might occur, is minimal. When turning to the *necessity entrepreneurs*, these are more likely to run standard low-margin and low-added-value businesses mainly based on imitative strategies. Therefore, the absence of any particular attribute or a firm's brand to protect against competitors makes registering trademarks an unlikely practice among this group.

---

[9]GEM data suffers from severe drawbacks, such as the limited numbers of covariates or the impossibility of comparing its figures with data from official international statistics such as Eurostat or the OECD. Fortunately, other cross-country datasets for the European area also allow to obtain accurate proxies for opportunity and necessity entrepreneurs. We refer here to the *European Community Household Panel* (ECHP), the *European Union Statistics on Income and Living Conditions* (EU-SILC) or the *European Working Conditions Survey* (EWCS), the last being the one we use in the present study.

To sum up, both approaches, either that of economists or business scholars, allow us, on the basis of existing data sources, to identify useful proxies of *Kirznerian* entrepreneurs (i.e. *self-employed with employees* and *opportunity entrepreneurs*) and less (or none) entrepreneurial forms of self-employment (i.e. *dependent self-employed workers* and *necessity entrepreneurs*).

3. Data and variables

3.1. Dependent variables: trademarks and patents

The World Intellectual Property Organization (WIPO) offers global statistics on different intellectual property indicators: patents, trademarks, utility models and industrial designs. Our main dependent variables are based on registered trademarks and patents at the country level provided by the WIPO. To make fairer comparisons between countries, these figures are adjusted by GDP, as usual (see e.g. WIPO 2017). GDP data are derived from the World Bank national accounts data and OECD National Accounts data files.

In particular, our dependent variables are the registered trademarks and patents per constant 2010 US\$ billion GDP for the periods 2010 and 2015. Both variables are generated for both periods at the country level for 33 European countries, which yields 66 observations. Table 1 shows this information for the countries in our sample.[10]

3.2. Focal variables: occupational status, start-up motivation and expenditure on R&D

As argued in our background section, trademark-filing activities are expected to relate to some particular groups within self-employment, whereas patent registration practices seem to be associated with R&D efforts. Therefore, our focal variables must be defined accordingly.

However, due to data limitations, identifying the existing heterogeneity within the self-employed workforce is not straightforward. Precisely to overcome this issue, we use data from the Fifth and Sixth waves of the *European Working Conditions Survey* – EWCS 2010 and 2015 – (Eurofound 2012, 2016, 2018), which are the first waves in the EWCS series allowing the identification of certain categories. This survey is carried out every five years by the EU Agency *Eurofound* (*European Foundation for the Improvement of Living and Working Conditions*) and offers key work-related information on 44,000 workers (including both employees and self-employed individuals) covering 35 European countries.[11] To this end, these workers are interviewed about several working condition aspects, including physical environment, workplace design, working hours, work organisation and social relationships in the workplace. Depending on country size and national arrangements, the sample ranges from 1,000 to 4,000 workers per country.

Conditional on self-classification, the EWCS 2010 and 2015 allow us to create two separate classifications of self-employed workers from more to less entrepreneurial

---

[10]Detailed definitions of all our country-level and individual variables are presented, respectively, in Tables A1 and A2 in the Appendix.

[11]This set includes the EU-28 together, five candidate countries (Albania, the Former Yugoslav Republic of Macedonia, Montenegro, Serbia and Turkey) and two EFTA countries (Norway and Switzerland).

Table 1. Patents, trademarks and Gross Domestic Expenditure on R&D (GERD) for 33 European countries.

Country	Patents per constant 2010 US$ billion GDP				Trademarks per constant 2010 US$ billion GDP				GERD PPS per inhabitant at constant 2005 prices			
	Rank#	2010	Rank#	2015	Rank#	2010	Rank#	2015	Rank#	2006–10	Rank#	2011–15
Austria	9	11.7	7	17.2	8	217.4	10	203.4	6	793.4	3	942.7
Belgium	12	10.4	10	12.5	15	152.0	16	155.3	10	563.6	9	682.9
Bulgaria	21	4.2	29	1.9	4	275.4	5	360.9	31	48.9	30	79.9
Croatia	29	1.7	33	0.9	31	50.1	30	86.1	23	111.5	27	104.2
Cyprus	17	5.7	16	7.8	3	389.1	3	661.8	25	101.9	28	102.8
Czech Republic	26	2.8	21	4.9	24	126.0	23	142.7	17	263.7	15	385.3
Denmark	8	12.2	8	16.3	20	134.4	17	153.2	5	803.7	6	863.6
Estonia	20	4.3	20	5.2	6	245.7	4	411.2	19	193.1	17	291.0
Finland	2	26.0	2	28.2	22	132.0	18	152.6	3	1,006.7	4	906.0
France	7	12.6	9	15.8	27	97.7	29	92.1	11	558.9	11	596.1
Germany	4	20.7	5	23.4	13	182.1	14	163.2	7	744.3	5	890.6
Greece	28	2.1	28	2.0	32	47.6	31	76.6	21	137.3	25	142.7
Hungary	19	4.4	22	4.4	25	110.1	21	145.1	20	154.3	20	200.3
Ireland	15	7.5	17	7.6	19	139.6	27	100.7	12	478.1	12	530.8
Italy	10	11.7	13	9.1	14	168.9	20	149.7	16	295.9	16	306.5
Latvia	13	10.2	15	7.9	11	193.2	8	210.8	29	76.1	29	94.4
Lithuania	27	2.2	24	3.1	18	139.7	12	198.9	22	113.9	23	160.7
Luxembourg	5	17.4	3	25.9	1	586.8	2	695.3	4	989.8	7	802.0
Macedonia	32	1.3	32	1.1	16	147.8	32	52.5	33	40.0	33	40.0
Malta	14	8.8	12	9.5	2	431.0	1	1082.6	24	111.3	21	168.0
Netherlands	6	17.1	6	19.7	9	204.0	13	183.8	9	568.0	10	654.2
Norway	18	5.6	18	6.6	33	32.8	33	34.8	8	657.2	8	700.0
Poland	23	3.3	19	5.7	21	133.6	19	151.6	26	86.3	24	146.0
Portugal	31	1.3	30	1.6	10	197.8	7	212.3	18	262.6	19	254.1
Romania	25	2.8	26	2.1	29	96.3	25	108.4	32	48.6	32	48.0
Serbia	24	2.9	27	2.0	26	99.7	26	102.1	30	71.8	31	70.9
Slovakia	30	1.6	31	1.6	28	96.9	24	124.6	27	84.2	22	165.7
Slovenia	11	11.6	11	12.3	7	223.5	9	204.2	14	375.3	13	519.9
Spain	22	3.3	23	4.0	12	187.4	11	200.1	15	309.2	18	285.3
Sweden	3	21.7	4	23.6	17	145.1	15	160.6	1	1,018.8	2	1,007.4
Switzerland	1	28.3	1	35.0	5	266.2	6	270.4	2	1,013.8	1	1,089.7
Turkey	33	1.2	25	2.2	30	64.0	28	95.7	28	77.0	26	112.0
United Kingdom	16	6.8	14	7.9	23	127.3	22	145.1	13	455.9	14	463.5
33 European countries		*9.2*		*10.4*		*139.4*		*146.3*		*392.8*		*436.5*

Notes: Countries' population sizes are used as supranational weights to ensure that larger (smaller) countries weigh heavier (weaker) when calculating aggregated figures at the European level (i.e. for our 33 European countries). *Data sources*: WIPO IP Statistics Database, Eurostat, World Bank national accounts data, and OECD National Accounts data files.

forms. The *first classification of self-employed workers* combines the information collected by two different questions. *First*, the individuals in the survey are asked about their main activity status: self-employed with employees, self-employed without employees, employed or other. *Second*, an additional question is asked to those respondents who previously indicated being self-employed without employees, i.e. whether his/her firm generally has more than one client. Based on this information, we classify self-employed workers within our dataset from more to less entrepreneurial in (1) self-employed with employees; (2) independent own-account self-employed (i.e. self-employed without employees answering positively to the question about whether his/her firm generally has more than one client); and (3) dependent self-employed worker (i.e. self-employed without employees answering negatively to the question about whether his/her firm generally has more than one client). For the clarity of our exposition, we will refer hereafter to this classification as *occupational status within self-*

employment. Our final sample includes men and women aged 18 to 65 who are classified as self-employed individuals. All individuals working part-time, i.e. working under 15 h per week, are excluded. The final dataset, after removing cases with missing data for any of the relevant variables, yields 8,535 observations for 33 countries.[12]

The *second classification of self-employed workers* is created by means of a *third* question, which is asked to those respondents who previously indicated being self-employed either with or without employees, i.e. whether he or she became self-employed mainly through personal preference, because he or she had no other alternatives for work, because of a combination of both reasons, or because of neither of these reasons. As this question was only used within the EWCS series in 2015, a subdataset is, hence, generated by excluding data from the EWCS 2010. Our subdataset, when using data from the EWCS 2015, yields 4,345 observations for 33 countries. Based on this information, we classify the observed set of self-employed workers within our dataset into (1) opportunity entrepreneur, (2) hybrid opportunity-necessity entrepreneur, (3) necessity entrepreneur and (4) entrepreneur for other reasons. Categories 1, 2 and 3 are ordered from more to less entrepreneurial form of self-employment. Category 4, however, is assumed to have, by definition, a heterogeneous composition. For clarification purposes, we will refer henceforth to this classification as *start-up motivation*.

For the 33 European countries in our sample, this micro-level information is turned into macro-level data by estimating the share of self-employed workers belonging to the different categories included within both classifications presented above. In this sense, to ensure that these figures accurately reflect the population of self-employed workers in each country, post-stratification weights provided by the EWCS are used. This process yields only 64 observations, which is precisely the size of our final dataset.[13] Table 2 shows the new data generated.

To capture the presence and commitment to technological effort and innovation activities in each of the considered economies, our regressions also include the 5-year average Gross Domestic Expenditure on R&D (GERD) for periods 2006–10 and 2011–15. This indicator includes expenditures by business enterprises, higher education institutions, as well as government and private non-profit organisations.[14] To make fairer comparisons between countries, Eurostat provides this information expressed as *Purchasing Power Standards* (PPS) per inhabitant at constant 2005 prices.[15] Table 1 also shows figures regarding this indicator for the 33 European countries in our sample.

3.3. Control variables

With the aim of controlling for the possible effects of different sector compositions of the economies under study, the empirical models control for the share of self-employed individuals working in high-technology industry and knowledge-intensive services for the 33 European countries in our sample. To this end, we use Eurostat aggregations of

---

[12]Albania and Montenegro are excluded during this process.
[13]The EWCS did not collect information for Serbia and Switzerland in 2010.
[14]GERD has been widely used within entrepreneurship literature as a measure of technological commitment in a particular economy (see e.g. Van Stel, J.M. Millán, and Román 2014).
[15]PPS is the technical term used by Eurostat for the common (artificial) currency in which national accounts aggregates are expressed when adjusted for price-level differences using PPPs. Thus, PPPs can be interpreted as the exchange rate of the PPS against the €.

Table 2. Occupational status within self-employment and start-up motivation for 33 European countries.

Country	Occupational status 2010			Occupational status 2015			Start-up motivation [a] 2015			
	1 SEwE	2 IOA	3 DSEW	1 SEwE	2 IOA	3 DSEW	1 Opp	3 Hyb	3 Nec	4 Oth
Austria	42.9	51.1	6.0	37.4	51.5	11.1	40.7	15.2	30.1	14.1
Belgium	40.1	59.0	0.9	43.6	50.2	6.1	79.0	5.9	7.8	7.3
Bulgaria	38.8	48.6	12.6	37.7	58.1	4.2	67.4	10.9	21.7	0
Croatia	46.8	41.1	12.1	39.7	44.5	15.8	34.2	24.8	38.6	2.4
Cyprus	36.2	48.0	15.8	35.9	53.2	10.9	74.4	13.2	11.9	0.5
Czech Republic	32.8	57.2	10.1	32.6	62.3	5.0	51.3	30.3	17.2	1.3
Denmark	58.9	38.6	2.5	36.7	60.3	3.0	83.3	12.3	4.5	0
Estonia	36.5	57.8	5.7	62.4	30.1	7.5	56.7	15.7	20.6	7.0
Finland	25.3	66.1	8.6	36.8	50.5	12.7	80.0	12.4	6.1	1.5
France	28.1	68.7	3.2	43.9	51.9	4.3	68.8	17.4	10.2	3.6
Germany	43.1	52.5	4.4	58.8	37.8	3.5	61.9	21.5	12.9	3.8
Greece	23.8	65.2	11.0	37.1	51.9	11.0	50.4	24.7	23.1	1.8
Hungary	39.7	54.4	6.0	34.0	49.0	17.0	44.2	23.9	20.5	11.4
Ireland	30.7	60.0	9.3	37.8	50.5	11.7	67.5	10.5	21.0	1.0
Italy	31.3	62.4	6.3	32.1	61.1	6.8	63.4	18.5	16.3	1.8
Latvia	43.0	44.3	12.7	48.0	40.6	11.5	42.7	21.3	32.5	3.5
Lithuania	31.3	50.2	18.5	39.9	46.5	13.6	63.8	14.2	21.3	0.7
Luxembourg	45.7	49.8	4.5	31.7	58.3	10.1	72.8	14.0	9.3	3.9
Macedonia	31.2	53.9	15.0	33.6	49.6	16.8	28.1	19.1	50.3	2.5
Malta	39.7	54.3	6.0	27.8	61.9	10.3	67.1	15.9	14.2	2.8
Netherlands	25.9	66.2	8.0	27.8	67.9	4.3	76.4	12.1	8.0	3.5
Norway	29.4	66.0	4.6	34.5	55.6	9.9	69.8	14.6	14.0	1.7
Poland	15.1	71.4	13.5	36.6	50.2	13.1	47.7	23.0	20.3	9.1
Portugal	23.6	68.9	7.5	31.8	48.2	20.0	44.3	18.3	35.3	2.1
Romania	13.1	62.9	24.0	29.1	46.1	24.8	50.4	12.8	36.9	0
Serbia	n.a.	n.a.	n.a.	24.1	57.0	18.9	32.6	12.3	54.2	0.9
Slovakia	20.6	63.7	15.8	22.8	60.0	17.2	69.7	12.4	16.2	1.7
Slovenia	49.9	48.1	2.1	31.6	51.7	16.7	60.2	17.5	17.4	5.0
Spain	37.0	59.6	3.3	33.4	60.5	6.1	52.6	17.9	27.3	2.3
Sweden	26.8	72.7	0.5	30.5	62.6	6.9	87.6	7.3	5.1	0
Switzerland	n.a.	n.a.	n.a.	45.6	47.3	7.0	61.5	22.1	11.2	5.2
Turkey	25.9	62.4	11.7	23.0	42.0	34.9	53.6	6.9	38.5	1.0
United Kingdom	27.7	62.9	9.3	20.0	66.7	13.4	74.5	8.9	14.7	1.9
33 European countries	*30.8*	*61.4*	*7.9*	*35.5*	*52.3*	*12.1*	*60.8*	*20.4*	*15.7*	*3.1*

Notes: SEwE = self-employed with employees, IOA = independent own-account self-employed worker, DSEW = dependent self-employed worker, Opp = opportunity entrepreneur, Hyb = hybrid opportunity-necessity entrepreneur, Nec = necessity entrepreneur, Oth = entrepreneur for other reasons; To ensure that these figures accurately reflect the population of self-employed workers in each country, post-stratification weights provided by the EWCS are used. The design weights are calibrated by comparing the EWCS with Eurostat's Labour Force Survey with regard to respondents' gender, age, region, occupation and sector of economic activity. Countries' population sizes are used as supranational weights to ensure that larger (smaller) countries weigh heavier (weaker) when calculating aggregated figures at the European level (i.e. for our 33 European countries); [a] The information about entrepreneurship reasons is only available within the EWCS 2015.
Data source: EWCS 2010, 2015 and Eurostat.

the manufacturing industry and services sector according to technological intensity based on NACE at the two-digit level.[16] Again, post-stratification weights provided by the EWCS are used to ensure that these figures accurately reflect each country's sector composition.

---

[16]Eurostat aggregations based on 'Statistics on high-tech industry and knowledge-intensive services' (sometimes referred to as simply 'high-tech statistics') can be found at https://ec.europa.eu/eurostat/cache/metadata/Annexes/htec_esms_an3.pdf.

Finally, in order to control for the business cycle and some structural differences among countries, the empirical models also include the 5-year average unemployment rates for the periods 2006–10 and 2011–15, which we collect from Eurostat, and a period 2015 (vs. 2010) dummy.

4. Results

4.1. Descriptive analysis

We aim to explore the relationship between different statistics on IPR indicators and some particular groups within the self-employment workforce. Our hypotheses formulation is based on the assumption that these groups are good proxies for entrepreneurs in the Kirznerian sense and other less entrepreneurial forms of self-employment, respectively. In this sense, one important advantage of our country-level entrepreneurship dataset presented in Table 2 is that we have access to the microdata information that was used for the macrodata generation process. Thus, we can use all the individual-based information within the EWCS to characterise those self-employed individuals belonging to each occupational status and start-up motivation we use in the analysis. Table 3 compares these groups.

We first explore occupational status within self-employment. Approximately 32.6%, 57.2% and 10.2% of our sample are, respectively, self-employed with employees, independent own-account self-employed and dependent self-employed workers. In this sense, the self-employed with employees are, in our sample, most often male and most often with a partner and with children. Moreover, they have the highest educational attainment, earnings and ability to make ends meet. Finally, they also work the longest hours and feel the healthiest. These figures suggest the appropriateness of this self-employment category in order to capture Kirznerian entrepreneurs. When comparing independent own-account self-employed and dependent self-employed workers, the latter group is lower-educated, older and more likely to have worse health perception. Furthermore, they work longer hours and, conversely, have lower earnings and are less able to make ends meet. Finally, they are also less likely to work in high-tech industry and knowledge-intensive services. These figures suggest the appropriateness of using dependent self-employed workers as a proxy for the least entrepreneurial form of self-employment. As expected, independent own-account workers show up as an intermediate category where many (but not all) can be examples of Kirznerian entrepreneurs.

When concentrating on start-up motivation (only available for the EWCS 2015), a similar characterisation of our relevant groups is revealed. However, the proportions of belonging to these groups vary substantially with respect to those obtained for our occupational statuses. In particular, 61.5% of our sample report being opportunity entrepreneurs. We observe, inter alia, that this group is in our sample most often male, higher-educated, and most often with a better health perception. Moreover, they have the highest earnings and ability to make ends meet. Finally, they are also the most likely to work in high-tech industry and knowledge-intensive services. These attributes suggest the appropriateness of this category in order to capture Kirznerian entrepreneurs. Regarding their necessity

Table 3. Descriptive statistics for occupational status within self-employment and start-up motivation in the EWCS.

	Occupational status						Start-up motivation [b]							
	1 Self-employed with employees 2010, 2015		2 Independent own-account worker 2010, 2015		3 Dependent self-employed worker 2010, 2015		1 Opportunity entrepreneur 2015		2 Hybrid opportunity-necessity entrepreneur 2015		3 Necessity entrepreneur 2015		4 Entrepreneur for other reasons 2015	
# observations	N = 2,780		N = 4,881		N = 874		N = 2,670		N = 652		N = 909		N = 114	
% observations	32.6%		57.2%		10.2%		61.5%		15%		20.9%		2.6%	
Variables	Mean	SD	Mean	SD	Mean	SD	Mean	SD	Mean	SD	Mean	SD	Mean	SD
Educational attainment														
Basic education [a]	0.059		0.114		0.222		0.058		0.060		0.188		0.052	
Secondary education [a]	0.598		0.613		0.638		0.598		0.635		0.632		0.681	
Tertiary education [a]	0.343		0.272		0.140		0.344		0.305		0.180		0.267	
Job characteristics														
Years of tenure in present job (1–53)	13.53	9.85	12.54	10.37	14.70	12.48	14.09	10.56	12.18	10.49	12.70	11.36	15.13	11.97
Working hours (15–98)	49.5	13.3	46.0	15.3	44.2	16.3	46.2	13.4	45.0	13.7	44.5	15.5	42.6	16.0
Net monthly earnings – PPP $ of 2015 (1–55,210)	2,884	2,454	1,950	1,733	1,471	1,509	2,545	2,578	1,984	1,422	1,440	1,115	2,021	1,380
Sector composition														
High-tech industry and knowledge-intensive services [a]	0.035		0.038		0.035		0.048		0.041		0.017		0.026	
Demographic characteristics														
Female [a]	0.293		0.372		0.368		0.332		0.351		0.399		0.422	
Immigrant [a]	0.107		0.101		0.097		0.111		0.113		0.115		0.121	
Age (18–65)	44.46	10.50	44.24	11.10	46.24	11.54	45.67	10.77	44.83	10.97	46.02	11.18	46.35	10.85
Cohabiting [a]	0.773		0.709		0.722		0.725		0.710		0.698		0.733	
Children under 14 [a]	0.341		0.308		0.251		0.299		0.299		0.275		0.241	
Health (1–5)	4.05	0.73	3.98	0.78	3.80	0.79	4.08	0.73	3.96	0.75	3.77	0.79	3.97	0.80
Ends meet (1–6)	4.24	1.16	3.70	1.31	3.35	1.34	4.16	1.17	3.71	1.22	3.18	1.34	4.05	1.32

N = 8,535; [a] Dummy variable; [b] The information about entrepreneurship reasons is only available within the EWCS 2015.
Data source: EWCS 2010, 2015.

entrepreneurs' counterparts, this group accounts for 20.9% of our sample. These self-employed workers present the lowest educational attainment levels and least often work in high-tech industry and knowledge-intensive services. Furthermore, they have the lowest earnings and are the least able to make ends meet. Hence, this category seems to be confirmed as a good proxy for the least entrepreneurial form of self-employment. Finally, the groups of hybrid entrepreneurs and entre- preneurs for other reasons account for 15% and 2.6% of our sample. Their intermediate positions in terms of education levels, earnings, ability to make ends meet and likelihood to work for high-tech industry and knowledge- intensive services suggest these categories may also collect a certain proportion of Kirznerian entrepreneurs.

4.2. Multivariate analysis

The estimation results are presented in Tables 4 and 5. Table 4 in subsection 4.2.1 shows the results from four specifications as regards patents and their covariates. Similarly, Table 5 in subsection 4.2.2 shows the results from four specifications aimed to present trademarks and their covariates. As regards estimation methods, we opted for estimating by means of OLS models and adjusted the standard errors for intra- countries correlation by clustering in those models where more than one EWCS wave was involved. The following structure is used to present our results. First, average predicted values of our dependent variables are indicated at the top of each specifica- tion. Below, each model is presented in a three-column format, where marginal effects and t-statistics are reported. Thus, within each specification, the first column shows the absolute marginal effects associated with all covariates. The second column also refers to marginal effects but is expressed in relative terms (with respect to average predicted values of our dependent variables). The third column presents t-statistics associated with marginal effects. Finally, the following information is reported at the bottom of each specification: (i) use of post-stratification weights, (ii) R-squared, (iii) sample size and (iv) periods involved.

4.2.1. Results for patents

Table 4 shows the estimation results from four specifications.

Models 1A-1B explore the relationship between patents and occupational status within self-employment, whereas models 2A-2B investigate the association between patents and start-up motivation. All models incorporate our measure of R&D effort, our control for sector composition and our control for business cycle. Models 1B and 2B correct for the possible presence of representation issues using post-stratification weights in our measures for occupational status, start-up motivation and sector com- position. Finally, models 1A-1B also include a period dummy given that two different periods, i.e. 2010 and 2015, are involved.

In line with what was predicted by our general hypothesis, our results show how none of our measures for occupational status and start-up motivation seem to be statistically associated with patent registration activities at the country level. We associ- ate this absence of relationship with the existing rather low propensity to patent within the SME and self-employment framework (Blind et al. 2006; Leiponen and Byma 2007;

Table 4. Results for patents – *linear regression models (OLS)*.

# Model	1A			1B			2B			2C		
Average predicted patents per constant 2010 US$ billion GDP (y)	9.14			9.11			10.04			10.03		
Independent variables (x)	$\frac{dy}{dx}$	$\frac{dy/dx}{y}\%$	t-statistic	$\frac{dy}{dx}$	$\frac{dy/dx}{y}\%$	t-statistic	$\frac{dy}{dx}$	$\frac{dy/dx}{y}\%$	t-statistic	$\frac{dy}{dx}$	$\frac{dy/dx}{y}\%$	t-statistic
Focal variables												
Occupational status within self-employment												
1 Share of self-employed with employees (13.1–62.4)	0.076	0.83	1.64	0.047	0.52	1.05	0.052	0.52	1.16	0.053	0.53	1.17
2 Share of independent own-account self-employed workers (30.1–62.7)	0.015	0.17	0.39	0.020	0.21	0.45	0.141	1.41	1.06	0.148	1.47	1.04
3 Share of dependent self-employed workers (ref.) (0.5–34.9)												
Start-up motivation												
1 Share of opportunity entrepreneurs (28.1–87.6)												
2 Share of hybrid opportunity-necessity entrepreneurs (5.9–30.3)												
3 Share of necessity entrepreneurs (ref.) (4.5–54.2)												
4 Share of entrepreneurs for other reasons (0–14.1)							-0.069	-0.69	-0.26	0.044	0.44	0.18
R&D effort												
GERD PPS per inhabitant at constant 2005 prices (40.0–1,089.7)	0.021	0.22	7.16 ***	0.021	0.23	7.60 ***	0.024	0.24	6.64 ***	0.023	0.23	7.02 ***
Control variables												
Sector composition												
Share of high-tech industry and knowledge-intensive services (2.3–11.7)	-0.293	-3.21	-1.08	-0.195	-2.14	-0.83	-0.621	-6.18	-1.31	-0.601	-6.00	-1.61
Business cycle												
Unemployment rate (3.0–33.8)	-0.115	-1.26	-1.15	-0.100	-1.10	-0.92	-0.137	-1.36	-1.11	-0.144	-1.44	-1.14
Period												
2015 [a]	0.968	10.59	1.23	0.958	10.51	1.20						
Post-stratification weights for entrepreneurship variables used	No			Yes			No			Yes		
R-squared	0.90			0.89			0.92			0.92		
# observations	64						33					
Periods	2010, 2015						2015					

[a] Dummy variable. For continuous variables, *dy/dx* captures absolute marginal effects whereas [(dy/dx)/y]% refers to marginal effects, but expressed in relative terms with respect to predicted probabilities. In the context of dummy variables, these reflect the impact for a discrete change of the dummy variable from 0 to 1; * $0.1 > p \geq 0.05$; ** $0.05 > p \geq 0.01$; *** $p < 0.01$; For models 1A-1B, the maximum correlation is −0.495 (between GERD and Unemployment rate), and the VIFs values (from model 1B) range from 1.07 to 1.49. For models 2A-2B, the maximum correlation is −0.564 (between Share of opportunity entrepreneurs and Unemployment rate), and the VIFs values (from model 2B) range from 1.32 to 1.78. Thus, multicollinearity does not pose a concern.

Data source: WIPO IP Statistics Database, Eurostat, World Bank national accounts data, OECD National Accounts data files, and EWCS 2010, 2015.

Table 5. Results for trademarks – *linear regression models (OLS).*

# Model	3A			3B			4A			4B		
Average predicted trademarks per constant 2010 US\$ billion GDP (y)	201.4			200.4			221.8			221.8		
Independent variables (x)	$\frac{dy}{dx}$	$\frac{dy/dx}{y}\%$	t-statistic	$\frac{dy}{dx}$	$\frac{dy/dx}{y}\%$	t-statistic	$\frac{dy}{dx}$	$\frac{dy/dx}{y}\%$	t-statistic	$\frac{dy}{dx}$	$\frac{dy/dx}{y}\%$	t-statistic
Focal variables												
Occupational status within self-employment												
1 Share of self-employed with employees (13.1–62.4)	5.79	2.87	3.08 ***	5.23	2.61	3.84 ***	6.07	2.74	2.58 ***	6.40	2.89	2.63 ***
2 Share of independent own-account self-employed workers (30.1–62.7)	3.01	1.50	2.25 **	3.93	1.96	2.23 **	0.49	0.22	0.12	3.16	1.42	0.84
3 Share of dependent self-employed workers (ref.) (0.5–34.9)												
Start-up motivation												
1 Share of opportunity entrepreneurs (28.1–87.6)							11.82	5.33	1.39	11.59	5.23	1.36
2 Share of hybrid opportunity-necessity entrepreneurs (5.9–30.3)												
3 Share of necessity entrepreneurs (ref.) (4.5–54.2)												
4 Share of entrepreneurs for other reasons (0–14.1)												
R&D effort												
GERD PPS per inhabitant at constant 2005 prices (40.0–1,089.7)	−0.11	−0.06	−0.76	−0.10	−0.05	−0.72	−0.32	−0.14	−1.36	−0.29	−0.13	−1.41
Control variables												
Sector composition												
Share of high-tech industry and knowledge-intensive services (2.3–11.7)	−9.43	−4.68	−0.62	−13.80	−6.89	−1.01	5.99	2.70	0.22	−4.62	−2.08	−0.25
Business cycle												
Unemployment rate (3.0–33.8)	−10.01	−4.97	−1.85 *	−10.59	−5.29	−1.82 *	−8.34	−3.76	−1.45	−8.87	−4.00	−1.35
Period												
2015 [a]	73.94	36.71	1.62	73.16	36.50	1.55						
Post-stratification weights for entrepreneurship variables used	No			Yes			No			Yes		
R-squared	0.64			0.63			0.63			0.62		
# observations	64						33					
Periods	2010, 2015						2015					

[a] Dummy variable. For continuous variables, dy/dx captures absolute marginal effects whereas [(dy/dx)/y]% refers to marginal effects, but expressed in relative terms with respect to predicted probabilities. In the context of dummy variables, these reflect the impact for a discrete change of the dummy variable from 0 to 1; * 0.1 > p ≥ 0.05; ** 0.05 > p ≥ 0.01; *** p < 0.01; For models 3A-3B, the maximum correlation is −0.495 (between GERD and Unemployment rate), and the VIFs values (from model 3B) range from 1.07 to 1.49. For models 4A-4B, the maximum correlation is −0.564 (between Share of opportunity entrepreneurs and Unemployment rate), and the VIFs values (from model 4B) range from 1.32 to 1.78. Thus, multicollinearity does not pose a concern.

Data source: WIPO IP Statistics Database, Eurostat, World Bank national accounts data, OECD National Accounts data files, and EWCS 2010, 2015.

Thomä and Bizer 2013; Flikkema, De Man, and Castaldi 2014), discussed above in our background section. As an illustration, only 7% of the total self-employed in our sample have 10 or more employees and only 2% have 50 or more employees. Hence, these self-employed are hardly engaged in patent-related activities and, as a result, patents do not seem to be revealed as a convenient measure of innovation for self-employed workers (as happens for SMEs; Kleinknecht 2000).

In contrast, our results consistently show a robust association at the country level between expenditures on R&D and patent registration, as predicted in the preceding sections. In particular, average predicted patents per constant 2010 US$ billion GDP are observed to increase by 0.21% (model 1B) with each PPS per inhabitant unit of increase in GERD. In light of this relationship, an important association is revealed between patents and (Schumpeterian) R&D-intensive and technology-oriented industrial activities.

Finally, as for our control variables, none of our controls for sector composition, business cycle and period show any statistically significant association with patent registration.

4.2.2. Results for trademarks

Table 5 shows the estimation results from four specifications.

The relationship between trademarks and occupational status within self-employment is investigated in Models 3A-3B, whereas models 4A-4B explore the association between trademarks and start-up motivation.

In line with what was stated by our general hypothesis, our results show how both categories of self-employed workers which better capture Kirznerian entrepreneurs, i.e. self-employed with employees and opportunity entrepreneurs, are positively and statistically associated with trademark registration at the country level. Similarly, independent own-account self-employed workers, which can also capture a certain amount of Kirznerian entrepreneurs, are also found to be positively and statistically associated with trademark registration. Specifically, average predicted trademarks per constant 2010 US$ billion GDP are observed to increase by 2.6% (model 3B), 2% (model 3B) and 2.9% (model 4B) with each unitary increase in the share of self-employed with employees, independent own-account self-employed workers, and opportunity entrepreneurs, respectively.[17]

We associate this result with the better ability of trademark indicators to capture the 'softer' non-technological types of innovation, i.e. service, marketing and organisational innovation, which are more probable within the SME framework and self-employment framework (Flikkema, De Man, and Castaldi 2014), as discussed previously. Therefore, an important association is revealed between trademarks and the relative weight of Kirznerian entrepreneurs in a given economy.

Conversely, we find no relevant association at the country level between expenditures on R&D and trademark registration. This absence of a link between both indicators can be explained by the existing relationship between R&D efforts and technology-oriented

---

[17]The reference categories for occupational status and start-up motivation are, respectively, dependent self-employed workers and necessity entrepreneurs. Therefore, each unitary increase in the share of self-employed with employees and opportunity entrepreneurs lead, respectively, to a unitary decrease in the share of dependent self-employed workers and necessity entrepreneurs.

firms, for which the propensity to register trademarks (patents) is low (high) (Amara, Landry, and Traoré 2008; Block et al. 2015a).

Regarding our control variables, we only find a negative relationship between unemployment rate and trademark registration, i.e. those economies with lower unemployment seem to register trademarks with higher likelihood (models 3A-3B). In contrast, neither our control for sector composition nor our period dummy shows any association with trademark registration.

4.2.3. Robustness checks

We perform several robustness checks. *First*, although we present only a few models in Tables 4 and 5, a complete stepwise regression approach (in which models incorporate covariates one by one) was followed, which serves as a robustness check for the results obtained in previous models. *Second*, as noted in subsection 4.2, we adjusted the standard errors for intra-countries correlation by clustering in those models where more than one EWCS wave was involved (models 1A-1B and 3A-3B). These approaches indicate no major changes relative to simple pooled regressions. *Third*, the robustness of our t-statistics was verified by re-estimating them from variance–covariance matrices of the coefficients obtained by bootstrapping. *Fourth*, the results are not sensitive to the use of dependent variables adjusted by population (instead, GDP). *Fifth*, the results are also robust to the use of two alternative proxies for Kirznerian entrepreneurs, i.e. self-employed with employees and opportunity entrepreneurs. *Sixth*, our results remain stable when using measures for occupational status and start-up motivation which are corrected for representation issues using post-stratification weights (models B). *Seventh*, the results are also not sensitive to the use of GERD adjusted for GDP (instead, population and PPP) and a more restrictive definition of high-tech manufacturing industries.[18] *Finally*, the results are also robust to the restriction of our geographical framework to the EU-28 area. All results regarding these robustness checks are available upon request.

5. Conclusions

This work assesses the appropriateness of trademark data as a source of qualitative information on the self-employed workforce within a particular country or region. More specifically, this paper investigates the possible existence of an association between trademark data and relative weight of Kirznerian entrepreneurial activities over total self-employment in a given economy. To this end, we use country-level information for 33 European countries during the periods of 2010 and 2015. Our empirical results suggest that trademarks present a stronger association with Kirznerian entrepreneurs' activity in a given economy than patents.

This evidence has important implications for scholars, practitioners and policy-makers. From an academic perspective, this paper lies at the intersection of

---

[18]This more restrictive definition excludes those industries classified by 'Eurostat high-tech statistics' as only medium-high (and not strictly high) technology manufacturing industries. We refer here to the following NACE rev. 2 codes: 20 = Manufacture of chemicals and chemical products; 27 = Manufacture of electrical equipment; 28 = Manufacture of machinery and equipment not elsewhere classified; 29 = Manufacture of motor vehicles, trailers and semi-trailers; and 30 = Manufacture of other transport equipment.

entrepreneurship, innovation and industrial organisation. For entrepreneurship literature, our results *first* confirm the need to consider self-employment as a heterogeneous or multifaceted group (Carrasco 1999; Burchell, Deakin, and Honey 1999; Reynolds et al. 2002; Grilo and Thurik 2008; Van der Zwan, Thurik, and Grilo 2010) and, *second*, suggest a strong association between trademark data and the presence of Kirznerian entrepreneurs in a given economy. Finally, from an innovation and industrial organisation perspective, there is an emerging body of literature supporting the links between trademarks and innovation (Mendonça, Pereira, and Godinho 2004; Flikkema, De Man, and Castaldi 2014; Block et al. 2015b), to which the present paper contributes. In this regard, trademarks are revealed as a unique (and still under-exploited) source of information for the analysis of innovation behaviour and industrial dynamics. For practitioners, this study stresses the importance of trademarks for opportunity-driven business development. Finally, from a public policy perspective, our results underline the risk of using a unique recipe when defining instruments for self-employment promotion. By ignoring the existing heterogeneity, prescriptions might be beneficial for certain forms of self-employment and harmless – or even harmful – for other types.

Our paper has some limitations, the more serious one being, perhaps, data availability and, in particular, our rather low number of observations. In addition, this work is exploratory in scope and, hence, its results can only be presented in an associative manner. Therefore, it remains unclear what the exact mechanisms behind our findings are. Undoubtedly, for finer-grained evidence and a better-tailored policy approach, better data availability is simply essential. In this sense, there are reasons to be optimistic, as the production and availability of reliable and internationally comparable statistics able to capture the existing heterogeneity within self-employment are expected to grow in the short term. Thus, the European Union Labour Force Survey *ad hoc* module 2017 (EU-LFS AHM 2017) on self-employment, which is expected to be ready for scientific purposes in 2019, incorporates particular sub-modules specifically designed to identify dependent self-employed workers (sub-module 1) and opportunity vs. necessity entrepreneurs (sub-module 2). Moreover, the former sub-module is planned to be permanently incorporated into the survey from 2019 onwards, which means a forthcoming availability of information extracted from some 1.8 million interviews throughout participating countries[19] each quarter. Future research will benefit from these new data.

Acknowledgments

The authors would like to thank the guest editor, Jörn Block, and two anonymous reviewers for their insightful comments that contributed substantially to the development of this paper. This paper is part of Serhiy Lyalkov's doctoral dissertation, which has been written under the framework of the *PhD Program in Economics, Business, Finance and Computer Science* at the University of Huelva and the International University of Andalusia, Spain.

Disclosure statement

No potential conflict of interest was reported by the authors.

---

[19]The EU-28, two candidate countries (the Former Yugoslav Republic of Macedonia and Turkey) and three EFTA countries (Iceland, Norway and Switzerland).

Funding

This work was supported by the Spanish Ministry of Economy and Competitiveness (Ministerio de Economía y Competitividad) under Grants number ECO2017-86305-C4-2-R and ECO2017-86402-C2-2-R; Regional Government of Andalusia (Junta de Andalucía) through Research Group SEJ-487 (Spanish Entrepreneurship Research Group – SERG); and University of Huelva through Research and Transfer Policy Strategy (Estrategia de Política de Investigación y Transferencia) 2018.

ORCID

Serhiy Lyalkov (iD) http://orcid.org/0000-0003-2570-0217
Mónica Carmona (iD) http://orcid.org/0000-0002-9790-3323
Emilio Congregado (iD) http://orcid.org/0000-0001-7409-0799
Ana Millán (iD) http://orcid.org/0000-0001-8195-1729
José María Millán (iD) http://orcid.org/0000-0002-5884-8106

References

Acs, Z. J., P. Braunerhjelm, D. B. Audretsch, and B. Carlsson. 2009. "The Knowledge Spillover Theory of Entrepreneurship." *Small Business Economics* 32 (1): 15–30. doi:10.1007/s11187-008-9157-3.

Acs, Z. J., and M. Sanders. 2012. "Patents, Knowledge Spillovers, and Entrepreneurship." *Small Business Economics* 39 (4): 801–817. doi:10.1007/s11187-011-9322-y.

Alba-Ramirez, A. 1994. "Self-Employment in the Midst of Unemployment: The Case of Spain and the United States." *Applied Economics* 26 (3): 189–204. doi:10.1080/00036849400000001.

Allred, B., and W. Park. 2007. "The Influence of Patent Protection on Firm Innovation Investment in Manufacturing Industries." *Journal of International Management* 13 (2): 91–109. doi:10.1016/j.intman.2007.02.001.

Amara, N., R. Landry, and N. Traoré. 2008. "Managing the Protection of Innovations in Knowledge-Intensive Business Services." *Research Policy* 37 (9): 1530–1547. doi:10.1016/j.respol.2008.07.001.

Aparicio, S., D. Urbano, and D. B. Audretsch. 2016. "Institutional Factors, Opportunity Entrepreneurship and Economic Growth: Panel Data Evidence." *Technological Forecasting and Social Change* 102: 45–61. doi:10.1016/j.techfore.2015.04.006.

Audretsch, D. B., W. Bönte, and P. Mahagaonkar. 2012. "Financial Signaling by Innovative Nascent Ventures: The Relevance of Patents and Prototypes." *Research Policy* 41 (8): 1407–1421. doi:10.1016/j.respol.2012.02.003.

Audretsch, D. B., and M. P. Feldman. 1996. "R&D Spillovers and the Geography of Innovation and Production." *American Economic Review* 86 (3): 630–640.

Baroncelli, E., C. Fink, and B. S. Javorcik. 2005. "The Global Distribution of Trademarks: Some Stylized Facts." *The World Economy* 28 (6): 765–782.

Baroncelli, E., E. Krivonos, and M. Olarreaga. 2007. "Trademark Protection or Protectionism?." *Review of International Economics* 15 (1): 126–145. doi:10.1111/roie.2007.15.issue-1.

Blind, K., E. Edler, R. Frietsch, and U. Schmoch. 2006. "Motives to Patent." *Research Policy* 35 (5): 655–672. doi:10.1016/j.respol.2006.03.002.

Block, J. H., G. De Vries, J. H. Schumann, and P. G. Sandner. 2014. "Trademarks and Venture Capital Valuation." *Journal of Business Venturing* 29 (4): 525–542. doi:10.1016/j.jbusvent.2013.07.006.

Block, J. H., C. O. Fisch, A. Hahn, and P. G. Sandner. 2015a. "Why Do SMEs File Trademarks? Insights from Firms in Innovative Industries." *Research Policy* 44 (10): 1915–1930.

Block, J. H., K. Kohn, D. Miller, and K. Ullrich. 2015b. "Necessity Entrepreneurship and Competitive Strategy." *Small Business Economics* 44 (1): 37–54. doi:10.1007/s11187-014-9589-x.

Brahem, M., S. El Harbi, and G. Grolleau. 2013. "What Drives Trademarks Registration among Tunisian Clothing Firms? an Econometric Investigation." *International Journal of Intellectual Property Management* 6 (1–2): 1–14. doi:10.1504/IJIPM.2013.053447.

Branstetter, L., R. Fishman, and F. Foley. 2006. "Do Stronger Intellectual Property Rights Increase International Technology Transfer? Empirical Evidence from US Firm-Level Panel Data." *The Quarterly Journal of Economics* 121 (1): 321–349. doi:10.1093/qje/121.1.321.

Burchell, B., S. Deakin, and S. Honey. 1999. "The Employment Status of Individuals in Non-Standard Employment." Employment Relations Research Series No. 6. London: Department of Trade and Industry.

Burke, A., and S. Fraser. 2012. "Self-Employment: The Role of Intellectual Property Right Laws." *Small Business Economics* 39 (4): 819–833. doi:10.1007/s11187-011-9336-5.

Carrasco, R. 1999. "Transitions to and from Self-Employment in Spain: An Empirical Analysis." *Oxford Bulletin of Economics and Statistics* 61 (3): 315–341. doi:10.1111/obes.1999.61.issue-3.

Cassiman, B., and R. Veugelers. 2006. "In Search of Complementarity in Innovation Strategy: Internal R&D and External Knowledge Acquisition." *Management Science* 52 (1): 68–82. doi:10.1287/mnsc.1050.0470.

Corrado, C., C. Hulten, and D. Sichel. 2005. "Measuring Capital and Technology: An Expanded Framework." *Measuring Capital in the New Economy.* edited by C. Corrado, J. Haltiwanger, and D. Sichel, 11–46. Chicago, IL: University of Chicago Press. https://www.nber.org/chapters/c0202.pdf

Dahlqvist, J., and J. Wiklund. 2012. "Measuring the Market Newness of New Ventures." *Journal of Business Venturing* 27 (2): 185–196. doi:10.1016/j.jbusvent.2010.12.001.

De Rassenfosse, G. 2016. "An Assessment of How Well We Account for Intangibles." *Industrial and Corporate Change* 26 (3): 517–534. doi:10.1093/icc/dtw034.

De Vries, G., E. Pennings, J. H. Block, and C. O. Fisch. 2017. "Trademark or Patent? the Effects of Market Concentration, Customer Type and Venture Capital Financing on Start-Ups' Initial IP Applications." *Industry and Innovation* 24 (4): 325–345. doi:10.1080/13662716.2016.1231607.

Earle, J. S., and Z. Sakova. 2000. "Business Start-Ups or Disguised Unemployment? Evidence on the Character of Self-Employment from Transition Economies." *Labour Economics* 7 (5): 575–601. doi:10.1016/S0927-5371(00)00014-2.

Eichhorst, W., M. Braga, U. Mühlberger, M. Gerard, T. Horvath, M. Kahanec, M. Kahancová, et al. 2013. "Social Protection Rights of Economically Dependent Self-Employed Workers." Policy Department A - Economic and Scientific Policy, European Parliament, Brussels: European Parliament. http://www.europarl.europa.eu/RegData/etudes/etudes/join/2013/507449/IPOL-EMPL_ET%282013%29507449_EN.pdf

Eurofound. 2012. *Fifth European Working Conditions Survey – Overview Report.* Luxembourg: Publications Office of the European Union. https://www.eurofound.europa.eu/sites/default/files/ef_publication/field_ef_document/ef1182en.pdf

Eurofound. 2016. *Sixth European Working Conditions Survey – Overview Report.* Luxembourg: Publications Office of the European Union. https://www.eurofound.europa.eu/sites/default/files/ef_publication/field_ef_document/ef1634en.pdf

Eurofound. 2018. "European Working Conditions Survey Integrated Data File, 1991–2015. [Data Collection]." 6th Edition. UK Data Service. SN: 7363, doi: 10.5255/UKDA-SN-7363-6.

Farre-Mensa, J., D. Hegde, and A. Ljungqvist. 2017. "What Is a Patent Worth? Evidence from the US Patent 'Lottery'." NBER Working Paper Series No. 23268. Cambridge, MA: National Bureau of Economic Research. doi: 10.3386/w23268.

Ferreira, J. J., A. Fayolle, C. Fernandes, and C. Raposo. 2017. "Effects of Schumpeterian and Kirznerian Entrepreneurship on Economic Growth: Panel Data Evidence." *Entrepreneurship & Regional Development* 29 (1–2): 27–50. doi:10.1080/08985626.2016.1255431.

Fink, C., B. S. Javorcik, and M. Spatareanu. 2005. "Income-Related Biases in International Trade: What Do Trademark Registration Data Tell Us?" *Review of World Economics* 14 (1): 79–103. doi:10.1007/s10290-005-0016-x.

Flikkema, M., A.-P. De Man, and C. Castaldi. 2014. "Are Trademark Counts a Valid Indicator of Innovation? Results of an In-Depth Study of New Benelux Trademarks Filed by SMEs." *Industry and Innovation* 21 (4): 310–331. doi:10.1080/13662716.2014.934547.

Greenhalgh, C., and M. Rogers. 2012. "Trade Marks and Performance in Services and Manufacturing Firms: Evidence of Schumpeterian Competition through Innovation." *Australian Economic Review* 45 (1): 50–76. doi:10.1111/j.1467-8462.2011.00665.x.

Grilo, I., and R. Thurik. 2008. "Determinants of Entrepreneurial Engagement Levels in Europe and the US." *Industrial and Corporate Change* 17 (6): 1113–1145. doi:10.1093/icc/dtn044.

Haeussler, C., D. Harhoff, and E. Mueller. 2014. "How Patenting Informs VC Investors: The Case of Biotechnology." *Research Policy* 43 (8): 1286–1298. doi:10.1016/j.respol.2014.03.012.

Helmers, C., and M. Rogers. 2010. "Innovation and the Survival of New Firms in the UK." *Review of Industrial Organization* 36 (3): 227–248. doi:10.1007/s11151-010-9247-7.

Herz, B., and M. Mejer. 2016. "On the Fee Elasticity of the Demand for Trademarks in Europe." *Oxford Economic Papers* 68 (4): 1039–1061. doi:10.1093/oep/gpw035.

Hsu, D. H., and R. H. Ziedonis. 2013. "Resources as Dual Sources of Advantage: Implications for Valuing Entrepreneurial-Firm Patents." *Strategic Management Journal* 34: 761–781. doi:10.1002/smj.2013.34.issue-7.

Hyytinen, A., and P. Rouvinen. 2008. "The Labour Market Consequences of Self-Employment Spells: European Evidence." *Labour Economics* 15 (2): 246–271. doi:10.1016/j.labeco.2007.02.001.

ILO. 2003. "The Scope of the Employment Relationship. Report V." Paper presented at the International Labour Conference, 91st Session, Geneva. http://www.ilo.org/public/english/standards/relm/ilc/ilc91/pdf/rep-v.pdf

Jaffe, A. B. 1986. "Technological Opportunity and Spillovers of R&D: Evidence from Firms' Patents, Profits and Market Value." *American Economic Review* 76 (5): 984–999.

Kanwar, S. 2006. "Innovation and Intellectual Property Rights." Centre for Development Economics Working Paper. No. 142. Department of Economics, Delhi School of Economics. http://cdedse.org/pdf/work142.pdf

Kirzner, I. M. 1973. *Competition and Entrepreneurship.* Chicago, IL: University of Chicago Press.

Kirzner, I. M. 2009. "The Alert and Creative Entrepreneur: A Clarification." *Small Business Economics* 32 (2): 145–152. doi:10.1007/s11187-008-9153-7.

Kleinknecht, A. H. 2000. "Indicators of Manufacturing and Service Innovation: Their Strengths and Weaknesses." In *Innovation Systems in the Service Economy. Measurement and Case Study Analysis,* edited by J. Stanley Metcalfe and I. Miles, 169–186. Dordrecht: Kluwer Academic Publishers.

Krasnikov, A., S. Mishra, and D. Orozco. 2009. "Evaluating the Financial Impact of Branding Using Trademarks: A Framework and Empirical Evidence." *Journal of Marketing* 73 (6): 154–166. doi:10.1509/jmkg.73.6.154.

Kuhn, P. 2000. "Editor's Note." *Labour Economics* 7 (5): 463–469. doi:10.1016/S0927-5371(00)00010-5.

Leiponen, A., and J. Byma. 2007. "If You Cannot Block, You Better Run: Small Firms, Cooperative Innovation and Appropriation Strategies." *Research Policy* 38 (9): 1478–1488. doi:10.1016/j.respol.2009.06.003.

Linder, S. B. 1961. *An Essay on Trade and Transformation.* Uppsala: Almqvist & Wiksell. Accessed February 3 2019. https://ex.hhs.se/dissertations/221624-FULLTEXT01.pdf

Llerena, P., and V. Millot. 2013. "Are Trade Marks and Patents Complementary or Substitute Protections for Innovation." Bureau d'économie théorique et appliquée (BETA). Document de Travail n 2013 - 01. Strasbourg: Université de Strasbourg. http://www.beta-umr7522.fr/productions/publications/2013/2013-01.pdf

Malmberg, C. 2005. "Trademark Statistics as Innovation Indicators? A Micro Study." CIRCLE Electronic Working Paper Series 2005/17. CIRCLE - Center for Innovation, Research and

Competences in the Learning Economy, Lund University. http://portal.research.lu.se/portal/files/4643553/4407256.pdf

Mangani, A. 2007. "Measuring Variety and Quality of Products with Trademarks." *International Economic Journal* 21 (4): 613–631.

Mendonça, S. 2012. "Trademarks as a Telecommunications Indicator for Industrial Analysis and Policy." In *Telecommunication Economics*, edited by A. M. Hadjiantonis and B. Stiller, 33–41. Heidelberg: Springer. doi:10.1007/978-3-642-30382-1_6.

Mendonça, S., T. S. Pereira, and M. M. Godinho. 2004. "Trademarks as an Indicator of Innovation and Industrial Change." *Research Policy* 33 (9): 1385–1404. doi:10.1016/j.respol.2004.09.005.

Millán, A., and J. M. Millán. 2017. "Disclosing 'Masked Employees' in Europe: Job Control, Job Demands and Job Outcomes of 'Dependent Self-Employed Workers'". Paper presented at XII Jornadas de Economía Laboral. University of Valladolid, Spain, July 5 –7.

Millán, A., J. M. Millán, and C. Román. 2018. "Are False Own-Account Workers Less Job Satisfied than True Ones?" *Applied Economics Letters* 25 (13): 945–950. doi:10.1080/13504851.2017.1388902.

Millán, J. M., E. Congregado, and C. Román. 2014a. "Persistence in Entrepreneurship and Its Implications for the European Entrepreneurial Promotion Policy." *Journal of Policy Modeling* 36 (1): 83–106. doi:10.1016/j.jpolmod.2013.10.001.

Millán, J. M., E. Congregado, and C. Román. 2014b. "Entrepreneurship Persistence with and without Personnel: The Role of Human Capital and Previous Unemployment." *International Entrepreneurship and Management Journal* 10 (1): 187–206. doi:10.1007/s11365-011-0184-1.

Muehlberger, U., and S. Bertolini. 2008. "The Organizational Governance of Work Relationships between Employment and Self-Employment." *Socio-Economic Review* 6 (3): 449–472. doi:10.1093/ser/mwm026.

OECD. 2014. *The Employment Outlook", Chapter 4.* Paris: OECD. doi:10.1787/empl_outlook-2014-en.

OECD. 2019a. "OECD Structural and Demographic Business Statistics (Database)." https://doi.org/10.1787/sdbs-data-en

OECD. 2019b. "Self-Employment Rate (Indicator)." https://doi.org/10.1787/fb58715e-en

Parchomovsky, G., and P. Siegelman. 2002. "Towards an Integrated Theory of Intellectual Property." *Virginia Law Review* 88 (7): 1455–1528. doi:10.2307/1073990.

Parker, S. C. 2018. "*The Economics of Entrepreneurship*". Cambridge University Press. https://doi.org/10.1017/9781316756706

Reynolds, P., S. M. Camp, W. D. Bygrave, E. Autio, and M. Hay. 2002. *Global Entrepreneurship Monitor 2001 Executive Report.* Babson Park/London: Babson College and London Business School. http://unpan1.un.org/intradoc/groups/public/documents/un/unpan002481.pdf

Román, C., E. Congregado, and J. M. Millán. 2011. "Dependent Self-Employment as a Way to Evade Employment Protection Legislation." *Small Business Economics* 37 (3): 363–392. doi:10.1007/s11187-009-9241-3.

Román, C., E. Congregado, and J. M. Millán. 2013. "Start-Up Incentives: Entrepreneurship Policy or Active Labour Market Programme?" *Journal of Business Venturing* 28 (1): 151–175. doi:10.1016/j.jbusvent.2012.01.004.

Sandner, P. G., and J. H. Block. 2011. "The Market Value of R&D, Patents and Trademarks." *Research Policy* 40 (7): 969–985.

Schautschick, P., and C. Greenhalgh. 2016. "Empirical Studies of Trade Marks – The Existing Economic Literature." *Economics of Innovation and New Technology* 25 (4): 358–390. doi:10.1080/10438599.2015.1064598.

Schumpeter, J. A. 1912. "*Theorie der Wirtschaftlichen Entwicklung* [The Theory of Economic Development]." Leipzig: Dunker & Humblot. Translated by Dedvers Opie. Cambridge, MA: Harvard University Press, 1934.

Schumpeter, J. A. 1942. *Capitalism, Socialism and Democracy.* New York: Harper & Row.

Shane, S. 2009. "Why Encouraging More People to Become Entrepreneurs Is Bad Public Policy." *Small Business Economics* 33 (2): 141–149. doi:10.1007/s11187-009-9215-5.

Srinivasan, R., G. L. Lilien, and A. Rangaswamy. 2008. "Survival of High Tech Firms: The Effects of Diversity of Product–Market Portfolios, Patents, and Trademarks." *International Journal of Research in Marketing* 25 (2): 119–128. doi:10.1016/j.ijresmar.2007.12.005.

Stewart, A., and J. Stanford. 2017. "Regulating Work in the Gig Economy: What are the Options?" *The Economic and Labour Relations Review* 28 (3): 420–437. doi:10.1177/1035304617722461.

Sundqvist, S. K., K. Kylheiko, O. Kuivalainen, and J. W. Cadogan. 2012. "Kirznerian and Schumpeterian Entrepreneurial-Oriented Behavior in Turbulent Export Markets." *International Marketing Review* 29 (2): 203–219.

Supiot, A. 2001. *Beyond Employment. Changes in Work and the Future of Labour Law in Europe.* Oxford: Oxford University Press.

Thomä, J., and K. Bizer. 2013. "To Protect or Not to Protect? Modes of Appropriability in the Small Enterprises Sector." *Research Policy* 42 (1): 35–49.

Thumm, N. 2004. "Strategic Patenting in Biotechnology." *Technology Analysis & Strategic Management* 16 (4): 529–538. doi:10.1080/0953732042000295829.

Van der Zwan, P., R. Thurik, and I. Grilo. 2010. "The Entrepreneurial Ladder and Its Determinants." *Applied Economics* 42 (17): 2183–2191. doi:10.1080/00036840701765437.

Van Stel, A., J. M. Millán, and C. Román. 2014. "Investigating the Impact of the Technological Environment on Survival Chances of Employer Entrepreneurs." *Small Business Economics* 43 (4): 839–855. doi:10.1007/s11187-014-9565-5.

Varsakelis, N. 2001. "The Impact of Patent Protection, Economy Openness and National Culture on R&D Investment: A Cross-Country Empirical Investigation." *Research Policy* 30 (7): 1059–1068. doi:10.1016/S0048-7333(00)00130-X.

Von Mises, L. 1952. "Profit and Loss." In *Planning for Freedom and Other Essays and Addresses* 3rd ed., edited by L. von Mises, 108–149. South Holland: Libertarian Press.

Wennekers, S., A. van Stel, M. Carree, and R. Thurik. 2010. "The Relationship between Entrepreneurship and Economic Development: Is It U-Shaped?" *Foundations and Trends in Entrepreneurship* 6 (3): 167–237. doi:10.1561/0300000023.

WIPO. 2017. *World Intellectual Property Indicators 2017.* Geneva: World Intellectual Property Organization. http://www.wipo.int/edocs/pubdocs/en/wipo_pub_941_2017.pdf

Appendix: Variable definitions

Table A1. Country-level variables.

Variable	Description
Dependent variables	
Trademarks per constant 2010 US$ billion GDP	Registered trademarks per constant 2010 US$ billion GDP. Data correspond to total trademark registrations, direct and via the *Madrid system*, expressed in equivalent class counts. This variable is generated for the periods 2010 and 2015 (*Data sources:* WIPO IP Statistics Database & World Bank national accounts data, and OECD National Accounts data files).
Patents per constant 2010 US$ billion GDP	Patent grants per constant 2010 US$ billion GDP. Data correspond to total patent grants registrations, direct and *Patent Cooperation Treaty* national phase entries, expressed in equivalent class counts. This variable is generated for the periods 2010 and 2015 (*Data sources:* WIPO IP Statistics Database & World Bank national accounts data, and OECD National Accounts data files).
Focal variables	
Occupational status within self-employment [a]	
1 Share of self-employed with employees	% of self-employed workforce who declare being self-employed with employees. This variable is generated for the years 2010 and 2015 (*Data source:* EWCS).
2 Share of independent own-account self-employed workers	% of self-employed workforce who declare being self-employed without employees and answer positively to the question on whether he/she generally has more than one client or customer. This variable is generated for the years 2010 and 2015 (*Data source:* EWCS).
3 Share of dependent self-employed workers	% of self-employed workforce who declare being self-employed without employees and answer negatively to the question on whether he/she generally has more than one client or customer. This variable is generated for the years 2010 and 2015 (*Data source:* EWCS).
Start-up motivation [a]	
1 Share of opportunity entrepreneurs	% of self-employed workforce who declare having become self-employed mainly through own personal preferences. This variable is generated for the year 2015 (*Data source:* EWCS).
2 Share of hybrid opportunity-necessity entrepreneurs	% of self-employed workforce who declare having become self-employed due to a combination of both reasons: own personal preferences and no other alternatives for work. This variable is generated for the year 2015 (*Data source:* EWCS).
3 Share of necessity entrepreneurs	% of self-employed workforce who declare having become self-employed because had no other alternatives for work. This variable is generated for the year 2015 (*Data source:* EWCS).
4 Share of entrepreneurs for other reasons	% of self-employed workforce who declare having become self-employed due to neither of these previous reasons. This variable is generated for the year 2015 (*Data source:* EWCS).
R&D effort	
GERD PPS per inhabitant at constant 2005 prices	5 years average Gross Domestic Expenditure on R&D expressed as Purchasing Power Standards – PPS – per inhabitant at constant 2005 prices. This variable includes expenditure on research and development by business enterprises, higher education institutions, as well as government and private non-profit organisations. This variable is generated for the periods 2006–10 and 2011–15 (*Data source:* Eurostat).
Control variables	
Sector composition [a]	

(*Continued*)

Table A1. (Continued).

Variable	Description
Share of high-tech industry and knowledge-intensive services [a]	% of self-employed workforce who declare working in high-technology industry and knowledge-intensive services, as defined by Eurostat aggregations based on 'Statistics on high-tech industry and knowledge-intensive services'. It includes all workers whose codes of main activity of the local unit of the business, by means of the Nomenclature of Economic Activities (NACE rev. 2, 2008) at 2-digit level, are 20 = Manufacture of chemicals and chemical products; 21 = Manufacture of basic pharmaceutical products and pharmaceutical preparations; 26 = Manufacture of computer, electronic and optical products; 27 = Manufacture of electrical equipment; 28 = Manufacture of machinery and equipment not elsewhere classified; 29 = Manufacture of motor vehicles, trailers and semi-trailers; 30 = Manufacture of other transport equipment; 59 = Motion picture, video and television programme production, sound recording and music publishing activities; 60 = Programming and broadcasting activities; 61 = Telecommunications; 62 = Computer programming, consultancy and related activities; 63 = Information service activities; and 72 = Scientific research and development (*Data source:* EWCS).
Business cycle	
Unemployment rate	5 years average unemployment rates. This variable is generated for the periods 2006–10 and 2011–15 (*Data sources:* Eurostat, ILO).
Period	
2015	Dummy equals 1 for observations corresponding to the period 2015 and 0 for observations corresponding to the period 2010 (*Data source:* EWCS).

[a] Two variants of these variables are used in our regressions: (i) uncorrected for the possible presence of over or under-representation of certain groups, and (ii) corrected for the possible presence of representation issues using post-stratification weights.

Table A2. Individual-level variables.

Variable	Description
Occupational status within self-employment	
1 Self-employed with employees	Dummy equals 1 for workers who declare being self-employed with employees.
2 Independent own-account self-employed worker	Dummy equals 1 for individuals who declare being self-employed without employees and answer positively to the question on whether he/she generally has more than one client or customer.
3 Dependent self-employed worker	Dummy equals 1 for individuals who declare being self-employed without employees and answer negatively to the question on whether he/she generally has more than one client or customer.
Start-up motivation	
1 Opportunity entrepreneur	Dummy equals 1 for workers who declare having become self-employed mainly through own personal preferences. This variable is only available for wave 2015.
2 Hybrid opportunity-necessity entrepreneur	Dummy equals 1 for workers who declare having become self-employed due to a combination of both reasons: own personal preferences and no other alternatives for work. This variable is only available for wave 2015.
3 Necessity entrepreneur	Dummy equals 1 for workers who declare having become self-employed because had no other alternatives for work. This variable is only available for wave 2015.
4 Entrepreneur for other reasons	Dummy equals 1 for workers who declare having become self-employed due to neither of these reasons. This variable is only available for wave 2015.
Educational attainment	
Basic education	Dummy equals 1 for workers with less than lower secondary education (ISCED-1997, 0–1).
Secondary education	Dummy equals 1 for workers with, at least, lower secondary education but non-tertiary education (ISCED-1997, 2–4).
Tertiary education	Dummy equals 1 for workers with tertiary education (ISCED-1997, 5–6).
Job characteristics	
Years of tenure in present job	Number of years of experience in the company or organisation.
Working hours	Working hours per week.
Net monthly earnings – PPP $ of 2015	Average net earnings in recent months. The variable is defined in PPP $ of 2015.
Sector composition	
High-tech industry and knowledge-intensive services	Dummy equals 1 for individuals who declare working in high-technology industry and knowledge-intensive services, as defined by Eurostat aggregations based on 'Statistics on high-tech industry and knowledge-intensive services'. It includes all workers whose codes of main activity of the local unit of the business, by means of the Nomenclature of Economic Activities (NACE rev. 2, 2008) at 2-digit level, are 20 = Manufacture of chemicals and chemical products; 21 = Manufacture of basic pharmaceutical products and pharmaceutical preparations; 26 = Manufacture of computer, electronic and optical products; 27 = Manufacture of electrical equipment; 28 = Manufacture of machinery and equipment not elsewhere classified; 29 = Manufacture of motor vehicles, trailers and semi-trailers; 30 = Manufacture of other transport equipment; 59 = Motion picture, video and television programme production, sound recording and music publishing activities; 60 = Programming and broadcasting activities; 61 = Telecommunications; 62 = Computer programming, consultancy and related activities; 63 = Information service activities; and 72 = Scientific research and development.
Demographic characteristics	
Female	Dummy equals 1 for females.
Immigrant	Dummy equals 1 for citizens of a different country of that of residence.
Age	Age reported by the worker.
Cohabiting	Dummy equals 1 for individuals cohabiting with spouse/partner.
Children under 14	Dummy equals 1 for individuals cohabiting with any son or daughter aged under 14.
Health	Variable ranging from 1 to 5. The scale refers to the level of health declared by the worker. It equals 1 for individuals whose health is very bad and 5 for individuals whose health is very good.
Ends meet	Variable ranging from 1 to 6. The scale refers to the household ability to make ends meet. It equals 1 for households which make ends meet very easily and 6 for households which make ends meet with great difficulty.

Data source: EWCS.

Overlap in external technology search locations and the breadth of IPR assets: lessons from the Security Software Industry

Szabolcs Szilárd Sebrek

ABSTRACT

This study examines the effect of intellectual property rights (IPR) on firms' geographic overlap strategy of external technology search (ETS) compared to rivals. I reveal that firms are able to realise less intensity of geographic overlap in ETS locations compared to competitors and that this outcome is a function of the breadth of their upstream (generality of patents) and downstream (diversification of trademarks) IPR tools. Accordingly, I conclude that both covariates influence the spatial isolation of ETS vis-à-vis competitors. The effect of generality of patents on isolation, however, is more pronounced in comparison with diversification of trademarks at strategic technology alliances, meanwhile the reverse scenario is true at acquisitions. I also reveal relevant findings about resource-rich organisations defined as those with the broadest portfolio of such up- and downstream IPR assets within the industry.

1. Introduction

Past literature on open innovation highlights the imperative role of knowledge and technology seeking for firms (Kim and Kogut 1996; Rosenkopf and Nerkar 2001). Such organisational behaviour that aims to source externally generated knowledge is more pronounced if the focal industry undergoes a rapid technological change (Chung and Alcácer 2002), and if technology development exhibits a clear pattern for complexity due to technological interdependencies (Dodgson 1989). Prior research indicates a strong correspondence between external technology search (ETS) and geography owing to the significant variation in innovative activity that can take place across regions within the same country (Almeida and Kogut 1999; Saxenian 1994), and to the specific factors that can be tapped at distinct locations (Cantwell 1989). Such crucial external factors can even be accessed from resource-poor firms if they are located in resource-rich areas that promote investment in technology innovation (Forman, Goldfarb, and Greenstein 2008).

At the same time, however, there exists another argument that can trigger a geographically isolated realisation of ETS from rival entities. As knowledge spillovers can be captured from geographically proximate competitors (Jaffe, Trajtenberg, and Henderson 1993), a defensive argument concentrates on firms' interest in protecting their own technological knowledge from rivals by a means of locating apart and avoiding geographic clustering (Shaver and Flyer 2000). As a matter of fact, studies recognise that firms can perceive the balance of knowledge in- and outflows (Cassiman and Veugelers 2002), and corresponding to possible knowledge spillover benefits, they can actively shape location strategies to preserve or augment their technical capabilities vis-à-vis rivals in the industry (Alcácer and Chung 2007).

Drawn from prior literature, firms can correspondingly notice the importance of ETS for their competitiveness, the manner by which relevant technology is spatially dispersed, and the limited number of locations where technology is presumably accessible. Furthermore, firms can discern the relevance of self-defence against non-deliberate knowledge outflows during their explorative undertakings. The central topic of this article is to merge geography and active location strategies, which has remained scant until now in the received openness literature. Thus, the first question is: Can we observe the strategic value of location choices in ETS and any corresponding patterns in varying intensity of geographic overlap? This raises the second question: What drives the intensity of geographic overlap in open innovation activities between firms?

In this paper, I explore these issues through distinguishing firms' relative resources in intellectual property rights (IPR) at upstream and downstream levels. Consequently, I resort to patents and trademarks as both are quintessential technological and marketing resources, respectively (Zhou et al. 2016), that can enhance the competitive advantage of the firm due to being nonsubstitutable and costly to imitate (Barney 1991; Castanias and Helfat 1991). Further still, such assets can advantageously influence firms' ability to adapt and to exploit new opportunities (Tripsas 1997; King and Tucci 2002). This standpoint is based on the breadth of these protected assets, captured by the generality of patents and the diversification of trademarks, which influences the firm's competitive position in ETS associated with open innovation compared to its within-industry rivals.

In this context, I formulate the following three research hypotheses: 1. (2.) Firms with more general (diversified) stock of patents (trademarks) are more likely to have less intensity of geographic overlap in external technology search locations compared to rivals; 3. Resource-rich firms that achieve parity and score high either on the generality of patent or on the diversification of trademark, are more likely to have high intensity of geographic overlap in ETS locations with each other, conditioned by multiple contacts in the market niches of the focal industry.

I empirically test these propositions on a unique dataset that is built upon the worldwide Security Software Industry (SSI). The practise of external technology search in SSI is a widespread activity because (i) it is a technology-based industry with enhanced product innovation, (ii) competition is fierce implied by low entry barriers and a high hazard rate of firm exit, (iii) new lucrative product categories proliferate, and (iv) the design of a security software system is a complex undertaking (Giarratana 2004; Giarratana and Fosfuri 2007; Fosfuri, Giarratana, and Sebrek 2018).

Two distinct mechanisms of ETS are examined: acquisitions and strategic technology alliances that correspond to acquiring and sourcing – two crucial inbound processes defined by Dahlander and Gann (2010). To this end, I assembled a comprehensive dataset of three years between 2000 and 2002. As the hypothesised relationships are inherently dyadic, I built up the sample of dyadic pairs of firms for which I incorporated 57 (51) security software firms in the sample on strategic technology alliances (acquisitions) that performed at least two ETS in the study period. I use the quadratic assignment procedure that permits me to analyse the sampled firms' geographic dispersion of ETS in a dyadic fashion. To study the hypothesised links with more precision, following Alcácer (2006) I apply three units of geographical classification: clusters, countries and economic regions.

My empirical results suggest that both IPR-based core covariates – patent generality and trademark diversification – support a lower extent of geographic overlap in external technology search compared to rivals. However, they play different roles depending on the type of the search activity, as trademarks support such an isolation process more than patents at acquisitions, while for patents the reverse case holds regarding strategic technology alliances. Other interesting findings are linked to resource-rich firms whose operationalisation was done separately both for patents and trademarks. The results imply that a high intensity of spatial overlap vis-à-vis similar research-rich competitors is achieved, only if both firms exhibit multimarket contact in the niches of the industry in question. The results associated with strategic technology alliances reveal that the significance of this effect depends on the level of geographic gradation applied.

This work links together several branches in the literature, such as openness of external technology search and the geographic component of firm strategy. I was able to demonstrate the strategic value of location choices where firms' breadth of upstream and downstream intellectual property rights play an indispensable role. An important contribution of the study is that it jointly incorporates technology alliances and acquisitions as key external knowledge and technology channels for organisations. By constructing a detailed dataset on partners' location of SSI incumbents, I assess that the intensity of geographic overlap in external technology search compared to rivals is a direct consequence of resource differentials in the breadth of firms' IPR-related assets. In addition, the study can enhance our understanding of firms' location patterns of ETS by applying a diverse geographical classification. Furthermore, I follow prior research that considers trademarks as important assets for firm strategy (e.g. Block et al. 2015; Fosfuri, Giarratana, and Luzzi 2008; Fosfuri and Giarratana 2009; Mendonça, Santos Pereira, and Godinho 2004). This paper offers a value addition in terms of measurement as it directly captures the diversification dimension of this downstream IPR asset. Finally, this paper joins with the line of academic enquiries (Block et al. 2014; De Vries et al. 2017; Helmers and Rogers 2010; Zhou et al. 2016) that mutually considers patents and trademarks in studying openness.

2. Theoretical background

The ability to compete in high-technology industries depends on the acquisition of competitive knowledge, implying, that a firm has to attain experience with the underlying science and related technological fields (Kim and Kogut 1996). Some of these newly acquired capabilities help the firm to respond rapidly to market changes and allow for expansion during windows of opportunity (Kim and Kogut 1996). Studying patenting activity in optical disc technology, Rosenkopf and Nerkar (2001) show that exploration spanning organisational boundaries consistently generates higher impact on subsequent technological evolution, thereby it can provide for the explorer organisation a competitive advantage within the industry and an option to diversify. Resorting to external exploration is desirable as technological evolution is generated by communities of organisations

(Rosenkopf and Tushman 1998). For instance, the evolution of products with the under-lying components can be viewed as the result of variation, selection and retention processes that take place by a broad community of organisational actors (Rosenkopf and Nerkar 1999). This feature influences a firm's technological trajectory and makes all industrial actors mutually interdependent.

To maintain or enhance competitive edge, firms might be motivated to employ ETS for search of new capabilities, and presumably to recombine those newly acquired or accessed capabilities with existing skills. This motive has been termed technology or knowledge seeking, and such organisational search behaviour can be more prevalent if a firm competes in a technology-intensive industry (Chung and Alcácer 2002). One can expect some firms to value locations' traits that reflect the level of localised technical activity. The uniqueness of a location relies much on location-specific factors that can nurture technologies not available elsewhere (Cantwell 1989). Even a relatively resource-poor firm but one that is situated in a resource abundant location can considerably improve chances to realise investment in innovative processes (Forman, Goldfarb, and Greenstein 2008). Tapping localised technology sources is greatly enhanced by frequent inter-partner inter-action as relevant knowledge can be tacit and the prerequisite of its transfer depends on physical propinquity (Kogut and Zander 1992). This idea that firms seeking new knowledge have to approach the target locations is reaffirmed by Almeida and Kogut (1999). They demonstrate that localised knowledge builds upon cumulative ideas within regional bound-aries, and as knowledge is frequently tacit that knowledge resides with engineers of a particular geographic community. For instance, science parks attract large enterprises that through spatial proximity enable them to satisfy their knowledge needs and to facilitate the transfer of tacit knowledge (le Duc and Lindeque 2018). Cantwell and Janne (1999) bring evidence that firms emanating from leading technical centres are also likely to pursue technological strategies in which they geographically differentiate their innovative activities abroad. In contrast to firms from more laggard technical centres whose primary interest relies on catch-up, they are primarily focused on sourcing more diverse technical knowl-edge. Studying inward FDI into the United States, Chung and Alcácer (2002) make a parallel inference, arguing that knowledge seeking takes place not only among technical laggards, but is also ubiquitous among technically leading firms.

Acknowledging the potential for higher added value and nonredundant knowledge to be captured from geographically distant organisations, a defensive argument puts emphasis on geographically isolating external technology search vis-à-vis competitors. Certain industries are based upon technical competition, which may force all participants to seek spillovers from competitors. The study by Shaver and Flyer (2000) argues that firms with the best technologies have strong motivation to geographically distance themselves, otherwise their technologies with other key resources spill over to competitors which become stronger and eventually endanger the competitive position of the former. Chung and Alcácer (2002) arrive to a similar conclusion in connection with foreign technologically leading flagship firms as they opt to spatially isolate themselves from existing clusters in the United States to prevent outward knowledge spillovers to rivals. Such unwanted outgoing knowledge spillover can occur as the level of knowledge in- and outflows is not exogenous to the firm, but the recipient firm can affect the extent of incoming spillovers through a deliberate innovation strategy (Cassiman and Veugelers 2002). In a related paper, Alcácer and Chung (2007) recognise that firms are active entities in making decisions upon location strategies in terms of net spillover benefits they may obtain, and thus are aware of the possible cost of outward spillovers. Using information on European inventions and data about firms and location, Giarratana and Mariani (2014) show that firms conducting research projects in locations with high levels of absorptive capability in a specific technology risk internal knowledge spillovers.

2.1. IPR assets and geographic overlap in ETS

The management literature on openness emphasises the strategic value of ETS locations choices that serve as key assumptions to the theory laid down. First, firms assign the importance of ETS in high-tech environments. Second, knowledge and technology are not concentrated but geographically dispersed, and there is a limited number of best locations for certain advanced types of knowledge and technology. Last, firms might apply self-defence from unintended knowledge spillover by diverging ETS from rivals. Therefore, ceteris paribus, there must be strong competition for the most attractive locations, implying that some firms should be able to exert an expelling effect or to first break-in into such locations; put differently, these firms should be able to reach a lower extent of geographic overlap through an isolation process in ETS locations *vis-à-vis* rivals. This represents a research gap in the open innovation management literature that I attempt to fill.

In turn, what moves the above process? This paper posits that an organisational strategy to flock with or to enjoy a position of spreading ETS geographically more extensively than within-industry competitors relates closely to firm resources. Namely, upstream and downstream organisational resources in intellectual property rights can potentially act as driving forces for firms to geographically isolate their external technology search networks. To this point, I examine patents and trademarks, the two types of IPR tools that, respectively, represent technological and marketing resources (Zhou et al. 2016). Both protected assets constitute as rare, not easily substitutable, costly and difficult to imitate internal organisational resources that may be key to the firm's acquisition and maintenance of sustainable, competitive advantage (Barney 1991; Castanias and Helfat 1991). Preexisting assets with these qualities can positively affect firms' ability to adapt and to exploit new opportunities (Tripsas 1997; King and Tucci 2002). In deriving the hypotheses, I utilise to the breadth of the endowments in patents and trademarks instead of the pure stock of such protected assets, proposing that resource differentials between firms affect the degree of geo-graphic overlap in their ETS channels. A broader portfolio of protected assets can better support openness in search activities, taking into consideration a potentially significant geographic variation in innovative activity (Almeida and Kogut 1999), reuse of existing capabilities to generate inventions (Strumsky and Lobo 2015), constraints on firm resources (Garriga, Von Krogh, and Spaeth 2013), evaluation difficulties of partners' resources and prospects (Reuer and Lahiri 2013), costs of identifying external knowl-edge inputs (Salge et al. 2013), and overall hidden costs (Cassiman and Valentini 2016).

Overall, firms with larger breadth of upstream and downstream IPR assets are expected to achieve less intensity of geographic overlap in ETS locations against their rivals because they can keep competitors out of strategically valuable locations (e.g. by breaking-in first or expelling rivals) or because they attempt to isolate themselves to diminish unintended knowledge spillovers and defend their competitive advantage.

3. Hypotheses

3.1. *Upstream resources: generality of patents*

A more general, industry-core patent portfolio (i.e. a stock of patented inventions with widespread impact) provides greater resilience and latitude in ETS which lowers the extent of geographic overlap *vis-à-vis* competitors for several reasons.

The first reason is strategic. Patents normally symbolise firms' technological capabilities (Giarratana and Torrisi 2010), assist with building a positive technological image (Blind et al. 2006; Veer and Jell 2012), and help open innovation activities (Zobel, Balsmeier, and Chesbrough 2016). A firm with a portfolio of more general stock of industry-specific patents is more effective at applying competitive pressures to rivals in forming ETS links. Particularly, exhibiting variety in the generality dimension, patents look more attractive for generating knowledge flows in the eyes of potential partners, thus the focal firms can easily approach those firms that are located in capability rich areas. By a related consideration, owning a more general patent portfolio of widespread impact can signal a technology leader position in the industry (Garud and Kumaraswamy 1993) which might offer a possibility for exploiting this reputation of a technology champion, enabling the leader to create a spatially divergent set of technology search locations with respect to less capable rivals. Therefore, less-capable competitors will prove to be less attractive candidates which reduces their opportunities to break into a geographically divergent set of locations. An additional source of advantage is that a more general industry-core patent portfolio might render potential partners a necessary knowledge overlap, facilitating broader partner selection with complementary patents and technologies. This can be an important aspect for geographically distant R&D collaborations that entail difficulties to evaluate others' resources and prospects (Reuer and Lahiri 2013).

The second reason is defensive and also indicates a lower extent of geographic overlap in technology search networks. Establishing multiple technological cooperations involves risk for the firm to infringe upon patents held by other entities. However, a more general patent portfolio of the searcher organisation through stronger bargaining power increases the likelihood of avoiding litigation or establishing friendly agreements with potential litigators. Through studying the semiconductor sector, Hall and Ziedonis (2001) and Ziedonis (2004) demonstrate that when there is a fragmented market for technologies, patent portfolios help resolve hold-up problems via the use of cross-licensing agreements. Consequently, a more general patent portfolio can shield the firm against IPR-related litigations and therefore may potentially dismantle legal barriers of geographically spreading ETS more extensively than the network of rivals with less general portfolios.

Third, firms with a more general patent portfolio obtain a different kind of benefit whereby, compared with and against competitors, they enjoy a geographic divergence of their technological search channels. A more general knowledge base creates a higher potential absorptive capacity (Lane and Lubatkin 1998; Zahra and George 2002) that extends an organisation's possibility to value and assimilate external knowledge. This component increases the overall level of absorptive capacity that allows firms to manage external knowledge flows more efficiently, and, consequently, stimulate innovative outcomes (Escribano, Fosfuri, and Tribo 2009). This leads to less information asymmetry when evaluating the quality of the skills of potential partners or acquisition targets that operate in a different segment of the industry. Lower expected costs due to higher absorptive capacity give the firm more freedom for trial and error experimentation. Therefore, a firm incurs less search costs of ETS which permits spatial divergence augmentation of its open innovation locations compared to rivals.

Finally, a more general patent portfolio provides more universal skills that can increase knowledge coordination in ETS links. Improved knowledge coordination contributes to the better exploitation of synergies and to the rate of organisational learning (Zollo and Winter 2002). Furthermore, a more general knowledge base with enhanced learning potential can promote a 'connect and develop' strategy that leverages external capabilities in order to enrich the connecting firm's innovation portfolio (Sakkab 2002), and can permit the reuse of existing capabilities to generate inventions (Strumsky and Lobo 2015).

As a result, by taking into account all the positive consequences of a more general patent portfolio for ETS associated with open innovation, I hypothesise the following:

HYPOTHESIS 1. *Firms with a more general preexisting stock of patents will have less intensity of geographic overlap in external technology search locations compared to rivals.*

3.2. Downstream resources: diversification of trademarks

The next proposition suggests that firms with more diversified complementary or downstream assets to product commercialisation have strong incentives to spread external technology search in the geographic space and build up beneficial positions against rivals. Teece (1986) argues that, in almost all cases, the successful commercialisation of an innovation requires complementary assets and that the ownership of such assets can position the innovator advantageously. Correspondingly, the lack of those assets can force a technology entrepreneur to sell its technology instead of commercialisation (Gans and Stern 2003; Arora and Ceccagnoli 2006). For instance, brand advertising can contribute to the creation of stronger downstream assets either by greater brand loyalty due to higher perceived customer differentiation (Lancaster 1984) or by elevating entry barriers to competitors when the brand acts as a reference in its category (Kapferer 1997).

An efficient form of creating downstream assets is through registering trademarks that secure legal marketing protection (Fosfuri, Giarratana, and Luzzi 2008) and technological investments by boosting the rate of appropriability (Block et al. 2015; Flikkema, De Man, and Castaldi 2014; Mendonça, Santos Pereira, and Godinho 2004). Differentiation is largely enhanced by trademarks that permit customers to distinguish a firm and its offerings from those of the competitors (Mendonça, Santos Pereira, and Godinho 2004; Fosfuri and Giarratana 2009) which reduces simultaneously their search costs (Cohen 1991). Trademarks key to the scope of operation is a signal of conscious investments into a firm's own brands, reputation for perceived quality, customer loyalty and distribution channels (Mendonça, Santos Pereira, and Godinho 2004; Block et al. 2015). Investment into trademarks provides good protection of marketing efforts as a strong brand along with reputation for quality transforms into an intangible asset that is not easily imitable by competitors. Linking this with the fact that an efficacious way to own markets is to own brands (Aaker 1991), trademark registration represents valuable efforts to develop and strengthen a business. Relatedly, Gao and Hitt (2012) have found that trademarks represent a signal of new product development capacity. Trademarks also protect brands against low-priced copycats as the aggrieved party can seek legal remedies for any market advantage enjoyed by the copycat due to confusion, mistake or deception (Warlop, Ratneshwar, and van Osselaer 2005). In consequence of the vantage-point for a successful commercialisation that emanates from several marketing- and reputation-related advantages, firms with a more diversified portfolio of trademarks seem more attractive to target organisations and can enjoy more freedom in selecting open innovation partners, as opposed to weaker rivals whose ETS activities would be expelled or limited. A diversified trademark portfolio might signal ample relevant marketing information about the firm, which is crucial in cases of geographically distant R&D collaboration and difficulty when determining would-be peers' resources and prospects (Reuer and Lahiri 2013).

Past research points out correspondence between a firm's own trademarks and its pecuniary features. For instance, Fosfuri and Giarratana (2009) find that filed trademarks relevant to the industry in question imply larger financial firm value. Prior studies also detect that trademarks strongly correlate with company sales (Seethamraju 2003), stock market value (Smith and Parr 2000), firm value (Sandner and Block 2011), cash flow, Tobin's q and return on assets (Krasnikov, Mishra, and Orozco 2009). As a consequence, one can expect a more diversified stock of trademarks concentrated in the focal industry to contribute more to the financial soundness of the firm compared to rivals that possess a less diversified portfolio. This implies that the focal firm has more resources for non-local search and can also become more attractive for potential partners due to larger investment freedom. In effect, more available resources to allocate can increase the geographic divergence of technology search channels compared with competitors that have a scarcity of such downstream assets.

Furthermore, a more diversified trademark holding generally encompasses brands from a broad range of product categories. To achieve wide product scope, the organisation had to undergo a continuous and repeated sequence of changes that identify the underlying organisational routines of this group of firms (Sorenson et al. 2006). Such firms might have presumably developed the ability to accommodate new technologies due to former expansions and the acumen to analyse the potential use of a technology due to the experience with a wide range of products (Fosfuri, Giarratana, and Sebrek 2018). Additionally, a diversified brand portfolio can prove to be beneficial from cost-efficiency considerations. For example, Cohen and Klepper (1996) find that the returns on R&D are closely dependent on the range of a firm's output because fixed costs related to R&D activities can be better spread and thus absorbed with more business applications. These organisational traits on firms with a diverse set of brands may involve a spatially divergent external search compared to their rivals.

Based on the above, the consequences of a more diversified trademark portfolio for ETS associated with open innovation leads to the next hypothesis:

HYPOTHESIS 2. *Firms with a more diversified preexisting stock of trademarks will have less intensity of geographic overlap in external technology search locations compared to rivals.*

3.3. Resource richness, its parity and multimarket contacts

To this point, the arguments of Hypotheses 1 and 2 suggest that differences in the degree of breadth of upstream and downstream IPR assets influence the outcomes of competitive contests between pairs of firms at external technology search. As a consequence, large resources differentials prevent weaker rivals to occupy similar geographic locations in ETS. Nevertheless, these inquires do not permit drawing precise conclusions on ETS location strategies, if both firms of a given pair score high either on the generality of patent or on the diversification of trademark. Studying the ETS location behaviour of such intra-industry resource-rich firms is of prime interest in contrast to medium value firm pairs, for instance, which according to theory established in the prior two hypotheses are only able to apply less extensive ETS due to the limitations of their IPR resources.

Therefore, questions regarding equally resource-rich firms remain unanswered: If both members of a firm pair reach parity in the breadth of key IPR assets, then both rivals may equally break into valuable locations. Therefore, a more spatially similar ETS network would develop. I propose that such a process is moderated by the existence of a high extent of market overlap between the firms that they develop within their focal industry. Indeed, Sirmon, Grove and Hitt (2008) found that the degree of parity in the resources held by the two rivals moderates the relationship between resource management and outcomes of competitive contests.

The precondition of multipoint competition is an organisational strategy in which the firm broadens its product portfolio and diversifies within its own industry (Giarratana and Fosfuri 2007; Li and Greenwood 2004). Firms having stakes in many product categories can enjoy different kinds of positional advantages like increased stability in a more uncertain business environment (Dobrev, Kim, and Carroll 2002), more strategic latitude for managers to hedge their bets (Sorenson 2000), increased entry barriers against newcomers (Lancaster 1990), beneficial positions at technology acquisitions (Fosfuri, Giarratana, and Sebrek 2018), higher survival chances (Dowell 2006; Giarratana and Fosfuri 2007) and better overall performance (Barroso and Giatarrana 2013; Zahavi and Lavie 2013). Furthermore, consumers might find it convenient to buy on the idea of one-stop shopping (Siggelkow 2003), and should consumer preference be positively correlated, a product bundling strategy might be implemented (Gandal, Markovich, and Riordan 2005).

In the model, I propose that if both members of a firm dyad are resource-rich in the breadth of their upstream or downstream IPR assets, and there is a high overlap of within-industry market niches, then it augments the convergence of their open innovation locations. I highlight three reasons that help explain such a competitive outcome. First, firms develop common interests for the same types of new technologies and knowledge as they operate in similar market segments serving the same groups of customers. This results in targeting a geographically similar network of external technology search which is more conspicuous if specific skills or technology can only be accessed in a limited number of locations.

The second reason is strategic and relates to the possibility of mutual forbearance. Multiplicity of contacts makes competitors recognise their interdependence, and hence advances the possibility of collusion (Karnani and Wernerfelt 1985). This leads to a more conscious coordination, development of information about each other and to a reduced intensity of market competition (Boeker et al. 1997). Mutual forbearance between two firms with high level of multimarket contacts is a stable strategy as it is buttressed with a lower rate of exit from the competitor's market (Baum and Korn 1999). Furthermore, if the mutual forbearance agreement breaks, namely if overly aggressive rivalry is not undermined, then multimarket contacts widen the scope for punishing attempts of technology expropriation, knowledge dissipation or reverse engineering. Such retaliation can be realised in those market niches where the aggressor has more to lose than the responder (Bernheim and Whinston 1990), or the cost of defense is likely to be relatively low (Karnani and Wernerfelt 1985). One effective way to counter-attack is if the threatened firm starts to sell products applying predatory pricing in core, cash-cow niches of the aggressor where it can achieve the starkest possible retaliation on the attacking firm. Therefore, multimarket contacts with rivals facilitate a higher extent of ETS overlap due to less fear of negative spillover balance. Instead of a lengthy litigation process, it can directly provide the opportunity for retaliation on cash-cow niches of the deviating rival. In addition, similarly to our notion of resource parity, Li and Greenwood (2004) found that similarity between firms facilitates rivals to capture more pecuniary benefits of multimarket contacts through mutual forbearance.

Third, the resource-partitioning model of organisational ecology demonstrates that the width of product portfolio through distinct forms of group identity development process shapes differently the adherence to quality, production methods, and clinging to customers and communities (Negro, Visentin, and Swaminathan 2014; Carroll and Swaminathan 2000; Swaminathan 2001). Consequently, to alleviate competitive threat posed by specialist firms, resource-rich, wide market-scoped generalists' ETS might be affected by their competitive interdependence and collective identity that would eventually permit a more mutually supportive behaviour in ETS for this class of organisations. These arguments lead to the last hypotheses:

HYPOTHESIS 3a(b). *If both members of a firm-pair are resource-rich in their generality of patents (diversification of trademarks), and exhibit multiple contacts in their market niches, then they will have more intensity of geographic overlap in ETS locations with each other.*

4. Data and methodology

4.1. Sample construction

To test these ideas, I resort to the Security Software Industry (SSI) which has its technological origins in the 1970s due to large investments made by the US government in military projects related to security of data transmissions. As a result, a sound scientific background in cryptography and encryption emerged through the involvement of large ICT firms and university departments which manifested in a historical, USPTO-registered patent stock. This process created a publicly available source of knowledge spillovers that benefited enormously the birth of the SSI with a clear commercial focus at the turn of 1980s and 1990s. At that time, several favourable environmental factors supported the industry's evolution such as the fabulously growing PC market, the development of the Internet accompanied with the need towards secure Internet-based financial transactions. Consequently, the worldwide sales of security software products between 1997 and 2002 tripled from USD2.2 billion to USD6.9 billion (IDC 2000, 2003). Rising demand enlarged the spectrum of market supply which embraced not only basic products of encryption such as firewall or antivirus programmes, but comprehensive and advanced security services linked to protection of operating systems and applications, network security management packages, and sensible data and hardware protection (Giarratana and Fosfuri 2007).

The emergence of new market niches altogether with fierce market competition spurred widespread trademark issuance in SSI that enables firms to forge brand protection, to take advantage of superior product quality reputation and to forge customer loyalty, which ultimately enhances the commercialisation potential of the trademark issuer. Table 1 exemplifies the various motives and applications of trademark issuance in the sector.

A notable technical characteristic of the industry pertains to the mathematical crypto algorithm that is the principal component of a security software product through transforming plain text data into cipher text, and what it can be strongly protected by patents. The task of crypto algorithm is to execute the encryption and decryption processes of the data, and its quality in terms of security level and speed of mathematical calculations is a decisive factor to provide competitive advantage for the owner organisation (Giarratana 2004). For instance, the US Patent 5,768,373 filed on 6 May 1996 by Symantec Corp. is directed towards providing a secure method to access data when the user has lost or forgotten the user password. The patent description employing several block diagrams explains that the decryption of an access key gives

Table 1. SSI trademarks with the scope of application filed by prominent security software producers.

Objective of the trademark from goods and services heading	Registrant	Filing date	Serial number	Emblematic design or the object of legal protection
Brand protection with logo	Security Dynamics	23 August 1996	75,154,776	SecurityDynamics
Brand name protection through an image	Symantec	27 August 1997	75,347,874	SYMANTEC.
Protection of a specific service	Verisign	22 April 1997	75,279,016	'NETSURE'
Protection of a specific product category	Security Dynamics	11 January 1996	75,041,170	'SOFTID'
Product/service protection through using an image	Security Dynamics	5 December 1996	75,208,517	ACE SERVER
Slogan protection	Symantec	25 April 1997	75,281,282	'VIRTUALLY ANYWHERE'
Logo to provide recognisable designations	Checkpoint Systems	14 November 1996	75,197,809	

Source: My collections from the USPTO database.

access to data and that two encrypted versions of the access key are created. If the password is forgotten access to data is accomplished by decrypting the second encrypted version of the access key via the private key, from the public-private key pair, which is required to be stored at a remote site. A further illustrative example is the US Patent 6,141,420 filed by Certicom Corp. on 29 January 1997 which applies an elliptic curve cryptosystem method instead of integer calculus, performing the encoding-decoding process more quickly while requiring less computer space expressed in bits (Giarratana 2004).

There are several industry traits that emphasise the importance of external technology search for security software manufacturers. First, product innovation plays a major role accompanied by the proliferation of lucrative new product categories (The Economist 2002). Second, it is a technology-based industry with continuous innovation where the complexity of a security software system requires incorporating problem solutions from distinct technological areas, for instance mathematics, hardware engineering, software development and network design (Giarratana 2004). Third, competition is intense implying low entry barriers, paucity of first-mover advantages for survival and a high hazard rate of firm exit (Giarratana and Fosfuri 2007). Therefore, I believe that the worldwide SSI proves an ideal setting to study firms' collocation patterns of external technology search.

To verify the hypotheses, I constructed a comprehensive data set tracing SSI firms' locations for acquisitions and strategic technology alliances on a global basis. I discovered the population of SSI organisations via security software product introduction data from Infotrac's General Business File ASAP and PROMT database (former Predicast) that, from a large set of trade journals, magazines and other specialised press (e.g. eWeek, PC Magazine, PR Newswire, Telecomworldwire), reports several categories of events classified by industrial sectors. This data source is the more recent version of the former Predicast database and was applied in various studies (e.g. Pennings and Harianto 1992; Fosfuri, Giarratana, and Luzzi 2008). I searched for all press articles that reported a 'Product announcement', a 'New software release' and a 'Software evaluation' in SSI at SIC Code 73726 (Encryption Software Sector) from 1980 to 2002. These steps determined that the first product was introduced in 1989.

Prior contributions point at the pivotal role that acquisitions (Haspeslagh and Jemison 1991; Hitt et al. 1996; Pisano 1991; Vermeulen and Barkema 2001; Cassiman and Colombo 2006) and strategic technology alliances (Dussauge, Garrette, and Mitchell 2000; Hamel 1991; Kumar and Nti 1998; Lane and Lubatkin 1998) can play when external sources of knowledge and technology have become relevant. Therefore, I take into consideration these inter-organisational mechanisms to study ETS patterns of firms. Resorting to the same Infotrac database, I downloaded all the articles for SSI firms that report an acquisition and an alliance event under SIC 73726. For all types of events, I carefully read the text of business news, and removed the equivocal events from the sample. Considering alliance texts, I selected only those events for the variable strategic technology alliance where partners are involved in combined innovative activities or exchange of technologies (Hagedoorn and Duysters 2002). Hence, equivocal cases or marketing alliances were excluded. It is worth noting that acquisitions are often used to increase CEO power or to penetrate in a new and untapped geographic market (especially at older sunk-cost industries). Notwithstanding, an acquisition in SSI has primarily a technology or knowledge acquisition orientation, as target organisations can have a valuable (protected) technology or employ skilled software engineers. For instance, Cisco Systems, a firm that is heavily interested in the network, content and web security business, uses a considerable part of its profits to purchase firms with R&D capabilities (Shapiro and Varian 1999).

I studied all the security software firms that realised at least two external technology searches during the 3-year span 2000–2002. By this period, SSI developed into a mature industry where the use of the above two mechanisms became ubiquitous. The sample on strategic technology alliances (acquisitions) consists of 57 (51) security software firms that are undoubtedly the leading players in the industry. In constructing the database, I made firm dyads as the unit of analysis which was motivated by the following reasons: it captures a firm's relative position, it provides a consistent comparison across organisations, and it efficiently reflects the competitive engagements of firms (Alcácer 2006; Baum and Korn 1999; Chen 1996; Sirmon, Gove, and Hitt 2008). Table 2 offers descriptive statistics on the different types of ETS that the sampled firms realised across the entire study period.

4.2. Dependent variables

Following Alcácer's study (2006), I apply a similar measure for the construction of the dependent variable. This location index (LOCI) allows for comparing the geographic convergence or dispersion of ETS networks to any two sample firms (i and j) in giving an in-between value of complete coincidence or total dissimilarity. The sign i' is a 1xn row vector while j denotes an nx1 column vector. Each element, of i_l or j_l takes on either 1 or 0, depending on whether the given firm has realised an ETS activity in location l. From the viewpoint of firm i, the LOCI$_{ij}$ measure is a percentage value of ETS locations overlapped by both firms, mathematically:

$$LOCI_{ij} = \frac{i' * j}{i' * i} = \frac{\sum_{l=1}^{l=n} i_l * j_l}{\sum_{l=1}^{l=n} i_l * i_l}.$$

The LOCI measure is dyadic by construction and varies theoretically from 0 (dispersion) to 1 (similarity). If the index reaches its maximum value 1, it means that firm j explored exactly the same geographical sites as firm i. In the reversed case, firm i and j don't share any geographically coinciding locations in their explorative undertakings, and so the index takes the value of zero. Alcácer's index is a quite precise and convenient way to compare the location choices of any two sample firms, as it represents a multidimensional relationship with a single value, and the interpretation is intuitive. Additionally, the index weighs only those elements that equal 1 and it is independent of the number of elements in the vectors, in contrast to correlation or covariance which 'vary when more null elements are added to the vectors (Alcácer 2006, 1461)'. Ultimately, the LOCI measure inherently is not

Table 2. Descriptive statistics on the types of ETS.

Type of ETS	Number of firms	Total number of ETS	Mean	SD	Min	Max
Acquisitions	51	252	4.94	3.53	2	13
Strategic technology alliances	57	430	7.54	7.16	2	34

symmetric for firm pairs i-j and j-i owing to the scale applied in the denominator that is always related to the focal firm. In fact, this feature reflects competitive asymmetry (Chen 1996) by recording differently the presence in geographic factor markets for participants in a given firm dyad.

To calculate LOCI, first, I had to identify the exact location of all organisations with which the sample SSI firms had ETS links. For firm i, I considered the acquired firms by i, and its technology alliance partners. Second, I had to devise an appropriate policy with regard to possible geographic divisions because isolation patterns of ETS grasped by the location index might be sensitive to units of geographical classification. Let's consider a Southern California security software maker that through locating ETS within a geographically limited territory, for example only in the neighbouring counties, might obtain increasingly higher values for LOCI compared to the same rivals if there is an increased size of geographic units. As a result, I apply a similar geographic gradation to that of Alcácer (2006), for which I determine the value of LOCI for three geographic levels: clusters, countries and economic regions. Operationally, clusters are equal to US counties, or equally sized official geographic units outside of the US; country level refers to independent states or US states; and an economic region is related to a group of countries that culturally or economically share common traits. The involvement of the spatially greater regions can amplify our understanding of ETS location patterns as cluster level may overestimate the extent of geographic extension of an ETS network, assigning a biased lower value to the LOCI index. Nonethless, a cluster-level measure for LOCI can provide a more sophisticated insight of location choices because some firms may concentrate ETS to a geographically limited area.

I identified all actual geographic locations properly through the Geographic Names Information System for US locations and the Getty Thesaurus of Geographic Names for foreign, non-US locations. Finally, I calculate the LOCI value for all geographic levels considering the type of ETS activities separately (acquisition or strategic technology alliances). Consequently, I obtained six LOCI measures depending on geographic gradation and activity type. Table 3 summarises the dyadic level location indices by the type of ETS activities (acquisition and strategic technology alliances) calculated at the cluster and country levels, whereas Table 4(a,b) show the geographic profile of the two ETS channels at the cluster level.

4.3. Estimation procedures

I hypothesise that the location of boundary-spanning external technology search vis-à-vis rivals is generated by the function $LOCI_{ij} = x^{T}_{ij} \beta + \varepsilon_{ij}$, where the dependent variable is the location index for the convergence or dispersion of technology exploration networks, x_{ij} is the set of explanatory dyadic variables, β is a vector of parameters to be estimated, and ε_{ij} is an error term. One econometric challenge involves the fact that dyadic data are assumed not to consist of independent observations, but rather have varying amounts of dependence on one another which can lead to autocorrelation in the error terms (Krackhardt 1988). The lack of such independence is best illustrated by a firm that purposefully decides to separate its ETS allocation from the rest of competitors due to some unknown reasons. The result introduces a chain of positive autocorrelation for all dyadic observation related to the deviating firm which can generate small standard errors and thus inflated t-statistics

(Alcácer 2006). Additionally, the existing row or column interdependence can bias ordinary-least-squares (OLS) tests of significance (Krackhardt 1988). To contend with this problem of bias, I use a method based on Krackhardt (1988), who proposes a nonparametric solution called the Quadratic Assignment Procedure (QAP) that provides unbiased tests for regression coefficients. The QAP algorithm proceeds by first performing an OLS regression on the original data set. Then the rows and columns of the dependent variable matrix are permuted to provide a new, scrambled matrix. The OLS regression

Table 3. Descriptive statistics on the LOCI measure at dyadic level.

	Cluster level		Country level	
	AQU	STA	AQU	STA
Mean	0.444	0.379	0.586	0.495
S.d.	0.345	0.315	0.328	0.305
Min	0	0	0	0
Max	1	1	1	1

Table 4. (a) Geographic profile of ETS activities for strategic technology alliances (at the cluster level). (b) Geographic profile of ETS activities for acquisitions (at the cluster level).

County	N. of STA	%	Country
(a)			
Santa Clara	99	23%	USA
San Mateo	44	10%	USA
Middlesex	39	9%	USA
King	30	7%	USA
Westchester	28	7%	USA
Tokyo	20	5%	Japan
Toronto	20	5%	Canada
San Francisco	19	4%	USA
Alameda	17	4%	USA
New York	17	4%	USA
Etela-Suomen	14	3%	Finland
Suffolk	10	2%	USA
Fulton	9	2%	USA
Baden-Wurttemberg	9	2%	Germany
Number of different locations at cluster level			39

County	N of AQU	%	Country
(b)			
Santa Clara	41	16%	USA
Middlesex	35	14%	USA
Alameda	34	13%	USA
San Mateo	28	11%	USA
King	16	6%	USA
Toronto	13	5%	Canada
San Francisco	12	5%	USA
Etela-Suomen	11	4%	Finland
San Diego	8	3%	USA
Fulton	6	2%	USA
Erie	5	2%	USA
Essex	4	2%	USA
Los Angeles	4	2%	USA
Philadelphia	4	2%	USA
Number of different locations at cluster level			34

Source. My elaborations spawn from the use of Infotrac's General Business File ASAP and PROMPT database.

calculation is then repeated with the new dependent variable. The programme stores coefficient estimates and R^2 values. Next, another permutation of the dependent variable is drawn that is subjected to a new OLS regression whose coefficients and R-square values are again stored. This permutation-regression step is repeated 500 times that yields a reference, empirical sampling distribution for the stored betas of independent variables under the null hypothesis of no relationship between the independent variables and the dependent variable. In the end, one can compare each actual coefficient of the first OLS regression with the empirical distribution to reject the null hypothesis at an extremely high or low percentile.

4.4. Independent variables

I controlled for the generality of a firm's upstream intellectual property right-related assets with the *patentgenerality* variable. Patents have been used extensively in the innovation literature to measure technological capabilities (e.g. Henderson and Cockburn 1994) and provide externally validated measures of innovative success that closely resonate to a firm's level of technological competence (Narin, Noma, and Perry 1987). I only considered the fundamental technological classes pertaining to the SSI which include the 380, 382, 705, 709, 713 and 726 three-digit patent classes (Giarratana 2004). The *patentgenerality* variable is the Jaffe-Trajtenberg index of generality which is essentially a one minus Herfindhal index on forward citations of patents in three-digit SIC codes (Trajtenberg, Jaffe, and Hall 2000). By construction, it can vary between 0 and 1 (maximum portfolio generality) with high generality scores representing wide-spread impact in a wide range of fields (Trajtenberg, Jaffe, and Hall 2000). This variable is for 1998, as lagged by two years with respect to the dependent variables, and was built upon the NBER/Case Western patent database.

To grasp the downstream intellectual property right breadth of the sampled firms I resorted to the USPTO database (see De Vries et al. 2017; Giarratana and Fosfuri 2007) and downloaded exclusively the annual number of live software trademarks. To obtain only software-related trademarks for the focal organisations, I followed the method of Fosfuri, Giarratana, and Luzzi (2008) in which I applied a search algorithm through strings of words to the text of the trademark description of goods and services. The second core variable, *trademarkdiversification* is the one minus Herfindhal index on the industrial class trade-mark codes from the yearly set of LIVE software trademarks of a firm. Similarly to *patentgenerality*, this variable is within the range 0–1 (maximum width of trademark portfolio) and lagged by two years.

To be able to test H3a and H3b, I created two multiplicative measures referred to as *RRF_PATGEN*MMC* and *RRF_TMDIV*MMC*. *RRF_PATGEN* and *RRF_TMDIV* stand for resource-rich firms in the breadth of patents and trademarks, respectively. Both are dummy variables and display 1 if the firm's *patentgenerality* or *trademarkdiversification* value belongs to the top 33%, respectively. For robustness checks, I also created these two dummy variables considering top 10, 15% and 25% values. Results in Tables 6 and 7 involve RRF variables on 10% and 33%. *MMC* is the abbreviation for multimarket contact, and demonstrates how many common SSI niches are shared by the two firms in a given firm dyad. The value of MMC for a firm can vary between 1 and 6, as any product launched by a security software producer can be classified into one of the six product niches: authentication digital signature, antivirus, data and hardware protection, firewalls, utility software, and network security and management (Giarratana 2004; Giarratana and Fosfuri 2007). Portfolio broadening built upon active presence in these niches is a notable product strategy in SSI (Fosfuri, Giarratana, and Sebrek 2018).

4.5. Controls

I introduce a set of controls that may be an alternate explanation for firms' external technology search behaviour. Experience in the market is captured by the number of years a firm is competing in SSI (*Age in market*) where it enhances firm survival (Giarratana and Fosfuri 2007). This variable is the difference between a firm's entry year and the current year. I account for any possible distortion of a firm's scale through the variable *Sales in software business* which is the logarithm of the share of LIVE software trademarks on the total LIVE trademarks multiplied by the firm sales (the source of this latter: Bureau Van Dijk's Osiris). To grasp its possible impact on the dependent variable, I inserted a subsidiary control constructed at country level that is one minus Herfindhal index on the geographic extension of sampled firms' subsidiary locations. Higher extent of industry competition at firm entry was found to deteriorate survival options for security software makers (Giarratana and Fosfuri 2007). To control for different industry conditions at the time of entry I employ a measure of organisational population density at the time a firm enters the market (*Density delay*), as initial competition conditions can exert lasting effects on the extent of overlap in technology search locations.

Firms' core business can influence the way ETS is spatially distanced or converged from competitors because a firm's core sector could exhibit common patterns in searching external knowledge and technology. Moreover, SSI can also host *de alio* companies as implied by Giarratana (2008). Hence, I employ three dummies that address the core business of the sampled organisations: *Hardware* (SIC code 357), *Software* (SIC 737), or *Electronics* (SIC 359-370). Data on firm core business was taken from Bureau Van Dijk's Osiris and Hoover's. In addition, I implement in the QAP regressions a geographical dummy that takes the value of 1 if the headquarter of a firm is situated in *North America* (0 otherwise). Dummies on firms' technological background and place of origin were also introduced by Alcácer (2006) in his study on subsidiary location choices.

Given that I employ a dyadic dataset, all independent and control variables similarly to the dependent variable are also dyadic: either differences from the focal firm's perspective, or dummies with a value of 1 if both firms in a given dyad share the same feature described in the discussion of the proxy variable. To construct the database, I applied a pairing algorithm using the statistical software package *R*. According to the number of firms involved, the data table on which I perform the QAP regressions consist of 3192 (2550) lines for strategic technology alliances (acquisitions). To alleviate potential endogeneity problems between firm resources and locations choices of ETS, a two-year lag of independent and control variables with the location index is applied. Table 5 provides the basic descriptive statistics for the independent variables and controls.

Table 5. Simple statistics of variables for QAP estimations.

Independent variables	STA				AQU			
	Mean	SD	Min	Max	Mean	SD	Min	Max
Core variables								
Patentgenerality	0.13	0.21	0	0.83	0.14	0.21	0	0.83
Trademarkdiversification	0.26	0.28	0	0.84	0.29	0.29	0	0.84
Controls								
Age in market	1.23	2.22	0	8	1.29	2.28	0	8
Sales in software business	4.55	2.31	0	7.69	4.49	2.40	0	7.69
Subsidiary	0.73	0.34	0	0.98	0.75	0.33	0	0.98
Density delay	127.23	46.61	12	256	126.12	47.76	12	256
Hardware[a]	0.07	0.26	0	1	0.12	0.33	0	1
Software[a]	0.82	0.38	0	1	0.80	0.40	0	1
Electronics[a]	0.05	0.23	0	1	0.08	0.27	0	1
North America[a]	0.91	0.29	0	1	0.96	0.20	0	1
Niche width[b]	2.91	1.98	1	6	3.14	1.83	1	6

Source. My elaborations spawn from the use of various data sources that embrace Infotrac's General Business File ASAP and PROMPT, US Patent and Trademark Office, NBER/Case Western, Compustat and Osiris databases.
Notes. [a] denotes dummy variables. [b] The niche width variable serves as the basis for the calculation of the dyadic multimarket contact variable.

5. Results and discussion

I run regressions using Multiple Regression Quadratic Assignment Procedure with the above covariates. The dependent variable is the location index (LOCI) of external technology search whose construction varies either by ETS type or geographic unit. Models 1 and 2 of Table 6 present the results of QAP estimation for strategic technology alliances on cluster and country levels. Taking into consideration the conceptualisation of the hypotheses, one must expect negative signs for the IPR-based variables of theoretical interest. The results indicate that a more general preexisting stock of industry-specific patents (*patentgenerality*) expands the geographic isolation of strategic technology alliances vis-à-vis rivals. *Trademarkdiversification* also enjoys explanatory power at strategic technology alliances causing less intensity of spatial overlap compared to rivals. Independently of the geographic units, both core variables take the expected signs, therefore corroborate H1 and H2 for strategic technology alliances.

In Model 1 and 2, the level of the resource-rich firm (RRF) dummy variables is on 33%. The multiplicative variable between resource-rich firms in the generality of patent stock and multimarket contact (*RRF_PATGEN*MMC*) is positive and significant both at cluster (Model 1 of Table 6) and country level (Model 2 of Table 6), confirming H3a for STA. This finding suggests that a high spatial overlap vis-à-vis similar resource-rich competitors in the generality of patent assets is achieved, only if both firms exhibit a high rate of multimarket contact in SSI niches. The *RRF_TMDIV*MMC* multiplicative variable is positive, significant at cluster but not country level which does not fully buttress H3b. Therefore, the flocking strategy of resource-rich rivals in the diversification of their trademark assets, with vast common market scope, is sensitive based on the level of geographic gradation applied. Perhaps diversification of trademarks of multipoint competitors only spurs more ETS overlap within smaller districts of a greater economic unit that result in some sort of scope economies benefits from a commercialisation point of view. These may not be obtained or may be too expensive or cost-inefficient if the range of ETS is extended. As robustness checks, Models 3 and 4 apply the 10% level for the construction of RRF variables, thus influencing the values of the multiplicative variables. Results of core variables are qualitatively unchanged.

Table 6. Results of QAP estimation (cluster and country level) for strategic technology alliances.

Type of search activity	STA		STA		STA		STA	
Geographic unit	Cluster level		Country level		Cluster level		Country level	
Models	1		2		3		4	
Core variables								
Patentgenerality	−0.2497	(0.01)**	−0.2606	(0.002)**	−0.2497	(0.002)**	−0.2606	(0.004)**
Trademarkdiversification	−0.1445	(0.034)*	−0.1519	(0.036)*	−0.1445	(0.046)*	−0.1519	(0.024)*
RRF_PATGEN*MMC	0.0467	(0.022)*	0.0435	(0.014)*	0.1059	(0.048)*	0.1059	(0.032)*
RRF_TMDIV*MMC	0.0521	(0.012)*	0.0247	(0.102)	0.1	(0.04)*	0.0396	(0.192)
Controls								
Age in market	0.0071	(0.402)	0.0039	(0.482)	0.0071	(0.352)	0.0039	(0.454)
Sales in sw. buss. (logs)	−0.0044	(0.326)	−0.0015	(0.424)	−0.0044	(0.294)	−0.0015	(0.442)
Subsidiary	−0.0544	(0.154)	−0.1021	(0.038)*	−0.0544	(0.17)	−0.1021	(0.04)*
Density delay	0.0012	(0.122)	0.001	(0.212)	0.0012	(0.13)	0.001	(0.182)
Hardware[a]	−0.0837	(0.232)	−0.0684	(0.252)	0.13	(0.164)	0.0631	(0.31)
Software[a]	−0.0487	(0.18)	−0.0065	(0.456)	−0.0648	(0.094)†	−0.013	(0.414)
Electronics[a]	0.0187	(0.448)	−0.0558	(0.292)	0.1232	(0.23)	−0.0116	(0.45)
North America[a]	0.0214	(0.334)	−0.0146	(0.436)	0.0214	(0.37)	−0.0162	(0.4)
MMC	0.018	(0.148)	0.0194	(0.074)†	0.0351	(0.008)**	0.0289	(0.01)*
RRF_PATGEN	−0.0392	(0.344)	−0.0934	(0.138)	−0.3156	(0.138)	−0.3315	(0.082)†
RRF_TMDIV	−0.0625	(0.234)	−0.0366	(0.274)	−0.2774	(0.074)†	−0.0832	(0.302)
Constant	0.3524	(0.336)	0.4774	(0.342)	0.3513	(0.372)	0.4731	(0.324)
Observations	3192		3192		3192		3192	
Level of RRF	**33%**		**33%**		**10%**		**10%**	
e(R2)	0.2835	(0.000)**	0.2757	(0.000)**	0.262	(0.000)**	0.2692	(0.000)**
e(F)	137.44	(0.000)**	122.07	(0.000)**	112.9	(0.000)**	118.98	(0.000)**

Notes. Dependent variable: LOCI of focal firm *i* with respect to reference firm *j*, data on dependent variables for 2000–2002. Independent and control variables are for 1998. † indicates $p < 0.1$. * indicates $p < 0.05$. ** indicates $p < 0.01$. Values in parentheses are pseudo p-values. [a] denotes dummy variables.

As far as it concerns the control variables, only a few play a role in developing a geographically dispersed or concentrated ETS network in the STA sample of the Security Software Industry. The *subsidiary* variable proves to be negative and significant exclusively at the country level (Model 2). This suggests that a more geographically extended subsidiary network with respect to a rival (giving high value of the subsidiary control for this particular firm pair) causes divergence in STA ETS locations. *Software* firms with similarities in technological background exhibit an isolation pattern in STA ETS, but such an effect is observable only at cluster level with a 10% RRF level and is significant only at the margin. The multimarket contact variable is positive and significant in Models 3 and 4, and partially significant in Model 2. This implies that those security software manufacturers that exhibit high rate of multimarket contact with each other, tend to develop a geographically similar STA network. It is worth noting that the RRF dummy is negative and significant on 10% in only two cases: the *RRF_PATGEN* on country level in Model 4 and the *RRF_TMDIV* on cluster level in Model 3. This finding might indicate that resource-rich firms may aspire to flee from similar competitors. Interestingly, differences in size do not exert a significant effect on the extent of geographic convergence or divergence of STA vis-à-vis rivals.

Models 5 and 6 of Table 7 present the results of QAP estimation for acquisitions on cluster and country levels. A more general preexisting stock of industry-specific patents (*patentgenerality*) expands the geographic isolation of acquisitions in relation to rivals. *Trademarkdiversification* also enjoys explanatory power at acquisitions causing less

Table 7. Results of QAP estimation (cluster and country level) for acquisitions.

Type of search activity	AQU		AQU		AQU		AQU	
Geographic unit	Cluster level		Country level		Cluster level		Country level	
Models	5		6		7		8	
Core variables								
Patentgenerality	−0.2639	(0.004)**	−0.2448	(0.022)*	−0.2639	(0.008)**	−0.2448	(0.02)*
Trademarkdiversification	−0.2334	(0.004)**	−0.2682	(0.004)**	−0.2334	(0.006)**	−0.2682	(0.002)**
RRF_PATGEN*MMC	0.094	(0.004)**	0.0818	(0.000)**	0.0955	(0.072)†	0.1321	(0.022)*
RRF_TMDIV*MMC	0.0554	(0.042)*	0.0798	(0.000)**	0.0996	(0.05)*	0.0911	(0.042)*
Controls								
Age in market	0.0005	(0.496)	−0.0031	(0.446)	0.0005	(0.474)	−0.0031	(0.432)
Sales in sw. buss. (logs)	−0.0015	(0.422)	−0.0044	(0.354)	−0.0015	(0.484)	−0.0044	(0.342)
Subsidiary	−0.0166	(0.43)	0.0235	(0.402)	−0.0166	(0.406)	0.0235	(0.368)
Density delay	0.0006	(0.368)	0.0005	(0.38)	0.0006	(0.372)	0.0005	(0.376)
Hardware[a]	0.029	(0.386)	−0.0364	(0.344)	0.0637	(0.244)	0.0021	(0.486)
Software[a]	−0.0624	(0.13)	0.0193	(0.344)	−0.0639	(0.126)	0.015	(0.382)
Electronics[a]	0.0909	(0.244)	−0.0064	(0.45)	0.1357	(0.218)	0.0433	(0.394)
North America[a]	−0.0198	(0.496)	−0.0256	(0.472)	−0.0159	(0.48)	−0.0189	(0.498)
MMC	0.0551	(0.002)**	0.03	(0.042)*	0.0661	(0.000)**	0.0418	(0.002)**
RRF_PATGEN	−0.4052	(0.000)**	−0.3211	(0.000)**	−0.4351	(0.076)†	−0.596	(0.032)*
RRF_TMDIV	−0.1465	(0.08)†	−0.3028	(0.000)**	−0.2945	(0.082)†	−0.3035	(0.05)*
Constant	0.4167	(0.364)	0.5616	(0.37)	0.384	(0.298)	0.5222	(0.23)
Observations	2550		2550		2550		2550	
Level of RRF	**33%**		**33%**		**10%**		**10%**	
e(R2)	0.3628	(0.000)**	0.3835	(0.000)**	0.3276	(0.000)**	0.3376	(0.000)**
e(F)	176.5	(0.000)**	167.24	(0.000)**	153.88	(0.000)**	147.07	(0.000)**

Notes. Dependent variable: LOCI of focal firm *i* with respect to reference firm *j*, data on dependent variables for 2000–2002. Independent and control variables are for 1998. † indicates $p < 0.1$. * indicates $p < 0.05$. ** indicates $p < 0.01$. Values in parentheses are pseudo p-values. [a] denotes dummy variables.

intensity of spatial overlap compared to rivals. Independently of the geographic units used for the analysis, both core variables take the expected signs which lends strong support for H1 and H2 for acquisitions.

In Model 5 and 6, the level of the resource-rich firm (RRF) dummy variables is on 33%. The multiplicative variable between resource-rich firms in the generality of patent stock and multimarket contact (*RRF_PATGEN*MMC*), is positive and significant both at cluster (Model 5 of Table 7) and country level (Model 6 of Table 7) confirming H3b. This finding suggests that a high spatial overlap at acquisitions regarding similar resource-rich competitors in the generality of patent assets is achieved, only if both firms exhibit a high rate of multimarket contact in SSI niches. The *RRF_TMDIV*MMC* multiplicative variable is also positive, significant on cluster and country levels, buttressing H3b. Therefore, resource-rich rivals in the diversification of their trademark assets with high market overlap follow a flocking strategy in their acquisition locations. As robustness checks, Models 7 and 8 apply the 10% level for the construction of RRF variables which demonstrates the results of core variables remain qualitatively unchanged.

With regard to the control variables, only few play a role in developing a lower or higher extent of geographic overlap in acquisition ETS locations with respect to another firm in the Security Software Industry. The multimarket contact variable is positive and significant in Models 5–8. This implies that those security software manufacturers that exhibit a high rate of multimarket contact with each other, tend to develop a geographically similar acquisition network. It is worth noting that the RRF dummy of both types is negative and significant at least on 10% through all models of Table 7. This finding indicates that resource-rich firms may aim to augment the divergence of acquisition locations from similar competitors; a notable difference in acquisition location strategy from the subpopulation of resource-rich firms with a high degree of multimarket contact. As to the other control variables, neither difference in size or in the geographic extension of subsidiary network produces a significant effect on the extent of geographic convergence or divergence of acquisitions vis-à-vis rivals.

In addition and available upon request, I examined whether the models applied in Tables 6 and 7 are over-specified by the joint inclusion of IPR covariates, RRF dummy variables and these latter's interaction with multimarket contact. Via the introduction of core covariates, and RRF variables and their interaction with MMC separately in any model, render the results unchanged.

5.1. Sensibility tests

Table 8 reports a sensibility test for changes in the Location Index at cluster level. For instance, if I use coefficient estimates of Model 1 of Table 6, and make a two standard deviation increase on the mean value of *patentgenerality* and *trademarkdiversification*, the value of the location index for strategic technology alliances decreases by 38.7% and 30.4%, respectively. As a possible explanation for this finding, I conjecture that fear from reverse engineering, technological knowledge expropriation and losses of key employees by a rival's hiring policy manifest in the *patentgenerality* variable. Collectively, these factors drive stronger isolation of STA network from competitors than *trademarkdiversification*. When repeating the same analysis on country level, the decrease in LOCI for STA is less by 7.8% for patents (equalling −30.9%), and 6% for trademarks (equalling −24.4%); understandably, firms strive more to maximise isolation when competing in a smaller geographic area.

The same sensibility test shown also by Table 8 was repeated with *patentgenerality* and *trademarkdiversification* for acquisitions (coefficients taken from Model 5 of Table 7) causing a decrease in LOCI of 36% and 43.2%, respectively. As with this case, *trademark-diversification*'s impact is stronger (compared with the STA sample) and I surmise that for the acquirer-searcher organisation's commercialisation purposes, the greatest possible augmentation of acquisition location divergence from rivals leads to the best outcome. Probably, the acquirer organisation already possesses important downstream assets that might help launch the target's technologies or products into the market. In a positive case, both parties could benefit. The acquirer can have access to key knowledge or technologies

Table 8. Sensibility test for changes in the Location Index (cluster level).

Core variables	SD	STA Coeff.[a]	Δ in LOCI	SD	AQU Coeff.[a]	Δ in LOCI
Patentgenerality	0.29	−0.2497	−38.7%	0.30	−0.2639	−36.0%
Trademark diversification	0.40	−0.1445	−30.4%	0.41	−0.2334	−43.2%

Notes. I made a two standard deviation increase on the mean value of the core variables to observe the change in the value of the dependent variable (location index). [a] Coefficient estimates for strategic technology alliances (acquisitions) come from Model I (V) of Table 6 (7).

to assimilate into its own products or to the target's products that the acquirer intends to commercialise under its own brands. In turn, the owners of the target organisation can earn profits on the sale.

I performed further sensitivity checks on the two multiplicative variables. First, I resorted to STA data from Model 1 of Table 6. If firms i and j are both resource-rich in the generality of patents (diversification of trademarks) and achieved wide market overlap, the location index of firm i with respect to firm j increases by 0.19 (0.21), 0.23 (0.26) and 0.28 (0.31) for having 4, 5 and 6 common niches, respectively. Then, I repeated the same exercise using acquisition data from Model 5 of Table 7. If firms i and j are both resource-rich in the generality of patents (diversification of trademarks) and achieved wide market overlap, the location index of firm i with respect to firm j increases by 0.38 (0.22), 0.47 (0.28) and 0.56 (0.33) for having 4, 5 and 6 common niches, respectively. I conjecture that at technology alliances, patents induce less than trademarks the flocking of multipoint resource-rich competitors due to more concerns over the efficiency of retaliation potential for knowledge leakage. Meanwhile, the reverse scenario might be true at acquisitions where patents drive more than trademarks the flocking strategy due to less expropriation concerns.

Comparing models of Tables 6 and 7 through R-square values reveals that there is no significant variation introduced by the modification of the level of analysis from cluster to country. To validate the findings on core variables, I performed further unreported robustness checks by adding regions as another, more ample geographic unit, and by changing the level of RRF to 15% and 25%. Regarding these cases, the results remained broadly consistent.

6. Conclusions

According to prior contributions (Chung and Alcácer 2002; Kim and Kogut 1996; Rosenkopf and Nerkar 2001), this research started with the premise that external technology and knowledge search is an important mechanism for firms. Former research also discussed a strategy of self-defence from unintended knowledge spillover (Shaver and Flyer 2000; Alcácer and Chung 2007), predicting divergence of ETS from rivals. However, a varying intensity of geographic overlap in ETS channels must critically depend on firm resources. In this paper, I have investigated empirically the role of the breadth of upstream and downstream intellectual property right tools on influencing the spatial dissimilarity of ETS networks of firms compared to rivals. Notably, I studied how much firms share the extent of geographic overlap in ETS locations given the investments made in the generality of patents and the diversification of trademarks. Using the Security Software Industry as a test-bed, the empirical results suggest that the larger breadth of both IPR-based core covariates supports a lower extent of geographic overlap in external technology search compared to rivals. They play, however, somewhat different roles depending on the type of the search activity: patents buttress more than trademarks such a divergence at technology alliances, while for acquisitions the reverse mechanism prevails. Other remarkable findings are connected to resource-rich firms whose operationalisation was done separately for both patents and trademarks, and designated entities whose breadth of patents or trademarks scored highly. According to the results, a high intensity of spatial overlap vis-à-vis similar research-rich competitors is achieved, only if both firms exhibit multimarket contact in the niches of the focal industry. The findings associated with strategic technology alliances, however, are sensitive to the level of geographic gradation used.

Although there is an ample literature on open innovation, it has not been empirically linked to geographic considerations. The main contribution of my work is that I provide one of the first attempts to bring together ETS approaches and the geographic components of firm strategy. Additionally, the present study connects with a fairly recent but growing body of literature that addresses the challenges in open innovation. Specifically, earlier contributions have primarily focused on intentional knowledge leakage (Ritala et al. 2015), fear of imitation in absorptive capacity-rich locations (Giarratana and Mariani 2014), constraints on firm resources (Garriga, Von Krogh, and Spaeth 2013), hidden costs of openness (Cassiman and Valentini 2016), substantial under- or over-performance (Alexy, Bascavusoglu-Moreau, and Salter 2016), and negative internal attitudes (de Araújo Burcharth, Knudsen, and Sondergaard 2014). My study discloses an additional challenge for firms to conduct effective ETS against rivals in the face of the breadth of IPR resources. This research adds some empirical contributions, too. First, a notable trait of this study is that it jointly involves acquisitions and strategic technology alliances as crucial external knowledge and technology sources for business organisations. Second, in observance to the research line hallmarked by contributions from Block et al. (2015), Fosfuri, Giarratana, and Luzzi (2008), Fosfuri and Giarratana (2009) and Mendonça, Santos Pereira and Godinho (2004) that promote trademarks as strategic assets, this study focuses on the diversity dimension offering a value addition.

The findings of this study offer several implications for management practise. The general message of this paper for practising managers is that firms having broad IPR-related resources can be better positioned in the quest for external knowledge and technology. It is an important factor to have in mind as there is strong competition for external partners that can be located in distinct geographical areas. Firms better equipped with a large breadth of key IPR assets can themselves set the pace of competition that eventually crowds out rivals from crucial technology input factor markets. The results stress the indispensable role of internal IPR policy for firms to be able to approach partners that might have a different knowledge background. This is underpinned by the meaningful impact of patent generality which might motivate senior management to develop a suitable portfolio with a more ample spectrum. In addition, the study also highlights how a diversified trademark portfolio can buttress a competitive advantage at ETS contests against rivals in an innovative setting. Its implication for management practise refers to boosting organisational ability to produce a portfolio of trademarks with a diversified nature. One option is by hiring trademark experts that can shorten the IPR-grant process whereby promoting external technology search. Last, managers of resource-rich entities should not necessarily worry about knowledge spillovers by their resource-rich rivals as flocking with them in ETS locations occurs solely in case of multimarket contacts in the niches of the industry. Specifically, when fear of negative spillover balance is of concern, effective managers should put more emphasis on conscious efforts against knowledge expropriation, for instance through secrecy or the practise of mutual forbearance with retaliation potential.

This study also sends important messages for policymakers. For instance, richer firms in terms of the breadth of IPR resources tend to source technical diversity through various channels of ETS in which they are willing to make a widespread geographical exploration.

This is a good piece of news for economic decision-makers of technologically laggard regions. If those regions are developed with an appropriate economic policy, the opportunity to nurture local firms with specialised expertise will be created. Sooner or later these local enterprises can connect with and potentially assimilate into a broad industrial network. The beneficial outcome will be increased profits via new business opportunities with a larger community of firms.

This study is not exempt from limitations. The single-industry nature of data (with limited technology focus) applied in the analyses demands the results are examined in other technology-based contexts. However, characteristics of the Security Software Industry like the overall focus on product innovation, the fierce nature of competition and the product complexity of security software systems (Giarratana 2004) can easily compare to other young and technology-based environments. Further limitations stem from the relatively short time window of the current study which could be widened and thus improved in the future research.

Acknowledgments

The author is grateful to Joern H. Block (special issue coeditor) and two anonymous reviewers for their excellent guidance and feedback. My appreciation also goes to Juan Alcácer, Marco S. Giarratana, Keld Laursen, Toke Reichstein, and seminar participants at the 2018 annual European Academy of Management Conference (Iceland) that have commented on earlier drafts. I also thank Betsabé Perez Garrido for computational assistance and Gregory De La Piedra for language assistance. I gratefully acknowledge financial support from the Hungarian National Research, Development and Innovation Office (PD16-121037).

Disclosure statement

No potential conflict of interest was reported by the author.

Funding

This work was supported by the Hungarian National Research, Development and Innovation Office [PD16-121037].

References

Aaker, D. A. 1991. *Managing Brand Equity: Capitalizing on the Value of a Brand*. New York: Free Press.

Alcácer, J. 2006. "Location Choices across the Value Chain: How Activity and Capability Influence Collocation." *Management Science* 52 (10): 1457–1471. doi:10.1287/mnsc.1060.0658.

Alcácer, J., and W. Chung. 2007. "Location Strategies and Knowledge Spillovers." *Management Science* 53 (5): 760–776. doi:10.1287/mnsc.1060.0637.

Alexy, O., E. Bascavusoglu-Moreau, and A. J. Salter. 2016. "Toward an Aspiration-Level Theory of Open Innovation." *Industrial and Corporate Change* 25 (2): 289–306. doi:10.1093/icc/dtw003.

Almeida, P., and B. Kogut. 1999. "Localization of Knowledge and the Mobility of Engineers in Regional Networks." *Management Science* 45 (7): 905–917. doi:10.1287/mnsc.45.7.905.

Arora, A., and M. Ceccagnoli. 2006. "Patent Protection, Complementary Assets, and Firms' Incentives for Technology Licensing." *Management Science* 52 (2): 293–308. doi:10.1287/mnsc.1050.0437.

Barney, J. B. 1991. "Firm Resources and Sustained Competitive Advantage." *Journal of Management* 17 (1): 99–120. doi:10.1177/014920639101700108.

Barroso, A., and M. S. Giarratana. 2013. "Product Proliferation Strategies and Firm Performance: The Moderating Role of Product Space Complexity." *Strategic Management Journal* 34 (12): 1435–1452. doi:10.1002/smj.2013.34.issue-12.

Baum, J. A. C., and H. J. Korn. 1999. "Dynamics of Dyadic Competitive Interaction." *Strategic Management Journal* 20 (3): 251–278. doi:10.1002/(SICI)1097-0266(199903)20:3<251::AID-SMJ23>3.0.CO;2-H.

Bernheim, B. D., and M. D. Whinston. 1990. "Multimarket Contact and Collusive Behavior." *The RAND Journal of Economics* 21 (1): 1–26. doi:10.2307/2555490.

Blind, K., J. Edler, R. Frietsch, and U. Schmoch. 2006. "Motives to Patent: Empirical Evidence from Germany." *Research Policy* 35 (5): 655–672. doi:10.1016/j.respol.2006.03.002.

Block, J. H., G. De Vries, J. H. Schumann, and P. Sandner. 2014. "Trademarks and Venture Capital Valuation." *Journal of Business Venturing* 29 (4): 525–542. doi:10.1016/j.jbusvent.2013.07.006.

Block, J. H., C. O. Fisch, A. Hahn, and P. G. Sandner. 2015. "Why Do SMEs File Trademarks? Insights from Firms in Innovative Industries." *Research Policy* 44 (10): 1915–1930. doi:10.1016/j.respol.2015.06.007.

Boeker, W., J. Goodstein, J. Stephan, and J. P. Murmann. 1997. "Competition in a Multimarket Environment: The Case of Market Exit." *Organization Science* 8 (2): 126–142. doi:10.1287/orsc.8.2.126.

Cantwell, J. 1989. *Technological Innovation and Multinational Corporations.* Oxford, UK: Basil Blackwell.

Cantwell, J., and O. Janne. 1999. "Technological Globalisation and Innovative Centres: The Role of Corporate Technological Leadership and Locational Hierarchy." *Research Policy* 28 (2–3): 119–144. doi:10.1016/S0048-7333(98)00118-8.

Carroll, G. R., and A. Swaminathan. 2000. "Why the Microbrewery Movement? Organizational Dynamics of Resource Partitioning in the U.S. Brewing Industry." *American Journal of Sociology* 106 (3): 715–762. doi:10.1086/318962.

Cassiman, B., and M. G. Colombo, Eds. 2006. *Mergers & Acquisitions: The Innovation Impact.* Cheltenham, UK: Edward Elgar Publishing.

Cassiman, B., and G. Valentini. 2016. "Open Innovation: Are Inbound and Outbound Knowledge Flows Really Complementary?" *Strategic Management Journal* 37 (6): 1034–1046. doi:10.1002/smj.2375.

Cassiman, B., and R. Veugelers. 2002. "R&D Cooperation and Spillovers: Some Empirical Evidence from Belgium." *American Economic Review* 92 (4): 1169–1184. doi:10.1257/00028280260344704.

Castanias, R. P., and C. E. Helfat. 1991. "Managerial Resources and Rents." *Journal of Management* 17 (1): 155–171. doi:10.1177/014920639101700110.

Chen, M.-J. 1996. "Competitor Analysis and Interfirm Rivalry: Toward a Theoretical Integration." *Academy of Management Review* 21 (1): 100–134. doi:10.5465/amr.1996.9602161567.

Chung, W., and J. Alcácer. 2002. "Knowledge Seeking and Location Choice of Foreign Direct Investment in the United States." *Management Science* 48 (12): 1534–1554. doi:10.1287/mnsc.48.12.1534.440.

Cohen, D. 1991. "Trademark Strategy Revisited." *The Journal of Marketing* 55 (3): 46–59. doi:10.1177/002224299105500305.

Cohen, W. M., and S. Klepper. 1996. "A Reprise of Size and R&D." *The Economic Journal* 106 (437): 925–951. doi:10.2307/2235365.

Dahlander, L., and D. M. Gann. 2010. "How Open Is Innovation?" *Research Policy* 39 (6): 699–709. doi:10.1016/j.respol.2010.01.013.

de Araújo Burcharth, A. L., M. P. Knudsen, and H. A. Søndergaard. 2014. "Neither Invented nor Shared Here: The Impact and Management of Attitudes for the Adoption of Open Innovation Practices." *Technovation* 34 (3): 149–161. doi:10.1016/j.technovation.2013.11.007.

De Vries, G., E. Pennings, J. H. Block, and C. Fisch. 2017. "Trademark or Patent? the Effects of Market Concentration, Customer Type and Venture Capital Financing on Start-Ups' Initial IP Applications." *Industry and Innovation* 24 (4): 325–345. doi:10.1080/13662716.2016.1231607.

Dobrev, S. D., T. Y. Kim, and G. R. Carroll. 2002. "The Evolution of Organizational Niches: US Automobile Manufacturers, 1885–1981." *Administrative Science Quarterly* 47 (2): 233–264. doi:10.2307/3094805.

Dodgson, M., Ed. 1989. *Technological Strategy and the Firm: Management and Public Policy.* London: Longman.

Dowell, G. 2006. "Product Line Strategies of New Entrants in an Established Industry: Evidence from the US Bicycle Industry." *Strategic Management Journal* 27 (10): 959–979. doi:10.1002/(ISSN)1097-0266.

Dussauge, P., B. Garrette, and W. Mitchell. 2000. "Learning from Competing Partners: Outcomes and Durations of Scale and Link Alliances in Europe, North America and Asia." *Strategic Management Journal* 21 (2): 99–126. doi:10.1002/(ISSN)1097-0266.

The Economist. 2002. *A Survey of Digital Security: Securing the Cloud.* October 26.

Escribano, A., A. Fosfuri, and J. A. Tribo. 2009. "Managing External Knowledge Flows: The Moderating Role of Absorptive Capacity." *Research Policy* 38 (1): 96–105. doi:10.1016/j.respol.2008.10.022.

Flikkema, M., A. P. De Man, and C. Castaldi. 2014. "Are Trademark Counts a Valid Indicator of Innovation? Results of an In-Depth Study of New Benelux Trademarks Filed by SMEs." *Industry and Innovation* 21 (4): 310–331. doi:10.1080/13662716.2014.934547.

Forman, C., A. Goldfarb, and S. Greenstein. 2008. "Understanding the Inputs into Innovation: Do Cities Substitute for Internal Firm Resources?" *Journal of Economics & Management Strategy* 17 (2): 295–316. doi:10.1111/j.1530-9134.2008.00179.x.

Fosfuri, A., and M. S. Giarratana. 2009. "Masters of War: Rivals' Product Innovation and New Advertising in Mature Product Markets." *Management Science* 55 (2): 181–191. doi:10.1287/mnsc.1080.0939.

Fosfuri, A., M. S. Giarratana, and A. Luzzi. 2008. "The Penguin Has Entered the Building: The Commercialization of Open Source Software Products." *Organization Science* 19 (2): 292–305. doi:10.1287/orsc.1070.0321.

Fosfuri, A., M. S. Giarratana, and S. S. Sebrek. 2018. "Resource Partitioning and Strategies in Markets for Technology." *Strategic Organization.* doi:10.1177/1476127018791329.

Gandal, N., S. Markovich, and M. Riordan. 2005. "Ain't it "Suite"? Bundling in the PC Office Software Market." Unpublished manuscript.

Gans, J. S., and S. Stern. 2003. "The Product Market and the Market for "Ideas": Commercialization Strategies for Technology Entrepreneurs." *Research Policy* 32 (2): 333–350. doi:10.1016/S0048-7333(02)00103-8.

Gao, G., and L. M. Hitt. 2012. "Information Technology and Trademarks: Implications for Product Variety." *Management Science* 58 (6): 1211–1226. doi:10.1287/mnsc.1110.1480.

Garriga, H., G. Von Krogh, and S. Spaeth. 2013. "How Constraints and Knowledge Impact Open Innovation." *Strategic Management Journal* 34 (9): 1134–1144. doi:10.1002/smj.2013.34.issue-9.

Garud, R., and A. Kumaraswamy. 1993. "Changing Competitive Dynamics in Network Industries: An Exploration of Sun Microsystems' Open Systems Strategy." *Strategic Management Journal* 14 (5): 351–369. doi:10.1002/(ISSN)1097-0266.

Giarratana, M. S. 2004. "The Birth of a New Industry: Entry by Startups and the Drivers of Firm Growth. The Case of Encryption Software." *Research Policy* 33 (5): 787–806. doi:10.1016/j.respol.2004.01.001.

Giarratana, M. S. 2008. "Missing the Starting Gun: De Alio Entry Order in New Markets, Inertia and Real Option Capabilities." *European Management Review* 5 (2): 115–124. doi:10.1057/emr.2008.7.

Giarratana, M. S., and A. Fosfuri. 2007. "Product Strategies and Survival in Schumpeterian Environments: Evidence from the US Security Software Industry." *Organization Studies* 28 (6): 909–929. doi:10.1177/0170840607075267.

Giarratana, M. S., and M. Mariani. 2014. "The Relationship between Knowledge Sourcing and Fear of Imitation." *Strategic Management Journal* 35 (8): 1144–1163. doi:10.1002/smj.2014.35.issue-8.

Giarratana, M. S., and S. Torrisi. 2010. "Foreign Entry and Survival in a Knowledge-Intensive Market: Emerging Economy Countries' International Linkages, Technology Competences, and Firm Experience." *Strategic Entrepreneurship Journal* 4 (1): 85–104. doi:10.1002/(ISSN)1932-443X.

Hagedoorn, J., and G. Duysters. 2002. "External Sources of Innovative Capabilities: The Preferences for Strategic Alliances or Mergers and Acquisitions." *Journal of Management Studies* 39 (2): 167–188. doi:10.1111/joms.2002.39.issue-2.

Hall, B. H., and R. H. Ziedonis. 2001. "The Patent Paradox Revisited: An Empirical Study of Patenting in the U.S. Semiconductor Industry 1979–1995." *The RAND Journal of Economics* 32 (1): 101–128. doi:10.2307/2696400.

Hamel, G. 1991. "Competition for Competence and Inter-Partner Learning within International Strategic Alliances." *Strategic Management Journal* 12 (S1): 83–103. doi:10.1002/(ISSN)1097-0266.

Haspeslagh, P., and D. Jemison. 1991. *Managing Acquisitions: Creating Value Through Corporate Renewal*. New York: Free Press.

Helmers, C., and M. Rogers. 2010. "Innovation and the Survival of New Firms in the UK." *Review of Industrial Organization* 36 (3): 227–248. doi:10.1007/s11151-010-9247-7.

Henderson, R., and I. Cockburn. 1994. "Measuring Competence? Exploring Firm Effects in Pharmaceutical Research." *Strategic Management Journal* 15 (S1): 63–84. doi:10.1002/(ISSN)1097-0266.

Hitt, M. A., R. E. Hoskisson, R. A. Johnson, and D. D. Moesel. 1996. "The Market for Corporate Control and Firm Innovation." *Academy of Management Journal* 39 (5): 1084–1119.

International Data Corporation (IDC). 2000. *Security Software Market Analysis*. Annual Report.

International Data Corporation (IDC). 2003. *Security Software Market Analysis*. Annual Report.

Jaffe, A., M. Trajtenberg, and R. Henderson. 1993. "Geographic Localization of Knowledge Spillovers as Evidenced by Patent Citations." *The Quarterly Journal of Economics* 108 (3): 577–598. doi:10.2307/2118401.

Kapferer, J.-N. 1997. *Strategic Brand Management: Creating and Sustaining Brand Equity Long Term*. London: Kogan Page.

Karnani, A., and B. Wernerfelt. 1985. "Multiple Point Competition." *Strategic Management Journal* 6 (1): 87–96. doi:10.1002/(ISSN)1097-0266.

Kim, D.-J., and B. Kogut. 1996. "Technological Platforms and Diversification." *Organization Science* 7 (3): 283–301. doi:10.1287/orsc.7.3.283.

King, A. A., and C. L. Tucci. 2002. "Incumbent Entry into New Market Niches: The Role of Experience and Managerial Choice in the Creation of Dynamic Capabilities." *Management Science* 48 (2): 171–186. doi:10.1287/mnsc.48.2.171.253.

Kogut, B., and U. Zander. 1992. "Knowledge of the Firm, Combinative Capabilities, and the Replication of Technology." *Organization Science* 3 (3): 383–397. doi:10.1287/orsc.3.3.383.

Krackhardt, D. 1988. "Predicting with Networks: Nonparametric Multiple Regression Analysis of Dyadic Data." *Social Networks* 10 (4): 359–381. doi:10.1016/0378-8733(88)90004-4.

Krasnikov, A., S. Mishra, and D. Orozco. 2009. "Evaluating the Financial Impact of Branding Using Trademarks: A Framework and Empirical Evidence." *Journal of Marketing* 73 (6): 154–166. doi:10.1509/jmkg.73.6.154.

Kumar, R., and K. O. Nti. 1998. "Differential Learning and Interaction in Alliance Dynamics: A Process and Outcome Discrepancy Model." *Organization Science* 9 (3): 356–367. doi:10.1287/orsc.9.3.356.

Lancaster, K. 1984. "Brand Advertising Competition and Industry Demand." *Journal of Advertising* 13 (4): 19–30. doi:10.1080/00913367.1984.10672913.

Lancaster, K. 1990. "The Economics of Product Variety: A Survey." *Marketing Science* 9 (3): 189–206. doi:10.1287/mksc.9.3.189.

Lane, P. J., and M. Lubatkin. 1998. "Relative Absorptive Capacity and Interorganizational Learning." *Strategic Management Journal* 19 (5): 461–477. doi:10.1002/(ISSN)1097-0266.

le Duc, N., and J. Lindeque. 2018. "Proximity and Multinational Enterprise Co-Location in Clusters: A Multiple Case Study of Dutch Science Parks." *Industry and Innovation* 25 (3): 282–307. doi:10.1080/13662716.2017.1355230.

Li, S. X., and R. Greenwood. 2004. "The Effect of Within-Industry Diversification on Firm Performance: Synergy Creation, Multi-Market Contact and Market Structuration." *Strategic Management Journal* 25 (12): 1131–1153. doi:10.1002/(ISSN)1097-0266.

Mendonça, S., T. Santos Pereira, and M. M. Godinho. 2004. "Trademarks as an Indicator of Innovation and Industrial Change." *Research Policy* 33 (9): 1385–1404. doi:10.1016/j.respol.2004.09.005.

Narin, F., E. Noma, and R. Perry. 1987. "Patents as Indicators of Corporate Technological Strength." *Research Policy* 16 (2–4): 143–155. doi:10.1016/0048-7333(87)90028-X.

Negro, G., F. Visentin, and A. Swaminathan'. 2014. "Resource Partitioning and the Organizational Dynamics of 'Fringe Banking'." *American Sociological Review* 79 (4): 680–704. doi:10.1177/0003122414537644.

Pennings, J. M., and F. Harianto. 1992. "The Diffusion of Technological Innovation in the Commercial Banking Industry." *Strategic Management Journal* 13 (1): 29–46. doi:10.1002/(ISSN)1097-0266.

Pisano, G. P. 1991. "The Governance of Innovation: Vertical Integration and Collaborative Arrangements in the Biotechnology Industry." *Research Policy* 20 (3): 237–249. doi:10.1016/0048-7333(91)90054-T.

Reuer, J. J., and N. Lahiri. 2013. "Searching for Alliance Partners: Effects of Geographic Distance on the Formation of R&D Collaborations." *Organization Science* 25 (1): 283–298. doi:10.1287/orsc.1120.0805.

Ritala, P., H. Olander, S. Michailova, and K. Husted. 2015. "Knowledge Sharing, Knowledge Leaking and Relative Innovation Performance: An Empirical Study." *Technovation* 35: 22–31. doi:10.1016/j.technovation.2014.07.011.

Rosenkopf, L., and A. Nerkar. 1999. "On the Complexity of Technological Evolution: Exploring Coevolution within and across Hierarchical Levels in Optical Disc Technology." In *Variations in Organization Science: In Honor of D. T. Campbell*, edited by J. A. C. Baum and W. McKelvey, 169–183. Thousand Oaks, CA: Sage.

Rosenkopf, L., and A. Nerkar. 2001. "Beyond Local Search: Boundary-Spanning, Exploration, and Impact in the Optical Disk Industry." *Strategic Management Journal* 22 (4): 287–306. doi:10.1002/(ISSN)1097-0266.

Rosenkopf, L., and M. L. Tushman. 1998. "The Coevolution of Community Networks and Technology: Lessons from the Flight Simulation Industry." *Industrial and Corporate Change* 7 (2): 311–346. doi:10.1093/icc/7.2.311.

Sakkab, N. Y. 2002. "Connect & Develop Complements Research & Develop at P&G." *Research Technology Management* 45 (2): 38–45. doi:10.1080/08956308.2002.11671490.

Salge, T. O., T. Farchi, M. I. Barrett, and S. Dopson. 2013. "When Does Search Openness Really Matter? A Contingency Study of Health-Care Innovation Projects." *Journal of Product Innovation Management* 30 (4): 659–676. doi:10.1111/jpim.2013.30.issue-4.

Sandner, P. G., and J. Block. 2011. "The Market Value of R&D, Patents, and Trademarks." *Research Policy* 40 (7): 969–985. doi:10.1016/j.respol.2011.04.004.

Saxenian, A. 1994. *Regional Advantage: Culture and Competition in Silicon Valley and Route 128.* Cambridge, USA: Harvard University Press.

Seethamraju, C. 2003. "The Value Relevance of Trademarks." In *Intangible Assets: Values. Measures and Risks*, edited by J. R. M. Hand and B. Lev, 228–247. New York: Oxford University Press.

Shapiro, C., and H. R. Varian. 1999. *Information Rules: A Strategic Guide to the Network Economy.* Boston: Harvard Business School Press.

Shaver, J. M., and F. Flyer. 2000. "Agglomeration Economies, Firm Heterogeneity, and Foreign Direct Investment in the United States." *Strategic Management Journal* 21 (12): 1175–1193. doi:10.1002/(ISSN)1097-0266.

Siggelkow, N. 2003. "Why Focus? A Study of Intra-Industry Focus Effects." *The Journal of Industrial Economics* 51 (2): 121–150. doi:10.1111/1467-6451.00195.

Sirmon, D. G., S. Gove, and M. A. Hitt. 2008. "Resource Management in Dyadic Competitive Rivalry: The Effects of Resource Bundling and Deployment." *Academy of Management Journal* 51 (5): 919–935. doi:10.5465/amj.2008.34789656.

Smith, G. V., and R. L. Parr. 2000. *Valuation of Intellectual Property and Intangible Assets*. 3rd ed. New York: John Wiley & Sons.

Sorenson, O. 2000. "Letting the Market Work for You: An Evolutionary Perspective on Product Strategy." *Strategic Management Journal* 21 (5): 577–592. doi:10.1002/(ISSN)1097-0266.

Sorenson, O., S. McEvily, C. R. Ren, and R. Roy. 2006. "Niche Width Revisited: Organizational Scope, Behavior and Performance." *Strategic Management Journal* 27 (10): 915–936. doi:10.1002/(ISSN)1097-0266.

Strumsky, D., and J. Lobo. 2015. "Identifying the Sources of Technological Novelty in the Process of Invention." *Research Policy* 44 (8): 1445–1461. doi:10.1016/j.respol.2015.05.008.

Swaminathan, A. 2001. "Resource Partitioning and the Evolution of Specialist Organizations: The Role of Location and Identity in the U.S. Wine Industry." *Academy of Management Journal* 44 (6): 1169–1185.

Teece, D. 1986. "Profiting from Technological Innovation: Implications for Integration, Collaboration, Licensing and Public Policy." *Research Policy* 15 (6): 285–305. doi:10.1016/0048-7333(86)90027-2.

Trajtenberg, M., A. Jaffe, and B. Hall. 2000. "The NBER/Case Western Patents Data File: A Guided Tour." Unpublished manuscript.

Tripsas, M. 1997. "Unraveling the Process of Creative Destruction: Complementary Assets and Incumbent Survival in the Typesetter Industry." *Strategic Management Journal* 19 (S1): 119–142.

Veer, T., and F. Jell. 2012. "Contributing to Markets for Technology? A Comparison of Patent Filing Motives of Individual Inventors, Small Companies and Universities." *Technovation* 32 (9–10): 513–522. doi:10.1016/j.technovation.2012.03.002.

Vermeulen, F., and H. Barkema. 2001. "Learning through Acquisitions." *Academy of Management Journal* 44 (3): 457–476.

Warlop, L., S. Ratneshwar, and S. M. J. Van Osselaer. 2005. "Distinctive Brand Cues and Memory for Product Consumption Experiences." *International Journal of Research in Marketing* 22 (1): 27–44. doi:10.1016/j.ijresmar.2004.02.001.

Zahavi, T., and D. Lavie. 2013. "Intra-Industry Diversification and Firm Performance." *Strategic Management Journal* 34 (8): 978–998. doi:10.1002/smj.2013.34.issue-8.

Zahra, S. A., and G. George. 2002. "Absorptive Capacity: A Review, Re-Conceptualization, and Extension." *Academy of Management Journal* 27 (2): 185–203.

Zhou, H., P. G. Sandner, S. L. Martinelli, and J. H. Block. 2016. "Patents, Trademarks, and Their Complementarity in Venture Capital Funding." *Technovation* 47: 14–22. doi:10.1016/j.technovation.2015.11.005.

Ziedonis, R. H. 2004. "Don't Fence Me In: Fragmented Markets for Technology and the Patent Acquisition Strategies of Firms." *Management Science* 50 (6): 804–820. doi:10.1287/mnsc.1040.0208.

Zobel, A. K., B. Balsmeier, and H. Chesbrough. 2016. "Does Patenting Help or Hinder Open Innovation? Evidence from New Entrants in the Solar Industry." *Industrial and Corporate Change* 25 (2): 307–331. doi:10.1093/icc/dtw005.

Zollo, M., and S. G. Winter. 2002. "Deliberate Learning and the Evolution of Dynamic Capabilities." *Organization Science* 13 (3): 339–351. doi:10.1287/orsc.13.3.339.2780.

Trademark or patent? The effects of market concentration, customer type and venture capital financing on start-ups' initial IP applications

Geertjan De Vries, Enrico Pennings, Joern H. Block and Christian Fisch

ABSTRACT
We analyse the initial IP applications of 4,703 start-ups in the U.S., distinguishing between trademark and patent applications. Our empirical results show that start-ups are more likely to file for trademarks instead of patents when entering markets with a higher market concentration. Furthermore, we find that start-ups that are primarily active in business-to-consumer markets instead of business-to-business markets are more likely to file trademarks. Finally, the involvement of a venture capitalist (VC) affects the initial IP application. VC-backed start-ups are more likely than other start-ups to file initial IP in the form of trademarks rather than patents. This paper contributes to research on the use of IP rights in start-ups and to the literature on new venture strategy.

1. Introduction

Intellectual property rights (IPRs) constitute a crucial set of assets and resources for start-ups and influence new venture strategy. Traditionally, research on the role of IPRs for small firms and start-ups has been patent-focused (e.g. Blind et al. 2006; De Rassenfosse 2012). Recently, research on trademarks has gained momentum and has established that trademarks are a similarly important form of IPR, particularly for start-ups. Like patents, trademarks have been found to be positively related to firm valuations (Sandner and Block 2011; Greenhalgh and Rogers 2012), firm survival (Srinivasan, Lilien, and Rangaswamy 2008; Helmers and Rogers 2010) and venture capital (VC) funding (Block et al. 2014).

Despite these similarities, trademarks and patents differ in important ways. Most notably, trademarks and patents reflect different protection intentions: Patents refer to the technological aspects of a firms' business model, whereas trademarks relate to marketing aspects, such as the commercialisation of an invention or the protection of a firm's brands (Mendonça, Pereira, and Godinho 2004; Srinivasan, Lilien, and Rangaswamy 2008). Thus, a common argument for why firms file patents versus trademarks is that firms which are active in R&D-intensive and technology-oriented industries will typically file for patent protection, whereas firms that are active in advertising-intensive, consumer-related and service-related industries are more likely to file for trademark protection (Amara, Landry, and Traoré 2008; Block et al. 2015).

So far, however, little empirical research exists with regard to the antecedents of a start-up's initial IP decision and IP strategy.[1] For start-ups, the decision about their initial IP is grounded in their overall innovation and new venture strategy, particularly whether it is more technology- or more marketing-oriented (e.g. Sandner and Block 2011; Block et al. 2014).

A start-up's initial IP decision and its first activities represent the starting point of a path-dependent process in the evolution of a new venture strategy. Innovation, entrepreneurship and business model-related activities are characterised by path dependency (Redding 2002; Garnsey, Stam, and Heffernan 2006; Thrane, Blaabjerg, and Møller 2010; Valorinta, Schildt, and Lamberg 2011; Greve and Seidel 2015): past events or decisions influence future events and decisions (i.e. future decisions are conditioned by historical events) (Coombs and Hull 1998; Sydow, Schreyögg, and Koch 2009). The founder's initial decisions shape his or her start-up's evolution, and have a long-lasting impact on its organisation, business model and strategy; this phenomenon is known as founder imprinting (e.g. Nelson 2003; Hsu and Lim 2014; Boling, Pieper, and Covin 2016). Thus, a start-up's initial IPR decision – to trademark or to patent – reflects, and at the same time influences, the evolution of the start-up as well as its business model and strategy. As a result of these initial decisions, start-ups can become constrained, overly focused on some particular dimensions of strategy, or even locked-in with regard to their strategy and IPR applications (Sydow, Schreyögg, and Koch 2009; Thrane, Blaabjerg, and Møller 2010). Thus, a start-up's initial IPR application has far-reaching implications, and is therefore a highly relevant area of investigation from both a theoretical and practical point of view.

We examine the initial IPR application (trademark or patent) of 4,703 U.S. start-ups between 1998 and 2007. Our results show that, as market concentration increases, start-ups are more likely to file trademarks instead of patents as their initial IP rights. Second, we find that start-ups focusing on business-to-consumer (B2C) markets are more likely to file for trademarks compared to start-ups serving business-to-business (B2B) markets. Third, we find that the involvement of a VC firm leads to a higher likelihood of filing the initial IP in the form of a trademark instead of a patent.

Our findings contribute to the literature on small firms' and start-ups' IPR usage (e.g. Amara, Landry, and Traoré 2008; Thomä and Bizer 2013; Flikkema, De Man, and Castaldi 2014). To date, the existing literature has investigated the motives of small- and medium-sized enterprises and start-ups when filing IPRs and the resulting effects. However, the initial decision of filing a trademark or a patent has not been assessed thus far. Our study also contributes to the broader literature on new venture strategy (Carter et al. 1994; McGee, Dowling, and Megginson 1995; Lee, Lim, and Tan 1999) and its evolution (e.g. Garnsey, Stam, and Heffernan 2006). Filing patents can be associated with differentiation strategies based on technology (Arundel 2001; Blind et al. 2006; Veer and Jell 2012), whereas

---

[1]Throughout the paper, a start-up's 'initial IP decision' refers to whether a start-up files a trademark or a patent as its first IPR.

trademarks can be associated with marketing-based differentiation strategies (Mendonça, Pereira, and Godinho 2004; Srinivasan, Lilien, and Rangaswamy 2008; Flikkema, De Man, and Castaldi 2014). Thus, our study investigates the antecedents of filing trademarks or patents as an initial IP right, while also providing information on whether a start-up's overall strategy is more technology- or marketing-oriented.

Finally, our study contributes to the growing literature on the relationship between IPRs and VC financing. This literature shows that start-ups filing patents have a higher likelihood of receiving VC funds in the first place (Cao and Hsu 2011; Haeussler, Harhoff, and Müller 2012; Hoenen et al. 2014) and that patents show a positive relationship with subsequent start-up valuations by VCs (Lerner 1994; Baum and Silverman 2004; Hsu and Ziedonis 2008). Recent research further shows that, in addition to patents, VCs also value trademarks for their protection and signalling value (Block et al. 2014). VCs are active investors with strong control rights. They advise start-up firms, shaping their strategies and business models (Sahlman 1990; Schefczyk and Gerpott 2001; Gompers and Lerner 2004). This influence most likely has an additional effect on the start-up's initial IP decisions. However, to date, we know little about this particular influence of VCs. Our study helps close this knowledge gap and contributes to the discussion on how VCs influence start-ups' strategies (Hellmann and Puri 2002; Bertoni, Colombo, and Grilli 2011) and how they drive start-ups' IPR applications.

The remainder of the paper is structured as follows: Section 2 provides background information on the motives for filing trademarks and patents and develops our hypotheses. Section 3 describes our data and variables. Section 4 presents the descriptive and multivariate results, which are then discussed in Section 5. Section 6 presents the conclusions of our study and details limitations and avenues for future research.

2. Conceptual framework and hypotheses

2.1. Start-ups' motives for filing trademarks and patents

A firm's motives for filing trademarks or patents are multifold and have sparked a considerable amount of research (e.g. Cohen, Richard, and Walsh 2000; Blind et al. 2006; Flikkema, De Man, and Castaldi 2014; Block et al. 2015). Briefly summarised, the reasons to file a patent can be grouped into protection, blocking, reputation, exchange and incentive motives (Blind et al. 2006). Similarly, trademarks are filed for protection, reputation and exchange reasons. Blocking and incentive motives do not apply for trademarks (Block et al. 2015).

2.1.1. Protection motives

The core function of both patents and trademarks is to protect IP assets (Cohen, Richard, and Walsh 2000; Block et al. 2015). The fundamental difference between patents and trademarks is that patents protect a firm's technological assets and capabilities (e.g. Blind et al. 2006; Thomä and Bizer 2013). By contrast, trademarks protect a firm's marketing assets. By protecting symbols and names, trademarks are supposed to distinguish a firm and its products or services from competitors in the eyes of the firm's customers (Mendonça, Pereira, and Godinho 2004; Fosfuri and Giarratana 2009). Trademarks provide the legal basis for brands and indicate a firm's willingness to protect its brands against competitors (Mendonça, Pereira, and Godinho 2004; Sandner and Block 2011).

2.1.2. Reputation motives

Another important motive for filing patents and trademarks is building a reputation (e.g. Blind et al. 2006; Block et al. 2015).[2] Trademarks help build a reputation with customers. They reduce the search costs of customers by signalling a higher product quality via brands (Srinivasan, Lilien, and Rangaswamy 2008). In contrast to trademarks, patents represent the technological capabilities of a firm and help build a positive technological image with customers and other stakeholders (e.g. Blind et al. 2006; Veer and Jell 2012).

2.1.3. Exchange motives

Exchange motives refer to facilitating a relationship with external partners to acquire funding or licensing income. Trademarks indicate a start-up's marketing orientation (Srinivasan, Lilien, and Rangaswamy 2008; Block et al. 2014). In this manner, they can increase a start-up's attractiveness to external investors and reduce funding costs (e.g. Ramello and Silva 2006; Srinivasan, Lilien, and Rangaswamy 2008). The same can be true for patents, which indicate a start-up's technological and innovation capabilities to potential capital providers (e.g. De Rassenfosse 2012; Veer and Jell 2012).

Based on these differences between trademarks and patents regarding protection, reputation and exchange motives, we now develop hypotheses on how market concentration, customer type and VC funding influence start-ups' initial IP applications.

2.2. Hypotheses

2.2.1. Market concentration and start-ups' initial IP applications

Market concentration describes the sum of the market share of the largest firms that are active within a particular market (e.g. Domowitz, Hubbard, and Petersen 1986; Harris 1998). We argue that market concentration influences a start-up's initial decision of filing a trademark or a patent. The argumentation is twofold.

First, market concentration and entry barriers are interconnected (Caves and Porter 1977; McAfee, Mialon, and Williams 2004). Markets with a low concentration oftentimes also have low entry barriers. In such markets, it is relatively easy for start-ups to become operational. Trademarks and branding play an important role in this regard, given that they help the start-up to pursue a product quality-based differentiation strategy and communicate its unique selling proposition to customers (Srinivasan, Lilien, and Rangaswamy 2008). In markets with low entry barriers, start-ups tend to rely more heavily on trademarks as a basic branding instrument to create a competitive advantage (Abimbola 2001). In markets with high concentration, the situation is different. Incumbents have a strong and powerful position, and entry barriers are often high (Besanko et al. 2010). To enter such markets, innovation (often radical or disruptive) is needed. Therefore, patents play an important role in the start-up's market entry strategy, given that they support the start-up in appropriating returns on innovations (Arundel 2001; Thomä and Bizer 2013). When entering a concentrated market, a patent will exclude incumbent firms from the use of a start-up's technological knowledge and thus helps capture some initial market share (Blind et al. 2006). Without the strong protection of the core knowledge of a start-up, it becomes more difficult to pose a credible threat to incumbent firms that are in control of the resources within an

---

[2]In the context of trademarks, Block et al. (2015) refer to the reputation motives as 'marketing motives.'

industry. Prior research shows that start-ups with protected novel technical knowledge can indeed pose a great threat to established, powerful incumbents (Abernathy and Clark 1984; Henderson 1993; Hill and Rothaermel 2003).

Second, a high market concentration often implies low competition (e.g. Domowitz, Hubbard, and Petersen 1986; Harris 1998).[3] Overall, the filing of a trademark should become more relevant when customers have several similar firms to choose from in their purchasing decisions. When market concentration is low, there exist more competing firms and a start-up's needs to build visibility and increase its reputation by branding. As described above, trademarks, being the legal anchor of brands, represent a powerful tool that can be used to build a strong link between the start-up and its customers. That is, trademarks enable a start-up to differentiate itself from its competitors (e.g. Mendonça, Pereira, and Godinho 2004; Sandner and Block 2011).

Taking these two lines of arguments, we propose the following:

Hypothesis 1: Start-ups in less concentrated markets are more likely than start-ups in highly concentrated markets to file the initial IP in the form of a trademark rather than a patent.

2.2.2. Customer type (B2C vs. B2B markets) and start-ups' initial IP applications

The main customer type is another important market characteristic that influences a start-up's initial IP decisions. Here, we distinguish between start-ups that primarily operate in B2C markets and start-ups that primarily operate in B2B markets. The main customers of start-ups in B2C markets are end customers, whereas start-ups in B2B markets primarily serve business customers.

Prior marketing research has found considerable differences between B2B and B2C markets (Edwards, Gut, and Mavondo 2007). For example, it has been found that end customers rely more on brands as quality signals compared to business customers. Building on this finding, we argue that the signalling function of trademarks should be of higher importance in B2C markets than in B2B markets (Ahmed and D'Astous 1995; Edwards, Gut, and Mavondo 2007). The reason is that business customers in B2B markets are often experts themselves and can judge product quality without having to rely on a product brand as a signal for product quality. Moreover, they mostly engage in long-term customer relationships, reducing the need for signalling through brands. In B2C markets, a patent might be a more valuable quality signal than trademarks, given that having a patent shows that a start-up has strong innovation and technology capabilities.

Thus, we formulate the following hypothesis:

Hypothesis 2: Start-ups that primarily serve end customers are more likely than start-ups that primarily serve business customers to file the initial IP in the form of a trademark rather than a patent.

2.2.3. VC funding and start-ups' initial IP applications

VCs are active investors who not only provide funding, but also spend a considerable amount of time advising and monitoring the management of the start-ups in their portfolios. VCs often have a powerful role in the start-ups' supervisory boards and have the ability to fire

---

[3]Although a higher market concentration oftentimes also corresponds to a higher competition or market power, this notion does not have to be true for every market. Because the market concentration used in this study only focuses on the top firms within a market, the remaining competitors in a market are not accounted for. Hence, there is some debate surrounding this subject (e.g. Schmalensee 1989).

the members of a start-up's management team. Prior research shows that VCs influence and shape a start-up's strategy (Sahlman 1990; Schefczyk and Gerpott 2001; Gompers and Lerner 2004). We argue that the involvement of a VC is likely to shift a start-up's focus from the development towards the commercialisation of its inventions.

The extant literature shows that VCs find early stage start-ups to be overly focused on the development of their inventions. VCs are of the opinion that start-ups should be consumer-oriented and conduct market analysis (Hisrich 1989; Hills, Hultman, and Miles 2008). When deciding to invest, VCs set milestones that a start-up needs to achieve to receive subsequent rounds of funding. In early stages, such milestones are directed towards market orientation, making the product more consumer-friendly and acquiring initial consumers who are willing to buy the product (Berkery 2008). Accordingly, the involvement of a VC is likely to shorten a start-up's time-to-market and speed up the professionalisation of marketing activities compared to non-VC-funded start-ups (Hellmann and Puri 2000, 2002). VCs only have a limited time period in which to turn a start-up into a functioning company that can either be sold through an IPO or through a trade sale to an incumbent. Thus, VCs seek to bring a product to market as early as possible. The filing of a trademark is likely to be one of the initial steps taken in the commercialisation process, securing the start-up's brand name and protecting its future marketing efforts (Sandner and Block 2011).

Hence, we derive the following hypothesis:

Hypothesis 3: Start-ups funded by VCs are more likely than start-ups not funded by VCs to file the initial IP in the form of a trademark rather than a patent.

3. Data

3.1. Data sources and sample

To construct our sample, we used Thomson Reuters' VentureXpert database and retrieved information on all U.S.-based start-ups that received VC funding in the period from 1998 to 2007 (11,808 firms). We were unable to take into account data beyond 2007 due to the lengthy process surrounding patent applications and the successive granting of international patent protection (Greenhalgh and Rogers 2010).

We defined the start-up's market by the six-digit NAICS code available from VentureXpert. For each NAICS classification, we used COMPUSTAT to calculate the three-year averages of R&D and advertising intensity over our sample period (1998–2007). COMPUSTAT data are commonly used in existing studies to calculate such measures (e.g. Chauvin and Hirschey 1993; Waring 1996). Additionally, we obtained data on market concentration, which is published by the U.S. Census Bureau every five years. The competition data from the U.S. Census Bureau is reliable, given that each firm in the U.S. is required by law to respond to the U.S. Census Survey (e.g. Ali, Klasa, and Yeung 2009).

We obtained information regarding the trademarks and patents of the sampled firms through a semi-manual process. The trademark applications were obtained from the United States Patent and Trademark Office (USPTO) (see also Graham et al. 2013). The U.S. Patent applications were obtained from PATSTAT, one of the most comprehensive databases on patents to date. The extent of IP activities could be determined for 10,128 of the start-ups in our sample (85.7%). Imperfect matches were verified through the industry and location records available from VentureXpert. Excluding start-ups that filed a first trademark or patent prior to 1998 and excluding observations with missing data on other variables reduced our sample to 6,095 firms. The final sample includes 4,703 firms that filed a trademark or patent between 1998 and 2007 and 2,022 firms that filed neither a trademark nor a patent.

3.2. Variables

Our dependent variable is the binary variable *trademark or patent*, indicating whether a start-up filed its first IP application in the form of a trademark (=1) or a patent (=0). We use the respective application dates because they closely relate to the point in time when the start-up made its IP decision and are not blurred by the publication process.

Regarding our independent variables, we measured *market concentration* as the sum of the market share of the four largest firms that are active within a particular NAICS class, also known as the C4 ratio (e.g. Domowitz, Hubbard, and Petersen 1986; Harris 1998). Because concentration data are published every 5 years by the U.S. Census Bureau, we used the C4 ratio that was published in 1997 (2002) for the start-ups in our sample that had applied for an initial IP right up until 2002 (2007).[4] A start-up's main customer type was captured by three dummy variables. The dummy variable *Customer type: B2C* captures whether a start-up is primarily active in B2C markets, whereas the dummy variable *Customer type: B2B* indicates that a start-up is primarily active in B2B markets. The dummy *Customer type: other* captures whether firms had multiple or other main customer types. The data were obtained from VentureXpert. Finally, we included a dummy variable (*VC dummy*) indicating whether the start-up received VC funding up until the date of its first IP application (coded as 1) or not (coded as 0). Note that this variable could only be calculated for firms that filed for trademarks or patents.

We include a wide range of control variables. First, we control for the average *industry R&D intensity* and the average *industry advertising intensity*, which are calculated for each individual market in COMPUSTAT over the three years prior to a start-up's initial IP application. It is important to control for these factors because start-ups that operate in research-intensive industries are more likely to file patent applications (Griliches 1998). Such industries are likely to be science-based. Similarly, a higher industry advertising intensity may be related to a more trademark-oriented IP strategy (Mendonça, Pereira, and Godinho 2004).

Second, we control for *start-up age* in years at the date of a start-up's first IP application. To control for the resource endowment of a company, we include the variable money *received (log.)*, which captures the total amount of VC funding a firm collected until 2007. Third, given that IP protection regimes or mechanisms may vary across different industry types (Amara, Landry, and Traoré 2008; Dushnitsky and Shaver 2009), we include six *industry dummies*, categorised by VentureXpert: 'biotechnology', 'communications and media', 'computer related', 'medical/health/life science', 'non-high-technology' and 'semiconductors/other electronics'. To control for time trends in trademark or patent applications, we use 10 *application year dummies* to indicate the year in which the start-up applied for its first IP. Time-related shifts in environmental, managerial or legal conditions may affect IP applications (Kortum and Lerner 1999). Finally, possible regional influences are controlled for

---

[4]An alternative to using the C4 ratio would be to use a convex function of the market share such, as a Herfindahl–Hirschman index. However, we were not able to compute such an index with the data available.

by 17 U.S. region dummies because the type and degree of regional technology orientation (e.g. Silicon Valley, New England) may affect IP behaviour (Audretsch and Feldmann 1996).

4. Analysis

4.1. Descriptive results

Table 1 presents the descriptive statistics for our sample, including firms that did not file a trademark or patent. Of the 4,703 start-ups in our sample that filed an IPR, 60.8% filed for a trademark first instead of a patent. This preference could be explained by the slightly broader applicability of trademarks, which is potentially relevant for both the technology- and service-related markets, whereas patents are especially relevant in technology-based markets (Greenhalgh and Rogers 2006; Block et al. 2015).

We find considerable variation in the market concentration. Although the average concentration is 36.2%, the market with the lowest concentration is dental services (NAICS classification = 621210), with a C4 ratio of 0.7%. By contrast, the market with the highest concentration is the manufacturing of space vehicles (NAICS classification = 336,414), with a C4 ratio of 91.6%. To assess potential differences between firms that filed an IPR and firms that did not, Table 1 shows the mean values of the two samples. With regard to market concentration, there exist only small differences between the two samples. Regarding main customer type, Table 1 shows that most start-ups in our sample operate in B2B markets: 60.3% of start-ups operate in B2B markets, whereas only 12.9% of start-ups operate in B2C markets. The B2B share, however, is significantly higher among firms that file IPRs. With regard to VC financing, we observe that 40.3% of the start-ups in our sample had received VC funding *before* applying for their first IP right. Note that this variable cannot be calculated if a firm did not file a trademark or patent application.

Regarding our control variables, we observe an average industry R&D intensity of 13.5% of sales and an average advertising intensity of 1.4% of sales. Both measures are right-skewed (e.g. maximum R&D intensity is 2,456.7%). As a robustness check, we correct for this phenomenon by taking only those NAICS sectors into account for which we have R&D and advertising intensity information for at least five firms (which resulted in a mean industry R&D intensity of 11.5% and a maximum value of 38.9%). Finally, the average start-up's age was 3.3 years and it received 18.5 million USD (log = 2.919) until 2007. Because of the skewed nature of this variable, we include the variable in logged form. Note that this variable shows a comparatively large difference between firms that filed an IPR and firms that did not. The reason is that, for those start-ups that did not file an IP application, the firm age from the year 2007 was taken. Finally, the industry dummies show that most of our firms (46.9%) are active in computer-related industries such as computer software and services and internet-related activities. There exist considerable differences regarding industry between firms that filed an IPR and firms that did not. For example, 19.3% of the firms that did not file an IPR belong to the non-high-technology category, whereas only 10.4% of the firms that did file an IPR belong to this category. Concerning a start-up's customer type, we find that start-ups are most likely to sell to end consumers in the medical and life science industry (37.8%) and in the non-high-tech industry (35.1%).

Table 1. Descriptive statistics and comparison of firms that filed no IPR at all and firms that filed a patent and/or a trademark.

Variable	Total sample (mean)				Firms that filed NO IPR		Firms that filed an IPR		Diff. (sig.)
	Mean	N	Min	Max	Mean	N	Mean	N	
Dependent variable									
Trademark or patent[a]	0.608	4,703	0	1	–	–	0.608	4.703	–
Independent variables									
Market concentration[b]	36.18	6,095	0.7	91.6	35.42	1,392	36.40	4,703	-0.981*
Main customer type: B2B	0.603	6,095	0	1	0.552	1,392	0.618	4,703	-0.066***
Main customer type: B2C	0.129	6,095	0	1	0.137	1,392	0.127	4,703	0.011
Main customer type: other	0.268	6,095	0	1	0.310	1,392	0.256	4,703	0.055***
Received VC before application[a]	0.403	4,703	0	1	–	–	0.403	4,703	–
Control variables									
Industry R&D intensity[a]	13.46	6,095	0	2,456,7	10.83	1,392	14.243	4,703	-3.411
Industry advertising intensity[a]	1.385	6,095	0	32.40	1.287	1,392	1.415	4,703	-0.128**
Age at application (log.)[a]	1.203	6,095	0	1.691	2.470	1,392	0.828	4,703	1.642***
Money received (log.)	2.919	6,095	-3.507	9.126	3.024	1,32	2.888	4,703	0.136***
Industry: biotechnology	0.063	6,095	0	1	0.058	1,392	0.065	4,703	-0.006
Industry: comm. and media	0.139	6,095	0	1	0.134	1,392	0.141	4,703	-0.007
Industry: computer-related	0.469	6,095	0	1	0.436	1,392	0.479	4,703	-0.043***
Industry: med./health/life sci.	0.113	6,095	0	1	0.103	1,392	0.116	4,703	-0.013
Industry: non-high-technology	0.124	6,095	0	1	0.193	1,392	0.104	4,703	0.088***
Industry: semicon./other elec.	0.090	6,095	0	1	0.075	1,392	0.095	4,703	-0.019**
Only included in selection equation									
Time since first VC round (log.)	1.743	6,095	0	3.555	1.862	1,392	1.559	4,703	0.279***
Actors invested in the start-up	5.456	6,095	1	29	5.645	1,392	5.400	4,703	0.245**

Note. For firms that did not file IPR, these variables are calculated until 31 December 2007.
[a]Values only exist if a firm filed a trademark or patent.
[b]Calculated until the first IPR application.
$*p < 0.1$; $**p < 0.05$; $***p < 0.01$.

Table 2. Correlations and variance inflation factors (VIF) for start-ups that filed a trademark or patent.

Variable	(1)	(2)	(3)	(4)	(5)	(6)	(7)	(8)	(9)	(10)	(11)	(12)	(13)	VIF
1. Trademark or patent														1.19
2. Market concentration	−0.09*													1.15
3. Main customer type: B2C	0.05*	−0.08*												1.17
4. Main customer type: other	−0.03*	0.01	−0.23*											1.14
5. Received VC before application	0.13*	0.01	−0.03	0.01										1.25
6. Industry R&D intensity	−0.03*	0.00	0.00	−0.01	−0.02									1.02
7. Industry advertising intensity	0.05*	0.16*	0.09*	−0.02	0.00	−0.01								1.11
8. Age at application (log.)	0.18*	−0.04*	−0.01	0.02	0.54*	−0.02	−0.03*							1.26
9. Money received (log.)	−0.06*	0.06*	0.01	−0.08*	0.13*	−0.02	−0.02	0.01						1.14
10. Industry: biotechnology	−0.14*	0.08*	0.01	0.10*	−0.04	0.11	−0.05*	−0.05*	0.03*					1.49
11. Industry: computer-related	0.23*	−0.08*	−0.04*	−0.09*	0.02	−0.02	0.07*	0.00	−0.09*	−0.24*				2.37
12. Industry: medical/health/life sci.	−0.16*	−0.07*	0.12*	0.09*	−0.06*	−0.02	−0.09*	−0.05*	0.01	−0.09*	−0.34*			1.78
13. Industry: non-high-technology	0.09*	−0.12*	0.13*	0.01	0.04*	0.00	0.01	0.18*	−0.03*	−0.10*	−0.35*	−0.13*		1.70
14. Industry: semicon./other electronics	−0.20*	0.24*	−0.10*	−0.05*	−0.03*	−0.01	0.03*	−0.07*	0.06*	−0.08*	−0.30*	−0.11*	−0.12*	1.63

Notes. $N = 4{,}703$. VIFs are estimated based on Model 7 (Table 4).
*$p < 0.05$.

Table 3. Probit regression (incl. Heckman model) with the dependent variable: Trademark (=1) or patent (=0).

Variable	Hyp.	Model 1	Model 2	Model 3	Model 4	Model 5	Model 6
Outcome equation							
Industry R&D intensity		−0.000	−0.000*	−0.000	−0.000	−0.000*	−0.000*
		(0.000)	(0.000)	(0.000)	(0.000)	(0.000)	(0.000)
Industry advertising intensity		0.034**	0.041***	0.031**	0.034**	0.037**	0.037**
		(0.014)	(0.016)	(0.013)	(0.013)	(0.015)	(0.015)
Age at application (log.)		0.341***	0.343***	0.359***	0.223***	0.242***	0.202***
		(0.053)	(0.049)	(0.050)	(0.077)	(0.071)	(0.028)
Money received (log.)		−0.009	−0.009	−0.009	−0.024*	−0.023*	−0.025*
		(0.013)	(0.013)	(0.013)	(0.013)	(0.014)	(0.014)
Market concentration	H1 (+)		−0.003*			−0.003*	−0.003*
			(0.002)			(0.002)	(0.002)
Main customer type: B2C	H2 (+)			0.242***		0.239***	0.235***
				(0.070)		(0.069)	(0.072)
Main customer type: other				0.053		0.052	0.047
				(0.049)		(0.050)	(0.052)
Received VC before application	H3 (+)				0.243***	0.248***	0.259***
					(0.055)	(0.055)	(0.044)
Industry dummies		Yes	Yes	Yes	Yes	Yes	Yes
Year dummies		Yes	Yes	Yes	Yes	Yes	Yes
Region dummies		Yes	Yes	Yes	Yes	Yes	Yes
Selection equation[a]							
Industry R&D intensity[b]		0.000	0.000	0.000	0.000	0.000	–
		(0.000)	(0.000)	(0.000)	(0.000)	(0.000)	–
Industry advertising intensity[b]		0.009	0.009	0.009	0.010	0.010	–
		(0.032)	(0.032)	(0.032)	(0.032)	(0.032)	–
Age at application (log.)[b]		−1.526***	−1.526***	−1.525***	−1.527***	−1.527***	–
		(0.086)	(0.086)	(0.086)	(0.086)	(0.086)	–
Money received (log.)		0.024	0.024	0.024	0.023	0.024	–
		(0.020)	(0.020)	(0.020)	(0.020)	(0.020)	
Market concentration[b]		−0.000	−0.000	−0.000	−0.000	−0.000	–
		(0.004)	(0.004)	(0.004)	(0.004)	(0.004)	–
Main customer type: B2C		−0.200**	−0.200**	−0.214**	−0.208**	−0.213**	–
		(0.090)	(0.090)	(0.090)	(0.088)	(0.090)	–
Main customer type: other		−0.235***	−0.235***	−0.238***	−0.236***	−0.237***	–
		(0.055)	(0.055)	(0.054)	(0.055)	(0.055)	–
Time first fund. round (log.)		0.419***	0.419***	0.419***	0.415***	0.415***	–
		(0.072)	(0.072)	(0.071)	(0.071)	(0.071)	–
Actors invested in the start-up		−0.049***	−0.049***	−0.050***	−0.049***	−0.049***	–
		(0.006)	(0.006)	(0.006)	(0.005)	(0.006)	–
Industry dummies		Yes	Yes	Yes	Yes	Yes	Yes
Year dummies		Yes	Yes	Yes	Yes	Yes	Yes
Observations		6,095	6,095	6,095	6,095	6,095	4,703
NAICS sectors		390	390	390	390	390	333
Rho (Wald-test)		−0.223*	−0.225*	−0.252**	−0.066	−0.096	–
LR-test (vs. Model 1)		–	6.134**	14.213***	27.469***	47.873***	–

Notes. Standard errors are clustered on six-digit NAICS sectors (in parentheses). Reference group for IP application year: 2001; reference U.S. region: 'Silicon Valley'; reference industry: 'communications and media.'
[a]The variable *Received VC before application* as well as the application year dummies could not be included in the selection equation because values only exist if a firm filed a trademark or patent.
[b]Calculated until the first IPR application. For firms that did not file IPR, these variables are calculated until 31 December 2007.
*p < 0.1; **p < 0.05; ***p < 0.01.

THE ROLE OF TRADEMARKS

Table 2 shows the correlations and variance inflation factors (VIFs). The directions of the reported correlations are in line with our hypothesised effects. The VIFs are below 2.5, indicating that multicollinearity is unlikely to pose a problem in our estimations.

4.2. Multivariate results

Table 3 shows the results of several Probit regressions with the dependent variable *trademark or patent*. Focusing only on firms that filed a trademark or patent might introduce a selection bias. The descriptive statistics (Table 1) reveal differences between start-ups that filed an IP application and start-ups that did not. To correct for this selection bias, we estimate a two-step Heckman Probit model (Heckman 1979; Heckman, LaLonde, and Smith 1999). Model 1 only includes the control variables. In the selection equation, we include all variables of the outcome equation, with the exception of variables that can only be estimated if a company filed an IPR (i.e. whether a company received VC funding before the IP application and the application year dummies). Because specifying a sufficient selection equation requires additional variables that are not included in the outcome equation, we additionally include the time elapsed since first funding round (log.) and the number of investors. Both variables have a significant impact and should influence a start-up's decision to file an IPR or not, while not necessarily influencing the decision of filing a trademark or a patent. A significant Rho coefficient, which quantifies the correlation between the error terms of the selection and the outcome equation, indicates that a selection bias is present.

Model 1 includes all of the control variables. All models include standard errors clustered at the NAICS level. The independent variables are entered subsequently in the following models. Model 2 includes market concentration, which shows a positive and significant effect ($p < 0.1$). As hypothesised in H1, an increase in market concentration leads to a higher likelihood of filing the first IP right in the form of a trademark instead of a patent. This effect also persists if all variables are entered jointly in Model 6 ($p < 0.1$), thus lending support for H1. Customer-type dummy variables are added in Model 3. The results show that a focus on B2C markets instead of B2B markets leads to a higher likelihood of filing trademarks instead of patents as a first IP right ($p < 0.01$ in Model 3 or $p < 0.01$ in Model 6). This finding supports H2 and is in line with our argument that start-ups active in B2C markets use trademarks or brands to differentiate themselves from their competitors from an end customer's perspective. Finally, in Model 4, we introduce the VC dummy variable. The coefficient shows that start-ups funded by VCs are more likely to file their first IP right in the form of a trademark than a patent ($p < 0.01$). This finding provides support for our third hypothesis, H3. All variables are entered simultaneously in Model 5. The results of the independent variables remain unchanged. However, the Rho coefficient becomes insignificant, indicating that a sample selection should not bias the estimation. Therefore, we also estimate Model 5 without accounting for a potential selection effect. Again, the results regarding the main independent variables remain largely unchanged (Model 6).

With regard to the control variables, the results show that R&D intensity has no effect on the choice between a trademark and patent, whereas a higher advertising intensity promotes trademark applications. Additionally, industry differences emerge: for example, compared to the reference category 'communications and media', firms in 'biotechnology', 'medical/life sciences' and 'semiconductors/other electronics' are more likely to file patents, whereas trademarks are more likely to be filed by firms active in 'computer-related' and

Table 4. Propensity score matching analysis of a potential VC selection effect.

Matching algorithm	N treatment group	N control group	Average treatment effect	Standard error	t-statistic
Nearest neighbour matching (replacement)	1,889	2,807	0.059	0.219	2.71
Nearest neighbour matching (no replacement)	1,889	1,889	0.010	0.013	7.38
Kernel matching	1,889	2,807	0.063	0.017	3.73
Radius matching	1,889	2,807	0.132	0.015	8.73

Notes. Sample includes start-ups that filed a trademark or patent only.
*$p < 0.1$; **$p < 0.05$; ***$p < 0.01$.

'non-high-technology' industries. Finally, younger start-ups are more likely to file for patents rather than trademarks as their first IP right. This effect is in line with existing studies that indicate that start-ups tend to be overly focused on their inventions instead of showing a greater market orientation during the early stages of their venture (Hisrich 1989; Wortman, Spann, and Adams 1989).

4.3. Additional analyses and robustness checks

The estimated effect of VC funding before filing an initial IP right may suffer from a selection bias. Start-ups that received VC funding before filing an initial IP right might differ structurally from other start-ups (e.g. with regard to the start-up's business models, age and economic conditions). Propensity score matching is a method of correcting this selection bias (Rosenbaum and Rubin 1983), comparing the initial IP rights of VC-backed start-ups (treatment group) to the initial IP rights of start-ups that are not VC-backed but are otherwise as similar as possible (control group).

The propensity scores were estimated by a Probit regression on the VC dummy. All available variables used in our main analysis were included as independent variables in this estimation. On the basis of the estimated propensity scores, VC-backed start-ups (treatment group) were matched with start-ups that had not yet received any VC funds (control group). The results show that VC-backed start-ups were on average 5.9–13.2% more likely to file the initial IP in the form of a trademark rather than a patent. The size of the effect differs with the matching algorithm used (see Table 4).

Our R&D and advertising industry intensity measures are strongly right-skewed. This phenomenon is mostly because some industry sectors only include a few individual firms that drive the intensity measures. As a robustness check, we account for this phenomenon by only including sectors with at least five firms, thereby reducing the skewness of these measures. This step reduces our sample to 3,966 start-ups that are active in 216 different NAICS classifications. The regression results, presented in Table 5 (Model 2), show a negatively significant effect of R&D intensity while also showing a highly significant and positive effect of advertising intensity on trademark applications. All other results remain unchanged.

Next, we exclude firms that filed a trademark and patent application within a period of six months. Given that the filings occurred in such a short period of time, there may be no clear preference for either a trademark or a patent. Furthermore, this exclusion reduces a potential bias due to errors or delays in the recording of the application dates or due to the differences between the filing systems of patents and trademarks. This step reduces our

Table 5. Robustness checks.

Variable	Model 1 Main model (=Model 7, Table 4)	Model 2 R&D and adver- tising intensity based on at least five firms	Model 3 TM and patent application >6 months apart	Model 4 Controlling for additional VC information
Industry R&D intensity	−0.000	−0.010**	−0.000*	−0.001**
	(0.000)	(0.004)	(0.000)	(0.000)
Industry advertising intensity	0.038**	0.051***	0.040*	0.071**
	(0.015)	(0.019)	(0.020)	(0.030)
Age at application (log.)	0.205***	0.218***	0.235***	0.071
	(0.028)	(0.031)	(0.034)	(0.060)
Market concentration	−0.003*	−0.003*	−0.004**	−0.003**
	(0.002)	(0.002)	(0.002)	(0.002)
Main customer type: B2C	0.235***	0.158**	0.293***	0.340**
	(0.072)	(0.076)	(0.073)	(0.167)
Main customer type: other	0.052	0.026	0.067	0.025
	(0.051)	(0.053)	(0.050)	(0.112)
Received VC before application	0.246***	0.243***	0.272***	
	(0.044)	(0.052)	(0.051)	
Round characteristics				
Round number				0.011
				(0.044)
Syndicate size				−0.011
				(0.042)
Funding amount (log.)				0.149***
				(0.053)
VC characteristics				
VC experience (log.)				0.073*
				(0.039)
VC age (log.)				−0.133
				(0.084)
Investor type dummies	No	No	No	Yes
Start-up development dummies	No	No	No	Yes
Industry dummies	Yes	Yes	Yes	Yes
Year/region dummies	Yes	Yes	Yes	Yes
Observations	4,703	3,966	3,891	1,811
NAICS sectors	333	216	319	207
Pseudo R^2	0.127	0.133	0.176	0.115

Notes. Standard errors are clustered on six-digit NAICS sectors (in parentheses). Reference group for IP application year: 2001; reference U.S. region: 'Silicon Valley'; reference industry: 'communications and media.'
*$p < 0.1$; **$p < 0.05$; ***$p < 0.01$.

sample to 3,891 start-ups that are active in 319 NAICS sectors. As reported in Model 3 of Table 5, the results regarding our hypothesised effects remain similar to the results from our main analyses.

Finally, the VentureXpert database contains additional information on the VC funding of the sampled firms which can be grouped into round characteristics and VC characteristics. Because this information is only available for firms that received VC funds, our sample is reduced to 1,811 observations. For example, VCs categorise a start-up as being in a specific venture stage, differentiating as to whether a start-up is still working on its first prototype or if it is already in a later venture stage, working on initial sales, expanding its market share or, ultimately, looking for an exit. Furthermore, we are able to control for the funding stage (round number), the amount of VC funds received, the number of investors involved, the VCs' experience and maturity levels and the different types of VC investors (VC firm, business angel, corporate investor, financial institution, governmental investor). Each specific

VC actor type operates under a different set of incentives and may therefore influence the start-up's management in a different manner (Sorenson and Stuart 2008; Dushnitsky and Shapira 2010). Even when controlling for these variables, the effects of our independent variables market concentration ($\beta = -0.015$, $p < 0.05$) and customer type: B2C ($p < 0.01$) remain unchanged, thus further underlining the robustness of our results.

5. Discussion of results

Prior research has investigated the link between market structure and appropriability conditions or regimes (Teece 1986; Arora 1997; Leiponen and Byma 2009). Based on Schumpeter (1950) and Arrow (1962), it is argued that a temporary monopoly granted by patents stimulates innovation and improves the appropriability of innovation rents. Market power provides a strong incentive to invest in R&D, which then increases the need for IP protection and patenting. Thus, markets with a high concentration and incumbents with high market power are characterised by high R&D investments and high patenting. Start-up entrants are aware of these phenomena and build on patents rather than trademarks as a pathway to enter such concentrated markets. Prior research has indicated that patents function as a stronger exclusion right than trademarks, given that patents can be used as an effective means to block competitors, whereas trademarks cannot (Block et al. 2015). Although a patent can exclude firms from the use of a start-up's technological knowledge, a trademark does not have such a strong exclusion power. Competitors can circumvent the trademark by conducting their business under a different brand name. Our findings that start-ups in highly concentrated markets are more likely to file patents rather than trademarks as initial IP rights is in line with this argumentation.

Our findings on the effect of market concentration on initial IP filings are also in line with Sutton (2007), who classifies R&D and advertising as endogenous sunk costs. He further argues that the investments needed to reach incumbents' economies of scale constitute exogenous sunk cost that entrants need to carry or overcome. Entry barriers and market concentration are determined by endogenous and exogenous sunk costs. Through our market concentration variable, we indirectly examine how exogenous sunk costs influence start-ups' initial IP decisions. We find that start-ups that are attempting to enter markets with high entry barriers and high exogenous sunk costs (resulting from economies of scale) file for patents rather than trademarks as first IP rights. To enter such markets, an entry strategy based on patented technological knowledge can pose a strong and credible threat to incumbents (Abernathy and Clark 1984; Henderson 1993; Hill and Rothaermel 2003). Trademarks, in turn, are more valuable in markets with differentiated goods, where exogenous sunk costs and market entry barriers are low. In such markets, they help the start-up to build and maintain strong visibility among the large number of firms that are active in the market.

Previous studies find that VCs influence the start-up's financial performance (Schefczyk and Gerpott 2001; Fitza, Matusik, and Mosakowski 2009), professionalisation (Hellmann and Puri 2002), time-to-market (Hellmann and Puri 2000), growth rate (Davila, Foster, and Gupta 2003) and survival chances (Manigart, Baeyens, and Van Hyfte 2002). Our findings add to this literature, showing that VCs also influence the IP management or IP strategy of start-ups, increasing the likelihood of filing the initial IP in the form of trademarks rather than patents. VCs are active investors with strong control rights who advise and monitor the start-ups in which they invest (Sahlman 1990; Gompers and Lerner 2004). VCs exert pressure on the start-up to commercialise its knowledge and inventions by setting mile-stones related to market orientation and/or initial revenues (Hisrich 1989; Hellmann and Puri 2000, 2002; Berkery 2008). Filing a trademark can be interpreted as a first step towards commercialisation and can be such a milestone.

However, our finding that VC funding increases the likelihood of trademarks rather than patents as initial IP rights can also reflect a selection effect. In that case, VCs do not actively push start-ups towards trademarking but rather have a preference for investing in start-ups that are close to the commercialisation of a product. Trademarks are a signal or an indicator of a start-up's market orientation and revenue potential (Sandner and Block 2011). Unfortunately, our data do not allow us to disentangle the selection from the treatment effect, and we cannot establish the exact direction and mechanism of how VCs influence trademarking as opposed to patenting.

6. Conclusions

We analyse the determinants of the initial filing of a trademark or patent for 4,703 start-ups in the U.S. Our results show that market concentration, customer type and VC funding influence this decision. Start-ups are more likely to file a trademark instead of a patent as their initial IP rights when operating in markets with a low concentration, when being active in B2C instead of B2B markets and when having received VC funding beforehand.

Our findings have practical implications for both start-ups and policy-makers. For start-ups, our results suggest that venture capitalists take an active role in new ventures: they not only provide funding, but also push start-ups towards the swifter commercialisation and marketing of their inventions. This is because VCs typically seek to bring a product to market as early as possible. Our results show that firms that received VC support are more likely to file trademarks as their initial IP rights than other start-ups. Hence, VC providers not only select innovative firms, but also influence these firms' strategies, pushing them towards the rapid commercialisation and marketing of their products (Colombo and Grilli 2010; Samila and Sorenson 2010). Start-ups seeking money from VCs should be aware of this influence and should take this into account when considering the pros and cons of VC financing. While a greater market orientation and focus on marketing might be useful and highly appreciated for certain ventures and entrepreneurs, start-ups that are still further away from the commercialisation phase in their innovation process might find this influence disturbing and distracting.

With respect to policy-makers attempting to improve start-ups' IPR usage, our study provides useful information about the sectors and conditions under which trademarks are typically preferred over patents as the initial IP rights, and vice versa. This information can be used to design and/or improve initiatives intended to strengthen start-ups' IPR usage, which is one of the main goals of policy-makers aiming to foster innovative entrepreneur-ship and the evolution of innovative start-ups (Block, Fisch, and van Praag, forthcoming; European Commission 2015).

Our paper has several limitations that provide guidance for further research. First, our empirical analysis only considers the very initial IPR applications of start-ups and excludes subsequent filings. It might be that start-ups decide to file both a patent and a trademark in close succession, and do not place much thought on whether to file a trademark or a patent first. Although studying follow-up filings and their determinants is a promising endeavour for future research, we account for the filing of a trademark and patent within 6 months of each other in our robustness checks. The primary results remain unchanged. Second, our data-set is constructed from several different data sources. IP data are gathered through a matching process relying on the manual creation of company name patterns that were used to extract information on trademark and patent filings. Although this method was cross-validated with records in the USPTO trademark register, we cannot completely rule out possible mismatches or the potential failure to include relevant IP applications in our data-set. Third, it still remains unclear what the exact mechanisms behind our findings are. As illustrated above, it is unclear whether our conclusion that VC-backed start-ups rely more on trademarks than on patents is due to a selection or a treatment effect. In other words: we do not know whether VCs push their start-ups to file for trademarks, or whether VCs actively select start-ups that have short-term revenue potential and are anyway close to filing a trademark, regardless of the VC's involvement. Finally, our paper only considers two particular formal IP protection mechanisms, namely patents and trademarks. However, the previous literature shows that other formal IP protection mechanisms are generally of lower importance for small firms (e.g. Arundel 2001; Leiponen and Byma 2009).

Disclosure statement

No potential conflict of interest was reported by the authors.

References

Abernathy, W. J., and K. B. Clark. 1984. "Innovation: Mapping the Winds of Creative Destruction." *Research Policy* 14 (1): 3–22.
Abimbola, T. 2001. "Branding as a Competitive Strategy for Demand Management in SMEs." *Journal of Research in Marketing & Entrepreneurship* 3 (2): 97–106.
Ahmed, S. A., and A. D'Astous. 1995. "Comparison of Country-of-origin Effects on Household and Organizational Buyers' Product Perceptions." *European Journal of Marketing* 29 (3): 35–51.
Ali, A., S. Klasa, and E. Yeung. 2009. "The Limitations of Industry Concentration Measures Constructed with Compustat Data: Implications for Finance Research." *Review of Financial Studies* 22 (10): 3839–3871.
Amara, N., R. Landry, and N. Traoré. 2008. "Managing the Protection of Innovations in Knowledge-Intensive Business Services." *Research Policy* 37 (9): 1530–1547.
Arora, A. 1997. "Patents, Licensing, and Market Structure in the Chemical Industry." *Research Policy* 26 (4–5): 391–403.
Arrow, K. 1962. "Economic Welfare and the Allocation of Resources for Invention." In *The Rate and Direction of Inventive Activity*, edited by R. Nelson, 609–626. Princeton, NJ: Princeton University Press.
Arundel, A. 2001. "The Relative Effectiveness of Patents and Secrecy for Appropriation." *Research Policy* 30 (4): 611–624.
Audretsch, D. B., and M. P. Feldmann. 1996. "R&D Spillovers and the Geography of Innovation and Production." *The American Economic Review* 86 (3): 630–640.
Baum, J. A. C., and B. S. Silverman. 2004. "Picking Winners or Building Them? Alliance, Intellectual, and Human Capital as Selection Criteria in Venture Financing and Performance of Biotech Start-ups." *Journal of Business Venturing* 19 (3): 411–436.
Berkery, D. 2008. *Raising Venture Capital for the Serious Entrepreneur*. New York: McGraw-Hill.
Bertoni, F., M. G. Colombo, and L. Grilli. 2011. "Venture Capital Financing and the Growth of High-tech Start-ups: Disentangling Treatment from Selection Effects." *Research Policy* 40 (7): 1028–1043.

Besanko, D., D. Dranove, M. Shanley, and S. Schaefer. 2010. *Economics of Strategy*. New York: Wiley.

Blind, K., J. Edler, R. Frietsch, and U. Schmoch. 2006. "Motives to Patent: Empirical Evidence from Germany." *Research Policy* 35 (5): 655–672.

Block, J. H., C. O. Fisch, and M. van Praag. Forthcoming. "The Schumpeterian Entrepreneur: A Review of the Empirical Evidence on the Antecedents, Behaviour and Consequences of Innovative Entrepreneurship." *Industry and Innovation*. http://www.tandfonline.com/doi/abs/10.1080/1366 2716.2016.1216397.

Block, J. H., G. De Vries, J. H. Schumann, and P. Sandner. 2014. "Trademarks and Venture Capital Valuation." *Journal of Business Venturing* 29 (4): 525–542.

Block, J. H., C. O. Fisch, A. Hahn, and P. Sandner. 2015. "Why do SMEs File Trademarks? Insights from Firms in Innovative Industries." *Research Policy* 44 (10): 1915–1930.

Boling, J. R., T. M. Pieper, and J. G. Covin. 2016. "CEO Tenure and Entrepreneurial Orientation within Family and Nonfamily Firms." *Entrepreneurship Theory and Practice* 40 (4): 891–913.

Cao, J, and P. H. Hsu. 2011. *The Informational Role of Patents in Venture Capital Financing*. Working paper (SSRN Working Paper Series). Rochester, NY: SSRN.

Carter, N. M., T. M. Stearns, P. D. Reynolds, and B. A. Miller. 1994. "New Venture Strategies: Theory Development with an Empirical Base." *Strategic Management Journal* 15 (1): 21–41.

Caves, R. E., and M. E. Porter. 1977. "From Entry Barriers to Mobility Barriers: Conjectural Decisions and Contrived Deterrence to New Competition." *The Quarterly Journal of Economics* 91 (2): 241–262.

Chauvin, K. W., and M. Hirschey. 1993. "Advertising R&D Expenditures and the Market Value of the Firm." *Financial Management* 22 (4): 128–140.

Cohen, W. M., R. N. Richard, and J. P. Walsh. 2000. *Protecting their Intellectual Assets: Appropriability Conditions and Why US Manufacturing Firms Patent (or not)*. Working Paper. Cambridge, MA: National Bureau of Economic Research.

Colombo, M. G., and L. Grilli. 2010. "On Growth Drivers of High-tech Start-ups: Exploring the Role of Founders' Human Capital and Venture Capital." *Journal of Business Venturing* 25 (6): 610–626.

Coombs, R., and R. Hull. 1998. "Knowledge Management Practices' and Path-Dependency in Innovation." *Research Policy* 27 (3): 237–253.

Davila, A., G. Foster, and M. Gupta. 2003. "Venture Capital Financing and the Growth of Startup Firms." *Journal of Business Venturing* 18 (6): 689–708.

De Rassenfosse, G. 2012. "How SMEs Exploit Their Intellectual Property Assets: Evidence from Survey Data." *Small Business Economics* 39 (2): 437–452.

Domowitz, I., R. G. Hubbard, and B. C. Petersen. 1986. "Business Cycles and the Relationship between Concentration and Price-cost Margins." *The RAND Journal of Economics* 17 (1): 1–17.

Dushnitsky, G., and Z. Shapira. 2010. "Entrepreneurial Finance Meets Organizational Reality: Comparing Investment Practices and Performance of Corporate and Independent Venture Capitalists." *Strategic Management Journal* 31 (9): 990–1017.

Dushnitsky, G., and J. M. Shaver. 2009. "Limitations to Interorganizational Knowledge Acquisition: The Paradox of Corporate Venture Capital." *Strategic Management Journal* 30 (10): 1045–1064.

Edwards, R., A. M. Gut, and F. Mavondo. 2007. "Buyer Animosity in Business to Business Markets: Evidence from the French Nuclear Tests." *Industrial Marketing Management* 36 (4): 483–492.

European Commission. 2015. *Evaluation of IPorta*. Accessed June 9, 2016. file:///D:/Users/Administrator/Downloads/NB0214001ENN_002.pdf

Fitza, M., S. F. Matusik, and E. Mosakowski. 2009. "Do VCs Matter? The Importance of Owners on Performance Variance in Start-up Firms." *Strategic Management Journal* 30 (4): 387–404.

Flikkema, M., A. De Man, and C. Castaldi. 2014. "Are Trademark Counts a Valid Indicator Of Innovation? Results of an In-depth Study of New Benelux Trademarks Filed by SMEs." *Industry and Innovation* 21 (4): 310–331.

Fosfuri, A., and M. S. Giarratana. 2009. "Masters of War: Rivals' Product Innovation and New Advertising in Mature Product Markets." *Management Science* 55 (2): 181–191.

Garnsey, E., E. Stam, and P. Heffernan. 2006. "New Firm Growth: Exploring Processes and Paths." *Industry and Innovation* 13 (1): 1–20.

Gompers, P. A., and J. Lerner. 2004. *The Venture Capital Cycle*. Cambridge, MA: MIT Press.

Graham, S. J. H., G. Hancock, A. C. Marco, and A. F. Myers. 2013. "The USPTO Trademark Case Files Dataset: Descriptions, Lessons, and Insights." *Journal of Economics & Management Strategy* 22 (4): 669–705.

Greenhalgh, C., and M. Rogers. 2006. "The Value of Innovation: The Interaction of Competition, R&D and IP." *Research Policy* 35 (4): 562–580.

Greenhalgh, C., and M. Rogers. 2010. *Innovation, Intellectual Property, and Economic Growth.* Princeton, NJ: Princeton University Press.

Greenhalgh, C., and M. Rogers. 2012. "Trade Marks and Performance in Services and Manufacturing Firms: Evidence of Schumpeterian Competition through Innovation." *Australian Economic Review* 45 (1): 50–76.

Greve, H. R., and M. D. L. Seidel. 2015. "The Thin Red Line between Success and Failure: Path Dependence in the Diffusion of Innovative Production Technologies." *Strategic Management Journal* 36 (4): 475–496.

Griliches, Z. 1998. *R&D and Productivity: The Econometric Evidence.* Chicago, IL: University of Chicago Press.

Haeussler, C., D. Harhoff, and E. Müller. 2012. *To Be Financed or Not: The Role of Patents for Venture Capital Financing.* Working Paper. Mannheim: ZEW-Centre for European Economic Research.

Harris, M. S. 1998. "The Association between Competition and Managers' Business Segment Reporting Decisions." *Journal of Accounting Research* 36 (1): 111–128.

Heckman, J. J. 1979. "Sample Selection Bias as a Specification Error." *Econometrica* 47 (1): 153–161.

Heckman, J. J., R. J. LaLonde, and J. A. Smith. 1999. "The Economics and Econometrics of Active Labor Market Programs." In *Handbook of Labor Economics*, vol. 3 (part 2), edited by O. Ashenfelder and D. Cards, 1865–2097. Amsterdam: Elsevier.

Hellmann, T., and M. Puri. 2000. "The Interaction between Product Market and Financing Strategy: The Role of Venture Capital." *Review of Financial Studies* 13 (4): 959–984.

Hellmann, T., and M. Puri. 2002. "Venture Capital and the Professionalization of Start-up Firms: Empirical Evidence." *The Journal of Finance* 57 (1): 169–197.

Helmers, C., and M. Rogers. 2010. "Innovation and the Survival of New Firms in the UK." *Review of Industrial Organization* 36 (3): 227–248.

Henderson, R. 1993. "Underinvestment and Incompetence as Responses to Radical Innovation: Evidence from the Photolithographic Alignment Equipment Industry." *The RAND Journal of Economics* 24 (2): 248–270.

Hill, C. W. L., and F. T. Rothaermel. 2003. "The Performance of Incumbent Firms in the Face of Radical Technological Innovation." *Academy of Management Review* 28 (2): 257–274.

Hills, G. E., C. M. Hultman, and M. P. Miles. 2008. "The Evolution and Development of Entrepreneurial Marketing." *Journal of Small Business Management* 46 (1): 99–112.

Hisrich, R. D. 1989. "Marketing and Entrepreneurship Research Interface." In *Research at the Marketing/Entrepreneurship Interface*, edited by G. Hills, R. W. LaForge, and B. J. Parker, pp. 3–17. Chicago, IL: University of Illinois.

Hoenen, S., C. Kolympiris, W. Schoenmakers, and N. Kalaitzandonakes. 2014. "The Diminishing Signaling Value of Patents between Early Rounds of Venture Capital Financing." *Research Policy* 43 (6): 956–989.

Hsu, D. H., and K. Lim. 2014. "Knowledge Brokering and Organizational Innovation: Founder Imprinting Effects." *Organization Science* 25 (4): 1134–1153.

Hsu, D. H., and R. H. Ziedonis. 2008. "Patents as Quality Signals for Entrepreneurial Ventures." *Academy of Management Proceedings* 2008 (1): 1–6.

Kortum, S., and J. Lerner. 1999. "What is behind the Recent Surge in Patenting?" *Research Policy* 28 (1): 1–22.

Lee, K. S., G. H. Lim, and S. J. Tan. 1999. "Dealing with Resource Disadvantage: Generic Strategies for SMEs." *Small Business Economics* 12 (4): 299–311.

Leiponen, A., and J. Byma. 2009. "If You Cannot Block, You Better Run: Small Firms, Cooperative Innovation, and Appropriation Strategies." *Research Policy* 38 (9): 1478–1488.

Lerner, J. 1994. "The Importance of Patent Scope: An Empirical Analysis." *The Rand Journal of Economics* 25 (2): 319–333.

Manigart, S., K. Baeyens, and W. Van Hyfte. 2002. "The Survival of Venture Capital Backed Companies." *Venture Capital – An International Journal of Entrepreneurial Finance* 4 (2): 103–124.

McAfee, R. P., H. M. Mialon, and M. A. Williams. 2004. "What is a Barrier to Entry?" *The American Economic Review* 94 (2): 461–465.

McGee, J. E., M. J. Dowling, and W. L. Megginson. 1995. "Cooperative Strategy and New Venture Performance: The Role of Business Strategy and Management Experience." *Strategic Management Journal* 16 (7): 565–580.

Mendonça, S., T. S. Pereira, and M. M. Godinho. 2004. "Trademarks as an Indicator of Innovation and Industrial Change." *Research Policy* 33 (9): 1385–1404.

Nelson, T. 2003. "The Persistence of Founder Influence: Management, Ownership, and Performance Effects at Initial Public Offering." *Strategic Management Journal* 24 (8): 707–724.

Ramello, G. B., and F. Silva. 2006. "Appropriating the Signs and Meaning: The Elusive Economics of Trademark." *Industrial and Corporate Change* 15 (6): 937–963.

Redding, S. 2002. "Path Dependence, Endogenous Innovation, and Growth." *International Economic Review* 43 (4): 1215–1248.

Rosenbaum, P. R., and D. B. Rubin. 1983. "The Central Role of the Propensity Score in Observational Studies for Causal Effects." *Biometrika* 70 (1): 41–55.

Sahlman, W. A. 1990. "The Structure and Governance of Venture Capital Organizations." *Journal of Financial Economics* 27 (2): 473–521.

Samila, S., and O. Sorenson. 2010. "Venture Capital as a Catalyst to Commercialization." *Research Policy* 39 (10): 1348–1360.

Sandner, P. G., and J. H. Block. 2011. "The Market Value of R&D, Patents and Trademarks." *Research Policy* 40 (7): 969–985.

Schefczyk, M., and T. J. Gerpott. 2001. "Management Support for Portfolio Companies of Venture Capital Firms: An Empirical Study of German Venture Capital Investments." *British Journal of Management* 12 (3): 201–216.

Schmalensee, R. 1989. "Inter-Industry Studies of Structure and Performance." In *Handbook of Industrial Organization*, edited by R. Schmalensee and R. Willig, 951–1009. Amsterdam: North Holland.

Schumpeter, J. A. 1950. *Capitalism, Socialism, and Democracy*. New York: Harper & Row.

Sorenson, O., and T. E. Stuart. 2008. "Bringing the Context Back in: Settings and the Search for Syndicate Partners in Venture Capital Investment Networks." *Administrative Science Quarterly* 53 (2): 266–294.

Srinivasan, R., G. L. Lilien, and A. Rangaswamy. 2008. "Survival of High Tech Firms: The Effects of Diversity of Product–Market Portfolios, Patents, and Trademarks." *International Journal of Research in Marketing* 25 (2): 119–128.

Sutton, J. 2007. *Sunk Costs and Market Structure*. Cambridge, MA: MIT Press.

Sydow, J., G. Schreyögg, and J. Koch. 2009. "Organizational Path Dependence: Opening the Black Box." *Academy of Management Review* 34 (4): 689–709.

Teece, D. J. 1986. "Profiting from Technological Innovation: Implications for Integration, Collaboration, Licensing and Public Policy." *Research Policy* 15 (6): 285–305.

Thomä, J., and K. Bizer. 2013. "To Protect or Not to Protect? Modes of Appropriability in the Small Enterprise Sector." *Research Policy* 42 (1): 35–49.

Thrane, S., S. Blaabjerg, and R. H. Møller. 2010. "Innovative Path Dependence: Making Sense of Product and Service Innovation in Path Dependent Innovation Processes." *Research Policy* 39 (7): 932–944.

Valorinta, M., H. Schildt, and J. A. Lamberg. 2011. "Path Dependence of Power Relations, Path-Breaking Change and Technological Adaptation." *Industry and Innovation* 18 (8): 765–790.

Veer, T., and F. Jell. 2012. "Contributing to Markets for Technology? A Comparison of Patent Filing Motives of Individual Inventors, Small Companies and Universities." *Technovation* 32 (9–10): 513–522.

Waring, G. F. 1996. "Industry Differences in the Persistence of Firm-Specific Returns." *The American Economic Review* 86 (5): 1253–1265.

Wortman, M. S., M. S. Spann, and M. Adams. 1989. "The Interface of Entrepreneurship and Marketing: Concepts and Research Perspectives." In *Research at the Marketing/Entrepreneurship Interface*, edited by G. Hills, R. W. LaForge, and B. J. Parker, 117–137. Chicago, IL: University of Illinois.

Index